Professional PHP6

Continues

Professional
PHP6

Professional
PHP6

Ed Lecky-Thompson
Steven D. Nowicki
Thomas Myer

WILEY

Wiley Publishing, Inc.

Professional PHP6

Published by
Wiley Publishing, Inc.
10475 Crosspoint Boulevard
Indianapolis, IN 46256
www.wiley.com

Copyright © 2009 by Wiley Publishing, Inc., Indianapolis, Indiana

Published by Wiley Publishing, Inc., Indianapolis, Indiana

Published simultaneously in Canada

ISBN: 978-0-470-39509-7

Manufactured in the United States of America

10 9 8 7 6 5 4 3 2 1

Library of Congress Cataloging-in-Publication Data

Lecky-Thompson, Ed.
　　Professional PHP6 / Ed Lecky-Thompson, Steven D. Nowicki, Thomas Myer.
　　　　p.　cm.
　　Includes index.
　　ISBN 978-0-470-39509-7 (pbk.)
　　　　1. PHP (Computer program language)　2. Web sites—Design.　I. Nowicki, Steven D.　II. Myer,
　　Thomas.　III. Title.
　　QA76.73.P224L423　2009
　　006.7'6—dc22

2009004148

To Marie, for being my drinking buddy
— Ed Lecky-Thompson

To Hope, for loving me anyway
— Tom Myer

About the Authors

Ed Lecky-Thompson was a founding partner of Brandspace before starting his own interactive agency in 2003. Currently, he heads up U.K. digital specialists Galileo (www.galileodm.com), where he runs thriving digital relationship marketing and online public relations accounts for top blue chips (including Microsoft and a major U.S. financial services group). He has written several books on PHP over the past five years, as well as writing for *php | architect magazine*. Ed was nominated for a New Media Age Effectiveness Award in 2004 for his work with First Leisure Corporation as head of new media.

Steven D. Nowicki is a senior software developer at AdKnowledge, Inc., and has more than 13 years of experience with software development and technology management in New York, London, and Los Angeles. He has been the lead software architect for several multimillion-dollar Web applications and dozens of large-scale, mission-critical PHP implementations, including enterprise resource planning, CRM systems, and high-volume analytics. This is his third book on PHP.

Thomas Myer is a technical book author, consultant, and Web developer. In 2001, he founded Triple Dog Dare Media in Austin, Texas. Triple Dog Dare Media focuses its attention on helping companies create CodeIgniter-based applications such as content management, portals, and eCommerce systems. He is the author of *No Nonsense XML Web Development with PHP* (Sitepoint, 2004) and *Lead Generation on the Web* (O'Reilly, 2007). His newest book is *Professional CodeIgniter* (Wrox, 2008). He has also authored dozens of technical and business articles for IBM DeveloperWorks, Amazon Web Services, AOL, *Darwin Magazine*, and others.

Credits

Acquisitions Editor
Jenny Watson

Development Editor
Kevin Shafer

Technical Editor
Ben Schupak

Production Editor
Rebecca Coleman

Copy Editor
Luann Rouff

Editorial Manager
Mary Beth Wakefield

Production Manager
Tim Tate

Vice President and Executive Group Publisher
Richard Swadley

Vice President and Executive Publisher
Barry Pruett

Associate Publisher
Jim Minatel

Project Coordinator, Cover
Lynsey Stanford

Proofreader
Publication Services, Inc.

Indexer
J & J Indexing

Acknowledgments

The authors would like to extend their thanks to the PHP, Linux, Apache, MySQL and PostgreSQL development communities for creating and maintaining such great products, and with such a wealth of supporting documentation. It's their sheer flexibility and extensibility as packages that makes them viable for the enterprise in the first place; and that's why this book has been made possible.

We'd like to pass on our thanks to everyone at Wiley for their support during the book's development, including Sara Shlaer and Jenny Watson, and Kevin Shafer and Ben Schupak for their support and patience throughout 2008.

Also, a special thank-you to all those who bought *Professional PHP5*, and whose feedback (good and bad) has enabled us to create (it is hoped) an even better product in *Professional PHP6*.

Ed would like to thank everybody who's put up with him for the past twenty-seven years; and to acknowledge the patience of all of his team at Galileo, especially David, Steve and Greg. Thanks also to Annabel, Laurence, and Angie for being such great mentors.

Tom Myer would like to thank the PHP community for all the feedback, encouragement, and great conversations. You're the best — keep on codin'.

Contents

Contents

Contents

Contents

Contents

Contents

Contents

Part III: A Real-World Case Study

Contents

Contents

Contents

Introduction

Professional PHP6 was written for PHP developers who are interested in expanding and leveraging their development skills by taking advantage of the features of the sixth major release. This demographic is not set in stone, of course, because experienced .NET and Java 2 Enterprise Edition (J2EE) developers should catch on quickly, too. However, inexperienced PHP developers (or those with no software development experience) are highly encouraged to start with *Beginning PHP6, Apache, MySQL 6 Web Development* (Wiley, 2009).

What Does This Book Cover?

The beauty of PHP is its accessibility and shallow learning curve. Virtually anyone with basic computing knowledge can pick it up and start putting together simple, dynamic Web sites. Indeed, it is qualities like these that have led to PHP powering more than 20 million Web sites across the globe, a figure that is growing by the thousands every day. However, that very accessibility has led to a lack of uniformity in development approach, and perhaps an absence of the application of industry-standard best practices. Put simply, a lot of PHP code *isn't that great*.

As a result, this book ventures beyond mere syntax and is designed to help you deliver better-quality software in a shorter amount of time. If you've ever been told not to use PHP because it's "not enterprise grade," then this book is for you, because you're about to learn how to prove such doubters wrong. Much of what you'll learn (although written with PHP6 in mind) is not limited to the PHP language. Many of the development techniques are directly translatable into other traditional high-level languages, and the skills you'll learn here will follow you the rest of your career.

Who Is This Book For?

This book covers some advanced techniques in PHP, so the book assumes that you have a solid grounding in the basics of PHP application development. You don't necessarily have to be familiar with PHP6 to get started, however. If you've been working in PHP5 until the recent launch of version 6, you'll be fine. Throughout the book, the authors have carefully ensured that any differences between PHP6 and PHP5 are highlighted prominently. If you're still plodding along with PHP4, don't worry — you won't be left behind either — just be sure that you start right at the beginning.

To sum it up, the authors assume that you have what might be called a *working knowledge* of PHP. If you have that and are eager to learn how you can become a true PHP *professional*, then this book is for you.

You might be a Web developer for a big software company. Your company may have been working in PHP for years, or maybe it's eager to take the first steps away from .NET, Java, and other Web development platforms in an effort to discover the myriad of benefits associated with PHP.

You may be a lone (or "almost lone") Web professional in an otherwise nontechnical company, assigned the task of implementing some huge project — perhaps a staff intranet or new corporate Web presence — looking for an appropriate development platform.

You may just be curious. Perhaps you're a student in university or college who's eager to supplement what you're learning in school with some professional code and project-management techniques plucked straight from the world of commercial Web development.

You might have a background in .NET or Java, and you may have heard good things about PHP and how its latest incarnation finally makes it a truly credible professional Web development environment. Perhaps you're skeptical, and you want to see whether what you've heard about PHP6 is true.

Whoever you are, as long as you know the basics of PHP and are eager to learn a whole lot more from people who not only know PHP inside and out, but also love using it and get paid for doing so, then this book is for you.

What You Need to Use This Book

Here's the minimum that you'll need to get the most from this book:

❑ A development workstation (running Windows, Mac OS X, or Linux, with a basic text editor or development environment of your choice) and a Web browser to try out the examples

❑ An installation of PHP and Apache, which needs to be configured roughly in line with the setup detailed in Appendix D

❑ Most of the examples in this book also require an installation of a database compatible with PHP Data Objects (PDO) — examples are written for MySQL or PostgreSQL

Ideally, you should also try to secure the following:

❑ An Internet connection, as numerous URLs are scattered throughout this book, and you'll undoubtedly want to go see them

❑ A lot of free time, an open mind, and a willingness to try new things

How This Book Is Structured

This section outlines the structure of the book; check the table of contents for more detail. Although you should feel free to dip in and out of the chapters to get information on a topic as and when you need it, if you're not familiar with object-oriented programming (OOP) development, or, more important, how it is implemented in PHP6, you should definitely start by reading Part I. The rest of the book makes use of these techniques from cover to cover, so it's vital for you to have the basic grounding in OOP before trying to press on with the trickier stuff.

Part I: Fundamentals of Professional Development

The book starts by outlining basic OOP concepts — both the theory behind them and their practical application and implementation in PHP6. This is of vital importance, as understanding the rest of this book is absolutely dependent on having a thorough understanding of OOP. Indeed, you'll notice that not a single line of procedural code appears anywhere within these pages. If you have a good grounding in .NET or J2EE, you won't need to spend long here — just enough time to see how PHP implements standard OOP patterns.

The book then looks at other tools made available by PHP6 (but rarely used by less-experienced developers), including namespaces, collections, iterators, and collections, and shows their usefulness in common design patterns.

Naturally, no professional title would be complete without a discussion of databases and their roles in enterprise application development. By introducing PDO in Chapter 7, the discussion can also introduce PostgreSQL, the database of choice for the examples in this book (although most of the concepts you'll meet are entirely database-agnostic, meaning they will work perfectly with MySQL, SQL Server, and other database platforms).

Part II: Learning Advanced Development Techniques

Because the first part of the book deals exclusively with the ins and outs of high-end PHP6 techniques, the second section is much more philosophical, teaching you how best to approach common software development challenges by using those techniques. This is sometimes called *software architecture* — the effective design of well-built software.

Among other topics, you'll be introduced to Object Relation Mapping (ORM), event-driven programming (EDP), logging and debugging techniques, how to communicate with users, session management, authentication, and designing and developing Web services.

Crucially, two quite meaty chapters on the most high-level aspects of technical design are included, as well as a discussion of the various PHP development frameworks on the market (and the pros and cons of each), and why using a framework makes sense in the first place. This is important, as one of those frameworks has been chosen for the examples shown in the rest of the book.

Part III: A Real-World Case Study

There's no substitute for trying something out yourself. Since the previous two parts of the book covered the theory, this third section is about putting it all into practice.

Rather than dive in, you'll learn some project-management fundamentals first, as well as how the systems and network architecture will underpin it. You will then put to use the software architecture and advanced development techniques you learned in the first two sections by rapidly building the application from the ground up using an MVC framework.

Having built the application, you'll learn the importance of quality assurance (QA) and testing, and how to approach it on a medium- to large-scale project, as well as an often overlooked topic: how to actually get your project live (otherwise known as *deployment*).

Part IV: Pushing PHP to Its Limits

The final section of the book is about providing you (as an aspiring PHP professional) with some truly impartial advice from developers just like you — people who have been there, done that, and bought the T-shirt.

As such, this section includes four "hot topics" that are the subject of much online and offline debate among those who use PHP every day of their working lives. With some dispassionate analysis, you'll be equipped with the hard facts you need to know in order to make your own decisions, as well as form educated opinions of your own.

You'll learn about PHP-driven content management systems (CMSs) and content management frameworks (CMFs), both off-the-shelf and home-grown. You'll be shown how PHP can play a starring role in powering high-traffic or high-availability Web sites such as Flickr and Facebook. You'll also learn how to convince skeptical colleagues or clients that PHP can easily take on the might of .NET and Java, and win hands down. Most important of all, you'll take a look at the career path that might lie ahead for you as a PHP professional — a look, it is hoped, that will convince you to stick with the language for a long time to come.

Appendixes

The appendixes are home to some important topics that wouldn't neatly fit into any of the previous four sections. In Appendix A you'll learn about version control — why it's important and how to implement it on a large project using CVS or Subversion (SVN). In Appendix B you'll meet a number of PHP development integrated development environments (IDEs), enabling you to cast aside your rusty, old text editor in favor of a slicker, PHP-tailored solution.

Appendix C provides a discussion about how to performance-tune your PHP applications to get the most out of them (even on slower server hardware), while Appendix D offers a simple cheat sheet for setting up PHP and Apache on Linux, Mac OS X, and Windows.

The Bigger Picture

We sincerely hope that you'll help us, the authors, in raising the bar concerning the quality of software found in both professional production environments and in projects found on the Internet. Professionally and philosophically, none of us codes alone, so maybe together we can help to make our existence just a little bit better.

Conventions

To help you get the most from the text and to keep track of what's happening, we've used a number of conventions throughout the book.

> **Boxes like this one hold important, not-to-be forgotten information that is directly relevant to the surrounding text.**

Tips, hints, tricks, and asides to the current discussion are offset and placed in italics like this.

As for styles in the text:

- ❏ We *italicize* important words when we introduce them.
- ❏ We show keyboard strokes like this: Ctrl+A.
- ❏ We show filenames, URLs, and code within the text like so: `persistence.properties`
- ❏ We present code in two different ways:

```
In code examples, we highlight new and important code with a gray background.
```

```
The gray highlighting is absent from code that's less important in the present
        context, or has been shown before.
```

Source Code

As you work through the examples in this book, you may choose to enter all the code manually or use the source code files that accompany the book. All the source code used in this book is available for download at `www.wrox.com`. When you're at the site, locate the book's title (either by using the Search box or by using one of the title lists) and click the Download Code link on the book's detail page to obtain all the source code for the book.

Because many books have similar titles, you may find it easiest to search by ISBN; this book's ISBN is 978-0-470-39509-7.

After you download the code, just decompress it with your favorite compression tool. Alternately, go to the main Wrox code download page at `www.wrox.com/dynamic/books/download.aspx` to see the code available for this book and all other Wrox books.

Errata

We make every effort to ensure that there are no errors in the text or in the code. However, no one is perfect, and mistakes do occur. If you find an error in one of our books (such as a spelling mistake or a faulty piece of code), we would be very grateful for your feedback. By sending in errata, you may save another reader hours of frustration and, at the same time, you will be helping us provide even higher-quality information.

To find the errata page for this book, go to www.wrox.com and locate the title using the Search box or one of the title lists. Then, on the book details page, click the Book Errata link. On this page, you can view all errata that has been submitted for this book and posted by Wrox editors. A complete book list, including links to each book's errata, is also available at www.wrox.com/misc-pages/booklist.shtml.

If you don't spot "your" error on the Book Errata page, go to www.wrox.com/contact/techsupport and complete the form there to send us the error you have found. We'll check the information and, if appropriate, post a message to the book's errata page, and fix the problem in subsequent editions of the book.

p2p.wrox.com

For author and peer discussion, join the P2P forums at p2p.wrox.com. The forums are a Web-based system for you to post messages relating to Wrox books and related technologies, and to interact with other readers and technology users. The forums offer a subscription feature to e-mail you topics of interest of your choosing when new posts are made to the forums. Wrox authors, editors, other industry experts, and your fellow readers are present on these forums.

At http://p2p.wrox.com you will find a number of different forums that will help you not only as you read this book, but also as you develop your own applications. To join the forums, just follow these steps:

1. Go to p2p.wrox.com and click the Register link.

2. Read the terms of use and click Agree.

3. Complete the required information to join, as well as provide any optional information you choose, and click Submit.

4. You will receive an e-mail with information describing how to verify your account and complete the joining process.

   You can read messages in the forums without joining P2P, but in order to post your own messages, you must join.

After you join, you can post new messages and respond to messages that other users post. You can read messages at any time on the Web. If you would like to have new messages from a particular forum e-mailed to you, click the "Subscribe to this Forum" icon by the forum name in the forum listing.

For more information about how to use the Wrox P2P, be sure to read the P2P FAQs for answers to questions about how the forum software works, as well as many common questions specific to P2P and Wrox books. To read the FAQs, click the FAQ link on any P2P page.

Part I

Fundamentals of Professional Development

Introduction to Object-Oriented Programming

Object-oriented (OO) software development can be a confusing topic for developers who create primarily procedural code, but it doesn't need to be. In this chapter, you'll explore some of the basic theory behind OO, and learn its (sometimes daunting) multisyllabic terminology. You'll also learn why you should be interested in OO techniques, how they can greatly improve the speed with which you develop complex applications, and see the ease with which you can modify those applications.

The next few chapters expand on the ideas presented here and familiarize you with some slightly more advanced topics. If you have already had exposure to OO development outside of PHP 6, you can probably skip this chapter and the next. However, this material serves as a good review, so it is recommended that you read it through.

What Is Object-Oriented Programming?

Object-oriented programming (OOP) requires a different way of thinking about how you construct your applications. Objects enable you to more closely model in code the real-world tasks, processes, and ideas that your application is designed to handle. Instead of thinking about an application as a thread of control that passes chunks of data from one function to the next, an OOP approach enables you to model the application as a set of collaborating objects that independently handle certain activities.

As an analogy, when a house is being constructed, the plumbers deal with the pipes, and the electricians deal with the wires. The plumbers don't need to know whether the circuit in the bedroom is 10 amps or 20 amps. They must concern themselves only with their own activities. A general contractor ensures that each subcontractor is completing the work that needs to be accomplished, but isn't necessarily interested in the particulars of each task. An OOP approach is similar in that each object hides from the others the details of its implementation. How it does its job is irrelevant to the other components of the system. All that matters is the service that the object is able to provide.

The concepts of classes and objects, and the ways in which you can leverage these ideas in the development of software, are the fundamental ideas behind OOP. This is, in a sense, the opposite of procedural programming, which is programming using functions and global data structures. As you'll see, an OO approach provides significant benefits over procedural programming and (with the new implementation of OO support that first appeared in PHP5, and was further improved in PHP6) some large performance boosts as well.

OOP Advantages

One of the main benefits of OOP is the ease with which you can translate individual business requirements into individual modules of code. Because an OOP approach enables you to model your application based on the idea of real-world objects, you can often identify a direct correlation between people, things, and concepts, and equivalent classes. These classes have the same properties and behaviors as the real-world concepts they represent, which helps you to quickly identify what code must be written and how different parts of the application must interact.

A second benefit of OOP is code reuse. You frequently need the same types of data in different places in the same application. For example, an application that enables a hospital to manage its patient records would definitely need a class called `Person`. A number of people are involved in patient care — the patient, the doctors, the nurses, hospital administrators, insurance claims people, and so on. At each step in the care of the patient, that patient's record requires a note about which person was performing a given action (such as prescribing medicine, cleaning wounds, or sending a bill to an insurance carrier) and verifying that the person is allowed to perform that action. By defining a generic class called `Person` that encompasses all the properties and methods common to all these people, you get an enormous amount of code reuse that isn't always possible in a procedural approach to programming.

What about other applications? How many applications can you think of that, at some point, handle information about individuals? Probably quite a few. A well-written `Person` class could easily be copied from one project to another with little or no change, instantly giving you all the rich functionality required for dealing with information about people that you developed previously. This is one of the biggest benefits of an OO approach — the opportunities for code reuse within a given application, as well as across different projects.

Another OOP advantage comes from the modularity of classes. If you discover a bug in your `Person` class, or you want to add to or change the way that class functions, you have only one place to go. All the functionality of that class is contained in a single file. Any processes of the application that rely on the `Person` class are immediately affected by changes to it. This can vastly simplify the search for bugs, and makes the addition of features a relatively painless task.

A Real-World Example

They might seem trivial in a smaller application, but in a more complex software architecture, the benefits of modularity can be enormous. One of the authors of this book worked on a project involving more than 200,000 lines of procedural PHP code. Easily, 65 percent of the time spent fixing bugs was devoted to uncovering where certain functions were located and determining which data interacted with which functions. A subsequent rewrite of that software in an OO architecture resulted in dramatically less code. Had the application been implemented in such a manner in the first place, it would have resulted in not only less development time from the outset, but also the discovery of fewer bugs (the smaller the amount of code, the fewer the opportunities for problems) and a faster turnaround time on bug fixes.

Because an OO approach easily lends itself to a system of clearly documenting the structure of an application (see Chapter 2), learning the structure of an existing application is much easier when you are new to the development team. In addition, you have a framework to aid you in determining the appropriate location for new functionality you might develop.

Larger projects often have a multimember software development team, usually composed of programmers with varying degrees of ability. Here, too, an OO approach has significant benefits over a procedural approach. Objects hide the details of their implementation from the users of those objects. Instead of needing to understand complex data structures and all the quirks of the business logic, junior members of the team can (with just a little documentation) begin using objects created by more experienced members. The objects themselves are responsible for triggering changes to data or the state of the system.

When the large application mentioned previously was still written using procedural code, new members of the software development team often took up to two months to learn enough about the application to be productive. After the software was rebuilt using objects, new members of the team usually took no more than a couple of days to begin making substantial additions to the code base. They were able to use even the most complex objects quickly because they did not need to fully understand the particulars of how the functionality contained within those objects was implemented.

Now that you have a good idea about why you should consider using an OO paradigm as your programming method of choice, you should read the next few sections to gain a better understanding of the fundamental concepts behind OO. If all goes well, through the course of the next two chapters you will begin to see the benefits of this approach for yourself.

Understanding OOP Concepts

This section introduces the primary concepts of object-oriented programming and explores how they interact; Chapter 3 looks at the specifics of implementing them in PHP6. This chapters covers the following topics:

- ❑ *Classes* — The "blueprints" for an object and the actual code that defines the properties and methods

- ❑ *Objects* — Running instances of a class that contain all the internal data and state information needed for your application to function

- ❑ *Inheritance* — The ability to define a class of one kind as being a subtype of a different kind of class (much the same way a square is a kind of rectangle)

- ❑ *Polymorphism* — Allows a class to be defined as being a member of more than one category of classes (just as a car is "a thing with an engine" and "a thing with wheels")

❑ *Interfaces* — A way of specifying that an object is capable of doing something without actually defining how it is to be done (e.g., a dog and a human are "things that walk," but they do it very differently)

❑ *Encapsulation* — The ability of an object to protect access to its internal data

If any of these terms seem difficult to understand, don't worry. The material that follows will clarify everything. Your newfound knowledge may even completely change the way you approach your software development projects.

Classes

In the real world, objects have characteristics and behaviors. A car has a color, a weight, a manufacturer, and a gas tank of a certain volume. Those are its characteristics. A car can accelerate, stop, signal for a turn, and sound the horn. Those are its behaviors. Those characteristics and behaviors are common to all cars. Although two particular cars in the same parking lot may have different colors, all cars have a color. Using a construct known as a *class*, OOP enables you to establish the idea of a car as being something with all those characteristics. A class is a unit of code (composed of variables and functions) that describes the characteristics and behaviors of all the members of a set. A class called Car would describe the properties and methods common to all cars.

In OO terminology, the characteristics of a class are known as its *properties*. Properties have a name and a value. Some allow their value to be changed; others do not. For example, in the Car class, you would probably have such properties as color and weight. Although the color of the car can be changed by giving it a new paint job, the tare weight of the car (without cargo or passengers) is a fixed value.

Some properties represent the *state* of the object. State refers to those characteristics that change because of certain events but are not necessarily directly modifiable on their own. In an application that simulates vehicle performance, the Car class might have a property called velocity. The velocity of the car is not a value that can be changed on its own, but rather is a by-product of the amount of fuel being sent to the engine, the performance characteristics of that engine, and the terrain over which the car is traveling.

The behaviors of a class are known as its *methods*. Methods of classes are syntactically equivalent to functions found in traditional procedural code. Just like functions, methods can accept any number of parameters, each of any valid data type. Some methods act on external data passed to them as parameters, but they can also act on the properties of their object, either using those properties to inform actions made by the method (such as when a method called accelerate examines the remaining amount of fuel to determine whether the car is capable of accelerating) or to change the state of the object by modifying values such as the velocity of the car.

Objects

To begin with, you can think of a class as a blueprint for constructing an object. In much the same way that many houses can be built from the same blueprint, you can build multiple instances of an object from its class; but the blueprint doesn't specify details such as the color of the walls or the type of flooring. It merely specifies that those things will exist. Classes work much the same way. The class specifies the behaviors and characteristics the object will have, but not necessarily the values of those characteristics. An object is a concrete entity constructed using the blueprint provided by a class. The idea of *a* house is analogous to a class. *Your* house (a specific instance of the idea of a house) is analogous to an object.

With a blueprint in hand and some building materials, you can construct a house. In OOP, when you use the class to build an object, this process is known as *instantiation*. Instantiating an object requires two things:

❑   A memory location into which to load the object. This is automatically handled for you by PHP.

❑   The data that will populate the values of the properties. This data can come from a database, a flat text file, another object, or some other source.

A class can never have property values or state. Only objects can. You must use the blueprint to build the house before you can give it wallpaper or vinyl siding. Similarly, you must instantiate an object from the class before you can interact with its properties or invoke its methods. Classes are manipulated at design time when you make changes to the methods or properties. Objects are manipulated at run-time when values are assigned to their properties, and their methods are invoked. The problem of when to use the word *class* and when to use the word *object* is something that often confuses those new to OOP.

After an object is instantiated, it can be put to work implementing the business requirements of the application. Let's look at exactly how to do that in PHP.

Creating a Class

Starting with a simple example, save the following in a file called `class.Demo.php`:

```php
<?php

  class Demo {

  }

?>
```

There you have it — the `Demo` class. Although not terribly exciting just yet, this is the basic syntax for declaring a new class in PHP. Use the keyword `class` to let PHP know you're about to define a new class. Follow that with the name of the class and braces to indicate the start and end of the code for that class.

> *It's important to have a clearly defined convention for organizing your source code files. A good rule to follow is to put each class into its own file and to name that file `class.[ClassName].php`.*

You can instantiate an object of type `Demo` like this:

```php
<?php

  require_once('class.Demo.php');

  $objDemo = new Demo();

?>
```

To instantiate an object, first ensure that PHP knows where to find the class declaration by including the file containing your class (class.Demo.php in this example); then invoke the new operator and supply the name of the class, followed by opening and closing parentheses. The return value of this statement is assigned to a new variable, objDemo in this example. Now you can invoke the $objDemo object's methods and examine or set the value of its properties — if it actually has any.

Even though the class you've created doesn't do much of anything just yet, it's still a valid class definition.

Adding a Method

The Demo class isn't particularly useful if it isn't able to do anything, so let's look at how you can create a method. Remember, a method of a class is basically just a function. By coding a function inside the braces of your class, you're adding a method to that class. Here's an example:

```php
<?php

class Demo {
    function sayHello($name) {
      print "Hello $name!";
    }
}

?>
```

An object derived from your class is now capable of printing a greeting to anyone who invokes the sayHello method. To invoke the method on your $objDemo object, you need to use the operator -> to access the newly created function:

```php
<?php

require_once('class.Demo.php');

$objDemo = new Demo();

$objDemo->sayHello('Steve');

?>
```

The object is now capable of printing a friendly greeting. The -> operator is used to access all methods and properties of your objects.

For readers who have had exposure to OOP in other programming languages, note that the -> operator is always used to access the methods and properties of an object. PHP does not use the dot operator (.) in its OO syntax at all.

Adding a Property

Adding a property to your class is just as easy as adding a method. You simply declare a variable inside the class to hold the value of the property. In procedural code, when you want to store some value, you assign that value to a variable. In OOP, when you want to store the value of a property, you also use a variable. This variable is declared at the top of the class declaration, inside the braces that bracket the class's code. The name of the variable is the name of the property. If the variable is called `$color`, you will have a property called `color`.

Open the `class.Demo.php` file and add the following highlighted code:

```php
<?php

class Demo {
    public $name;

    function sayHello() {
      print "Hello $this->name!";
    }
  }
?>
```

This new variable, called `$name`, is all you have to do to create a property of the `Demo` class called `name`. To access this property, you use the same `->` operator as that of the previous example, along with the name of the property. The rewritten `sayHello` method shows how to access the value of this property.

Create a new file called `testdemo.php` and add the following:

```php
<?php

require_once('class.Demo.php');

$objDemo = new Demo();
$objDemo->name = 'Steve';

$objAnotherDemo = new Demo();
$objAnotherDemo->name = 'Ed';

$objDemo->sayHello();
$objAnotherDemo->sayHello();

?>
```

Save the file and then open it in your Web browser. The strings "Hello Steve!" and "Hello Ed!" print to the screen.

The keyword `public` is used to let the class know that you want to have access to the following variable from outside the class. Some member variables of the class exist only for use by the class itself and should not be accessible to external code; these variables are declared as `private` or `protected` (more on that later). In this example, you want to be able to set and retrieve the value of the property `name`. Note that the way the `sayHello` method works has changed. Instead of taking a parameter, it now fetches the `name` value from the property.

You use the variable `$this` so that the object can get information about itself. You might have multiple objects of a class, for example, and because you don't know in advance what the name of an object variable will be, the `$this` variable enables you to refer to the current instance.

In the previous example, the first call to sayHello prints "Steve" and the second call prints "Ed". This is because the $this variable allows each object to access its own properties and methods without having to know the name of the variable that represents it in the exterior application. Previously, you learned that some properties influence the action of certain methods, such as the example in which the accelerate method of the Car class needs to examine the amount of fuel remaining. The code inside accelerate would use code such as $this->amountOfFuel to access this property.

> *When accessing properties, you need only one $. The syntax is $obj->property, not $obj->$property. This fact often causes confusion for those new to PHP. The property variable is declared as public $property and accessed using $obj->property.*

In addition to the variables that store the values for the properties of the class, other variables may be declared for use by the internal operations of the class. Both kinds of data are collectively referred to as the class's *internal member variables*. Some of these are accessible to code outside the class in the form of properties. Others are not accessible and are strictly for internal housekeeping. For example, if the Car class needed to get information from a database for whatever reason, it might keep a database connection handle in an internal member variable. This database connection handle is obviously not a property of the car, but rather something the class needs to carry out certain operations.

Protecting Access to Member Variables

As the previous example shows, you can set the value of the name property to just about anything you want — including an object, an array of integers, a file handle, or any other nonsensical value. However, you don't get an opportunity to do any sort of data validation or update any other values when the name property is set.

To work around this problem, always implement your properties in the form of functions called get[property name] and set[property name]. Such functions are known as *accessor methods*, and are demonstrated in the following example.

Change class.Demo.php as shown here:

```php
<?php
class Demo {
    private $_name;

    public function sayHello() {
      print "Hello " . $this->getName() . "!"
    }

    public function getName() {
      return $this->_name;
    }

    public function setName($name) {
      if(!is_string($name) || strlen($name) == 0) {
        throw new Exception("Invalid name value!");
      }

      $this->_name = $name;
    }
}
?>
```

Edit `testdemo.php` as shown here:

```php
<?php

require_once('class.Demo.php');

$objDemo = new Demo();
$objDemo->setName('Steve');
$objDemo->sayHello();

$objDemo->setName(37); //would trigger an error

?>
```

As you can see, the member access level of `name` has changed from `public` to `private` and has been prefixed with an underscore. The underscore is a recommended naming convention to indicate private member variables and functions; however, it is merely a convention — PHP does not require it. The keyword `private` protects code outside the object from modifying this value. Private internal member variables are not accessible from outside the class. Because you can't access these variables directly, you're forced to use the `getName()` and `setName()` accessor methods to obtain this information, ensuring that your class can examine the value before allowing it to be set.

In this example, an exception is thrown if an invalid value is supplied for the `name` property. Additionally, the `public` access specifier for the functions has been added. Public is the default visibility level for any member variables or functions that do not explicitly set one, but it is good practice to always explicitly state the visibility of all the members of the class.

A member variable or method can have three different levels of visibility: public, private, and protected. *Public members* are accessible to any and all code. *Private members* are accessible only to the class itself. These are typically items used for internal housekeeping, and might include such things as a database connection handle or configuration information. *Protected members* are available to the class itself and to classes that inherit from it. (Inheritance is defined and discussed in detail later in this chapter.)

By creating accessor methods for all your properties, you make it much easier to add data validation or new business logic, or make other changes to your objects later. Even if the current business requirements for your application involve no data validation of a given property, you should still implement that property with `get` and `set` functions so that you can add validation or business logic functionality in the future.

> *Always use accessor methods for your properties. Changes to business logic and data validation requirements in the future will be much easier to implement.*

Initializing Objects

For many of the classes you will create, you will need to do some special setup when an object of that class is first instantiated. You might need to fetch some information from a database or initialize some property values, for example. By creating a special method called a *constructor*, implemented in PHP using a function called `_construct()`, you can perform any activities required to instantiate the object. PHP will automatically call this special function when instantiating the object.

For example, you could rewrite the Demo class in the following way:

```php
<?php
class Demo {
  private $name;

  public function __construct($name) {
    $this->name = $name;
  }
  function sayHello() {
    print "Hello $this->name!";
  }
}
?>
```

The _construct function will be automatically invoked when you instantiate a new object of class Demo. Note that you will need to update testdemo.php to pass the name in the constructor, rather than in the setter method.

In PHP 4, object constructors were functions with the same name as the class. PHP version 5 changed this to use a unified constructor scheme. For backward compatibility, PHP first looks for a function called __ construct, but if none is found, it will still look for a function with the same name as the class (public function Demo () in the preceding example). While this backward compatibility has been maintained in PHP 6, there is no guarantee it will be preserved in future versions.

If you have a class that does not require any special initialization code to be run, you don't need to create a constructor. As you saw in the first version of the Demo class, PHP automatically does what it needs to do to create that object. Create a constructor function only when you need one.

Destroying Objects

The object variables that you create are removed from system memory when the requested page has completed running, when the variable falls out of scope, or when it is explicitly set to null. In PHP 6, you can trap the destruction of the object and take actions when that happens. To do so, create a function called __destruct with no parameters. Before the object is destroyed, this function is called automatically, if it exists.

Calling this function gives you the opportunity to perform any last-minute clean-up (such as closing file handles or database connections that might have been opened by the class), or any other last-minute housekeeping that might be needed before the object is destroyed.

The following example fetches the properties of an object from a database. If any properties of the object are changed, they are automatically saved back to the database when the object is destroyed. This eliminates the need to explicitly call a save method. The destructor also closes the open database connection handle.

As with most of the database examples in this book, this one uses PostgreSQL as its platform. The authors firmly believe that the advanced features, transaction support, and robust stored procedure mechanism of PostgreSQL make it a superior alternative to MySQL and other open-source relational database management systems (RDBMSs) for large-scale enterprise software development. If you don't have a PostgreSQL environment at your disposal, or if you prefer MySQL (as many do), feel free to make the appropriate modifications for the database platform you use.

Create a table called `"widget"` using the following SQL statement:

```
CREATE TABLE "widget" (
  "widgetid" SERIAL PRIMARY KEY NOT NULL,
  "name" varchar(255) NOT NULL,
  "description" text
);
```

Insert some data:

```
INSERT INTO "widget" ("name", "description")
VALUES('Foo', 'This is a footacular widget!');
```

Create a file called `class.Widget.php` and enter the following code:

```php
<?php

class Widget {

    private $id;
    private $name;
    private $description; private $hDB;
    private $needsUpdating = false;

    public function __construct($widgetID) {
        //The widgetID parameter is the primary key of a
        //record in the database containing the information
        //for this object

        //Create a connection handle and store it in a private member variable
        //This code assumes the DB is called "parts"
        $this->hDB = pg_connect('dbname=parts user=postgres');
        if(! is_resource($this->hDB)) {
            throw new Exception('Unable to connect to the database.');
        }

        $sql = "SELECT \"name\", \"description\" FROM widget WHERE widgetid =
                $widgetID";
        $rs = pg_query($this->hDB, $sql);
        if(! is_resource($rs)) {
            throw new Exception("An error occurred selecting from the database.");
        }

        if(! pg_num_rows($rs)) {
            throw new Exception('The specified widget does not exist!');
        }
        $data = pg_fetch_array($rs);
        $this->id = $widgetID;
```

```
        $this->name = $data['name'];

        $this->description = $data['description'];
    }

    public function getName() {
        return $this->name;
    }

    public function getDescription() {
        return $this->description;
    }

    public function setName($name) {
        $this->name = $name;
        $this->needsUpdating = true;
    }
    public function setDescription($description) {
        $this->description = $description;
        $this->needsUpdating = true;
    }

    public function __destruct() {
        if($this->needsUpdating) {

            $sql = 'UPDATE "widget" SET ';
            $sql .= "\"name\" = '" . pg_escape_string($this->name) . "', ";
            $sql .= "\"description\" = '" .
            pg_escape_string($this->description) . "'";
            $sql .= "WHERE widgetID = " . $this->id;

            $rs = pg_query($this->hDB, $sql);
        }

        //We're done with the database. Close the connection handle.
        pg_close($this->hDB);
    }
}
?>
```

The constructor to this object opens a connection to a database called parts using the default super-user account postgres. This connection handle is preserved in a private member variable for use later. The ID value passed as a parameter to the constructor is used to construct a SQL statement that fetches the information for the widget with the specified primary key in the database. The data from the database is then assigned to private member variables for use with the get and set functions. Note that if anything should go wrong, the constructor throws exceptions, so be sure to wrap any attempts to construct a Widget object in try... catch blocks.

The two accessor methods, getName() and getDescription(), enable you to fetch the values of the private member variables. Similarly, the setName() and setDescription() methods enable you to assign a new value to those variables. Note that when a new value is assigned, the needsUpdating value is set to true. If nothing changes, then nothing needs to be updated.

To test this, create a file called testWidget.php with the following content:

```php
<?php

require_once('class.Widget.php');

  try {
    $objWidget = new Widget(1);
    print "Widget Name: " . $objWidget->getName() . "<br>\n";

    print "Widget Description: " . $objWidget->getDescription() . "<br>\n";
    $objWidget->setName('Bar');
    $objWidget->setDescription('This is a bartacular widget!');

  } catch (Exception $e) {
     die("There was a problem: " . $e->getMessage());
  }

?>
```

Access this file in your Web browser. The first time it runs, the output should be something like the following:

```
Widget Name: Foo
Widget Description: This is a footacular widget!
```

Any subsequent call should display as follows:

```
Widget Name: Bar
Widget Description: This is a bartacular widget!
```

Look at how powerful this technique can be. You can fetch an object from the database, change a property of that object, and automagically write the changed information back to the database with just a few lines of code in testWidget.php. If nothing changes, you don't need to go back to the database, so you save load on the database server and improve the application's performance.

Users of the object do not necessarily need to understand its internals. If a senior member of the software development team wrote the Widget class, he or she could give this object to a junior member, who perhaps doesn't understand SQL as well, and the junior member of the team could put this object to use without any knowledge whatsoever of where the data comes from or how to save changes to it. In fact, you could change the data source from a PostgreSQL database to a MySQL database or even an XML file without the junior team member ever knowing or having to touch any of the code that uses this class.

Inheritance

If you were creating an application to handle inventory at a car dealership, you would probably need classes such as Sedan, PickupTruck, and MiniVan that would correspond to the same types of automobiles in the dealer's inventory. Your application would need not only to show how many of these items you have in stock, but also to report on the characteristics of these vehicles so that the salespeople could give the information to customers.

A sedan is a four-door car, and you would probably want to record the back-seat space and the trunk capacity. A pickup truck doesn't have a trunk, but does have a cargo bed with a certain capacity, and the truck itself has a towing capacity (the maximum weight of any cargo that can be safely carried). For a minivan, you would probably need to list the number of sliding doors (either one or two) and the number of seats inside.

However, each of these vehicles is really just a different type of automobile, and as such would share a number of characteristics in your application (such as color, manufacturer, model, year, vehicle identification number, and so on). To ensure that each of the classes has these same properties, you could just copy the code that creates those properties into each of the files containing your class definitions. As mentioned earlier in this chapter, one of the benefits of an OOP approach is code reuse. Therefore, of course, you don't need to copy code, but instead can reuse the properties and methods of these classes through a process called *inheritance*. Inheritance is the ability for one class to assume the methods and properties of a parent class.

Inheritance enables you to define a base class, in this case `Automobile`. You can say that other classes are also a type of `Automobile`, and as such have all the same properties and methods that all `Automobiles` have. Because a `Sedan` is an `Automobile`, it therefore automatically inherits everything defined by the `Automobile` class without your having to copy any code. That way, you need to write only the additional properties and methods of the `Sedan` class that are not shared by all automobiles. In other words, the only work left for you to do is define the differences; the similarities between the classes are inherited from the base class.

The ability to reuse code is one benefit, but there's a second major advantage to using inheritance. Suppose that you have a class called `Customer` with a method `buyAutomobile`. This method would take one parameter, an object of class `Automobile`, and its internal operations would print the paperwork needed to document the sale, and decrement the car in question from the inventory system. Because all `Sedans`, `PickupTrucks`, and `MiniVans` are `Automobiles`, you can pass objects of these classes to a function expecting an `Automobile`. Because the three specific types inherit from the more generic parent class, you know that they will all have the same base set of properties and methods. As long as you need only the methods and properties common to all `Automobiles`, you can accept objects of any class that inherits from `Automobile`.

Consider the example of cats. All cats share some properties. They eat, sleep, purr, and hunt. They also have shared properties — weight, fur color, whisker length, and running speed. However, lions have a mane of a certain length (at least, the male lions do), and they growl. Cheetahs have spots. Domesticated cats have neither of these things, yet all three animals are cats.

In PHP you specify that a class is a subset of another by using the keyword `extends`, which tells PHP that the class you are declaring should inherit all the properties and methods from its parent class, and that you are adding functionality or providing some additional specialization to that class.

If you had to design an application to handle zoo animals, you'd probably need to have classes `Cat`, `Lion`, and `Cheetah`. Before writing any code, plan your class hierarchy in Unified Markup Language (UML) diagrams so you have something to work from when you write the code and the documentation of those classes. (UML is examined in more detail in Chapter 2, so don't worry if you don't completely understand what's shown here.) Your class diagram should indicate a parent class `Cat`, with subclasses `Lion` and `Cheetah` inheriting from it. Figure 1-1 shows that diagram.

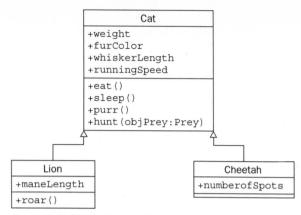

Figure 1-1: Class diagram for cats

Both the `Lion` and `Cheetah` classes inherit from `Cat`, but the `Lion` class also implements the property `maneLength` and the method `roar()`, whereas `Cheetah` adds the property `numberOfSpots`.

The `Cat` class, `class.Cat.php`, should be implemented as follows:

```php
<?php

class Cat {
    public $weight;          //in kg
    public $furColor;
    public $whiskerLength;
    public $maxSpeed;        //in km/hr
    public function eat() {
        //code for eating...
    }

    public function sleep() {
        //code for sleeping...
    }

    public function hunt(Prey $objPrey) {
        //code for hunting objects of type Prey
        //which we will not define...
    }

    public function purr() {
        print "purrrrrrr..." . "\n";
    }
}
?>
```

This simple class sets up all the properties and methods common to all cats. To create the `Lion` and `Cheetah` classes, you could copy all the code from the `Cat` class to classes called `Lion` and `Cheetah`. However, this generates two problems.

First, if you find a bug in the Cat class, you must remember to fix it in the Lion and Cheetah classes as well. This creates more work for you, not less (and creating less work is supposed to be one of the primary advantages of an OO approach).

Second, imagine that you had a method of some other class (maybe CatLover) that looked like this:

```php
public function petTheKitty(Cat $objCat) {
   $objCat->purr();
}
```

Although petting a lion or cheetah may not be a terribly safe idea, they will purr if they let you get close enough to do so. You should be able to pass an object of class Lion or Cheetah to the petTheKitty() function.

Therefore, you must take the other route to create the Lion and Cheetah classes, which is to use inheritance. By using the keyword extends and specifying the name of the class that is extended, you can easily create two new classes that have all the same properties as a regular cat but provide some additional features. Consider this example, which you can type into class.Lion.php:

```php
<?php
   require_once('class.Cat.php');

   class Lion extends Cat {
      public $maneLength; //in cm

      public function roar() {
         print "Roarrrrrrrrr!";
      }
   }
?>
```

That's it! With the Lion class extending Cat, you can now do something like the following:

```php
<?php
   include('class.Lion.php');

   $objLion = new Lion();
   $objLion->weight = 200;    //kg = \s450 lbs.
   $objLion->furColor = 'brown';
   $objLion->maneLength = 36; //cm = \s14 inches
   $objLion->eat();
   $objLion->roar();
   $objLion->sleep();
?>
```

As shown here, you can invoke the properties and methods of the parent class Cat without having to rewrite all that code. Remember that the extends keyword tells PHP to automatically include all the functionality of a Cat, along with any Lion-specific properties or methods. It also tells PHP that a Lion object is also a `Cat` object, and you can now call the `petTheKitty()` function with an object of class `Lion` even though the function declaration uses `Cat` as the parameter hint:

```php
<?php
  include('class.Lion.php');

  $objLion = new Lion();
  $objPetter = new CatLover();
  $objPetter->petTheKitty($objLion);
?>
```

In this way, any changes you make to the `Cat` class are automatically inherited by the `Lion` class. Bug fixes, changes to function internals, or new methods and properties are all passed along to the subclasses of a parent class. In a large, well-designed object hierarchy, this can make bug fixing and the addition of enhancements very easy. A small change to one parent class can have a large effect on the entire application.

In this next example, you'll see how a custom constructor can be used to extend and specialize a class. Create a new file called `class.Cheetah.php` and enter the following:

```php
<?php
  require_once('class.Cat.php');

  class Cheetah extends Cat {
    public $numberOfSpots;

    public function __construct() {
      $this->maxSpeed = 100;
    }
  }
?>
```

Enter the following code into `testcats.php`:

```php
<?php
require_once('class.Cheetah.php');

  function petTheKitty(Cat $objCat) {
    if($objCat->maxSpeed < 5) {
      $objCat->purr();
    } else {
      print "Can't pet the kitty - it's moving at " .
             $objCat->maxSpeed . " kilometers per hour!";
    }
  }
  $objCheetah = new Cheetah();
  petTheKitty($objCheetah);

  $objCat = new Cat();
  petTheKitty($objCat);
?>
```

The Cheetah class adds a new public member variable called numberOfSpots and a constructor that did not exist in the parent Cat class. Now, when you create a new Cheetah, the maxSpeed property (inherited from Cat) is initialized to 100 kilometers per hour (roughly 60 miles per hour), which is the approximate maximum speed of a cheetah over short distances. Note that because a default value for the Cat class isn't specified, the maxSpeed evaluates as 0 (actually, null) in the petTheKitty() function. As those who have ever had a house cat know, the amount of time they spend sleeping means that their maximum speed probably is approaching 0!

By adding new functions, properties, or even constructors and destructors, the subclasses of a parent class can easily extend their functionality and, with a minimum amount of code, add new features and capabilities to your application.

When you can say that one class is a special type of some other class, use inheritance to maximize the potential for code reuse and increase the flexibility of your application.

Overriding Methods

Just because a child class inherits from a parent class doesn't mean that the child class necessarily needs to use the parent class's implementation of a function. For example, if you were designing an application that needed to calculate the area of different geometric shapes, you might have classes called Rectangle and Triangle. Both of these shapes are polygons, and as such these classes will inherit from a parent class called Polygon.

The Polygon class will have a property called numberOfSides and a method called getArea. All polygons have a calculable area; however, the methods for calculating that area can be different for different types of polygons. (A generic equation exists for the area of any polygon, but it is often less efficient than the shape-specific equations for the simple polygons being used here.) The formula for the area of a rectangle is w * h, where w is the width of the rectangle and h is the height. The area of a triangle is calculated as 0.5 * h * b, where h is the height of a triangle with base b. Figure 1-2 shows the area of two types of polygon.

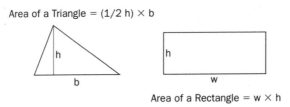

Area of a Triangle = (1/2 h) × b

Area of a Rectangle = w × h

Figure 1-2: Area of two polygons

For each subclass of Polygon that you create, you will probably want to substitute an equation for the default implementation of the area method with one specific to the type of polygon class. By redefining that method for the class, you can provide your own implementation.

In the case of the `Rectangle` class, you would create two new properties, `height` and `width`, and override the `Polygon` class's implementation of the `getArea()` method. For the `Triangle` class, you would probably add properties to store information about the three angles, the height, and the length of the base segment, and override the `getArea()` method. By using inheritance and overriding methods of the parent class, you can allow the subclasses to specialize their implementations of those methods.

A function that takes a `Polygon` as a parameter and needs to print the area of that polygon will then automatically call the `getArea()` method of the subclass of `Polygon` that was passed to it (that is, `Rectangle` or `Triangle`). This capability for an OOP language to automatically determine at run-time which `getArea()` method to call is known as *polymorphism*. Polymorphism is the ability of an application to do different things based on the particular object it is acting on. In this case, that means invoking a different `getArea()` method.

> *Override a method in a subclass when the parent class's implementation is different from that required by the subclass. This allows you to specialize the activities of that subclass.*

Sometimes you want to retain the implementation provided by the parent class, but also perform some additional activities in the method of the subclass. For example, if you have an application that manages a nonprofit organization, you would probably have a class called `Volunteer` that would have a method called `signUp()`; this method would enable the volunteer to sign up for a community service project and add the user to the list of volunteers for that activity.

You might, however, have some users with restrictions (such as a criminal background) that should prevent them from signing up for certain projects. In this case, polymorphism enables you to create a class called `RestrictedUser` with an overridden `signUp()` method that first checks the restrictions on the user account against the properties of the project, preventing users from signing up if their restrictions do not allow them to volunteer for a particular activity. If their restrictions do not prohibit them from participating, then you should invoke the actions of the parent class to complete their registration.

When you override methods of the parent class, you do not necessarily need to completely rewrite the method. You can continue to use the implementation provided by the parent, but add additional specialization for your subclass. In this way, you can reuse code and also provide customizations as required by the business rules.

The capability of one class to inherit the methods and properties of another class is one of the most compelling features of an OO system, and one that enables you to gain an incredible level of efficiency and flexibility in your applications.

In the following example, you'll create two classes — `Rectangle` and `Square`. A square is a special kind of rectangle. Anything you can do with a rectangle you can do with a square; however, because a rectangle has two different side lengths and a square has only one, you need to do some things differently.

Create a file called `class.Rectangle.php` and add the following code:

```php
<?php

class Rectangle {
    public $height;
    public $width;

    public function __construct($width, $height) {
        $this->width = $width;
        $this->height = $height;
    }

    public function getArea() {
        return $this->height * $this->width;
    }

}
?>
```

This is a fairly straightforward implementation of a class to model a rectangle. The constructor takes parameters for the width and height, and the area function calculates the area of the rectangle by multiplying them together.

Now, take a look at `class.Square.php`, shown here:

```php
<?php
    require_once('class.Rectangle.php');

    class Square extends Rectangle {
        public function __construct($size) {
            $this->height = $size;
            $this->width = $size;
        }

        public function getArea() {
            return pow($this->height, 2);
        }

    }
?>
```

This code overrides both the constructor and the `getArea()` method. For a rectangle to be a square, all four sides must be of the same length. As a result, you need only one parameter for the constructor. If more than one parameter is passed to the function, any values after the first parameter are ignored.

> *PHP does not raise an error if the number of parameters passed to a user-defined function is greater than the number of parameters established in the function declaration. In a few cases, this is actually desired behavior. If you'd like to learn more, see the PHP documentation of the built-in* `func_get_args()` *function.*

The `getArea()` function also was overridden. The implementation in the `Rectangle` class would have returned a perfectly correct result for the `Square` objects. The method was overridden to improve application performance (although, in this case, the performance benefit is minuscule).

It is faster for PHP to fetch one property and compute its square than to fetch two properties and multiply them together.

By overriding constructors, destructors, and methods, you can alter aspects of how subclasses operate.

Preserving the Parent's Functionality

Sometimes you want to preserve the functionality provided by the parent. You don't need to completely override the function; you just need to add something to it. You could copy all the code from the parent method into the subclass's method, but as you've already seen, OOP offers you better ways of doing this than just copying lines of code.

To call the functionality provided by the parent, use the syntax parent::[function name]. When you just want to add additional behavior to a method, first you call parent::[function name] and then add your additional code. When extending a function in this way, always call the method on the parent before doing anything else. Doing so ensures that any changes to the operation of the parent won't break your code.

> Because the parent class may be expecting the object to be in a certain state, or may alter the state of the object, overwrite property values, or manipulate the object's internal data, always invoke the parent method before adding your own code when extending an inherited method.

The following example has two classes: Customer and SweepstakesCustomer. A supermarket has an application that, from time to time, switches which class is being used in the cash register application when certain promotions are run. Each customer who comes in has his or her own ID value (which comes from a database), as well as a customer number (which indicates how many customers have come to the supermarket before him or her). For these sweepstakes, the millionth customer wins a prize.

Create a file called class.Customer.php and add the following code:

```php
<?php

    class Customer {
    public $id;
    public $customerNumber;
    public $name;

    public function __construct($customerID) {
       //fetch customer infomation from the database
       //
       //We're hard coding these values here, but in a real application
       //these values would come from a database
       $data = array();
       $data['customerNumber'] = 1000000;
       $data['name'] = 'Jane Johnson';

       //Assign the values from the database to this object
       $this->id = $customerID;
       $this->name = $data['name'];
       $this->customerNumber = $data['customerNumber'];
    }
  }
?>
```

Now create a file called `class.SweepstakesCustomer.php` and enter this code:

```php
<?php
  require_once('class.Customer.php');

  class SweepstakesCustomer extends Customer {
    public function __construct($customerID) {
      parent::__construct($customerID);

      if($this->customerNumber == 1000000) {
        print "Congratulations $this->name! You're our " .
"millionth customer!" .
               "You win a year's supply of frozen fish sticks! ";
      }

    }

  }
?>
```

How Inheritance Works

The `Customer` class initializes values from the database based on the customer ID. You would most likely retrieve the customer ID from a loyalty program swipe card such as the type available at most larger grocery store chains. With the customer ID, you can fetch the customer's personal data from the database (just hard-coded in this example), along with an integer value representing how many customers have entered the store before that customer. Store all this information in public member variables.

The `SweepstakesCustomer` class adds a bit of extra functionality to the constructor. You first invoke the parent class's constructor functionality by calling `parent::_construct` and passing to it the parameters it expects. You then look at the `customerNumber` property. If this number is the millionth, you inform this customer that he or she has won a prize.

To see how to use this class, create a file called `testCustomer.php` and enter the following code:

```php
<?php

  require_once('class.SweepstakesCustomer.php');
  //since this file already includes class.Customer.php, there's
  //no need to pull that file in, as well.

  function greetCustomer(Customer $objCust) {
    print "Welcome back to the store $objCust->name!";
  }

  //Change this value to change the class used to create this customer object
  $promotionCurrentlyRunning = true;
  if ($promotionCurrentlyRunning) {
```

```
    $objCust = new SweepstakesCustomer(1000000);
  } else {
    $objCust = new Customer(1000000);
  }

  greetCustomer($objCust);

?>
```

Run `testCustomer.php` in your browser with the `$promotionCurrentlyRunning` variable set first to `false` and then to `true`. When the value is `true`, the prize message is displayed.

Interfaces

Sometimes you have a group of classes that are not necessarily related through an inheritance-type relationship. You may have totally different classes that just happen to share some behaviors in common. For example, both a jar and a door can be opened and closed, but they are in no other way related. No matter the kind of jar or the kind of door, they both can carry out these activities, but there is no other common thread between them.

What Interfaces Do

You see this same concept in OOP as well. An *interface* enables you to specify that an object is capable of performing a certain function, but it does not necessarily tell you how the object does so. An interface is a contract between unrelated objects to perform a common function. An object that implements this interface is guaranteeing to its users that it is capable of performing all the functions defined by the interface specification. Bicycles and footballs are totally different things, but objects representing those items in a sporting goods store inventory system must be capable of interacting with that system.

By declaring an interface and then implementing it in your objects, you can hand completely different classes to common functions. The following example demonstrates the rather prosaic door-and-jar analogy.

Create a file called `interface.Openable.php`:

```php
<?php

  interface Openable {
    public function open();
    public function close();
  }

?>
```

Just as you name your class files `class.[class name].php`, you should use the same convention with interfaces and call them `interface.[interface name].php`.

You declare the interface `Openable` using a syntax similar to that of a class, except that you substitute the word `interface` for the word `class`. An interface does not have member variables, and it does not specify an implementation of any of its member functions.

Because no implementation is specified, you declare these functions to be `abstract`. Doing so tells PHP that any class implementing this interface is responsible for providing an implementation of the functions. If you fail to provide an implementation of *all* the abstract methods of an interface, PHP will raise a run-time error. You may not selectively choose some of the abstract methods to implement; you must provide implementations of them all.

How Interfaces Work

The `Openable` interface is a contract with other parts of the application that says any class implementing this interface will provide two methods, called `open()` and `close()`, that take no parameters. With this agreed-upon set of methods, you can allow very different objects to pass into the same function without the need for an inherited relationship to exist between them.

Create the following file, called `class.Door.php`:

```php
<?php

require_once('interface.Openable.php');

class Door implements Openable {

    private $_locked = false;

    public function open() {
      if($this->_locked) {
        print "Can't open the door. It's locked.";
      } else {
        print "creak...<br>";
      }
    }

    public function close() {
      print "Slam!!<br>";
    }

    public function lockDoor() {
      $this->_locked = true;
    }
    public function unlockDoor() {
      $this->_locked = false;
    }

  }
?>
```

Now create a file called `class.Jar.php`:

```php
<?
require_once('interface.Openable.php');

class Jar implements Openable {
  private $contents;
  public function __construct($contents) {
```

```
      $this->contents = $contents;
   }

   public function open() {
      print "the jar is now open<br>";
   }

   public function close() {
      print "the jar is now closed<br>";
   }
}
?>
```

To use these files, create a new file called `testOpenable.php` in the same directory:

```
<?php
   require_once('class.Door.php');
   require_once('class.Jar.php');

   function openSomething(Openable $obj) {
      $obj->open();
   }

   $objDoor = new Door();
   $objJar = new Jar("jelly");

   openSomething($objDoor);
   openSomething($objJar);
?>
```

Because both the `Door` class and the `Jar` class implement the `Openable` interface, you can pass both to the `openSomething()` function. Because that function accepts only something that implements the `Openable` interface, you know that you can call the functions `open()` and `close()` within it. However, you should not attempt to access the `contents` property of the `Jar` class or utilize the `lock()` or `unlock()` functions of the `Door` class within the `openSomething()` function, because that property and those methods are not part of the interface. The interface contract guarantees that you have `open()` and `close()` and nothing else.

By using interfaces in your application, you can allow completely different and unrelated objects to talk to each other with a guarantee that they will be able to interact on the terms specified in the interface. The interface is a contract to provide certain methods.

Encapsulation

As mentioned earlier in this chapter, objects enable you to hide the details of their implementation from users of the object. You do not need to know whether the `Volunteer` class mentioned earlier stores information in a database, a flat text file, an XML document, or another data-storage mechanism in order to be able to invoke the `signUp()` method. Similarly, you do not need to know whether the information about the volunteer contained within the object is implemented as single variables, an array, or even other objects.

This ability to hide the details of implementation is known as *encapsulation*. Generally speaking, encapsulation refers to two concepts: protecting a class's internal data from code outside that class, and hiding the details of implementation.

The word *encapsulate* literally means to place in a capsule, or outer container. A well-designed class provides a complete outer shell around its internals, and presents an interface to code outside the class that is wholly separated from the particulars of those internals. By doing so, you gain two advantages:

❑ You can change the implementation details at any time without affecting code that uses your class.

❑ Because you know that nothing outside your class can inadvertently modify the state or property values of an object built from your class without your knowledge, you can trust the state of the object and the value of its properties to be valid and to make sense.

The member variables of a class and its functions have a visibility. *Visibility* refers to what can be seen by code outside the class. As mentioned earlier in this chapter, *private* member variables and functions are not accessible to code outside the class and are used for the class's internal implementation. *Protected* member variables and functions are visible only to the subclasses of the class. *Public* member variables and functions are usable by any code, inside or outside the class.

Generally speaking, all internal member variables of a class should be declared private. Any access needed to those variables by code outside the class should be done through an accessor method. You don't let someone who wants you to try a new food blindfold and force-feed you; you need to be able to examine the item and determine whether you want to allow it into your body. Similarly, when an object wants to allow code outside it to change properties or in some other way affect its internal data, by encapsulating access to that data in a public function (and by keeping the internal data private), you have the opportunity to validate the changes and accept or reject them.

For example, if you are building an application for a bank that handles details of customer accounts, you might have an `Account` object with a property called `totalBalance` and methods called `makeDeposit()` and `makeWithdrawal()`. The total balance property should be read-only. The only way to affect the balance is to make a withdrawal or a deposit. If the `totalBalance` property were to be implemented as a public member variable, you could write code that would increase the value of that variable without having to actually make a deposit. This approach, obviously, would be bad for the bank.

Instead, you should implement this property as a private member variable and provide a public method called `getTotalBalance()`, which returns the value of that private member variable. Because the variable storing the value of the account balance is private, you can't manipulate it directly; and because the only public methods that affect the account balance are `makeWithdrawal()` and `makeDeposit()`, you have to actually make a deposit if you want to increase the value of your account.

By allowing you to hide the details of implementation and protect access to internal member variables, an object-oriented software development approach gives you a flexible, stable application.

> *Encapsulation of internal data and method implementations enables an object-oriented software system to protect and control access to data and hide the details of implementation.*

Changes to OO in PHP 6

Support for objects in PHP goes all the way back to PHP 3. There was never any intention of supporting the idea of classes or objects, but some limited support was added, almost as an afterthought, to provide "syntactic sugar" (to use Zeev Suraski's phrase) for associative arrays. Object support in PHP was originally designed as a convenient way of grouping data and functions, but only a small subset of the features traditionally associated with a full-blown object-oriented programming language was included. As PHP grew in popularity, the use of an OO approach became increasingly common in large applications. However, the poor internal implementation became limiting.

Most notably, there was no support for real encapsulation. You could not specify member variables or methods to be private or protected. Everything was public — which, as you've seen, can be problematic.

Additionally, there was no support for abstract interfaces or methods. Methods and member variables could not be declared static. There were no destructors. All these concepts are familiar to anyone with a background in another OOP language, and the lack of these features in PHP's object model could make the transition from a language such as Java (which does support all these ideas) to PHP difficult. For those who have previous experience with PHP 4, Table 1-1 lists some of the new features in the PHP

Table 1-1: Object Model Evolution from PHP 4 to PHP 5 and 6

New Feature	Benefit
Private, protected member variables and methods	Real encapsulation and data protection are now possible in PHP.
Improved dereferencing support	Statements such as `$obj->getSomething()->doSomething()` are now possible.
Static member variables and methods	Methods that can be called statically are now clearly identifiable. Class-level constants help control pollution of the global namespace.
Unified constructors	All class constructors are now called `__construct()`. This helps with encapsulation of overridden subclass constructors, and makes it easier to alter inheritance when multiple classes are involved in a tree of inheritance.
Destructor support	Through the `__destruct()` method, classes in PHP can now have destructors. This feature allows actions to be carried out when the object is destroyed.
Support for abstract classes and interfaces	You can define required methods in a parent class while deferring implementation to a subclass. Abstract classes can't be instantiated; only their non-abstract subclasses can.
Parameter type hints	You can specify the class for function parameters that are expecting an object. `function foo(Bar $objBar) {...` allows you to be sure that the data type of the parameter is what you expect.

object model that appeared starting in PHP 5. For those already familiar with OOP in PHP 5, little has changed in version 6.

Summary

In this chapter, you explored the concept of object-oriented programming (OOP). A class was shown as a blueprint for creating objects. Objects are run-time bundles of data and functions created from a class definition. They have characteristics, called *properties*, and behaviors, called *methods*. Properties can be thought of as variables, and methods as functions.

Some classes share a common parent type. For example, squares (children) are a type of rectangle (parent). When you declare a class to be a subtype of a parent class, it inherits the methods and properties of the parent. You have the option to override inherited methods. You can completely re-implement the method, if you so choose, or continue to use the parent's implementation but also add specializations particular to the subclass (or not override the method at all).

Encapsulation is an important concept to OOP. It refers to the capability of a class to protect access to its internal member variables and shield users of that class from the particulars of its implementation. Member methods and properties have three levels of visibility: private, protected, and public. Private members can be used only by the class's internal operations. Protected members are visible to subclasses. Public members can be used by code outside the class.

Object-oriented (OO) support in PHP received a major overhaul with the introduction of PHP 5 and the Zend Engine 2. New features and significant performance improvements since PHP version 5, and further enhanced in PHP 6, make PHP a real OOP language.

Chapter 2 discusses the Unified Modeling Language (UML), a system for diagramming OO software architecture that will provide you with the tools for describing and planning the architecture of even the most complex applications.

Unified Modeling Language (UML)

2

If you're the only programmer working on a small project, drawing a small sketch of the application on paper or keeping the design completely in your mind is often sufficient. A solo programmer can usually complete a project without any problems this way.

Suppose, however, that you were to get a larger project requiring two developers. You're the one who's responsible for designing the system, and the second developer is there to help you write the code. How would you communicate the design of this system to the other person? You could describe in words what classes were necessary, and provide a description of how the system functions both for the end user and internally. After a while, you might end up with a lot of text describing the system. If you imagine a larger project, it quickly becomes clear that describing a large software system purely in words is not practical; and if you created diagrams of your own design, then you would have the added task of explaining your system of notation to the other members of the team.

The Unified Modeling Language (UML) was designed to solve this problem. UML is primarily a language of standardized diagrams, each of which lends itself to describing a particular area of software design. UML gives everyone the same way of "speaking" about a system, and provides a powerful method of visualizing it.

In this chapter, you'll work through the design and development of a hypothetical band-tracking system called BandSpy. In the process, you'll learn about UML diagrams and where they fit into the process.

Requirements Gathering

Here's the hypothetical scenario for this chapter. A client from a record company has contacted you to develop a Web-based system to track the bands that the client represents. During an initial phone conversation, the client explains that BandSpy should enable Web users to view details about the different bands the company represents, and check out upcoming concerts. Someone from the record company should be able to add new bands to the system, edit existing band information, and book new concert performances for the bands. Although your conversation with the client is informal, it begins a key part of the software design: the *requirements-gathering* phase. In this phase, you'll want to determine exactly what the software needs to do to satisfy its users.

Interviewing the Client

Speaking on the phone, you arrange to meet with the client. After some quality get-to-know-you time, the meeting progresses to a further discussion of the system. The attendees of the meeting are Bill (the owner of the company), Jane (the operations manager), and Tom (the company "computer guy").

During your initial interviews, getting a feel for the roles of the people who are involved is important. You can infer that the people attending the meeting have some interest in how the software works. That interest, however, may or may not always be beneficial to the outcome of the project.

The key person to identify during requirements gathering is the person who has detailed knowledge of the *domain* — the area that the software will model. That could include someone who previously did manually what the software will now automate, or it could be someone who knows how the business works and what the software must do to correctly model it. This person is often referred to as a *domain expert*.

Over the course of the interview, Jane does most of the talking. She describes what they're hoping the system can accomplish and how the company currently handles this process. It's a good bet that Jane is your domain expert. During further interviews, speaking to her directly will be useful. Bill stays quiet most of the time; he probably has other matters to attend to. Tom mentions that he'll be the one actually entering the data into the system. You note that you may have to devote a little time to explaining the use of the administration tools to him.

During the course of the meeting you take notes on what Jane says the system must do, and you come out with the following list:

❑   Users can visit the BandSpy Web site and browse information about bands. Band information includes the type of band, musicians in the band, and what instruments they play.

❑   Users can view information about upcoming performances that might include one or multiple bands.

❑   A site administrator can add new information about bands.

❑   A site administrator can edit existing band information.

❑   A site administrator can add a new performance. Adding a new performance includes booking a venue and generating tickets. Separate third-party companies handle both the venue booking and the tickets. These companies have reservation systems that you will need to notify via the BandSpy software.

Now that you have a list of requirements, it's time to start putting the UML diagrams to work.

Use Case Diagrams

Use case diagrams show the system from the task-oriented perspective of a user. One use case represents a task the user is trying to accomplish with the system. Figure 2-1 shows a very simple use case diagram for users visiting the BandSpy site and browsing band information.

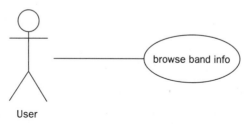

Figure 2-1: A simple use case diagram

The stick figure is called an *actor*, and the bubble is the *use case*. The line indicates that this actor can perform the connected use case. In use case diagrams, the actor is usually a role associated with a person, although it can represent an external system that acts upon your system.

Notice that the use case "browse band info" is rather general. A high level of detail isn't necessary here. You just want to be able to cover all the use cases the system should be capable of handling. If necessary, use cases can be broken down into their separate *scenarios*. A scenario is the sequence of steps comprising the use case. For example, the scenario for the previous use case is as follows:

1. The user goes to the BandSpy Web site.

2. The user navigates the site using the menu.

3. The user examines band/musician/concert information.

Figure 2-2 shows the use case diagram for the administrative tasks.

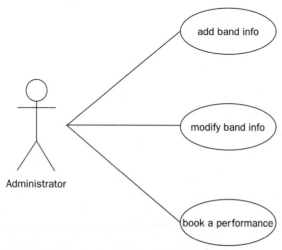

Figure 2-2: Use case diagram for the administrator tasks

The administrative use cases are the separate tasks that the administrator might attempt when using the BandSpy system. The client has mentioned that he would like the administrative section of the site to require a password-protected login. Because logging into the system can be thought of as a task itself, you can use an `include` to show that this use case is part of all three other use cases. Figure 2-3 shows the use of an `include`, indicated by a dashed line.

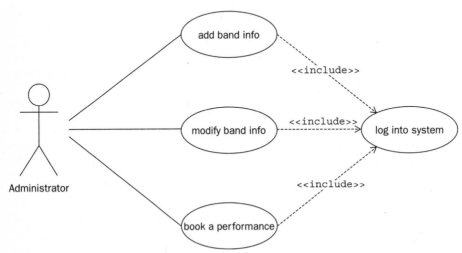

Figure 2-3: Indicating an include in a use case diagram

Multiple actors may appear within a use case diagram. Often, different actors may share a use case. Figure 2-4 shows the completed use case diagram for the BandSpy system. Because both the administrator and the regular users can look up band information, they share that use case. Additionally, the use case shows the nonhuman actor (the venue booking system) performing the task of updating information about an upcoming performance.

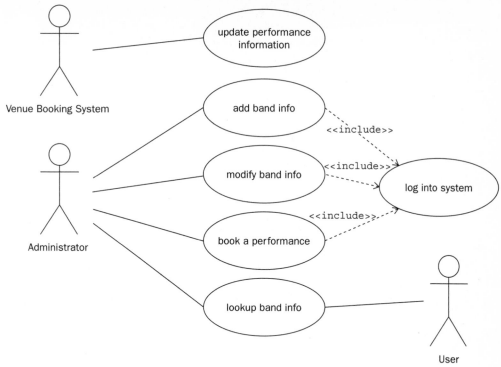

Figure 2-4: Showing multiple actors sharing a common task

Class Diagrams

Although the use case diagrams provide a useful way to express what capabilities the system will have for various actors, they do little to explain the inner workings of the software. This is the point at which you can start using the other UML diagrams, as well as your knowledge of objects, to define those inner workings in more detail.

Modeling the Domain

After the interviews with the client are complete, and the use cases have been finalized, you can move on to the process of designing the software to model the domain. One thing that this means is developing the system so that its classes are closely modeled after what they represent in real life. For instance, in this example application, users can see information about different types of musicians, so it's probably a good idea to have a Musician class or, even better, a Musician interface that all different types of musicians can implement.

Class diagrams are probably the most important diagrams to use and understand. They provide a good balance of detail and flexibility. They provide a description of the domain you're modeling, and allow a varying level of detail — from a very high level to very specific — about the exact methods and properties of a class. In addition, they're useful for describing interesting object-oriented (OO) concepts such as design patterns, which are covered in Chapter 4.

Figure 2-5 shows the basics of a class diagram. The top box in the rectangle shows the name of the class. The middle box shows its *attributes,* and the bottom box shows its *operations.* In PHP, the terms "attributes" and "operations" translate to member variables and methods, respectively, in the Musician class.

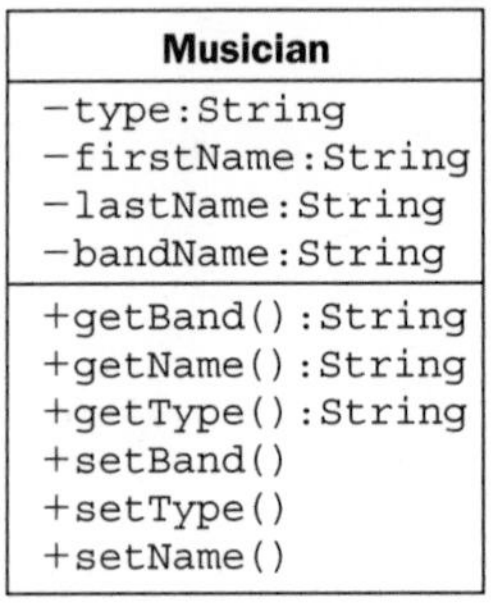

Musician
−type:String −firstName:String −lastName:String −bandName:String
+getBand():String +getName():String +getType():String +setBand() +setType() +setName()

Figure 2-5: A class diagram

The attribute types are indicated after the colon. In this simple example, all the attribute types are strings. The minus sign (−) says that the attributes are private members of the class. The plus sign (+) in front of the operations indicates that they are public. If an operation returns a value, its type is shown after the colon. Again, in this example, they are all strings.

The following is the PHP code for Musician shown in the class diagram. Type this into a file called class.Musician.php:

```php
class Musician {

    private $last;
    private $first;
    private $bandName;
    private $type;

    function __construct($last, $first, $musicianType) {
            $this->last = $last;
            $this->first = $first;
            $this->type = $musicianType;
    }

    public function getName() {
            echo $this->first . $this->last;
    }

    public function getBand() {
            echo $this->bandName;
    }

    public function getMusicanType() {
            echo $this->type;
    }

    public function setName($first, $last) {
            $this->first = $first;
```

```
            $this->last = $last;
    }

    public function setBand($bandName) {
            $this->bandName = $bandName;
    }
    public function setMusicianType($musicianType) {
            $this->type = $musicianType;
    }
}
```

Relationships

If your application had only one class, it might not be particularly helpful to draw diagrams. Because the BandSpy system requires more than one class, you must think about how the objects will interact with one another. In the previous example, strings were used as the data type for all the member variables. Generally, this is not a good idea. If a musician were a part of a band, then it would make sense that you would want more than just the name of the band. For example, you might want the other members of the band, what genre of music they play, and so on. This type of thinking will guide you during the design phase of your software. Certain member variables will require a higher degree of complexity, and therefore must be broken out into their own classes.

Associations

If you take a look at Figure 2-6, you can see that the bandName attribute moved over into an attribute of the Band class. In addition, note that this diagram does not show every attribute and method in the classes.

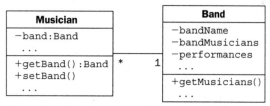

Figure 2-6: Associating the Musician and Band classes

When using class diagrams, you need to show only what is important in the context of the diagram. Simple accessor methods for private member variables are assumed, and hence left out. When a class diagram is incomplete, you can use ellipses (. . .) to show that certain information is intentionally omitted.

The line connecting the two classes is a type of relationship known as an *association*. For this example, the association is one-to-many — one Band may have many Musicians, or, conversely, many Musicians can be in one Band, as denoted by the * and 1 beneath the association.

The association line can also show *navigability*. In this example, the line without any arrowheads shows that you can move in both directions, also known as *bi-directional navigability*. In other words, each class has an internal reference to the other one. If the association allows you to navigate in only one direction, it is referred to as *unidirectional navigability*. Figure 2-7 shows the relationship between the Musician class and the Instrument class. The Musician class has access to any Instruments in its internal collection, but the Instrument is not aware of which Musician possesses it.

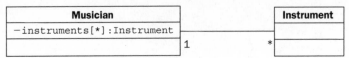

Figure 2-7: Unidirectional navigability

Realizations and Generalizations

As mentioned previously, creating a `Musician` interface that all other musician type classes could implement would be a better idea. This way, you can derive other classes (such as `Guitarist` and `Drummer`) that follow the rules governing how `Musician` behaves in your system. As long as you follow the contract of the `Musician` interface, you can have confidence that your derived classes will play along correctly.

When you want to indicate an interface and the classes that implement it, you show a relationship between them called a *realization*. A dashed line shows a realization, with a hollow arrowhead at the end pointing to the interface. Interfaces in UML diagrams are similar to standard class diagrams, but are shown using the word *interface* in guillemots above the interface name. Figure 2-8 displays two classes, `Drummer` and `Guitarist`, implementing the `Musician` interface.

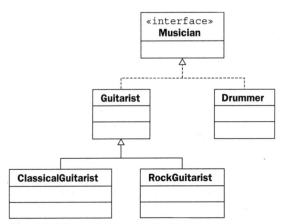

Figure 2-8: Indicating generalization and realization

When you want to indicate inheritance either from an abstract class or from another concrete one, you can use a generalization. A *generalization* is identical to a realization, except that the line is not dashed. Figure 2-8 also shows the subclassing of `Guitarist` to create the `RockGuitarist` and `ClassicalGuitarist` classes.

Composites

Often, the useful relationships of classes are not based on associations or inheritance, but rather on the way classes are grouped. Consider the example of a drum set. In this example application, the `Instrument` interface is implemented in a concrete class such as `Guitar` or `Piano`, as shown in Figure 2-9. In addition, the `DrumSet`, `Drum`, and `Cymbal` classes implement it as well. The new notation of the lines with the black diamonds indicates that the `DrumSet` is a *composite* of the `Drum` and `Cymbal` classes. One instance of `DrumSet` will contain instances of the `Drum` and `Cymbal` classes.

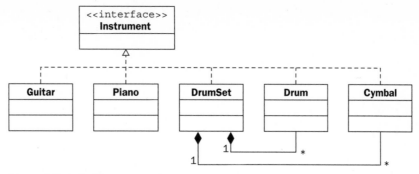

Figure 2-9: Indicating composites

A composite is a strict relationship characterized by two rules. First, the parts of a composite may not be shared elsewhere. In other words, an instance of Drum belonging to an instance of DrumSet may not belong to any other DrumSet. The second rule is that when an instance of DrumSet is deleted, its composite parts should also be deleted.

A more general type of composite is called an *aggregate*. The notation for an aggregate is the same as a composite, except that the diamond is hollow. Aggregates are allowed to share instances of other classes, and therefore are not required to delete them when they themselves are deleted.

Implementation

Now that you've covered the basics of class diagrams, take a look at a bit of sample code based on some of the concepts just covered. Save all of this code into a single file called test_music.php:

```php
<?php

interface Band {
    public function getName();
    public function getGenre();
    public function addMusician(Musician $musician);
    public function getMusicians();
}

interface Musician {
    public function addInstrument(Instrument $instrument);
    public function getInstruments();
    public function assignToBand(Band $band);
    public function getMusicianType();
}

interface Instrument {
    public function getName();
    public function getCategory();
}

class Guitarist implements Musician {
    private $last;
```

```php
    private $first;
    private $musicianType;
    private $instruments;
    private $bandReference;

    function __construct($first, $last) {
      $this->last = $last;
      $this->first = $first;
      $this->instruments = array();
      $this->musicianType = "guitarist";
    }

    public function getName() {
      return $this->first . " " . $this->last;
    }

    public function addInstrument(Instrument $instrument) {
      array_push($this->instruments, $instrument);
    }

    public function getInstruments() {
      return $this->instruments;
    }

  public function getBand() {
      return $this->bandReference;
  }

  public function assignToBand(Band $band) {
    $this->bandReference = $band;
  }

  public function getMusicianType() {
      return $this->musicianType;
  }

  public function setMusicianType($musicianType) {
    $this->musicianType = $musicianType;
  }

}

class LeadGuitarist extends Guitarist {
  function __construct($last, $first) {
        parent::__construct($last, $first);
        $this->setMusicianType("lead guitarist");
  }
}

class RockBand implements Band {
  private $bandName;
  private $bandGenre;
  private $musicians;
```

```php
    function __construct($bandName) {
      $this->bandName = $bandName;
      $this->musicians = array();
      $this->bandGenre = "rock";
    }

  public function getName() {
      return $this->bandName;
  }

  public function getGenre(){
      return $this->bandGenre;
  }

  public function addMusician(Musician $musician){
      array_push($this->musicians, $musician);
      $musician->assignToBand($this);
  }

  public function getMusicians() {
      return $this->musicians;
  }
}

class Guitar implements Instrument {

  private $name;
  private $category;

    function __construct($name) {
      $this->name = $name;
      $this->category = "guitar";
    }

  public function getName() {
      return $this->name;
  }

  public function getCategory() {
      return $this->category;
  }
}

// Test Objects
$band = new RockBand("The Variables");
$bandMemberA = new Guitarist("Jack", "Float");
$bandMemberB = new LeadGuitarist("Jim", "Integer");

$bandMemberA->addInstrument(new Guitar("Gibson Les Paul"));
$bandMemberB->addInstrument(new Guitar("Fender Stratocaster"));
$bandMemberB->addInstrument(new Guitar("Hondo H-77"));
```

```
$band->addMusician($bandMemberA);
$band->addMusician($bandMemberB);

foreach($band->getMusicians() as $musician) {
  echo "Musician ".$musician->getName() . "<br>";
  echo "is the " . $musician->getMusicianType() . "<br>";
  echo "in the " . $musician->getBand()->getGenre() . " band <br>";
  echo "called " . $musician->getBand()->getName() .. "<br>";

  foreach($musician->getInstruments() as $instrument) {
    echo "And plays the " . $instrument->getName() . " ";
    echo $instrument->getCategory() . "<br>";
  }
  echo "<p>";
}
?>
```

Although this example is fairly simple, it illustrates an important aspect of object-oriented programming (OOP). Notice how no conditional branching occurs when the objects are tested at the end. You don't need to find out what type of Musician or Instrument you're dealing with before calling its methods. Because the rules of the interface were followed, you can trust that the objects will all respond appropriately and uniquely to their implementation. As discussed in Chapter 1, this is what's referred to as *polymorphism*. Anytime you need to add another type of Musician, you can just write the new class, defining its behavior behind the standard Musician interface.

Activity Diagrams

Jane mentioned in an earlier meeting that the BandSpy application will need to hook into two other third-party systems — the ticketing system and the venue reservation system — when a new performance is added. To understand the order of events necessary to accomplish this task, you can draw an *activity diagram*. Activity diagrams are good in any situation when you need to understand the flow of activities going on within a use case. In this example, the use case is the BandSpy administrator booking a performance.

Further conversations with Jane reveal that the BandSpy system will have to not only send a message to the venue reservation system, but also receive information back from both systems. The venue system will send a confirmation that the venue is available, and the ticketing system will transmit ticketing information (such as pricing). If the administrator attempts to book a venue on a date or time that is not available, the venue system will indicate that fact to BandSpy. The administrator will be notified and may try to book another date.

Figure 2-10 shows the activity diagram for the process described here. Activity diagrams begin with a solid black circle called the *starting point*. From there, the flow of the process follows the arrows (known as *transitions*) into rounded rectangles representing *activities*.

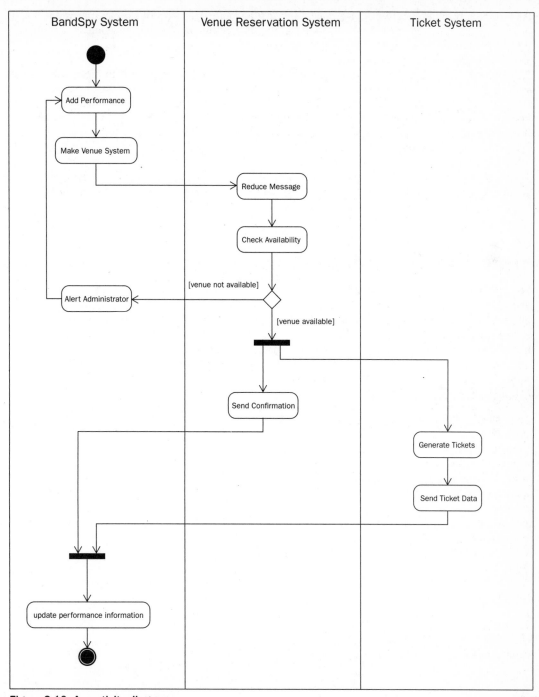

Figure 2-10: An activity diagram

A black hollow diamond indicates a *decision point*. As the name suggests, the flow of transitions is split, based on some decision or condition. In the diagram, the decision is whether the venue is available on the requested date.

After the decision, a large black bar called a *fork* splits the flow to two different activities. In the venue system, a confirmation is generated and sent back to the BandSpy system, where the ticket system is fired up to start generating tickets for the event. Information from both the ticket system and the venue system is sent back to BandSpy, where it meets up in another black bar called a *join*. The join indicates that both external systems messages must reach the join for the activity diagram to proceed to its final step: storing and updating information about the new performance.

The three large rectangles dividing the activities particular to each system are called *swimlanes*. Although swimlanes are not mandatory, they often help to clarify the diagram when multiple systems are involved.

Sequence Diagrams

You may have noticed that the BandSpy application has a hierarchy of classes. `Band` classes contain `Musicians` that have `Instruments` that may be composites of other `Instruments`. During the use of the application, messages are relayed through the object relationships. You can think of method calls as a kind of message that one object might call on another. For example, if an instance of `Band` needed to know what `Instruments` its `Musicians` were playing, it would send a message to call `getInstruments()` to all its `Musicians`. Another way of saying this is that `Band` is calling the `getInstruments()` method on all its `Musicians`.

It's useful to visualize how messages move between different objects, and UML provides another diagram that's designed to represent that movement: the *sequence diagram.*

Sequence diagrams can usually be tied to an individual use case. The previous discussion on use cases contained a general "browse band info" use case. To illustrate the sequence diagram, you can break the "browse band info" use case down into more specific cases. Figure 2-11 shows some more specific use cases for the "User" actor.

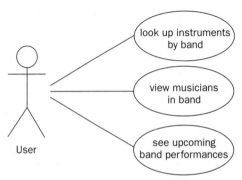

Figure 2-11: More specific use cases for the User

For the "lookup instruments by band" use case, the sequence diagram should show all the objects involved and the messages passed between them to complete the tasks. Figure 2-12 shows the sequence diagram.

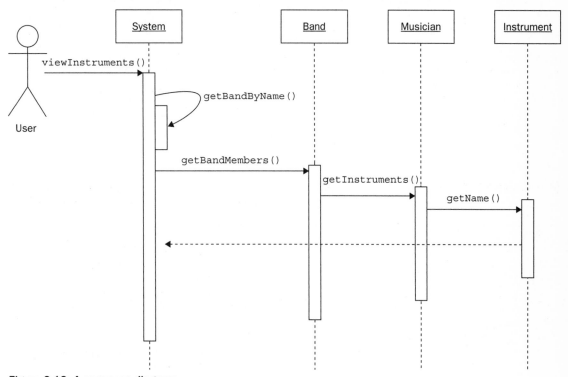

Figure 2-12: A sequence diagram

The boxes at the top show the instances of objects involved in the sequence. In general, a box with an underlined name denotes an instance, rather than a class. The dashed line descending from the object is the object's *lifeline*. In this case, the lifeline doesn't indicate the creation or deletion of any of your objects — before this use case was acted upon, all the objects were already there. However, it is possible to indicate the instantiation of an object by using a "create" message and a large X at the bottom of the object's lifeline to show its deletion.

The vertical rectangle shows the object's *activation* — that is, the time during which the object is involved in the execution of a particular operation. Time in this case is represented vertically, so the longer an object's activation (denoted by the length of the rectangle that represents it), the longer it is involved in the operation.

Another object in the application, the System object, is introduced in this diagram. In the BandSpy application, the System object will receive all messages from the Web GUI, rather than allow it to interact directly with your other objects. This way, the application has a single point of entry.

Arrows indicate messages. They're named with the corresponding method names of the objects, but it's okay to be less formal about it and just use a non-methodlike name for the message. Taking the messages step by step, the sequence is as follows:

1. A user requests to see all instruments of a particular band by typing in the band's name.

2. The `System` object looks up the band reference by performing a *self-call* on its own utility method.

3. The `System` object uses the found band reference and calls the `getBandMembers` method on it.

4. The `Band` object calls the `getInstruments` method of its assigned musicians.

5. The `Musician` object calls the `getName` method on each of its assigned instruments.

6. The `Instrument` names are returned to the system object for display to the user.

State Diagrams

State diagrams are handy when you want to show the changes to a single object's state during its life cycle. State changes can be simple differences in member variables, or more complex behavior such as polling for a response from an external source.

In BandSpy, the `Performance` class has a life cycle that's worth documenting with a state diagram. When a new `Performance` object is created, it must contact the venue reservation system and await a confirmation. If the response from the venue system says the reservation is good, the performance must be permanently stored. If the reservation is not accepted, the `Performance` object should inform the system and then be destroyed. In Figure 2-13, a state diagram shows the various states for the object.

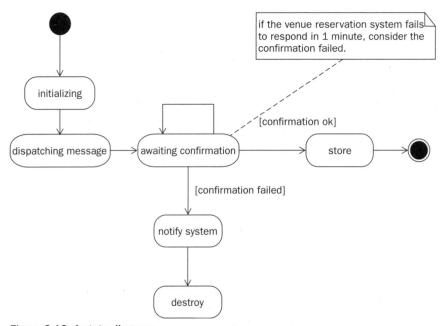

Figure 2-13: A state diagram

The solid circle shows the start of the object's life cycle, and arrows indicate transitions from one state to another. After the new `Performance` is initialized and dispatches a message to the venue system, the awaiting confirmation state polls until it receives a message back from the venue system.

One new symbol in Figure 2-13 is a *note* indicating that the awaiting confirmation state should wait one minute to receive a reply from the venue system. A note can be used in any UML diagram where you want to add extra information such as this.

Component and Deployment Diagrams

The last diagram discussed in this chapter is the *component diagram,* which provides a high-level, abstract view of your software. For the BandSpy component diagram, the majority of the code is reduced to a single component on the Web server. Technically, elements such as the Web server are parts of another UML diagram called a *deployment diagram.* Deployment diagrams show some of the physical elements of your application's infrastructure (such as the different servers on which your application runs).

In Figure 2-14, the large cube-shaped boxes are called *nodes.* Think of a node as a separate piece of physical hardware, or, in a more conceptual sense, as a defined, separate system of software such as a Web browser.

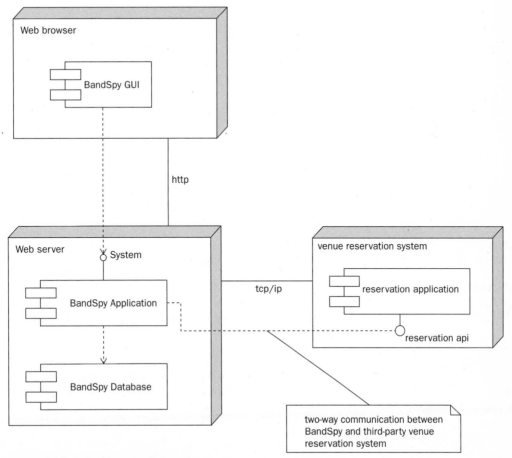

Figure 2-14: A deployment diagram

The components are the smaller rectangles within the nodes. Dashed arrows are *dependencies*. The BandSpy Web GUI is dependent upon the BandSpy application on the Web server. The reverse is not true, however; another client could access the system. Solid lines show a connection between nodes — for example, the Web browser communicating over HTTP.

The small circles are a kind of shorthand to show an interface. As mentioned earlier, this example application has a single `System` interface that all clients must use. Another interface is shown within the venue reservation system node. The company that manages the system has provided you with a list of the public methods you can use. You don't need to know any of the inner workings of the venue system; you just need to know the methods of the Application Programming Interface (API) used in the reservation system.

Summary

UML provides you with a standardized, flexible language to design and model your software. This chapter discussed the following UML diagrams:

❑   Use case diagrams

❑   Class diagrams

❑   Activity diagrams

❑   Sequence diagrams

❑   State diagrams

❑   Component and deployment diagrams

You also learned some concepts about software architecture, such as domain modeling and gathering requirements.

Remember, using every diagram is not necessary. The use case and class diagrams are almost always useful, but the other diagrams are not worth drawing for every class or use case in your software. You need an activity diagram only if you want to get a better idea of the processes within a single use case. Use a state diagram if you have an object whose state changes in a complex way during one or more use cases and you need to make clear how it will work. A few sequence diagrams are usually necessary, but don't try to diagram every message passed between every instance in your application.

Chapter 4 discusses software design patterns, which are a way of describing reusable object relationships that you can use to solve various problems in software development. Because each design pattern is described with a UML class diagram, you're in good shape to learn about them when you get to that chapter.

Chapter 3 starts to look at how you actually implement the concepts examined in this chapter and in Chapter 1 to make functioning PHP code. You will be using class diagrams to describe the code you will write, so you'll start to get a sense for how they're used and why they're an important tool to leverage when designing the application architecture.

3

Putting Objects to Work

Now that you have gained a good understanding of object-oriented (OO) basics from Chapter 1, let's push on with a slightly more complex look at how you can build a real application using OO techniques.

The sample application in this chapter is a contact manager that is intended to manage data about individuals and organizations, and to enable users to look up and edit contact information associated with them. The discussion in this chapter is designed to present you with a good grounding in the issues behind creating working OO applications. Along the way, this chapter also demonstrates how the major principles behind the OO paradigm (such as code reuse, encapsulation, inheritance, and, of course, abstraction) can be applied.

Creating the Contact Manager

A contact management application enables the user to track individuals and organizations, their contact information (such as address, e-mail, and phone number), and the relationships between them. This is basically what Microsoft Outlook's address book does.

Here's a quick, high-level description of what you might expect from this sort of program:

❑　The application will track information about individuals and organizations in a database, and display it on a Web page.

❑　Contacts can have zero or more addresses, e-mail addresses, and phone numbers.

❑　An individual has just one employer (an organization).

❑　An organization has zero or more employees (individuals).

You can now take a look at how to begin putting together this solution using UML. One caveat, however, should be made clear before you begin. This chapter demonstrates how, while designing an application, your thinking might evolve as you discover new and better ways of implementing the solution. As a result, the chapter should be read more as a progressive evolution and development of the sample application, rather than as a straightforward listing of its code. A concrete example such as this can help you gain a better understanding of how the principles of object-oriented programming (OOP) work.

The Contact Manager UML Diagrams

Fire up the UML diagramming application of your choice and create a new file called ContactManager.
[extension], where [extension] is the default file extension for your application (for example, .dia for diagrams created using Dia, and so on).

First, create classes for the different kinds of contact information that you want to represent. For this sample application, these are address, e-mail address, and phone number classes — but you could create classes for whatever type of contact information you require. Table 3-1 shows the sample application properties.

Table 3-1 Contact Information Classes

Class	Properties
Address	street1
	street2
	city
	state
	zip (zip code)
	type (home, work, and so on)
Email	email
	type
PhoneNumber	number
	extension
	type

These classes just store and display data, so you don't need to define any methods at this time, and the third sections of the class symbols are empty. The properties are all public, so they're prefixed with a plus sign. Figure 3-1 shows the current UML representation of these classes.

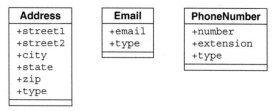

Figure 3-1: Basic contact types

Next, you should map out the `Individual` and `Organization` classes. An individual has a first name, a last name, an employer, a job title, a unique identifier (the `id` field from the database), and a collection (of e-mails, addresses, and phone numbers). You must also be able to add contact types. Figure 3-2 shows the UML diagram with the `Individual` class.

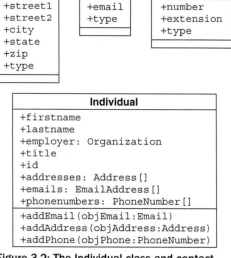

Figure 3-2: The Individual class and contact types

An organization has a name, a unique identifier, collections of contact types (much as an individual does), methods to add them, and a collection of employees. Figure 3-3 shows the UML diagram with the Organization class.

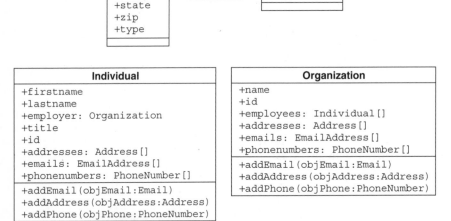

Figure 3-3: The Individual and Organization contact types

The diagram shows the Individual and Organization classes sharing a lot of the same properties and methods. This is generally an indication that you could save yourself a lot of work and improve the flexibility of your application by using inheritance. You can create another class (Entity, in this example) in which you combine the features common to the Individual and Organization classes, and then enable them to share the same code. In a UML diagram, you indicate properties and methods only on the class that actually implements them. In this case, you must move all the common properties and methods of the Individual and Organization classes to the symbol representing the Entity class, as shown in Figure 3-4. You repeat them in the child class (child classes inherit members from their parent classes) only if the child overrides the implementation.

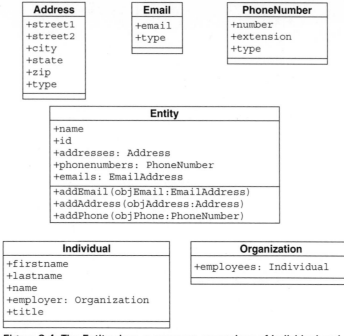

Figure 3-4: The Entity class, a common superclass of Individual and Organization

In this case, the name property of the Entity class is overridden in the Individual class. When you retrieve the name property of an Individual, you'll return "lastname, firstname". This way, you can hand the Organization or Individual classes to a function that will just print a name without having to use separate functions.

UML also defines symbols to indicate relationships. In this example, you need something to show that the Individual and Organization classes inherit from the Entity class. As you have seen, the UML specification calls this relationship *generalization,* and indicates it by an open-headed arrow that points from the child class(es) to the parent class, as shown in Figure 3-5.

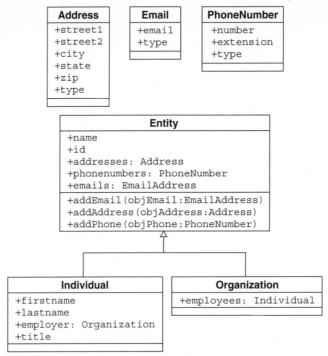

Figure 3-5: Generalization, indicated by an open-headed arrow

Now it's clear that the `Individual` and `Organization` classes inherit from the `Entity` class. Using connectors to indicate inheritance makes it easy to glance at the diagram and see how the classes relate to one another.

There's another type of connection you need to show — the `Entity` class, which uses the `Address`, `Email`, and `PhoneNumber` classes. The UML specification calls this relationship a *composite*, and you indicate it by using a black diamond on the end of the line attached to the user of the class, as shown in Figure 3-6. The classes being used also have a property called *multiplicity* (that is, how many of them are used). In this example, an entity may have zero, one, or more of any of the contact types, so you write `0..*` on the connector line closest to the item being used to indicate that a class may have 0 or more of the class to which it points.

Figure 3-6 also shows that notation. By revealing this relationship in the diagram, you can clearly see which parts of the application will be affected by a change to another part. Here, a change to the `Email`, `Address`, or `PhoneNumber` classes will have an impact on the `Entity`, `Individual`, and `Organization` classes.

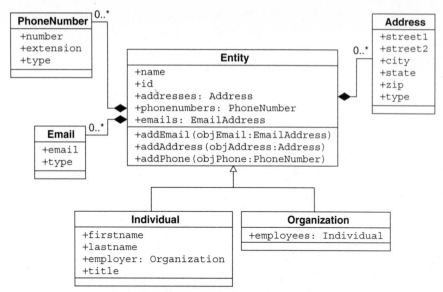

Figure 3-6: Composite, indicated by using a black diamond on the end of the line

An `Entity` has a `PhoneNumber`, an `Email`, and an `Address`; and in all three cases, it may have zero or more of that item. Because `Individual` and `Organization` inherit from `Entity`, both of these also have zero or more of the contact types.

This is the basic structure of the application as understood so far. Of course, you could make plenty of improvements to it by thinking of how you actually begin implementing it in real life. There are a few important points to note regarding this. In the next section, you'll work on the application. More UML is shown a little later in this chapter to give you a clear idea of what the final product looks like.

Recall from the encapsulation discussion in Chapter 1 that it's always a good idea to protect your data in private member variables, and to use accessor methods to provide access to those properties. Also recall that using __get and __set makes this process a bit easier. You can see just by looking at the class diagrams shown earlier in this chapter that all your classes have fairly simple property requirements. Because you know about inheritance and how to use it to your advantage in PHP, you can remove the functionality from being tied to just the `Entity` class, and create a class that will enable you to reuse its code in other classes — in effect, adding another layer of abstraction to facilitate better use of the functions common to all the classes. This parent class will be called `PropertyObject`.

In the real world, you would probably also want to add a layer of abstraction when dealing with data as a matter of good practice. To this end, creating a `DataManager` class is probably a good idea. One more thing to consider is that, at present, you have no unified facility for data validation, so you need an interface for anything that can be validated. Quickly, here's the code for the interface:

```php
<?php
    interface Validator {
       public function validate();
    }
?>
```

Name the file `interface.Validator.php`. Now put it to some use with the new `PropertyObject` class, which is shown in the next section.

The PropertyObject Class

The code that follows shows how to integrate the `Validator` interface with the `PropertyObject` class. Enter the code in a file called `class.PropertyObject.php`:

```php
<?php
require_once('interface.Validator.php');

abstract class PropertyObject implements Validator {

    protected $propertyTable = array();   //stores name/value pairs
                                          //that hook properties to
                                          //database field names
    protected $changedProperties = array(); //List of properties that
                                            //have been modified

    protected $data;                        //Actual data from
                                            //the database

    protected $errors = array();          //Any validation errors
                                          //that might have occurred
    public function __construct($arData) {
        $this->data = $arData;
    }

    public function __get($propertyName) {
        if(!array_key_exists($propertyName, $this->propertyTable)) {
            throw new Exception("Invalid property \"$propertyName\"!");
        }
        if(method_exists($this, 'get' . $propertyName)) {
            return call_user_func(
                    array($this, 'get' . $propertyName));
        } else {
            return $this->data[$this->propertyTable[$propertyName]];
        }
    }

    public function __set($propertyName, $value) {
        if(!array_key_exists($propertyName, $this->propertyTable)) {
            throw new Exception("Invalid property \"$propertyName\"!");
        }
        if(method_exists($this, 'set' . $propertyName)) {
            return call_user_func(
                            array($this, 'set' . $propertyName),
                            $value);
        } else {

            //If the value of the property really has changed
            //and it's not already in the changedProperties array,
            //add it.
```

```
                    if($this->propertyTable[$propertyName] != $value &&
                        !in_array($propertyName, $this->changedProperties)) {
                            $this->changedProperties[] = $propertyName;
                    }
                    //Now set the new value
                    $this->data[$this->propertyTable[$propertyName]] = $value;
            }
        }

    public function validate() {

        }
    }
?>
```

Take a closer look at what's happening here. You've created four protected member variables. Protected member variables are visible only to subclasses of a class; they aren't visible to the code that uses those objects.

$propertyTable will contain a mapping of human-readable property names to field names in your database. A common naming convention for database fields involves the use of a prefix to indicate data type. For example, entities.sname1 might be a field in the table entities of type string, containing the first name. However, sname1 isn't a terribly friendly name for an object property, so it's useful to provide a mechanism to translate database field naming conventions to friendly property names.

$changedProperties is an array that stores a list of the names of the properties that have been modified.

$data will be an associative array of database field names and values. The array will be supplied to the constructor with the data structure coming directly from pgsql_fetch_assoc(). This approach makes constructing a useful object directly from a database query a lot easier, as you'll see shortly.

The last member variable, $errors, will contain an array of field names and error messages in the event that the validate method (required by the Validate interface) should fail.

The class is declared abstract for two reasons. First, the PropertyObject class on its own is not very useful. The classes that extend PropertyObject still have some work to do before you can use its methods. Second, you have not provided an implementation of the required method validate(). Because you are still labeling that method abstract in PropertyObject, you must also label the class itself abstract, forcing all inheriting classes to implement that function. Anything that attempts to use classes that extend PropertyObject, but not implement the function, will cause a run-time error.

Next you see the greatly simplified constructor. The constructor merely accepts the associative array that will most likely be populated from a database query, and assigns it to the protected member variable $data. Most subclasses of PropertyObject will need to override the constructor and do something a little more interesting.

Finally, note the internals of the __get() and __set() accessor methods. Because you are storing data in the $data member, you must be able to map property names to the actual field names in the database. The lines containing the following code are doing just that:

```
$this->data[$this->propertyTable[$propertyName]]
```

By fetching and assigning values to the $data member using their database field names, rather than their property names, you are implementing a form of data persistence.

If the workings of the $data and $propertyTable members aren't clear to you yet, don't worry. They will be as soon as you see an example.

The Contact Type Classes

Now that you have the PropertyObject class, you can start putting it to some use. The files that follow are for the Address, Email, and PhoneNumber classes.

In the code, you'll see a reference to a class called DataManager, which will be a wrapper class for all the database functions you need to use. This wrapper enables you to have one central place for all your data-interaction code. You'll examine that class very soon.

Enter the code that follows (the Address class) into a file called class.Address.php:

```php
<?php
  require_once('class.PropertyObject.php');

  class Address extends PropertyObject {

    function __construct($addressid) {
      $arData = DataManager::getAddressData($addressid);

      parent::__construct($arData);

      $this->propertyTable['addressid'] = 'addressid';
      $this->propertyTable['id'] = 'addressid';
      $this->propertyTable['entityid'] = 'entityid';
      $this->propertyTable['address1'] = 'saddress1';
      $this->propertyTable['address2'] = 'saddress2';
      $this->propertyTable['city'] = 'scity';
      $this->propertyTable['state'] = 'cstate';
      $this->propertyTable['zipcode'] = 'spostalcode';
      $this->propertyTable['type'] = 'stype';
    }

  function validate() {
    if(strlen($this->state) != 2) {
      $this->errors['state'] = 'Please choose a valid state.';
    }

    if(strlen($this->zipcode) != 5 &&
       strlen($this->zipcode) != 10) {
        $this->errors['zipcode'] = 'Please enter a 5- or 9-digit zip code';
    }

    if(!$this->address1) {
        $this->errors['address1'] = 'Address 1 is a required field.';
    }
```

```
        if(!$this->city) {
            $this->errors['city'] = 'City is a required field.';
        }

        if(sizeof($this->errors)) {
          return false;
          } else {
            return true;
          }
        }

    function __toString() {
        return $this->address1 . ', ' .
                $this->address2 . ', ' .
                $this->city . ', ' .
                $this->state . ' ' . $this->zipcode;
    }


}

?>
```

Because the `PropertyObject` class took care of so much of the work, only two methods in the `Address` class needed to be implemented (a `__toString()` implementation was thrown in just for fun). In the constructor, you see for the first time how the `$propertyTable` array works. The list of properties required in the class was specified in the `Address` class UML diagram created during the initial architecture of the application (in the beginning of this chapter).

Based on the properties of this object, you can also make some decisions about the structure of the database table. Generally, you need one field for each property; and because this class has to relate back to the `Entity` class, you need to store some reference to the parent `Entity`. Use the following SQL statement to create the `Entity` and `Address` tables:

```sql
CREATE TABLE "entity" (
  "entityid" SERIAL PRIMARY KEY NOT NULL,
  "name1" varchar(100) NOT NULL,
  "name2" varchar(100) NOT NULL,
   "type" char(1) NOT NULL
);

CREATE TABLE "entityaddress" (
  "addressid" SERIAL PRIMARY KEY NOT NULL,
  "entityid" int,
  "saddress1" varchar(255),
  "saddress2" varchar(255),
  "scity" varchar(255),
  "cstate" char(2),
  "spostalcode" varchar(10),
  "stype" varchar(50),
   CONSTRAINT "fk_entityaddress_entityid"
     FOREIGN KEY ("entityid") REFERENCES "entity"("entityid")
);
```

A properly named database field indicates its data type by using a one-character prefix, letting you know what kind of data goes in the field. Having naming conventions is just as important for database design as it is for your code.

The propertyTable array is set up in the Address class to map friendly property names (such as city, state, and zip code) to the less friendly database field names (such as scity, cstate, and spostalcode). Note that you can map multiple property names to the same database field name in propertyTable. This mapping enables you to refer to the primary key of the address by either $objAddress->addressid or $objAddress->id.

What's incredibly exciting about the Address class is that the overwhelming majority of the code is spent implementing business logic and data validation. There's almost no extraneous code here. Its sole responsibility is to populate itself and validate its own contents. Everything else is left up to the DataManager class (which you'll see in detail shortly) and the PropertyObject.

Following is the code for the Email class, which should look very familiar. Enter it into a file called class.EmailAddress.php:

```php
<?php

require_once('class.PropertyObject.php');

class Email extends PropertyObject {

    function __construct($emailid) {

        $arData = DataManager::getEmailData($emailid);

        parent::__construct($arData);

        $this->propertyTable['emailid'] = 'emailid';
        $this->propertyTable['id'] = 'emailid';
        $this->propertyTable['entityid'] = 'entityid';
        $this->propertyTable['email'] = 'semail';
        $this->propertyTable['type'] = 'stype';
    }

    function validate() {
        if(!$this->email) {
            $this->errors['email'] = 'You must set an email address.';
        }

        if(sizeof($this->errors)) {
            return false;
        } else {
            return true;
        }
    }

    function __toString() {
        return $this->email;
    }
}
?>
```

This file has very little ancillary code; it's just fetching the code from the database and setting up the `propertyTable`. Everything else is data validation. Again, the UML diagram was the guide to deciding on the properties of the `Email` class and the structure of the corresponding database table.

The database table for the `entityemail` table looks like this:

```
CREATE TABLE "entityemail" (
 "emailid" SERIAL PRIMARY KEY NOT NULL,
 "entityid" int,
 "semail" varchar(255),
 "stype" varchar(50),
  CONSTRAINT "fk_entityemail_entityid"
    FOREIGN KEY ("entityid") REFERENCES "entity"("entityid")
);
```

The `PhoneNumber` class works very much like `Address` and `Email`. Here's the code to enter into `class.PhoneNumber.php`:

```php
<?php
  require_once('class.PropertyObject.php');

  class PhoneNumber extends PropertyObject {

function __construct($phoneid) {
      $arData = DataManager::getPhoneNumberData($phoneid);

      parent::__construct($arData);

      $this->propertyTable['phoneid'] = 'phoneid';
      $this->propertyTable['id'] = 'phoneid';
      $this->propertyTable['entityid'] = 'entityid';
      $this->propertyTable['number'] = 'snumber';
      $this->propertyTable['extension'] = 'sextension';
      $this->propertyTable['type'] = 'stype';

    }

    function validate() {
      if(!$this->number) {
        $this->errors['number'] = 'You must supply a phone number.';
      }

      if(sizeof($this->errors)) {
        return false;
      } else {
        return true;
      }
    }

    function __toString() {
      return $this->number .
            ($this->extension ? ' x' . $this->extension : '');
    }
  }
?>
```

And here's the SQL statement to create the `entityphone` table:

```
CREATE TABLE "entityphone" (
  "phoneid" SERIAL PRIMARY KEY NOT NULL,
  "entityid" int,
  "snumber" varchar(20),
  "sextension" varchar(20),
  "stype" varchar(50),
   CONSTRAINT "fk_entityemail_entityid"
     FOREIGN KEY ("entityid") REFERENCES "entity"("entityid")
);
```

The DataManager Class

Let's now take a look at that `DataManager` class. It and the other database code samples in this chapter (and in the rest of this book) use PostgreSQL, although a class like this would work just as well with MySQL, Oracle, or any other RDBMS. Chapter 6 examines a more sophisticated way of handling database abstraction, but for now let's keep it simple using the PHP PostgreSQL functions.

The primary responsibility of the `DataManager` class is to put all the data access code into a single location, making it much easier to change the database type or connection parameters later. All the class's methods have been declared static because the class doesn't rely on any member variables. Note the use of the static function variable in `getConnection()`. This is used to ensure that only one database connection is open during a single page request. A lot of overhead is associated with establishing a database connection, so eliminating unnecessary connections helps to improve performance. Create a file called `class.DataManager.php` and enter the following class code:

```php
<?php

require_once('class.Entity.php'); //this will be needed later
require_once('class.Individual.php');
require_once('class.Organization.php');

class DataManager {

    private static function _getConnection() {
        static $hDB;

        if(isset($hDB)) {
            return $hDB;
        }

        $hDB = pg_connect("host=localhost port=5432 " .
                          "dbname=[your db name] user=[your user name]
                          password=[your password]")
            or die("Failure connecting to the database!");
        return $hDB;
    }

    public static function getAddressData($addressID) {
        $sql = "SELECT * FROM \"entityaddress\" WHERE\"addressid\" = $addressID";
        $res = pg_query(DataManager::_getConnection(), $sql);
```

```
        if(! ($res && pg_num_rows($res))) {
            die("Failed getting address data for address $addressID");
        }

        return pg_fetch_assoc($res);
    }

    public static function getEmailData($emailID) {
        $sql = "SELECT * FROM \"entityemail\" WHERE\"emailid\" = $emailID";
        $res = pg_query(DataManager::_getConnection(), $sql);
        if(! ($res && pg_num_rows($res))) {
            die("Failed getting email data for email $emailID");
        }

        return pg_fetch_assoc($res);
    }

    public static function getPhoneNumberData($phoneID) {
        $sql = "SELECT * FROM \"entityphone\" WHERE \"phoneid\" = $phoneID";
        $res = pg_query(DataManager::_getConnection(), $sql);
        if(! ($res && pg_num_rows($res))) {
            die("Failed getting phone number data for phone $phoneID");
        }

        return pg_fetch_assoc($res);
    }
}
?>
```

The `DataManager` class provides the data structures used to populate the `$data` member of your `PropertyObject` subclasses. Separate functions return the data for each of the types. You'll be adding a few new functions to this class a bit later in this chapter. Note that the values supplied to `pg_connect` do not need the square brackets. All of the values in the square brackets (including the brackets themselves) should be replaced with the appropriate connection details for your server.

All the methods of this class are declared to be *static*. Remember that static methods are those requiring all member variables to be static, too. You don't need to instantiate static classes to use their methods. There are several scenarios in which this makes sense. Consider a class called `Math` that exposes methods such as `squareRoot()`, `power()`, and `cosine()`, and has properties including the mathematical constants e and pi. All instances of this class perform the same math. The square root of 2 doesn't change; 4 raised to the third power will always be 64; and the two constants are, well, constant. There's no need to create separate instances of this class because its state and properties never change. A class called `Math` implemented in this manner should allow for all its functions to be called statically.

The `DataManager` class is much the same. All the functions are self-contained. No nonstatic member variables are present for the functions to interact with. The class exposes no properties. You can invoke the methods of the class using the static method operator `::` as a result. Because all the methods you've created are static, you need never instantiate the object with `$obj = new DataManager()` and then call methods using syntax such as `$obj->getEmail()`. Instead, you can use the simple syntax `DataManager::getEmail()`.

The Entity, Individual, and Organization Classes

With all the supporting classes in place, you can move on to the core of the application: the `Entity` class and its subclasses.

First, ensure that you're updating your UML diagram as you make changes to the object hierarchy so that you keep track of what you (or the development team) are doing. You've created the `PropertyObject` class and made all your classes inherit from it, with one exception — the new `DataManager` class, which does not inherit from anything, but rather merely provides data abstraction functionality. The `PropertyObject` implements an abstract interface called `Validator`. Figure 3-7 shows the updated diagram.

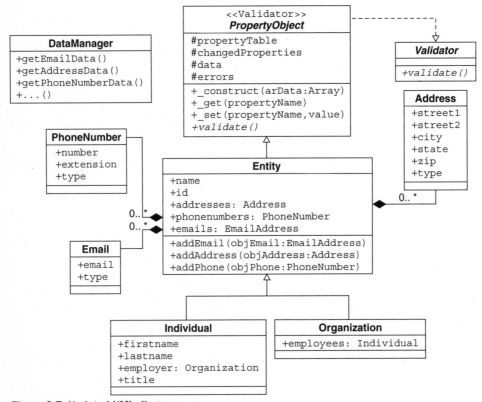

Figure 3-7: Updated UML diagram

Now you can begin to develop the `Entity`, `Individual`, and `Organization` classes. The following code shows the fully implemented `Entity` class called `class.Entity.php`:

```php
<?php

    require_once('class.PropertyObject.php');
    require_once('class.PhoneNumber.php');
    require_once('class.Address.php');
    require_once('class.EmailAddress.php');

    abstract class Entity extends PropertyObject {
      private $_emails;
      private $_addresses;
      private $_phonenumbers;

      public function __construct($entityID) {
        $arData = DataManager::getEntityData($entityID);

        parent::__construct($arData);

        $this->propertyTable['entityid'] = 'entityid';
        $this->propertyTable['id'] = 'entityid';
        $this->propertyTable['name1'] = 'sname1';
        $this->propertyTable['name2'] = 'sname2';
        $this->propertyTable['type'] = 'ctype';
        $this->_emails = DataManager::getEmailObjectsForEntity($entityID);
        $this->_addresses = DataManager::getAddressObjectsForEntity($entityID);
        $this->_phonenumbers = DataManager::
                getPhoneNumberObjectsForEntity($entityID);
      }

      function setID($val) {
        throw new Exception('You may not alter the value of the ID field!');
      }

      function setEntityID($val) {
        $this->setID($val);
      }

      function phonenumbers($index) {
        if(!isset($this->_phonenumbers[$index])) {
          throw new Exception('Invalid phone number specified!');
        } else {
          return $this->_phonenumbers[$index];
        }
      }

      function getNumberOfPhoneNumbers() {
        return sizeof($this->_phonenumbers);
      }
```

```php
    function addPhoneNumber(PhoneNumber $phone) {
      $this->_phonenumbers[] = $phone;
    }

    function addresses($index) {
      if(!isset($this->_addresses[$index])) {
        throw new Exception('Invalid address specified!');
      } else {
        return $this->_addresses[$index];
      }
    }

    function getNumberOfAddresses() {
      return sizeof($this->_addresses);
    }

    function addAddress(Address $address) {
      $this->_addresses[] = $address;
    }

    function emails($index) {
      if(!isset($this->_emails[$index])) {
        throw new Exception('Invalid email specified!');
      } else {
          return $this->_emails[$index];
      }
    }

    function getNumberOfEmails() {
      return sizeof($this->_emails);
    }

    function addEmail(Email $email) {
      $this->_emails[] = $email;
    }

    public function validate() {
      //Add common validation routines
    }
  }
?>
```

By moving all the accessor method functionality to the parent `PropertyObject` class, you simplify the `Entity` class and ensure that it is focused only on the code required to implement an entity.

The `Entity` class is declared abstract because it isn't useful on its own. All entities are either `Individuals` or `Organizations`. You do not want to be able to instantiate objects of class `Entity`. Declaring it abstract prevents the class from being instantiable.

You've added requests to a few new functions of the `DataManager::getEntityData()` and `get[x]ObjectsForEntity()`. `getEntityData()` returns the data required to instantiate an entity, just as functions you've already seen do for the contact types. The following shows the code for the new functions in `class.DataManager.php`:

```
// top of file omitted for brevity
   ...
     die("Failed getting phone number data for phone $phoneID");
   }
    return pg_fetch_assoc($res);
  }
  public static function getEntityData($entityID) {
    $sql = "SELECT * FROM \"entity\" WHERE \"entityid\" = $entityID";
    $res = pg_query(DataManager::_getConnection(),$sql);
    if(! ($res && pg_num_rows($res))) {
      die("Failed getting entity $entityID");
    }
    return pg_fetch_assoc($res);
  }
?>
```

To add the `get[x]ObjectsForEntity()` functions, place the following code at the end of `class.DataManager.php`, just after the `getEntityData` function:

```
  public static function getAddressObjectsForEntity($entityID) {
    $sql = "SELECT \"addressid\" from \"entityaddress\" WHERE " .
        "\"entityid\" = $entityID";
    $res = pg_query(DataManager::_getConnection(), $sql);
    if(!$res) {
      die("Failed getting address data for entity $entityID");
    }
    if(pg_num_rows($res)) {
      $objs = array();
      while($rec = pg_fetch_assoc($res)) {
        $objs[] = new Address($rec['addressid']);
      }
      return $objs;
    } else {
      return array();
    }
  }

  public static function getEmailObjectsForEntity($entityID) {
    $sql = "SELECT \"emailid\" from \"entityemail\"
        WHERE \"entityid\" = $entityID";
    $res = pg_query(DataManager::_getConnection(), $sql);
    if(!$res) {
      die("Failed getting email data for entity $entityID");
    }

    if(pg_num_rows($res)) {
      $objs = array();
```

```
        while($rec = pg_fetch_assoc($res)) {
          $objs[] = new EmailAddress($rec['emailid']);
        }
        return $objs;
      } else {
      return array();
      }
  }

  public static function getPhoneNumberObjectsForEntity($entityID) {
      $sql = "SELECT \"phoneid\" from \"entityphone\" " .
            "WHERE \"entityid\" = $entityID";
      $res = pg_query(DataManager::_getConnection(), $sql);

      if(!$res) {
        die("Failed getting phone data for entity $entityID");
      }

      if(pg_num_rows($res)) {
        $objs = array();
      while($rec = pg_fetch_assoc($res)) {
          $objs[] = new PhoneNumber($rec['phoneid']);
        }
        return $objs;
      } else {
      return array();
      }
  }
}
```

These functions take an entity ID value. They query the database to determine whether any e-mails, addresses, or phone numbers exist for the entity in question. If they do, then the functions build an array of `EmailAddress`, `Address`, or `PhoneNumber` objects by passing each ID to the constructor for the appropriate object type. This array is then passed back to the `Entity` object, where it is stored in the appropriate private member variable.

With the `Entity` class doing all the heavy lifting, the remaining work is fairly simple. You just need to implement the `Individual` and `Organization` classes. Create a file called `class.Individual.php` and enter the following:

```php
<?php

require_once('class.Entity.php');
require_once('class.Organization.php');

class Individual extends Entity {

  public function __construct($userID) {
    parent::__construct($userID);

    $this->propertyTable['firstname'] = 'name1';
    $this->propertyTable['lastname'] = 'name2';
  }
```

```php
    public function __toString() {
      return $this->firstname . ' ' . $this->lastname;
    }

    public function getEmployer() {
      return DataManager::getEmployer($this->id);
    }

    public function validate() {
      parent::validate();

      //add individual-specific validation
    }

  }
?>
```

That's short and sweet. Inheritance makes this easy. The `Individual` class sets up a few new properties that make accessing the first and last name of the individual easier, instead of having to use the rather ugly `name1` and `name2` properties defined in the `Entity` class. It also defines a new method, `getEmployer()`, which requires a new function in the `DataManager`. You get to that function as soon as you have your `Organization` class, which is shown in the following code. Create a file called `class.Organization.php` and enter this code into it:

```php
<?php

require_once('class.Entity.php');
require_once('class.Individual.php');

class Organization extends Entity {

  public function __construct($userID) {
    parent::__construct($userID);
    $this->propertyTable['name'] = 'name1';
  }

  public function __toString() {
    return $this->name;
  }

  public function getEmployees() {
    return DataManager::getEmployees($this->id);
  }

  public function validate() {
    parent::validate();
    //do organization-specific validation
  }

}

?>
```

Again, this is a fairly simple class, thanks to the power of inheritance. You declare a property called `name` that makes it easier to obtain the one and only name that an organization has (the `sname2` property goes unused for organizations).

To add the functions `getEmployer()` and `getEmployees()` to the `DataManager` class, append the following code to the end of `class.DataManager.php`:

```php
public static function getEmployer($individualID) {
    $sql = "SELECT \"organizationid\" FROM \"entityemployee\" " .
        "WHERE \"individualid\" = $individualID";
    $res = pg_query(DataManager::_getConnection(),$sql);
    if(! ($res && pgsql_num_rows($res))) {
        die("Failed getting employer info for individual $individualID");
    }

    $row = pgsql_fetch_assoc($res);

    if($row) {
        return new Organization($row['organizationid']);
    } else {
        return null;
    }
}

public static function getEmployees($orgID) {
    $sql = "SELECT \"individualid FROM \"entityemployee\" " .
        "WHERE \"organizationid\" = $orgID";
    $res = pgsql_query(DataManager::_getConnection(), $sql);

    if(! ($res && pgsql_num_rows($res))) {
        die("Failed getting employee info for org $orgID");
    }
    if(pgsql_num_rows($res)) {
        $objs = array();
        while($row = pgsql_fetch_assoc($res)) {
            $objs[] = new Individual($row['individualid']);
        }
        return $objs;
    } else {
        return array();
    }
}
```

These two functions rely on the presence of a table called `entityemployee`, shown in the following code. This table relates individuals to the organizations by which they are employed. For example, employees of the same company would have different individual IDs, but the same organization IDs.

```sql
CREATE TABLE "entityemployee" (
  "individualid" int NOT NULL,
  "organizationid" int NOT NULL,
  CONSTRAINT "fk_entityemployee_individualid"
```

```
      FOREIGN KEY ("individualid") REFERENCES "entity"("entityid"),
   CONSTRAINT "fk_entityemployee_organizationid"
      FOREIGN KEY ("organizationid") REFERENCES "entity"("entityid")
);
```

One last function is needed to make the entire system work — the `DataManager` method for listing all the entities in the database. It's called `getAllEntitiesAsObjects()` and it finishes all the work you need to do on your objects. Add this method to `class.DataManager.php`:

```php
public static function getAllEntitiesAsObjects() {
  $sql = "SELECT \"entityid\", \"type\" from \"entity\"";
  $res = pgsql_query(DataManager::_getConnection(), $sql);
  if(!$res) {
    die("Failed getting all entities");
  }

  if(pgsql_num_rows($res)) {
    $objs = array();
    while($row = pgsql_fetch_assoc($res)) {
      if($row['type'] == 'I') {
        $objs[] = new Individual($row['entityid']);
      } elseif ($row['type'] == 'O') {
        $objs[] = new Organization($row['entityid']);
      } else {
        die("Unknown entity type {$row['type']} encountered!");
      }
    }
    return $objs;
  } else {
    return array();
  }
}
```

`DataManager` enables you to enumerate over all the contacts in your system. It examines the value of the `ctype` field in the `entity` table to determine whether the entry is an `Individual` or an `Organization`, and then instantiates an object of the appropriate type and adds it to the array that the function returns.

Making Use of the System

By now, you can see the real power of an OOP approach. The following code, called `test.php`, will display a view of all the contacts in your database, including all their contact details:

```php
<?php

require_once('class.DataManager.php'); //everything gets included by it

function println($data) {
  print $data . "<br>\n";
}
```

```php
$arContacts = DataManager::getAllEntitiesAsObjects();

foreach($arContacts as $objEntity) {

  if(get_class($objEntity) == 'Individual') {
    print "<h1>Individual - {$objEntity->__toString()}</h1>";
  } else {
    print "<h1>Organization - {$objEntity->__toString()}</h1>";
  }

  if($objEntity->getNumberOfEmails()) {
    //We have emails! Print a header
    print "<h2>Emails</h2>";

    for($x=0; $x < $objEntity->getNumberOfEmails(); $x++) {
      println($objEntity->emails($x)->__toString());
    }
  }

  if($objEntity->getNumberOfAddresses()) {
    //We have addresses!
    print "<h2>Addresses</h2>";

    for($x=0; $x < $objEntity->getNumberOfAddresses(); $x++) {
      println($objEntity->addresses($x)->__toString());
    }
  }

  if($objEntity->getNumberOfPhoneNumbers()) {
    //We have phone numbers!
    print "<h2>Phones</h2>";

    for($x=0; $x < $objEntity->getNumberOfPhoneNumbers(); $x++) {
      println($objEntity->phonenumbers($x)->__toString());
    }
  }

  print "<hr>\n";

} //End foreach

?>
```

You can enter the data into your own tables, because that will help you to figure out how everything goes together. You may want to try to imitate the results shown in Figure 3-8 (by navigating to test.php in your browser).

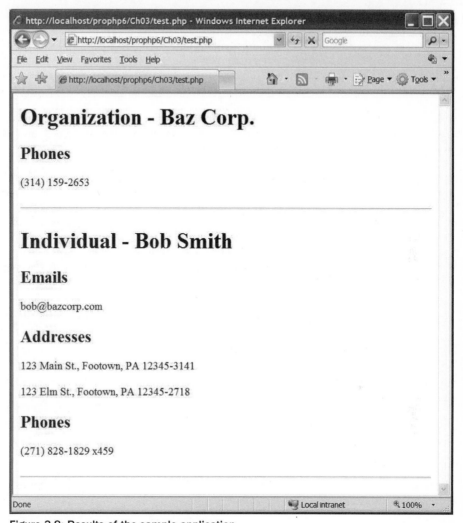

Figure 3-8: Results of the sample application

In only 50 lines of code (including blank lines), you can display nearly everything there is to show about the entities in your system. Employer and employees aren't shown here; again, that is an exercise for you to try. The line that calls the `get_class` function in `test.php` will give you some ideas for figuring out which class you're dealing with so that you'll know whether to call `getEmployer()` on an `Individual`, or `getEmployees()` on an `Organization`.

Summary

UML diagrams are an essential tool for planning complex (and even not so complex) applications. Properly designed diagrams enable you to document intricate systems in a clearer way than text alone allows. When you use class diagrams as part of your routine software development process, it is much easier to see how your classes and database tables should be designed.

Take full advantage of the OO features in PHP6 to help you rapidly develop applications and establish a code base that's easier to maintain, offers a greater degree of flexibility and extensibility, and reduces the total volume of code required to implement the business requirements.

By separating the software architecture into a business logic layer (like the `Individual` class) and a data access layer (like the `DataManager` class), you make it easy to change the underlying data source, table structure, or queries without disrupting the rest of the application. Objects that are responsible for implementing business logic aren't cluttered with the data access mechanism, the presence of which can confuse and obscure the business rules.

Chapter 4 takes a look at a new way of thinking about software architecture that improves code reusability and maintainability, and provides a different level of abstraction when designing classes.

Design Patterns

In previous chapters of this book, you learned that objects can descend from parent objects via inheritance. You've also seen how objects can contain references to other objects (such as a `DrumSet` object holding `Drum` objects). In general, the technique of composing an object from other objects is referred to as *object composition*.

Both inheritance and object composition are powerful tools in designing object-oriented (OO) software, and allow for a wide variety of design choices. Of course, having many choices does not always make decisions easier. How would you design your application so that it's easy to maintain and extend? How would you write a component that the other members of your team could use through a simple interface? When writing software, you can solve certain problems on your own using your experience, intelligence, luck, large doses of caffeinated beverages, or any combination of the above.

You've probably reused existing code of your own to solve a problem. Perhaps you have a standard script for connecting to a database. Design patterns are a bit different in that they are not simply about reusing code; they are more abstract and generalized than that. The same design pattern can show up in completely different types of software. Design patterns are about reusing ideas for organization and composition, not just repurposing the same execution. After you know a pattern, you should be able to recognize where it would be useful. Then you can go ahead and implement it — knowing that it's an accepted solution.

A design pattern is a specific way of solving a particular problem. In this book, it represents the way an object or set of objects is structured, how they collaborate and communicate with other objects in the pattern. Each pattern has a descriptive name (such as `Observer` or `Observable`), and each pattern has a specific design that can be shown in a class diagram.

Patterns can be confusing at first. If this initial description doesn't seem clear, don't be concerned. You'll be working through five different patterns in this chapter, building on some of the code you saw in the last few chapters.

The Composite Pattern

You've already had a little experience with one pattern — the composite — from the `Instrument` interface in Chapter 2. Take a look at the class diagram again in Figure 4-1.

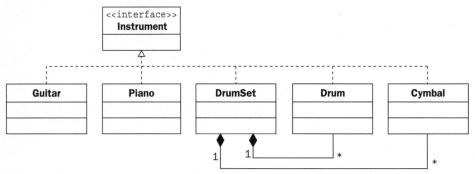

Figure 4-1: Use case diagram indicating composites

Figure 4-1 shows that a `DrumSet` object can be composed of both `Drum` and `Cymbal` objects. `Drum` and `Cymbal` can be thought of as *children* of the `DrumSet` object. A `DrumSet` can be composed of any number of `Drums` and `Cymbals`. Notice, though, that both `DrumSet` and its children are all of the same type — namely, `Instrument`. When a client object interacts with `DrumSet`, it does so through the same interface as it would to interact with its children. This relationship is known as the *composite pattern*.

Figure 4-2 shows the general case for the composite.

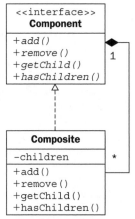

Figure 4-2: General case for the composite

The composite pattern has two parts: the Component abstract class and the Composite, which is a concrete implementation of the Component class. All Composite objects descend from the abstract Component class. Any Component can contain other Components. A Component containing other components can be thought of as a Composite. A Component with no children can be thought of as an empty Composite.

> *Some implementations of* Composite *make a distinction between* Composite *objects and* Leaf *objects.* Leaf *objects are* Components *that can't contain children. To simplify this example, all* Components *have the ability to be a* Composite.

Moving back from the general case, it will be necessary to make a change in the design and switch the Instrument interface to an abstract class. Interfaces and abstract classes are similar because neither one can be used directly to instantiate an object. The key difference is that an abstract class can have some fully implemented methods, whereas interfaces just have method declarations.

Use abstract classes when you want to maintain the same methods in all your subclasses but have some general functionality that can be shared by the subclasses. Use interfaces when the implementations will differ across most or all of the methods in subclasses. Figure 4-3 shows the new class diagram. Note that abstract class diagrams are indicated with italics.

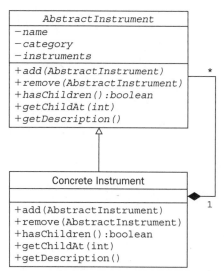

Figure 4-3: New class diagram

The association line indicates that each concrete instance of AbstractInstrument may contain any number (including zero) of other instances of AbstractInstrument.

Implementation

The following PHP code shows the implementation of the composite pattern:

```
<html>
<body>
<head>
<style>
body {font : 12px verdana; font-weight:bold}
td {font : 11px verdana;}
</style>
</head>

<?php

abstract class AbstractInstrument {

  private $name;
  private $category;
  private $instruments = array();

  public function add(AbstractInstrument $instrument) {
     array_push($this->instruments, $instrument);
  }

  public function remove(AbstractInstrument $instrument) {
     array_pop($this->instruments);
  }

  public function hasChildren() {
    return (bool)(count($this->instruments) > 0);
  }

  public function getChild($i) {
    return $instruments[i];
  }

  public function getDescription() {
    echo "- one " . $this->getName();
    if ($this->hasChildren()) {
      echo " which includes:<br>";
      foreach($this->instruments as $instrument) {
        echo "<table cellspacing=5 border=0><tr><td>     
              </td><td>-";
        $instrument->getDescription();
        echo "</td></tr></table>";
      }    }
  }

  public function setName($name) {
    $this->name = $name;
  }
```

```php
  public function getName() {
    return $this->name;
  }

  public function setCategory($category) {
    $this->category = $category;
  }

  public function getCategory() {
    return $this->category;
  }
}

class Guitar extends AbstractInstrument {
  function __construct($name) {
    parent::setName($name);
    parent::setCategory("guitars");
  }
}

class DrumSet extends AbstractInstrument {
  function __construct($name) {
   parent::setName($name);
   parent::setCategory("drums");
  }
}

class SnareDrum extends AbstractInstrument {
  function __construct($name) {
    parent::setName($name);
    parent::setCategory("snare drums");
  }
}

class BaseDrum extends AbstractInstrument {
  function __construct($name) {
    parent::setName($name);
    parent::setCategory("base drums");
  }
}

class Cymbal extends AbstractInstrument {
  function __construct($name) {
    parent::setName($name);
    parent::setCategory("cymbals");
  }
}

$drums = new DrumSet("tama maple set");
$drums->add(new SnareDrum("snare drum"));
$drums->add(new BaseDrum("large bass drum"));
```

```
$cymbals = new Cymbal("zildjian cymbal set");
$cymbals->add(new Cymbal("small crash"));
$cymbals->add(new Cymbal("large high hat"));
$drums->add($cymbals);

$guitar = new Guitar("gibson les paul");

echo "List of Instruments: <p>";
$drums->getDescription();
$guitar->getDescription();

?>

</body>
</html>
```

Notice that all the concrete instruments (such as `DrumSet` and `Guitar`) descend from the `AbstractInstrument` class. Also notice that all the subclasses inherit the implemented methods in the abstract class. To implement the `getDescription()` method, the current instrument is checked to see whether it has children. If it does, then the method is called recursively until it travels through the entire tree. Figure 4-4 shows the output from `composite.php`.

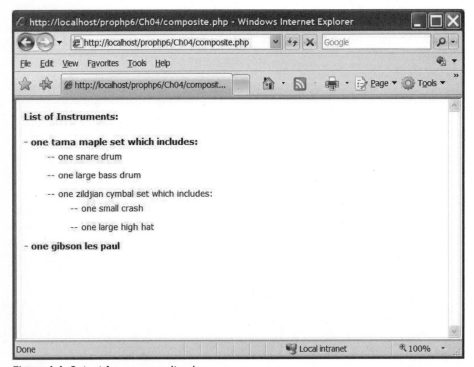

Figure 4-4: Output from composite.php

This code listing exhibits several combined class definitions, code demonstrating the use of those classes, and inline HTML. This is done strictly as a means of keeping this book from becoming excessively long. In your code, you will want to have a separate file for each class, and separate the business logic from the class definitions. You'll learn more about a design pattern for doing this in Chapter 13.

Historically (in PHP 4), the & symbol caused the object (in this case, of type `AbstractInstrument`) to be passed by reference:

```
public function add(AbstractInstrument & $instrument) {
```

This is important because otherwise an entirely new local copy would be used within the function. However, because PHP 6 automatically passes objects by reference, the & is not required. For the purposes of this discussion, this behavior is desired because you actually want to work on the original object, rather than a copy of it. Figure 4-5 shows the *object diagram* for the previous code after the instruments and their child instruments have been assembled. Object diagrams are similar to class diagrams, except that they show instances of objects indicated with their names underlined. In addition, they represent the object relationships in the system at a point in time.

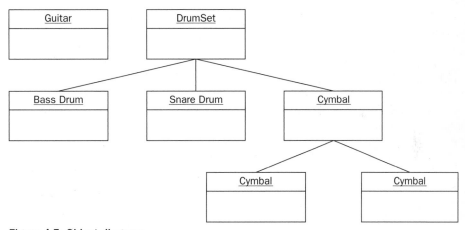

Figure 4-5: Object diagram

In this example, the concrete instrument classes don't really differ in great detail, except for overriding the `getDescription()` method in the `Guitar` class. Consider, though, if you needed to add methods to contact a manufacturer to get stocking information. If each manufacturer had a favored way to receive contact from the system, you could specify that in a `contact()` method. You would first add an abstract method to `AbstractInstrument`, and then you would implement it in each subclass. Adding the abstract method ensures that you won't forget to implement it in the subclasses. If you don't, you'll get an error.

If you were certain that no additional functionality needed to be added to your instruments, you could just create a `GenericInstrument` class that inherited from `AbstractInstrument`. This way, when you created, say, a cymbal, you would use the following:

```
$cymbals = new GenericInstrument("zildjian cymbal set");
```

The key point here is that anyone or anything accessing the `Instrument` interface (be it you, another programmer, or another part of the application) doesn't need to know how it was implemented. Calling `getDescription()` returns a description of the tree structure of an `Instrument` whether it has children or not, or its children have children, and so on. The caller of the method doesn't need to know whether it has children.

Because the interface is the same for all instrument objects but they do not respond in the same way, the instrument objects can be thought of as *polymorphic*. The basic description of polymorphism is *same interface, different implementation* or, more generally, *same interface, different behavior*.

Considerations

The composite pattern described here is very flexible. There are no constraints on which instrument may have children. Consider adding the following line:

```
$cymbals->add(new Cymbal("large high hat"));
$drums->add($cymbals);
$cymbals->add($drums);
$guitar = new Guitar("gibson les paul");
```

Adding the `drums` to the `cymbals` that already belong to drums creates a circular reference. When calling `getDescription()`, a line like this can crash a Web server. You might want to safeguard against such mistakes. One strategy would be to check during the `add()` method to see whether the instrument being added already contains a reference to the one calling the method. If so, you could report an error.

You also might want to experiment with groups of instruments that cannot have things added to them. One option is to individually go to each class definition and override the `add()` method so that it does nothing. Another option is to create a new abstract class from which all single instruments descend. This abstract class could have an `add()` method that either does nothing or reports an error. This is more in keeping with the composite pattern discussed previously, in which two classes descend from `Component`. One is a `Leaf` that cannot have children, and the other is a `Composite` that can. The class diagram for this is shown in Figure 4-6.

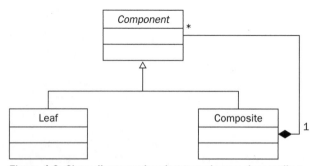

Figure 4-6: Class diagram showing two classes descending from `Component`

One other consideration is constraining certain instruments from being added to composites. Perhaps you don't want to allow a `Guitar` object to be added to a `DrumSet`. In that case, you could define certain legal types based on the `category` attribute for subject-verb agreement: Implementing any or all of these features would be worthwhile to try on your own.

The Observer Pattern

Often, you'll have data in your application that changes over time. For example, suppose you have some GUI components that are required to show this data and then update the data when it changes. How would you handle it? One solution might be to pass the newly updated data to a method of the GUI component so that it could redraw the information. A problem with this approach is remembering to do that each time the data is updated. What if it's not clear how often the data will be updated, and whether you want the GUI to update automatically when it does?

The *observer pattern* solves this problem by using two interfaces: `Observer` and `Observable`. As the name suggests, the `Observer` "watches" the `Observable` to see whether it changes.

> *Keeping the theme of human senses, an* `Observer` *is sometimes called a* `Listener`, *but for this chapter, we'll stick with the former name.*

In its most basic implementation, the `Observable` can add `Observers`. `Observable` is then responsible for notifying them if anything about its state has changed, and the `Observer` is responsible for reacting to the change. In this example, the data is the `Observable` and the GUI components are the `Observers`. If the data changes, those changes will automatically be reflected in any GUI component that is an `Observer` of the data. Figure 4-7 demonstrates the observer pattern.

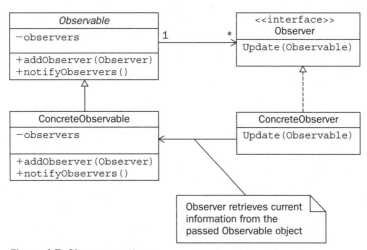

Figure 4-7: Observer pattern

Widgets

Continuing with the previous example, you'll use the observer pattern to handle displaying price information for some of the instruments within graphical elements on a Web page. First, you must define some simple graphical components. These components will be basic HTML table structures whose functionality will be contained within an object. Such components are often referred to using the all-purpose term of *widgets*.

The widgets must display the same instrument information. For this example, that information is just the instrument's name and price.

Designing the Widgets

A graphical widget will have two responsibilities. It needs to draw its own HTML so that it can be seen on a Web page, and it needs to update the data it displays. You may have noticed (from Figure 4-7) that an `Update` method is defined in the `Observer` interface.

Each widget is an `Observer`. The item being observed is the data representing the instrument name and price information. The data source is `Observable`.

All widgets, then, should implement the `Observer` interface. In addition, each one should descend from an abstract class that defines some shared functionality between widget objects. This is an example of using interfaces and abstract classes together. Because the `update()` method is the same for all widgets, it can be implemented in the `abstract` class. The class diagram is shown in Figure 4-8.

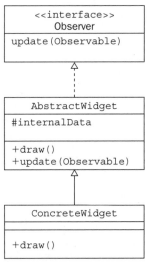

Figure 4-8: abstract class diagram

Now, all concrete implementations of widgets will descend from the `AbstractWidget` class. The `AbstractWidget` class, in turn, implements the `Observer` interface. Notice that the `update()` method in the class diagram for `AbstractWidget` is not shown in italics. This means that the method is actually implemented at that point. The # symbol indicates that the `internalData` property is protected. That means subclasses of `AbstractWidget` have access to it. If it were private, subclasses would not be able to access it.

Take a look at the following `Widget` code, in a file called `abstract_widget.php`:

```php
<?php
interface Observer {
  public function update(Observable $subject);
}

abstract class Widget implements Observer {
  protected $internalData = array();
  abstract public function draw();
  public function update(Observable $subject) {
    $this->internalData = $subject->getData();
  }
}

class BasicWidget extends Widget {

  function __construct() {

  }

  public function draw() {
    $html = "<table border=1 width=130>";
    $html .= "<tr><td colspan=3 bgcolor=#cccccc>
                <b>Instrument Info<b></td></tr>";
    $numRecords = count($this->internalData[0]);
    for($i = 0; $i < $numRecords; $i++) {
      $instms = $this->internalData[0];
      $prices = $this->internalData[1];
      $years = $this->internalData[2];
      $html .= "<tr><td>$instms[$i]</td><td> $prices[$i]</td>
          <td>$years[$i]</td></tr>";
    }
    $html .= "</table><br>";
    echo $html;
  }
}

class FancyWidget extends Widget {

  function __construct() {

  }

  public function draw() {
```

```php
        $html = "<table border=0 cellpadding=5 width=270>
            <tr><td colspan=3 bgcolor=#cccccc>
            <b><span>Our Latest Prices<span><b>
            </td></tr>
            <tr><td><b>instrument</b></td>
            <td><b>price</b></td><td><b>date issued</b>
            </td></tr>";

    $numRecords = count($this->internalData[0]);

    for($i = 0; $i < $numRecords; $i++) {

        $instms = $this->internalData[0];
        $prices = $this->internalData[1];
        $years = $this->internalData[2];
        $html .= "<tr><td>$instms[$i]</td><td>
                    $prices[$i]</td><td>$years[$i]
                </td></tr>";
    }

    $html .= "</table><br>";
    echo $html;

    }}
?>
```

There are two concrete `Widget` implementations: `FancyWidget` and `BasicWidget`. Both implement the `draw()` method required from the `abstract` parent class they extend, yet the implementations are different. Both also inherit the `update()` method from the parent class.

You might be wondering about the benefit of using the `Observer` interface when you could just put the single method in the subclasses anyway. Earlier PHP versions provided no direct way to ensure that a method parameter was of a certain type. A feature that first appeared in PHP 5 called *class type hints* serves as a way of guaranteeing that the correct type of object is passed as an argument. In the following function declaration, the reference passed as an argument must be of type `Observer`, or you get an error:

```php
    public function addObserver(Observer $observer) {
```

If a particular method takes an `Observer` as an argument (as is the case with the `Observable` `addObserver()` method), you know it's safe to pass a `Widget` to it. That's because all `Widget` objects are of type `Observer`. All widgets descend from the `AbstractWidget`, which implements `Observer`. Thus, the widgets themselves are also that type.

Another question arises: Why not just require the method `addObserver()` to take a `Widget`? That way, you could also do away with the `Observer` interface. Suppose, however, that you wanted to create another type of `Observer` that wasn't a `Widget`. Then the class type hint would prevent you from passing any other type of object to the `addObserver()` method.

The DataSource

The `DataSource` object encapsulates the name, price, and date of issue for a group of musical instruments. It's also the `Observable` object. The key methods in `Observer` are `addObserver()` and `notifyObservers()`. Any `Observer` (in this case, any `Widget`) that needs to "watch" the `DataSource` can be added to it using `addObserver()`. The following code comprises `observable.php`:

```php
<?php
abstract class Observable {

  private $observers = array();

   public function addObserver(Observer $observer) {
        array_push($this->observers, $observer);
   }

   public function notifyObservers() {
      for ($i = 0; $i < count($this->observers); $i++) {
        $widget = $this->observers[$i];
        $widget->update($this);
      }
   }

}

class DataSource extends Observable {

  private $names;
  private $prices;
  private $years;

  function __construct() {
        $this->names = array();
        $this->prices = array();
        $this->years = array();

  }

  public function addRecord($name, $price, $year) {
        array_push($this->names, $name);
        array_push($this->prices, $price);
        array_push($this->years, $year);
        $this->notifyObservers();

  }

  public function getData() {
        return array($this->names, $this->prices, $this->years);
  }
}
?>
```

The `addRecord()` method enables you to add a new instrument to the internal storage of the `DataSource` object. Notice, though, that the `addRecord()` method does one more thing:

```php
$this->notifyObservers();
```

Any time the `DataSource` object has its internal data altered, it notifies all its observers. Observers are added using the previously mentioned `addObserver()` method. After an observer is added, it's stored in the internal `$observers` array. When `notifyObservers()` is called, the method iterates through the `$observers` array, calling the `update()` method for each `Observer` stored in the array.

The sole parameter of the `update` method is a copy of the `Observable` object itself:

```php
$widget->update($this);
```

This allows the `Widget` (the `Observer`) to get a copy of the most current state of the `DataSource` (the `Observable`). Note that the `Widget` is passed by value — a copy of `DataSource`, rather than the actual reference. This way, the `DataSource`'s internal information is not shared.

Connecting Observer and Observable

Now that you've done all the difficult work up front, the payoff is an easy-to-use and flexible system for connecting an `Observer Widget` to the `Observable DataSource`. Take a look at the following example, in a file called `widget.php`:

```php
<?php
require_once("observable.php");
require_once("abstract_widget.php");

$dat = new DataSource();
$widgetA = new BasicWidget();
$widgetB = new FancyWidget();

$dat->addObserver($widgetA);
$dat->addObserver($widgetB);

$dat->addRecord("drum", "$12.95", 1955);
$dat->addRecord("guitar", "$13.95", 2003);
$dat->addRecord("banjo", "$100.95", 1945);
$dat->addRecord("piano", "$120.95", 1999);

$widgetA->draw();
$widgetB->draw();

?>
```

All you have to do is create your `DataSource` and `Widget` objects. Then you can add the `Widget` objects as observers of the `DataSource`. Now you're free to add as many records as needed to the `DataSource` object, not concerning yourself about updating the widgets — it all happens automatically. Finally, when you call `draw()` on the widgets, they will display themselves with the correct data.

If you were designing a desktop application, you could include a redraw() *function in the* update() *method of the* Observer. *This way, you wouldn't need to call* draw() *explicitly, but instead have the component redraw itself automatically in response to the* DataSource *being updated. In a purely server-side Web application, there's no way to redraw a component unless you reload the page.*

Another cool feature of the observer pattern is that you can define multiple DataSources. You just tell the DataSource which widget you want listening to it, and you can reuse the same widget for different DataSources. Figure 4-9 shows the result of running the previous code.

Instrument Info		
drum	$12.95	1955
guitar	$13.95	2003
banjo	$100.95	1945
piano	$120.95	1999

Our Latest Prices		
instrument	price	date issued
drum	$12.95	1955
guitar	$13.95	2003
banjo	$100.95	1945
piano	$120.95	1999

Figure 4-9: Result of running widget.php

Considerations

The observer pattern is useful when you have a source of data that you would like to connect to different representations. The examples in this chapter have used a simple DataSource object, but you can create more complex data sources, such as ones that retrieve data from a database or an XML file. You could design a Widget that could observe either an XML DataSource or a database DataSource. As long as the DataSource object had the same interface, it wouldn't matter how it retrieved its data.

The Widgets in this example are coded to display a table with three columns (as shown in Figure 4-9), but they could be more flexible. If you want to get creative, try redesigning them so that they can display an arbitrary number of columns. You could also try using a little helper object instead of the arrays to transfer the information between Observable and Observer.

The Decorator Pattern

The two concrete widgets created for the observer pattern have a different appearance. If you needed to add a new style of widget, you would subclass Widget and implement the draw() method to write the HTML. For example, say that you needed to add a feature to all existing widgets, such as a border. You could go into each draw() method and add some more HTML to each, but then the border would be hard-coded and all widgets would be forced to have a border.

Alternatively, you could create a new set of subclasses of existing concrete widgets that implemented the border in the `draw()` method. If you had only two widgets (as in the `Observer` example), this might be an option — you would end up with four widgets. However, if you had five widgets to start with, it might not seem so appealing. Suddenly you have a lot of widget classes to worry about.

There is another way to handle situations like this, one that doesn't require you to create a new subclass for every widget to which you want to add a border: Using the *decorator pattern* enables you to add features or functionality to existing objects without using inheritance. Figure 4-10 shows the class diagram for the decorator pattern.

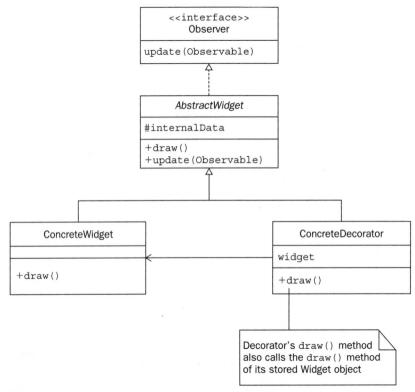

Figure 4-10: Class diagram for the decorator pattern

The class diagram indicates that `Decorators` are a type of `Widget`, too. This is good, because you don't want to change the way you access a `Widget`, whether it's decorated or not. Take a look at the code of the following `Decorator` (saved as `border_decorator.php`) that draws a border around a `Widget`:

```php
<?php
require_once("abstract_widget.php");

class BorderDecorator extends Widget {

  private $widget;

  function __construct(Widget $widget) {
    $this->widget = $widget;
  }

  public function draw() {

    echo "<table border=0 cellpadding=1 bgcolor=#3366ff>";
    echo "<tr bgcolor=#ffffff><td>";
    $this->widget->draw();
    echo "</td></tr></table>";

  }

  public function update(Observable $subject) {
    $this->widget->update($subject);
  }

}
?>
```

This example moves all the classes and interfaces into their own files, and uses `require_once` to import them. The `draw()` method generates some HTML to draw a table. Notice that in the middle of drawing this border table, the `draw()` method calls the `draw()` method of the `Widget` that was passed in the constructor. Because of this, the `Widget` gets some extra "decoration" around it — namely, the border. An example of how you use the `Decorator` follows:

```php
$widgetA = new BorderDecorator(new BasicWidget());
```

After the decorator pattern is set up, you need only to pass it a `Widget` object. Then you can use the decorated `Widget` exactly the same way as you would a regular one. Figure 4-11 shows the `BasicWidget` object with the `BorderDecorator` applied to it.

Instrument Info		
drum	$12.95	1955
guitar	$13.95	2003
banjo	$100.95	1945
piano	$120.95	1999

Figure 4-11: BasicWidget
with the BorderDecorator
applied

Implementation

There are some small (but important) changes in the implementation of the `Widget` objects to accommodate the decorator pattern. First, the protected `InternalData` array in the abstract `Widget` class (`abstract_widget.php`) has been changed to a private reference to the `DataSource` object stored in the `$subject` variable, as shown here:

```
abstract class Widget implements Observer {

  private $subject;

  abstract public function draw();

  public function update(Observable $subject) {
        $this->subject = $subject;
  }

  public function getSubject() {
        return $this->subject;
  }
}
```

Next, during the implemented `draw()` methods in each concrete `Widget` class, the `Widget` accesses its subject by calling its inherited `getSubject()` method:

```
public function draw() {
    $data = $this->getSubject()->getData();
    $numRecords = count($data[0]);
    $html = "<table border=1 width=130>";
    $html .= "<tr><td colspan=3 bgcolor=#cccccc>
                    <b>Instrument Info<b></td></tr>";
    for($i = 0; $i < $numRecords; $i++) {
        $instms = $data[0];
        $prices = $data[1];
        $years = $data[2];
        $html .= "<tr><td>$instms[$i]</td><td> $prices[$i]
                    </td><td>$years[$i]</td></tr>";
    }
    $html .= "</table>";
    echo $html;

}
```

Finally, because the `Decorator` class is what is actually assigned as an observer of the `DataSource` object, it must, in turn, pass the `DataSource` down to its `Widget` object when the `Decorator`'s `update()` method is called. This allows the `Widget` object to have access to the data:

```
public function update(Observable $subject) {
  $this->widget->update($subject);
}
```

Using the Decorator

After you've done the work developing the `Decorator` classes, you'll find that it is a very flexible and powerful pattern. Not only is it easy to use, but different `Decorators` can be combined to give multiple effects to the same widget. `Decorators` can even be applied in different order. Another `Decorator` class follows. Save the file as `closebox_decorator.php`:

```php
<?php require_once("abstract_widget.php");

class CloseBoxDecorator extends Widget {

  private $widget;

  function __construct(Widget $widget) {
    $this->widget = $widget;
  }

  public function draw() {
    print '<table border=0 cellspacing=1 bgcolor="#666666">';
    print '<tr bgcolor=#666666>';
    print '<td align=right>';
    print '<table width=10 height=10 bgcolor="cccccc">';
    print '<tr><td><b>x</b></td></tr>';
    print '</table>';
    print '</td>';
    print '</tr>';
    print '<tr bgcolor=#ffffff>';
    print '<td>';

    $this->widget->draw();

    print '</td>';
    print '</tr>';
    print '</table>';
   }

  public function update(Observable $subject) {
    $this->widget->update($subject);
  }
 }
}
```

The preceding `Decorator` applies a simple menu bar with a closed box on it. Combining the two `Widgets` with the two `Decorators` is easy. Save the following file as `decorator.php`:

```php
<?php
require_once("abstract_widget.php");
require_once("closebox_decorator.php");
require_once("border_decorator.php");
require_once("observable.php");

$dat = new DataSource();
$widgetA = new BasicWidget();
$widgetB = new FancyWidget();
```

```
$widgetB = new BorderDecorator($widgetB);
$widgetB = new CloseBoxDecorator($widgetB);

$widgetA = new CloseBoxDecorator($widgetA);
$widgetA = new BorderDecorator($widgetA);

$dat->addObserver($widgetA);
$dat->addObserver($widgetB);

$dat->addRecord("drum", "$12.95", 1955);
$dat->addRecord("guitar", "$13.95", 2003);
$dat->addRecord("banjo", "$100.95", 1945);
$dat->addRecord("piano", "$120.95", 1999);

$widgetB->draw();
echo "<br>";
$widgetA->draw();
?>
```

Notice that the first Widget has its Decorators applied in one order, and the second has them applied in the opposite order. Figure 4-12 shows the result of this code.

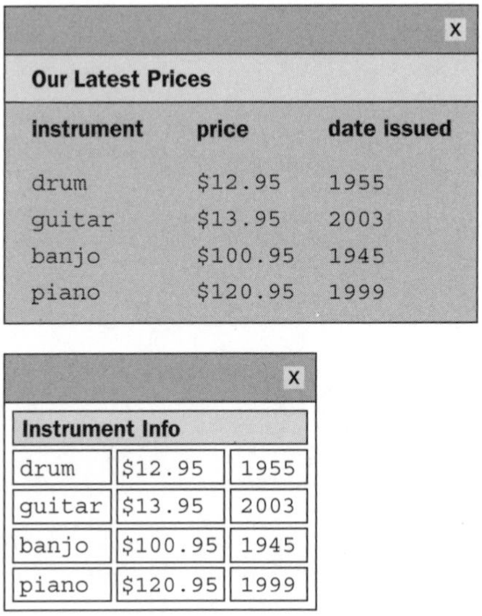

Figure 4-12: Result of code for decorator.php

Considerations

The Decorators in this section all have hard-coded color values. There's no reason that you can't alter them to be more flexible. The BorderDecorator class can be changed to allow for a specified border width and color. You can use some JavaScript to make the CloseBoxDecorator actually hide itself when the Close box is clicked. To increase maintainability of the code, you can (and probably should) use a templating system to divorce the HTML markup from the class definition.

Remember that the decorator pattern need not be limited to purely graphical elements. In the case of the `Widgets`, the decorator pattern generated additional HTML to alter their look. You could instead have a data structure of some kind and use a `Decorator` to add additional information to it. For example, if you had a fragment of XML, you could use a `Decorator` to embed it in a larger XML structure.

The Facade Pattern

The best way to understand the *facade pattern* is to look at a component diagram of a system before and after using a facade.

Figure 4-13 shows the front end of a Web site communicating with an application on the Web server. On the right side of the diagram, the front-end code is accessing various objects in the application. On the left, showing the facade, the front end communicates only with the facade object, which in turn delegates responsibilities to the internal objects.

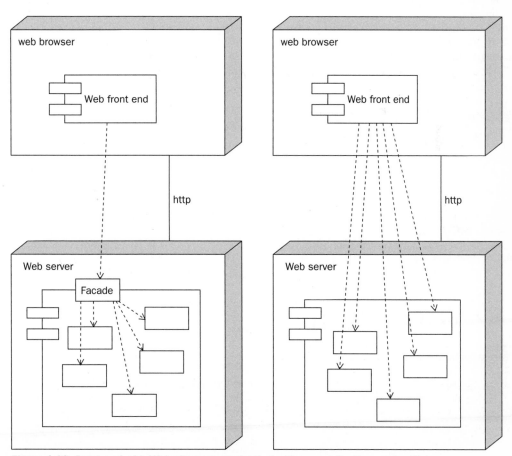

Figure 4-13: Front end of a Web site communicating with an application on the Web server

Suppose that you designed a small Web application. Over time, your client kept adding new features to it, and gradually the number of classes in the application increased. Certain pages on your Web site started building up many calls to the various objects. Such pages might resemble the following example:

```
$dbManager = new DBManager();
$userArray = $dbManager->getNewUsers();
$emailer = new Emailer();
$stats = new StatLog();

for ($i = 0; $i < count($userArray[$i]; $i++) {

  $user = $userArray[$i];
  $userPref = $user->getMailPreference();
  $userMail = $user->getEmail();

  if ($userPref == true) {
        $emailer->sendMailToUser($userMail);
  } else {
        $stats->storeUnmailedUser($user->getID());
  }
}
}
```

The preceding hypothetical code would send an e-mail to new users who indicated they want to receive mail. If they don't want to receive mail, their userID would be sent to a part of the application that manages statistics about users. Although this code isn't too ugly, if you had to mix in large amounts of HTML and get information back to report to the user, it might become unwieldy. Following is another version of using the facade pattern:

```
Application::mailNewUsers();
```

Now, any time this functionality is required, the front end just requests it from the facade (in this case, the Application class). All messages from the front end of the site go through the Application class and never interact directly with the other objects in the system. The Application object's methods can be static because you don't even need an instance of the Application class.

Notice that the client of the Application class doesn't need to know how it works internally. One good result of this (in addition to cleaner code) is that it enables a separation of front-end presentation and back-end functionality. The less your application is tied up in a particular presentation of HTML, the more likely it is to be reusable elsewhere. There's more discussion of this good design practice in Chapter 13.

The Builder Pattern

If you look back at the composite pattern, you'll notice that the objects that made up the composite were manually created, as shown in the following example:

```
$drums = new DrumSet("tama maple set");
$drums->add(new SnareDrum("snare drum"));
$drums->add(new BaseDrum("large bass drum"));
```

```
$cymbals = new Cymbal("zildjian cymbal set");
$cymbals->add(new Cymbal("small crash"));
$cymbals->add(new Cymbal("large high hat"));
$drums->add($cymbals);
```

The code creating this DrumSet composite is not particularly complex, but what if you needed to create Instrument or Instrument composite objects for many different Musician objects, and those Musician objects in turn were composites of a Band object?

It wouldn't be impossible to write out the code that created the new objects and then added them, although it might start to get tedious if you had several bands with several musicians in them, each with their own set of instruments. If you needed to create bands in response to the actions of a user (perhaps through a GUI), then it might start to get difficult — especially if you had to hard-code each type of band, with the required musicians and instruments.

Implementation

Say that you were required to create a wizard that generated a Band for an end user. The user would choose from a list of genres (for example, rock, country, salsa, heavy metal, and so on), and the resulting Band would be returned, assembled with its musicians and their instruments. Figure 4-14 shows the class diagram for the *builder pattern*.

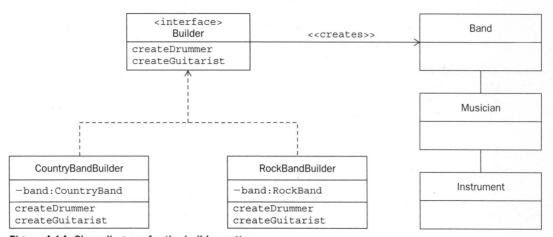

Figure 4-14: Class diagram for the builder pattern

For this example, the builder pattern creates Bands that have only two types of Musicians — guitarists and drummers:

```php
<?php

interface Builder {
    public function buildDrummer();
    public function buildGuitarist();
}
?>
```

Each time a concrete builder class is instantiated, it creates a `Band` object. Take a look at the following code for the `RockBandBuilder` class:

```php
<?php

require_once("interface_builder.php");
require_once("class_rockband.php");
require_once("class_musician.php");
require_once("class_instrument.php");

class RockBandBuilder implements Builder {

  private $band;

  function __construct($name) {
        $this->band = new RockBand($name);
  }

  public function getBand() {
        return $this->band;
  }

  public function buildDrummer() {
        $musician = new Musician("rock drummer");
        $drumset = new Instrument("rock drum kit");
        $drumset->add(new Instrument("cymbal"));
        $drumset->add(new Instrument("bass drum"));
        $drumset->add(new Instrument("snare drum"));
        $musician->addInstrument($drumset);
        $this->band->addMusician($musician);
  }

  public function buildGuitarist() {

        $musician = new Musician("rock guitarist");
        $guitar = new Instrument("electric guitar");
        $musician->addInstrument($guitar);
        $this->band->addMusician($musician);
  }

}
?>
```

Note how the implementation of the constructor in `RockBandBuilder` creates a `RockBand`. Similarly, the constructor of `CountryBandBuilder` creates a `CountryBand`, as shown next, in the file `countryband_builder.php`:

```php
<?php
require_once("interface_builder.php");
require_once("class_musician.php");
require_once("class_countryband.php");
require_once("class_instrument.php");

class CountryBandBuilder implements Builder {
```

```php
        private $band;

        function __construct() {
                $this->band = new CountryBand();
        }

        public function getBand() {
                return $this->band;
        }

        public function buildDrummer() {

                $musician = new Musician("washboard player");
                $drumset = new Instrument("washboard");
                $musician->addInstrument($drumset);
                $this->band->addMusician($musician);

        }

        public function buildGuitarist() {

                $musician = new Musician("country guitarist");
                $guitar = new Instrument("acoustic guitar");
                $musician->addInstrument($guitar);
                $this->band->addMusician($musician);
        }
}
?>
```

Check out the buildDrummer() method from RockBandBuilder. Now compare it to the one from CountryBandBuilder. Notice how each method creates not only the Musician object, but also the instruments for that musician. Because of the Builder interface, both Builders are required to implement the buildDrummer() and buildGuitarist() methods, but they each construct a Musician in a completely different way, including the Instrument objects belonging to that musician.

You may have noticed that the Musician and Instrument classes are no longer subclassed into specific subtypes such as Guitarist. This demonstrates that Builders can be implemented to create different objects (as in the constructor), or the same objects with different parameters and operations (as in the buildDrummer() method).

The Director

Builder patterns have one final important aspect, called the Director. The Director is responsible for calling the methods of the Builder to create the finished product, which, in this case, is a Band object. In this example, the Director will be the Application object similar to the one described in the discussion of the facade pattern. The Application class follows in a file called application.php:

```php
<?php

class Application {

  public static function createBand(Builder $builder) {
```

```
            $builder->buildGuitarist();
            $builder->buildDrummer();

            return $builder->getBand();

        }
    }
    ?>
```

The `Application` class has one method, `createBand`, which takes a `Builder` as its argument. The `Application` then calls the `create` methods of the passed `Builder` object. Note two important points here. First, the `Application` decides which methods of the `Builder` it wants to call. Second, it doesn't care which type of `Builder` is passed to it.

Finally, here is how you would use the `Application` (also known as the `Director`) and `Builder` together. Simply create an instance of the appropriate `Builder` object and pass it to the `createBand` method of the `Application`:

```
$builder = new RockBandBuilder();
$band = Application::createBand($builder);
```

The `Application` object and `Builder` work together to build the correct `Band` object step by step. The `Band` object is manipulated and stored in the `Builder` until it's requested by the `getBand` method.

Considerations

The builder pattern is useful for assembling composites and hierarchical object structures such as the `Band->Musician->Instrument` one. Although having the builder return a completed object is useful, don't forget that the `Band` object returned by the builder is still the same as any `Band` object you might have created by hand. That means that it can still be altered after its construction.

The `Director` class can be modified to allow for more than one creation method. In the case of the `Application` object, you had only one method, `createBand`, but having methods that called different configurations using the same builder is possible. For example, you could have methods such as `createTrio`. By passing different `Builder` objects, the same method would assemble either a rock trio or a country trio.

Summary

This chapter demonstrated five different design patterns:

❑ Composite

❑ Observer

❑ Decorator

❑ Facade

❑ Builder

Although each pattern handles a different design issue, one feature is common to them all. After the work to develop and implement the pattern is finished, the code to actually use it is very simple and flexible. Patterns enable developers and software designers to share complex ideas with just a single term. They're also reusable ideas. The same design pattern can be a solution in very different types of software. Often, you'll see design patterns incorporated into a language or framework — so if you know about them, you'll understand how they are supposed to work within that language.

The five patterns presented here are just a small subset of the design patterns that exist. You should continue to explore design patterns on your own — they're a great tool for a serious developer. The seminal text on design patterns is *Design Patterns: Elements of Reusable Object-Oriented Software*, by Erich Gamma, Richard Helm, Ralph Johnson, and John M. Vlissides (Addison-Wesley, 1994). The book uses C++ and the somewhat obscure language Smalltalk for most of its examples, but the design patterns they describe are applicable to developers in any language. The book is sufficiently influential — it is usually known as the "GOF" book, short for "gang of four," referring to the four authors. The professional PHP developer can benefit from an understanding of the power of design patterns and from specific examples of them when planning any application architecture.

Chapter 5 looks at the `Collection` class, the first in a series of utility classes this book discusses that you can use as part of your application development toolkit.

5

Collections

Now that you've learned the ins and outs of object-oriented (OO) application design in PHP, you might be tempted to dive in and start coding your application. With your new-found knowledge, you're certainly ready to do just that, but you will almost certainly be taking the longest route to get there. There are a number of shortcuts you can take along the way, in the form of a series of utilities and reusable classes that together comprise an immensely powerful, easy-to-use development toolkit. This book introduces you to some useful toolkit components, piece by piece, and shows you (with real-world examples) just how useful it can be. The first class in your toolkit is called `Collection`, and that's what you'll meet in this chapter.

The `Collection` class is an OO replacement for the traditional `array` data type. Much like an array, it contains member variables, although those variables tend to be other objects, rather than simpler data types such as strings, integers, and so forth. The class then provides simple methods to enable you to add member variables, remove them, and fetch them for use in applications. As you'll see in this chapter, it has numerous advantages over using a simple array for storing a series of instantiated objects.

As with many of the chapters in this book, in this chapter you will not only utilize the code for the class itself, but also see exactly how it is put together, based on original design requirements that will be determined. Along the way, topics such as lazy instantiation using callbacks are discussed, as well as how to put the `Collection` class to use, and what possible improvements could be made to it in the future.

Purpose of the Collection Class

Applications frequently have objects that contain a group of other objects. For example, if you were building an application for a university's registrar's office, you would need to have a `Student` class and a `Course` class. A `Student` object would probably have more than one `Course` object associated with it. The most obvious way to construct this would be to have an array of `Course` objects as a member variable of the `Student` object, as shown here:

```
/* student class */
class Student {
  public $courses = array();
  // ... other methods/properties
}

/* using the student class */
$objStudent = new Student(1234); //constructor not shown above
foreach($objStudent->courses as $objCourse) {
  print $objCourse->name;
}
```

Of course, if the most obvious approach were the best possible approach, this book wouldn't require this chapter. The previous method has a few problems:

❑   Exposing the array of `Course` objects as a public member variable breaks encapsulation. There is no opportunity to validate changes to the array, or to change the state of the `Student` object, should that be necessary.

❑   It's not obvious from this implementation how the courses will be indexed in the array, and how to traverse that array to find a specific `Course` object in which you might be interested.

❑   Most important, to ensure that the courses array is available to any code that might want to use the `Student` object, you must pull up all the course information from the database at the same time as the student information. This means that even if you want to print only the student's name, you must fetch all the information about courses, unnecessarily increasing load on the database server and bogging down the entire application.

The `Collection` class is designed to solve all these problems. It provides an OO wrapper around an array, and implements a mechanism that enables *lazy instantiation*. Lazy instantiation defers creation of the members of the collection until they are actually needed. It's called "lazy" because the object determines on its own when to instantiate its component objects, rather that create them when it is instantiated. When you create a `Student` object, the `Course` objects should not be created at the same time. Only when you first attempt to access the courses should they be created, and this should happen automatically without requiring you to do anything special.

The functional requirements of the `Collection` class are as follows:

1.   Establish a wrapper around an array of objects.

2.   Provide methods to add, remove, and fetch the member objects in a predictable, obvious way.

3.   Enable you to easily determine how many member objects exist in the collection.

4.   Enable you to use lazy instantiation to save system resources.

Designing the Collection Class

Before writing any code, you should ensure that you've carefully planned the classes you'll create. Based on the written functional requirements in items 1, 2, and 3 from the previous list, you can establish a class diagram that looks something like Figure 5-1.

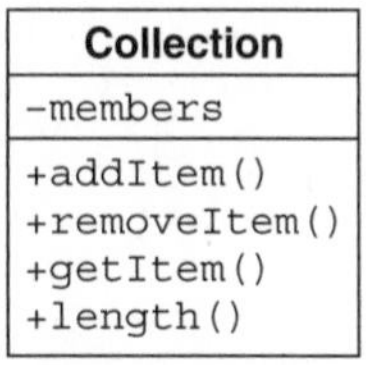

Collection
−members
+addItem() +removeItem() +getItem() +length()

Figure 5-1: Class diagram

To handle the operations to add, remove, and get members "in a predictable, obvious way," users of this object must be allowed to specify a useful key name when adding the objects. The key works just like a string index in an associative array, specifying the location in the collection into which the member object of the collection will be stored. This key can then be used for retrieving or removing the object later. To use the previous example of the registrar's office application, the key for each course might be the course code (for example, CS101 for a beginning computer science class). In some cases, you won't have a meaningful key value to use. In this situation, the collection should be able to determine a valid key on its own. Figure 5-2 shows the updated UML diagram.

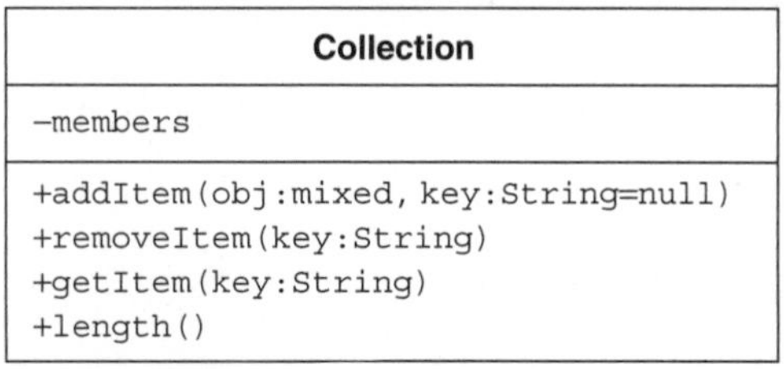

Collection
−members
+addItem(obj:mixed, key:String=null) +removeItem(key:String) +getItem(key:String) +length()

Figure 5-2: Updated UML diagram

The obj parameter to addItem() is the item being added to the collection. This item is usually an object, but it can be any valid data type. The key parameter to addItem(), removeItem(), and getItem() is a string (optional in addItem()) representing the key.

Later in this chapter, after the basic code for manipulating the collection's contents has been established, you'll refer to this diagram to see how the lazy instantiation code will work. One final thing to note here is that length() simply returns the number of items currently in the collection.

Collection Class Basics

Based on the UML diagram in Figure 5-2, the skeleton for the `Collection` class looks like this:

```php
<?php
class Collection {

  private $_members = array();

  public function addItem($obj, $key = null) {
  }

  public function removeItem($key) {
  }

  public function getItem($key) {
  }

  public function length() {
  }

}
?>
```

Later in this chapter, the discussion will assume the code is in a file called `class.Collection.php`. The `$_members` variable provides a location in which to store the objects that are members of the collection. `addItem()` enables you to add a new object to the collection. `removeItem()` removes an object. `getItem()` returns the object, and `length()` returns the number of items in the collection. The `Collection` class does not require a constructor.

The addItem Method

When adding a new object to the collection, that object is inserted into the `$_members` array, at the location specified by `$key`. If no key is provided, you'll allow PHP to pick one. If an attempt is made to add an object to the collection using a key that already exists, an exception should be thrown to prevent inadvertent overwriting of information:

```php
class Collection {

  private $_members = array();
  public function addItem($obj, $key = null) {
    if($key) {

      //Throw exception if this key is already in use.
      if(isset($this->_members[$key])) {
        throw new KeyInUseException("Key \"$key\" already in use!");
      } else {
        $this->_members[$key] = $obj;
      }
```

```
    } else {
      $this->_members[] = $obj;
    }

  }

}
```

As with most of the subclasses of `Exception` used in this book, `KeyInUseException` has no body, and instead inherits everything from the default `Exception` class that ships with PHP 6:

```
class KeyInUseException extends Exception { }
```

The `KeyInUseException` class provides a means of letting users of the object know when they might be overwriting information by specifying the same key more than once. The value of the key is used as the index in the `$_members` array. If no key is specified, PHP picks a numeric index for this element. In either case, the object is inserted into the array at that location.

Subclasses of `Collection` can override the `addItem()` method with a type hint that ensures that the items being added are of the correct type for the desired collection. Here's an example:

```
<?php
class CourseCollection extends Collection {
  public function addItem(Course $obj, $key = null) {
    parent::addItem($obj, $key);
  }
}
?>
```

Using this technique, with very little code you can create subclasses that enforce a data type for the members of the collection.

The removeItem and getItem Methods

The `removeItem()` and `getItem()` methods take a key as a parameter, which indicates what items are being removed or fetched. An exception should be thrown if an invalid key is supplied:

```
public function removeItem($key) {
    if(isset($this->_members[$key])) {
      unset($this->_members[$key]);
    } else {
      throw new KeyInvalidException("Invalid key \"$key\"!");
    }
  }

  public function getItem($key) {
    if(isset($this->_members[$key])) {
      return $this->_members[$key];
    } else {
      throw new KeyInvalidException("Invalid key \"$key\"!");
    }
  }
```

The InvalidKeyException class is just as simple as the KeyInUseException class:

```
class KeyInvalidException extends Exception { }
```

Other Methods

Because the $key parameter to the addItem() method is optional, you won't necessarily know the key used for each item in the collection. A function called keys() enables you to provide a listing of those keys to any external code that might need it. The keys will be returned as an array:

```
public function keys() {
    return array_keys($this->_members);
}
```

You might want to know how many items are in the collection. The sizeof PHP function returns the number of elements in an array, so you'll use that to implement your length() method:

```
public function length() {
    return sizeof($this->_members);
}
```

Because getItem() throws an exception if an invalid key is passed, you need to have a means of determining whether a given key exists in the collection. The exists() method enables you to check before calling getItem():

```
public function exists($key) {
    return (isset($this->_members[$key]));
}
```

This approach enables you to either use a try ... catch block to trap for invalid keys, or call the exists() method before calling getItem(), depending on which method is more convenient.

Now that you've added all the basic methods to the class, you can move on to see how the Collection class is used.

Using the Collection Class

To use the Collection class as it stands now, create a file called class.Collection.php and save the code for the Collection class in it. Create files for the KeyInvalidException and KeyInUseException classes. Be sure to add require_once statements to the top of class.Collection.php to pull in those exception classes. Save the following code in testCollection.php:

```php
<?php
require_once('class.Collection.php');

/* a silly class for testing */
class Foo {
    private $_name;
    private $_number;
```

```php
    public function __construct($name, $number) {
      $this->_name = $name;
      $this->_number = $number;
    }
    public function __toString() {
      return $this->_name . ' is number ' . $this->_number;
    }
}

$colFoo = new Collection();
$colFoo->addItem(new Foo("Steve", 14), "steve");
$colFoo->addItem(new Foo("Ed", 37), "ed");
$colFoo->addItem(new Foo("Bob", 49));

$objSteve = $colFoo->getItem("steve");

print $objSteve; //prints "Steve is number 14"
$colFoo->removeItem("steve"); //deletes the 'steve' object

try {
  $colFoo->getItem("steve"); //throws KeyInvalidException
} catch (KeyInvalidException $kie) {
  print "The collection doesn't contain anything called 'steve'";
}

?>
```

This example may not be particularly interesting yet, but it should give you some idea of how the Collection class is used. The next section discusses how to handle lazy instantiation, which is one of the primary benefits of this class.

Implementing Lazy Instantiation

Recall that lazy instantiation refers to the ability of the Collection class to defer creation of its members until such time as they are needed. In the registrar's application discussed at the beginning of this chapter, a Student object has multiple Course objects associated with it. When you want to use a Student object to display the name of a student, you do not need any of the information about that student's courses. However, for the sake of a consistent interface, the Course objects should be available as member variables of the Student object.

To keep things simple when displaying a list of courses for a given student, the software interface should allow you to write code like this:

```php
<?php

  $objStudent = StudentFactory::getStudent(12345); //12345 is the student ID
  print "Name: " . $objStudent->name . "<br>\n";
  print "Courses: <br>\n";
  foreach($objStudent->courses as $objCourse) {
    print $objCourse->coursecode . " - " . $objCourse->name . "<br>\n";
  }

?>
```

For now, it's enough to know that the StudentFactory is a class with a static method getStudent that returns a new student object, given the ID as a parameter. It does all the heavy lifting in the database. You should assume that the Student class constructor takes care of populating the list of courses; but if you just have a listing of students by name (as in the next example), you shouldn't have to incur the overhead of fetching the unwanted courses. Again, assume the StudentFactory is a class that creates Student objects by interrogating the database for you. In this case, you retrieve a collection of students by searching by their last name:

```php
<?php

    $colStudents = StudentFactory::getByLastName("Smith");
    print "<h1>Students With the Last Name 'Smith'</h1>";
    foreach($colStudents as $objStudent) {
        print $objStudent->name . "<br>\n";
    }
?>
```

In this case, getting the course information would be totally unnecessary because you're merely displaying the name, but how can you keep the simple interface of the Student class without forcing the database activity?

You could add methods such as $objStudent->loadCourses() that would populate the collection and have to be called before interacting with the courses collection, but that isn't terribly intuitive, and it clutters the interface. You could do something like the following:

```
CourseFactory::getCoursesForStudent($objStudent)
```

That would return a collection of courses for a given student, but again, it's not obvious to someone who just joined your development team that such a function must be called to get the Course objects for a given student.

There is a better way, and it involves using callbacks.

Callbacks

If you've ever done any JavaScript programming and assigned some activity to happen in the onclick event for some object, you've used a callback. A *callback* is a nifty programming trick in which you tell the application to perform a function when some event happens. That event is out of your control — you don't necessarily know when it will happen. You tell the application to take care of performing that function if and when the event takes place.

Many times in JavaScript, an onSubmit event handler is created for a form that allows client-side data validation to happen if the user tries to submit that form. You don't know when the user is going to submit the form, or even whether the user will do that at all. After the event handler is specified, the JavaScript engine takes care of the rest. You can also use this technique in server-side application development.

When you're designing the Student class for the registrar's application, you don't know whether or when the course collection will be accessed by the code that uses the class. Because fairly significant overhead is associated with getting the Course objects, this is a great time to take advantage of a callback. You need to be able to tell the course collection, "If someone tries to talk to you, you need to populate yourself first."

However, because the Collection class is a generic member of the reusable toolkit, you don't want to hard-code the name of a function inside the class (this obviously limits the reusability of the class), and you don't want to have to create a new subclass of Collection every time you want to use it (because this is creating more work for you, not less). Instead, you should be able to supply the name of a procedural function, or supply a reference to an object and specify the method on that object that you want to call to populate the collection. To do so, you need to understand a special built-in PHP function.

Using call_user_func

When you want to call a function, you usually invoke the literal name of the function. However, PHP also enables you to call functions (and methods on objects) using string variables. The following is perfectly valid PHP code:

```
<?php
  $myFunc = "pow";
  print $myFunc(4, 2); //prints 16, or pow(4, 2)
?>
```

PHP evaluates the variable name and executes the function with that name. This works for compiled-in core functions, as well as user-defined functions. You can perform the same trick with a method of an object, as shown here:

```
<?php
  $myMethod = 'sayHello';
  $obj = new Person();
  $obj->$myMethod();
?>
```

Assuming that you have a class called Person with a method called sayHello(), this would work just fine. (You can also invoke static methods that way — that is, Person::$myMethod().)

The only problem with this trick is that it's not at all obvious that $obj->$myMethod() is calling $obj->sayHello(). This would be even more confusing if the value of $myMethod were passed in as a parameter to some wrapper function. PHP provides a built-in method for doing the same thing, in a manner a little less confusing and far more transparent.

The function call_user_func() takes one mandatory parameter to define the function to be called, and zero or more additional parameters to be passed as parameters to the user-defined function. The function definition is as follows:

```
mixed call_user_func ( callback function [, mixed parameter [, mixed ...]])
```

The value of the `callback function` parameter takes one of three forms:

❑   `string $functionName` — A string corresponding to the name of the procedural function to be called

❑   `array(object $object, string $functionName)` — An array consisting of an instantiated object and a string corresponding to the name of the method to be called on that object

❑   `array(string $className, string $functionName)` — An array consisting of the name of a class and a string corresponding to the name of a *static* method of that class

Here are a few examples of using this function:

```php
<?php

class Bar {

  private $_foo;

  public function __construct($fooVal) {
    $this->_foo = $fooVal;
  }

  public function printFoo() {
    print $this->_foo;
  }

  public static function sayHello($name) {
    print "Hello there, $name!";
  }

}


//procedural function - not part of the Bar class
function printCount($start, $end) {
  for($x = $start; $x <= $end; $x++) {
    print "$x ";
  }
}

/* ex. 1 */
//prints 1 2 3 4 5 6 7 8 9 10
call_user_func('printCount', 1, 10);

/* ex. 2 */
//calls $objBar->printFoo()
$objBar = new Bar('elephant');
call_user_func(array($objBar, 'printFoo'));


/* ex. 3 */
//calls Bar::sayHello('Steve')
```

```
call_user_func(array('Bar', 'sayHello'), 'Steve');

/* ex. 4 */
//This throws a fatal error "Using $this when not
//in object context" because the function call
//is Bar::printFoo, which is not a static method
call_user_func(array('Bar', 'printFoo'));

?>
```

The first example of calling `call_user_func` is straightforward. You pass the name of the procedural function as a string, and supply the two parameters it expects.

In the second example, you pass an array as the first parameter. Because the first element of that array is an object, the method `printFoo()` is invoked on that object.

In the third and fourth examples, the first element in the array is a string. Therefore, PHP attempts to statically invoke the method on the specified class. If the method doesn't exist, or relies on nonstatic class variables (that is, `$this`), then you will encounter a fatal run-time error. This is what happens in the last line when you try to statically invoke `printFoo()`.

> **Terminology reminder: static methods are those that do not rely on nonstatic class member variables and can be invoked without first instantiating an object of that class. The invocation syntax is** `ClassName::methodName()`. **The keyword** `$this` **is not available to statically invoked methods.**

Implementing a Callback

You can use `call_user_func` to create a callback in one of your classes. By creating a method that allows the same types of parameters as `call_user_func`, you can allow code outside your class to specify a function or method to be invoked when certain events in your class happen.

To create a callback in one of your classes, take the following steps:

1. Determine which events will be raised by your class.

2. For each of those events, create an `on[EventName]` method that takes two parameters:

    ❑   The name of the function

    ❑   Optionally, an object (an instantiated object variable) or class name (a string)

3. For each event, create a private member variable in your class that will store those parameters as a string (if no object or class name was provided), or as an array (if the second parameter had a value).

4. At each point in the class where these callbacks should be triggered, query the private member variable created in Step 3 to see whether it has been set. If so, call `call_user_func()`, passing in the value of that variable.

The following example shows how to create an onspeak() event in a class called Dog. Create a function called onspeak() that takes a function name as a string and optionally, an object or class name. Construct the string or array that should be passed to call_user_func(), and test the value to ensure that it's callable. If it is, then store the value in a private member variable for later use. Have a look at the bark() method to see how this value is used:

```php
<?php
class Dog {
  private $_onspeak;

  public function __construct($name) {
    $this->_name = $name;
  }

  public function bark() {
    if(isset($this->_onspeak)) {
      if(! call_user_func($this->_onspeak)) {
        return false;
      }
    }

    print "Woof, woof!";
  }

  public function onspeak($functionName, $objOrClass = null) {
    if($objOrClass) {
      $callback = array($objOrClass, $functionName);
    } else {
      $callback = $functionName;
    }

    //make sure this stuff is valid
    if(!is_callable($callback, false, $callableName)) {
      throw new Exception("$callableName is not callable " .
                          "as a parameter to onspeak");
      return false;
    }

    $this->_onspeak = $callback;
  }
} //end class Dog

//procedural function
function isEveryoneAwake() {
  if(time() < strtotime("today 8:30am") ||
    time() > strtotime("today 10:30pm")) {
    return false;
  } else {
    return true;
  }
}

$objDog = new Dog('Fido');
$objDog->onspeak('isEveryoneAwake');
```

```php
$objDog->bark(); //polite dog

$objDog2 = new Dog('Cujo');
$objDog2->bark(); //always barks!

//Throws exception when onspeak is called.
$objDog3 = new Dog('Lassie');
$objDog3->onspeak('nonExistentFunction', 'NonExistentClass');
$objDog3->bark();
?>
```

The `isEveryoneAwake()` function checks to see whether the current time is between 8:30 A.M. and 10:30 P.M. If so, return `true`, allowing the dog to bark. If not, return `false`, keeping the dog silent. (If only real dogs could be programmed with callbacks.) This approach works only for `$objDog` because `$objDog2` did not have the callback set.

Note the use of the `is_callable()` function in `onspeak()`. This is another built-in PHP function, as is `call_user_func()`. It's basically a sanity check on the parameters passed to the `onspeak()` method. When you pass in the parameters to `$objDog3->onspeak()`, the nonexistent function and class will cause an exception to be thrown.

The setLoadCallback Method in the Collection Class

Now that you've seen how callbacks can work, you need to understand how to put them to work in the `Collection` class to give it one of its more important advantages — lazy instantiation.

Consider the `Student` class from the registrar's application. You want to be able to keep the very simple interface you saw at the beginning of the chapter, in which the courses are a member variable of the `Student` object, but you shouldn't have to suffer the overhead of fetching the course list every time you fetch a `Student` object. Instead, you need to enable a callback on the `Collection` class that will tell it to call some function before allowing any external code to interact with it.

Each call to `addItem()`, `getItem()`, `length()`, `exists()`, and `keys()` should first ensure that the collection has been loaded, and if not, invoke any callback functions that might be specified. The function specified in the callback is responsible for populating the collection. You also need some sort of flag to indicate whether the callback has been invoked. This flag will prevent unnecessarily repeated attempts to load a collection that has already been loaded, because that could have a detrimental impact on performance.

The following code shows the complete `Collection` class with the modifications necessary to implement the lazy instantiation capabilities of this class (shown highlighted):

```php
<?php
class Collection {

  private $_members = array();   //collection members
  private $_onload;              //holder for callback function
  private $_isLoaded = false;    //flag that indicates whether the callback
                                 //has been invoked
```

```php
public function addItem($obj, $key = null) {

    $this->_checkCallback();        //_checkCallback is defined a little later

    if($key) {

        //Throw exception if this key is already in use.
        if(isset($this->_members[$key])) {
            throw new KeyInUseException("Key \"$key\" already in use!");
        } else {
            $this->_members[$key] = $obj;
        }

    } else {
        $this->_members[] = $obj;
    }

}


public function removeItem($key) {

    $this->_checkCallback();

    if(isset($this->_members[$key])) {
        unset($this->_members[$key]);
    } else {
        throw new KeyInvalidException("Invalid key \"$key\"!");
    }

}

public function getItem($key) {

    $this->_checkCallback();

    if(isset($this->_members[$key])) {
        return $this->_members[$key];
    } else {
        throw new KeyInvalidException("Invalid key \"$key\"!");
    }

}


public function keys() {
    $this->_checkCallback();
    return array_keys($this->_members);
}


public function length() {
    $this->_checkCallback();
```

```php
        return sizeof($this->_members);
    }

    public function exists($key) {
        $this->_checkCallback();
        return (isset($this->_members[$key]));
    }

    /**
     * Use this method to define a function to be
     * invoked prior to accessing the collection.
     * The function should take a collection as a
     * its sole parameter.
     */
    public function setLoadCallback($functionName, $objOrClass = null) {

        if($objOrClass) {
            $callback = array($objOrClass, $functionName);
        } else {
            $callback = $functionName;
        }

        //make sure the function/method is valid
        if(!is_callable($callback, false, $callableName)) {
            throw new Exception("$callableName is not callable " .
                                "as a parameter to onload");
            return false;
        }
        $this->_onload = $callback;

    }


    /**
     * Check to see if a callback has been defined and if so,
     * whether or not it has already been called. If not,
     * invoke the callback function.
     */
    private function _checkCallback() {

        if(isset($this->_onload) && !$this->_isLoaded) {
            $this->_isLoaded = true;
            call_user_func($this->_onload, $this);
        }

    }

}
?>
```

The setLoadCallback() function enables you to supply the name of a function and optionally, the name of a class or object variable that will be invoked to populate this collection. If a callback is supplied to the collection, then the $_onload private member variable is populated with the string or array to be passed to call_user_func. Note that, just as in the example using the Dog class previously, there's a bit of sanity checking to ensure that the callback is callable.

All the other methods of the `Collection` class have had the line `$this->checkLoadCallback()` added as the first line in the function declaration. Adding this line forces the collection to check for the existence of an as-yet uninvoked callback, and will cause that function to be called. Before calling the callback function, you set a flag to ensure that you call that function only once. Note the check for `$this-> isLoaded`. Any function used as a load callback with the `Collection` class should expect exactly one parameter, which will be of type `Collection`. A reference to the current collection (using the `$this` variable) is passed to the callback function with the following line:

```
call_user_func($this->_onload, $this)
```

This enables the callback function to operate directly on the collection object that caused the function to be invoked. The example that follows shows how this would work in a real situation.

Create a class called `NightClub`. This class has a `name` property and a collection of `Singer` objects. Sometimes you just need to display the name of the club. Sometimes you want to do something with the collection of singers. As a result, you use the `setLoadCallback()` method of the collection object to ensure that you don't execute any unnecessary code.

Here are the `NightClub` and `Singer` classes. Name the file `club_singer.php`:

```php
<?php
require_once("class.Collection.php");

class Singer {
  public $name;

  public function __construct($name) {
    $this->name = $name;
  }
}

class NightClub {
  public $name;
  public $singers;

  public function __construct($name) {
    $this->name = $name;
    $this->singers = new Collection();
    $this->singers->setLoadCallback('loadSingers', $this);
  }

  public function loadSingers(Collection $col) {
    print "(We're loading the singers!)<br>\n";
    //these would normally come from a database
    $col->addItem(new Singer('Frank Sinatra'));
    $col->addItem(new Singer('Dean Martin'));
    $col->addItem(new Singer('Sammy Davis, Jr.'));
  }
}
?>
```

Note the `print` statement in the `loadSingers()` method. Having this here is just for demonstration purposes. Run the following code (you can add it to the bottom of the previous code, if you wish), and you'll see that the `print` statement does not appear on the screen:

```php
<?php
$objNightClub = new NightClub('The Sands');
print "Welcome to " . $objNightClub->name . ".<br>\n";
?>
```

Now try it again, this time doing something with the `$singers` collection:

```php
<?php
$objNightClub = new NightClub('The Sands');
print "Welcome to " . $objNightClub->name . ".<br>\n";
print "We have " . $objNightClub->singers->length() . " singers " .
        "for your listening pleasure this evening.";
?>
```

Running this should result in the following output:

```
Welcome to The Sands.
(We're loading the singers!)
We have 3 singers for your listening pleasure this evening.
```

As you can see, this makes using the `singers` collection extremely easy. If you were to create the `NightClub` class, you could hand that class off to a more junior member of your software development team, who could then use that class to display the screen output shown in the example without any knowledge of how or when that collection was loaded. In addition, you ensure that the application isn't taking up any more system resources than are absolutely necessary.

The next section returns to the registrar's office example and shows how to put all this to good use in a real-world application.

Using the Collection Class

As already mentioned previously in this chapter, the registrar's office application involves a class called `Student` that contains a collection of `Course` objects. Both classes are fairly simple. The UML class diagram is shown in Figure 5-3.

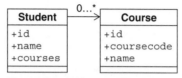

Figure 5-3: UML class diagram

Of course, a Course should also have a collection of students, but the code will be quite similar, so after you've seen how to implement the courses collection for the Student class, you can update the UML diagram and add the necessary code to support the students collection on the Course class.

For the Collection class, we'll use the code exactly as it appears in the example with the NightClub object previously, so if you've already created that class you don't need to make any changes. If you haven't already created a file containing that class and you want to try the example out for yourself, do so now.

From the UML diagram shown in Figure 5-3, you can see that the Course class is quite simple, having only a name, a course code, and an ID. The course code is the course identifier, such as CS101 for a beginning computer science class. The name is the full name of the course. The ID is the numeric primary key from the database. In a real application, you would probably want to have access to a list of prerequisites (another collection), a syllabus outline, information about the instructor, and so on. Again, these are left as an exercise for you to complete on your own.

Have a look at the code:

```php
<?php
class Course {
    private $_id;
    private $_courseCode;
    private $_name;

    function __construct($id, $courseCode, $name) {
        $this->_id = $id;
        $this->_courseCode = $courseCode;
        $this->_name = $name;
    }

    public function getName() {
        return $this->_name;
    }

    public function getID() {
        return $this->_id;
    }

    public function getCourseCode() {
        return $this->_courseCode;
    }

    public function __toString() {
        return $this->_name;
    }
}
?>
```

According to the class diagram, a course has two properties: $id and $name. Because this part of the application should not allow the name or ID of the class to be modified, private member variables are used to store those values, and the getID() and getName() methods retrieve them. When you build the parts of the application that do allow these values to be modified (the course administration tools), you can add `setID()` and `setName()` methods. These methods should probably utilize some sort of security mechanism to ensure that no unauthorized individuals are modifying properties of a course.

This code also includes a `__toString()` method. This "magic" method can be defined by any object in PHP 6. It enables you to write code like this:

```
print "This course is called " . $objCourse . "<br>";
```

`$objCourse` is obviously not a string, but because the special `__toString()` method has been defined, PHP will use the return value of that method when attempting to coerce the variable from an object to a string.

Because the `courses` collection should only ever consist of `Course` objects, create a subclass of `Collection` called `CourseCollection`. Override the `addItem()` method to include a type hint that allows only `Course` objects to be added to the collection:

```php
<?php
require_once('class.Collection.php');

class CourseCollection extends Collection {
  public function addItem(Course $obj, $key = null) {
    parent::addItem($obj, $key);
  }
}
?>
```

This enables PHP to do some type checking to ensure that everything in the courses collection is exactly what you expect it to be — a `Course` object.

The `Student` class has the properties `$id` and `$name`, which represent the unique identifier and name of that student, respectively. It must also have a property called `$courses`, which is a collection of the courses for which the student is currently registered:

```php
<?php
class Student {
  private $_id;
  private $_name;

  public $courses;

  public function __construct($id, $name) {
    $this->_id = $id;
    $this->_name = $name;

    $this->courses = new CourseCollection();
    $this->courses->setLoadCallback('_loadCourses', $this);
  }

  public function getName() {
    return $this->_name;
  }
```

```php
    public function getID() {
        return $this->_id;
    }

    private function _loadCourses(Collection $col) {
        $arCourses = StudentFactory::getCoursesForStudent($this->_id, $col);
    }

    public function __toString() {
        return $this->_name;
    }


}
?>
```

Just as in the `Course` class, implement the `$id` and `$name` properties as private member variables and provide `getID()` and `getName()` functions. For now, leave the `$courses` member as a public member variable. Note the creation of a `__toString()` method for this class also. This makes it a little bit easier to display the most common string representation of any object (in this case, the name of the student).

In the constructor, call `setLoadCallback()` and pass in the name of the loading method `_loadCourses()` and a reference to the object where that method exists (namely, `$this`).

The `_loadCourses()` method takes a `Collection` as its only parameter, as required by the `setLoadCallback()` function, and uses a static method of the `StudentFactory` class (discussed next). This method requires the ID of the student and is passed a `Collection` object into which to load the courses.

The `StudentFactory` class contains two static methods that do all the work of loading the student and course information in the database. For this application, three tables must be created in your database: `student`, `course`, and `studentcourse`. The purpose of the first two tables should be fairly obvious — to store the basic information about the students and the courses. The third table has two fields: `studentid` and `courseid`. It creates the association between students and courses.

The following SQL statements are for PostgreSQL (the preferred database server for the examples in this book); but with only minor modifications, it would also work for most RDBMSs:

```sql
CREATE TABLE "student" (
  "studentid" SERIAL NOT NULL PRIMARY KEY,
  "name" varchar(255)
);

CREATE TABLE "course" (
  "courseid" SERIAL NOT NULL PRIMARY KEY,
  "coursecode" varchar(10),
  "name" varchar(255)
);

CREATE TABLE "studentcourse" (
  "studentid" integer,
```

```
    "courseid" integer,
     CONSTRAINT "fk_studentcourse_studentid"
        FOREIGN KEY ("studentid")     REFERENCES "student"("studentid"),
     CONSTRAINT "fk_studentcourse_courseid"
        FOREIGN KEY ("courseid")
  REFERENCES "course"("courseid")
  );

  CREATE UNIQUE INDEX "idx_studentcourse_unique" ON
    "studentcourse"("studentid", "courseid");
```

Be sure that the foreign keys are created and don't overlook the unique constraint of the `studentcourse` table. A student should not be able to register twice for the same course, and this constraint enforces this fact at the database level.

Insert some sample data into each of the three tables. Statements like the following should work for the purposes of this exercise:

```
  INSERT INTO "student"(name) VALUES('Bob Smith');     -- studentid 1
  INSERT INTO "student"(name) VALUES('John Doe');      -- studentid 2
  INSERT INTO "student"(name) VALUES('Jane Baker');    -- studentid 3

  INSERT INTO "course"("coursecode", "name")
      VALUES('CS101', 'Intro to Computer Science');    -- courseid 1
  INSERT INTO "course"("coursecode", "name")
      VALUES('HIST369', 'British History 1945-1990'); -- courseid 2
  INSERT INTO "course"("coursecode", "name")
      VALUES('BIO546', 'Advanced Genetics');           -- courseid 3

  INSERT INTO "studentcourse"("studentid", "courseid") VALUES(1, 1);
  INSERT INTO "studentcourse"("studentid", "courseid") VALUES(1, 2);
  INSERT INTO "studentcourse"("studentid", "courseid") VALUES(1, 3);
  INSERT INTO "studentcourse"("studentid", "courseid") VALUES(2, 1);
  INSERT INTO "studentcourse"("studentid", "courseid") VALUES(2, 3);
  INSERT INTO "studentcourse"("studentid", "courseid") VALUES(3, 2);
```

The last six statements should be adjusted, depending on the `studentid` and `courseid` values that result from the `insert` statements into `student` and `course`.

With the database tables created and populated with sample data, you can write and test the `StudentFactory` class. This class has two static methods: `getStudent()` and `getCoursesForStudent()`. The former is responsible for creating a `Student` object, given a student ID. The latter populates the `courses` collection for a given student.

The following code does not demonstrate the use of any particular database functions, so some pseudocode is standing in for the calls to actual database functions. Chapter 6 shows you how to use the PHP Data Objects (PDO) database abstraction functions. For now, you should feel free to substitute the explicit calls to pg_connect, pg_query, and so on (or whatever the appropriate PHP functions are for your database type):

```php
<?php
class StudentFactory {

  public static function getStudent($id) {
    $sql = "SELECT * from \"student\" WHERE \"studentid\" = $id";
    $data = $db->select($sql); //pseudo code. Assume it returns an
                               //array containing all rows returned
                               //by the query.

    if(is_array($data) && sizeof($data)) {
      return new Student($data[0]['studentid'], $data[0]['name']);
    } else {
      throw new Exception("Student $id does not exist.");
    }
  }

  public static function getCoursesForStudent($id, $col) {
    $sql = "SELECT \"course\".\"courseid\",
                   \"course\".\"coursecode\",
                   \"course\".\"name\"
            FROM \"course\", \"studentcourse\" WHERE
                   \"course\".\"id\" =
                    \"studentcourse\".\"courseid\" AND
                    \"studentcourse\".\"studentid\" = $id";

    $data = $db->select($sql);  //same pseudo code in getStudent()

    if(is_array($data) && sizeof($data)) {
      foreach($data as $datum) {
        $objCourse = new Course($datum['courseid'], $datum['coursecode'],
                                $datum['name']);
        $col->addItem($objCourse, $objCourse->getCourseCode());
      }
    }

  }
}
?>
```

The getStudent() method returns a new Student object populated with the appropriate data. If no student exists in the database with that ID, then an exception is thrown. All calls to StudentFactory::getStudent() should be wrapped in a try...catch statement.

The getCoursesForStudent() method is passed the $courses collection from within _loadCourses(). The database query selects all the data from the course table, employing an implicit JOIN to the studentcourse table to get the courses associated with the specified student.

Based on the data returned from the database (if any), new Course objects are added to the collection. Note that you are using the coursecode value as the key when adding the Course to the courses collection.

Because all objects in PHP 6 are passed by reference, you are able to alter the contents of the collection from within getCoursesForStudent(), and see those changes manifest in the $courses variable of the Student object. If the phrase "passed by reference" doesn't mean much to you, see the discussion in Chapter 4 on the difference between function parameters passed by value versus those passed by reference.

To finally put all this good stuff to some use, try the following code:

```php
<?php
$studentID = 1; //use a valid studentid value from your student table

try {
   $objStudent = StudentFactory::getStudent($studentID);
} catch (Exception $e) {
   die("Student #$studentID doesn't exist in the database!");
}

print $objStudent . ($objStudent->courses->exists('CS101') ? ' is ' : ' is not ') .
 'currently enrolled in CS101';
//displays: "Bob Smith is enrolled in CS101"
?>
```

In a deployed application, you should do something a bit more graceful than an abrupt termination of the application if the specified student isn't found, but this gives you an idea of why that try...catch statement must be used.

After getting $objStudent, this code displays a simple message letting you know whether this student is enrolled in CS101. Upon invoking the exists() method, the courses collection is populated from the database, courtesy of StudentFactory. Because the course code was used as the key when adding Course objects to the collection, you can use the course code ('CS101') as the parameter to exists().

Improving the Collection Class

You might be wondering how you could possibly improve the Collection class. How could it be more powerful, useful, or exciting? Well, the problem is that you don't yet have a simple way to iterate over the entire collection — displaying a list of the courses, for example. Right now, you can jump directly only to those items that you already know are in the collection. Obviously, you don't always know what the contents of the collection are before you set out to use it, so you need a way to write code like this:

```php
<?php
$objStudent = StudentFactory::getStudent(1);
foreach($objStudent->courses as $objCourse) {
   print $objStudent . ' is currently enrolled in ' . $objCourse . '<br>\n";
}
?>
```

If you were to try to run that code now, you would either get an error or see nothing at all (depending on the error_reporting level) because $objStudent->courses is not an array (it's a Collection). In PHP 4, the only data type that could be used as the operand of a foreach statement was an array. With the release of PHP 5 (and still in PHP 6), you have two new built-in interfaces, `Iterator` and `IteratorAggregate`, that enable you to use `foreach` on objects, as long as they implement those interfaces.

Summary

The `Collection` class is a very useful OO alternative to the traditional array, and one that you can usefully employ in virtually any application you might build. It provides careful management of its members and a consistent API that makes it easy to write code that uses the class.

Subclassing `Collection` and overriding the `addItem()` method to include a type hint on the first parameter enables you to control the type of objects that are added to the collection. Although not strictly necessary, this approach provides an extra level of error checking.

By wrapping all calls to `addItem()`, `getItem()`, and `removeItem()` in `try...catch` blocks, you have complete control over any errors that may occur in those methods. Be sure to handle these errors with something a bit more graceful than the call to `die()` shown in the examples.

Callbacks are an incredibly powerful technique that you can use to implement lazy instantiation, which conserves system resources and ensures that you're manipulating only the data that it is absolutely necessary to manipulate. When you have a complex hierarchy of objects, you can use callbacks to automatically handle the instantiation of child objects, and defer the creation of those not absolutely necessary for the current application activity. Be sure that you understand how this works and see whether you can find other uses for this technique.

Chapter 6 introduces a powerful database abstraction extension that is the authors' preferred way to access relational databases and avoid some of the pitfalls associated with using the native PostgreSQL (or MySQL, or Oracle, or whatever) functions for PHP.

6

Database Abstraction
with PDO

Virtually every serious Web application you'll build will use some sort of data-storage mechanism. Such data storage is typically used to store application settings, user registrations, dynamic content — more or less anything in your application that will be *dynamic* (that is, it could change at some stage, either as a result of something one of your users does or as a result of a change in the business that owns the application).

For all but the very smallest applications, the accepted choice for data storage tends to be a relational database management system (RDBMS). The benefits are clear: scalability, ease of interrogation, reliability, resilience, integrity of data — the list goes on. It's also a virtual necessity should you ever desire something other than PHP to get its hands on your data. By using a platform-agnostic container for your data, you're not limiting yourself artificially should you, for example, ever determine that a .NET application might need to use that data, too.

Indeed, so prolific is the combination of "PHP-and-a-database" that virtually all beginners' books introduce the MySQL database in the very first chapter. The acronym LAMP (Linux, Apache, MySQL, and PHP) has cropped up in recent years — and searching Google for the phrase "PHP and MySQL" yields more than 2 million hits.

Unfortunately, as with so much in PHP, the way most people learn to work with databases in their early years of PHP education is rarely considered best practice. Building applications that are scalable, extensible, easy to port, and easy to maintain requires a different approach.

In this chapter, you'll learn just that. You'll start off with a recap of PHP's database support, as well as remind yourself how database connectivity has been handled in PHP since its introduction many years ago. By considering hypothetical examples, you'll learn about the limitations of this approach. Then, you'll meet PHP Data Objects (PDO) and learn how PDO can provide a more enterprise-ready approach.

PHP and Databases

PHP has enjoyed widespread support for RDBMSs since the early days of PHP 3. Whereas some older Web application development technologies (notably PERL) were not purpose-built, and some other technologies (notably Java) have far wider appeal outside of Web development, PHP specializes in building database-driven Web applications.

PHP's Database Support

Out of the box, PHP can support more than 20 different RDBMSs, and individual vendors frequently release their own extensions to PHP. All the popular flavors are catered to, including, perhaps most importantly, the big four: MySQL, Oracle, SQL Server, and PostgreSQL.

Despite its utility, database support in PHP is considered an *extension*. This means it is not considered part of the core language and, as a result, must be enabled either during compilation (on UNIX platforms), or at run-time (on Windows platforms) by enabling the appropriate DLL in `php.ini`.

The technique for enabling each supported RDBMS varies in any given installation of PHP. The following URLs address the ever-useful `php.net` reference site:

❑   *MySQL* — `http://uk.php.net/manual/en/mysql.installation.php`

❑   *PostgreSQL* — `http://uk.php.net/manual/en/pgsql.installation.php`

❑   *MS SQL Server* — `http://uk.php.net/manual/en/mssql.installation.php`

❑   *Oracle* — `http://uk.php.net/manual/en/oci8.setup.php`

You can easily determine what database support is enabled in your own installation of PHP by using the `phpinfo()` statement.

Fire up your favorite text editor and start a new PHP document called `phpinfo.php`. Enter the following:

```php
<?php
  phpinfo();
?>
```

Now fire up your Web browser and point it at the script you just created. With luck, you'll see a full breakdown of PHP's configuration. Using your browser's search functionality, look for the string `mysql`, `postgresql`, `mssql`, or `oci8`, as appropriate. If you find a section with that title, then chances are good that your build of PHP has support for that database enabled.

If not, it's time to re-install. Luckily, you'll find information on that in Appendix D, where you'll be introduced to the best-practice installation of PHP and Apache on Linux, Mac OS X, and even Windows.

PHP and PostgreSQL

This is the first chapter in this book that covers database connectivity. Virtually every subsequent chapter will feature it in some capacity — hardly surprisingly when you consider this is a book about enterprise-grade development in PHP.

That's why it's essential to understand this important topic right here and now. The database platform you choose for your project comes down to a number of important factors, and a true professional will almost certainly end up working with all four of the platforms mentioned previously at some point in his or her career.

Having said that, there will be moments where the choice is wide open, and it comes down to personal preference. The authors of this book prefer PostgreSQL in such circumstances. It's free, fast, well supported, extensible, scalable, and reliable, and sports an enterprise-grade feature set that pips MySQL to the post. There's no doubt this view goes against the grain, but, then again, so does the idea of PHP in the enterprise in the first place.

The important point here is that you realize that this is a *personal preference*; ultimately, *it does not matter*. Computer-related religious wars over anything (operating systems, languages, Web servers, databases) are deeply tiresome and are the hallmark of the spotty teenaged programmer, not a professional. For every so-called expert who advocates platform X, you'll find another who advocates platform Y, and who can probably do so every bit as eloquently.

So, to be blunt, *get over it*. This chapter (and, indeed, the rest of this book) will demonstrate to you why properly developed PHP applications are "database agnostic" — just as they are "Web-server agnostic" and "operating-system agnostic." This book isn't about "LAMP" or "LAPP"; if you took the nomenclature to its natural conclusion, this book is really about "XXXP" — that is, just PHP.

However, where you find examples in this book, they will be in PostgreSQL. You'll find more information about its installation and configuration in Appendix D. If this choice bothers you intensely, the authors implore you to bite your tongue for the purposes of the broader education this book provides — and then go ahead and use *whatever you like* in your own projects. As this chapter and the next demonstrate, you won't have to change very much to make the switch.

Recap

Let's recap how database connectivity in PHP has worked since the dawn of time. The following assumes a working installation of PHP, with PostgreSQL support enabled, and a working installation of PostgreSQL on the same box.

Create a new database in PostgreSQL at your console as follows:

```
$ /usr/local/pgsql/bin/createdb chaptersix
CREATE DATABASE
```

This syntax assumes PostgreSQL is installed on a Linux or other UNIX platform in the directory `/usr/local/pgsql`. If you're running on Windows or Mac OS X, this might well be different. The PostgreSQL installer might have added the bin directory to your path. If this is the case, you can just enter `createdb chaptersix`.

The `CREATE DATABASE` message indicates that the database was created successfully from the console. That's great, but your application must be able to connect to that database. Your application won't run from the console, so it will need its own login credentials to authenticate. Therefore, create a new user called `chaptersix` that can connect to your new database:

```
$ /usr/local/pgsql/bin/createuser -P chaptersix
Enter password for new role:
Enter it again:
Shall the new role be a superuser? (y/n) n
Shall the new role be allowed to create databases? (y/n) n
Shall the new role be allowed to create more new roles? (y/n) n
CREATE ROLE
```

At the first prompt, enter a password for the new role. For the purposes of this test, let's keep that as `chaptersix` as well. Not exactly secure, but it'll do fine for test purposes.

Naturally, the latter three prompts should elicit a response in the negative. This isn't any special kind of user; it needs minimum privileges as a result.

You now have an empty database, and login credentials for your application to use. Let's create a sample table:

```
$ /usr/local/pgsql/bin/psql chaptersix
Welcome to psql 8.2.4, the PostgreSQL interactive terminal.

Type:  \copyright for distribution terms
       \h for help with SQL commands
       \? for help with psql commands
       \g or terminate with semicolon to execute query
       \q to quit

chaptersix=# CREATE TABLE "user" (
chaptersix(# "id" SERIAL PRIMARY KEY NOT NULL,
chaptersix(# "username" character varying(32),
chaptersix(# "password_hash" character varying(32),
chaptersix(# "first_name" character varying(64),
chaptersix(# "last_name" character varying(64));
NOTICE:  CREATE TABLE will create implicit sequence "user_id_seq" for serial column
    "user.id"
NOTICE:  CREATE TABLE / PRIMARY KEY will create implicit index "user_pkey" for
    table "user"
CREATE TABLE
```

In case it's not clear from this snapshot, here's what you're entering at the PostgreSQL console:

```
CREATE TABLE "user" (
"id" SERIAL PRIMARY KEY NOT NULL,
"username" character varying(32),
"password_hash" character varying(32),
"first_name" character varying(64),
"last_name" character varying(64));
```

Because the user you created was unprivileged, it was created with no access rights to the table you just created. You must tell PostgreSQL that it's OK for the user called `chaptersix` to access the database called `chaptersix`, and that this user has full read/write access to the relations in that database.

Assuming you're still in your PostgreSQL console session (and you will be unless you've exited it by typing \q and pressing Enter), you can run the following two SQL statements to set the privileges that you need:

```
chaptersix=# GRANT ALL PRIVILEGES ON "user" TO "chaptersix";
GRANT
chaptersix=# GRANT ALL PRIVILEGES ON "user_id_seq" TO "chaptersix";
GRANT
```

Notice that you must grant privileges on both the database table and the sequence associated with it.

Finally, for the purposes of this exercise, let's put some data into the table you created. PostgreSQL allows you to do that en masse using the COPY statement, but for entering dummy data, it is fussy. Instead, let's just use some old-fashioned INSERT statements to put four test rows into the database, as shown here:

```
INSERT INTO "user"("username", "password_hash", "first_name", "last_name")
  VALUES('ed', md5('berkhamsted'), 'Ed', 'Lecky-Thompson');
INSERT INTO "user"("username", "password_hash", "first_name", "last_name")
  VALUES('steve', md5('newyork'), 'Steve', 'Nowicki');
INSERT INTO "user"("username", "password_hash", "first_name", "last_name")
  VALUES('marie', md5('leicester'), 'Marie', 'Ellis');
INSERT INTO "user"("username", "password_hash", "first_name", "last_name")
  VALUES('harriet', md5('cambridge'), 'Harriet', 'Frankland');
```

Assuming it all went in without errors, you should see four instances of the following message:

```
INSERT 0 1
```

You're finished with the PostgreSQL console now. You can exit it by typing \q and pressing Enter.

Now you have a database set up, a user configured, and a test table with data all set up. It's time to refamiliarize yourself with how PHP works with the database. Fire up your text editor and bang out the following code. Call it dbtest.php and place it somewhere in your Web server's document root:

```php
<?php
$objHandle = pg_connect("host=localhost port=5432 dbname=chaptersix user=chaptersix
                         password=chaptersix");

if (!$objHandle) {
  echo "An error occurred connecting.\n";
  exit;
}
$objResult = pg_query($objHandle, "SELECT * FROM \"user\"");
if (!$objResult) {
  echo "An error occurred querying.\n";
  exit;
};
$arRowHash = pg_fetch_all($objResult);
for ($i=0; $i>=sizeof($arRowHash)-1; $i++) {
        print "Row $i<br />\n";
```

```
            foreach ($arRowHash[$i] as $key = $value) {
                    print " - Column $key, value $value<br />\n";
            };
    };
    pg_close($objHandle);
    ?>
```

Point your Web browser at the previous code, and you'll see the following output:

```
Row 0
- Column id, value 1
- Column username, value ed
- Column password_hash, value fb097067945b57d5943bf9a49b7b7f12
- Column first_name, value Ed
- Column last_name, value Lecky-Thompson
Row 1
- Column id, value 2
- Column username, value steve
- Column password_hash, value 369389d19e24204b4927e30dd7c39efc
- Column first_name, value Steve
- Column last_name, value Nowicki
Row 2
- Column id, value 3
- Column username, value marie
- Column password_hash, value 16ba4bec9c54a088c9762527601b355a
- Column first_name, value Marie
- Column last_name, value Ellis
Row 3
- Column id, value 4
- Column username, value harriet
- Column password_hash, value efa93cabd5de7d42d6a31d41c33043ab
- Column first_name, value Harriet
- Column last_name, value Frankland
```

If you find yourself getting one of the deliberately trapped error messages instead, check your PHP error log to find out why. You might have forgotten to set permissions correctly, or you might not have started PostgreSQL to allow TCP/IP connections from external data sources. See Appendix D for the PostgreSQL setup you need.

It is hoped that all went well, and that the previous code seems pretty straightforward. It certainly shouldn't be something you haven't met before.

There are essentially four procedural functions being called here: `pg_connect`, `pg_query`, `pg_fetch_all`, and `pg_close`. They do pretty much what their names suggest they do. The prefix `pg_` indicates that they are PostgreSQL-specific functions; in a similar vein, MySQL-specific functions begin `mysql_`, Oracle's begin `oci_`, and SQL Server's begin `mssql_`.

The Problem

This state of affairs is, frankly, a mess. PHP is pretty much unique in that it has almost no predefined classes. Almost every method exists in a sort of global namespace. It's not part of a parent class, meaning it's really a "function." This is a throwback from PHP 3, for which OOP support was, shall we say, limited. It means that every database PHP wants to support creates at least 30 or so functions in this global namespace.

It gets worse. Check out the syntax for mysql_query and pg_query. You'd expect it to be the same, right? Wrong, as shown here:

```
resource mysql_query ( string $query [, resource $link_identifier ] )
resource pg_query ( resource $connection , string $query )
```

That's right. Despite being essentially identical in functionality, these two methods take their parameters in a *different order*.

This adds to a difficult situation. PHP has excellent database *support* (in terms of the breadth and depth of platforms supported), but an appalling *implementation* (mainly for historical reasons). As a result of this messy inconsistency, PHP database-driven applications built in this officially sanctioned way become a major headache to maintain — and an impossibility to scale or port.

Wrapper Classes

To address this disparity, as well as to bring some sense of order to the myriad database functions created in the global namespace, various third-party developers have, in recent years, attempted to create *wrapper classes* around these database methods.

A good example is MDB2, which is part of the PEAR repository. (See http://pear.php.net/package/ MDB2 for more information and comprehensive documentation.)

A typical session with MDB2 might look like the following. No need to try this out — it's just an illustration:

```php
<?php
require_once 'MDB2.php';
$dsn = 'pgsql://chaptersix:chaptersix@localhost/chaptersix';

$mdb2 = MDB2::factory($dsn);

if (PEAR::isError($mdb2)) {
    echo ($mdb2-getMessage().' - '.$mdb2-getUserinfo());
}

$query = 'SELECT * FROM "user"';
$result = $mdb2-query($query);

if (PEAR::isError($result)) {
    echo ($result-getMessage().' - '.$result-getUserinfo());
    exit();
}
while ($array = $result-fetchRow()) {
    var_dump($array);
};
$result-free();
?>
```

You can probably guess the output. All such classes do is provide an interface to the existing PHP global methods — but with some degree of consistency between platforms.

As a PEAR class, this means that this MDB2 package is semi-official — but the emphasis there is on "semi." It's just not quite pervasive enough, meaning that the choice of wrapper in use in any given project (if, indeed, one has been used at all) can be unpredictable. How many of you have chanced upon a legacy PHP project with some class called DatabaseConnection or similar? Perhaps this is something the original author brewed himself or herself?

Summing Up

To recap the problem: PHP's database support is a chronic mess — a hodgepodge of static methods inside the global namespace that have arisen from the language growing too quickly by too many authors over the past several years.

The mess manifests itself as an inconsistency in approach, which makes portability between databases a virtual nonstarter. Some may argue "this doesn't matter" — but don't be fooled. It does matter. You may be confident in your choice of RDBMS now, but what if its manufacturer is bought out by a big corporation that decides to stop developing it? What if a new release of that same RDBMS changes the way it works? Portability — and consistency — matters. That's why Java has Java Database Connectivity (JDBC), and .NET has ADO.NET. Even the much criticized Coldfusion has something along these lines, in the form of Coldfusion Data Sources.

Finally, as with so much in PHP, a well-meaning (but ill-advised) cabal of third-party developers have attempted to tackle the problem themselves — and made it somewhat worse. Virtually every PHP developer has recognized that the by-the-book approach is out of kilter with common sense; but every one has had his or her own unique approach, leading to an array of amateur classes to provide cleaner interfaces to PHP's database functions. Some are good, some are less than good, but none is official, and, hence, none has achieved widespread usage.

Mercifully, PHP 6 has brought us a solution.

Database Abstraction

The approach just discussed is generally described as *database abstraction*. At the simplest level, what this involves is any technique that decreases the number of points at which database-specific code occurs.

By decreasing the frequency of such touchpoints, the application becomes easier to maintain (because less code is required for simple database operations) and more portable (because the number of places where code may need changing is reduced), thus simplifying migration.

What's Needed

What is required is a universal, officially PHP-sanctioned approach for database abstraction. What is needed is something that achieves the goals of consistency and portability, while providing a universally accepted approach around which all developers can unite.

Given that other platforms such as .NET and Java 2 Enterprise Edition (J2EE) already have established mechanisms for database abstraction, something similar to their admittedly rather slick approach would be advisable, too.

Introducing PDO

Thankfully, as of PHP 5.2 (and, by implication, PHP 6), the PHP community has been gifted with PHP Data Objects (PDO).

PDO provides a database-agnostic mechanism for connecting to, reading, and manipulating myriad RDBMS platforms in PHP. It enables developers to assume a consistent approach across each database platform, easing portability and scalability, as well as eliminating the need for fly-by-night third-party abstraction layers.

Getting Started with PDO

For PHP developers familiar with the traditional database connectivity methods, PDO will seem at first a little unusual in its approach. In fact, its particular techniques are often seen in other development platforms and their abstraction layers. Other platforms such as .NET, J2EE, and even PERL practically insist upon the use of their respective abstraction layers. PHP is virtually unique in recommending in official documentation using techniques for "raw" connectivity. As a result, what is probably second nature to developers working in other languages seems especially unusual to PHP developers new to PDO.

Don't worry, however. There's a solid rationale behind every aspect of the PDO approach; and as you meet the layer throughout the rest of this chapter, it will soon become apparent why certain techniques and approaches have been adopted.

Enabling PHP Support

Earlier in this chapter, you were reminded how to enable database support within PHP:

❑ On UNIX platforms, by compiling in the relevant library during installation

❑ On Windows platforms, by enabling the appropriate DLL in `php.ini`

Unfortunately, simply enabling database support for your RDBMS of choice does not enable PDO itself, nor does it enable PDO support for that platform. As such, you must further configure PHP to enjoy PDO connectivity to the database of your choice.

There is one "gotcha" to be aware of. PDO support does not *replace* traditional PHP database support. It merely provides an additional interface to it. As a result, you must still enable base support for your database platform. Following is a checklist:

❑ Enable base PostgreSQL support — `with-pgsql`

❑ Enable PDO support — `enable-pdo=shared`

❑ Enable PostgreSQL on PDO — `with-pdo-pgsql=/usr/local/pgsql`

Full instructions on enabling PDO and the necessary support for your RDBMS can be found at www.php.net/manual/en/pdo.installation.php. You may also consult Appendix D, where a best-practice PHP and Apache installation enabling PostgreSQL support with PDO can be found for the Mac, Windows, and Linux platforms.

Connecting and Disconnecting

The best way to check whether your PHP installation is correctly configured to work with PDO and the database platform of your choice is to try to make a quick connection.

For now, you won't do any work with PDO — just connect and disconnect right away:

```
<?php
$strDSN = "pgsql:dbname=chaptersix;host=localhost;port=5432;user=chaptersix;
        password=chaptersix";

// Let's connect
try {
  $objPDO = new PDO($strDSN);
  print "Successfully connected ....\n";
} catch (PDOException $e) {
  echo "An error occurred connecting: " . $e->getMessage() . "\n";
  exit(0);
}

// Let's disconnect
$objPDO = NULL;
print "Successfully disconnected.\n";

php?>
```

This example uses the same test PostgreSQL database you populated earlier in this chapter. If you still have it set up and working, you should see the following output:

```
Successfully connected .... Successfully disconnected.
```

If something's not right, you should see an error message such as the following generated by PDO:

```
An error occurred connecting: SQLSTATE[08006] [7] FATAL: database "chaptersix"
    does not exist
```

The message comes straight from the RDBMS in question, so it is hoped that it is relatively easy to track down. Again, if the example earlier in this chapter was working for you, and you have PDO support enabled correctly, there's no reason why this example shouldn't fire off without any problems.

Working with PDO

Since you're now connected successfully to a simple PostgreSQL database via PDO, it's time to get into a bit more detail about what's going on under the hood.

The PDO Class

You probably noticed in the previous example that there's no "connect" method in PDO, nor is there any "disconnect" method. This is quite deliberate. The act of instantiating a new instance of the global PDO class establishes a connection to the database. Disconnecting happens automatically at the end of the script or, alternatively, when the class is destroyed by setting it to null.

As a result, connecting to the database is a simple as the following:

```
$objPDO = new PDO($strDSN);
```

Disconnecting is as simple as this:

```
$objPDO = NULL;
```

As such, the PDO class itself is best described as a symbolic representation of a database connection; an instance of the class can only exist once a connection has been established.

You'll doubtlessly notice the single parameter you are passing to the constructor of the PDO class. This is known as a *database source name (DSN)*. This is a concatenated string that describes the protocol, hostname, username, password, port, and database name. In some cases, other parameters can be passed, and in other cases, parameters can be omitted and the default assumed (such as in the case of TCP/IP port, which in the case of PostgreSQL is usually 5432).

PDO supports a handful of formats for valid DSN strings, but the following is the most common:

```
protocol:key=value;key=value;key=value [etc]
```

Here, protocol refers to the PDO driver to use — pgsql for PostgreSQL, mysql for MySQL, mssql for MS SQL Server, and oci for Oracle.

Each key/value pair is used to specify a particular attribute for the connection. They are many and varied, but the following are most commonly used:

❑ host — Hostname of the database (or IP address)

❑ user — Username

❑ password — Password (plain text)

❑ port — TCP/IP port (only supported if not connecting to localhost)

❑ dbname — Database name

For a full list of parameters for the database of your choice, refer to the PHP manual's database of supported drivers at www.php.net/manual/en/pdo.drivers.php. After choosing your driver, you will see a list of supported parameters enumerated.

Executing Queries

So far, you've learned how to connect and disconnect using the PDO driver, and you should understand how to pass connection parameters to customize your connection.

Now you can see how to execute a simple query using your instantiated PDO object. The following snippet of code should be inserted between your simple connection and disconnection code:

```
// Let's interrogate the database
$i = 0;
$strQuery = "SELECT * FROM \"user\"";
$objStatement = $objPDO-query($strQuery);
foreach ($objStatement as $arRow) {
        print "Row $i<br />\n";
        foreach ($arRow as $key = $value) {
                if (!is_numeric($key)) print " - Column $key, value
                $value<br />\n";
        };
        $i++;
};
```

If all goes well, then you should be able to see exactly the same output you generated earlier in the chapter using procedural database connectivity.

It's worth taking a little time to understand what's happening here. It will make your life considerably easier when you get into the more advanced material later in this chapter.

The `query()` method of the PDO class quickly and "unfussily" executes the query specified and returns an instantiated class of type `PDOStatement`. The beauty of the `PDOStatement` class is that it implements the interface known as `Traversible`; that means it supports direct iteration. Therefore, you can execute a `foreach()` statement on an instance without worrying about how the class works under the hood.

Well, that is, almost. Iterating over the class results in associative arrays, each one equaling one row of output; but each associative array entry contains both `key/value` and `index/value` data. That's why you need the `is_numeric()` clause to filter out the `index/value` stuff — try removing it and see what happens.

The preceding illustrates two points. First, it is hoped that it shows you that interrogating a database using PDO need not necessarily be any more code-intensive than using procedural code. Second, it also demonstrates that this quick-and-dirty approach doesn't exactly give you much flexibility.

What would happen if, rather than iterate directly over the `PDOStatement` object returned directly, you intercepted it, and worked with it in a little more detail?

The PDOStatement Class

The PDOStatement class represents a single statement to be executed against a given session within PDO, both *before* the query in question has been executed and *afterward*.

Instances of PDOStatement are never created directly. Instead, the PDO class itself provides the prepare() method, which generates an instance of PDOStatement. In turn, the mechanisms for interrogating the return data held by PDOStatement are considerably more sophisticated than simply using direct iteration over the class instance.

Modify the preceding block of code to read as follows:

```
// Let's interrogate the database
$i = 0;
$strQuery = "SELECT * FROM \"user\"";
$objStatement = $objPDO-prepare($strQuery);
$objStatement-execute();
while ($arRow = $objStatement-fetch(PDO::FETCH_ASSOC)) {
        print "Row $i<br />\n";
        foreach ($arRow as $key = $value) {
                print " - Column $key, value $value<br />\n";
        };
        $i++;
};
```

Refresh the page. You should see a familiar sight — yes, that's right, exactly the same output as before.

However, you're being a little smarter here by making two big changes. First, rather than call the query() method of the PDO class, you're calling the prepare() method. The key difference is that although an instance of PDOStatement is being returned, the query is not yet being executed. In the preceding example, you're executing the query more or less immediately; but as you'll see shortly, by separating out the preparation of the statement and the execution of the query, you're allowing yourself an opportunity to further manipulate the statement prior to execution.

The second big change you're making is to use the fetch() method of PDOStatement to fetch each row returned by the database one at a time, rather than use foreach() to iterate over the instance of PDOStatement itself. This gives you the flexibility to pass a parameter — a constant, namely PDO::FETCH_ASSOC. This means the data returned is an associative array containing only key/value data — not mixed with index/value data as before.

Notice, too, that it's easy to return just one row at a time. The fetch() method returns false as soon as there are no further rows to return. A similarly structured method fetchAll() enables you to return all rows at once in a single array of associative arrays.

Prepared Statements

One of the core uses of prepared statements is to provide a convenient mechanism to pass variable parameters into SQL queries.

A classic example is a scenario in which you may want to retrieve information on a particular row or rows by using a WHERE clause. Naturally, this is technically possible without using any SQL-specific techniques:

```
// Let's interrogate the database
$i = 0;
$strUsername = 'ed';
$strQuery = "SELECT * FROM \"user\" WHERE username = '$strUsername'";
$objStatement = $objPDO-prepare($strQuery);
$objStatement-execute();
while ($arRow = $objStatement-fetch(PDO::FETCH_ASSOC)) {
        print "Row $i<br />\n";
        foreach ($arRow as $key = $value) {
                print " - Column $key, value $value<br />\n";
        };
        $i++;
};
```

As you'd expect, this code returns just the row you want — in the example data, the row for the user named 'ed'.

In the preceding example, though, you are relying on PHP to merge the variable parameter (in this case, the username) with the hard-coded SQL (the statement). An alternative approach is to use the database engine to undertake the "merge." Try the following:

```
// Let's interrogate the database
$i = 0;
$strUsername = 'ed';
$strQuery = "SELECT * FROM \"user\" WHERE username = :username";
$objStatement = $objPDO-prepare($strQuery);
$objStatement-bindParam(':username', $strUsername, PDO::PARAM_STR);
$objStatement-execute();
while ($arRow = $objStatement-fetch(PDO::FETCH_ASSOC)) {
        print "Row $i<br />\n";
        foreach ($arRow as $key = $value) {
                print " - Column $key, value $value<br />\n";
        };
        $i++;
};
```

The results should be exactly the same — only data about the username 'ed' is returned. In this case, as promised, the SQL engine is undertaking the merge.

Notice that the SQL query string being passed to the prepare() method contains an unquoted parameter prefixed with a colon — namely, :username. This indicates to the PDO engine that you plan to fill that in a bit later.

The bindParam() method does just that — takes a variable and passes it to the PDO engine, telling it where to tie it into the original SQL statement. The constant PDO::PARAM_STR tells the PDO engine that the parameter being passed is a string. This is important, because the onus is on the PDO engine and the RDBMS to apply the quotes necessary to construct the final SQL.

The `bindValue()` method works similarly, but it won't accept a PHP variable as a parameter — it wants a hard-coded value instead. Similarly, `bindParam()` will fail if you try to pass it a hard-coded value — it wants a variable passed by reference.

There are four key benefits to this approach.

First (and foremost) is the benefit of abstraction. If MS SQL Server likes its parameterization to be represented using square brackets (`[` and `]`), and PostgreSQL likes single quotes (`'` and `'`), then a natural barrier to portability is introduced. By having PDO and the database itself handle such database-specific nuances, this particular barrier is removed.

The second issue is the particularly hot topic of security — specifically, vulnerability to SQL injection attacks. Web-based applications that pass HTTP POST or GET parameters toward a database as statement input parameters are particularly vulnerable to such an attack. Input parameters can be manipulated adversely in an attempt to execute malicious queries other than those originally intended. For more information, see the informative Wikipedia article at `http://en.wikipedia.org/wiki/SQL_injection`.

One solution to avoiding SQL injection is *escaping* — that is, pre-parsing HTTP POST and GET parameters to escape any characters with special meaning in SQL (such as square brackets and apostrophes). This is not foolproof, however, especially when using unusual non-ASCII character sets such as Unicode.

It also introduces a portability problem — compare databases that escape apostrophes using a backslash (`\'`) versus those that escape by using double-entry (`''`).

Using parameterized prepared statements closes this issue down once and for all. The escaping of values (including the encapsulation in delimiters as needed) is handled entirely by PDO and the database itself. The onus is therefore no longer on the developer to mitigate against SQL injection throughout — which, on a large project, can be a serious boon, even to an experienced developer.

Finally, there is the issue of performance. By using a single prepared statement, the underlying database can be made aware that a popular query (such as the example shown earlier) in an application is, in fact, structurally the same throughout, with only a parameter or set of parameters changing each time. This enables the database's own caching and memory-management techniques to self-optimize to allow those queries to execute as quickly as possible each time. When parameters are passed in outside of the database engine's consciousness, such optimizations cannot occur.

Write-Only Statements

In the previous examples, you've learned how to use PDO to extract data from the database using SELECT statements; but, naturally, not all statements result in data being returned — UPDATE, DELETE and INSERT statements spring to mind.

Your technique should be much the same as before, however:

```
$strQuery = "INSERT INTO \"user\"("username", "password") VALUES
                          (:username, :password)";
$strUsername = 'newuser';
$strPassword = 'mypassword'
$objStatement = $objPDO->prepare($strQuery);
$objStatement->bindParam(':username', $strUsername, PDO::PARAM_STR);
$objStatement->bindParam(':password', $strPassword, PDO::PARAM_STR);
$blSuccess = $objStatement-execute();
```

Notice that you capture the return parameter when executing the query. This enables you to perform some very basic error checking regarding whether the execution was successful. This isn't really sufficient for an enterprise-grade application, as you might expect. Later in this chapter, you'll learn about some of PDO's purpose-built error-handling techniques.

Transactions and Committals

As you'd probably expect, by default, PDO assumes that write operations to the database should commit automatically. In the previous example, the insertion into the database happens right away — as soon as the execute() statement is called against the PDOStatement object.

Naturally, this isn't always desirable. Most databases provide support for transactions, meaning that multiple database operations can be committed in a single operation and cancelled wholesale should some condition be (or not be) met. The classic example is one of a monetary transfer between two bank accounts. The withdrawal of money from the sender account and the receipt of money in the recipient account must happen *atomically* — that is, either *both* must occur or *neither* should occur. In other words, if, having deducted the money from the sender account, a failure occurs that prohibits the crediting of the recipient's account, then the original operation removing money from the sender should be cancelled, too.

Control of transactions takes place against instances of the PDO class — not PDOStatement. Three operations are possible: starting a new transaction, committing (completing) a transaction, and rolling back (canceling) a transaction. These are accomplished using the beginTransaction(), commit(), and rollBack() methods of PDO. Have a look at the following snippet of code:

```
<?php
$objPDO = new PDO($strDSN);
$objPDO-setAttribute(PDO::ATTR_ERRMODE, PDO::ERRMODE_EXCEPTION);

try {

  // begin the transaction
  $objPDO-beginTransaction();

  $objPDO-exec($strQuery1);
  $objPDO-exec($strQuery2);

  // commit the transaction
  $objPDO-commit();
```

```
    } catch (Exception $e) {

      // rollback the transaction
      $objPDO-rollBack();

      echo "Failed: " . $e-getMessage();
    }
    ?>
```

This example assumes a connection is made to the DSN described by $strDSN. In turn, a transaction commences, which encapsulates two interdependent queries described by $strQuery1 and $strQuery2.

Should any error occur at any stage, an exception will be generated, thus preventing the execution of any further code. All those transactions that have been executed since the transaction being initiated will be rolled back (that is, undone).

Transactions are a huge topic in and of themselves, and a complete discussion is outside the scope of this chapter. However, you will undoubtedly encounter them again throughout your programming career, so it is hoped that this section has proven a useful primer.

Constants

Throughout this chapter, you have seen numerous references to static constants exposed by the PDO class — such as PDO::PARAM_STR, PDO::ERRMODE_EXCEPTION, PDO::FETCH_ASSOC, and more.

These constants are used to define column data types, specify different fetch modes, set operational properties and attributes, and change row retrieval cursor behavior.

A full list of constants can be found at www.php.net/manual/en/pdo.constants.php.

Handling Errors

Any enterprise-grade application needs exceptional exception handling (pun intended). Although you can mitigate against errors caused by everyday events (such as users failing to enter a password correctly) by using simple techniques in your PHP code, it's also a good idea to ensure that you're coping gracefully with any unexpected eventualities that might arise as a result of your application's communication with your underlying database. This would include failing to connect to the database in the first place; failed authentication; missing relations (tables and/or columns), constraint violations; and more — anything your PHP couldn't know about on its own.

How you handle the existence of an error is up to you — but *graceful degradation* is the goal. In Chapter 20, you'll learn more about quality assurance and its importance in your application. The mechanism you use to handle exceptions in your application plays a big part in achieving a high degree of quality.

By default, PDO operates in what is called *silent mode*. This means errors won't be detected if you don't explicitly look for them using the errorCode() and errorInfo() methods on either (or both) PDO or PDOStatement.

The `errorCode()` method will return a five-character error code — for example, `45S02`, which reflects what is known as the `SQLSTATE` of the last operation on the PDO instance or `PDOStatement` instance, as appropriate. Your database of choice should provide a list of `SQLSTATE` values in its own documentation; PostgreSQL provides one at `www.postgresql.org/docs/8.2/static/errcodes-appendix.html`.

The `errorInfo()` method will return a little more detail. A three-element array is your reward. The first element contains the same information as `errorCode()`; the second contains any driver-specific (e.g., PostgreSQL-specific) error code; and the third contains a human-readable error message from the database itself.

Both of these methods are useful, but it does require you (as a developer) to test for an error at virtually every stage. This isn't really appropriate for production-grade applications and will quickly result in unwieldy code. You should instead tell PDO to throw an exception whenever it encounters a problem — and trap that exception yourself. This gives you the power to handle that error with whatever leniency or severity you deem appropriate as a developer. However, it does place the onus on you to ensure that every single possible error is caught. Any uncaught exceptions will cause a big, ugly PHP error — not something you want your users to see.

You can tell PDO to work in this way by using the following:

```
$objPDO-setAttribute(PDO::ATTR_ERRMODE, PDO::ERRMODE_EXCEPTION);
```

This needs to be called more or less immediately after instantiating the PDO class, before you even try the first query preparation.

Any PDO usage, then, must be wrapped inside `try/catch` pairs. Here's a complete example you can try for yourself:

```php
<?php
$strDSN = "pgsql:dbname=chaptersix;host=localhost;port=5432;user=chaptersix;
                    password=chaptersix";

// Let's connect
try {
  $objPDO = new PDO($strDSN);
  $objPDO-setAttribute(PDO::ATTR_ERRMODE, PDO::ERRMODE_EXCEPTION);


// Let's interrogate the database
$i = 0;
$strQuery = "SELECT * FROM \"udser\"";
$objStatement = $objPDO-prepare($strQuery);
$objStatement-execute();
while ($arRow = $objStatement-fetch(PDO::FETCH_ASSOC)) {
        print "Row $i<br />\n";
        foreach ($arRow as $key = $value) {
                print " - Column $key, value $value<br />\n";
        };
        $i++;
};

// Let's disconnect
```

```
$objPDO = NULL;

} catch (PDOException $e) {
  echo "An error occurred connecting: " . $e-getMessage() . "<br />\n";
  list($strCode, $strCode2, $strInfo) = $objPDO-errorInfo();
  print "PDO: - Code was '$strCode',<br /> - Driver code was '$strCode2',<br /> -
      Info string was '$strInfo'";
  if ($objStatement instanceof PDOStatement) {
        list($strCode, $strCode2, $strInfo) = $objStatement-errorInfo();
        print "<br /><br />PDO Statement: - Code was '$strCode',<br /> - Driver
              code was '$strCode2',<br /> - Info string was '$strInfo'";
  };
  exit(0);
}


php?>
```

Run this code (which contains a deliberate error), and you should see something like this:

```
An error occurred connecting: SQLSTATE[42P01]: Undefined table: 7 ERROR:
                            relation "udser" does not exist
PDO: - Code was '00000',
- Driver code was '7',
- Info string was 'ERROR: relation "udser" does not exist'

PDO Statement: - Code was '42P01',
- Driver code was '7',
- Info string was 'ERROR: relation "udser" does not exist'
```

It is hoped that this kind of verbosity makes it very easy to see the error you've trapped — you've made an honest typo. Fix it, refresh, and you should see some very familiar output.

This example has fallen over and died when trapping the error. Naturally, in your enterprise-grade, real-world application, you'll want to be a bit smarter than this. Rather than simply dump the information available to you to the screen, you'd be wise to use a `switch()` statement or similar to make some decision regarding what error message to display — if, indeed, you display one at all.

One final word of warning: Don't tell the user too much. Not only is this tiresome and useless from a usability point of view (why would the user care what table is missing?), but it also exposes your database schema to the outside world. From a security perspective, that's best avoided.

Advanced PDO Techniques

So far, you've learned about the basics of PDO. It is hoped that you're now confident how to use it in your projects in place of traditional procedural connectivity or third-party unofficial wrapper classes.

There are a few topics that are still worth covering, though. Don't expect too much detail here — they're big topics in their own right, and some of them you'll meet in more detail later in this book. However, by scratching the surface of each here, you can learn why you should not be tempted to revert back to bad habits as the complexity of your projects increases.

Large Objects

There's some debate in programming circles over whether it's a good idea to store large objects in a database. The term *large object (LOB)* typically refers to any one columnar value of a given row exceeding around 4,098 bytes.

This could be plain text. For example, you could be storing a complex piece of HTML representing the body of an HTML e-mail in a database. It could equally be binary data. For example, you may want to store a large user-uploaded image in a database.

The reason for the debate is the enormous processing burden involved in storing and making available what is essentially a chunk of unstructured data in a structured environment. Consider, for example, displaying a user-uploaded image in the course of rendering a Web page. If that Web page could simply retrieve that image from the file system of a Web server, then that's easy. If, however, that Web page must retrieve the image from a PHP script, which, in turn, must retrieve binary data from a database, then that's not so easy.

A compromise solution is often achievable, however. For example, you could use the database to store a "master copy" of such large objects, but then use offline generation scripts to create a file-system-stored cache. This gives you the best of both worlds: using a single database to store all variable data, but using a file system and simple Web server to serve up static content.

The mechanism by which large objects are stored in databases varies from platform to platform. Mercifully, each PDO driver knows the best way to get that data to and from the database and takes care of it for you.

The PDO::PARAM_LOB constant represents a neat way of treating large object return data from a PDO-supported database, as shown in the following example. This represents the code to a script that might be used to dump images straight into HTML <img> tags:

```php
<?php
$db = new PDO($strDSN);

$stmt = $db-prepare("SELECT \"bindata\" FROM \"jpeg_image\" WHERE id = :imageid");
$stmt-bindParam(':imageid', $_GET["id"], PDO::PARAM_INT);
$stmt-execute();
$stmt-bindColumn(1, $binData, PDO::PARAM_LOB);
$stmt-fetch(PDO::FETCH_BOUND);

header("Content-Type: image/jpeg");
fpassthru($binData);
exit(0);
?>
```

If you named this script dumpimage.php, you might invoke it using an image tag that looks like this:

```
<img src="dumpimage.php?id=12345" />
```

Notice that you bind the input parameter representing the image identifier in the normal way, taking care to tell PDO that it must be an integer by using the constant PDO::PARAM_INT. Also notice, though, that you use a method of PDOStatement called bindColumn(). This has the unusual behavior of allowing subsequent invocations of fetch() to populate given PHP variables without further notice.

In this case, using bindColumn() tells PDO that the first (leftmost) column of its return data should be fed into a PHP variable $binData — one feeding per row called using fetch(). By specifying a data type of PDO::PARAM_LOB, the fetch() method will store that data in that variable using PHP's closest approximation of a large object — namely, a *stream*.

A file stream in PHP can be sent straight to standard output using fpassthru() — and this is exactly what you use to dump the image binary data straight to the browser, taking care to first issue a suitable MIME type as a header.

It's worth noting that PHP assumes you're using a database's preferred large object metaphor. If you're not (for example, if you are storing Base64 encoded data as a string), then this technique will fail. In PostgreSQL, large objects are implemented using object identifier (OID) references and are largely taken care of by the database "behind the scenes." More reading than you could ever wish for can be found at www.postgresql.org/docs/8.1/static/largeobjects.html.

Database-Specific Functions

PDO does its best to emulate behavior (or gracefully fail) when a specific request cannot be fulfilled on the database platform in use. Indeed, certain database behavior is unarguably peculiar to that specific platform. It would, therefore, be asinine for PDO to attempt to provide universal implementation, only for it to fail on 19 out of 20 RDBMSs.

For this reason, certain methods of the PDO and PDOStatement classes are only available when PDO has been instantiated using a particular driver.

For example, the creation of large objects (as just discussed) in PostgreSQL is achieved through the allocation of a new OID from the central large object repository, which spans multiple tables and databases, and is therefore essentially unique per-installation. This behavior is niche to say the least, and, as such, PDO exposes a PostgreSQL-only method, PDO::pgsqlLOBCreate(), to achieve it. See www.php.net/manual/en/function.pdo-pgsqllobcreate.php for the full syntax.

This is a sensible approach. However good PDO's intentions may be, perfect database abstraction is something of a pipe dream, as you'll see in the next section. When methodology truly is unique to a particular platform, the developers have allocated a unique method to achieve it.

Hence, individual driver-specific methods and constants can be located on the PDO drivers' function references found at www.php.net/manual/en/pdo.drivers.php. Be sure to consult it if your database of choice is often prone to nonconformist tendencies.

Persistent Connections

Generally speaking, a new TCP/IP connection to the database is formed whenever an instance of the PDO class is created as an object. In turn, this connection is closed when that object is destroyed.

For high-traffic connections, this may not always be preferable. Using persistent connections means PHP will keep the established connection open after the script terminates. When the script runs again in another session, an existing idle connection will be "hijacked" for immediate use. It's like keeping the phone permanently dialed to your favorite pizza place, and then just lifting the handset to your ear when you get hungry.

This provides performance benefits. Because there is overhead associated with opening and closing sockets, by keeping those connections open, that overhead is eliminated.

Using persistent connections is easy, as shown here:

```php
<?php
$objPDO = new PDO($strDSN, NULL, NULL,array(
    PDO::ATTR_PERSISTENT = true
));
?>
```

Notice the blank parameters after the DSN. If you're populating the username and password in the DSN, then these parameters (normally used for specification of username and password) are not required. The fourth parameter (an array of driver-specific parameters) features the parameter PDO::ATTR_ PERSISTENT set to true.

Note one drawback, and one prerequisite. The drawback is that those connections are "reserved" by PHP, meaning other applications (including command-line PHP scripts you may have to regularly perform batch jobs on) can't use those connections to talk to your database. The prerequisite is that in order to maintain the connection beyond the script execution, PHP must be running as a Web server module — not a CGI script. If you follow the installation instructions in Appendix D, however, then this shouldn't be an issue.

Stored Procedures

Many database platforms support *stored procedures*. This means that certain common procedures and functions can be coded into the database schema — rather than developed in the application development language (such as PHP). As a result, for example, methods such as getNearestStore() can be called directly from SQL syntax — rather than having to construct multiple queries to achieve the same effect in PHP.

There are certain advantages to this approach. Some RDBMSs are able to cache the data sets involved in calls to stored procedures intelligently. As a result, subsequent calls to these stored procedures are able to enjoy performance benefits. In addition, should other platforms (perhaps .NET applications or PERL scripts) need to access the same data and execute those same procedures, there are code savings to be realized.

Calling a stored procedure is no different from calling any SQL statement. The syntax depends on the RDBMS in question. MySQL uses the CALL() statement; PostgreSQL simply invokes the function as if it were built in. Passing parameters is achieved in exactly the same way, as shown here:

```php
$iUserID = 12345;
$objStatement = $objPDO-prepare("SELECT getNearestStore(:userid)");
$objStatement-bindParam(":userid", $iUserID, PDO::PARAM_INT);
// call the stored procedure
$objStatement-execute();
```

Keep in mind that stored procedures severely limit database portability — one of the key aims of the PDO project. To that end, use them sparingly and judiciously.

Singleton Instantiation

On a typical PHP project, only one connection to one database is required. For that reason, instantiating multiple instances of the PDO class shouldn't happen in a given request — after all, one instance equals one connection.

This can be a tricky rule to stick to, though. You'll notice as you start to build increasingly sophisticated projects that your database access requirements are split across multiple classes. If each method of each class needs access to your database, how do you share access to a single connection across each of those classes?

The answer is a *singleton class,* a class with a single factory method that returns an instance of PDO for your application. This method is pretty smart. It figures out whether or not an instance of PDO has already been returned to your application. If one hasn't, then it creates a new instance of PDO and returns a reference to it. If it has, then it returns a reference to the existing instance:

```php
<?php
class PDOFactory {

    public static function GetPDO($strDSN, $strUser, $strPass, $arParms) {
        $strKey = md5(serialize(array($strDSN, $strUser, $strPass, $arParms)));
        if (!($GLOBALS["PDOS"][$strKey] instanceof PDO)) {
            $GLOBALS["PDOS"][$strKey] = new PDO($strDSN,
                                    $strUser, $strPass, $arParms);
        };
        return($GLOBALS["PDOS"][$strKey]);
    }


}
?>
```

This class enables you to create new instances of PDO without ever worrying about duplicate connections. Provided that the DSN, username, password, and parameter array are identical on each occasion, you'll never get a duplicate — just the original.

Therefore, in your code, look for the following:

```
$objPDO = new PDO($strDSN, NULL, NULL, array(PDO::ATTR_PERSISTENT => true));
```

Instead of the preceding syntax, use the following:

```
$objPDO = PDOFactory::GetPDO($strDSN, NULL, NULL, array(PDO::ATTR_PERSISTENT =>
    true));
```

The effect is the same — you get an instance of the PDO object — but you're guaranteed not to get more than one per script execution, regardless of the class from which you request the instance.

Limitations of PDO

So far in this chapter, you've seen PDO in something of a positive light — a simple, straightforward, and officially sanctioned mechanism that can provide uniform database abstraction in your PHP applications, regardless of your choice of RDBMS.

In the aim of true portability between platforms, though, it is fair to say that PDO has its limitations. Understanding and recognizing where it can (and cannot) help you is the hallmark of a true PHP professional. As you'll see in subsequent chapters, there are techniques well beyond the realm of database abstraction that can ease portability and scalability.

Query Syntax

Consider the following SQL query:

```
SELECT TOP 10 * FROM [user]
```

Now consider this query:

```
SELECT * FROM "user" LIMIT 10;
```

These two queries are obviously different on the surface. As you may have guessed, however, they result in identical output when executed in their respective databases. The first query is Transact-SQL, and hence compatible with MS SQL Server and Sybase. The latter is PostgreSQL — or indeed MySQL.

However, the differences run deeper. Consider the following:

```
SELECT * FROM user
```

Now consider this:

```
SELECT * FROM "user"
```

Both the former and the latter are perfectly permissible in MySQL. However, only the latter is permissible in PostgreSQL because "user" is a reserved word, so quotation marks are required — not optional. By now you have no doubt spotted the argument. Although SQL allows a great deal of commonality between various RDBMSs, each dialect of SQL is subtly different. PDO can accommodate minor differences such as escaping and enquoting, but it can't accommodate fundamental differences in syntax.

Such shortcomings naturally limit portability — the whole purpose of PDO.

Feature Emulation

Similarly, certain RDBMSs support entire feature sets absent in others. A case in point is transaction support — notably absent in older versions of MySQL, as well as flat-file databases such as SQLite and Access.

PDO will do its best to emulate software-level features not inherent in the RDBMS in question. When it can't do this, unfortunately, it will rarely throw an error — instead, it just won't work. A good example is PDO::lastInsertID() — a useful method designed to return the auto-incremented numeric identifier assigned from the last INSERT statement executed by your application. Regrettably, if your database driver doesn't support this method, then you may not get a meaningful or consistent result.

The moral of the story here is to be *very sure* that your RDBMS supports what you are trying to do before you try to do it. If it doesn't, then you may not find an error is thrown as you would expect; rather, PDO may try to be helpful and end up thoroughly confusing in the process.

Non-SQL Data Sources

Finally, it's worth touching on the concept of a *data source*. PDO assumes that any data source your application may use will be a traditional, off-the-shelf database (such PostgreSQL or Oracle), or a flat-file solution (such as Access or SQLite). Increasingly, however, this isn't always the case; applications frequently make use of remote data sources run over Web services of one form or another.

A good example would be a business that starts out small — maybe running a single PostgreSQL or MySQL database — and then decides to franchise out its business model. The same code that powered that small business may be required to be rolled out across the franchise, but instead of using a simple installation of an RDBMS, make use of central Web services that provides access to the same approximate model of data on a distributed basis.

In such a scenario, PDO falls short of expectations. There is no mechanism to port from using a traditional database with PDO to using a more distributed model such as that described here. Writing your own PDO drivers is certainly possible, but not in PHP. Patches in C++ to the PHP core are required, with all the inherent difficulties associated with maintainability.

Beyond PDO

There's one final point worth making — and that is that PDO does *not* write SQL for you. This is quite deliberate. Refer to the PDO documentation at www.php.net/manual/en/intro.pdo.php and you'll clearly see that PDO advertises itself as "data access abstraction," rather than "database abstraction."

This might sound like semantics, but the distinction is important. PDO still requires you to possess a near-encyclopedic knowledge of the RDBMS of your choice — its peculiarities, specific features, and limitations. This is arguably not a bad thing, but you may well find yourself frustrated at having to write and rewrite repetitive SQL statements to do simple things such create, read, update, and delete entities.

Fret not. In Chapter 7, you'll learn about Object Relation Mapping (ORM) and how it can save you a whole heap of time by constructing common SQL queries on your behalf.

Summary

This important chapter introduced you to PHP Data Objects (PDO). You learned how PDO can play an important role in guaranteeing your application's portability and scalability across seemingly disparate database platforms.

You started off with a recap of PHP's basic database support by creating, connecting to, reading, and manipulating a simple PostgreSQL database. By considering hypothetical examples, you saw how PHP's built-in procedural database access limits the scalability and portability of your application; and even saw how well-meaning (but ultimately fruitless) efforts by third parties have already attempted to address the problem.

You were introduced to "the official way" to undertake database access in PHP6 — namely, PDO. From the ground up, you learned how to recreate the simple data access techniques you were used to in PHP 4 and 5 using preferred PHP techniques.

Finally, you were given a crash course in some of the advanced mechanisms PDO makes available to developers, with a view to learning each technique in greater detail later in the book. You were also shown some of PDO's limitations (not insignificant in some cases), which demonstrate that it only goes some of the way in addressing the issues at hand.

Chapter 7 is of equal importance. You'll be introduced to Object Relation Mapping (ORM), which enables you to write even less SQL when building common database applications. It's something you've probably bumped into before without even realizing it, but the power of PDO enables it to go one step further than it has done historically. Your newly found knowledge of PDO will give you a newly found appreciation of what ORM can do for your applications, and why it's so important.

Part II

Learning Advanced Development Techniques

7

Object Relation Mapping

Chapter 6 introduced you to PHP Data Objects (PDO), which provides a form of simple database abstraction to enable a greater degree of portability, scalability, and ease of maintenance for enterprise-grade PHP applications.

The tail end of the chapter, however, described some of the limitations of PDO. As you discovered, PDO never generates SQL statements for you; it still relies on you, as the developer, to craft every one from scratch. That's sometimes quite desirable, especially for performance reasons; but more often than not, it ends up violating a golden rule of enterprise level development: *Don't Repeat Yourself* (DRY, for short).

In this chapter, you'll see how even relatively simple applications that use databases to hold business data run the risk of code repetition, with the myriad risks associated with it. You'll see how the use of a further degree of abstraction, Object Relation Mapping (ORM), can minimize the amount of code you must write to achieve the most common database operations.

By gaining an understanding of the principles behind ORM, when you're introduced to a key part of your enterprise PHP 6 toolkit, `DataBoundObject`, you'll understand not just what it does, but also how it works under the hood. This is an important chapter, so don't move on until it has fully sunk in.

Types of Classes

The first few chapters of this book provided you with a crash course in the principles behind object-oriented programming (OOP). Your take on those chapters will have depended on whether you are familiar with objects in other development languages such as Java 2 Enterprise Edition (J2EE) and .NET. If you are, it is hoped that you breezed through those first few pages and gained an understanding of "how PHP does it." If you aren't, then it is hoped that you are now fully versed in not only how to write OOP code in PHP, but also why you *should*.

In this chapter, you will be dealing with a particular kind of class, though — a *business class*. For that reason, it's worth understanding the differences between the various types of classes you'll encounter (or write) in your PHP programming career. After all, you must be able to identify when the ORM model (which applies only to business classes) is actually appropriate to use.

Utility Classes

One of the first guiding principles of OOP development is that "everything should be an object." In other words, the idea of using procedural code — that is, including functions inside the global namespace — should be consigned to your mental wastebasket.

This leaves developers with something of a conundrum. If you're not allowed to have sets of functions anymore, then where do you put all those useful bits of code that do things such as encryption, sending e-mails, doing math, and so forth?

The answer is that you wrap them inside a *helper class* (also called a *utility class*). In this way, you group together methods with a common purpose inside a single class, usually (though not always) as static methods. For example, a single global function called `EncryptString()` might instead be replaced by a static method in a class called `Encryption`, and hence be invoked using `Encryption::EncryptString()` instead.

PHP is one of relatively few modern development languages that has such niche methods in the global namespace — that is, outside of a class of any descriptions. True proponents of OOP in PHP often decry this fact and vigorously write wrapper classes to attempt to eliminate the need for global methods — for example, a class called `String` such that `$objString->getLength()` may be used instead of `strlen($strVar)`.

This book does not go quite that far. After all, the authors quite like writing `base64_encode($s)` instead of `Convert.ToBase64String(System.Text.Encoding.ASCII.GetBytes(s))` (a tip of the hat to .NET there); but you will certainly find that this book does advocate grouping together common developer-authored methods into single classes.

It's worth stating that these classes are normally "data stateless." That is, they do not create, read, update, or delete in external data sources, such as file systems, Web services or, crucially, databases. Should you find yourself needing a class to do just that, then a business class is a far better bet.

Business Classes

As a rule, a *business class* is a class (or a *business object*, once it's been instantiated) that represents a single (usually changeable) entity that your application is designed to support. Note that the word "business" is misleading — after all, not all applications are written for a business — but these classes most definitely do represent "things" that are created, read, updated, or deleted by your application.

Developers often cite the example of an e-commerce site, which has users who generate orders, which consist of a shopping cart full of products, and a credit card transaction used to pay for that cart of products. In that one sentence you can find five potential business classes:

- ❑ A class `User` that represents a user on the site
- ❑ A class `Order` that represents an order placed by a "user"

❑   A class `Product` that represents a product a "user" may buy as part of his or her "order"

❑   A class `Cart` that represents a temporary storage area for products that may (or may not) form an "order" at some point in the future

❑   A class `CardPayment` that represents a credit card payment used to pay for an "order"

As you can see, each of these five classes has a semantic meaning outside the inner workings of the application itself. You could easily explain to a nontechnical suit within the business what a "user" or "order" is without too much difficulty. That's where the phrase "business object" comes from, although some use the term *domain object*.

Business Objects in Detail

Now that you broadly understand what a business object is, and where you might use one in your application, it's worth taking a look at how you might implement one in practice. In this section, you'll see the evolution of a simple class designed to represent a user on a system.

The Design

Before pressing keys on the keyboard, it's useful to design the class on paper. The `User` class represents a single registered user in this hypothetical application. As a simple application, only a few fields are prompted for at registration:

❑   First name

❑   Last name

❑   Username

❑   Password (which is stored encrypted)

❑   E-mail address

You may want to store a few more pieces of information about each user, though:

❑   Date of last login

❑   Time of last login

❑   Date account was created

❑   Time account was created

With this design in mind, you can easily fashion an early prototype for your class.

Prototyping

You can now build a very simple class that represents the design. The following source code demonstrates an early prototype of the User class — you might want to call it `userv1.phpm` to distinguish it from later versions you'll build this chapter:

```php
<?php

class User {

        private $FirstName;
        private $LastName;
        private $Username;
        private $Password;
        private $EmailAddress;

        private $DateLastLogin;
        private $TimeLastLogin;
        private $DateAccountCreated;
        private $TimeAccountCreated;


        public function __call($strFunction, $arArguments) {

                $strMethodType = substr($strFunction, 0, 3);
                $strMethodMember = substr($strFunction, 3);
                switch ($strMethodType) {
                        case "set":
                                return($this->SetAccessor($strMethodMember,
                                        $arArguments[0]));
                                break;
                        case "get":
                                return($this->GetAccessor($strMethodMember));
                };
                return(false);
        }

        private function SetAccessor($strMember, $strNewValue) {
                if (property_exists($this, $strMember)) {
                        if (is_numeric($strNewValue)) {
                                eval('$this->' . $strMember . ' = ' . $strNewValue
                                        . ';');
                        } else {
                                eval('$this->' . $strMember . ' = "' . $strNewValue
                                        . '";');
                        };
                } else {
                        return(false);
                };
        }

        private function GetAccessor($strMember) {
                if (property_exists($this, $strMember)) {
```

```
                    eval('$strRetVal = $this->' . $strMember . ';');
                    return($strRetVal);
            } else {
                    return(false);
            };
        }

    }

?>
```

Naturally, the newly created prototype class is of little use without some PHP to test it out. Here's a quick example you can quickly call up in your Web browser:

```php
<?php

        require("userv1.phpm");

        $objUser = new User();
        $objUser->setFirstName("Ed");
        $objUser->setLastName("Lecky-Thompson");
        $objUser->setUsername("ed");

        print "First name is " . $objUser->getFirstName() . "<br />";
        print "Last name is " . $objUser->getLastName() . "<br />";
        print "Username is " . $objUser->getUsername() . "<br />";

?>
```

Try the preceding little bit of code. You'll need to save it in the same directory as the class — and it is hoped that you'll see the following fairly predictable output:

```
First name is Ed
Last name is Lecky-Thompson
Username is ed
```

You're already doing a few fairly clever things here, so it's worth stepping through the class step-by-step to ensure that it all makes sense to you.

First of all, notice that all the member variables discussed earlier in the chapter are being declared as private, not public:

```
        private $FirstName;
        private $LastName;
        private $Username;
        private $Password;
        private $EmailAddress;

        private $DateLastLogin;
        private $TimeLastLogin;
        private $DateAccountCreated;
        private $TimeAccountCreated;
```

This is a good practice. The member variables are not something you want outside code to touch or inspect directly, as it wrests control away from where the magic can happen — that is, your class. Therefore, you use *accessor* methods. These methods enable you to access each member variable via an aptly named method, as you saw in the previous test. For example, to get the "last name" property (a member variable called `LastName`), you use a method called `getLastName()`. Similarly, to set it you would use `setLastName()`.

However, with so many member variables, it would be a pain to have to write two accessor methods for each — so you don't. You make use of a PHP feature called *object overloading*, which enables you to describe the behavior that PHP should exhibit when your code calls a method that doesn't (on the face of it) exist.

The two physical methods, `SetAccessor()` and `GetAccessor()`, provide a useful "map" between all your virtual accessor methods and the behavior you want when those accessor methods are used. In this case, nothing clever happens. The methods simply provide a public interface to public member variables and use PHP's `eval()` function to write PHP code on-the-fly; but as you'll see shortly, these two methods provide a useful "trap" in which other code may be executed as part of your setting and getting.

Adding Data Binding

Your class works, and you've written a short test to prove that to yourself. You've even saved yourself maintenance headache by defining overloaded virtual accessor methods. If you need to add an extra member variable in the future, then you simply add it to the class definition, with no extra code required.

Crucially, however, your class lacks something — data binding. Right now, as soon as you create a new user, it exists only for the lifetime of that HTTP request. Assuming your users' registrations are to last a while longer than that, you'll need to store your users in a database.

Naturally, the way to do that is to create a database table (or *relation*) that matches (or *maps to*) your *object*. Suddenly, the title of this chapter — "Object Relation Mapping" — makes a bit of sense.

Before you create a table, you must create a database to hold it. If you followed Chapter 6 to the letter, then this task is unlikely to present you with any problems:

```
$ /usr/local/pgsql/bin/createdb chapterseven
CREATE DATABASE
```

Next, create a user of the same name to access the database:

```
$ /usr/local/pgsql/bin/createuser -P chapterseven
Enter password for new role:
Enter it again:
Shall the new role be a superuser? (y/n) n
Shall the new role be allowed to create databases? (y/n) n
Shall the new role be allowed to create more new roles? (y/n) n
CREATE ROLE
```

As before, open the PostgreSQL console to create the relevant database table:

```
$ /usr/local/pgsql/bin/psql chapterseven
Welcome to psql 8.2.4, the PostgreSQL interactive terminal.

Type:  \copyright for distribution terms
       \h for help with SQL commands
       \? for help with psql commands
       \g or terminate with semicolon to execute query
       \q to quit

chapterseven=# CREATE TABLE "system_user" (
chapterseven(# "id" SERIAL PRIMARY KEY NOT NULL,
chapterseven(# "first_name" character varying(64),
chapterseven(# "last_name" character varying(128),
chapterseven(# "username" character varying(32),
chapterseven(# "md5_pw" character varying(32),
chapterseven(# "email_address" character varying(128),
chapterseven(# "date_last_login" date,
chapterseven(# "time_last_login" time,
chapterseven(# "date_account_created" date,
chapterseven(# "time_account_created" time
chapterseven(# );
NOTICE:  CREATE TABLE will create implicit sequence "system_user_id_seq" for
         serial column "system_user.id"
NOTICE:  CREATE TABLE / PRIMARY KEY will create implicit index "system_user_pkey"
         for table "system_user"
CREATE TABLE
chapterseven=#
```

The final step is to give the user 'chapterseven' full access to the table 'system_user'. Therefore, you would use the following while still in the PostgreSQL console:

```
chapterseven=# GRANT ALL PRIVILEGES ON "system_user" TO "chapterseven";
GRANT
chapterseven=# GRANT ALL PRIVILEGES ON "system_user_id_seq" TO "chapterseven";
GRANT
```

You're all set. There's no need to create any test data. The test code you will meet later in this chapter creates a test entry for you.

Data Requirements

Before meeting any more code, it's worth considering in some detail exactly what you want out of your data-bound User class.

Ever heard of "CRUD"? It stands for "create, read, update, and delete" — and it refers to the four most common data operations you will typically perform on a data-bound object:

❑　*Create* — Obviously, you want to be able to create new instances of users in your database table by creating a new instance of the class. Typically, you'll set some attributes using the various accessor methods, and then call some sort of method to commit the new object to the database, generating an appropriate INSERT statement in the process.

❏ *Read* — You'll also be interested in being able to create new instances of the `User` object that represent exiting users in the database. For example, you may know that you're interested in a user with the `'id'` of 345 — perhaps in common parlance referred to as "user 345." You'll need some mechanism of instantiating the class with that identifier, populating its properties so they mirror that of the underlying database table entry, and enabling the user of accessor methods to retrieve those properties.

❏ *Update* — In the same vein as the reading capabilities defined earlier, you'll want your business object to allow for the updating of an existing user's current properties. Therefore, having instantiated a new user in exactly the same way described previously, you'll want to provide accessor methods to enable properties to be updated and, crucially, a mechanism to commit all those changes to the database.

❏ *Delete* — Finally, there will be times when the user in question will never be needed again, so the underlying database table entry will never be needed again. Therefore, a mechanism is needed to destroy the object and underlying database table entry, provided that the object instance in question represented a bona fide database entry.

Relation Mapping

You will have noticed in the example prototype class that you provided virtual accessor methods to every property of the `User` object — for example, `SetFirstName()`, `SetLastName()`, `GetFirstName()`, `GetLastName()`, and so forth.

This is a good practice. Some alternative approaches you may have seen in the past use generic methods called `GetField()` and `SetField()`, which take the name of a database column as a string parameter. While this is suitably flexible, it is less than ideal. The purpose of database abstraction of any kind is to remove programmer dependency on underlying database knowledge. This approach requires knowledge of database column names, which may not necessarily be the same as your member variable names. For example, compare `SetFirstName()` versus `SetField("first_name")`.

Indeed, it is often undesirable to use the same name for a member attribute and database column name. Many RDBMSs frown upon the use of capital letters in relation names, yet using capitalization in PHP variable and member names can greatly increase readability, particularly when capitalizing the first letter of each discrete English word in your variable name (a technique known as *StudleyCaps*).

As a result, there must be some mechanism in your data-bound business object to *map* column names to class member variables. This way, when your class executes `INSERT`, `UPDATE`, `SELECT`, and `DELETE` statements, it can easily translate between column names and database table column names, and vice versa.

A Working Business Object

Based on the previous discussion, the next step is to construct a fully working version of your original prototype, which binds itself to your underlying database, but, on the surface, works almost exactly the same way.

The key word there is *almost*. You'll notice changes to the addition of a constructor that allows the invoker to pass a numeric identifier, if known. This enables the class to be instantiated to represent an existing user in the database, rather than a brand-new one. This identifier is then stored in a new member variable, `'id'`. The constructor also sets up the relation map, which maps relation names to member variable names.

In addition, notice the use of a `Save()` method to commit changes (`INSERT` or `UPDATE`, as required); and a `MarkForDeletion()` method to allow destruction.

Meet the Code

You can enter the following code for the class and save it as `userv2.phpm`. It's a long piece of code, so be careful to ensure that you don't accidentally introduce any carriage returns or linefeeds where code spans the width of this book's page:

```php
<?php

class User {

        private $ID;
        private $objPDO;
        private $strTableName;
        private $arRelationMap;
        private $blForDeletion;

        private $FirstName;
        private $LastName;
        private $Username;
        private $Password;
        private $EmailAddress;

        private $DateLastLogin;
        private $TimeLastLogin;
        private $DateAccountCreated;
        private $TimeAccountCreated;

        public function __construct(PDO $objPDO, $id = NULL) {
                $this->strTableName = "system_user";
                $this->arRelationMap = array(
                        "id" => "ID",
                        "first_name" => "FirstName",
                        "last_name" => "LastName",
                        "username" => "Username",
                        "md5_pw" => "Password",
                        "email_address" => "EmailAddress",
                        "date_last_login" => "DateLastLogin",
                        "time_last_login" => "TimeLastLogin",
                        "date_account_created" => "DateAccountCreated",
                        "time_account_created" => "TimeAccountCreated");
                $this->objPDO = $objPDO;
                if (isset($id)) {
                        $this->ID = $id;
                        $strQuery = "SELECT ";
                        foreach ($this->arRelationMap as $key => $value) {
                                $strQuery .= "\"" . $key . "\",";
```

```php
        }
        $strQuery = substr($strQuery, 0, strlen($strQuery)-1);
        $strQuery .= " FROM " . $this->strTableName . " WHERE
                    \"id\" = :eid";
        $objStatement = $this->objPDO->prepare($strQuery);
        $objStatement->bindParam(':eid', $this->ID,
                                    PDO::PARAM_INT);
        $objStatement->execute();
        $arRow = $objStatement->fetch(PDO::FETCH_ASSOC);
        foreach($arRow as $key => $value) {
                $strMember = $this->arRelationMap[$key];
                if (property_exists($this, $strMember)) {
                        if (is_numeric($value)) {
                                eval('$this->' . $strMember . ' =
                                    ' . $value . ';');
                        } else {
                                eval('$this->' . $strMember . ' =
                                    "' . $value . '";');
                        };
                };
        };
    };
}

public function Save() {
        if (isset($this->ID)) {
                $strQuery = 'UPDATE "' . $this->strTableName . '" SET ';
                foreach ($this->arRelationMap as $key => $value) {
                        eval('$actualVal = &$this->' . $value . ';');
                        if (isset($actualVal)) {
                                $strQuery .= '"' . $key . '\" = :$value, ";
                        };
                }
                $strQuery = substr($strQuery, 0, strlen($strQuery)-2);
                $strQuery .= ' WHERE "id" = :eid';
                unset($objStatement);
                $objStatement = $this->objPDO->prepare($strQuery);
                $objStatement->bindValue(':eid', $this->ID,
                                    PDO::PARAM_INT);
                foreach ($this->arRelationMap as $key => $value) {
                        eval('$actualVal = &$this->' .
                                $value . ';');
                        if (isset($actualVal)) {
                                if ((is_int($actualVal)) ||
                                    ($actualVal == NULL)) {
                                        $objStatement->bindValue
                                    (':' . $value, $actualVal, PDO::PARAM_INT);
                                } else {
                                        $objStatement->bindValue
                                    (':' . $value, $actualVal, PDO::PARAM_STR);
                                };
                        };
                };
```

```php
                        $objStatement->execute();
            } else {
                    $strValueList = "";
                    $strQuery = 'INSERT INTO "' . $this->strTableName . '"(';
                    foreach ($this->arRelationMap as $key => $value) {
                            eval('$actualVal = &$this->' . $value . ';');
                            if (isset($actualVal)) {
                                    $strQuery .= '"' . $key . '", ';
                                    $strValueList .= ":$value, ";
                            };
                    }
                    $strQuery = substr($strQuery, 0, strlen($strQuery) - 2);
                    $strValueList = substr($strValueList, 0,
                                    strlen($strValueList) - 2);
                    $strQuery .= ") VALUES (";
                    $strQuery .= $strValueList;
                    $strQuery .= ")";
                    unset($objStatement);
                    $objStatement = $this->objPDO->prepare($strQuery);
                    foreach ($this->arRelationMap as $key => $value) {
                            eval('$actualVal = &$this->' . $value . ';');
                            if (isset($actualVal)) {
                                    if ((is_int($actualVal)) ||
                                        ($actualVal == NULL)) {
                                            $objStatement->bindValue
                        (':' . $value, $actualVal, PDO::PARAM_INT);
                                    } else {
                                            $objStatement->bindValue
                        (':' . $value, $actualVal, PDO::PARAM_STR);
                                    };
                            };
                    }
                    $objStatement->execute();
                    $this->ID = $this->objPDO->lastInsertId
                                        ($this->strTableName . "_id_seq");
            }
    }

    public function MarkForDeletion() {
            $this->blForDeletion = true;
    }

    public function __destruct() {
            if (isset($this->ID)) {
                    if ($this->blForDeletion == true) {
                            $strQuery = 'DELETE FROM "' .
                                $this->strTableName . '" WHERE "id" = :eid';
                            $objStatement = $this->objPDO->prepare($strQuery);
                            $objStatement->bindValue
                                (':eid', $this->ID, PDO::PARAM_INT);
                            $objStatement->execute();
                    };
            }
```

```php
        }

        public function __call($strFunction, $arArguments) {

                $strMethodType = substr($strFunction, 0, 3);
                $strMethodMember = substr($strFunction, 3);
                switch ($strMethodType) {
                        case "set":
                                return($this->SetAccessor
                                        ($strMethodMember, $arArguments[0]));
                                break;
                        case "get":
                                return($this->GetAccessor($strMethodMember));
                };
                return(false);
        }

        private function SetAccessor($strMember, $strNewValue) {
                if (property_exists($this, $strMember)) {
                        if (is_numeric($strNewValue)) {
                                eval('$this->' . $strMember .
                                        ' = ' . $strNewValue . ';');
                        } else {
                                eval('$this->' . $strMember .
                                        ' = "' . $strNewValue . '";');
                        };
                } else {
                        return(false);
                };
        }

        private function GetAccessor($strMember) {
                if (property_exists($this, $strMember)) {
                        eval('$strRetVal = $this->' . $strMember . ';');
                        return($strRetVal);
                } else {
                        return(false);
                };
        }

}

?>
```

Ensuring Requirements Are Met

The preceding piece of code is pretty daunting, and the longest piece of code you have met in this book so far. Don't worry; you will learn how it works in more detail in the following sections. For now, it's important to try it out to ensure that it fulfills all of the requirements you drafted previously — namely, CRUD (create, read, update, and delete).

Create

Try out the following piece of code. You'll need `userv2.phpm` (created previously) and `pdofactory`.`phpm` (found in Chapter 6) in order for it to work.

```php
<?php

        require("userv2.phpm");
        require("pdofactory.phpm");

        print "Running...<br />";

        $strDSN = "pgsql:dbname=chapterseven;host=localhost;port=5432";
        $objPDO = PDOFactory::GetPDO($strDSN, "chapterseven", "chapterseven",
                array());
        $objPDO->setAttribute(PDO::ATTR_ERRMODE, PDO::ERRMODE_EXCEPTION);
        $objUser = new User($objPDO);

        $objUser->setFirstName("Steve");
        $objUser->setLastName("Nowicki");
        $objUser->setDateAccountCreated(date("Y-m-d"));

        print "First name is " . $objUser->getFirstName() . "<br />";
        print "Last name is " . $objUser->getLastName() . "<br />";

        print "Saving...<br />";

        $objUser->Save();

        print "ID in database is " . $objUser->getID() . "<br />";

?>
```

It is hoped that you see the following output:

```
Running...
First name is Steve
Last name is Nowicki
Saving...
ID in database is 1
```

Take a look at the database, too. You should be able to see the following entry:

```
chapterseven=# SELECT first_name, last_name, date_account_created FROM
 "system_user" WHERE id=1;
 first_name | last_name | date_account_created
------------+-----------+----------------------
 Steve      | Nowicki   | 2008-05-26
(1 row)
```

Notice that you didn't specify every column, but it didn't matter. Because other columns had no NOT NULL constraints, they were effectively optional and were left blank.

Read

Here's a much simpler piece of code that makes use of the record you just inserted:

```php
<?php

        require("userv2.phpm");
        require("pdofactory.phpm");

        print "Running...<br />";

        $strDSN = "pgsql:dbname=chapterseven;host=localhost;port=5432";
        $objPDO = PDOFactory::GetPDO($strDSN, "chapterseven", "chapterseven",
                array());
        $objPDO->setAttribute(PDO::ATTR_ERRMODE, PDO::ERRMODE_EXCEPTION);

        $objUser = new User($objPDO, 1);
        print "First name is " . $objUser->getFirstName() . "<br />";


?>
```

The output should be exactly what you would expect:

```
Running...
First name is Steve
```

By passing in an ID of '1' to the object, it is automatically populated with the data from the table represented by that ID — in this case, your good friend Steve.

Update

Here's another piece of code you can try that demonstrates updating Steve's entry in the database:

```php
<?php
        require("userv2.phpm");
        require("pdofactory.phpm");

        print "Running...<br />";

        $strDSN = "pgsql:dbname=chapterseven;host=localhost;port=5432";
        $objPDO = PDOFactory::GetPDO($strDSN, "chapterseven", "chapterseven",
                array());
        $objPDO->setAttribute(PDO::ATTR_ERRMODE, PDO::ERRMODE_EXCEPTION);

        $objUser = new User($objPDO, 1);
        $objUser->setFirstName("Steven");
        $objUser->Save();

?>
```

Give this a shot. You won't see much output of interest, but you should see that the underlying database table has been updated, and that Steve is now called Steven, as shown here:

```
chapterseven=# SELECT first_name, last_name, date_account_created FROM
                     "system_user" WHERE id=1;
 first_name | last_name | date_account_created
------------+-----------+----------------------
 Steven     | Nowicki   | 2008-05-26
(1 row)
```

You could have made more than one update in this session — one column, all of them, or anything in between.

Delete

Here's one final piece of code for you to try before you discover how the underlying class works:

```php
<?php

        require("userv2.phpm");
        require("pdofactory.phpm");

        print "Running...<br />";

        $strDSN = "pgsql:dbname=chapterseven;host=localhost;port=5432";
        $objPDO = PDOFactory::GetPDO($strDSN, "chapterseven", "chapterseven",
                                array());
        $objPDO->setAttribute(PDO::ATTR_ERRMODE, PDO::ERRMODE_EXCEPTION);
        $objUser = new User($objPDO, 1);
        $objUser->MarkForDeletion();

?>
```

Run this one in your browser. Again, you won't see output of much interest, but you should observe that in the underlying database, Steve has firmly disappeared:

```
chapterseven=# SELECT first_name, last_name, date_account_created FROM
                     "system_user" WHERE id=1;
 first_name | last_name | date_account_created
------------+-----------+----------------------
(0 rows)
```

That's enough practice. Now it's time for some theory.

Understanding How It Works

It is hoped that you've demonstrated to yourself by now that the class works and works well. It's a big piece of code, but the code that makes use of the class is small and lightweight. This is crucial in best-practice PHP: Keep things in reusable classes, and keep the complexity away from your general application logic.

The following discussion assumes an understanding of how the first version of the class presented earlier in this chapter works in practice. If that didn't make sense, then it would be good to review that material before continuing.

New Member Variables

You should notice that the following member variables have been added to the class:

```
private $ID;
private $objPDO;
private $strTableName;
private $arRelationMap;
private $blForDeletion;
```

All these member variables have been declared as private, as they have no place being accessed or modified from outside the class itself.

The member variable $ID, as you might expect, stores the unique identifier assigned to the row in the database table. It's assumed throughout the class that this is numeric, that it increments automatically, and that it's called 'id' in the table. If not, then it should be easy enough to adapt the class as needed.

An instance of the PDO object is stored in $objPDO. This is passed in for the first time in the constructor, and retained as a member variable throughout the lifetime of the class. In your own applications, you will probably want to make use of the PDOFactory class to generate a singleton instance of the PDO object, in order to avoid redundant multiple connections to the same DSN. That instance can then be passed into your business classes as (and when) you instantiate them.

Because the table name cannot be assumed from the name of the class (in this case, for example, the name of the class is 'User', but the table is called 'system_user'), it is necessary to make use of a member variable solely to store the name of the corresponding database table. This is set inextricably in the constructor.

An associative array, $arRelationMap, is used to map table names (as the array key) to member variable names (as the array value). Member variable names are stored without the leading dollar sign. Again, this is set in the constructor.

Finally, a simple Boolean flag is used to indicate whether or not the object has been marked for permanent destruction. When set to true, the destructor of the class will invoke a physical deletion in the underlying database. In practice, of course, enterprise-class applications rarely call for business records to be permanently destroyed (for reasons such as adoption of the Sarbanes-Oxley Act). However, you may decide to vary the behavior in the destructor — for example, to set a 'disabled' flag on the record or somehow otherwise prohibit its future inclusion in general selections.

Constructor

The addition of a standard constructor enables several operations to be automatically executed upon instantiation of an object of the class.

First and foremost, the table name and relation map as described previously are defined. Although hard-coded here, in more complex applications these may be stored in separate PHP structures, or even XML, to ease maintainability.

The constructor allows for an instance of the PDO object to be passed in, which is stored by reference in the object's cluster of member variables. It also allows an ID (a numeric identifier that represents an existing user) to be passed, although this is made firmly optional. However, if one has been passed, then the database is immediately interrogated to retrieve the current columnar values of that record. Those columnar values are then used to populate the member variables representing the properties of the business object.

This interrogation is performed by progressively constructing a SELECT statement. First, the keyword SELECT is appended to with a list of column names separated by commas. The final vestigial comma is then discarded. The keyword FROM is then appended, followed by the table name, and a WHERE clause demanding the record represented by the ID value in question. Note the use of parameterized query parameters in the WHERE clause; sadly, this technique cannot reliably be used to populate table and column (relation) names.

With the query then executed, the results are used to progressively populate the properties of the class using the relevant accessor methods. The class can then be considered 'loaded', and any subsequent calls to 'get' accessor methods will yield the expected value.

Save() Method

The Save() method is an additional method provided to enable you, as a developer, to commit changes you have made to the class in memory to the underlying database.

This is a semi-smart method, in that it figures out whether it needs to build an INSERT statement (as indeed it will if this is a new object and hence no ID is yet allocated), or whether to build an UPDATE statement if this is an existing object. Either way, parameterized query syntax is used for columnar values (but not table or column names).

In the event that an INSERT statement is generated, PDO's lastInsertId() method is used to capture the ID of the row just inserted. When working with PostgreSQL, this method must be passed the name of the sequence associated with the table's ID, usually in the form tablename_id_seq. Having been determined, this ID is then stored in the "ID" property of the object and can be retrieved using getID() just like any other property.

MarkForDeletion() Method

This accessor method enables the class object to be marked for permanent deletion upon destruction. The threat is carried through by the destructor.

Destructor

The destructor does nothing other than to delete the underlying database table entry in the event that the object has been marked for destruction using the MarkForDeletion() method.

Limitations

By now, it is hoped that you have worked your way through the class and, using the examples supplied here, have proven to yourself that it does actually work. Furthermore, the benefits should be clear. A relatively complex class means that your application code can be kept lightweight, simple, and portable.

There are a few limitations to this approach, though.

Impact on the Database

When instantiating the class with an existing ID for reading, updating, or deleting, a SELECT query is automatically executed to transfer the contents of the underlying database table entry directly into the class object. This is usually, but not always, desirable.

Consider a hypothetical method in a factory class that produces a collection or array of User objects. For example, your Product class may well have a method called GetOrderingUsers() that will return all those users who have ordered that product. The result may be an array of a hundred or so User objects. That's all well and good, but how likely are you to need all 100 of those objects at once? Hardly at all — it's far more likely that you will paginate over them five or so at a time.

By simply creating the object with an existing ID, however, you are forcing a SELECT query to be generated. As a result, in the previous example, 100 SELECT queries will hammer the database in one go, rendering 95 of them totally redundant.

Database queries are expensive, so anything that can be done to minimize them should (and must) be done.

Unnecessary Queries

When creating a brand-new instance of a User, the INSERT statement that is built is reasonably smart in that it includes only those columns that have been set; don't set (for example) the 'date created' property, and it won't be included in the INSERT statement.

Unfortunately, this technique is dependent on the use of the isset() method to determine whether or not a property has been assigned a value. That's fine when dealing with a brand-new object; but when working with an existing User, every property is assigned a value as it is read from the database. As a result, isset() simply replies "yes!" when called; therefore, a call to Save() will yield an UPDATE statement that updates every column in the table — whether it has actually been changed or not. Not only is this wasteful, it can also have undesirable effects if other applications connected to the database commit changes to other columns between the initial SELECT and the final UPDATE being executed.

Code Duplication

Finally, read the class source code again. How much of that class is actually specific to the User object and/or its underlying table? Not a great deal.

As a result, this complex code is going to end up being duplicated repeatedly for every business object in your application, which disregards the well-respected philosophy of DRY (*Don't Repeat Yourself*).

A Smarter Approach

Notice that you've been building something of a straw man throughout this chapter — that is, building something up only to tear it down again in one fell swoop. Don't worry. You'll see in this section that 80 percent of the code you've written so far can be reused to form a third version of your business object, along with a portable, reusable, generic class you can add to your toolkit.

Lazy Instantiation

You saw in the previous section how the immediate execution of a SELECT query upon instantiation can exert unnecessary stress on the underlying database. A remedy to this particular problem is what is known as *lazy instantiation*.

This means that the class is wired to accept exactly the same input parameters to its constructor as before, but is engineered to delay behavior resulting from that instantiation until the last possible moment.

In practice, this means deliberately delaying the SELECT query until the very first 'get' accessor call is executed. At that point, it is possible to infer accurately that the query is absolutely necessary and execute it immediately. Thereafter, it need not be executed again for the lifetime of the class.

Property Monitoring

The issue of the overly zealous UPDATE statement needlessly firing against all columns should be easy to fix. All that is required is to maintain a register of columns (in the form of an array stack) that have been updated since the class was first instantiated.

At the point at which the Save() method is called, this register can be consulted such that the UPDATE statement that is built is deliberately curtailed to include only those columns that have been modified.

Reusability

Finally, the easiest way to encourage portability and minimize (or even eliminate) unnecessary code duplication is to deliberately abstract away the code that is not specific to the business object in question.

That code can then be placed into an *abstract class*, which can be *extended* for each unique case, the extension containing only what is particular to the entity in question — in this case, a User.

DataBoundObject Class

With all of this in mind, this section introduces you to a new class, DataBoundObject, that takes the bulk of the code you've already written and places it in an abstract, reusable package that you can subclass for your own business objects.

It also addresses the two other key limitations of the second version of the User class you've created — namely, the impact on the underlying database and the perils of unnecessarily aggressive queries.

Design

Before jumping in at the deep end and meeting the code, it's worth thinking about what's involved in producing a suitable reusable class to meet the agreed requirements.

By producing an *abstract class*, you are both providing final methods that child classes need not reproduce (and, optionally, via the `'final'` keyword, cannot overload), as well as declaring certain methods that *must* be implemented by the child.

It's worth considering, therefore, what methods and member variables are *generic* (that is, they can be defined in full in the abstract class) and those that are *class-specific* (and, therefore, something you expect the child class to define). Think of it as dividing assets following a divorce settlement; you're asking, *who gets what?*

In terms of member variables, the following from the original User class can remain in the abstract parent:

```
private $ID;
private $objPDO;
private $strTableName;
private $arRelationMap;
private $blForDeletion;
```

There's nothing class-specific about these member variables; therefore, they will form part of your new abstract class.

Conversely, consider the following:

```
private $FirstName;
private $LastName;
private $Username;
private $Password;
private $EmailAddress;

private $DateLastLogin;
private $TimeLastLogin;
private $DateAccountCreated;
private $TimeAccountCreated;
```

Between them, these comprise the User-specific member variables and should, therefore, reside firmly within the child class.

In terms of methods, all of the methods defined in the User class are already completely generic, relying as they do on other member variables that describe the table and its columns. However, some of the hard-coding of detail in the constructor must be moved into the child; and to this end, new abstract methods can be defined in the parent class for required implementation in the child.

With this in mind, it's time to meet the class itself.

The Code

Here's the class in all its glory. You should save this as `databoundobject.phpm`:

```php
<?php

abstract class DataBoundObject {

    protected $ID;
    protected $objPDO;
    protected $strTableName;
    protected $arRelationMap;
    protected $blForDeletion;
    protected $blIsLoaded;
    protected $arModifiedRelations;

    abstract protected function DefineTableName();
    abstract protected function DefineRelationMap();

    public function __construct(PDO $objPDO, $id = NULL) {
        $this->strTableName = $this->DefineTableName();
        $this->arRelationMap = $this->DefineRelationMap();
        $this->objPDO = $objPDO;
        $this->blIsLoaded = false;
        if (isset($id)) {
            $this->ID = $id;
        };
        $this->arModifiedRelations = array();
    }

    public function Load() {
        if (isset($this->ID)) {
                $strQuery = "SELECT ";
                foreach ($this->arRelationMap as $key => $value) {
                        $strQuery .= "\"" . $key . "\",";
                }
                $strQuery = substr($strQuery, 0, strlen($strQuery)-1);
                $strQuery .= " FROM " . $this->strTableName . " WHERE
                        \"id\" = :eid";
                $objStatement = $this->objPDO->prepare($strQuery);
                $objStatement->bindParam(':eid', $this->ID,
                                PDO::PARAM_INT);
                $objStatement->execute();
                $arRow = $objStatement->fetch(PDO::FETCH_ASSOC);
                foreach($arRow as $key => $value) {
                        $strMember = $this->arRelationMap[$key];
                        if (property_exists($this, $strMember)) {
                                if (is_numeric($value)) {
                                        eval('$this->' . $strMember .
                                                ' = ' . $value . ';');
                                } else {
                                        eval('$this->' . $strMember .
                                                ' = "' . $value . '";');
```

```php
                                                };
                                        };
                                };
                $this->blIsLoaded = true;
        };
}

public function Save() {
    if (isset($this->ID)) {
        $strQuery = 'UPDATE "' . $this->strTableName . '" SET ';
                        foreach ($this->arRelationMap as $key => $value) {
                                eval('$actualVal = &$this->' . $value . ';');
            if (array_key_exists($value, $this->arModifiedRelations)) {
                                $strQuery .= '"' . $key . "\" = :$value, ";
            };
                        }
        $strQuery = substr($strQuery, 0, strlen($strQuery)-2);
        $strQuery .= ' WHERE "id" = :eid';
        unset($objStatement);
                        $objStatement = $this->objPDO->prepare($strQuery);
        $objStatement->bindValue(':eid', $this->ID, PDO::PARAM_INT);
                        foreach ($this->arRelationMap as $key => $value) {
                                eval('$actualVal = &$this->' . $value . ';');
            if (array_key_exists($value, $this->arModifiedRelations)) {
                if ((is_int($actualVal)) || ($actualVal == NULL)) {
                    $objStatement->bindValue(':' . $value, $actualVal,
                                        PDO::PARAM_INT);
                } else {
                    $objStatement->bindValue(':' . $value, $actualVal,
                                        PDO::PARAM_STR);
                };
            };
                        };
        $objStatement->execute();
    } else {
        $strValueList = "";
        $strQuery = 'INSERT INTO "' . $this->strTableName . '"(';
        foreach ($this->arRelationMap as $key => $value) {
                        eval('$actualVal = &$this->' . $value . ';');
            if (isset($actualVal)) {
                if (array_key_exists($value, $this->arModifiedRelations)) {
                    $strQuery .= '"' . $key . '", ';
                    $strValueList .= ":$value, ";
                };
            };
                        }
        $strQuery = substr($strQuery, 0, strlen($strQuery) - 2);
        $strValueList = substr($strValueList, 0, strlen($strValueList) - 2);
        $strQuery .= ") VALUES (";
        $strQuery .= $strValueList;
```

```
        $strQuery .= ")";

        unset($objStatement);
        $objStatement = $this->objPDO->prepare($strQuery);
                    foreach ($this->arRelationMap as $key => $value) {
                        eval('$actualVal = &$this->' . $value . ';');
                        if (isset($actualVal)) {
            if (array_key_exists($value, $this->arModifiedRelations)) {
                if ((is_int($actualVal)) || ($actualVal == NULL)) {
                                            $objStatement->bindValue
                            (':' . $value, $actualVal, PDO::PARAM_INT);
                                } else {
                                            $objStatement->bindValue
                            (':' . $value, $actualVal, PDO::PARAM_STR);
                                    };
            };
                        };
                    }
        $objStatement->execute();
        $this->ID = $this->objPDO->lastInsertId($this->strTableName . "_id_seq");
    }
}

public function MarkForDeletion() {
    $this->blForDeletion = true;
}

public function __destruct() {
    if (isset($this->ID)) {
        if ($this->blForDeletion == true) {
            $strQuery = 'DELETE FROM "' . $this->strTableName . '" WHERE
                    "id" = :eid';
            $objStatement = $this->objPDO->prepare($strQuery);
            $objStatement->bindValue(':eid', $this->ID, PDO::PARAM_INT);
                    $objStatement->execute();
        };
    }
}

public function __call($strFunction, $arArguments) {

    $strMethodType = substr($strFunction, 0, 3);
    $strMethodMember = substr($strFunction, 3);
    switch ($strMethodType) {
        case "set":
            return($this->SetAccessor($strMethodMember, $arArguments[0]));
            break;
        case "get":
            return($this->GetAccessor($strMethodMember));
    };
    return(false);
```

```php
        }

        private function SetAccessor($strMember, $strNewValue) {
            if (property_exists($this, $strMember)) {
                if (is_numeric($strNewValue)) {
                    eval('$this->' . $strMember . ' = ' . $strNewValue . ';');
                } else {
                    eval('$this->' . $strMember . ' = "' . $strNewValue . '";');
                };
                $this->arModifiedRelations[$strMember] = "1";
            } else {
                return(false);
            };
        }

        private function GetAccessor($strMember) {
            if ($this->blIsLoaded != true) {
                $this->Load();
            }
            if (property_exists($this, $strMember)) {
                eval('$strRetVal = $this->' . $strMember . ';');
                return($strRetVal);
            } else {
                return(false);
            };
        }

    }

?>
```

As you can see, the code has become somewhat longer, so take even more care than you did before when entering this into your editor to ensure that no errant line breaks make their way in.

Example Implementation

Naturally, the abstract class isn't of much use without a corresponding implementation that matches your original — namely, a new version of the User object. You can call the following code userv3.phpm:

```php
<?php

class User extends DataBoundObject {

        protected $FirstName;
        protected $LastName;
        protected $Username;
        protected $Password;
        protected $EmailAddress;

        protected $DateLastLogin;
        protected $TimeLastLogin;
```

```php
        protected $DateAccountCreated;
        protected $TimeAccountCreated;

        protected function DefineTableName() {
                return("system_user");
        }

        protected function DefineRelationMap() {
                return(array(
                        "id" => "ID",
                        "first_name" => "FirstName",
                        "last_name" => "LastName",
                        "username" => "Username",
                        "md5_pw" => "Password",
                        "email_address" => "EmailAddress",
                        "date_last_login" => "DateLastLogin",
                        "time_last_login" => "TimeLastLogin",
                        "date_account_created" => "DateAccountCreated",
                        "time_account_created" => "TimeAccountCreated"));
        }
}

?>
```

That's all well and good, but you must also prove to yourself that the third version of your user object works exactly the same as your second version — at least in terms of its interface to the outside world. This all-in-one example showcases creation, reading, updating, and deletion.

```php
<?php
        require("pdofactory.phpm");
        require("databoundobject.phpm");
        require("userv3.phpm");

        print "Running...<br />";

        $strDSN = "pgsql:dbname=chapterseven;host=localhost;port=5432";
        $objPDO = PDOFactory::GetPDO($strDSN, "chapterseven", "chapterseven",
            array());
        $objPDO->setAttribute(PDO::ATTR_ERRMODE, PDO::ERRMODE_EXCEPTION);
        $objUser = new User($objPDO);

        $objUser->setFirstName("Steve");
        $objUser->setLastName("Nowicki");
        $objUser->setDateAccountCreated(date("Y-m-d"));

        print "First name is " . $objUser->getFirstName() . "<br />";
        print "Last name is " . $objUser->getLastName() . "<br />";

        print "Saving...<br />";

        $objUser->Save();

        $id = $objUser->getID();
```

```php
        print "ID in database is " . $id . "<br />";

        print "Destroying object...<br />";
        unset($objUser);

        print "Recreating object from ID $id<br />";
        $objUser = new User($objPDO, $id);

        print "First name is " . $objUser->getFirstName() . "<br />";
        print "Last name is " . $objUser->getLastName() . "<br />";

        print "Committing a change.... Steve will become Steven,
                Nowicki will become Nowickcow<br/>";
        $objUser->setFirstName("Steven");
        $objUser->setLastName("Nowickcow");
        print "Saving...<br />";
        $objUser->Save();
?>
```

Give this a shot, ensuring that you save it into the same directory as its required classes. You should see output similar to the following:

```
Running...
First name is Steve
Last name is Nowicki
Saving...
ID in database is 167
Destroying object...
Recreating object from ID 167
First name is Steve
Last name is Nowicki
Committing a change.... Steve will become Steven, Nowicki will become Nowickcow
Saving...
```

As you can see, the newly formed lightweight User class works exactly the same as your second version, but it is a great deal smaller and more portable and doesn't suffer from the same issues identified earlier in the chapter, as you'll prove to yourself throughout the following discussions.

Understanding How It Works

Because there's a great deal of similarity between the code, it is hoped that a quick run through it won't seem too frightening.

First and foremost, notice that the class is declared abstract:

```php
abstract class DataBoundObject {
```

This tells PHP to expect one or more *abstract methods* — methods that you will define but not implement in the parent class. This enables you to dictate the structure of those methods in terms of parameter quantity and order, as well as insist that any class that extends the abstract class *must* implement those methods.

Moving on, you'll see that a number of protected member variables are declared:

```
protected $ID;
protected $objPDO;
protected $strTableName;
protected $arRelationMap;
protected $blForDeletion;
protected $blIsLoaded;
protected $arModifiedRelations;
```

These non-class-specific variables link the object to the underlying relational database. Note the addition of a variable holding the database table name, as well as an associative array indicating which fields have been modified during the lifetime of the child object.

In addition, the member variables are declared *protected*. This means that, while not publicly accessible outside the class, they are available to child classes of the parent.

Two abstract methods are defined:

```
abstract protected function DefineTableName();
abstract protected function DefineRelationMap();
```

These methods must be implemented in the child class and are tasked simply with setting the table name and relation map.

The constructor actually calls upon those two methods, assuming (as it may rightly do) that the child class has implemented them:

```
public function __construct(PDO $objPDO, $id = NULL) {
        $this->strTableName = $this->DefineTableName();
        $this->arRelationMap = $this->DefineRelationMap();
        $this->objPDO = $objPDO;
        $this->blIsLoaded = false;
        if (isset($id)) {
                $this->ID = $id;
        };
        $this->arModifiedRelations = array();
}
```

You'll notice that the constructor, as before, takes an instance of PDO and, optionally, an identifier, which would indicate that the entity in question already exists in the database. The constructor also sets the 'loaded' state to false, indicating that no data has yet been drawn in from the underlying database. The array of modified relations is also reset.

The new Load() method draws on code that was previously in the constructor, used to populate the object with data from the database in the event that an identifier has been passed when instantiating the class. By placing such code in a separate method, it is no longer invoked automatically upon instantiation.

```php
public function Load() {
    if (isset($this->ID)) {
        $strQuery = "SELECT ";
        foreach ($this->arRelationMap as $key => $value) {
            $strQuery .= "\"" . $key . "\",";
        }
        $strQuery = substr($strQuery, 0, strlen($strQuery)-1);
        $strQuery .= " FROM " . $this->strTableName . " WHERE
                        \"id\" = :eid";
        $objStatement = $this->objPDO->prepare($strQuery);
        $objStatement->bindParam(':eid', $this->ID,
                                    PDO::PARAM_INT);
        $objStatement->execute();
        $arRow = $objStatement->fetch(PDO::FETCH_ASSOC);
        foreach($arRow as $key => $value) {
            $strMember = $this->arRelationMap[$key];
            if (property_exists($this, $strMember)) {
                if (is_numeric($value)) {
                    eval('$this->' . $strMember .
                            ' = ' . $value . ';');
                } else {
                    eval('$this->' . $strMember .
                            ' = "' . $value . '";');
                };
            };
        };
        $this->blIsLoaded = true;
    };
}
```

Once the loading is complete, the `'blIsLoaded'` flag is set to true. This prevents the class from unnecessarily invoking the Load() method for the remainder of the child object's lifetime.

The Save() method is virtually unchanged from the original data-enabled User class. The only key difference is the test to establish whether a given property has been modified or not:

```php
if (array_key_exists($value, $this->arModifiedRelations)) {
    $strQuery .= '"' . $key . "\" = :$value, ";
};
```

This way, if a given field has not been modified, then it will not be included in the UPDATE or INSERT statement that is generated. Naturally, this same test is applied when populating the prepared statement parameters:

```php
if (array_key_exists($value, $this->arModifiedRelations)) {
    if ((is_int($actualVal)) || ($actualVal == NULL)) {
        $objStatement->bindValue(':' . $value, $actualVal, PDO::PARAM_INT);
    } else {
        $objStatement->bindValue(':' . $value, $actualVal, PDO::PARAM_STR);
    };
};
```

Testing twice in this way is important; PDO will complain rigorously if you attempt to bind a value to a non-existent parameter.

The methods that mark for deletion, destructor, and 'call' overload method (__call()) all remain unchanged from the original User class.

The two accessor methods have been slightly adapted:

```php
private function SetAccessor($strMember, $strNewValue) {
        if (property_exists($this, $strMember)) {
                if (is_numeric($strNewValue)) {
                        eval('$this->' . $strMember . ' = ' .
                                $strNewValue . ';');
                } else {
                        eval('$this->' . $strMember . ' = "' .
                                $strNewValue . '";');
                };
                $this->arModifiedRelations[$strMember] = "1";
        } else {
                return(false);
        };
}
```

Notice now that the modified relations map is adjusted to indicate that the relation in question has been modified. This data is used by Save() to build a more concise UPDATE or INSERT statement as needed:

```php
private function GetAccessor($strMember) {
        if ($this->blIsLoaded != true) {
                $this->Load();
        }
        if (property_exists($this, $strMember)) {
                eval('$strRetVal = $this->' . $strMember . ';');
                return($strRetVal);
        } else {
                return(false);
        };
}
```

Finally, the 'get' accessor has had a small modification, as you can see from looking at the earlier code. The class is tested to determine whether the 'loaded' flag is set to true. If it is not, then the Load() method is called *before* attempting to evaluate and return the property.

What about the class itself? As shown in the code for userv3.phpm, it has become *much* smaller. Notice first that it subclasses from DataBoundObject:

```php
class User extends DataBoundObject {
```

As a result, your application must ensure that not only is a require() statement present for the class itself, but also, equally important, that one is present for the DataBoundObject class.

Individual member variables remain much the same:

```
protected $FirstName;
protected $LastName;
protected $Username;
protected $Password;
protected $EmailAddress;

protected $DateLastLogin;
protected $TimeLastLogin;
protected $DateAccountCreated;
protected $TimeAccountCreated;
```

Notice that the variables are declared 'protected' — this is important, as it permits the parent class to access and manipulate those variables directly.

Finally, you can see the implementation of the two all-important abstract methods:

```
protected function DefineTableName() {
        return("system_user");
}

protected function DefineRelationMap() {
        return(array(
                "id" => "ID",
                "first_name" => "FirstName",
                "last_name" => "LastName",
                "username" => "Username",
                "md5_pw" => "Password",
                "email_address" => "EmailAddress",
                "date_last_login" => "DateLastLogin",
                "time_last_login" => "TimeLastLogin",
                "date_account_created" => "DateAccountCreated",
                "time_account_created" => "TimeAccountCreated"));
}
```

These were declared in the parent class as abstract, so you are obliged in your child class to provide an implementation using the same method name (keeping in mind that PHP is case sensitive). Neither method takes any parameters. Instead, two simple values are returned — one is a string indicating the name of the underlying database table, and the other is a simple associative array mapping relation names to PHP member variables.

Benefits

Before closing, it's worth taking a minute to reflect on the benefits of the approach discussed in this chapter. What you've been able to do is construct a reusable, portable, PDO-enabled toolkit class that enables you to create data-bound business objects in moments.

Indeed, the example User class itself contains not a jot of SQL — it doesn't need to, as all of the standard CRUD (create, read, update, delete) methods can be generated for you on request. Not only is your code more lightweight, your application is also more portable. Should you later decide to port from, say, MySQL to PostgreSQL, or, indeed, the other way around, very little should need changing.

The "abstract class" approach is neat, too. You are not in the least bit limited as to what you can do in your child class. The previous example was simple, but naturally you can add your own methods, too — some of which will probably make use of SQL more complex than simple CRUD operations. In addition, there's nothing to stop you from delegating relation mapping to something a bit more readable than PHP — maybe an XML document, for example.

In a big project with 20 or more business objects, ORM starts to make a lot of sense. You'll wonder how you ever lived without it.

Summary

In this vital chapter, you were introduced to a further layer of database abstraction — that of object relation mapping (ORM). Having been introduced formally to the two varieties of classes you are likely to meet in the course of your enterprise-grade PHP projects (namely, business objects and utility classes), and having learned about the measures you can use to help identify each, you were introduced to a simple example of a stateless business object representing a hypothetical commercial entity.

With an understanding of how such a business object works on a functional level, but does not retain data, you were introduced to a traditional approach to retention by binding to a database relation — namely, a specific table within a relational database — and shown how it can enable and facilitate persistence of your object's properties in a manner largely suitable for an enterprise-grade project.

Finally, by recognizing the limitations of your business object, you built and examined a reusable, toolkit-ready enterprise class for the development of data-enabled objects in your own projects. By maintaining an identical interface to your business-specific class, you proved to yourself that a common business problem could be solved by abstracting away business-specific issues into subclasses of a toolkit-ready module.

In Chapter 8, you'll discover that PHP, despite being developed from the ground up as a procedural Web application development language, is ideally suited for developing event-driven applications as well.

8

Event-Driven Programming

Sometimes it is useful to think of an application in terms of *events* and how best to handle them, rather than look at that application's architectural design from a traditional object-oriented (OO) perspective. That's not to say that you must discard an OOP approach altogether to implement event handling, but rather that you build classes around the events relevant to the application. This approach is rather radical, but for many applications, you may find that it gives you a massively powerful mechanism for approaching the software architecture of the whole project.

Events occur pretty much all the time, and some of the best examples of event-driven programming are the applications you use every day, such as to manage e-mail or write text. For the end user of traditional desktop GUI applications, event handling is of paramount importance because these applications are designed to lurk around until the user does something, and then react accordingly. Of course, the same is now true for many Web-based applications.

Nearly all actions taken by a user, and even those taken by the applications themselves, can be thought of as an event. A rather contrived example of an event not initiated by a user is your machine's clock. If you wanted to create an application that performed various actions depending on the time, you could capture certain changes in time as an event, and bundle it off to a piece of code that deals with it accordingly.

Whatever needs to be done, applications have various ways to implement a solution, and PHP 6 is no different in this regard. There is, of course, no new extension or library to deal with events, because the way you deal with them is more about how you "think" about designing an application, rather than how you actually implement it. In other words, they need no special underlying technology. Let's take a look at one way to handle events in PHP.

Understanding Events

An event is any occurrence to which your application can react. You will almost certainly have already written applications that have handled events in some capacity or another. When something happens or some condition is suddenly met, deciding what action to take in your code (no matter how trivial) is a form of event handling. For example, imagine that you have implemented a database holding a number of records, and you want your customers to be able to work on those records via a Web interface. You would probably realize that the users must at least be able to view and update records, so your likely reaction would be to create functions to view and edit records.

Deciding which function to call depends entirely on the input provided by the user. Accordingly, the interface you develop needs to present the various options, and enable users to decide which ones they want. After the user has decided, the application must respond accordingly by calling the correct functions, which will handle the request.

Typically, you might create a home page with two buttons, one offering the option to view the records and another to edit them. The following code snippet might suffice as a mechanism to handle that choice:

```
switch($_GET['action']) {
  case "edit_record":
    edit_record();
  break;
  case "view_record":
    view_record();
  break;
}
```

As you can see, the previous snippet of code is designed to interpret information from $_GET (in other words, the user's request) and make a decision about what response to take, based on what the user has requested. That's it — you have handled an event that was fired by the simple action of a user clicking a button.

This principle stands for pretty much any event you could possibly imagine. For those of you who use Outlook or something similar, system-generated events are commonplace. Warnings about meetings and deadlines pop up all the time based on a specific event firing (for example, the system's clock reaching a certain time).

Of course, how you implement the code to handle events is up to you. Using a switch statement is not the only way; any sort of loop could enable you to respond to events. An if/else block would work just as well in the previous example.

You may be wondering what all the fuss is about events. After all, what you've seen so far seems simple enough. Why can't you just leave it at that? The problem with what has been discussed so far is that you could easily end up with a big mess if your application changes or grows after your initial development run. What starts off as a nice simple if statement could grow to monstrous proportions, rendering any attempts to understand it in the future very difficult indeed. This has obvious implications as your application's needs become more complex. Accordingly, you should use the simple methods alluded to previously only for very simple requirements, where you can be sure the code is at no time going to blossom into a full-blown enterprise application.

Using OOP to Handle Events

To implement effective event-driven solutions in your own PHP applications, it is best to take a step back and determine (from a high-level perspective) how these applications should behave. A more sophisticated approach to implementing events would enable you to more easily control their behavior exactly as you wish, should the need ever arise. Creating an OO solution to event-driven programming is the answer.

Not only will using classes and objects help you maintain uncluttered code, it also enables you to create an easily extensible architecture. Extensibility in application development is a worthy goal these days, so this is a good thing. There are plenty of other benefits, too, which are explored in some detail later in this chapter. Additionally, considering an OO approach should alert you to the fact that a design pattern might well exist that could fit the event-driven model quite well.

Let's build a picture of what is needed to implement proper event handling using an OO approach. You can then see whether a pattern (or patterns) exists that will fit this model appropriately.

Designing an Event-Driven Solution

There are three main steps to take when designing any event-driven application:

1. First determine how you will go about capturing the events the application must handle. This is difficult to discuss in an abstract manner, as your approach to capturing these events depends on exactly what type of events you're trying to capture.

2. You need a way of deciding how to go about handling the captured events. Depending on the specific application you are considering, there may be a number of questions worth posing at this early stage. For example, it's worth determining how many distinct sources will be sending events to your event handler. In addition, you must decide whether the application will handle just one class of event or a number of different classes, and if necessary, how handlers will effectively differentiate between them.

3. Finally, after you have determined the events applicable to your application and decided how they will be handled, you must design the handlers necessary to carry out whatever tasks the application requires in response to each event. The types of responses an event could elicit are almost unlimited — anything from directing users to a new page, to updating a record, to firing more events. All of these could be regarded as proper responses.

Effectively, what has just been described is the use of a reactor, or *dispatcher* class, to take an event and ensure that the correct handler deals with it. Let's explore this idea a little further.

In keeping with the initial example, let's assume that a user of this application will want to edit or view records of some form or another. You could expect a URL such as the following to be requested as a result of a user's input returned from a form:

```
http://myserver/interface.php?event=edit
```

It's fairly clear from the URL that the event being triggered is an `edit` event, whatever that may mean. By passing this event to the dispatcher class, that determines which handlers to call based on what is required from the application. After the dispatcher determines which handler to call (in this case, by checking the values associated with the `$_GET` or `$_POST` array keys), the actual processing of the request is done by the relevant handler, and not by the dispatcher.

The handlers themselves are an exercise in OOP in their own right. Indeed, one effective way to implement individual handlers in your application is to extend a generic parent `handler` class. Using inheritance makes implementing new handlers easy, as the functionality common to all event handlers can be kept hidden away inside the parent class. For example, code to establish database connections can be made available to subclasses of `handler` that may require access to such a connection.

You can begin by mapping the perceived course of actions for this example by drawing the activity diagram shown in Figure 8-1.

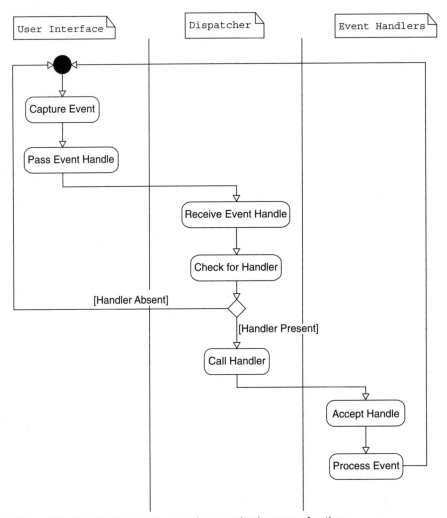

Figure 8-1: Activity diagram to map the perceived course of actions.

This is a pretty simple representation, but for the purposes of this example you needn't worry about the niceties behind the implementation. Admittedly, a virtually unlimited number of concerns could well be brought to bear here on the strength of this illustration — security, database, handler registration, and multiple event sources are just some of the valid considerations you might need to take into account at this stage.

Having said that, you are now equipped with a basic model to work from, so go ahead and look at the class diagram shown in Figure 8-2 that is derived from these perceived requirements.

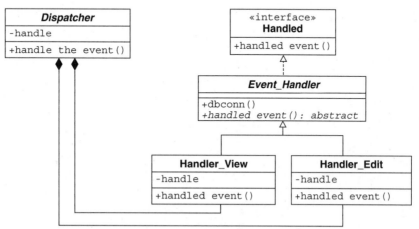

Figure 8-2: Class diagram derived from the perceived requirements.

There is no need to be too concerned about the code driving the user interface here, because choices concerning such matters are better made by the end user, not the software architect. Concentrate instead on representing in your class diagram the *dispatcher* and *handlers*. This application provides just the bare bones in terms of functionality. This example concentrates instead on the event-driven paradigm and the advantages derived from using it.

Implementing the Solution

Recall from the class diagram that you are making use of an interface to implement each event handler. The use of an interface to enforce the existence of certain methods within each handler is crucial to this example, and is good practice in general, as it standardizes the way in which your handlers are built. This is important, because your application may grow to the point at which third-party developers want to add functionality of their own. Having an interface promotes the "plug-and-play" aspect of your code — that is, makes your code more extensible.

Aside from being extensible, there are several other advantages yet to be gained. After presenting the classes in this section, the discussion examines how easy it is to implement fine-grained security using this model. First, let's look through the code class by class.

class.Dispatcher.php

To begin, the code for the `Dispatcher` class looks something like this:

```php
<?php
require_once('class.Event_Handler.php');
require_once('class.Handler_View.php');
require_once('class.Handler_Edit.php');

class Dispatcher
{

    private $handle;

    function __construct($event_handle){
        $this->handle = $event_handle;
    }

    function handle_the_event(){
        $name = "handler_{$this->handle}";
        if (class_exists("$name")){
            $handler_obj = new $name($this->handle);
            $response = $handler_obj->handled_event();
            return $response;
        }else{
            echo "I can't handle this!";
        }
    }
}
?>
```

Crucially, the constructor is responsible for capturing the event handle and retaining it within the class so that it can be used later to decide what action to take. The event handle may be needed as part of the event handler's processing, so let's pass this value on to any handlers you may call upon. Of course, the handlers might need additional information, too.

As part of this application, when querying the database for existing records, the user might want to return only records in a certain range. When this crops up, you can simply capture the delimiter parameters as part of the event, as demonstrated in the following URL:

```
http://myserver/interface.php?event=edit&first=2&last=7
```

It is a simple enough job to populate a suitable array (for example, `$event_parameters`) as part of the constructor. These values can then be passed on to the handler, which uses them to return records within only the specified range. Let's stick to simply sending the actual event handle for this example.

The `handle_the_event()` function relies on you and your development team sticking to a particular naming convention for any new event handler classes. If someone wanted to add functionality to this application, he or she would need to be aware that each handler's name is in the following form:

```php
class Handler_(Unique_Event_Handle)
{
    //Handle the event with handle Unique_Event_Handle
}
```

In this case, you have only two event handlers: `Handler_View` and `Handler_Edit`. The `handle_the_event()` method in our `Dispatcher` class checks whether the relevant handler exists within the PHP namespace before creating an instance of the pertinent handler object. If not, it confesses:

```
echo "I can't handle this!";
```

Notice that the instantiation of the handler passes the event handle into the constructor, in case it is needed. In the same way, you could pass an array of values here for use in the handler's processing, as shown here:

```
$handler_obj = new $name($this->handle);
```

Don't concern yourself too much with the action of the handler — you simply want to pass off any information that you collect in the dispatcher to the correct handler without having to worry about what it might actually be doing with that information.

The next step is to call the `handled_event()` method to extract any response from the handler that might have resulted from its handling of the event:

```
$response = $handler_obj->handled_event();
```

As you have already seen in the class diagram, both the existence and precise format of the `handled_event()` function is enforced through the use of an interface. The consequence of this is that the dispatcher can safely call the `handled_event()` method on its instantiated handler to retrieve a response, even if that method simply returns `NULL`. Once the response from the handler (if any) has been returned, the dispatcher's work is done.

Now, let's take a look at the handlers' side of things.

interface.Handled.php

The interface ensures that you implement the `handled_event()` function in any handler classes you might develop. As mentioned previously, this is important from the perspective of the dispatcher, but if you do intend to take on larger game, this is where you can enforce the existence of any other important methods that might be relevant to your event handlers. Such methods can then either be implemented in the parent handler and overridden by the children, or be simply declared abstract, passing the implementation off to the children handlers directly. As you can see from the following interface code, for this example you stick to simply requiring the existence of the `handled_event()` method:

```php
<?php
interface Handled {
  function handled_event();
}
?>
```

The `handled_event()` method itself is implemented either by the parent event handler class for your application or by its children. Let's look first at the parent event handler class.

class.Event_Handler.php

The parent event handler class is really more of a utility class specifying how to handle lower-level events that may occur in your application. In this specific example, it creates a database connection. The common_db.inc file contains a db_connect() function that creates a database connection — pretty straightforward stuff, and the implementation of such a method is left to you. However, if you are creating an application of any serious magnitude, the best way to approach such a challenge is to make use of a database abstraction layer, as explored in Chapter 6.

Of course, you may consider adding any number of appropriate methods here, depending on the nature of the problem you are solving. For now, here's the code for a simple class.Event_Handler.php:

```php
<?php
require_once ("interface.Handled.php");
require_once('common_db.inc');

abstract class Event_Handler
{
    function dbconn(){
        $link_id = db_connect('sample_db');
        return $link_id;
    }

    abstract function handled_event();
}
?>
```

Because you are unlikely to know what each event is going to do, you declare the handled_ event() function abstract so that the descendent handler classes can each implement it as they see fit. In order to allow this, you will notice that the whole class has been declared abstract. This has no real bearing on the application itself, because you will never directly instantiate this class — the dispatcher will figure out which descendent event handler to instantiate, and do so directly.

class.Handler_View.php

This descendent handler gives a quick demonstration of the type of code you can usefully execute within a typical handler. Notice how you are forced to give an implementation of handled_events(), as this has been declared as an abstract method in the parent handler class. The following code shows how to view a few records pulled straight from a database:

```php
<?php
require_once('class.Event_Handler.php');

class Handler_View extends Event_Handler
{
    private $handle;

    function __construct($event_handle){
        $this->handle = $event_handle;
    }

    function handled_event(){
        echo "The event, $this->handle, is now handled. <BR>
```

```
            It is, I promise!<BR><BR>Your records are as follows: <BR> <BR>";

        $id = parent::dbconn();
        $result = pg_query($id, "SELECT * FROM user");
        while($query_data = pg_fetch_row($result)) {
            echo "'",$query_data[1],"' is a ",$query_data[4],"<br>";
        }
    }
}
?>
```

Of course, the actual data being pulled out of here is irrelevant — this is just an example. If you want to try it out, however, simply hook this up to an example database of your own and query it as you like, changing the SQL statement.

Note that, in the constructor, the handler still holds onto the event handle passed to it, by saving it into a local private member variable. It's not actually used in this example, but it does demonstrate that you can get such parameters through to the handlers, if necessary.

class.Handler_Edit.php

Let's take a look at another descendent handler. This demonstration of an edit handler simply returns a message to the user when invoked:

```
<?php
require_once('class.Event_Handler.php');

class Handler_Edit extends Event_Handler {
    private $handle;

    function __construct($event_handle){
        $this->handle = $event_handle;
    }

    function handled_event(){
        echo "This is event $this->handle, which is now handled - no
            kidding! <BR>";
    }
}
?>
```

As usual, you capture the event handle and store it locally. In this case, the handler does actually use it as part of its event processing. Admittedly, the `handled_event()` method implementation is nothing special; it simply returns a message confirming that the event has been dealt with.

That's about it for setting things up. Let's now explore how easy it is to modify the application and get great results with little effort.

Implementing Security

Assume that you wanted to limit the functionality of the application depending on who was using it — which is not an uncommon requirement. An application with such a requirement could be something like a wiki, which should allow certain trusted sources to edit whatever they like, but limit others to only read (and not change) the content.

First, have the application create a new session after you have successfully validated the user. You can then populate the session variable with relevant details concerning who the user is. In this case, you use a session variable that contains the user's name. This means that you now have access to the current user's details from virtually anywhere in your application, including from within your event handlers. You can use this information to determine whether or not to allow the event to take place at all.

Add the following method to each of the descendent event handler classes whose use you wish to restrict. As you can see, the method simply checks the author's name currently held in the session, and if the name being offered isn't acceptable, the method will consider the user unauthorized to perform the requested action:

```php
function secure_handler(){
    if ($_SESSION['name'] == "David"){
        $this->handled_event();
    } else {
        echo "Sorry ${_SESSION['name']} you are not authorized!";
    }
}
```

You need to change one line in the dispatcher to ensure that only the secure method is used when handling the event. Open the file and find the following line:

```php
$response = $handler_obj->handled_event();
```

Change the preceding line as follows:

```php
$response = $handler_obj->secure_handler();
```

You also need to ensure that you keep to the design principles you first set out by ensuring that the existence of this method in the children handlers is enforced via the use of the interface. This means that the parent handler must at least contain an abstract representation of the `secure_handler()` function.

Add the following line to the interface:

```php
abstract function secure_handler();
```

There is no way to know precisely what level of permission each event will require; it may well differ from event to event. Accordingly, the parent event handler does not directly implement the secure handler itself. Instead, much in the same way as the regular handler method previously discussed, it passes responsibility for its implementation to its children, by again declaring the method abstract:

```php
abstract function secure_handler();
```

Each descendent event handler is now required to implement both a `handled_event()` and `secure_handler()` method as specified by the interface. To determine whether to allow the event to take place, each event handler's `secure_handler()` method could retrieve its own permission setting from a file held by the administrator. This file would, of course, be encrypted (or at least held somewhere secure), and would most likely be editable by the wiki administrator, such that he or she could change which handlers were available to which users.

Here is a little example user interface that would make use of the secure, event-oriented application:

```php
<?php
require_once ('class.Dispatcher.php');
session_start();


?>
<html>
    <head>
        <title>Secure, Event Driven Record Viewer!</title>
    </head>
    <body>
        <form method="GET" ACTION="<?=$_SERVER['PHP_SELF']?>">
            <input type="submit" name="event" value="View" />
            <input type="submit" name="event" value="Edit" />
        </form>
    </body>
</html>

<?php
function handle() {
    $event = $_GET['event'];
    $disp = new dispatcher($event);
    $disp->handle_the_event();
}

$_SESSION['name'] = "Horatio";

handle();
?>
```

The session variables would normally be set during the user's login, but for brevity's sake, let's assume that Horatio wants in — hence the reason this has been hard-coded. By way of example, let's check whether you can allow Horatio to use the edit function. You quite rightly expect the output shown in Figure 8-3 if Horatio clicks the Edit button.

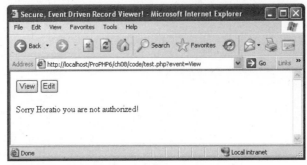

Figure 8-3: Output if Horatio clicks the Edit button.

As you can see, Horatio's attempts to edit records are stopped in their tracks, as only David may edit records.

The power of this approach should be making itself clearer now. You have seen security as an example of how easy it is to modify the application, but this approach can apply to any number of new requirements that might arise.

Pausing for Thought

Many issues must be carefully considered when designing a well-architected, enterprise-level, event-driven application. Improvements to your event-handling methodology could include some sort of handler registration, for example. This would mean that when a user logs onto a site (logging on, in this case, would be an event captured by the application), the application could automatically check which handlers are available to the user. This is achieved through the use of a default handler, which retrieves a list of the user's permissible handlers from a database and returns that information to the presentation layer.

Armed with this information, the presentation layer would know which buttons to render for the user. The administrator would get many buttons, whereas a visitor might have only one View button. If access is restricted to a View button, there is little chance that an untrusted user can maliciously modify anything to which he or she has no access.

A second issue to consider (albeit closely related to the first) before using this method for your next big contract is how to get the dispatcher to include the correct PHP project files in the first place. Because the dispatcher instantiates the event handlers, it must have the correct classes included. In this example, you simply included every handler class that you would need. For larger applications, this approach would be wasteful, because you might be including a hundred classes and only ever use one of them.

One way to rectify this issue is to mark certain handlers as being available by default, with the rest being made available on a per-user basis. Each user stored in the database would have (among other properties) a field containing a list of handlers available to that user. This information could be used to automatically include the relevant handlers in the dispatcher at the same time as the relevant buttons are being added to the user interface.

Finally, your various events may be fired by different entities, so you may want to consider adding functionality to determine what entity is invoking that event, and return an appropriate response based largely on that determination. This may be useful, for example, should you want to return some piece of data either in machine-readable XML format or in human-readable HTML, depending on which entity has invoked the event.

One design pattern that may interest you is the *reactor pattern*. This deals with multisource, enterprise-level event handling, and is definitely worth a look if you are serious about using events. Remember that a design pattern may exist that fits your requirements. The reactor pattern is very similar to what you have done in this chapter, but has added capabilities that enable your handlers to easily differentiate between event sources. For more information on this, see *Pattern-Oriented Software Architecture, Volume 2, Patterns for Concurrent and Networked Objects* by Douglas C. Schmidt, Michael Stal, Hans Rohnert, and Frank Buschmann (Wiley, 2000).

Summary

This chapter has served as an introduction to event-driven programming in PHP. You should now have a good idea of how the event-driven paradigm can be implemented using simple OOP.

Creating an event-driven application is a problem-specific business, and much attention should be paid to the environment in which the intended application will run. Event-driven programming has applications in many areas of computing, but good candidates are often those programs that have graphical user interfaces.

Finally, through the discussion in this chapter, you have seen how the power and elegance inherent in OOP can be effectively complemented by designing applications using an event-driven programming paradigm.

Chapter 9 takes a look at implementing an effective logging and debugging mechanism in your application, to aid you and your development team during both the development and the testing phases of your project.

9

Logging and Debugging

In every application you build, robust logging and debugging mechanisms can save you hours of effort trying to track down problems that might occur.

Logs can be used to help you analyze historical usage patterns that can't be obtained through the Web server log, such as server load, specific SQL statements that were executed, or application-specific messages that wouldn't otherwise be captured.

A debugging mechanism enables you to examine the values of variables, see which conditional loops are being executed, or otherwise determine the state of the application at run-time, without having to litter your code with `print` statements that need to be deleted before you deploy. After you've worked through the code in this chapter, you'll have a set of classes that should be a part of every project you work on.

Creating a Logging Mechanism

The primary purpose of logging is to enable you to see what the application was doing, or how it was performing, at some time in the past. A properly written log will enable you to do a historical analysis of system behavior to determine whether changes must be made.

Simple File Logging

The easiest way to handle logging is to write the information to a file. Usually, the user ID from which your Web server process is running does not have the access needed to write to the file system, except for a temporary directory (`/tmp` on most UNIX systems), which isn't necessarily the best location in which to keep important application log files. To allow the Web server user to be able to write to a file, create a dedicated directory in which to store your log files:

Create a folder above the document root of your application called logs *and ensure that the Web server user has write permissions to this folder. (Use* chmod 744 *and* chown nobody, *or the name of your Apache user, on UNIX systems. Windows users should consult the relevant documentation for your version of Windows).*

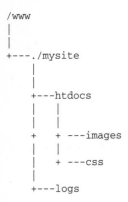

Example File System Layout

To write to a file in PHP, use fopen() to get a file handle and specify that you want to open the file for writing. Use fwrite() to write data to the file, and fclose() to close the file. The following code defines and then demonstrates a simple method called logMessage(), which uses these basic methods to write to a predefined log file:

```php
<?php

function logMessage($message) {
    $LOGDIR = '/www/mysite/logs/'; //chmod 744 and chown nobody
    $logFile = $LOGDIR . 'mysite.log';
    $hFile = fopen($logFile, 'a+'); //open for appending, create
                                    //the file if it doesn't exist
    if(! is_resource($hFile)) {
      printf("Unable to open %s for writing. Check file permissions.", $logFile);
      return false;
    }

    fwrite($hFile, $message);
    fclose($hFile);

    return true;
}

logMessage("Hello, log!\n");
?>
```

If you run this code, and you have all the permissions correctly set on the $LOGDIR directory, you should see the message Hello, log! in the mysite.log file. For the most rudimentary needs, this function might be sufficient; but for a real application, you'll want to track more than just the message. The log should be a "machine-parsable" file, meaning that you should be able to process the log data using a separate application that analyzes the information held within it. The log should include the date and time of each message, some sense of the severity or importance of the message, and some remark about which module of the application generated the message.

The Logger Class

The class in the following code sample provides an OO mechanism for generating a more detailed log file than that created using the code in the previous section. Create a file called `class.Logger.php`. This file will contain the `Logger` class, which enables you to write information in a tab-delimited format to a text file on the server, tracking the timestamp, the log level (which is the severity of the message), the message itself, and an optional module name. The module name can be any string that helps to identify which part of the application generated the message. The code for the `Logger` class is as follows:

```php
<?php

class Logger {

  private $hLogFile;
  private $logLevel;

  //Log Levels.  The higher the number, the less severe the message
  //Gaps are left in the numbering to allow for other levels
  //to be added later
  const DEBUG     = 100;
  const INFO      = 75;
  const NOTICE    = 50;
  const WARNING   = 25;
  const ERROR     = 10;
  const CRITICAL  = 5;

  //Note: private constructor.  Class uses the singleton pattern
  private function __construct() {

    //This is pseudo code that fetches a hash of configuration information
    //Implementation of this is left to the reader, but should hopefully
    //be quite straightforward.
    $cfg = Config::getConfig();

    /* If the config establishes a level, use that level,
       otherwise, default to INFO
    */
    $this->logLevel = isset($cfg['LOGGER_LEVEL']) ?
                            $cfg['LOGGER_LEVEL'] :
                            Logger::INFO;

    //We must specify a log file in the config
    if(! ( isset($cfg['LOGGER_FILE']) && strlen($cfg['LOGGER_FILE'])) ) {
      throw new Exception('No log file path was specified ' .
                    'in the system configuration.');
    }
```

```php
    $logFilePath = $cfg['LOGGER_FILE'];

    //Open a handle to the log file.  Suppress PHP error messages.
    //We'll deal with those ourselves by throwing an exception.
    $this->hLogFile = @fopen($logFilePath, 'a+');

    if(! is_resource($this->hLogFile)) {
      throw new Exception("The specified log file $logFilePath " .
                 'could not be opened or created for ' .
                 'writing.  Check file permissions.');
    }

    //Set encoding type to ISO-8859-1
    stream_encoding($this->hLogFile, 'iso-8859-1');
}

public function __destruct() {
  if(is_resource($this->hLogFile)) {
    fclose($this->hLogFile);
  }
}

public static function getInstance() {

  static $objLog;

  if(!isset($objLog)) {
    $objLog = new Logger();
  }

  return $objLog;
}

public function logMessage($msg, $logLevel = Logger::INFO, $module = null) {

  if($logLevel > $this->logLevel) {
    return;
  }

  /* If you haven't specifed your timezone using the
     date.timezone value in php.ini, be sure to include
     a line like the following.  This can be omitted otherwise.
  */
  date_default_timezone_set('America/New_York');

  $time = strftime('%x %X', time());
  $msg = str_replace("\t", ' ', $msg);
  $msg = str_replace("\n", ' ', $msg);

  $strLogLevel = $this->levelToString($logLevel);
```

```
        if(isset($module)) {
          $module = str_replace("\t", ' ', $module);
          $module = str_replace("\n", ' ', $module);
        }

        //logs: date/time loglevel message modulename
        //separated by tabs, new line delimited
        $logLine = "$time\t$strLogLevel\t$msg\t$module\n";
        fwrite($this->hLogFile, $logLine);
      }

    public static function levelToString($logLevel) {
      switch ($logLevel) {
        case Logger::DEBUG:
          return 'Logger::DEBUG';
          break;
        case Logger::INFO:
          return 'Logger::INFO';
          break;
        case Logger::NOTICE:
          return 'Logger::NOTICE';
          break;
        case Logger::WARNING:
          return 'Logger::WARNING';
          break;
        case Logger::ERROR:
          return 'Logger::ERROR';
          break;
        case Logger::CRITICAL:
          return 'Logger::CRITICAL';
          break;
        default:
          return '[unknown]';
      }
    }
  }
?>
```

This class should seem straightforward enough. Note that you create a private constructor to prevent having to open the file handle several times during the execution of a page request. The getInstance() method allows code that will use this class to get an instance of it. This is known as the *singleton* pattern, which you first saw in Chapter 4.

The first few lines of the file establish a number of logging level constants. These constants enable you to control what information is logged. While developing the first version of an application, for debugging purposes you'll probably want to log quite a bit of information to help you track down bugs. When the application is finally put into production, you'll want to log less information to save on system resources. Logging less information also increases the signal-to-noise ratio, meaning there is more useful information in a given number of lines of log information. When an application is running in a production environment, much of the debugging information you used during development will be of little use when trying to track down problems, which makes finding those problems in the log more difficult.

In the constructor, two pieces of information are pulled from a global array of configuration information: the name of the log file and the current debugging level. For this example, you can assume that there is only one log file per application. Later in this chapter, you'll look at ways to extend this class to provide even more functionality and greater flexibility regarding where information is logged.

Store the logging level in a private member variable that will be used later to determine which information is written to the log file. The log filename is checked to ensure that it has a value, and that the Web server user can actually open or create the log file for appending. The `a+` parameter to `fopen()` means "open this file for appending and if it doesn't exist, create it." Store the file handle as another private member variable. If, for any reason, you can't create a valid file handle, the constructor throws an exception.

Any attempt to call `Logger::getInstance()` should be wrapped in a `try...catch` block because of the possibility of failure arising from incorrect permissions on the log file, or lack of disk space on the volume on which it resides. In the event that this happens, the entire application should not cease to work because of the logger. You should catch this exception and take appropriate action, perhaps by sending an e-mail to a systems administrator. (See Chapter 11 for a robust e-mailing class you can use.)

This class also has a destructor that closes the file handle if it is open. If the file path wasn't valid, then the file handle will not be a valid resource. Even though the exception was thrown in the constructor, the destructor is still called when the object is de-allocated from memory. Therefore, some code has been added to ensure that yet another error isn't generated by trying to close a file handle that was never opened successfully in the first place.

The `getInstance()` method in the `Logger` class has a static variable that stores an instance of the class in between invocations of the `getInstance()` method. The first time the method is called, that variable will be `null`, resulting in the creation of a new instance of `Logger`. If the log file path is invalid, then the exception will bubble up to this method. On subsequent calls to this method, the variable will store the reference created during the first invocation, and that original instance will be returned. Using the singleton pattern here enables you to save the system resources required to open and close the file handle when creating and destroying instances of the `Logger` class.

The `logMessage()` method does all the hard work. It takes the message text, the logging level, and an optional module name. If the current systemwide logging level configuration parameter (assigned to the private member variable `$logLevel` in the constructor) is at least as large as the log level specified in the second parameter to this function, an entry in the log file is created. If the current application logging level is less than the level specified in the second parameter, then no entry is created. This enables you to control what is entered into the log.

For each message sent to the `logMessage()` method, a log level should be supplied indicating the severity of the message. For example, if you're printing just the contents of some variable to the log for debugging purposes, the second parameter to `logMessage()` should be `Logger::DEBUG`. Then, when deploying the code to the production server, you should set the `$cfg['LOGGER_LEVEL']` parameter to `Logger::WARNING` or higher. This will stop debug messages from being printed to the log, saving CPU cycles and restricting the content in the log to errors of varying severity.

`logMessage()` generates a timestamp on line 84 using PHP's `strftime()` function, which takes a format string as its first parameter and a UNIX timestamp as the second. The format string used in the code sample uses the system default short date representation (`%x`) and the system default time representation (`%X`). For example, on a server located in the United States, output from `strftime('%x %X', time())}`

is in the form 07/14/2008 03:55:25 (meaning July 14, 2008, at 3:55:25 in the morning). If your computer is located in other parts of the world, the date representation would be shown appropriately for your location (in this case, that would likely mean 14/07/2008).

> *If you want more control over the formatting of the timestamp in the log, see the documentation for the* strftime()*function at* www.php.net/strftime. *If your log requires higher time resolution than one second, you can use the* microtime()*function to get milliseconds. Again, see the documentation for more information on how to use this function.*

Note that PHP 6 is a bit stricter than previous versions about how it determines the current time zone. Web servers are often not in the same time zone as the programmer, and many servers do not have a correct time zone setting for the location they are in. As a result, every application should specify its time zone either in php.ini, or by using the date_default_timezone_set()function, with the latter option generally invoked as part of the application's configuration at the beginning of every page request (rather than on a function-specific basis, as shown in the example code).

After creating a textual representation of the timestamp, logMessage()must do some formatting of the message. Because you want to create a log file that is easily machine-readable, separate the fields on each line of the log with a tab (\t). Each log entry is separated by a newline character (\n). Because of this, you must remove any tabs or new lines that might exist in the message because these would corrupt the log file and make it difficult to parse with a log analyzer. Replace the tabs with four spaces (the default number of characters occupied by a tab in most text editors) and replace new lines with a space. If the $module parameter has a value, then the same replacements should be made. If you are logging information for which tabs and newline characters are meaningful and cannot be discarded, consider replacing them with the standard conventions of \t and \n, which would enable you to restore the original value when analyzing the data.

The only other thing of interest that happens here is the conversion of the numeric log level constant to a string. Because PHP sees the constants as their actual numeric value, there is no easy way to convert the name of a constant to a string representation of that constant name. As a result, the string representations are hard-coded into the method levelToString(). The switch statement loops through the constants and returns the name of the constant. Although the break statements are not technically necessary, they are added for clarity. Also not actually necessary is the declaration of this method as static, but because it doesn't depend on any of the member variables, and because you may find a need to print the log level in code outside this class, declaring the method static makes it easy to write code such as echo Logger::levelToString($cfg['LOGGER_LEVEL']), for example.

The following code sample shows how you might be able to use the Logger class in a real application:

```php
<?php
require_once('class.Config.php');
require_once('class.Logger.php');

//Again, the implementation of this class is left to the user, but an
//example of how it could work will be provided in the code download
//that accompanies the book on wrox.com
Config::addConfig('LOGGER_FILE', '/var/log/myapplication.log');
Config::addConfig('LOGGER_LEVEL', Logger::INFO);

$log = Logger::getInstance();
```

```
if(isset($_GET['fooid'])) {

    //not written to the log - the log level is too high
    $log->logMessage('A fooid is present', Logger::DEBUG);

    //LOG_INFO is the default so this would get printed
    $log->logMessage('The value of fooid is ' . $_GET['fooid']);

} else {

    //This will also be written, and includes a module name
    $log->logMessage('No fooid supplied',
                     Logger::CRITICAL,
                     "Foo Module");

    throw new Exception('No foo id!');
}
?>
```

If $_GET['fooid'] is set, then two calls to logMessage() are made, but only one message will actually be written to the file because of the configured logging level. The contents of the log will look something like the following:

```
03/17/04 03:58:42      Logger::INFO     The value of fooid is 25
```

Here you see the timestamp, the logging level of the message, and the message itself.

If $_GET['fooid'] is not set, then you will see the following log entry:

```
03/19/04 05:30:07    Logger::CRITICAL  No fooid passed from
         http://localhost/testLogger.php    Foo Module
```

In this case, the testLogger.php page failed to pass fooid to the page that invoked the logger, so the Logger::CRITICAL error was written to the file.

Extending the Logger Class

Logging to a text file is an incredibly useful way to store log data. There are literally thousands of utilities you can use to parse and analyze this data—from simple UNIX utilities (such as sed and grep) to fancy commercial log analysis software packages costing tens of thousands of dollars. Sometimes, however, a text file isn't the most convenient storage medium. You might want to use a relational database or integrate with your platform's system logger to centralize all your application logs. Additionally, the Logger class as developed thus far is capable of writing only to a single file, no matter where in the application it is invoked. There are several circumstances in which you might want to keep separate logs for different sections of an application, or for different tasks performed. In this section, you'll extend the Logger class to be able to integrate with any data storage medium and support multiple logs in a single application.

In Chapter 6 you learned how the PDO class can connect to a completely different database back end by a simple change to its connection string. By connecting with `"mysql:host=localhost;dbname=mydb"`, you can connect to a MySQL database running on the local machine and use to the database called `"mydb"`. To connect to a PostgreSQL database, the connection string looks like `"mysql:host=localhost;dbname=yourdb"`, which connects to a PostgreSQL database instance on the local machine and uses the database called `"yourdb"`. After a connection has been established using this common connection string syntax, everything else about the use of the PDO class is identical, regardless of which RDBMS you're connected to. You can use a very similar construct to enable your Logger class to connect to any kind of storage medium.

The goal of the enhanced Logger class is to use a similar syntax for establishing a connection to a storage medium for log data. Because you'll be able to use different storage media, you should also be able to store different logs for different parts of the application. The new Logger class should support some sort of "registry" of log connections. For example, you should be able to have a log called "errors" and one called "queries," which will store error messages and SQL statements, respectively. The following sample code represents what you should be able to do with the redesigned class:

```php
<?php

Logger::register('errors', 'file:///var/log/error.log');
Logger::register('app',
                 'pgsql://postgres@db/errors?table=applog&timestamp=dtlog&' .
                 'msg=smesg&level=slevel&module=smod');

$objQLog = Logger::getInstance('app');

$sql = "SELECT * FROM foo";
$objQLog->logMessage("Selecting all foos");

try {
  Database->getInstance()->select($sql);
} catch (DBQueryException $e) {
    $objErrLog = Logger::getInstance('errors');
    $objErrLog->logMessage($e->getMessage(), LOGGER_CRITICAL);
}
?>
```

Showing this code before showing the new class that drives it may be a little confusing, but sometimes it's easier to design a class by first knowing how you want to be able to use it. In a real application, you would put the first two lines in a globally included file. These two lines establish two different logs:

❑   app—The app log will store its log messages in a PostgreSQL database, in a table called `applog` using the field names specified for the timestamp, message, logging level, and module.

❑   errors—The error log will be a text file located in `/var/log/error.log`.

In the main part of the application, you would store most messages in the app log for later analysis. Any errors that occur will be stored in the errors log, which is a text file. A text file is used for the errors because one of the errors may be an inability to connect to the database.

Parsing the Connection String

The first step in creating the new `Logger` class is to be able to parse strings of the form `scheme://user:password@host:port/path?query#fragment`. Luckily, PHP provides an incredibly handy function for doing just that. The `parse_url()` function takes a string in this general form and returns an array containing the elements from the URL that exists. (The array keys are the same as the names used in the previous string.) If one or more of the elements do not exist, then no item with that key is added to the array (as opposed to having a `null` entry for that key.)

Consider the following example:

```
$url = "ftp://anonymous@ftp.gnu.org:21/pub/gnu/gcc"
$arParts = parse_url($url);
var_dump($arParts);

//prints out:
Array (
    [scheme] => ftp
    [user] => anonymous
    [host] => ftp.gnu.org
    [port] => 21
    [path] => /pub/gnu/gcc
)
```

Note that the password, query, and fragment keys do not appear in the array, because they do not appear in the URL.

Redesigning Logger to Use the Connection String

`Logger` will use the `scheme` part of this array to determine which logging back end to use. The `register()` method is used to establish a new connection, and takes a canonical name and a URL as parameters. Because the `register()` method was statically invoked in the sample code, you'll need to use some sort of intermediate function that allows both the `register()` and the `getInstance()` methods to talk to the same set of information.

The following code shows the new `register()` method and the reworked `getInstance()` and constructor. In fact, this code sample represents the entirety of the new `Logger` class. The parts that have changed are highlighted. Save these changes to `class.Logger-enhanced.php`:

```php
<?php

class Logger {
    private $hLogFile;
    private $logLevel;

    //Log Levels.  The higher the number, the less severe the message
    //Gaps are left in the numbering to allow for other levels
    //to be added later
    const DEBUG   = 100;
    const INFO    = 75;
    const NOTICE  = 50;
```

```
const WARNING   = 25;
const ERROR     = 10;
const CRITICAL  = 5;

//Note: private constructor.  Class uses the singleton pattern
private function __construct() {

}

public static function register($logName, $connectionString) {

  $urlData = parse_url($connectionString);

  if(! isset($urlData['scheme'])) {
    throw new Exception("Invalid log connection string $connectionString");
  }

  @include_once('Logger/class.' .
                $urlData['scheme'] . 'LoggerBackend.php');

  $className = $urlData['scheme'] . 'LoggerBackend';

  if(! class_exists($className)) {
    throw new Exception('No logging backend available for ' .
          $urlData['scheme']);
  }

  $objBack = new $className($urlData);

  Logger::manageBackends($logName, $objBack);
}

public static function getInstance($name) {
  return Logger::manageBackends($name);
}

private static function manageBackends(
                         $name,
                         LoggerBackend $objBack = null) {

  static $backEnds;

  if(! isset($backEnds)) {
    $backEnds = array();
  }

  if($objBack == null) {
    //we must be retrieving
    if(isset($backEnds[$name])) {
      return $backEnds[$name];
    } else {
```

```
            throw new Exception("The specified backend $name was not " .
                'registered with Logger.');
    }

} else {
    //we must be adding
    $backEnds[$name] = $objBack;
}
}

public static function levelToString($logLevel) {
    switch ($logLevel) {
        case Logger::DEBUG:
            return 'Logger::DEBUG';
            break;
        case Logger::INFO:
            return 'Logger::INFO';
            break;
        case Logger::NOTICE:
            return 'Logger::NOTICE';
            break;
        case Logger::WARNING:
            return 'Logger::WARNING';
            break;
        case Logger::ERROR:
            return 'Logger::ERROR';
            break;
        case Logger::CRITICAL:
            return 'Logger::CRITICAL';
            break;
        default:
            return '[unknown]';
    }
}
}

?>
```

In the preceding code, Logger pulls in the file that defines an abstract class called LoggerBackend, which serves as the base class for the classes that will do the actual work of writing to a given logging mechanism. Logger's constructor is now empty, but is still declared to be private to prevent its instantiation outside the getInstance() method.

The new static method, register(), is responsible for instantiating a LoggingBackend object based on the scheme part of the URL specified in the second parameter. To do so, it makes a call to parse_url() to determine the scheme. If no scheme was present in the URL, register() throws an exception. If the scheme is present, an attempt is made to include_once a file called Logger/class . [scheme]LoggerBackend.php, and the class contained therein is instantiated by passing the $urlData array. If the file isn't found, the code throws an exception. include_once is used here instead of require_once because if you use require_once and the file isn't found, a fatal exception is thrown, and application execution terminates.

If the specified `LoggerBackend` class is properly instantiated, the new instance is passed, along with the canonical name specified in the first parameter to `register()` to the private function `manageBackends()`. This function exists because all public methods of `Logger` are now static. As a result, the class can't use any member variables to store the instantiated back-end objects. `manageBackends()` contains a static variable that takes the place of a class member. If the function has two parameters, it stores the `LoggerBackend` object in the `$backEnds` array using the `$name` parameter as a key. If only one parameter is specified (the `$name` parameter), `manageBackends()` returns the `LoggerBackend` object stored in `$name` (if one exists).

The new `getInstance()` method no longer returns a `Logger` object, but instead returns an instantiated `LoggerBackend`. It does so by calling `manageBackends()` with only one parameter, the canonical name of the particular log requested. If the named log wasn't previously registered, or was unable to be instantiated during `register()`, `manageBackends()` throws an exception that will bubble up to `getInstance()`.

The LoggerBackend Class

The `manageBackends()`, `register()`, and `getInstance()` methods all interact with `LoggerBackend` objects. This class provides a *concrete constructor* (a construct that exists and is callable) and an abstract method called `logMesage()`, which you probably remember from the original `Logger` class. The latter method is unchanged in number and type of parameters from the code presented previously. However, in the `LoggerBackend` class, the `logMessage()` method is abstract—no actual function body exists, just the declaration of a function that must be implemented by classes that inherit from `LoggerBackend`. The constructor of the class takes the array output from `parse_url()` and stores it in a protected member variable. No other methods are defined by the `LoggerBackend` class.

Save the following as `Logger/class.LoggerBackend.php`:

```php
<?php
abstract class LoggerBackend {
  protected $urlData;

  public function __construct($urlData) {
    $this->urlData = $urlData;
  }

  abstract function logMessage($message, $logLevel = Logger::INFO, $module);
}
?>
```

The class itself should be declared abstract because it contains one abstract method and because there is no practical use for an instance of `LoggerBackend`. Only the subclasses of `LoggerBackend` will do any real work.

Subclassing LoggerBackend

In order for the new and improved `Logger` class to be able to do anything, you'll need to create at least one subclass of `LoggerBackend`. Because you already have some code that will log information to a file, this will be the easiest `LoggerBackend` subclass to create first.

Create a file called `class.fileLoggerBackend.php` (pay attention to capitalization in the filename) and enter the following code:

```php
<?php

require_once('class.LoggerBackend.php');

class fileLoggerBackend extends LoggerBackend {

  private $logLevel;
  private $hLogFile;

  public function __construct($urlData) {

    parent::__construct($urlData);

    $this->logLevel = Config::getConfig('LOGGER_LEVEL');

    $logFilePath = $this->urlData['path'];

    if(! strlen($logFilePath)) {
      throw new Exception('No log file path was specified ' .
                 'in the connection string.');
    }

    print "Logging data to $logFilePath";

    //Open a handle to the log file.  Suppress PHP error messages.
    //We'll deal with those ourselves by throwing an exception.
    $this->hLogFile = @fopen($logFilePath, 'a+');

    if(! is_resource($this->hLogFile)) {
    throw new Exception("The specified log file $logFilePath " .
                 'could not be opened or created for ' .
                 'writing.  Check file permissions.');
    }

    //Set encoding type to ISO-8859-1
    stream_encoding($this->hLogFile, 'iso-8859-1');

  }

  public function logMessage($msg, $logLevel = LOGGER_INFO, $module = null) {
    if($logLevel > $this->logLevel) {
      return;
    }

    /* If you haven't specifed your timezone using the
       date.timezone value in php.ini, be sure to include
       a line like the following.  This can be omitted otherwise.
    */
    date_default_timezone_set('America/New_York');
    $time = strftime('%x %X', time());
    $msg = str_replace("\t", '     ', $msg);
```

```
      $msg = str_replace("\n", ' ', $msg);

      $strLogLevel = Logger::levelToString($logLevel);

      if(isset($module)) {
        $module = str_replace("\t", '    ', $module);
        $module = str_replace("\n", ' ', $module);
      }

      //logs: date/time loglevel message modulename
      //separated by tabs, new line delimited
      $logLine = "$time\t$strLogLevel\t$msg\t$module\n";
      fwrite($this->hLogFile, $logLine);

    }
  }
?>
```

Much of this code should look familiar to you. It is taken nearly verbatim from the original Logger class. The fileLoggerBackend class will respond to logs registered with the file:// scheme. It writes the log to the file specified in the path component of the parse_url() array. To register a log of this type, the URL should be something like file:///var/log/app.log. Note that these components are file:// (ending in two forward slashes) and /var/log/app.log (starting with one forward slash). There are three initial forward slashes in the file scheme.

To use this back end, you can write code such the following (just like what you saw at the beginning of this section):

```
<?php
    require_once('class.Logger.php');
    Logger::register('app', 'file:///var/log/applog.log');
    $log = Logger::getInstance('app');
    $log->logMessage('This is a new log message!', LOGGER_CRITICAL, 'test');
?>
```

This registers a fileLoggerBackend with the Logger class called 'app', which writes to the file /var/log/applog.log.

Logging to a Database Table

You can use this same process of subclassing LoggerBackend to create a mechanism for logging to any conceivable data repository. The following code shows a PostgreSQL back end, but the same principles can be used to log to any database platform.

This class has a significantly longer constructor. The connection parameters and the names of the fields in the database to which the information is written should all be representable in the connection string, with sensible defaults for those items that can be optional. As a result, the code must check to see whether certain values are set before building up connection strings and field names. None of this code is very interesting, but all of it is included here to show how to parse the connection string to allow a flexible PostgreSQL logging mechanism. This code should be saved in Logger/class.pgsqlLoggerBackend.php:

```php
<?php

require_once('class.LoggerBackend.php');

class pgsqlLoggerBackend extends LoggerBackend {

  private $logLevel;
  private $hConn;
  private $table = 'logdata';
  private $messageField = 'message';
  private $logLevelField = 'loglevel';
  private $timestampField = 'logdate';
  private $moduleField = 'module';

  public function __construct($urlData) {

    parent::__construct($urlData);

    $this->logLevel = Config::getConfig('LOGGER_LEVEL');

    $host = $urlData['host'];
    $port = $urlData['port'];
    $user = $urlData['user'];
    $password = $urlData['pass'];
    $arPath = explode('/', $urlData['path']);
    $database = $arPath[1];

    if(!strlen($database)) {
      throw new Exception('pgsqlLoggerBackend: Invalid connection string.' .
                          'No database name was specified');
    }

    $connStr = '';
    if($host) {
      $connStr .= "host=$host ";
    }

    if($port) {
      $connStr .= "port=$port ";
    }
    if($user) {
      $connStr .= "user=$user ";
    }

    if($password) {
      $connStr .= "password=$password ";
    }
```

```php
    $connStr .= "dbname=$database";

    //Suppress native errors.  We'll handle them with an exception
    $this->hConn = pg_connect($connStr);

    if(! is_resource($this->hConn)) {
      throw new Exception("Unable to connect to the database using $connStr");
    }

    //Take the query string in the form var=foo&bar=blah
    //and convert it to an array like
    // array('var' => 'foo', 'bar' => 'blah')
    //Be sure to convert urlencoded values
    $queryData = $urlData['query'];
    if(strlen($queryData)) {
      $arTmpQuery = explode('&',$queryData);

      $arQuery = array();
      foreach($arTmpQuery as $queryItem) {
        $arQueryItem = explode('=', $queryItem);
        $arQuery[urldecode($arQueryItem[0])] = urldecode($arQueryItem[1]);
      }
    }

    /* None of these items is mandatory.  The defaults are
       established in the private member declarations at the top
       of the class. These variables establish the name of the
       table and the names of the fields within that table
       that store the various elements of the log entry.
    */

    if(isset($arQuery['table'])) {
      $this->table = $arQuery['table'];
    }

    if(isset($arQuery['messageField'])) {
      $this->messageField = $arQuery['messageField'];
    }
      if(isset($arQuery['logLevelField'])) {
      $this->logLevelField = $arQuery['logLevelField'];
    }

      if(isset($arQuery['timestampField'])) {
      $this->timestampField = $arQuery['timestampField'];
    }
    if(isset($arQuery['moduleField'])) {
      $this->logLevelField = $arQuery['moduleField'];
    }
  }


  public function logMessage($msg, $logLevel = Logger::INFO, $module = null) {
```

217

```php
        if($logLevel <= $this->logLevel) {

            $strLogLevel = Logger::levelToString($logLevel);

            $msg = pg_escape_string($msg);

            if(isset($module)) {
                $module = "'" . pg_escape_string($module) . "'";
            } else {
                $module = 'NULL';
            }

            $arFields = array();
            $arFields[$this->messageField] = "'" . pg_escape_string($msg) . "'";
            $arFields[$this->logLevelField] = pg_escape_string($logLevel);
            $arFields[$this->timestampField] = "CURRENT_TIMESTAMP";
            $arFields[$this->moduleField] = $module;

            $sql = 'INSERT INTO ' . $this->table;
            $sql .= ' (' . join(', ', array_keys($arFields)) . ')';
            $sql .= ' VALUES (' . join(', ', array_values($arFields)) . ')';

            pg_exec($this->hConn, $sql);
        }
    }
}
?>
```

In the constructor, the class parses out the query part of the URL to determine the table name and the names of the fields in which the log information is stored. The assumption is that the table will be created using a SQL statement such as the following. The field names don't matter (because they're configurable in the connection string), but the data types in your table should be the same (or compatible data types):

```sql
create table logdata (
    message text,
    loglevel smallint,
    logdate timestamp,
    module varchar(255)
);
```

To use the new PostgreSQL logger, the code should look something like the following:

```php
<?php

require_once('class.Config.php');
require_once('class.Logger-enhanced.php');

Config::addConfig('LOGGER_LEVEL', Logger::INFO);
```

```
Logger::register('app', 'pgsql://steve:pass@localhost/mydb?table=logdata');

$log = Logger::getInstance('app');

if(isset($_GET['fooid'])) {

  //not written to the log - the log level is too high
  $log->logMessage('A fooid is present', Logger::DEBUG);

  //LOG_INFO is the default, so this would get printed
  $log->logMessage('The value of fooid is ' .  $_GET['fooid']);

  } else {

  //This will also be written and includes a module name
  $log->logMessage('No fooid supplied',
                   Logger::CRITICAL,
                   "Foo Module");

    throw new Exception('No foo id!');
}
?>
```

The connection string passed to `Logger::register()` specifies a log called `app` that connects to a PostgreSQL database running on `localhost`. The `LoggerBackend` connects as the user `steve` to the database called `mydb`. The table into which the log entries are written is called `logdata`. Had you not specified any of these parameters, the defaults declared as the class's private member variables would have been used. Of course, this back end can easily be modified to support any type of database for which there is a PHP module (including MySQL and SQL Server).

This example used the native PostgreSQL functions, rather than leveraging PDO. You could also construct a PDO back end that could connect to any database for which drivers are available using the appropriately structured connection string passed to `Logger::register` in the form `pdo://user:pass@hostname/database?driver=[pdo driver name]`.

Creating a Debugging Mechanism

Although a logging mechanism as robust as the one you just created has nearly infinite possibilities for flexibility and storage, sometimes it's far more convenient to print debugging messages to the browser window, rather than have to pore through a big log file; but just as the `Logger` class was meant to prevent having dozens of `print` statements that must be manually deleted prior to deployment, the debugging mechanism enables the developer to print messages to the screen in such a way that they can easily be removed at deploy time.

The `Debugger` class stores the debug messages in the session, and then prints them out at the bottom of a screen at the end of a page request. This centralizes debug output into one location on the screen, making it easier to find the specific output for which you're looking. It also enables you to print large amounts of data without disturbing the structure of the user interface, and makes suppressing the debug output easy.

The reason you store this information in the session is because not every page request generates output. For example, when saving information to the database by posting a form, you should usually issue a 302 redirect to prevent data modification when a user presses the reload button on his or her browser. A 302 redirect refers to the HTTP response code issued by the browser when you issue code such as header('Location: [url]').

Debugger has two primary functions:

❑ The DEBUG function writes code to the debug array in the session with an optional key and debug level. The debug level works just like the logging level in the Logger class. The lower the logging level value, the higher its priority.

❑ The debug_print function should be invoked at the bottom of every page that generates output. It takes the array from the session and generates an HTML table containing the contents of the array. When it is finished printing, it removes the information from the session. This way, page requests that do not generate output will still have their debugging information preserved.

The code for this class is as follows. Call this class.Debugger.php:

```php
<?php

define('DEBUG_INFO', 100);
define('DEBUG_SQL', 75);
define('DEBUG_WARNING', 50);
define('DEBUG_ERROR', 25);
define('DEBUG_CRITICAL', 10);

session_start();

class Debugger {

  public static function debug($data, $key = null, $debugLevel = DEBUG_INFO) {

    if(! isset($_SESSION['debugData'])) {
      $_SESSION['debugData'] = array();
    }

    if($debugLevel <= Config::getConfig('DEBUG_LEVEL') ) {
      $_SESSION['debugData'][$key] = $data;
    }
  }

  public static function debugPrint() {

    $arDebugData = $_SESSION['debugData'];
    print Debugger::printArray($arDebugData);

    $_SESSION['debugData'] = array();

  }
```

```
    public static function printArray($var, $title = true) {

    $string = '<table border="1">';
    if ($title) {
        $string .= "<tr><td><b>Key</b></td><td><b>Value</b></td></tr>\n";
    }

    if (is_array($var)) {
       foreach($var as $key => $value) {
                   $string .= "<tr>\n" ;
           $string .= "<td><b>$key</b></td><td>";

           if (is_array($value)) {
               $string .= Debugger::printArray($value, false);
           } elseif(gettype($value) == 'object') {
               $string .= "Object of class " . get_class($value);
           } else {
               $string .= "$value" ;
           }

           $string .= "</td></tr>\n";
       }
    }

    $string .= "</table>\n";
    return $string;
  }

}
?>
```

The five constants defined at the top of the file define debugging levels that work in exactly the same way as the logging level constants in class.Logger.php. The debug() method expects to find an array called $cfg in the global namespace that contains an element DEBUG_LEVEL defining the current debug level for the whole application.

By default, the debug level is DEBUG_INFO, though the third parameter of debug() enables you to set it to any level. This way, you can display as much or as little debugging information as you want by simply altering $cfg['DEBUG_LEVEL'].

The $key parameter is an option label for the information in the debugging array. Though it is second in the parameter list, it will appear in the leftmost column of the table that is eventually produced by debugPrint().

The debugPrint() function just passes the debug information from the session to the printArray() method, which does all the real heavy lifting. After printing the debug information, debugPrint() then blows out the session array to clear the debug information for the next page view.

`printArray()` takes an array of at least one dimension and prints an HTML table that shows the contents of that array. Multidimensional arrays are properly handled. Objects have only their class name printed.

The following code shows how this class is used:

```php
<?php

    require_once('class.Debugger.php');
    require_once('class.Config.php');

    Config::addConfig('DEBUG_LEVEL', DEBUG_INFO);

    $myData = array();
    $myData[] = 'hello';
    $myData[] = array('name' => 'Bob',
                'colors' => array('red', 'green', 'blue'));

    Debugger::debug($myData, 'my data');
    $x = 5 + 8;
    Debugger::debug($x, 'x');

    Debugger::debugPrint();

?>
```

This example is easier to appreciate by looking at Figure 9-1, which shows the output from the `debugPrint()` function as rendered on the screen.

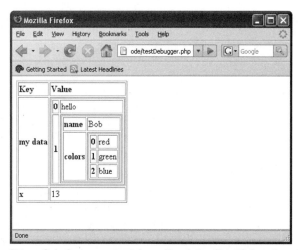

Figure 9-1: Screen output from the debugPrint() function

Summary

The `Logger` class can be extended to support logging information to virtually any conceivable data repository. Just create and use the back end that best supports your needs. For most uses, the `fileLoggerBackend` class should be the most appropriate, but there are some definite advantages to using a database.

The `Debugger` class gives you functionality similar to the `Logger` class, but enables the information to be displayed on the screen and stored in the session for display, even if the original page request contains no output.

In Chapter 10, you'll learn how you can use PHP 6 to write and interact with Web services, which enable you to interact with data and functionality provided by third parties.

10

Writing and Using Web Services

With the vast array of modules and PEAR packages available to you when building an application in PHP, it might seem like there's not much that PHP can't do for you to facilitate the implementation of fairly complex business requirements in a short period of time. From image manipulation and complex date/time arithmetic to transactional database interactions, PHP does, indeed, provide a lot right out of the box. However, there are a number of features you might want to provide in your application that you can't, either because you lack the data and obtaining it would be too onerous (for example, rolling your own search engine for the entire Web) or because the application logic is far more complex than your project's budget would allow (for example, creating an interactive geographic information systems application).

Thankfully, a number of application providers expose the functionality of their applications through an application programming interface (API) that allows for the exchange of data in a markup-free manner. Typically, this involves making a call via HTTP, using a request structured according to certain rules and markup formats, and receiving a response in a structured manner, typically XML but often in other formats as well (CSV, JSON, and so on). Because this response is structured data, rather than data containing HTML or other stylized output, you can use it and display it in any manner you like.

If your application is HTML, then you convert the output to HTML. If your application is Flash, then you can output in a manner most appropriate for your Flash application. Furthermore, your interaction with a Web service need not have any output to the user, but might be used instead to populate or augment data in your database (for example, using a geo-location service to get values for the latitude and longitude of a list of locations).

Leveraging a Web services API from another application enables you to create "mashups" of that application with your own data and functionality. This chapter describes several methods of interacting with Web services APIs, including some of the more popular commercial services such as Google and Yahoo!. You'll learn how you can combine data from them to create your own application. Finally, you'll learn how you can expose the features of your application to others so that they can take advantage of your application, and you'll discover how you can benefit from this approach as well.

There are numerous different standards for interacting with a Web services API. The term "Web services" in no way implies any one of them in particular. That term merely connotes the idea of a remote call into another application via HTTP. The actual nature of the communication is governed by one of several established data exchange protocols, typically overseen by the W3C. This chapter covers a few of the most popular protocols for Web services.

SOAP

Simple Object Access Protocol (SOAP) is the most robust of the Web services protocols, allowing for the discovery of application features, the automatic determination of data types, data validation capabilities, and complex request-and-response data structures. SOAP uses an XML schema for data exchange, usually layered over HTTP for the communications protocol (though there are mostly theoretical implementations using SMTP or other protocols for the communications layer).

The downside to all of this robustness is that the capability for a fairly complex (meaning flexible and potentially sophisticated) request-and-response structure means that the data structure is *necessarily* complicated (meaning difficult to understand and difficult to implement). As a result, a number of PHP packages have been developed that act as wrappers over the actual implementation of the XML data structures and HTTP interactions.

XML is a huge topic, and this chapter does not cover it in great detail. You should have a basic knowledge of XML in order to understand and use this chapter. If you're not familiar with XML but would like a good grounding, you might want to take a look at *Beginning XML, Fourth Edition* (Wiley, 2007). The next part of this chapter looks at how SOAP can be used to implement XML-based Web services in PHP 6.

SOAP and PHP 6

SOAP is a messaging protocol that is platform agnostic — that is, happy to use a variety of Internet protocols such as HTTP, SMTP, and even MIME. You already know that it makes use of XML as part of its information exchange methodology, and the only other thing to note here is that Web Service Description Language (WSDL) is also used to make your life easier. This discussion looks at how you can use the services that are to be accessed by SOAP. WSDL, as well as all other aspects of SOAP, are examined in more detail a little later in the chapter.

What does SOAP do? The simple answer is that it enables you to pass structured, typed data in a decentralized, distributed environment. This means that you can pass a request from a GNU/Linux server running a PHP application in your data center to a J2EE application on a Solaris machine on another continent, and expect a perfectly coherent response. Using SOAP, many of the data-conversion and systems-integration problems of the past are solved, and a remote procedure call mechanism that works for all platforms with a viable XML parser is available and well documented. (Currently, nearly every major platform that would be deployed in an enterprise capacity has XML parsing capabilities and an HTTP implementation available.)

Following are the different libraries that implement SOAP in PHP:

❑   The PHP 6 SOAP extension — Bundled with PHP 6

❑   PEAR::SOAP — http://pear.php.net/package/SOAP

❑   NuSOAP — http://sourceforge.net/projects/nusoap/

Depending on what you feel most comfortable with, you can choose whatever you like. For the purposes of this chapter, we'll look only at the use of the SOAP extension that is bundled with PHP 6. It has been completely revamped for PHP 6. Because it is implemented in C, it will be considerably faster than the other modules, which are implemented in earlier versions of PHP.

The PHP6 SOAP Extension

As of this writing, you must manually add the SOAP extension to the php.ini file, extension= php_soap.dll, for Windows, or compile with --enable-soap for Linux versions. In addition, note that a number of online sources say the SOAP extension is enabled by default, but the snapshot of PHP 6 currently being used does not have it enabled by default. By the time this book hits the shelves, the default policy may have changed, so take a look at the phpinfo() output of your PHP distribution to determine whether SOAP must be manually enabled.

There are a couple of things to note with regard to configuring SOAP in PHP 6. One of the biggest drawbacks to using SOAP is that you end up relying on the speed of your server's Internet connection because the SOAP client making the request must first download the WSDL document in order to know how to make a function call to the target service. Obviously, downloading a file over a slow connection (or perhaps more important, one with a high latency, or "ping time") could present the greatest bottleneck in terms of the time it takes for a given task to be executed.

The solution is provided in the form of PHP configuration settings, which enable you to specify whether you want to cache WSDL pages, where you want them cached, and how long you want to use that cached copy of the files. This means that your application's execution time is "charged" only once in order to download the WSDL; from then on, you use the cached version.

If you think that this will significantly enhance the performance of your application, you can add the following lines to your php.ini file (substituting whatever values you deem necessary):

```
; SOAP

;Boolean paramater to indicate whether caching should occur
soap.wsdl_cache_enabled = "1"

;directory where files are to be cached
soap.wsdl_cache_dir = "/tmp/wsdlcache"

;time, given in seconds, to use the cached copy - ttl = time to live
soap.wsdl_cache_ttl = "86400"
```

The functions provided with PHP 6 can nominally be divided into three categories. The main two are SoapClient and SoapServer functions, with the other category handling miscellaneous functions. Each of these is briefly examined in the next few sections, but for more comprehensive coverage, see the documentation at www.php.net/soap.

SoapClient Functions

In keeping with all things object-oriented, available SOAP functions are exposed through the use of SOAP objects, and you can instantiate a generic `SoapClient` object to work with as follows:

```
$client = new SoapClient (mixed wsdl [, array options]);
```

The first parameter can take either the `null` value (if you aren't using WSDL) or the Uniform Resource Identifier (URI) of the WSDL document to be used. The `options` parameter that follows should be passed as an array, and can be used to provide proxy settings or stipulate the SOAP specification to which the SOAP client should adhere. For example, to create a SOAP client that uses encoded SOAP messages and RPC style, you can use the following:

```
$client = new SoapClient(null,
    array('location' => "http://localhost/my_soap.php",
    'uri' => "http://my_uri/",
    'style' => SOAP_RPC, 'use' => SOAP_ENCODED));
```

After you have the SOAP client instantiated, several methods are provided by PHP 6 that you can call in the resulting client object. The more important of those methods are as follows:

❑ `__call` — Use this to make a SOAP call directly. Usually, you can simply call the SOAP functions as a `SoapClient` method, but this may come in handy for transmitting SOAP headers and footers, for example.

❑ `__getFunctions` — This exposes the functions provided by a given Web service.

❑ `__getLastRequest` — As the name implies, you can retrieve the previous request made by the SOAP client, but only if your `SoapClient` instance was created with the `trace` option set to `true` in the `options` array parameter.

❑ `__getLastResponse` — Similarly, you can use this to determine the previous response received by the SOAP client, provided that your `SoapClient` has the `trace` option enabled.

❑ `__getTypes` — This will return a list of SOAP types (that is, structures and objects defined and implemented by the Web service). It can be used only if your `SoapClient` was instantiated in WSDL mode (i.e., supplied with a WSDL URI as its first argument).

You will learn how to create and use a SOAP client a little later. For the moment, let's continue to explore the other SOAP functionality provided by PHP 6.

SoapServer Functions

Of course, accessing information from a client is not the only way developers use SOAP. Providing the server is high up on the Web service to-do list, and PHP 6 provides some methods to create SOAP servers.

As with the `SoapClient`, you have a constructor that can be used to create the `SoapServer` object as follows:

```
$server = new SoapServer (mixed wsdl [, array options])
```

You can either specify the WSDL document to use in the first parameter, or leave it as null. If the first option is null, you must set the uri option as part of the options array in much the same way as the SoapClient. Following are the available server methods:

❑ addFunction — This allows functions to be added to service SOAP requests.

❑ getFunctions — This returns a list of the functions available on the server.

❑ handle — This takes values from either the single soap_request parameter or, in its absence, the global variable $HTTP_RAW_POST_DATA, and deals with the given request, returning a response to the client.

❑ setClass — This allows PHP methods (and entire classes) to be added to the server in order to handle SOAP requests.

❑ setPersistence — Assuming that you have used setClass to add the server's functionality, this can be used to perpetuate data between requests in a session.

Miscellaneous Functions

The final few SOAP functions deal with a couple of different issues, the most important of which is exception handling. You can create a SoapFault object to return fault responses from the server as follows:

```
$fault = new SoapFault (string faultcode, string faultstring [,
    string faultactor [, mixed detail [, string faultname
    [, mixed headerfault]]]]);
```

If a SoapClient has its exceptions option set to 0, the requested method will return the SoapFault object on any failure. With this in mind, you can use the following function (just a function, not part of any class) to test whether a function call failed:

```
is_soap_fault ($methodresult)
```

This returns true if the result parameter passed in is, in fact, an instance of the SoapFault object.

Apart from these exception-related issues, PHP 6's SOAP extension also implements the SoapVar object, which can be used to set type properties when not in WSDL mode. It is instantiated like this:

```
$type = new SoapVar ( mixed data, int encoding [, string type_name [, string
type_namespace [, string node_name [, string node_namespace]]]]);
```

SoapHeader, as the name implies, enables you to pass raw SOAP headers between client and server. This can be done from either the _call() or the _handle() functions:

```
client->__call("myFunction", null, null,
    new SoapHeader('http://thenamespace.org/mynamespace/', 'myExample',
    'an example'));
```

Finally, you are also given the `SoapParam` object to pass name and value pairs as SOAP parameters from clients that are not in WSDL mode. For example, to supply parameters to a SOAP server's method call, you can say something like this:

```
$client->__call ("getSoapMethod", array(new SoapParam($value, "name")));
```

With that, you now have a brief idea of how the first bundled SOAP extension goes about using SOAP. You can use this to create an example SOAP client, as well as a simple SOAP server.

Making a SOAP Client

The examples in this section leverage the Web services functionality exposed by `Amazon.com`. You can use Amazon's SOAP API to fetch things such as prices, descriptions, images, and related items for anything being sold at `Amazon.com`. Notice that Amazon has made things quite easy in that it has provided the URI (see the following code snippet) for the appropriate WSDL document, which, as you know, will tell your SOAP client how to use the service.

Recall from earlier in the chapter that when you are creating a new `SoapClient` object, you can choose whether or not to use WSDL mode. Because you have a WSDL link, let's use it. Save this code to `soap.php`:

```
<?php
$client = new SoapClient(
"http://webservices.amazon.com/AWSECommerceService/AWSECommerceService.wsdl");
?>
```

That's pretty much it. If you had chosen not to use WSDL mode, or if it were not made available to you, you would have to add the array options such as location, URI, style, and so on.

Assuming that the Web service is working, then your work is done. From the Web site, you can click the Analyze WSDL link to see the service definitions, but let's instead use some of the native PHP 6 functions to determine how you can use this service.

The best way to do this is simply to dump the output of the `__getFunctions()` function to the screen, like so:

```
<?php
$client = new SoapClient(
"http://webservices.amazon.com/AWSECommerceService/AWSECommerceService.wsdl");
var_dump($client->__getFunctions());
?>
```

Save this code as `soap_functions.php` and navigate to it in your browser. You will see something similar to Figure 10-1.

```
array(23) {
  [0]=>
  unicode(29) "HelpResponse Help(Help $body)"
  [1]=>
  unicode(47) "ItemSearchResponse ItemSearch(ItemSearch $body)"
  [2]=>
  unicode(47) "ItemLookupResponse ItemLookup(ItemLookup $body)"
  [3]=>
  unicode(65) "BrowseNodeLookupResponse BrowseNodeLookup(BrowseNodeLookup $body)"
  [4]=>
  unicode(47) "ListSearchResponse ListSearch(ListSearch $body)"
  [5]=>
  unicode(47) "ListLookupResponse ListLookup(ListLookup $body)"
  [6]=>
  unicode(80) "CustomerContentSearchResponse CustomerContentSearch(CustomerContentSearch $body)"
  [7]=>
  unicode(80) "CustomerContentLookupResponse CustomerContentLookup(CustomerContentLookup $body)"
  [8]=>
  unicode(65) "SimilarityLookupResponse SimilarityLookup(SimilarityLookup $body)"
  [9]=>
  unicode(53) "SellerLookupResponse SellerLookup(SellerLookup $body)"
  [10]=>
  unicode(38) "CartGetResponse CartGet(CartGet $body)"
  [11]=>
  unicode(47) "CartCreateResponse CartCreate(CartCreate $body)"
  [12]=>
  unicode(38) "CartAddResponse CartAdd(CartAdd $body)"
  [13]=>
  unicode(47) "CartModifyResponse CartModify(CartModify $body)"
```

Figure 10-1: Listing available functions from Amazon.com's SOAP API

This output indicates that you have many methods available to you. The most immediately useful of these is ItemSearch. Before you can invoke any function in the Amazon SOAP API, you must sign up for a free Amazon Web Services (AWS) account by going to http://aws.amazon.com/ and clicking the Sign Up Now button to get a new account. Once you have an AWS access ID, you can query the server for the details of the books on PHP 6:

```php
<?php
$client = new SoapClient(
"http://webservices.amazon.com/AWSECommerceService/AWSECommerceService.wsdl");

$request = array(
                'SearchIndex' => 'Books',
                'Keywords' => 'PHP 6'
                );

$params = array(
                'AWSAccessKeyId' => '[your Amazon AWS Access Key]',
                'Operation' => 'ItemSearch',
                'Request' => $request
                );

$out = $client->ItemSearch($params);

foreach($out->Items->Item as $item) {
  print '<a href="' . $item->DetailPageURL . '">' .
        $item->ItemAttributes->Title . "</a><br>\n";
}
?>
```

Save this code as `php6_books.php` and navigate to it in your browser. If all is well, you will see something similar to Figure 10-2.

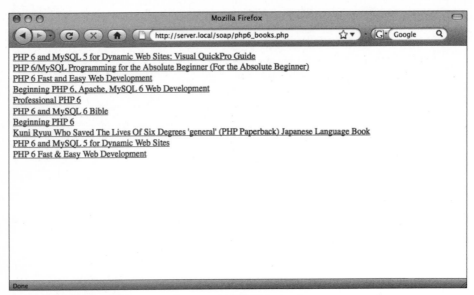

Figure 10-2: Output from an Amazon.com SOAP API search

By the time this book goes to press, there may be more or fewer search results for the specified query.

As you can see, you can easily get the details for any item in the Amazon product catalog with only a few lines of code. Of course, a little more is going on under the hood. Let's take a more detailed look at what's happening here.

Looking Under the Hood

Although the programming interface of PHP 6's SOAP extension is simple to use, a lot of work goes into ensuring that all communications are carried out correctly. Understanding the WSDL document's role in this is important, because this determines how communication will be carried out between client and server. Basically, you can think of WSDL as an extensible, XML-based means of defining Web services as a set of *endpoints* that can operate on *messages*.

This discussion examines in detail the WSDL document utilized in the previous example, and looks at the request and response SOAP messages that were passed between the client and server in order to get the book price.

The WSDL Document

A WSDL document is divided into various sections, which together make up the contract by which the clients and servers of this Web service must communicate. WSDL documents are structured to contain several major components, as well as some slightly less important ones. Not all of the following elements must be included in any given scenario:

❑   definitions — The root element. This defines the name and target namespaces.

❑   types — This describes the data types to be used. It is not required and defaults to the W3C XML Schema specification if no types are defined.

❑   message — This describes either a request or a response message.

❑   portType — This defines (or describes) an operation, which usually consists of the request and response messages together — a round-trip.

❑   bindings/operation — This describes how messages are to be transported. It contains elements such as binding and message coding style.

❑   service — As the name implies, this gives the address for the required service.

❑   documentation — This simply allows the service provider to provide a description of its service.

❑   import — This enables you to decouple your WSDL documents into different elements so that they can be stored in different documents to be imported as and when required.

This chapter doesn't spend much time discussing WSDL, but to take a more in-depth look at it, go to www.w3.org/TR/wsdl.

As you can see from the first piece of XML that follows, you define which version of XML you are using (1.0), and then declare the definitions element. The definitions element is always the root element, and defines the namespaces used in the document:

```
<?xml version="1.0" encoding="UTF-8"?>
<definitions xmlns=http://schemas.xmlsoap.org/wsdl/
xmlns:soap=http://schemas.xmlsoap.org/wsdl/soap/
xmlns:xs=http://www.w3.org/2001/XMLSchema
xmlns:tns=http://webservices.amazon.com/AWSECommerceService/2008-10-06
targetNamespace="http://webservices.amazon.com/AWSECommerceService/2008-10-06">
```

The next section of the Amazon WSDL document defines the various data types used in requests and responses. From the function listing in Figure 10-1, you can see that the function ItemSearch takes a single argument of type ItemSearch. The definition of this type can be found in the WSDL document:

```
<xs:element name="ItemSearch">
  <xs:complexType>

    <xs:sequence>

      <xs:element name="MarketplaceDomain" type="xs:string"
              minOccurs="0"/>
      <xs:element name="AWSAccessKeyId" type="xs:string" minOccurs="0"/>
      <xs:element name="SubscriptionId" type="xs:string" minOccurs="0"/>
      <xs:element name="AssociateTag" type="xs:string" minOccurs="0"/>
      <xs:element name="XMLEscaping" type="xs:string" minOccurs="0"/>
      <xs:element name="Validate" type="xs:string" minOccurs="0"/>
      <xs:element name="Shared" type="tns:ItemSearchRequest"
              minOccurs="0"/>
```

```
          <xs:element name="Request" type="tns:ItemSearchRequest"
                      minOccurs="0" maxOccurs="unbounded"/>

      </xs:sequence>
    </xs:complexType>
  </xs:element>
```

Note that the Request element (which is what was used in php6_books.php to provide the search query) is another custom data type, called ItemSearchRequest, and is specified in the WSDL file as follows:

```
<xs:complexType name="ItemSearchRequest">
      <xs:sequence>
          <xs:element name="Actor" type="xs:string" minOccurs="0"/>
          <xs:element name="Artist" type="xs:string" minOccurs="0"/>
          <xs:element name="Availability" minOccurs="0">
              <xs:simpleType>
                  <xs:restriction base="xs:string">
                      <xs:enumeration value="Available"/>
                  </xs:restriction>
              </xs:simpleType>
          </xs:element>
          <xs:element ref="tns:AudienceRating" minOccurs="0"
                                              maxOccurs="unbounded"/>
          <xs:element name="Author" type="xs:string" minOccurs="0"/>
          <xs:element name="Brand" type="xs:string" minOccurs="0"/>
          <xs:element name="BrowseNode" type="xs:string" minOccurs="0"/>
          <xs:element name="City" type="xs:string" minOccurs="0"/>
          <xs:element name="Composer" type="xs:string" minOccurs="0"/>
          <xs:element ref="tns:Condition" minOccurs="0"/>
          <xs:element name="Conductor" type="xs:string" minOccurs="0"/>
          <xs:element name="Count" type="xs:positiveInteger" minOccurs="0">
              <xs:annotation>
                  <xs:appinfo>
                      <aws-se:restricted
                         xmlns:aws-se=
                            "http://webservices.amazon.com/
                               AWS-SchemaExtensions">
                          <aws-se:excludeFrom>public</aws-se:excludeFrom>
                          <aws-se:excludeFrom>partner</aws-se:excludeFrom>
                      </aws-se:restricted>
                  </xs:appinfo>
              </xs:annotation>
          </xs:element>
          <xs:element name="Cuisine" type="xs:string" minOccurs="0"/>
          <xs:element ref="tns:DeliveryMethod" minOccurs="0"/>
          <xs:element name="Director" type="xs:string" minOccurs="0"/>
          <xs:element name="FutureLaunchDate" type="xs:string" minOccurs="0"/>
          <xs:element name="ISPUPostalCode" type="xs:string" minOccurs="0"/>
```

```
                <xs:element name="ItemPage" type="xs:positiveInteger" minOccurs="0"/>
                <xs:element name="Keywords" type="xs:string" minOccurs="0"/>
                <xs:element name="Manufacturer" type="xs:string" minOccurs="0"/>
                <xs:element name="MaximumPrice" type="xs:nonNegativeInteger"
                                        minOccurs="0"/>
                <xs:element name="MerchantId" type="xs:string" minOccurs="0"/>
                <xs:element name="MinimumPrice" type="xs:nonNegativeInteger"
                                        minOccurs="0"/>
                <xs:element name="MusicLabel" type="xs:string" minOccurs="0"/>
                <xs:element name="Neighborhood" type="xs:string" minOccurs="0"/>
                <xs:element name="Orchestra" type="xs:string" minOccurs="0"/>
                <xs:element name="PostalCode" type="xs:string" minOccurs="0"/>
                <xs:element name="Power" type="xs:string" minOccurs="0"/>
                <xs:element name="Publisher" type="xs:string" minOccurs="0"/>
                <xs:element name="ResponseGroup" type="xs:string" minOccurs="0"
                                        maxOccurs="unbounded"/>
                <xs:element name="ReviewSort" type="xs:string" minOccurs="0"/>
                <xs:element name="SearchIndex" type="xs:string" minOccurs="0"/>
                <xs:element name="Sort" type="xs:string" minOccurs="0"/>
                <xs:element name="State" type="xs:string" minOccurs="0"/>
                <xs:element name="TagPage" type="xs:positiveInteger" minOccurs="0"/>
                <xs:element name="TagsPerPage" type="xs:positiveInteger"
                                        minOccurs="0"/>
                <xs:element name="TagSort" type="xs:string" minOccurs="0"/>
                <xs:element name="TextStream" type="xs:string" minOccurs="0"/>
                <xs:element name="Title" type="xs:string" minOccurs="0"/>
                <xs:element name="ReleaseDate" type="xs:string" minOccurs="0"/>
        </xs:sequence>
    </xs:complexType>
```

Of course, you didn't create a data structure with all of these parameters. You only used the mandatory SearchIndex element and the Keywords element to define your search criteria. You can get very specific with the search criteria used, specifying publisher, price range, and other details. Clearly, some of these elements (such as Cuisine and MusicLabel) do not apply to books, but to other items in the Amazon product catalog.

Next in the WSDL document are the message elements. This section provides the request and response message names, and specifies the types they will use (refer to the documentation at www.php.net/manual/en/ref.soap.php for a list of what types are defined for use with the SOAP extension). These are the message definitions for the ItemSearch function:

```
<message name="ItemSearchRequestMsg">
  <part name="body" element="tns:ItemSearch"/>
</message>

<message name="ItemSearchResponseMsg">
  <part name="body" element="tns:ItemSearchResponse"/>
</message>
```

The `portType` element defines the function called `ItemSearch`, which consists of the input and output messages specified in the previous snippet:

```
<portType name="AWSECommerceServicePortType">
  [snip]

  <operation name="ItemSearch">
    <input message="tns:ItemSearchRequestMsg"/>
    <output message="tns:ItemSearchResponseMsg"/>
  </operation>

  [snip]
</portType>
```

The `portType` element's `name` attribute specifies which of the available bindings is to be used for the operations defined in each `portType` section. The `AWSECommerceServicePortType` is defined lower in the WSDL document in a `binding` element:

```
<binding name="AWSECommerceServiceBinding"
          type="tns:AWSECommerceServicePortType">
  <soap:binding style="document" transport=
          "http://schemas.xmlsoap.org/soap/http"/>

  [snip]

  <operation name="ItemSearch">
    <soap:operation soapAction="http://soap.amazon.com"/>
    <input>
      <soap:body use="literal"/>
    </input>
    <output>
      <soap:body use="literal"/>
    </output>
  </operation>

  [snip]

</binding>
```

The binding definition specifies the transport to be used in sending requests and receiving responses (in this case, HTTP, which is the most common SOAP transport protocol).

The binding name refers to a service that defines the specific URL to be used when sending requests to the remote server:

```
<service name="AWSECommerceService">
  <port name="AWSECommerceServicePort" binding=
        "tns:AWSECommerceServiceBinding">
    <soap:address location="http://soap.amazon.com/onca/soap?Service=
        AWSECommerceService"/>
  </port>
</service>
</definitions>
```

By looking through the WSDL document, you are able to determine the parameters needed by each function, and their return types. It is important to understand how to read a WSDL document so that you can more effectively debug communications problems and error message returned by the remote system. However, for normal operations, PHP enables you to avoid wading through a huge pile of XML by interpreting the WSDL document for you.

Let's now look at how requests and responses are formed. You should already have an idea from the WSDL document, but PHP can provide further assistance here.

The Request and Response Envelopes

The PHP 6 SOAP extension provides a couple of functions that can be used to look at the requests and responses from the client. Open the `php6_books.php` file from earlier in this chapter and modify it like this:

```php
<?php

$client = new SoapClient(
"http://webservices.amazon.com/AWSECommerceService/AWSECommerceService.wsdl",
array('trace' => 1));


$request = array(
            'SearchIndex' => 'Books',
            'Keywords' => 'PHP 6'
            );

$params = array(
            'AWSAccessKeyId' => '[your Amazon AWS Access Key]',
            'Operation' => 'ItemSearch',
            'Request' => $request
            );

$out = $client->ItemSearch($params);

foreach($out->Items->Item as $item) {
  print '<a href="' . $item->DetailPageURL . '">' . $item->ItemAttributes->Title .
      "</a><br>\n";
}

print "<pre>" . htmlentities(print_r($client->__getLastRequest(), true)) .
      "</pre>\n";
print "<pre>" . htmlentities(print_r($client->__getLastResponse(), true)) .
      "</pre>\n";
?>
```

This gives you the output shown in Figure 10-3.

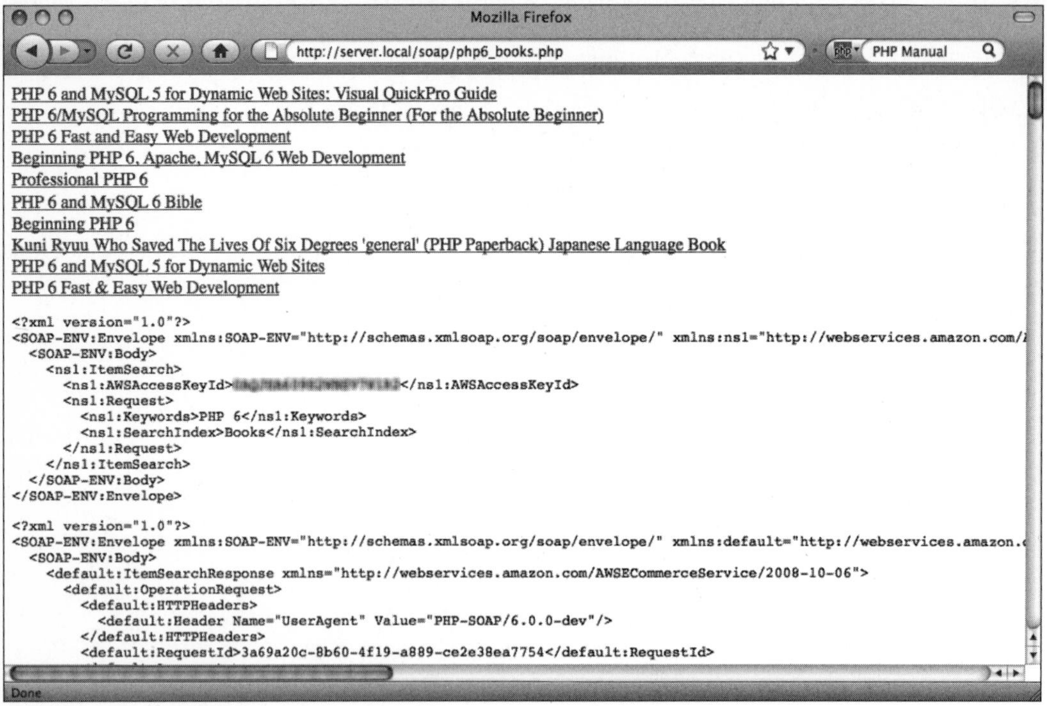

Figure 10-3: The request and response XML

Using this output, you can see exactly what was sent to the Web server and the full contents of the XML response it produced. You can quite easily relate how the message transmission was defined in the WSDL document to the actual XML produced by the SOAP extension. For example, you can see that the keywords and search index choices are sent as strings:

```xml
<?xml version="1.0"?>
<SOAP-ENV:Envelope xmlns:SOAP-ENV="http://schemas.xmlsoap.org/soap/envelope/"
    xmlns:ns1="http://webservices.amazon.com/AWSECommerceService/2008-10-06">
  <SOAP-ENV:Body>
    <ns1:ItemSearch>
      <ns1:AWSAccessKeyId>[Your Key]</ns1:AWSAccessKeyId>
      <ns1:Request>
        <ns1:Keywords>PHP 6</ns1:Keywords>
        <ns1:SearchIndex>Books</ns1:SearchIndex>
      </ns1:Request>
    </ns1:ItemSearch>
  </SOAP-ENV:Body>
</SOAP-ENV:Envelope>
```

Next, you have the response envelope (which is too long to reprint here) that is returned by the Web service server. Once again, you can relate it to the WSDL document quite easily. For example, among other things, you will notice that the title is part of the ItemAttributes element and is a string.

What has not yet been covered is what happens in the event that an invalid SearchIndex is specified, or some other error occurs. Of course, you must implement some sort of error handling. There are several ways to do this, and you can choose which methods work best for your application. As you might guess, you can use PHP 6's SOAP implementation to make things slightly more robust.

Exception Handling in the SOAP Client

Recall from an earlier discussion that a SoapFault object is readily available for your use. Open your soap.php file and modify it to use an invalid function name, as shown in the following code snippet (save it as soapfaults.php):

```php
<?php
$client = new SoapClient(
    "http://webservices.amazon.com/AWSECommerceService/
        AWSECommerceService.wsdl",
    array('trace' => 1, 'exceptions' => 0));

$request = array(
                'SearchIndex' => 'Books',
                'Keywords' => 'PHP 6'
                );

$params = array(
                'AWSAccessKeyId' => '[Your Key]',
                'Operation' => 'ItemSearch',
                'Request' => $request
                );

$out = $client->ItemSearchError($params);

if(is_soap_fault($out)) {
  print      "Something went wrong!<br>\n";
  print      $out->faultstring;
  exit;
} else {

  foreach($out->Items->Item as $item) {
    print '<a href="' . $item->DetailPageURL . '">'.
          $item->ItemAttributes->Title .
          "</a><br>\n";
  }

}
?>
```

Having the exceptions array option set to 0 means that the SoapClient object will automatically return a SoapFault object if something goes wrong. Use the is_soap_fault function to determine whether or not the returned value is a SoapFault object.

The SoapFault class exposes the properties faultcode (a number) and faultstring (a string), detailing the exact problem. You should get results similar to what is shown in Figure 10-4, explaining (quite correctly) that you have requested an invalid method.

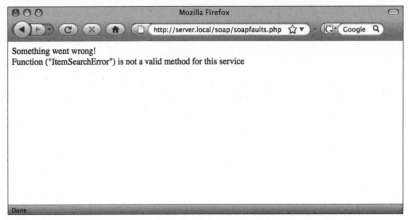

Figure 10-4: Checking for errors using the SOAP extension

If you prefer to use `try...catch` with PHP 6 exceptions, then set the `exceptions` parameter to 1. Obviously, there are plenty of ways to go about implementing exception handling, and you should pick the method that fits in with your application as a whole. The point of this section is simply to alert you to the available functionality.

Making a SOAP Server

Most often, you'll want to create a server that provides its clients with a useful service, which can be absolutely anything, ranging from book price quotes to employee information to domain name verification. In this section, you create a server that you can connect to with a client to receive a short message. This discussion uses a short WSDL document to describe how the two parts of the SOAP application can communicate. (You have already seen a WSDL document in action, so it won't be discussed again in detail.)

Creating and Registering Functions

This trivial example receives a `name` string from the client and returns a message to the effect that you should be glad SOAP is so reliable. Open a new code file called `soapserver.php`:

```php
<?php function sayHello($name){
    $salutation = "You, $name, will be delighted to know I am working!";
    return $salutation;
}

$server = new SoapServer ("greetings.wsdl");
$server->addFunction("sayHello");
$server->handle();
?>
```

Although this example is actually a simple "hello world" example, you do not have to go much further in terms of making something truly useful. For example, if you wanted a Web service to return results from a database, you would merely need to substitute a couple of functions that returned the relevant results into your SOAP server file, add the functions to the server, modify the WSDL quickly to reflect these changes, and away you go.

The preceding code has a function entitled `sayHello()`, which is the only method this fledgling service provides. The server can then be created referencing the `greetings.wsdl` document (which is defined in a moment), the `sayHello()` function added with the PHP 6 `addFunction()` method (discussed earlier in the section "Soapserver Functions"), and then `handle()` doing the hard work of processing the request and responding. That's all you need from the server's perspective.

Creating the WSDL Document

To make the service work nicely for a client, you just need to tell prospective clients how they can expect to communicate with the server via the WSDL document. The whole concept of WDSL is not rehashed here, but the following is a good example of what you can use with the simple Web service. Naturally, it is entitled `greetings.wsdl`:

```xml
<?xml version ="1.0" encoding ="UTF-8" ?>
<definitions name="greetings"
   targetNamespace="http://server.local/sayHello"
   xmlns:tns=" http://server.local/sayHello "
   xmlns:soap="http://schemas.xmlsoap.org/wsdl/soap/"
   xmlns:xsd="http://www.w3.org/2001/XMLSchema"
   xmlns:soapenc="http://schemas.xmlsoap.org/soap/encoding/"
   xmlns:wsdl="http://schemas.xmlsoap.org/wsdl/"
   xmlns="http://schemas.xmlsoap.org/wsdl/">

   <message name="sayHelloRequest">
    <part name="name" type="xsd:string"/>
   </message>
   <message name="sayHelloResponse">
    <part name="salutation" type="xsd:string"/>
   </message>

   <portType name="sayHelloPortType">
    <operation name="sayHello">
       <input message="tns:sayHelloRequest"/>
       <output message="tns:sayHelloResponse"/>
    </operation>
   </portType>

   <binding name="sayHelloBinding" type="tns:sayHelloPortType">
      <soap:binding style="rpc"
        transport="http://schemas.xmlsoap.org/soap/http"/>
      <operation name="sayHello">
        <soap:operation soapAction="" />
```

```xml
      <input>
        <soap:body use="encoded" namespace=""
          encodingStyle="http://schemas.xmlsoap.org/soap/encoding/" />
      </input>
      <output>
        <soap:body use="encoded" namespace=""
          encodingStyle="http://schemas.xmlsoap.org/soap/encoding/" />
      </output>
    </operation>
  </binding>
  <documentation>This is Wiley"s SOAP server Example</documentation>
  <service name="sayHelloService">
    <port name="sayHelloPort" binding="sayHelloBinding">
      <soap:address location="http://server.local/soap/soapserver.php"/>
    </port>
  </service>
</definitions>
```

With that, you're all set. Remember, though, that you must set the address location URI to the correct value for your setup.

Now, all that remains is to make use of the new server. The following file, called `soapclient.php`, does that:

```php
<?php $client = new SoapClient("greetings.wsdl");
print_r($client->sayHello("Steve"));
?>
```

Navigating to this file will give you the slightly terse (yet reasonably accurate) results displayed in Figure 10-5, varying according to which name you have substituted.

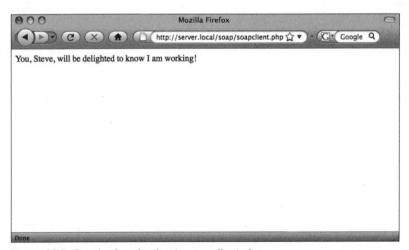

Figure 10-5: Result of navigating to soapclient.php

Clearly, this example is trivial and not terribly useful on its own, but it is hoped that it gives you some ideas about how to implement your own SOAP server. You can expose any aspect of your application that would be useful to others, or that you would like to access via Ajax or Flash. In a typical application using an MVC architecture, you would create a separate controller to handle the SOAP inputs and outputs, with the corresponding views rendered using the SOAP extension to create the XML output automatically. You are otherwise able to completely reuse the application logic encapsulated in the model classes, which enables you to create a Web services API for many of your applications with fairly little additional code or time investment.

While SOAP is the granddaddy of Web services, enabling fully automated discovery of data types, functions, and their return types, in practice, very little of this sort of automated discovery actually happens. In general, you know which functions you want, where to find them, and their return values. You know this from reading the API documentation, rather than writing code to discover this information automatically.

The complexity of the WSDL document for a large Web services API can be a barrier to understanding the functionality offered. Additionally, the step of downloading the WSDL file (even when it has been cached on the server's hard drive) adds additional computation time to each request. For many of the (generally fairly simple) requests you might make to a remote Web service (or services) that you might want to expose in your own application, the overhead of a SOAP request is overkill. Fortunately, there are alternative schemas for implementing Web service clients and servers. One of the most popular is called *Representational State Transfer (REST)*.

REST

First formally described by Roy Fielding (one of the principal authors of the HTTP specification) as part of his doctoral dissertation in 2000, REST takes an entirely different approach to Web services. Instead of using all of the overhead and complexity of SOAP's WSDL document and XML envelope structure, REST instead uses the primary HTTP verbs of GET, POST, PUT, and DELETE to request and manipulate resources, uniquely identified by a URL that clearly identifies the resource requested.

To show a very simple example of what a typical REST request might look like, consider an online bookstore application. To access the resource descriptor for a book with the ISBN 0470395097, you might use a URL such as http://example.com/books/0470395097. Typically, you would expect this to return an XML document with the details for the book, though nothing in the REST architecture defines the return data type. Such a URL could return an image, an HTML document, a CSV file, or any other data.type.

Because all REST operations follow a simple URL structure that identifies the resource to be created, read, updated, or deleted, you can fairly easily understand what it is you are getting by looking at the URL of the resource to be fetched. The easier-to-use REST interfaces use a neat and simple URL structure like that in the example. Others, such as the Amazon REST interface (which is discussed shortly), use slightly "uglier" syntax, involving query string parameters, but the basic idea is the same.

REST and PHP 6

Because REST is nothing more than simple HTTP interactions at its core, there isn't a PHP extension for REST as you have with SOAP. In fact, REST is an architecture design, not a protocol like SOAP is. The simplest way to implement REST in PHP is to use the `curl` extension to implement the client and server components yourself. You could go even more low-level and use the socket functions, but the `curl` extension makes things a lot easier.

The return value from the typical REST operation is usually (but not necessarily) an XML document. Let's use the `simplexml` extension to parse and manipulate the sent and received data. This is by far the easiest way to deal with XML in PHP 6.

> *If you're not already familiar with the functions in this extension, consult the documentation at* `http://php.net/simplexml`.

The SOAP extension uses the relatively complicated (but standardized) XML envelope structure and return values, which is predefined in the WSDL document. REST, conversely, drops the overhead and complexity of the envelope and WSDL file; but the trade-off is that the developer must get closer to the XML than is required with the SOAP extension. Understanding how to create and parse XML documents is an essential skill for the professional developer, and is necessary to understanding much of the discussion in the remainder of this chapter.

Implementing the REST Client

Let's return to the `Amazon.com` API for a REST example, as Amazon conveniently offers both SOAP and REST APIs. It is worth noting that the simpler REST interface accounts for more than 85 percent of the requests to the Amazon Web Services system, with SOAP only accounting for the remaining 15 percent. You will soon see why so many developers prefer the REST interface.

The complete documentation for the Amazon REST interface can be found at `http://aws.amazon.com/documentation/`. In brief, like the SOAP interface, the Amazon REST API requires you to obtain an AWS access ID. All requests are made from the same base URL, which (unlike the simpler URL structure in the previous pseudo-example) uses a parameterized query.

The following simple example shows how to do an `ItemSearch` for PHP 6 books using the REST API. Note that it uses the PHP `curl` extension, which must be enabled on your PHP installation. Enter the following code into `php6_books.php`:

```php
<?php

//Base URL for all AWS REST operations
define('AWS_BASE_URL',
       'http://ecs.amazonaws.com/onca/xml?Service=AWSECommerceService');
//AWS Access Key ID
define('AWS_ACCESS_KEY_ID', '[Your AWS Key]');

$params = array();
$params['Operation'] = 'ItemSearch';
$params['SearchIndex'] = 'Books';
```

```php
$params['Keywords'] = 'PHP 6';

//Construct the URL
$url = AWS_BASE_URL . '&AWSAccessKeyId=' . AWS_ACCESS_KEY_ID;
foreach($params as $name => $value) {
  //Need to URL encode in case there are spaces or other funny chars
  //in the values
  $value = urlencode(unicode_encode($value, 'ISO-8859-1'));
  $url .= "&$name=$value";
}


$hc = curl_init($url);
curl_setopt($hc, CURLOPT_RETURNTRANSFER, 1);
$xml = curl_exec($hc);

$out = new SimpleXMLElement($xml);

foreach($out->Items->Item as $item) {
  print '<a href="' . $item->DetailPageURL . '">' .
        $item->ItemAttributes->Title . "</a><br>\n";
}

?>
```

This code sample is fairly similar to the SOAP example of the same name, but it uses the far more familiar `curl` extension and basic XML processing, instead of the SOAP extension (with which many developers may not be familiar). Depending on how you have PHP configured, you could also simply use `file_get_contents($url)` to fetch the XML, if HTTP requests are allowed in that function (this is a `php.ini` setting). This example also has the benefit of enabling you to debug problems by simply entering the `$url` value into your Web browser and looking at the output in the browser window. The SOAP extension keeps you far enough away from the actual interactions with the remote server that debugging basic connection problems can often be difficult and time-consuming.

The returned XML structure lacks the outer envelope section of the SOAP transaction, but it is otherwise the same. Therefore, this examination does not include a discussion of the iteration over the `Items`, because the code is identical.

Making a REST Server

The creation of a service using the REST architecture is also much more straightforward than using the SOAP extension, which involves the registering of functions with the SOAP extension. The following example architecture uses the `$_SERVER` value `PATH_INFO` to fetch anything that might be in the query string after the name of the PHP file, but before the query string (that is, before the `?` in the URL):

```php
<?php

$DEFAULT_ACTION = 'badAction';

$pathInfo = isset($_SERVER['PATH_INFO']) ? $_SERVER['PATH_INFO'] : '';
```

```php
$pathParts = explode('/', substr($pathInfo, 1));
$action = isset($pathParts[0]) ? $pathParts[0] : $DEFAULT_ACTION;

if(function_exists($action)) {
  $action($pathParts);
} else {
  badAction();
}


//REST functions

function badAction($parts = null) {
  print 'The function specified is invalid';
}

function sayHello($parts) {
  $name = isset($parts[1]) ? $parts[1] : 'undefined';
  $xml = new SimpleXMLElement('<message>Hello, ' . $name . '</message>');
  header('Content-Type: text/xml');
  print $xml->asXML();
}

?>
```

To invoke the service, an example URL might be `http://server.local/rest/restserver.php/sayHello/Steve`, which would produce the following output:

```
<?xml version="1.0"?>
<message>Hello, Steve</message>
```

Note that the additional parameters have been supplied in the URL, rather than appending them to the query string. This is not essential, and you should feel free to use query string parameters if you prefer; but the cleaner URL structure is aesthetically pleasing, and makes the API simple to document.

Summary

The capability to leverage Web services enables you to include data and functionality from other applications, and provide additional, powerful features to your application that you might not otherwise be able to include. Exposing features of your application to others provides opportunities to increase the overall utility of your code, and possibly drive traffic to your Web site.

Chapter 11 takes a look at better ways for generating e-mail and other communications with your users.

11

Communicating with Users

The Web is a simple method of communication when you come right down to it. The end user requests a page, things happen in the background, and the Web server fires back some content in response. That's the HTTP protocol summed up in one, pithy sentence; but if you limit yourself simply to talking to users through the HTTP protocol, you're missing out on a very big part of what makes a truly impressive user interface.

In this chapter, you learn about the building blocks of user communication, and how it translates into a natural PHP object hierarchy. You'll see how you can extend and develop this hierarchy to support virtually any form of electronic communication. You'll also look at practical examples of implementing some functionality that PHP doesn't provide, and that you may find useful in your day-to-day development.

Perhaps most important, you'll learn why you should communicate with your users in the first place.

Why Communicate?

In the early days of the Web, long before PHP came onto the horizon, the user experience — that is, the emotional impact on the user of using your Web site — was largely unimportant. Content was key. In fact, content was all there was. The Web was little more than a magazine with convenient tabs for ease of turning the pages.

No more. The Web is increasingly accepted as a superb mechanism for implementing thin client applications, from the simple Webmail facilities of an entertainment portal to the sophisticated multi-user inventory control network of a big corporation. This sheer flexibility and reach is, after all, why you decided to learn PHP in the first place.

Unfortunately, the adoption of the Web as a means for implementing thin client solutions has been less than plain sailing. Many authors have omitted (perhaps with the best of intentions) providing modern-day equivalents of the key features that made thin client architectures of yesteryear usable.

One of the biggest of these is the capacity for communicating with users outside the context of the immediate user interface. Consider an abstract example. The immediate user interface of a telephone consists of the mouthpiece and earpiece, yet all telephones include ringers so that you know when a call is incoming. This is an example of *notifying* the user of an event.

A second example is the fax machine. Many fax machines print a delivery report when a fax has been sent successfully. This report is auxiliary to the keypad and LCD display, which constitute the immediate user interface, and is an example of keeping the user *informed*.

One final example. If you have ever applied for a bank loan over the phone, you have doubtlessly found that acquiring debt in a matter of minutes is remarkably easy (although, these days, perhaps not as easy as it was since the previous edition of this book). Still, the bank sends papers for you to sign to your registered home address. Even if you are approved in principle over the phone, the money doesn't go anywhere near your checking account until you sign and return the papers they sent you. This is an example of using communication with the user as a form of security, a form of *validation*.

There are other examples, but this chapter examines how those mentioned here have an impact on the real world, and how you act on them through OOP mechanisms.

Reasons to Communicate with Users

Notifying, informing, and validating — let's take these three examples and try applying them to the Web. In this way, you can discover why you might want your application to notify, inform, or validate your users.

Notification

A number of scenarios can arise in which you may want to notify your users of something through a means other than a Web browser. This issue is particularly relevant if you remember that HTTP is what is known as a *stateless* protocol. It is not particularly easy to get the Web browser to sit there and wait for something to happen before informing the user. You can do it in various ways, but none is particularly pretty.

Imagine that your application has a sophisticated reporting system that enables users to request that reports be generated on all manner of business details. Particularly if those reports are extremely SQL intensive, a strong argument can be made for generating those reports offline — that is, independently of the user's Web browser-initiated request. That way, the user is not presented with any excessively long HTTP request in order to view the report.

It is simply not realistic to guarantee that users will not give up and click the Stop button halfway through a two-minute wait for a page to be generated. In a real-world scenario, users would use the Web browser to order the report, doing so with the understanding that the system would notify them when the report is ready (probably by e-mail or some other mechanism).

In another example, imagine that a subscription Web site is set up to bill the user's credit card automatically every month on the first of the month. It wouldn't be terribly good customer service if, because the user's credit card had been declined during that month's billing process, the user were simply unable to log in to the Web site. Instead, you would issue what is sometimes known as an *exceptional notification* — a notification that occurs as a result of something out of the ordinary (typically, bad) happening. In this case, it would be in the form of an e-mail inviting the user to log on and provide details for another valid credit card.

Notification is not restricted to e-mail, of course. Operators of data centers all over the world have fallen in love with text message notifications to their cellular phones to advise them when vital servers or processes have fallen over, regardless of where they are at the time. These have largely replaced pagers outside the United States.

Information

Communicating information to users differs slightly from notification in that it is not necessarily event driven. Instead, it is a fully expected communication issued with the intent of updating the user about the status of something. Compare the arrival of the morning newspaper on your front porch with a sudden notice from the Emergency Alert System during a television show. You expect the newspaper's arrival, but the notice of impending blizzards in Tampa Bay come as a bit of a surprise.

A good example of keeping users informed is that of a weekly newsletter from a subscriber Web site. This could be something automatically generated by tabulating an extract of that week's news stories, or it could be something put together by an editorial team. Either way, you're keeping your users up-to-date.

Another good example is an order update from an online "e-tailer." If seven days have passed without the arrival of the books you ordered, you might be getting worried, and you would undoubtedly be reassured by an e-mail explaining that the books are still on order. Again, this is *not* a notification. Nothing has changed. Nothing is new. It's just a quick update for the purposes of reassurance.

This means of communication is perfectly adaptable to other information methods — fax, text message, snail mail, you name it. You'll see shortly that the various communications media you may previously have thought to be completely different are, in fact, virtually identical (at least from a software architecture perspective).

Validation

Validation is often a means of communicating once for the purpose of communicating again. You validate a destination address of some description so that you may reassure yourself of its accuracy should you need to use it again. Alternatively, you may have some piece of information your user wants, but to be doubly sure of the requesting user's identity, you will send that information only to the user's registered address.

The bank loan example earlier in this chapter represents the more serious side of things. After all, the bank wants to verify your correct address so that it can send the repo men in if your repayments are tardy. Numerous Web sites, however, validate e-mail addresses in this way for later direct marketing usage. The simple way to do this is to send out an activation link (usually presenting some kind of unique key stored against the user's record in the database) to the e-mail address offered by the user. The user must click the link to activate his or her membership.

Similar methods can be used to throw a rope to users who have forgotten their passwords, although it isn't usually either a good or feasible idea to reveal their passwords via e-mail. You shouldn't be storing user passwords unencrypted or in any reversible form, or transmitting them in plain text over e-mail. You can certainly provide them with a highly obfuscated link (generally of limited-time validity) for the purposes of gaining temporary access to your site so that they may set a new password.

In Europe (where it is increasingly common to communicate with Web site visitors via their cell phones as well as via e-mail), some sites send an activation code as a short text message to the cell phone number the user offered at registration. The user must then enter that activation code on the site to prove the validity of the number he or she provided.

As an aside, this Short Message Service (SMS) code-sending technique can actually be used as a poor man's form of second-layer authentication. Authentication on systems is generally provided by one or more of three keys. These are *something you are* (a fingerprint, iris scan, or even originating IP address), *something you know* (a password), and *something you have* (a key or a fob). Each of these is a *factor*. The accepted wisdom is for any system guarding any type of sensitive data to implement more than one of these mechanisms. By sending a unique code to a registered mobile phone upon entry of a username and password, that extra layer of protection is provided.

Thinking Outside the Web Browser

By realizing the potential of alternative communication mechanisms (particularly e-mail), you offer users a far more enhanced user experience on your site. In the next section, you'll explore how you can implement this in PHP (beyond the `mail()` function, of course).

> It's probably worth stressing that using the `mail()` function in PHP to send e-mail from your code is analogous to what a six-year-old's paper-cup phone is to digital telephony. It should never appear in serious production sites.

Types of Communication

Before you get down and dirty with some communication code, take a step back from the problem for a second. Doing so can give you a better grasp on the obvious outbound communication class hierarchy in front of you, which you will have to write yourself because PHP doesn't provide it. What do all communications have in common?

All Communications Have . . .

You can quite reasonably say that all communications have the following:

❑ *Recipients* — One or more people to receive the communication. This communication can be in the form of e-mail addresses, fax numbers, mobile phone numbers, postal addresses, post office boxes, pigeonholes, and so on.

❑ *A message* — The actual body of what you want to send. The message can be transmitted in plain text or HTML (for an e-mail), a letter-size bitmap (for a fax), 160 characters of text (for a text message), a stream of 11 KHz audio (for an automated phone call), and so on.

Not All Communications Have . . .

On the flip side, you must also understand the differences between the various types of communication. Not all communications have the following:

❑ *Subjects* — Typically, only e-mails have subjects.

❑ *Content variants* — E-mails these days are often sent with both HTML and plain-text versions entwined in one MIME package (more on this later).

❑ *Attachments* — These are e-mail and text-message specific.

❑ *Revealing of or differentiation between carbon and blind carbon recipients* — If you send a fax, text message, or letter to more than one person, no one will know who else received the message unless you make a list and add it in the body.

What About Recipients?

A recipient of an e-mail message is a totally different kind of recipient from a recipient of a text message. Take a look at the comparison shown in Table 11-1.

Table 11-1 Comparison of Recipients

Type of Communication	Recipient Component	Format
Email	Name	String
	Address	String following RFC822 specification
SMS text message to cell phone	Number	String, consisting of plus sign, country prefix, and local number
Fax	Number	String, consisting of telco-understood telephone number
Letter	Full name	String
	House number	Integer
	Street	String
	Town/city	String
	State	String
	Zip	String matching U.S. Postal Service ZIP format

Communication As a Class Hierarchy

There are many possibilities to consider if you are to construct a class hierarchy. You must understand that although communications have much in common, fundamental differences exist between one media form and another, as do totally different methods of addressing.

The Recipient Class: A Quick Test of OOP-Like Thinking

All messages have recipients (and often more than one). Given that these recipients are clearly more involved than strings, it would be nice to have a class to represent them with such useful methods as isValid() to determine whether the recipient is a valid one.

The difficulty is obvious. How are you to implement such a class effectively when so much variation in the data is required?

You could create a single Recipient class covering all possible scenarios, but this isn't particularly OOP-compliant because large numbers of member methods and variables are peculiar to one form of communication and irrelevant to others. The solution must be to have some kind of generic Recipient class, with each special case having a class in its own right; but how do you relate these special-case recipients to the master Recipient class?

First, reject the use of traditional class inheritance. Although technically feasible, it's still a misuse of OOP design. Superclasses (that is, classes that are extended to form subclasses) must be classes in their own right. Ford is a subclass of superclass Car, but although Ford may contain additional or even overloaded methods or member variables, certain characteristics of Car indicate that it is (or once was) an object of use in its own right. It has its own methods (such as Drive and Shift) and its own member variables (such as Registration and Color), and these are not likely to be overloaded. A recipient of a particular ilk (such as that for an e-mail) could have member variables and methods of its own just like the Ford, but it would not inherit any of them from a parent generic recipient superclass. For reasons that a glance at Table 11-1, shown previously, should make apparent, a generic recipient cannot have any useful member variables or methods. Accordingly, you must reject the use of class inheritance.

The answer becomes apparent if you consider the bigger picture. What is your communications framework likely to want from these recipient objects? In fact, you can limit it to just two methods that will be accessed by the communications framework: isValid() and getStringRepresentation(). These two would return a usable string representation of the framework, dependent on the context. Any other methods (setHouseNumber, for example) are for use by your application solely for populating the recipient. You can quite safely say that the communications framework will never touch them.

Therefore, the task can be summarized as follows: Create some means for a number of distinct classes representing recipients of different types of communications media to be universally accessed by an external framework of other classes, such that additional distinct classes may be added later without any modification to that external framework.

The solution is to create an *interface* for the generic recipient class (not really a class at all). That interface provides definitions for these two key methods (isValid() and getStringRepresentation()), which the individual recipient objects must provide exactly as shown.

Consider the following code snippet, which provides just such a generic interface. You may wish to save this code as recipient.phpm at this stage:

```php
<?php
interface Recipient {
    public function isValid();
    public function getStringRepresentation();
}
?>
```

You might be tempted to implement an abstract recipient class to almost exactly the same effect, but this would be bad design rearing its ugly head once more. Again, remember that the recipient as you understand it has no useful properties and no useful methods. It would be fatuous to try to extend it in any way that infers class status when you merely want to provide a common means for other classes to interface with a collection of unrelated classes. If you have doubts regarding the lack of commonality of the various recipient classes, refer to Table 11-1.

The EmailRecipient Class

Take a look at how to implement this. You won't reproduce every single type of recipient, so look at a simple one — the `EmailRecipient` class. You can save this code as `emailrecipient.phpm` — you'll need this too, throughout this chapter. Start it by declaring a class that implements the `Recipient` interface declared previously:

```
<?

class EmailRecipient implements Recipient {
```

Add some member variables to store important properties of your e-mail recipient. As shown in Table 11-1, an e-mail recipient has both a recipient name and a recipient address:

```
private $recipient_name;
private $recipient_address;
```

Now you must provide an implementation of every method declared in the `Recipient` interface. In fact, there are just two. The first will validate your recipient after it has been set up by whatever application is using it. Be careful when entering the regular expression checked by `preg_match()` — it needs to go on a single line in your editor:

```
    public function isValid() {
      if (preg_match("/[\<\>\r\n]{1,}/", $this->recipient_name)) {
        return(false);
      };
      if (preg_match("/^([A-Z0-9._%-]+)(\@)([A-Z0-9._%-]+)(\.)
                     ([A-Z0-9._%-]{2,4})$/i", $this->recipient_address)) {
        return(true);
      } else {
        return(false);
      };
    }
```

What's going on here is straightforward. A couple of regular expression matches are performed on the recipient. First, the recipient name is validated to ensure that it consists of one or more valid characters. Then the e-mail address is checked against a regular expression to ensure its conformity to RFC 822 format.

Next, you must provide some means to get an intelligent (that is, readily usable) string representation of your recipient:

```
public function getStringRepresentation() {
  $strMyRepresentation = "";
  if ($this->recipient_name) {
    $strMyRepresentation .= $this->recipient_name . " ";
  };
  $strMyRepresentation .= "<" . $this->recipient_address . ">";

  return($strMyRepresentation);
}
```

Because the readily accepted format for e-mail addresses is `First Name Last Name <user@example.com>`, that is the format used here.

The remainder of the class is dedicated to accessor methods — that is, methods to get and set the various properties of the e-mail recipient. As shown, you have provided an easy means to set all these within the constructor. For other recipients (such as those of a snail mail letter), doing this may be cumbersome:

```
public function __construct($strRecipientAddress, $strRecipientName = "") {
  $this->recipient_name = $strRecipientName;
  $this->recipient_address = $strRecipientAddress;
}
public function setRecipientName($strRecipientName) {
  $this->recipient_name = $strRecipientName;
}

public function setRecipientAddress($strRecipientAddress) {
  $this->recipient_address = $strRecipientAddress;
}

public function getRecipientName() {
  return($this->recipient_name);
}

public function getRecipientAddress() {
  return($this->recipient_address);
}
}
```

That concludes the e-mail recipient class, an implementation of the generic `Recipient` interface. If you wanted to save this as `emailrecipient.phpm` at this stage, no one would hold it against you.

Even though you haven't reached the communication framework yet, you can test this by using the following snippet of sample code. You might want to call this `test1.php` so that you can pull it up in a browser when you're done:

```
<?php
require("recipient.phpm");
require("emailrecipient.phpm");

$objEmailRecipient = new EmailRecipient("fiona@example.com", "Fiona Chow");
if ($objEmailRecipient->isValid()) {
```

```
    print "Recipient is valid! ";
    print "The string representation of this recipient would be: " .
        htmlentities($objEmailRecipient->getStringRepresentation());
} else {
    print "Recipient is not valid!";
};
?>
```

This yields the following output:

```
Recipient is valid! The string representation of this recipient would be:
Fiona Chow <fiona@example.com>
```

If you take a quick look at the EmailRecipient class in more detail, you can see just how simple it is. The two private member variables are specific to this class, as are the constructor and the (somewhat superfluous) setRecipientName and setRecipientAddress accessor methods and their (less superfluous) get counterparts.

Because you have declared this class to implement the Recipient interface, you are obliged to provide the two methods so described in that interface. If you do not, then PHP helpfully returns an error message.

In the getStringRepresentation method, you simply glue the pieces together to form a usable RFC822-compliant representation of the recipient's name and e-mail address. This is something you can drop straight into an SMTP session.

In the isValid method, you check the recipient's name for any bad characters that might confuse the SMTP server. Then you check the e-mail address for basic syntactical validity against a regular expression.

Other Implementations

You have just implemented an EmailRecipient class to encapsulate neatly the concept of e-mail recipients. Other types of communication have their own types of recipient, and each needs an implementation of the Recipient interface, too.

You can follow a very similar procedure to implement such alternative recipient types. First, ensure that sufficient member variables exist to hold every property of that recipient type, and that you have suitable Get and Set accessor methods to read and write to those member variables. Second, implement the mandatory methods required by the Recipient interface: the validator method and the string representation method.

The Communication Class

Even though recipients are different by nature, with streamlined interface access to any and all recipient objects, you can greatly simplify your communication class.

A communication object is literally that — a single communication by whatever method. We don't particularly mind which method, nor do we even allude to which ones are possible.

The communication class will never itself be instantiated. Instead, it will be extended by a class representing the particular form of communication to be used: EmailCommunication, SMSCommunication, and so forth.

Unlike the generic recipient construction, however, it will have useful methods of its own. For this reason, it really will be a genuine class and not just an interface. However, one method — send — will be declared as abstract so that it is implemented only in subclasses.

Subclasses of Communication may, of course, have methods and member variables of their own that supplement those of their superclass. A likely use for this would be methods that somehow manipulate the message property of Communication in some way. An example is a method in SMSCommunication in which to load a bitmap (.BMP) file to send as a cellular phone operator logo in place of a standard text message.

Storing Recipients Using a Collection

Whatever type of communication your class may represent, the preceding discussion should have made it clear that it will always have recipients of some sort or another. For that reason, a protected member variable (not private — it needs to be accessible by child objects) is needed to store such recipients. An array is an obvious choice, but it gives you little flexibility and requires a lot of coding on your part.

In Chapter 5, though, you were introduced to the concept of collections — essentially an object-oriented mechanism for storing groups of objects together as a single variable. The following class is a stripped-down, pared-back version of the Collection class you met in that chapter. It will make the rest of the code in this chapter a lot easier to follow. You should save the following as collection.phpm and keep it aside — you'll need it shortly:

```php
<?php
class Collection implements Iterator {

    protected $_members = array();    //collection members in a linear array
    protected $_keys = array();       //names of keys in numeric order to match
                                      //linear array
    protected $position = 0;          //current position

    public function __construct() {
        $this->position = 0;
        $this->_members = array();
        $this->_keys = array();
    }

    public function rewind() {
        $this->position = 0;
    }

    public function current() {
        return($this->_members[$this->position]);
    }

    public function addItem($obj, $key = NULL) {
        $this->_members[] = $obj;
        if (!$key) {
```

```
                            $key = sizeof($this->_members) - 1;
            };
            $this->_keys[] = $key;
            $this->position = sizeof($this->_members);
    }

    public function key() {
            return($this->_keys[$this->position]);
    }

    public function next() {
            ++$this->position;
    }

    public function valid() {
            return(isset($this->_members[$this->position]));
    }

    public function length() {
        return sizeof($this->_members);
    }

    public function exists($key) {
        // resolve key to index
        $idx = -1;
        for ($i=0; $i<=sizeof($this->_keys)-1; $i++) {
            if ($this->_keys[$i] = $key) {
                    $idx = $i;
            };
        }
        if ($idx == -1) {
            return(false);
        };
        return (isset($this->_members[$i]));
    }

}

?>
```

With the collections class in place, you can code up a communication class to make use of it.

The Communications Class Itself

Take a look at the following code, which you should save as `communication.phpm`. Note that it makes use of the simple collection class you just wrote in order to store its collection of recipients:

```
<?php

abstract class Communication {

    protected $arRecipientCollection;
    private   $strMessage;
```

```
protected $strErrorMessage;
protected $errorCode;

abstract public function send();
  public function __construct() {
  $this->strMessage = "";
}

public function addRecipient($objRecipient, $strIdentifier = "") {
  $strRecipient = $objRecipient->getStringRepresentation();
  if (!$strIdentifier) {
    $strIdentifier = $strRecipient;
  };
  $this->arRecipientCollection->addItem($objRecipient, $strIdentifier);
}
public function removeRecipient($strIdentifier) {
  $this->arRecipientCollection->removeItem($strIdentifier);
}
protected function _setMessage($strMessage) {
  $this->strMessage = $strMessage;
}

protected function _getMessage() {
  return($this->strMessage);
}

public function getErrorMessage() {
  return($this->strErrorMessage);
}

public function getErrorCode() {
  return($this->errorCode);
}
} ?>
```

As you can see, you declare the recipient collection as protected. This means that although it cannot be tinkered with from within your application's code, it *can* be tinkered with by subclasses of the Communication class — which is a good thing.

You probably have noticed how these examples brazenly add recipient objects passed to addRecipient to the recipient collection, even though you have absolutely no idea of what type that object is, and equally no idea of what type of collection arRecipientCollection is. You may assume that this is a recipe for run-time errors, but in fact it is the subclass that initializes the collection, and it will make it a collection of whatever it wants. As long as whatever is passed as a recipient object supports the interface developed earlier, and is of the same type as the type required by the subclass, there will be no problems.

Use the string representation of the object as a suitable key for the collection. The message property remains private and can be manipulated using _setMessage and _getMessage, accessible only from the subclass. Don't worry about the error message and error code member variables yet. You'll meet those a bit later.

How do you use this in practice? Quite simply, you extend it to form a useful subclass. In the next section, you'll take a look at `EmailCommunication`, which, as the name suggests, is used for sending a message to one or more `EmailRecipient` objects.

E-mailing Your Users

`EmailCommunication` is the subclass to `Communication`. First, you need some simple way of enforcing the recipient collection of the superclass to contain only `EmailRecipient` objects. You can do this by reworking the `Collection` class slightly to form a subclass called `EmailRecipientCollection`. This may, by definition, consist only of `EmailRecipient` members:

```php
<?php
class EmailRecipientCollection extends Collection {
  public function addItem(EmailRecipient $obj, $key = null) {
    parent::addItem($obj, $key);
  }
} ?>
```

Note that this offers no new functionality. It merely offers the enforcement, through *Class Type Hints,* of the class type to which new members must adhere.

With this class now understood by PHP and saved as `emailrecipientcollection.phpm`, you can implement the `EmailCommunication` class itself.

Building a Test Version

It's a good idea to first build an implementation of reduced functionality to test the OOP interfaces. After all, if you can get that right, the rest should be fairly straightforward. By using some strategic printouts, you can see what's going on and confirm that the logic works.

After you are certain the logic and, hence, the OOP integration and interfaces work correctly, you can concentrate on the implementation — that is, getting the e-mail out the door.

Start the class in a fairly standard manner, declaring it and its two properties: one a visible address and the other is a collection of visible carbon copy addresses. You do not need to worry about blind carbon copy addresses; they are not visible and therefore can be handled solely by the parent `Communication` class:

```php
<?php
class EmailCommunication extends Communication {

  private $objApparentPrimaryRecipient;          // Visible To: address
  private $arObjApparentSecondaryRecipients;     // Visible Cc: address(es)
```

Next, provide a means to set the primary recipient of the e-mail. Note that the class adds to the main recipient collection of the parent class (generic), while also setting the primary visible recipient (specific to the `EmailCommunication` class):

```php
public function setPrimaryRecipient($objRecipient) {
  if (!($this->arRecipientCollection->exists(
            $objRecipient->getStringRepresentation()))) {
    parent::addRecipient($objRecipient);
  };
  $this->objApparentPrimaryRecipient = clone $objRecipient;
}
```

The methods for adding and removing carbon copy (Cc:) recipients are much the same. Again, you manipulate both the parent collection and the local apparent recipients array:

```php
public function addCarbonRecipient($objRecipient) {
  if (!($this->arRecipientCollection->exists(
            $objRecipient->getStringRepresentation()))) {
    parent::addRecipient($objRecipient);
  };
  if (!($this->arObjApparentSecondaryRecipients->exists(
            $objRecipient->getStringRepresentation()))) {
    $this->arObjApparentSecondaryRecipients->addItem(
            $objRecipient, $objRecipient->getStringRepresentation());
  };
}

public function removeCarbonRecipient($objRecipient) {
  if ($this->arRecipientCollection->exists(
            $objRecipient->getStringRepresentation())) {
    parent::removeRecipient($objRecipient);
  };
  if ($this->arObjApparentSecondaryRecipients->exists(
            $objRecipient->getStringRepresentation())) {
    $this->arObjApparentSecondaryRecipients->removeItem(
            $objRecipient->getStringRepresentation());
  };
}
```

The same principle applies for adding and removing blind recipients, except that you do not touch the apparent recipients list:

```php
public function addBlindRecipient($objRecipient) {
  if (!($this->arRecipientCollection->exists(
        $objRecipient->getStringRepresentation()))) {
    parent::addRecipient($objRecipient);
  };
}

public function removeBlindRecipient($objRecipient) {
  if (!($this->arRecipientCollection->exists(
        $objRecipient->getStringRepresentation()))) {
    parent::removeRecipient($objRecipient->getStringRepresentation());
  };
}
```

Now turn your attention to the constructor, which must initialize the superclass collection to be a collection of the appropriate type, and the local collection of apparent recipients to be another collection of the same type (though not necessarily with the same contents). Note that you also call the parent class constructor when you're finished:

```
public function __construct() {
  // Superclass collection
  $this->arRecipientCollection = new EmailRecipientCollection();
  // Local collection of visible (CC:) recipients
  $this->arObjApparentSecondaryRecipients = new EmailRecipientCollection();
  parent::__construct();
}
```

Now comes the dummy `send` method, used to ensure that your class works correctly:

```
public function send() {
  print "ACTUAL RECIPIENTS<BR><BR>";
  foreach ($this->arRecipientCollection as $strRecipientIdentifier =>
      $objEmailRecipient) {
    print "NAME: " . $objEmailRecipient->getRecipientName() . "<BR>";
    print "EMAIL ADDRESS: " . $objEmailRecipient->
        getRecipientAddress() . "<BR>";
  };

  print "<BR><BR>APPARENTLY TO RECIPIENT<BR><BR>";
  print "NAME: " . $this->objApparentPrimaryRecipient->
      getRecipientName() . "<BR>";
  print "EMAIL ADDRESS: " . $this->
      objApparentPrimaryRecipient->getRecipientAddress() . "<BR>";

  print "<BR><BR>APPARENT SECONDARY RECIPIENTS<BR><BR>";
  foreach ($this->arObjApparentSecondaryRecipients as
      $strRecipientIdentifier => $objEmailRecipient) {
    print "NAME: " . $objEmailRecipient->getRecipientName() . "<BR>";
    print "EMAIL ADDRESS: " . $objEmailRecipient->
        getRecipientAddress() . "<BR>";
  };
  }
}
```

Let's examine the previous code in a bit more detail. First, notice the member properties:

```
private $objApparentPrimaryRecipient;       // Visible To: address
private $arObjApparentSecondaryRecipients; // Visible Cc: address(es)
```

These two member properties exist in addition to the master recipient list inherited from the `Communication` superclass. They represent a single `EmailRecipient` object representing to whom the e-mail is directly addressed (the "To:" line) and a collection of `EmailRecipients` representing any Carbon Copy (Cc:) addresses. These two member properties are not, strictly speaking, important in determining who gets the message. That is still handled by the collection in the superclass. However, they exist for the purpose of formatting the e-mail so that the "master" and "Cc:" recipients appear in the right place in the message headers.

The constructor method concerns itself with the setup of these two additional private member variables, and calls the superclass constructor for good measure.

The various methods used for adding and removing the master recipient, carbon copy recipients, and blind carbon copy recipients all work in much the same way. They check to see whether an object of that key (the key being the string representation of the recipient object) exists in the collection before performing the relevant operation. This is achieved using the `exists` method provided by the `collection` object.

Take a look at some test addresses just to prove that it works. You can then go back and look at the way you actually send the mail. To execute the following code, you need to `require()` all the classes developed so far in this chapter. Call this `test2.php` so you can see it in your Web browser:

```php
<?php
require("collection.phpm");
require("communication.phpm");
require("emailcommunication.phpm");
require("recipient.phpm");
require("emailrecipient.phpm");
require("emailrecipientcollection.phpm");
$objEmail = new EmailCommunication;
$objEmailRecipient = new EmailRecipient("ed@example.com",
    "Ed Lecky-Thompson");
$objEmailCCRecipient = new EmailRecipient("ted@example.com",
    "Ted Lecky-Thompson");
$objEmailBCCRecipient = new EmailRecipient("zed@example.com",
                        "Zed Lecky-Thompson");
$objEmail->setPrimaryRecipient($objEmailRecipient);
$objEmail->addCarbonRecipient($objEmailCCRecipient);
$objEmail->addBlindRecipient($objEmailBCCRecipient);
$objEmail->send(); ?>
```

Run the preceding code. You should get output like that shown here:

```
ACTUAL RECIPIENTS

NAME: Ed Lecky-Thompson
EMAIL ADDRESS: ed@example.com
NAME: Ted Lecky-Thompson
EMAIL ADDRESS: ted@example.com
NAME: Zed Lecky-Thompson
EMAIL ADDRESS: zed@example.com

APPARENTLY TO RECIPIENT

NAME: Ed Lecky-Thompson
EMAIL ADDRESS: ed@example.com

APPARENT SECONDARY RECIPIENTS

NAME: Ted Lecky-Thompson
EMAIL ADDRESS: ted@example.com
```

This looks pretty healthy. As you can see from the code, Ed is the main recipient of this e-mail, while Ted has been Cc'd, and Zed has been Bcc'd. When Ed receives the mail, he will be able to see his name on the To: line, and Ted's on the Cc: line. Ed won't know Zed got the mail. When Ted receives the mail, he will see much the same. Again, he won't know Zed was Bcc'd on this important message. When Zed receives the mail, he won't see his name anywhere, but he'll be able to deduce that he must have been Bcc'd on the original message.

The output from this dummy test implementation shows that the code is correct. The list of actual recipients displays all three genuine recipients of the e-mail. The primary recipient is correct, and the Cc'd recipient is listed correctly, too.

Getting the Message Across

You must do a couple of things to make the `EmailCommunication` class function properly.

First, you must get the body of the e-mail built and slotted into the `message` member variable. A simple, plain-text e-ail consists of two parts: the header and the body. Conveniently enough, the two are separated by nothing more complex than a blank line. The header contains the sender's address, the recipient's address, the subject, the Cc: addresses, and a myriad of other bits and pieces.

Now, add two member variables: one for the subject line and one for the sender. The sender can again be an `EmailRecipient` object because a sender has a name and an address, just like a recipient:

```
private $objApparentSender;  // Visible From: address
private $strSubjectLine;     // Subject line
```

The use of some basic methods will allow users of the class to set these properties.

For the time being, assume that you're dealing with purely plain text e-mails. You add a simple method to allow public setting of the message property. The message property is synonymous with the body of the e-mail, because the headers will be managed separately:

```
public function setSubject($strSubject) {
  $this->strSubjectLine = $strSubject;
}

public function setMessageBody($strMessageBody) {
  $this->_setMessage($strMessageBody);
}

public function setSender($objSender) {
  $this->objApparentSender = $objSender->__clone();
}
```

All that remains to do now is to convert the `send()` method into something that assembles a header and a body, glues them together, and spits them out to the Internet.

How do you go about doing that? The easiest way is with PEAR's `Net_SMTP` package, which gels quite neatly with this setup, and again provides a good example of why PEAR is so useful in avoiding reinventing the wheel in your application development. The `Net_SMTP` package may already be installed in your PHP setup. If not, install it in the usual way.

The basic syntax for using the Net_SMTP package is simple. You can feed it the assembled message as-is with no changes. Just tell it the operands to use when talking to the mail server. The minimum that the mail server requires is a sender and a list of recipients. The server doesn't look at your headers. This is why blind carbon copies work. Although the server is told to deliver the message to that recipient, the recipient is never listed anywhere in the headers.

The following example shows a basic usage of Net_SMTP, step by step, assuming that the completed message is in $full_message _content and that an array of recipients exists in $rcpt:

```
if (! ($smtp = new Net_SMTP("mail"))) {
    die("Unable to instantiate Net_SMTP object\n");
}
```

First, you instantiate a new instance of the Net_SMTP class with the name of your SMTP server, and die if you are unable to do so for some reason:

```
if (PEAR::isError($e = $smtp->connect())) {
    die($e->getMessage() . "\n");
}
```

Next, you ensure that you can connect to the SMTP server you just specified; if not, you die:

```
if (PEAR::isError($smtp->mailFrom("sender@example.com"))) {
    die("Unable to set sender\n");
}
```

In this case, the sender was set to be sender@example.com:

```
foreach($rcpt as $recipient) {
    if (PEAR::isError($res = $smtp->rcptTo($rcpt))) {
        die("Unable to add recipient: " . $res->getMessage() . "\n");
    }
}
```

Now loop through your array of recipients, adding each into the Net_SMTP class instance and dying if any single recipient proves impossible to add:

```
if (PEAR::isError($smtp->data($full_message_content))) {
    die("Unable to send data\n");
}
$smtp->disconnect();
```

Finally, you send your message and disconnect from the SMTP server.

Note that this example uses mail as the hostname of the remote SMTP server. If you're running on Linux or something similar, then you can probably stick a reference to the hostname mail in your /etc/hosts file pointing to 127.0.0.1 and everything will work fine out of the box. Otherwise, you must locate the nearest friendly SMTP server to relay for you, and use that instead.

Now take a look at the following finished EmailCommunication class, complete with an SMTP send through Net_SMTP:

```
class EmailCommunication extends Communication {
  private $objApparentSender;               // Visible From: address
  private $strSubjectLine;                  // Subject line
  private $objApparentPrimaryRecipient;     // Visible To: address
  private $arObjApparentSecondaryRecipients; // Visible Cc: address(es)


  public function __construct() {
    // Superclass collection
    $this->arRecipientCollection = new EmailRecipientCollection();
    // Local collection of visible (CC:) recipients
    $this->arObjApparentSecondaryRecipients = new EmailRecipientCollection();
    parent::__construct();
  }

  public function setPrimaryRecipient($objRecipient) {
    if (!($this->arRecipientCollection->exists(
              $objRecipient->getStringRepresentation()))) {
      parent::addRecipient($objRecipient);
    };
    $this->objApparentPrimaryRecipient = clone $objRecipient;
  }

  public function addCarbonRecipient($objRecipient) {
    if (!($this->arRecipientCollection->exists(
              $objRecipient->getStringRepresentation()))) {
      parent::addRecipient($objRecipient);
    };
    if (!($this->arObjApparentSecondaryRecipients->exists(
          $objRecipient->getStringRepresentation()))) {
      $this->arObjApparentSecondaryRecipients->addItem(
          $objRecipient, $objRecipient->getStringRepresentation());
    };
  }

  public function removeCarbonRecipient($objRecipient) {
    if ($this->arRecipientCollection->exists(
          $objRecipient->getStringRepresentation())) {
      parent::removeRecipient($objRecipient);
    };
    if ($this->arObjApparentSecondaryRecipients->exists(
          $objRecipient->getStringRepresentation())) {
      $this->arObjApparentSecondaryRecipients->removeItem(
          $objRecipient->getStringRepresentation());
    };
  }

  public function addBlindRecipient($objRecipient) {
    if (!($this->arRecipientCollection->exists(
```

```php
            $objRecipient->getStringRepresentation()))) {
      parent::addRecipient($objRecipient);
    };
  }

  public function removeBlindRecipient($objRecipient) {
    if (!($this->arRecipientCollection->exists(
          $objRecipient->getStringRepresentation()))) {
      parent::removeRecipient($objRecipient->getStringRepresentation());
    };
  }

  public function setSubject($strSubject) {
    $this->strSubjectLine = $strSubject;
  }

  public function setMessageBody($strMessageBody) {
    $this->_setMessage($strMessageBody);
  }

  public function setSender($objSender) {
    $this->objApparentSender = $objSender->__clone();
  }

  public function send() {

    // Establish headers
    $strHeaders .= "From: " .
        $this->objApparentSender->getStringRepresentation() . "\n";
    $strHeaders .= "To: " .
        $this->objApparentPrimaryRecipient->getStringRepresentation() . "\n";
    foreach ($this->arObjApparentSecondaryRecipients as $strRecipientIdentifier =>
          $objEmailRecipient) {
      $strHeaders .= "Cc: " . $objEmailRecipient->getStringRepresentation() . "\n";
    };
    $strHeaders .= "Date: " . date("D, M j H:i:s T Y O") . "\n";

    // Establish body
    $strBody = $this->_getMessage();

    // Pull together to form complete email, correctly formatted
    $strFullEmail = $strHeaders . "\n" . $strBody;


    if (! ($smtp = new Net_SMTP("mail"))) {
        $this->strErrorMessage = "Unable to instantiate Net_SMTP object";
        $this->errorCode = 1;
        return(false);
    }

    if (PEAR::isError($e = $smtp->connect())) {
        $this->strErrorMessage = $e->getMessage();
```

```
            $this->errorCode = 2;
            $smtp->disconnect();
            return(false);
        }

    if (PEAR::isError($smtp->mailFrom(
                $this->objApparentSender->getStringRepresentation()))) {
            $this->strErrorMessage = "Unable to set sender";
            $this->errorCode = 3;
            $smtp->disconnect();
            return(false);
        }

        // Send to each recipient
        foreach ($this->arRecipientCollection as $strRecipientIdentifier =>
                $objEmailRecipient) {
        $strThisAddress = $objEmailRecipient->getRecipientAddress();
        if (PEAR::isError($res = $smtp->rcptTo($strThisAddress))) {
            $this->strErrorMessage = "Unable to add recipient " . $strThisAddress;
            $this->errorCode = 4;
            $smtp->disconnect();
            return(false);
        };
        };

        if (PEAR::isError($smtp->data($strFullEmail))) {
            $this->strErrorMessage = "Unable to send data to server";
            $this->errorCode = 5;
            $smtp->disconnect();
            return(false);
        }
        $smtp->disconnect();
        return(true);


    }
};
```

Note a few things about this approach. First, when a recipient is added as the primary recipient or a member of the carbon copy (Cc:) list, you can add the recipient to the collection held in the parent superclass, and then clone the recipient object before adding to the list of apparent recipients. This step isn't vital, but it means that you can implement your own _clone()method in your EmailRecipient class, if you want, to modify the behavior taken when this copy is made.

Second, this example uses the error code and error message member variables of the Communication superclass. These are accessible through public functions. You can use these to debug your applications. E-mail can be an unpredictable phenomenon at times, and failure can occur through any number of scenarios, including a failure to reach the SMTP server, being denied permission to send e-mail to your particular IP address, or having a recipient be rejected outright by the SMTP server.

Third, the code date("D, M j H:i:s T Y O")is used to construct the e-mail header's date property. A quick glance at the PHP documentation reminds you that this produces a timestamp in the format Tue, Jul 20 22:58:58 BST 2004 +0100, which is the format required in e-mail headers.

To test the final working class, you can knock out some code like the following:

```
$objEmail = new EmailCommunication;
$objEmailRecipient = new EmailRecipient("ed@example.com", "Ed Lecky-Thompson");
$objEmailCCRecipient = new EmailRecipient("cc@example.com", "Ted Lecky-Thompson");
$objEmailSender = new EmailRecipient("info@example.com", "Test Sender");
$objEmail->setPrimaryRecipient($objEmailRecipient);
$objEmail->setSender($objEmailSender);
$objEmail->setMessageBody("Hello,\n\nThis is a short test email.\n\nGoodbye!");
$objEmail->setSubject("Test Subject");
$objEmail->addCarbonRecipient($objEmailCCRecipient);
$objEmail->addBlindRecipient($objEmailBCCRecipient);

if ($objEmail->send()) {
 print "DONE! All went well! Mail sent successfully.";
} else {
 print "Sorry, didn't send mail successfully.";
};
```

Being Smart with Templates

In Chapter 13 we talk about how separating application and display logic from each other through the model-view-controller (MVC) paradigm is generally an excellent idea, one well worth pursuing in your own application architecture.

Chapter 13 also covers a package called Smarty, which helps you do just that, and describes how useful it can be in traditional Web application implementation. Smarty has another use that is often overlooked: It can produce template-driven e-mail output.

As you know, nine times out of ten, the e-mails you send your users will be virtually the same. A few tags, or the first name after "Dear," or an account number might change, but not much else.

Splicing variables into strings is fine for smaller operations, but when those e-mails start to get bigger and more unwieldy, and even contain printed array structures, things will get tough. The solution is to use the TemplatedEmailCommunication class.

The TemplatedEmailCommunication class makes full use of Smarty. If you haven't read Chapter 13 yet, now would be an excellent time. You need to know how Smarty works in order to pull this off.

The class you're about to create actually extends EmailCommunication, so have that up and running first; and have Smarty installed and working, too:

```
class TemplatedEmailCommunication extends EmailCommunication {

  private $path_to_template_file;
  private $objSmarty;

  public function __construct($strPathToTemplateFile) {
    $this->objSmarty = new Smarty;
```

```
    $this->path_to_template_file = $strPathToTemplateFile;
    parent::__construct();
  }

  public function setParameter($strParameter, $strValue) {
    $this->objSmarty->assign($strParameter, $strValue);
  }

  public function parse() {
    $this->setMessageBody($this->objSmarty->fetch($this
->path_to_template_file));
  }
}
```

The preceding code is simple but effective. Now try the following code. It needs to point to a simple Smarty template, so first create a template file named `test.tpl` as follows:

```
Name: {$name}
Favorite Food: {$favefood}
```

Next, enter the PHP code that follows. Ensure that it resides in the same directory as your Smarty template, or modify the first line to point to the right path. You'll see that it's very similar to the last time you took `EmailCommunication` for a drive, but the differences in the code are highlighted for you:

```
$objEmail = new TemplatedEmailCommunication("test.tpl");
$objEmail->setParameter("name", "Ed");
$objEmail->setParameter("favefood", "Steak");
$objEmail->parse();
$objEmailRecipient = new EmailRecipient("ed@example.com", "Ed Lecky-Thompson");
$objEmailSender = new EmailRecipient("info@example.com", "Test Sender");
$objEmail->setPrimaryRecipient($objEmailRecipient);
$objEmail->setSender($objEmailSender);
$objEmail->setSubject("Test Subject");

if ($objEmail->send()) {
 print "DONE! All went well! Mail sent successfully.";
} else {
 print "Sorry, didn't send mail successfully.";
};
```

This produces the following output in the body of the sent e-mail:

```
Name: Ed
Favorite Food: Steak
```

As you can see, the `parse()` method constructed the body of the e-mail for you. Smarty parsed the template according to the two parameters you gave it; but rather than use the traditional `display()` method, you use `fetch()` to capture its output into a string. You then set the message body to be that string and you're all set to send the e-mail.

Note that by extending the `EmailCommunication` class, you've not only avoided reinventing the wheel with respect to recipient management and SMTP connectivity, but also kept the `TemplatedEmailCommunication` class down to just a few lines of code, making it much easier to tinker with.

Of course, what has been demonstrated here is but a small subset of what is possible with Smarty, but it does show just how easy Smarty is to adapt for e-mail.

Using MIME

You've probably noticed that so far this chapter has dealt almost exclusively with simple, plain text e-mails. These are easier to deal with, but inevitably, occasions will for arise for sending HTML e-mail, or maybe even templated HTML e-mail. And what about attachments? How do you handle those? MIME is the answer, and it is an enormous topic.

Mercifully, PEAR has it largely covered. See `http://pear.php.net/package/Mail_Mime` for more details. The suggested approach is to extend `EmailCommunication` to form `RichEmail Communication`, which sports additional methods such as `setHTMLContent`, `setPlainText Content`, `addAttachment`, and so forth.

This discussion will not go into more detail; but if you have the hang of this chapter, you can probably integrate MIME functionality into the classes you've already built without difficulty. Download and install the PEAR package from `http://pear.php.net/package/Mail_Mime` and read the documentation thoroughly. Constructing the relevant new `RichEmailCommunication` class should be straightforward enough.

You can find out more about MIME in the Usenet `comp.mail.mime` FAQ, the latest version of which is available in the newsgroup and is replicated across the Web, such as at `www.uni-giessen.de/faq/archiv/mail.mime-faq.part1-9/`.

Other Communication Subclasses

This chapter sticks firmly to e-mail simply because it's the most common form of communicating with users on the Web. It's free, and everyone knows the basics.

However, the whole point of the `Communication` class is that it can be extended to form virtually anything — a fax, an SMS, a voice call. This section describes a few ways you can go about implementing such facilities.

SMS Text Messaging

A number of gateway providers have sprung up in the last year or so who will send messages on your behalf for a small fee. Rather than use physical cellular phones to send the messages, they use direct links straight into the cellular networks, which saves time and money.

The interface is usually via SOAP (introduced in Chapter 10) or even just a simple HTTP POST. Search the Web for "SMS Gateways" if you're curious.

The more instant alternative is via a serial cable to your cellular phone, if your phone supports it. Again, the Web has more details on the API for communicating with your phone in this way. The trick is to treat it as though it were a modem; a Hayes-compatible AT command set is perfect for such communication. You can find more information at `www.cellular.co.za/sms_at_commands.htm`.

Fax

Rather than physically render a fax page and fire it down a modem, a far simpler solution is to use one of the many e-mail-to-fax gateways in existence today. Most of these will accept a TIFF or similar file e-mailed as an attachment to a special e-mail address, and send the fax on your behalf. By using PHP's built-in graphics functions, you should be able to compose a TIFF on the fly, e-mail it to such a catcher address, and create an instant, dynamically produced fax as a result.

An example of such a service is eFax. See www.efax.com for more information.

Other Considerations

Before wrapping up this chapter, there are a couple of other things worth considering. If you're building an enterprise-class application that makes use of user communications, such little details can make the difference between a really slick user experience (one that will make your users want to come back for more) and something half-baked.

Blocking Activity

Blocking refers to an activity in a piece of procedural code that must complete before any other code can complete. If that activity takes a while, well, then that's just tough — everything else must wait.

Sending e-mail is just such an activity. Sending an e-mail (as shown earlier in this chapter) is an intensive activity: making a connection to an SMTP server, waiting to be authenticated, passing the message body, and waiting for the server to accept. Depending on how busy the server is, this could take anywhere from a fraction of a millisecond to — wait for it — maybe four or five seconds.

Those four or five seconds are added to the HTTP request — there's no two ways about it. If your user's HTTP request has generated an e-mail, then that delay will be felt by that user before the e-mail is sent and the request fulfilled. At best, the user might think something's gone wrong; at worst, that user will hit the Stop button and give up.

Remember, too, that SMTP servers fail or become unavailable from time to time. If you're dependent on that server being available to implement some vital piece of functionality (a forgotten password e-mail, for example), then a SMTP server being down essentially makes that functionality unavailable, too.

It's not just e-mail. If you're sending SMS text messages using a GSM modem, what if someone yanks the power cord from that modem? If you're sending faxes, what if your fax service goes down? The list goes on.

Maintaining a Job Queue

The solution to this conundrum is actually delightfully simple. Go back to something you know *won't* block — or at least shouldn't. It's your database, and it probably forms the backbone of your application.

Create a simple table to hold the e-mails you need to send. It might look something like this:

```
CREATE TABLE "scheduled_email" (
    "id" SERIAL PRIMARY KEY NOT NULL,
    "subject_line" character varying(256) NOT NULL,
    "sender_name" character varying(256) NOT NULL,
    "sender_address" character varying(256) NOT NULL,
    "recipient_name" character varying(256) NOT NULL,
    "recipient_address" character varying(256) NOT NULL,
    "reply_to_name" character varying(256) NOT NULL,
    "reply_to_address" character varying(256) NOT NULL,
    "html_content" text,
    "text_content" text,
    "status" character varying(1) NOT NULL
);
```

It is hoped that most of these columns are self-explanatory. Perhaps the only one that requires explanation is the column named status.

The idea is simple. When you want to send an e-mail, don't connect to the SMTP server directly. Instead, create an entry in the table scheduled_email, setting the status flag to N — meaning "Not Processed Yet."

That's it — that's all your code does. All that is required is a simple INSERT statement into your database, something that should take only fractions of a second. The blocking problem disappears.

Of course, you still have to actually send the e-mail. That's where your processor script comes in. Write a simple piece of PHP code that looks for entries in the scheduled_email table whose status is N. Then, for each entry, send the e-mail via SMTP. For each e-mail processed, set its status to C for "Completed." That way, your script won't accidentally send it again the next time it runs.

That script must be placed in your system's scheduled task system — cron on Mac OS X and UNIX, and Scheduled Tasks on Windows. Set it to run once a minute, and process any entries "Not Processed Yet."

Be careful to ensure that only one copy of your script runs at a time, though. Otherwise, you might find that two instances of the script attempt to send the same e-mail for you. You can mitigate against this too, though. Consider setting the status of an e-mail to S (for "Started") before you start sending it. That way, even if two copies of your script begin running at the same time, there's no chance of them both attempting to send the same e-mail.

The net effect of what you're doing here is taking an unpredictable task (the act of sending an e-mail) and replacing it with something predictable (inserting a record into the database). The unpredictable task is kept offline, well away from the user's Web browser.

Deliverability

One of the very hottest topics of the past few years is spam and junk mail. Recent estimates suggest that as many as 75 percent of the literally hundreds of millions of e-mails sent through the Internet each day are spam. Not only does this provide an immense irritation to end users, it also wastes bandwidth and CPU clock cycles, both of which cost money.

As a result, efforts have been made to limit the deliverability of suspected spam wherever possible. The most prominent of these is the junk mail filter — not only the one built into most modern e-mail clients, but also those installed at the perimeters of major ISP e-mail infrastructures, as well as those of the major Web-based e-mail providers (such as Hotmail, Gmail, and Yahoo!).

These junk mail systems are becoming increasingly aggressive in determining what they believe to be spam. Of course, they use traditional Baysian algorithms to look at the subject line and message body for "spammy" words — "refinance," "pills," "meds," and so forth. The presence of such attributes add to a "score" — which, if it goes above a certain value, means that e-mail is junked. Increasingly, ISPs are also using sophisticated checks that, if passed, can rapidly detract from that score. As a result, legitimate senders can more reliably get e-mails through, even if they exhibit characteristics that could otherwise be considered "spammy."

For enterprise Web application builders, this is, of course, important. If you are, for example, sending regular e-mail newsletters, the last thing you want is for your e-mail to be junked as a false positive. This can happen more easily than you think. For example, if you were a major retail bank, an e-mail to your customers about a great mortgage offer could easily make it into junk.

With that in mind, what techniques can you use to help tell those junk mail filters that you're a legitimate sender — and that they should let you through (within reason) no matter what?

SPF Records

Sender Policy Framework (SPF) records allow the DNS records for the domain name from which the e-mail originates to be impregnated with additional information specifying which physical servers may send e-mails for that domain name.

This means that recipient e-mail servers can check quickly whether or not the sender domain name is likely to be legitimate, or whether it is spoofed. If it is legitimate, then a corresponding SPF record will "marry" that domain name to the originating server. This sort of match is not a characteristic usually associated with a spam e-mail. The sender domain is usually completely false or, at a minimum, has nothing to do with the originating mail server — especially given that so-called "open relays" are the source of 90 percent of spam e-mail.

More information can be found at `http://en.wikipedia.org/wiki/Sender_Policy_Framework`.

Sender ID

Sender ID is impregnated into the DNS records for the sending domain, just like an SPF record. The syntax is subtly different, but provides broadly the same purpose. It tells recipients about the domain name in question, and which servers might have been used to legitimately send e-mails through that domain. It differs from SPF records in its exact syntax and implementation. It is, for all intents and purposes, a competing product.

Most domains choose to implement both formats to ensure optimum compatibility. For more information, see `http://en.wikipedia.org/wiki/Sender_ID`.

Domain Keys and DKIM

Domain Keys Identified Mail (DKIM) provides a mechanism for e-mail dispatch systems to digitally sign an e-mail at the header level. This signature can be double-checked against the official DNS records for that domain to assess whether it is genuine.

Such a mechanism does not guarantee that the e-mail is not spam, but it does enable it to be traced back very easily. To this end, if an ISP receives too many complaints against a given domain, it can be blocked, along with its domain key. Hence, upon receiving an e-mail, an ISP can verify the authenticity of the sending domain, and consult its internal records to determine whether or not it has been previously reported as a spammer. If it has been, then the message will likely be rejected.

For more information, see http://en.wikipedia.org/wiki/DomainKeys_Identified_Mail.

Broadcast E-mail Providers

If all this sounds like a lot of hassle, you're right — it is. Standard SMTP from your own Web or application server is a tough way to go these days. All it takes is one overzealous user to hit the "This is spam" button, and your reputation goes down the drain. Unless you're prepared to sit around monitoring spam feedback loops — disputing each and every case that comes your way from ISPs — there is a better way.

A new breed of broadcast e-mail providers has sprung up in the past few years. These companies have one purpose and one purpose only: to send out (legitimate) bulk e-mail on behalf of their clients, as fast as possible, as cheaply as possible, and with as high a degree of deliverability as possible.

These broadcast e-mails are sent as part of marketing activity — for example, a weekly newsletter from your Web site — but there's no reason at all you couldn't use the same provider to send your triggered e-mails, too. That way, your triggered e-mails (such as order confirmations and so forth) will come from the same domain as your broadcast e-mails, with all the deliverability techniques described previously already established and in place.

The broadcast e-mail providers also take care of monitoring for you. They'll deal with any spam complaints, and monitor any particular e-mail copy that is frequently being junked. You can also avail yourself of some very sophisticated reporting on opens, click-throughs, and so forth.

Most of the broadcast e-mail providers provide an API to enable you to send such triggered e-mails from your own applications. A good example is eCircle, (www.ecircle.com/en/home.html), which provides synchronous and asynchronous APIs, and even PHP code samples. You can get more details at http://developer.ecircle-ag.com/. E-mails start at a few dollars per thousand, so as long as you aren't processing millions of e-mails per month, you'll find that the extra investment makes sense.

Summary

In this chapter, you learned about communicating with your users, not just through a Web browser, but through that most vital of modern media: electronic mail.

You were weaned off PHP's mail() function early on by looking at how communications with users can be represented in an elegant class hierarchy. You also created the EmailRecipient and EmailCommunication classes as part of that hierarchy, robust and stable enough for everyday use.

You learned how Smarty can play a big part in enabling you to produce template-driven e-mails, and about some of the more advanced possibilities for the class framework discussed.

In Chapter 12, you meet two of the most important concepts in building enterprise PHP applications: sessions and authentication.

12

Sessions and Authentication

Despite the advancements of PHP in recent years that have brought it to the full-featured, object-oriented (OO) Web application development platform it has become today, it still relies (as do all other languages of its ilk) on the basics. That is, it relies on the HTTP protocol, as well as the most basic building block of any kind of interactivity on the Web, the Common Gateway Interface (CGI) functionality that HTTP provides.

When people speak of HTTP, they often describe it as *stateless* — meaning that no "memory" is retained from one user's request to the next. The request is made via GET or POST, data is returned, and the request is completed — and, as far as the Web server is concerned, forgotten.

This characteristic isn't of much use if you're trying to build complex Web applications that emulate the functionality of their equivalent desktop counterparts. You must be able to keep track of users' previous actions (not just what they're doing right at this moment) in order to be able to produce meaningful output.

Thankfully, PHP provides a way around this: *sessions*. This technique enables you to maintain certain stateful information from one request by the user to the next. This leads very neatly to one of the most common and useful applications of session handling — that of authentication and user state persistence.

The first half of this chapter discusses PHP's built-in session-handling features. You'll see that although (on the surface) the functionality available to you may seem basic, it can be extended and adapted to provide an enormous degree of flexibility (including integrating with third-party databases). You'll also learn the ins and outs of session security so that you can devise session architectures that keep hackers at bay.

In the second half of the chapter, you'll learn how to apply this knowledge of session management to develop an essential component of your toolkit: a reusable, scalable, and highly secure session management and authentication class that can be deployed on almost any enterprise-grade PHP application.

Introduction to Sessions

Before getting into how sessions work in PHP and the benefits they can bring to your application, let's look at the broader concept of sessions in general. What are they, how do they work, and why are they so important?

How HTTP Works

Consider how a Web request actually works. When the user's Web browser makes a request, it presents (among other bits and pieces) the following core information to the Web server:

❑ Method of request (either GET or POST) and the protocol version used (1.0 or 1.1)

❑ The actual document required (for example, /index.php)

❑ The server hostname from which the document is being requested (which is important, because many Web sites are hosted on a single server with a single IP address)

❑ The GET or POST request parameters (for example, foo=bar, username=fred, password=letmein) in URL-encoded format

❑ The browser type (known as the *user agent* — essentially variant, platform, and version)

❑ Any cookies stored on the client's machine that have been previously issued by the server of which the client is now making a request

If you want to see this in action, telnet to port 80 on the Web server of your choice, and issue something that looks like the following:

```
GET /pub/WWW/TheProject.html HTTP/1.1
User-Agent: CERN-LineMode/2.15 libwww/2.17b3
Host: www.w3.org
```

The easiest way to do this is to paste this code into the text editor of your choice, manipulate it to your liking, and then paste it in one fell swoop at the console. In response to your request, the Web server will spit out an appropriate Web page, which you should be able to see in your telnet session.

You would not be dense if you struggled to see how this protocol could be anything but stateless — at the time of a given request, the server, after all, is completely unaware of what went on during a previous request.

This approach causes problems because although the Web server sees a user's requests as stateless, the user does not. The user remembers perfectly well what was done at the time of the last page requested and expects (rather reasonably) the Web server to do the same. A particularly good example of this is when a username and password are required to access a particular page resource. The user expects to enter this information once and only once. The application should remember the details and not ask for them again, should the user need to request a similarly restricted page on the site.

After all, this is generally how computers have worked for decades. Mirroring this functionality in your Web applications is vital for the sake of your users' collective sanity.

In the early days of the Web, this functionality was sometimes provided by the server's checking of the remote IP address of the connecting user against a database. When the user first logged in, the IP address was recorded, and subsequent requests (within a given time frame) from that IP were assumed to have come from the same user.

This was fine in an Internet with no firewalls, Network Address Translation (NAT), proxy servers, or other such pesky intrusions. Today's Internet is quite different, of course. Some consumer ISPs will actually present completely different external proxy server addresses with each request a user makes to your Web site — a side effect of their own proxy load-balancing technology.

Another common solution to the problem is to use HTTP authentication, which does not depend on a consistent IP address from request to request. If you've ever visited a Web site and been presented with a box that looks something like what is shown in Figure 12-1, then you've met HTTP authentication.

Figure 12-1: HTTP authentication dialog box

Provided from the very early days of the Web, HTTP authentication allows certain files and directories on Web servers to be restricted to a group of users. Traditionally, this user list was a simple plain-text file containing pairs of usernames and (barely) encrypted passwords; but recent advances have enabled Apache to directly consult a MySQL database for this information.

This method works well, and after you have issued a username and password for a given directory on a Web server, any subsequent requests to files in that directory or its subdirectories (whatever they may be) will be automatically presented to the Web server alongside that username and password.

This method is of little use when building PHP applications, however. It is rare to want to protect specific scripts, or even directories. Far more likely is the need to restrict functionality delineated in some way that is recognized and understood in PHP, but not necessarily in Apache. Even though replicating the HTTP headers required to emulate this functionality from within PHP itself is feasible, it's rarely desirable, for a number of reasons:

❑ You have almost no control over the appearance of this box, so it's not exactly a user-friendly approach.

❑ You can't ask for any other information (for example, to pose a security question such as "What is your mother's maiden name?")

❑ You can't store any information against the request other than the identity to which the user has logged in.

The list goes on. Thankfully, a third and far more desirable solution is available, and that is to use sessions.

Definition of a Session

Strictly speaking, a *session* is defined as a series of consecutive HTTP requests made at designated time intervals by a single user from a single computer on a single Web application.

The general methodology behind sessions is that the *first* request made by a user will generate a new session, should one not yet exist. Subsequent requests are considered to be *part* of that session, unless they are made outside some arbitrary time period (the *session timeout* period).

There is, therefore, a verifiable relationship between sessions and requests. Many requests can yield a single session, so a single session can belong to many requests. It's a one-to-many relationship, thinking in database terms. You'll see quite shortly that you can encapsulate this quite neatly in a class hierarchy.

A session is normally used to determine the currently connected user of an application, if any. After a user has successfully logged in for the first time, the application's database should record the user's user ID against that session, such that any subsequent requests proffering that session are understood to have been made by that user and no other.

The real meat of a session is the *session identifier*. This uniquely identifies the session, which may exist concurrently with hundreds of other user sessions. When a session ID is generated and sent to the client for the first time, it is important for the session identifier to be both unique and obscure enough that another, valid session ID could not easily be "invented" by a potentially hostile third party. For example, although issuing session numbers 1, 2, 3, 4, and so on, would certainly satisfy the requirement for uniqueness, it fails to satisfy the security side of the requirement, because a user who has been allocated session number 3 could simply suddenly claim to be session number 4 and potentially gain access to another user's account as a result.

Session identifiers are more often than not 32-character strings consisting of numbers and letters. This is how PHP's built-in session handling (discussed later in the chapter) generates session identifiers. The stumbling of one user across a valid session ID of another is unlikely, therefore, except through brute force — and later in this chapter you'll learn about a couple of easy ways to stop that from happening, too.

Perpetuation of a Session

With the first of the user's requests made and a session identifier generated for that request, you are faced with the challenge of ensuring that the session identifier in question is perpetuated with each subsequent request.

There are two ways to do this: URL rewriting and cookies. A good way to begin is to look at the principles of these without getting bogged down just yet in how PHP's own session handling works.

URL Rewriting

This is the simplest form of session perpetuation. It involves ensuring that every single link, form target, and JavaScript relocation is doctored to include the session identifier as a GET or POST parameter, as appropriate.

Consider the following example. Assume for the sake of argument that PHP has decided upon the following session identifier:

```
abcde1234567890abcde1234567890ab
```

Say that you want this session identifier to be issued with every subsequent request by the Web browser. Wherever you have anchor links in your HTML, you must arrange for PHP to doctor them so that

```
<A href="mybasket.php">Go to my basket</A>
```

becomes

```
<A href="mybasket.php?session_id=abcde1234567890abcde1234567890ab
">Go to my basket</A>
```

Obviously, you would not hard-code this into your HTML. Rather, you would work out some clever way to infuse your HTML on-the-fly with such session identifiers, probably using regular expressions.

It would also be necessary for PHP to doctor form targets, so that

```
<FORM method="POST" action="mybasket.php">
```

becomes

```
<FORM method="POST" action="mybasket.php">
<INPUT type="HIDDEN" name="session_id" value="abcde1234567890abcde1234567890ab">
```

Your PHP would even need to update any JavaScript you might have, to make

```
window.location.replace("index.php")
```

become

```
window.location.replace("index.php?session_id=abcde1234567890abcde1234567890ab")
```

Indeed, there may well be rare cases of URLs being missed and, consequently, the session lost. The really unpleasant part about URL rewriting is that if you lose the session on one request, it's lost forever, so thoroughness is essential; but this is not the only pitfall.

How do you bookmark pages in this way? If you bookmark the page you're on, you'll also record the session identifier, and this won't be valid next time you log in. Therefore, you have to manually scrub out the session identifier when you bookmark.

The biggest and most prevalent pitfall comes when people try to copy and paste links to their friends and colleagues. Joe User simply will not think to strip out the session identifier before he e-mails or instant messages a link to a page on your site to his friends, or sticks it on his Facebook page. As a result, when his friend clicks the link, one of two things will happen, depending on the level of security you've implemented. Either the friend will gain full access to the user's original login, or the system will freak out at a potential security breach because the user is claiming to be the rightful owner of a valid session without presenting other credentials associated with that session.

There is a better way, but it's not without its share of (largely unwarranted) controversy — using cookies.

Cookies

Although URL rewriting is (theoretically speaking) the simplest form of session perpetuation, using cookies is even simpler in terms of the amount of code required.

Cookies are little nuggets of information sent by a Web browser along with the HTML output of a page. The Web browser is instructed to record that information and then volunteer it with every subsequent request made to that Web server.

Much the same as variables, cookies have a name and a value. Some also have a validity (how long it lasts) and a scope (which server or servers should receive it). With each request to the Web server, the user's Web browser offers the name and value of any cookies within the scope of that Web server's domain that have yet to expire. Expired cookies are deleted automatically by the Web browser, but live cookies can also be instantly deleted by the Web server if necessary.

The implementation is simple. As with the previous example, assume that the session identifier is as follows:

```
abcde1234567890abcde1234567890ab
```

With the first request made by the user's Web browser in a session, this session identifier must be pushed to the user's Web browser so that the Web browser knows to offer it on subsequent requests. Accordingly, a cookie is sent to the user's Web browser instructing it to save the value `abcde1234567890abcde1234567890ab` to an appropriately named identifier.

With each subsequent request made to the Web server, PHP looks for a cookie offering a valid session identifier, with that validity remaining to be checked against some external set of rules and/or a database of valid sessions. If a valid session identifier has been offered as part of the cookies sent by the Web browser, PHP can assume this to be the correct session identifier and proceed with the script as normal. If none is offered, or that which is offered is deemed to be invalid, then a new session identifier is generated and, in turn, sent as a cookie, as in the previous step.

This cycle continues from request to request throughout the remainder of the user's session.

For the name for your cookie, you should stick with something easily identifiable such as `session_id`. The scope should be restricted to your own Web server (or, in a pinch, domain), and the validity equal to the maximum dwell time you think users will need on your site. For example, if you don't think a typical user will ever use the site for more than half an hour, setting a validity period of 30 minutes isn't a bad idea.

Historically, there has been controversy surrounding the privacy of the use of cookies. The bulk of that controversy has arisen from a mixture of the ignorance of those detractors, some instances of extraordinarily poor site design (often by agencies and brands that should know better), and perhaps some commercially unscrupulous site operators.

Despite the controversy, there is absolutely no reason for any user to fear a simple session identifier being issued through a cookie. However, do ensure that you restrict the scope of the cookie to your server and your server only, so that it is not inadvertently sent to any other sites that may attempt to use it for tracking purposes. In addition, it makes sense to post a clear and concise privacy policy on your Web site that explains to your users the purpose of the cookies you use, and the steps you have taken to safeguard users' privacy and security.

In addition, remember that cookies should only be used to store session identifiers, and never any data associated with that session. Such data, held on your server, is properly secured and kept away from prying eyes. A session identifier is meaningless outside the context of your application, so it puts little at risk. It's a bit like losing your house key. If you were dumb enough to attach a tag with your address to it, then you'd better get your locks changed pretty quickly. If you didn't, you have nothing to worry about.

Despite all this, some potential pitfalls do exist, as the next section explains.

Session Security

Is a session identifier really secure in itself? There are certainly a few risks associated with using session identifiers as the sole means of identifying logged-in users on your site, but, mercifully, there are countermeasures you can take to help minimize those risks.

Guessing at Valid Sessions

If a malicious visitor to your site happens to fashion a valid session identifier, he or she can hijack the session of another visitor. After all, if user A is making request after request using session identifier X, and then malicious user B comes along and uses session identifier X to make a request as well, your Web site will assume that user B is user A, and user B will have access to everything user A has access to, potentially exposing sensitive information.

For this scenario to be realized, the potential hacker needs to guess at a valid session identifier. How feasible is doing so in a real-world situation?

Consider your 32-character hexadecimal string. This could be generated in any number of ways, but assume that it is largely random. With 32 bytes, and 16 possible characters for each byte (a through f, and 0 through 9), you have 16^{32} possible combinations for your session identifier. That's a big number — too big to print here. It would take an awfully long time for a potential hacker to cycle through all possible session identifiers — 00000000000000000000000000000000, 00000000000000000000000000000001, 0000000 00000000000000000000000002, and so on, all the way up to ffffffffffffffffffffffffffffffff. Even if you could manage to test 100 per second by using multiple computers, it would take you 107,902,830,708,060,141,88 9,705,291,549 years. The Arizona Cardinals might have won the Super Bowl by then.

However, what if the identifier were not just random hexadecimal digits, but an MD5 serialization of a 10-digit number? If the hacker actually knew this fact, there would only be 10,000,000,000 combinations to cycle through, given that the MD5 hash of any given number is a constant answer. It would be a very trivial matter to knock up a script (perhaps even in PHP) to try an MD5 serialization of each number on a loop until it struck one that actually worked.

Consider what might happen if the user requested an "update my details" page (`mydetails.php`). This page behaves in one of two ways, depending on whether a valid session was issued with the request:

❑ If a valid session is issued and the session is known to be logged in, then the page displays the user's details, and allows the user to reset his or her password (among other things).

❑ If a valid session is not issued, then the page issues a 302 redirect to a login page (with a view that, once the correct username and password is given, a session is issued, and the user permitted to update his or her details as originally planned).

The mischievous script would have to iterate through these 10 billion combinations while making an HTTP request to `mydetails.php` with each one. If it gets a 302 redirect, it ignores it and moves on. If it gets the contents of the "my details" page, it resets the user's password to 12345 by submitting the form on the page, making a note of the username, and moving on to the next session.

Leave this running for a few weeks, and it can absolutely be guaranteed that the script would have chanced upon a few valid sessions during its run. It may even have alerted the hacker via e-mail or an SMS text message when it struck a user account whose password it managed to reset. Keep in mind that with a fast connection (and the ability to run multiple instances of this script across multiple servers), a really determined hacker can get through many thousands of session identifiers every second.

If the hacker *didn't* know how your session identifiers were formed, you would be fairly safe. Using a random number between two limits is a pretty bad idea, however, even if the hacker didn't know what those limits were. It would be a simple matter to write a script to bombard your site with cookie-less requests, each of which would generate a new session. Soon enough, the laws of probability would dictate that your hacker would be furnished with a complete database of all feasible MD5-encoded session identifiers (all 10 billion, in the previous example). The hacker wouldn't be able to reverse-engineer these to work out how they were formed, but doing so isn't necessary. The hacker can simply feed the list of pre-hashed identifiers into his or her brute-force script — something known as a *dictionary attack*.

The only way to prevent such analysis is to ensure that sessions are *single use*. This means that the same session identifier will never be generated twice, or at least not within a considerable time span of its first generation. A good way to do this is to construct your session identifier based on a combination of a random number *and* the current timestamp. That way, any script constructed to fish for a complete database of session identifiers will be practically useless, because its database of valid session identifiers will (theoretically) grow to near-infinity.

Obliterating Session Guessing

One simple way to completely obliterate session guessing is to send as a second cookie a *supplemental key* alongside the session identifier. This key would be completely random and generated at the time the session is formed. There would be no obvious link between the two. The key associated with that session would be stored in the database.

With each request, both the session identifier cookie and the session key cookie would be transmitted. Even if the session offered is valid, PHP would still check that the key transmitted matches the key originally issued and, if not, immediately cancel and invalidate the session. By canceling the session offered, any attempt to force further possible combinations of key against that session would be pointless, because the first wrong key issued would invalidate that session anyway. The only downside to this approach is that your legitimately logged-in user would be logged out as the session was cancelled, but it's better to be inconvenienced and safe than hacked.

For true randomness when generating such keys, try to avoid using any kind of randomization whose seed is based on the system clock. Using truly random seeds such as processor temperature, server process identifiers, and network interface statistics produce a more satisfactory random number. Sequential digits of pi also work well, provided you never use the same digit again.

Discovery of Valid Sessions

Discovery of valid sessions is a less prominent threat, but a more difficult one to protect against. Essentially, the risk is that a malicious third party can somehow gain access to the cookies on your legitimate user's machine, and use them to gain access to the user's session.

Unfortunately, this technique is not immune to the session key methodology discussed previously. If a hacker can gain access to the session cookie, the secondary key cookie is just as easily obtainable.

There are a few scenarios in which this could happen:

❏ A session cookie is "mis-issued" by your site so that its scope is broader than it needs to be. A malicious Web site within that overly broad scope then visited by the user would be made privy to that session cookie, too. The operators of that site could then use the cookie to hijack your session on the original site. The user does not even necessarily have to visit a malicious site. Literally millions of pieces of HTML spam e-mail every day are sent out containing images, the purpose of which is simply to cause its recipient to make a Web request, with the hope that session cookies from other poorly constructed sites will be offered accidentally.

❏ A physical intrusion to the machine could allow access to the cookies stored on it, from which data on valid sessions could be extracted.

❏ An intrusion to the machine that somehow modifies the HOSTS file could redirect traffic supposedly for your site's hostname to a third-party site. This third-party site may even relay the genuine data from your Web server, such that the user is none the wiser. It would, crucially, collect the session identifier for later use.

❏ A poorly configured network could allow session identifiers to be sniffed in HTTP traffic by malicious systems administrators on-site.

❑ A malicious employee of an ISP that employs proxy servers (transparent or otherwise) could easily enable transmitted session identifiers to be logged.

The first of these scenarios is easy to overcome. When issuing cookies from your site, always get the scope correct — same hostname, same protocol (HTTP or HTTPS), and same directory. This most basic of errors is exploited with such frequency only because of the frequency with which it is made in the first place.

A physical intrusion is almost impossible to guard against. Any physical exploitation is attributable more to lackluster physical security of the location from which the site is being accessed than to anything else. Good session practice (see the following section) can help minimize the risk of this kind of occurrence.

Another major problem is the modification of the HOSTS file of a machine allowing name servers to be overridden transparently. It is remarkable there are not more e-mail worms in circulation that exploit this, but it is only a matter of time. The HOSTS file exists on almost every variant of Windows imaginable, and on Mac OS X and other UNIX platforms, too. Unless a tight local administration rights policy has been set up, users can modify it themselves. An e-mail worm distributed as an attachment (as are most modern worms) exploiting this vulnerability would work as follows:

1. The user regularly visits www.myfictionalbank.com to use an online checking account management facility. This resolves to 10.123.123.123.

2. An attachment (which might be .vbs, .scr, .pif or any of the other numerous file extensions that still aren't universally blocked by e-mail clients) has a viral payload that creates an entry in your HOSTS file pointing to a malicious foreign IP address, which is actually a server owned by the hacker. The IP address is 192.168.123.123, and is probably located somewhere in Eastern Europe.

3. The next time the user logs into his or her online banking account, he or she enters www.myfictionalbank.com and appears to get the account login page as normal. In fact, the connection is being made to the malicious Web server. The malicious server, in turn, makes a real-time HTTP connection to the real bank's Web server and mirrors every request made by the user, as if a marionette. It retransmits all the data returned by the real bank's Web server. The only data not relayed back in this way is that generated when the user's session details (immediately after login) are instantly recorded by the malicious relay server, which then seizes control of the session, denying the real user any further access. In just a few seconds, several thousands of dollars of the user's hard-earned cash are on their way to Eastern Europe.

Of course, a scam like this wouldn't last long. The bank would get wind of it pretty quickly and block off the malicious server's IP address, or take other steps to make such a scam impossible; but it does serve to illustrate just how easily this kind of attack can be pulled off.

On-site exploitation is as big a threat as exploitation from Eastern Europe, particularly in big companies. Many corporate networks may be switched at their most central point, but when floor socket availability starts to get tight, most systems administrators slap in a hub. It's cheap and quick, and the two PCs on that hub can immediately sniff each other's traffic. If a savvy user is on the same hub as a colleague whose session the user wishes to seize, some simple traffic-sniffing software can retrieve those session identifiers.

Finally, keep in mind that many ISPs these days use transparent proxy servers. That is, all HTTP traffic is intercepted and relayed through a standard proxy server without the user's explicit knowledge (and without any kind of configuration required on the user's part). Ostensibly, this is to improve performance by caching commonly requested pages and images at the ISP so that they are only one hop away from the user. The more genuine reason is that ISPs are under increasing pressure in the current climate to maintain very detailed logs of the behavior of their customers on the Web. This is not for commercial reasons, but rather for the purpose of handing over this information to law enforcement agencies should they demand it. The potential for abuse of this facility is quite obvious. If cookies are logged, seizing them is a simple matter for a bored systems administrator.

Good Session Practice

As you have seen, physically obtaining the session identifier (and session key, if available) is very difficult to guard against. The most effective barriers to such exploitation are physical, political, or economic in nature. They certainly have nothing to do with PHP.

Nonetheless, you can do a few neat things in your code should you wish to minimize the risk of these theoretical exploits being put into practice.

Use Session Timeouts

First and foremost, use session timeouts. These are *not* the same as session expiration times. When issuing a cookie to a user, you will almost certainly give it an expiration time, but this does not guard against the user walking away from his or her computer and forgetting to log out. Using session timeouts involves recording the timestamp of each request against the session and then, with each subsequent request made against that session, measuring the time elapsed since the last request. If it exceeds five or ten minutes, you would be *strongly* advised to revoke the session and request the user to log in again.

This is a remarkably effective measure. Many of the attacks described earlier rely on being able to make use of a session perhaps only some moments after the user has finished with it. By reducing the window of opportunity to just a few minutes, you reduce the effectiveness of those attacks.

The implementation of session timeouts has nothing to do with cookies. Rather, the code you implement to handle sessions has responsibility for measuring the time elapsed between requests, and determining when to revoke a session because of a timeout. Later in this chapter, you'll find out about the HTTPSession class, which can do just that.

Use Low Expiry Times

Having a low expiration time in your session cookie does make sense. Users don't mind being asked to log in again occasionally, so setting an expiration time of an hour or so is fine. If you do this, be sure to build the rest of your application so that the interruption to the user is minimal. For example, if you are building a Webmail application, don't instruct your code to arbitrarily end a user's session if he or she is in the middle of sending out an e-mail message. Try to design sympathetically.

As mentioned previously, you will see how to effectively implement a low cookie expiration time later in this chapter.

Check User Agent Consistency

One simple check you can make involves recording the user's Web browser user agent against the session. This is the string issued by the Web browser identifying the manufacturer, browser name, version, and platform. It is by no means unique to that computer, but there are so many different browsers and browser versions in use that there is a strong chance that any two computers produce slightly different user agent strings.

By ensuring that subsequent requests against a session carry the same user agent as the original request, you provide an additional line of defense against session hijacking. Interestingly, the user agent string that Internet Explorer produces can be modified in the Windows registry. System administrators can take advantage of this fact by making their network's workstations have organization-specific user agent strings. This further strengthens the usefulness of this security mechanism.

Don't Be Afraid to Ask Users to Log in Again

If you're about to let the user place an order, or view and update his or her details, don't be afraid to ask for the username and password again. That way, should a hacker succeed in taking over a session, the damage that can be done will be limited to some degree. Many large commercial sites employ this practice, and the user will not be too irritated with this request if it is used judiciously.

Watch for Unusual Traffic

If you're feeling particularly brave, you could construct some algorithms to watch for unusual traffic against a particular session in order to determine multiple usage. How you define "unusual traffic" is open to debate, but you could, for example, raise an alarm if more than one request is made in any one-second period, and cancel the session as a result. Alternatively, you could map the physical navigation of your site to likely user paths, and ensure that the requests made by the user's session are following one of those paths.

For example, on an e-commerce site, should the user request the index of a particular product category with one request, it is exceedingly unlikely that he or she would then immediately select the View Product page for a product that falls *outside* that category. To do that, he or she must have accessed it from a bookmark or third-party link, or have typed in the URL. However, if your algorithms are not rock-solid, the false-positives rate could easily start to disgruntle your users.

Watch for Bizarre IP Address Variance

Although it is not legitimate to determine the validity of a session based on the consistency of the IP address, it is still possible to detect some possible break-in attempts by keeping an eye on its variance. Load-balancing proxy servers are likely to change the IP address with each request, but by how much? It is incredibly unlikely that anything but the last two octets would change. Certainly, the request would most definitely remain within the same net block (that is, the owner of the block would be consistent from request to request). An excellent way to check this is to consult RIPE, ARIN, and so on, in real time.

In your application, you would simply devise a low-overhead means of checking the net block owner, utilizing some kind of caching technology, if possible. If requests of the same session seem to be coming from different owners, it's worth raising the alarm and destroying the session.

Avoiding Storing Session Variables on the Client Side

One obvious benefit of sessions is the capability to associate the value of relevant variables to a session. These variables could be the contents of a shopping basket, or the population of a search form, for example.

Nevertheless, storing this information on the client side is best avoided. For one thing, this can get privacy activists very upset. For another, the value of those variables is open to modification outside the control of your code (either malicious or accidental).

Pumping that much data upstream with each HTTP request can be quite inefficient. Keep in mind that most broadband connections are asymmetric, meaning that they upload slower than they download. Therefore, if you are storing 16KB worth of session variables on the client side, that will add a second or so to each request. That may not sound like much, but it can quickly drive users crazy, so using cookies in this manner is not good practice.

All you need to store on the client side is the session identifier (and supplemental security key, if used). Store everything else on the server side somewhere, out of harm's reach, and associate those variables with the session identifier in question.

Consider Using a Second Security Factor

Some retail banks have started employing two-factor authentication for parts of their consumer online banking operations. This second factor usually takes the form of a smart card reader and a card issued to the customer by mail.

While most online banking operations can be undertaken without it (to limit inconvenience), certain crucial activities (usually, transferring money to a brand-new recipient) requires the entry of a one-time-use code generated by the card reader. This ensures that the operator of the bank has possession of the card reader itself. In many of the circumstances described earlier, this would be unlikely; hence, the opportunity for fraud is greatly reduced with only minimal inconvenience to the end user.

The lesson of this part of the chapter is that 100 percent security is always just out of reach. However, there are always steps you can take to minimize your own exposure.

How PHP Implements Sessions

PHP enables you to implement a highly effective session-management infrastructure in your applications, but you must do a lot of the difficult work yourself.

As you'll see in this section, PHP's built-in session handling isn't really appropriate for enterprise-class applications. Luckily, it has been made extensible enough to give you a head start when you're writing your own more robust solution.

Basic PHP Sessions

Enter the following code and save it as `firstpage.php`:

```php
<?php

session_start();
$_SESSION['favorite_artist'] = 'Tori Amos';

?>
Currently, my favorite artist is Tori Amos. It may also interest you to
know that my identifier for this browser session, as allocated by PHP, is
<?=session_id()?>.
<BR><BR>
<A href="secondpage.php">Go to the second page</A>
```

Now start a brand-new bit of code. Call this `secondpage.php`:

```php
<?php

session_start();

?>Having checked, I can tell you that my favorite artist is still
<?=$_SESSION['favorite_artist']?>. At the moment, my identifier for this
browser session, as allocated by PHP, is <?=session_id()?>.
<BR><BR>
<A href="firstpage.php">Go back to the first page</A>
```

Run the first of these and you should get some predictable output. Let's say that your favorite artist is Tori Amos, and PHP has given you a session identifier, as shown in the following output:

```
Currently, my favorite artist is Tori Amos. It may also interest you to know that
my identifier for this browser session, as allocated by PHP, is
balq167m1gor56oqjlc5e1dca2.
Go to the second page
```

You can see that the session identifier is 26 characters in length. PHP actually uses the full alphabet, as well as 0–9. This increases the number of possible session identifiers to 36^{26}. If you click the link to take you to the second page, you should see something that looks like this:

```
Having checked, I can tell you that my favorite artist is still Tori Amos. At the
moment, my identifier for this browser session, as allocated by PHP is
balq167m1gor56oqjlc5e1dca2.
Go back to the first page
```

Note two important things here. The session identifier is the same, and the second script seems to have remembered your musical preferences.

This result is obtained in a straightforward manner. First, use `session_start()` to tell PHP to enable sessions, well before the first character of HTML of the script. Using `session_start()` is important, because the session data sent to the Web browser must go in the HTTP headers, and the first use of any HTML (or even whitespace) precludes this from happening.

Second, register a session variable by adding to the `$_SESSION` global associative array (or *hash*). This can be placed anywhere in the script because it won't send anything to the Web browser. It just makes a note on the server side, as you will see shortly.

On the second page, call `session_start()` just as you did on the first to enable session management, but now you can read from `$_SESSION` just as you wrote to it on the first page. Lo and behold, the value `Tori Amos` has been successfully retained from one page to the next. This value has been inextricably associated with the session identifier, which explains why the server remembered it.

How does PHP remember the session identifier from the first page to the second? Take a look on your server in `/tmp`. Perform a directory listing using `ls` for all files starting with `sess_` (the word *sess* followed by an underscore):

```
$ cd /tmp
$ ls -la sess_*
```

It is hoped that you'll see a directory listing that looks something like this:

```
-rw-r--r-- 1 nobody users 33 2008-08-17 15:23 sess_balq167m1gor56oqjlc5e1dca2
```

Notice a file called `sess_`, followed by the session ID you were allocated in the previous example. Open it using the editor of your choice:

```
pico -w sess_balq167m1gor56oqjlc5e1dca2
```

You should see something that looks like this:

```
favorite_artist|s:9:"Tori Amos";
```

For those in Windows, PHP sessions are most likely to be stored in `C:\TEMP`, but it depends on how you have configured PHP and Apache (or your Web server of choice). If you can't find any, you can use Windows' built-in search functionality to find files beginning with `sess_` (session, and an underscore). Don't forget to include hidden files and folders. You can then open the session (once found) using Notepad or a similar text editor.

The output of the session file looks quite straightforward. It is hoped that you noticed the session variable you created and its contents in plain text in a simple "key-value" pair.

In fact, the format of what's on display might look eerily familiar. It's the output from the PHP function `serialize()`, a string representation of a PHP data structure.

Regardless of the complexity or size of the data structure you create in the `$_SESSION` variable, PHP will store its contents in this file by default. The location for storing such files, as well as how long they are stored, are all settings that can be altered in `php.ini`.

That's really all there is to native PHP sessions. Let's look now at some of their limitations to see why they can't be used in an enterprise environment.

Limitations of Basic PHP Sessions

There are a few key problems with implementing sessions in this manner, most of which relate to the way in which PHP stores its session data on disk.

What if you have multiple Web servers servicing your request with a load-balancer appliance round-robin dividing traffic between them? You would have to implement some kind of shared /tmp using NFS, which would be dreadfully slow.

Second, if you're running on a shared Web server (with a hosting company, for example), the directory listing of /tmp is readable by all, even if the contents of its files are not. Given that PHP uses the session identifiers as part of the filename, a malicious fellow user on that Web server could quite easily get a full listing of all the session identifiers created, as well as when they were created. This would once again open the door for easy session hijacks, as discussed earlier.

Third, this implementation of session handling is not very secure. Not one of the additional measures discussed earlier is employed for additional security, nor is it easily possible to employ them in this state. Therefore, as far as a secure environment for a production Web site using sessions is concerned, PHP session handling in its off-the-shelf state isn't really a viable option.

The fourth limitation is speed. By storing session data on disk, it becomes necessary for PHP to read and write to the disk with virtually every request. This can keep the disk very busy (unnecessarily busy, in fact), and slow down requests for all involved. Thus, the level of traffic that a single server can sustain is reduced, potentially increasing your exposure to higher hardware budgets.

Finally, given that you store the rest of your application's data in a database, you are bound to have times when you need to construct queries that consult both session variables and database tables in tandem. With session data totally exterior to the database, you must first extract that data using PHP and then inject it into an SQL statement. Serious performance implications are associated with this approach when compared to conducting a single SQL query to extract the data you need. On a production server, for example, this could become quite a serious issue. The solution to this problem is to integrate the PHP session management with a database.

Creating an Authentication Class

In the final part of this chapter, you'll learn how to adapt PHP's session-handling technology to talk to a PostgreSQL database, which will be used to store the session data hitherto stored on disk. At the same time, you'll put together a class to handle user authentication that you should be able to reuse on any project.

Connecting PHP Session Management to a Database

Getting PHP to use a database as opposed to the server's disk to store its data is far easier than you might expect. The following examples use PostgreSQL, but this method can easily be adapted to work with MySQL, XML flat files, or whatever you prefer.

The key to all this is just one PHP function: `session_set_save_handler`. If you take a look at the PHP manual reference entry for the function, you can see its syntax quite clearly:

```
bool session_set_save_handler ( string open, string close, string
read, string write, string destroy, string gc)
```

The idea is simple. You call this function *before* `session_start()` is used on any page that employs sessions. The function instructs PHP as to which custom functions to call when certain session behavior takes place (such as when a session is started, finished, read to, written from, or destroyed). There are certain requirements regarding the parameters passed into these methods, as well as the value they must return. These are outlined in some detail on the PHP manual page for `session_set_save_handler`, but the following sections cover the basics.

The open() Function

The `open()` function is called whenever `session_start()` is called. PHP passes two values: the path in which it thinks the session should be stored if it is to be saved on disk (which can be ignored for the purposes of this discussion) and the cookie name (for example, `PHPSESSID`) it is using for the session. It needs to return a `true` value in order for the session to be regarded by PHP as having been successfully created.

The close() Function

The `close()` function (not to be confused with the `destroy()` function) is called at what is effectively the end of the execution of any PHP script that uses session handling. For your purposes, it need do nothing other than return a `true` value, although it might be nice to close its database connection if it isn't going to be used anymore. In most production environments, you'll be using a globally accessible handle to a database that's already open for other purposes, so you'll no doubt have code in place to close it down again at the end of the script anyway. In practice, therefore, all this function needs to return is a `true` value.

The read() Function

The `read()` function is used whenever an attempt to retrieve a variable from the `$_SESSION` hash is made. It takes the session identifier as its sole operand, and expects a serialized representation of `$_SESSION` in its entirety to be returned. You won't actually be using this in your class because you'll be doing your own session variable handling.

The write() Function

The `write()` function is used whenever an attempt to change or add to `$_SESSION` is made. It takes the session identifier, followed by the preserialized representation of `$_SESSION`, as its two parameters. It expects `true` to be returned if the data is successfully committed. This method is called even if no session variables are registered, and it is the first time the generated session ID is revealed to you.

The destroy() Function

The `destroy()` function is called whenever the `session_destroy` function is used in code. It must return `true` upon execution.

The gc() Function

The `gc()` (garbage cleanup) function should be able to accept the "maximum lifetime of session cookies" parameter as its only operand and get rid of any sessions older than that lifetime. It should return `true` when it's done. This function appears to be called just before `open()` so that PHP rids itself of any expired sessions before they may be used.

Introducing the HTTPSession Class

The `HTTPSession` class is a convenient way of implementing an object-oriented approach to session management, as well as providing basic authentication methods for your applications. Here, you will implement your own methods to replace those of PHP, using the `session_set_save_handler()` method discussed previously.

It will be an entirely self-contained class that hides all of PHP's `session_` functions from your application's main body.

It also provides session variable handling, which bypasses PHP's own. Rather than store multiple variables in a single serialized hash, your methodology will use separate table rows for each variable. This could speed up access immensely. Note, however, that the previous session-handling instruction method was not designed to cope with class methods, so you have to be rather cunning in your implementation.

Database Schema

The class depends upon three tables existing. The SQL (PostgreSQL flavor) to recreate these tables is in the following code. Create a new database with these tables in them before you go any further.

You can customize the `user` table to suit your needs. You will probably want to store more than just first name and last name. Note that a column called `last_impression` has been included, too. This is used to store the time and date when the user last made an impression (that is, requested a page) against his or her session. This is used to calculate session timeouts.

```
CREATE TABLE http_session (
 "id" SERIAL PRIMARY KEY NOT NULL,
 "ascii_session_id" character varying(32),
 "logged_in" bool,
 "user_id" int4,
 "last_impression" timestamp,
 "created" timestamp,
 "user_agent" character varying(256)
);

CREATE TABLE "user" (
 "id" SERIAL PRIMARY KEY NOT NULL,
 "username" character varying(32),
 "md5_pw" character varying(32),
 "first_name" character varying(64),
 "last_name" character varying(64)
);
```

```
CREATE TABLE "session_variable" (
 "id" SERIAL PRIMARY KEY NOT NULL,
 "session_id" int4,
 "variable_name" character varying(64),
 "variable_value" text
);
```

As you can see, the sessions are stored as indexed by a standard serial ID, rather than by their PHP-generated session ID. This enables far faster indexing when you look at session variables (numbers always index better than strings).

It's worth creating a test user at this stage (e.g., username 'ed', password '12345'). You need to know the MD5 representation of this password to enter it into the database. Of course, in the real world, you'd have an application to do this, but for now here's the SQL you need to make the examples that follow work:

```
INSERT INTO "user"(username,md5_pw,first_name,last_name) VALUES
('ed','827ccb0eea8a706c4c34a16891f84e7b', 'Ed', 'Lecky-Thompson');
```

First, take a look at the complete code for the class `HTTPSession.phpm`. Don't worry. You'll go through it all, including how to tell `session_set_save_handler` to use class methods, right after you've tried it.

The Code: HTTPSession.phpm

Remember that you use the `phpm` extension to explicitly signify this as a class, rather than a template or an executable script in its own right.

Note that the long SQL statements in this class must be entered *on one line*; they must not wrap onto multiple lines. If you use the code available on www.wrox.com, you won't have a problem.

```php
<?php
  class HTTPSession {
    private $php_session_id;
    private $native_session_id;
    private $dbhandle;
    private $logged_in;
    private $user_id;
    private $session_timeout = 600;      # 10 minute inactivity timeout
    private $session_lifespan = 3600;    # 1 hour session duration

    public function __construct() {
      # Connect to database
      $this->dbhandle = pg_connect("host=db dbname=prophp6 user=ed")  or die
        ("PostgreSQL error:--> " . pg_last_error($this->dbhandle));
      # Set up the handler
      session_set_save_handler(
          array(&$this, '_session_open_method'),
          array(&$this, '_session_close_method'),
```

```
            array(&$this, '_session_read_method'),
            array(&$this, '_session_write_method'),
            array(&$this, '_session_destroy_method'),
            array(&$this, '_session_gc_method')
        );
        # Check the cookie passed - if one is - if it looks wrong we'll
        # scrub it right away
        $strUserAgent = $_SERVER["HTTP_USER_AGENT"];
        if ($_COOKIE["PHPSESSID"]) {
         # Security and age check
         $this->php_session_id = $_COOKIE["PHPSESSID"];
         $stmt = "select id from \"http_session\" where ascii_session_id =
'" . $this->php_session_id . "' AND ((now() - created) < ' " .
            $strUserAgent .$this->session_lifespan . " seconds') AND
            user_agent='" . "' AND ((now() - last_impression) <=
'".$this->session_timeout." seconds'
            OR last_impression IS NULL)";

         $result = pg_query($stmt);
         if (pg_num_rows($result)==0) {
             # Set failed flag
             $failed = 1;
             # Delete from database - we do garbage cleanup at the same time
             $maxlifetime = $this->session_lifespan;
             $result = pg_query("DELETE FROM \"http_session\"
               WHERE (ascii_session_id =
'". $this->php_session_id . "') OR (now() - created
               > '$maxlifetime seconds')");
             # Clean up stray session variables
             $result = pg_query("DELETE FROM \"session_variable\" WHERE
               session_id NOT IN (SELECT id FROM \"http_session\")");
             # Get rid of this one... this will force PHP to give us another
             unset($_COOKIE["PHPSESSID"]);
          };
        };

        # Set the life time for the cookie
        session_set_cookie_params($this->session_lifespan);
        # Call the session_start method to get things started
        session_start();
    }

    public function Impress() {
       if ($this->native_session_id) {
          $result = pg_query("UPDATE \"http_session\" SET last_impression = now()
          WHERE id = " . $this->native_session_id);
       };
    }

    public function IsLoggedIn() {
       return($this->logged_in);
    }
```

```
    public function GetUserID() {
      if ($this->logged_in) {
        return($this->user_id);
      } else {
        return(false);
      };
    }

    public function GetUserObject() {
      if ($this->logged_in) {
        if (class_exists("user")) {
          $objUser = new User($this->user_id);
          return($objUser);
        } else {
          return(false);
        };
      };
    }

    public function GetSessionIdentifier() {
      return($this->php_session_id);
    }

    public function Login($strUsername, $strPlainPassword) {
      $strMD5Password = md5($strPlainPassword);
      $stmt = "select id FROM \"user\" WHERE username = '$strUsername'
               AND md5_pw = '$strMD5Password'";
      $result = pg_query($stmt);
      if (pg_num_rows($result)>0) {
        $row = pg_fetch_array($result);
        $this->user_id = $row["id"];
        $this->logged_in = true;
        $result = pg_query("UPDATE \"http_session\" SET logged_in = true,
                  user_id = " . $this->user_id . " WHERE id = " .
                  $this->native_session_id);
        return(true);
      } else {
        return(false);
      };
    }

    public function LogOut() {
      if ($this->logged_in == true) {
        $result = pg_query("UPDATE \"http_session\" SET logged_in = false,
                  user_id = 0 WHERE id = " . $this->native_session_id);
        $this->logged_in = false;
        $this->user_id = 0;
        return(true);
      } else {
        return(false);
      };
    }
```

```
    public function __get($nm) {
      $result = pg_query("SELECT variable_value FROM session_variable WHERE
            session_id = " . $this->native_session_id . " AND
            variable_name = '" . $nm . "'");
      if (pg_num_rows($result)>0) {
        $row = pg_fetch_array($result);
        return(unserialize($row["variable_value"]));
      } else {
        return(false);
      };
    }

    public function __set($nm, $val) {
      $strSer = serialize($val);
      $stmt = "INSERT INTO session_variable(session_id, variable_name,
            variable_value) VALUES(" . $this->native_session_id .
", '$nm', '$strSer')";
      $result = pg_query($stmt);
    }

      private function _session_open_method($save_path, $session_name) {
      # Do nothing
      return(true);
    }

      private function _session_close_method() {
      pg_close($this->dbhandle);
      return(true);
    }

    public function _session_read_method($id) {
      # We use this to determine whether or not our session actually exists.
      $strUserAgent = $_SERVER["HTTP_USER_AGENT"];
      $this->php_session_id = $id;
      # Set failed flag to 1 for now
      $failed = 1;
      # See if this exists in the database or not.
      $result = pg_query("select id, logged_in, user_id from \"http_session\"
            where ascii_session_id = '$id'");
      if (pg_num_rows($result)>0) {
       $row = pg_fetch_array($result);
       $this->native_session_id = $row["id"];
       if ($row["logged_in"]=="t") {
         $this->logged_in = true;
         $this->user_id = $row["user_id"];
       } else {
         $this->logged_in = false;
       };
      } else {
       $this->logged_in = false;
```

```php
                # We need to create an entry in the database
                $result = pg_query("INSERT INTO http_session(ascii_session_id,
                        logged_in,user_id, created, user_agent) VALUES
                        ('$id','f',0,now(),'$strUserAgent')");
                # Now get the true ID
                $result = pg_query("select id from \"http_session\" where
                        ascii_session_id = '$id'");
                $row = pg_fetch_array($result);
                $this->native_session_id = $row["id"];
            };
            # Just return empty string
            return("");
    }
    public function _session_write_method($id, $sess_data) {
        return(true);
    }

    private function _session_destroy_method($id) {
        $result = pg_query("DELETE FROM \"http_session\" WHERE
                ascii_session_id = '$id'");
        return($result);
    }

    private function _session_gc_method($maxlifetime) {
        return(true);
    }


    }
?>
```

The Code: Testing the HTTPSession Class

Before going through the code, test the class for an imaginary user logging in and out. The following simple script shows the class in action:

```php
<?php
  require_once("HTTPSession.phpm");
  $objSession = new HTTPSession();
  $objSession->Impress();
?>
HTTPSession Test Page
<HR>
<B>Current Session ID: </B> <?=$objSession->GetSessionIdentifier();?><BR>
<B>Logged in? </B> <?=(($objSession->IsLoggedIn() == true) ?
"Yes" : "No")?><BR>
<BR><BR>
Attempting to log in ...
<?php
  $objSession->Login("ed","12345");
?>
<BR><BR>
```

```
<B>Logged in? </B> <?=(($objSession->IsLoggedIn() == true) ?
"Yes" : "No")?><BR>
<B>User ID of logged in user: </B> <?=$objSession->GetUserID();?><BR>

<BR><BR>
Now logging out...
<?php
  $objSession->Logout();
?>

<BR><BR>
<B>Logged in? </B> <?=(($objSession->IsLoggedIn() == true) ?
"Yes" : "No")?><BR>
<BR><BR>
```

After running this, you should see output similar to the following:

```
UserSession Test Page
Current Session ID: 51bd591g054sn3bp2dsur4pme3
Logged in? No

Attempting to log in ...

Logged in? Yes
User ID of logged in user: 1

Now logging out ...
Logged in? No
```

If you click Refresh in your Web browser several times, you should get the same output repeatedly. The session identifier is perpetuated, therefore remaining the same.

If you want to prove to yourself that the logged-in state of the session really is maintained, try commenting out the Logout line (which reads `<?php $objSession->Logout(); ?>`) and clicking Refresh. You should see that the Logged in? statement at the top of the page repeatedly returns Yes.

It's worth looking at the database, too. As soon as the user is logged in successfully, that flag is set against the session in the database table, and remains until either the session itself is deleted or the explicit LogOut method is called:

```
prophp5=# SELECT * FROM http_session ;
 id  |       ascii_session_id    | logged_in | user_id |      last_impression
     |          created          |           |                      user_agent

-----+---------------------------+-----------+---------+----------------------
-----+---------------------------+-----------+------------------------------------

 168 | 51bd591g054sn3bp2dsur4pme3 | f         |       0 |2008-02-23 07:31:04.33
4694 | 2008-02-23 06:54:31.802746 | Mozilla/4.0 (compatible; MSIE 6.0;
Windows NT 5.1; .NET CLR 1.1.4322)
(1 row)
```

Now try the session variable functionality:

```php
<?php
require_once("HTTPSession.phpm");

$objSession = new HTTPSession();
$objSession->Impress();

?>
HTTPSession Variable Test Page
<HR>
<B>Current Session ID: </B> <?=$objSession->GetSessionIdentifier();?><BR>
<B>Logged in? </B> <?=(($objSession->IsLoggedIn() == true) ? "Yes" :
"No")?><BR>
<BR><BR>
<B>Current value of TESTVAR:</B> [<?=$objSession->TESTVAR?>]<BR>
<BR><BR>
Setting TESTVAR to 'foo'
<BR><BR>
<?php
  $objSession->TESTVAR = 'foo';
?>
<B>Current value of TESTVAR:</B> [<?=$objSession->TESTVAR?>]<BR>
<BR><BR>
```

Run this (just once, for now) and you will see something like the following:

```
UserSession Variable Test Page

Current Session ID: 51bd591g054sn3bp2dsur4pme3
Logged in? No

Current value of TESTVAR: []

Setting TESTVAR to 'foo'
Current value of TESTVAR: [foo]
```

Click Refresh and you will see that the value of TESTVAR is perpetuated. The top current value statement will read foo as well:

```
UserSession Variable Test Page

Current Session ID: 51bd591g054sn3bp2dsur4pme3
Logged in? No

Current value of TESTVAR: [foo]

Setting TESTVAR to 'foo'
Current value of TESTVAR: [foo]
```

A quick glance at the `session_variable` table in the database shows what is actually stored:

```
prophp5=# SELECT * FROM session_variable;
 id | session_id | variable_name | variable_value
----+------------+---------------+----------------
  6 |        168 | TESTVAR       | s:3:"foo";
(1 row)
```

As you can see, using serialization to store the data follows PHP. However, unlike PHP, you use a new row for each variable. This enables more than one variable to be stored, separately serialized, against an individual session. With PHP's native session variable handling, all variables are lumped together in a single associative array that is then serialized. This can have very serious performance implications. Serialization and deserialization have a fair amount of overhead, and PHP is not the quickest language in the world when it comes to string processing — that honor probably goes to PERL. With this in mind, the decision is duly made to go against the grain on this occasion.

Clearly, the `HTTPSession` class is incredibly easy to use, but let's take a look at the class itself in more detail, to both understand the logic behind it and be fully equipped to deploy it in production applications.

How the HTTPSession Class Works

Start by looking at the private member variables of the class, shown in Table 12-1.

Table 12-1 Private Member Variables

Variable	Purpose
php_session_id	The 32-character PHP-generated session ID
native_session_id	The native session ID used to identify the session in the database. This is never sent to the Web browser, and is used only for the purpose of database entity relationships.
dbhandle	A database connection handle. In production environments, this would be declared elsewhere as a global resource, and the HTTPSession class would make use of it just like any other.
logged_in	Is this session a logged-in session? If this is true, then a user ID will be available.
user_id	The ID (from the database table) of the currently logged-in user
session_timeout	An inactivity timeout. If a period of time greater than this elapses between reported impressions, then the session is destroyed. Measured in seconds, so 600 = 10 minutes.
session_lifespan	The maximum age of the session. This is given to PHP for the purpose of setting the cookie, and is used in garbage cleaning SQL to keep the database free of dead sessions. Also measured in seconds, so 3600 = 1 hour.

The Constructor

You want your class to be plug-and-play. This enables the programmer to instantiate it once and forget about it.

The constructor does the following:

❑ Sets up the database connection. This would normally be handled by another class in a production environment.

❑ Tells PHP how to handle session events in the custom class (discussed in further detail shortly)

❑ Checks whether an existing session identifier is being offered by the client before PHP has a chance to get its hands on it (which would be the case if the user is in the middle of a session instead of starting a new one). It also performs various checks on age, inactivity, and the consistency of the reported HTTP user agent. If it fails, remove it altogether (and any garbage found) so that PHP can issue a new session from scratch.

❑ Sets up the session lifespan parameter (which PHP will obey when issuing the cookie itself)

❑ Tells PHP to go ahead and start the session in the normal way

Note the interesting syntax used for `session_set_save_handler`:

```
session_set_save_handler(
  array(&$this, '_session_open_method'),
  array(&$this, '_session_close_method'),
  array(&$this, '_session_read_method'),
  array(&$this, '_session_write_method'),
  array(&$this, '_session_destroy_method'),
  array(&$this, '_session_gc_method')
);
```

Although largely undocumented, parameters for this method do not necessarily have to be strings representing procedural function names within current PHP scope.

Instead, you may pass an array of two components. The first is a reference to an instance of a class (in this case, `&$this` refers to this instance of the class). The second is the name of the method of that class.

The session_read_method() Handler

Because the first method called by PHP's own session management after a valid session ID has been decided upon (through generation of a brand-new session or the presentation of a still-valid cookie by the Web browser), you use this method to ensure that the session database is kept fully up-to-date.

If the 32-character session identifier supplied by PHP does exist in the database, then the class member variables (`logged_in` and `user_id`) are updated against the database record. If it does not, then it is inserted with defaults in place.

The Impress() Function

This method touches the session to indicate that a new page impression has taken place. Generally, this method would be called on any page that uses the session class directly after it has been instantiated.

The last impression column in the database is used for determining session timeouts, so it is very important to call this method if you want a given page to count against a user's accrued inactivity timeout.

If you are using any form of an `include()` or `require()` statement at the top of your pages to include a library of code (or, indeed, other `include()` or `require()` statements), you might consider placing the session invocation and impression inside this file. That way, you won't ever forget to include them.

The IsLoggedIn() Function

This method simply reports from the private member variable whether this session has undergone a successful login in its lifespan that has not been rescinded by means of a `logout()`.

The GetUserID() and GetUserObject() Functions

If a user is logged in, then these two functions return, respectively, the ID of the logged-in user (from the user table defined in the database) and, if possible, an instantiated object of the user class, should one exist.

One has not been defined in this chapter because it is slightly outside the scope of session management, but you will almost certainly want to develop one for any serious production application because you will almost certainly frequently want to read and write the properties of your currently logged-in user.

The class assumes that your `User` class (however it works under the hood) is instantiated on the exterior using the user ID as the sole operand of the constructor. Therefore, this would work well with the discussion of `DataBoundObject` in Chapter 7, "Object-Relation Mapping," although you would additionally have to pass an instance of PDO that matches the database credentials used by the class.

The GetSessionIdentifier() Function

This method returns the 32-character PHP session identifier, rather than the internal (database) identifier. This is the property more likely to be used in applications because the internal identifier is only really meaningful to PostgreSQL, and is never exposed to the application or Web browser.

The _get() and _set() Overload Methods

Taking advantage of PHP 6's support for overloading the inspection and assignment of ostensibly public member variables, the overload methods provide their own session variable functionality. Quite simply, a variable for a given session is set by merely assigning a value to an appropriately named member variable of the session class. Likewise, it is read by simply reading it, as if it were a publicly declared member variable.

PHP will automatically realize that this is not a native member variable, and therefore call the relevant methods `_get()` or `_set()` to either get or set the value in the session variable table, respectively. This means that you can't use session variables with the same name as any of the methods or members of the session class. For example, a session variable name called `user_id` is out of the question.

Performance Considerations

Note that while the previous session class is database driven, it doesn't make use of PHP Data Objects (PDOs) which, as you discovered in Chapter 6, is most certainly the preferred mechanism for managing database communication in PHP 6.

This is a conscious decision. PDO has performance overhead. In isolation, they're miniscule (not noticeable to the human eye), but nevertheless, there is an overhead in providing that layer of abstraction in order to keep your code nice and clean — and if there's one thing that needs to run as fast as possible, it's session management. Don't forget that in a session-enabled application, *every single HTTP request* will invoke the session class, and, as a result, every single request will hit the database. If you also have the additional overhead of PDO in the way, those tiny fractions of seconds on each request will soon add up.

The solution is to bite your tongue, accept that architecturally it's not that "clean," but understand that it has a performance gain. After all, no one's going to use your Web site if it's slow as heck, even if it is very well built. Your users don't care about the architecture; they'll just see that the site is slow and never come back again.

Alternative Storage

Using a database to store session data is certainly attractive. It's scalable — you can add more servers using the same database server, or more database servers replicating between one another. It's easy to debug — if you're not sure why something isn't working, just look in the session tables. It makes writing queries easy — you can use your session tables in an INNER JOIN to write sleek, single SQL queries. It's also a darn sight faster than using flat files, which is PHP's default solution.

However, if raw speed is what you seek, then neither a disk nor a database is the way to go — memory is. If your application is going to be the next Facebook, this might be worth looking at. Memory is certainly superfast; and if you're using the same memory as your application server to store your session data, it'll be considerably faster than database or disk. Do keep in mind, though, that such an approach doesn't satisfy the scalability test entirely. You couldn't load-balance between multiple servers if they were all using their own memory to store session data — and memory is always lost should the server power down. It's also a pain to debug, because there's no easy human access to the memcached server, as there is with an SQL database's console.

If you'd like to experiment, though, feel free. It's another technique to add to your arsenal. The solution you're looking for is almost certain to use memcached. You can download it from www.danga.com/memcached/, but you'll also need the event notification library libevent from www.monkey.org/~provos/libevent/, which must be installed first.

memcached provides a sort of brain-dead key-value database server. Give it a key and a value, and it'll store that value against that key. Give it that key again, and it'll tell you the value you stored against it. That's it — no queries, no tables, no usernames and passwords, and certainly no clever stored procedures. Because it is simple, it is lightning fast, as you'll discover. Just start up the memcached server by telling it how much of your precious physical RAM it can eat (generally not more than 25 percent of what you have installed) and off you go.

PHP has (sort of) built-in support for reading and writing to a memcached server — see http://uk.php.net/manual/en/ref.memcache.php for more information. You must install a PECL module and tell php.ini about it first — but once you have, you'll see that simple methods are made available to connect to, disconnect from, read from, and write to a memcached server.

Some example code can be found at www.php.net/manual/en/function.session-set-save-handler.php, but the best approach is probably to amend the HTTPSession class in this chapter to support both database and memcached as a storage mechanism. That way, you can simply flip a switch to choose between database storage and memory storage, and keep your client-side code identical.

Putting It All Together

The HTTPSession class built in this chapter is a fully reusable, modular component. It can be easily included in virtually any project that requires maintaining session data, as well as support the authentication of registered users.

This discussion has provided an object-oriented interface to PHP's own session management and replaced its session variable functionality with a more flexible variant, whereby each variable is stored separately for the sake of speed and cleaner code.

Integration with your own applications should be most straightforward. You may find that you need to extend its functionality to suit your own needs, but because it is a self-contained class it is significantly easier than extending PHP's session management out of the box.

It's also worth pointing out that the only additional security mechanism incorporated from earlier in the chapter is the user agent check. Should you require firmer security, you may wish to explore integrating other security functionality, such as the IP variance analysis discussed earlier.

Summary

In this chapter, you learned about sessions: why they're useful, how to best implement them in your applications, and how to avoid some of the security pitfalls normally associated with them through some strategic security measures.

You also learned about PHP's traditional implementation of sessions, and why it is largely inadequate for professional software architects. You looked at how you can easily extend and adapt it to make it far more functional and scalable.

Finally, you used this knowledge to build a single, modular, self-contained HTTPSession class that can be easily integrated into your future applications. You also looked briefly at the performance considerations associated with using databases to store sessions, and explored the possibility of using memory-based storage as an alternative.

Speaking of future applications, you're almost ready to embark upon a case study. In the next couple of chapters, you'll learn how the tools you've amassed for your arsenal over the past 12 chapters are best used in the design of an application — a technique known as *application architecture.*

Chapter 13 discusses the fundamentals of sound application design — that is, faced with a set of functional requirements, how you can best apply best practice business analysis techniques to design a robust, scalable, and secure software architecture.

13

Application Architecture

When PHP first arrived on the scene in the latter half of the 1990s, a minor revolution took place. Highly interactive and feature-rich Web applications, once the exclusive preserve of large corporations able to commission expensive development shops or hire large in-house teams, were springing up left, right, and center. Suddenly, some seemingly sophisticated interactive Web content, which went well beyond the traditional (and now largely forgotten) guest book CGI script, was appearing in some very surprising places.

A driving factor behind this revolution was the enormous accessibility and shallow learning curve of PHP. It's not just that the "hello world" program was refreshingly easy to implement. Even traditionally complex procedures such as database integration became possible with just a few lines of code. This contrasted markedly with the notoriously fiddly PERL and the loudly trumpeted (but generally impenetrable) Java Servlet Engine.

The problem, however, was that this accessibility became quickly abused. In some cases, it resulted in complex applications being built by inexperienced development staff. In others, previously dedicated professionals (perhaps understandably) let their traditional values lapse slightly in the face of enormous temptation to take advantage of the simplicity PHP offered.

The risk associated with this kind of development is obvious. Such abuse has led to unmaintainable applications on a shocking scale, along with well-documented cases of instability, unreliability, and even exploitable security holes.

Although many programming languages such as Java and .NET enforce good programming practices through their design, PHP requires self-discipline. The difference between a seasoned PHP professional and a bedroom coder is exactly that — self-discipline. It's that self-discipline that necessitates good project planning; and a big part of project planning is *application architecture*.

In this chapter, you'll learn the basis of sound application architecture, and why something called *MVC* is a great methodology to use in your own programming. You'll build a useful toolkit for handling some core parts of the MVC principles, and learn how to use them in your applications.

Finally, you'll be introduced to two effective ways to implement the use of templates in your applications, and how to use templates alongside the MVC toolkit you've just met.

Introducing MVC

The *M* is for model, the *V* is for view, and the *C* is for controller — but what does it all mean? MVC is best described as what is often known as a *design pattern*, a description of a reusable solution to a recurring problem given a particular context. Design patterns exist so that the challenges faced when designing large-scale applications may be approached in a consistent manner. Best practices can be achieved by tackling the architecture in a tried-and-tested manner.

In this case, the problem is how to best separate the user interface of a program (the *view*), the business and utility classes that actually do the complex thinking (the *model*), and its inner processing and decision making (the *controller*) in such a way that they represent three distinct, separable components. The solution (as you might have guessed) is MVC.

Why is this approach needed?

First, separation yields interchangeability. By keeping three components separate, yet having them talk to one other in a consistent manner, you can swap any component out should you need to. For example, if you need to rebuild your Web application to work on PDAs instead of Web browsers, you can swap out your view component for one that renders content especially for the PDA, rather than the Web browser. If you need to accept data via voice input, rather than mouse clicks, you can swap out that same component for one that uses VoiceXML.

Second, debugging to catch hard-to-trace bugs, as well as maintenance programming after release, are made immeasurably simpler if there is a separation of logic in sensible places. The rationale behind using object-oriented programming (detailed in the first few chapters of this book) also applies here. It's much better to have a lot of small components that talk to each other than just a handful of huge, unwieldy files filled to the brim with code. A complex software architecture can be made a great deal simpler by separating components in this way.

Finally, you may wish to implement multiple controllers and views for your single-model application. To take the earlier example of PDAs, if you choose an MVC architecture, you can implement the necessary controllers and views to support traditional Web browsers, PDAs, cellular phones, voice, tablet PCs, and even legacy browsers — all of which will use the same model, even if they use different views and controllers. Without MVC, you'll find yourself unable to reuse the code behind the model, and you'll be burdened with all the problems associated with unnecessary duplication.

As you can see, MVC is a great design pattern, and one that you should endeavor to use whenever possible. The following sections examine each of the three components in turn, how they interact with one another, and, most important, where MVC sits in the context of Web application architecture in PHP.

The Model

The model is the very heart of your application. Generally speaking, it refers to the suite of classes you have developed to handle the various processes involved in your application's behavior. It concerns itself with retrieving the data behind the output (perhaps from a database), as well as manipulating data as a result of user input. It connects directly to the controller, and has no visibility to (nor sight of) the view. The controller supplies the model with its instructions; the view manipulates the data retrieved from the controller into human-usable output.

The key test to determine whether or not your model is compliant with all this is to ask yourself: *Is there anything Web-specific in my model classes?* If there is, then you're not doing it right. Talk of pages, user flow, navigations, cookies, sessions — all things related to the Web — should be firmly within your controllers. Anything to do with user input (or the presentation of output) should be within your view.

If you can take the classes that comprise your model and drop them into, say, a command-line application, a behind-the-scenes daemon, or even a desktop application without any changes being required, then you can be sure you're doing it right.

The View

The view is at the sharp end of the application. It presents data from the controller that the user has requested, or information that the controller considers the user needs to know. It enables the user to feed back to the controller by means of its user interface (typically, links and form input).

In practice, the view is comprised of a series of page templates in HTML, or whatever markup language is appropriate for the application in question — perhaps Wireless Markup Language (WML) for a mobile application, for example. There is typically limited back-end logic within the view to control things such as conditionals (whether things should or should not be displayed), dynamic content areas (e.g., showing a user's username in the navigation bar), and loops (for displaying tables of data). There should be no direct references to classes, and *certainly* no communication with databases.

Crucially, there is no direct link between the view and the model. In order for the view to access the heavy lifting contained within the model, the view must issue a command to the controller. The controller will then pass that message on to the model if it deems it necessary.

The Controllers

The third element of the MVC paradigm is the controller. This is best thought of as the owner of the user journey through your application. When a user requests a page, this request is passed through a controller. The controller will then pass data into (and retrieve data out of) the model as necessary, and then pass that information back to the user by way of the view.

The controller is, in effect, a form of abstraction. The view talks in terms of pages, navigations, clicks, form inputs, and so forth (very "Web" stuff), but the model talks in terms of getting properties, setting properties, performing tasks, and so on (very "business" stuff). There must be a translation layer between the two — and that's exactly what the controller does.

In practice, an application's controllers consist of a series of executable scripts (for the purposes of this book, PHP scripts) to which pages in the Web application may GET or POST. The controller decides what to do with each request based on the user's current page, the user's action on that page, conditions of the page (such as form input states), external conditions (session data, for example), and a myriad of other climatic factors. It will then communicate to and from the model as necessary, before directing the user to another view state.

Figure 13-1 shows the role of the controllers in your application.

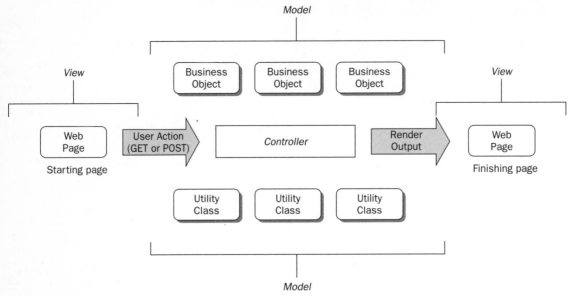

Figure 13-1 The model-view-controller (MVC) paradigm

MVC in Web Applications

MVC is not a new concept. Indeed, it is considered by some to be the evolution of the *input, processing, and output (IPO)* model, which was the best-practice model applied to the linear, text-only applications of yesteryear. The application of MVC in a Web context is relatively simple.

The model is represented by your suite of classes, assuming that you have followed an object-oriented approach in your application. In any Web language, these classes perform the core communication with any external data source, make critical application decisions, and perform parsing and processing on both input and output.

The view is represented by the Web browser, or rather what is displayed in it. Upon making a request (be it a simple request for a page or an instruction to update or query a database), the output determined by the model is actually displayed by the Web browser.

Perhaps confusingly, the controller is also represented by the Web browser, or, rather, the user's actions within it. Whether just a series of links or a complex form, the GET and POST requests made by the user's browser represent the effort to get data into the model in the first place. These actions are passed through the controller.

MVC in PHP

As discussed earlier, PHP's simplicity and accessibility can easily be abused to the point where applications become unmaintainable. Specifically, this abuse takes the form of combining model, view, and controller into a single PHP script. In fact, the term *script* is appropriate only in such an approach. In a proper MVC application, there are no scripts, only components.

How Not to Do It

Ask any inexperienced PHP developer to create a guest book application and he or she will probably come up with a single file. The file would be called `guestbook.php` and would handle both displaying existing entries and adding new ones to the database. Stepping through the code, it might look something like this:

1. Look at the GET parameters passed to it to determine which page of the guest book to show.

2. If no page is specified, then decide to show page 1.

3. See whether a parameter called `NewGuestBookEntry` has been passed. If so, check whether it conforms to various validity constraints (length and content) and enter it into the database. If not, write an error message and quit.

4. Get the current guest book entries from the database matching this page number.

5. Write them out in an HTML table (embedded right in the script).

6. Write out the HTML form pointing to this same script, allowing the user to add an entry.

This approach has a number of problems, quite apart from using GET instead of POST to effect a change in a database. (Strictly speaking, the associated RFC states that this is a bad idea.)

If you think back to the reasons in favor of MVC — such as interchanging controllers and views, ease of maintenance and initial development, and multiple simultaneous controllers and views — you can see that in all three cases we encounter difficulties.

Instead, let's take a look at a more mature approach to development that enables you to follow the MVC design pattern.

Getting It Right: An MVC Approach

The first rule of MVC in PHP is to *split up your files*. There are a number of possible approaches to this task, but many favor taking the step of actually using different file extensions to represent different roles in the MVC pattern, and then using `require_once` at the appropriate time to link them together.

The documented practice of naming files to be `included` or `required` with an extension `.inc` should not be followed, as it tells you nothing about the content of that file, and thus encourages role overlap between files.

You may wish to try something like what is shown in Table 13-1.

Table 13-1 A Suggested Approach to File-Naming

Extension	Component	Role
.php	Controller	Behavioral logic — the communications infrastructure between model and view
.phpm	Model	PHP classes — the heart of the application
.phtml	View	The rendering of both the results of the user's input and the interface to enable the user to make further input

The word "view" is a bit misleading because, of course, the Web browser is used not just to render output, but also to accept input. In this case, the view represents the user interface to your application — typically HTML.

If you are unsure as to what code should appear in which modules, you can rely on a few rules to ensure that you're following this methodology:

❑　.php (controllers) should never contain SQL queries or HTML.

❑　.phpm (classes) should never contain HTML.

❑　.phtml (templates) should never contain SQL queries, and only very basic PHP (for/if/while).

What you are accomplishing in this separation is a very primitive form of templating known as *native templating*. In such a setup, PHP is used to render the output of the application in a separate template file (in this case, the .phtml file). That output is decided upon by presentation of the user's input by the controller (the .php file) to the classes (the .phpm files).

This is implemented in practice as follows:

1. The .php file is the actual recipient of the GET or POST request (hence, there is no need to reconfigure Apache to support these new extensions).

2. The .php file is home to all require() statements needed to import the necessary classes that comprise the model (with each class stored in a .phpm file).

3. The .php controller examines the input in GET and POST parameters and determines a course of action. It passes that data (in either a raw or processed form) into methods of these classes that have been made available to it through inclusion in the previous step.

4. The classes in question parse the input data, update and query databases or other data sources as necessary, and return data to the .php file.

5. The .php file then examines the output from those classes. It may make decisions based on that output, deliver the output in some processed state, or simply deliver it as is. The delivery, however, is always performed through the construction of a single supervariable (usually a hash or an associative array) that contains, unformatted, the output you want to display to the user.

6. The `.php` file then `includes` the appropriate `.phtml` file, which effectively takes over execution.

7. The `.phtml` file recurses that supervariable, displaying it in whatever form is appropriate, and rendering whatever new user input components are required, such that the user is presented with the finished Web page.

This may sound more complex than it actually is; in fact, it is a remarkably simple process. You'll see some examples later in this chapter showing how this native templating is best implemented. For now, you'll take a look at a few toolkit classes that can help you in the quest to use an MVC design pattern in PHP by vastly simplifying some of the steps set out previously.

Later in this chapter, you'll learn how this toolkit integrates neatly with the native templating techniques just discussed.

The MVC Mini Toolkit

The mini toolkit you are about to meet makes sticking to an MVC design pattern a whole lot easier. The toolkit concerns itself only with the controller element of the MVC trio. You've already looked at the model side of things in Chapter 7. Later you'll meet an off-the-shelf PEAR package called Smarty that allows for an effective implementation of the view components.

Introducing the Toolkit

The mini toolkit enables you to handle the connection between view and model in a consistent, clean, and clear manner. The core of this is a request object that seeks to provide a more object-oriented perspective on the user's input into your application. As well as sporting the usual means for interrogating the user's input directly, it supports the concept of applying constraints to each parameter, such that you may easily specify in your code what you are and are not prepared to accept.

Such error-checking practices are almost certainly not new to you, of course. However, the concept of constraints enables you to separate the view and model by providing a universal approach to your controller development. Because the model may now assume that its input is within expected parameters, you can divorce cleanly such code from methods within the model, safe in the knowledge that it has been vetted by the controllers of your MVC design pattern.

This is an entirely appropriate approach. After all, sanity checks are not core to your model's functionality. By leaving responsibility for such checks well outside the model itself, you can also apply different rules for different controllers and different views talking to the same model. This is very much in keeping with the philosophy behind MVC.

You may want to extend or modify these classes to suit your own needs better. What is provided here is a very basic implementation. For example, you may want to examine the feasibility of adding methods to automatically perpetuate GET and POST variables using hidden form parameters, without having to turn to session variables. This may prove useful for the purposes of pagination forward and backward through a data set of search results, maintaining those search criteria with each request for a new page. Such functionality could easily be integrated into the request object itself. In Chapter 14, you'll meet a number of PHP frameworks that have already done just that.

In addition, the pre-packaged constraint types supplied here are not exhaustive. However, a quick glance at the code should make it quite clear how easily you can add your own, should your application require them.

Constants

You do need to define a number of constants in order for your classes to work seamlessly together. They define the three types of parameter (GET, POST, and Cookies), as well as the various types of constraint you can apply. As previously mentioned, you should feel free to define additional constraints that may suit your application, as long as you also remember to implement them in the Request class.

Examine the following code and save it in a file called constants.phpm:

```php
<?php // Constants

define(VERB_METHOD_COOKIE, 1);
define(VERB_METHOD_GET, 2);
define(VERB_METHOD_POST, 4);
define(CT_MINLENGTH, 1);
define(CT_MAXLENGTH, 2);
define(CT_PERMITTEDCHARACTERS, 3);
define(CT_NONPERMITTEDCHARACTERS, 4);
define(CT_LESSTHAN, 5);
define(CT_EQUALTO, 6);
define(CT_MORETHAN, 7);
define(CT_NOTEQUALTO, 8);
define(CT_MUSTMATCHREGEXP, 9);
define(CT_MUSTNOTMATCHREGEXP, 10);
?>
```

Note the two numbering schemes as an approach in defining these constants. These are an *exponential sequence* to define the three verbs of parameters offered in an HTTP request, and a purely *sequential sequence* to define the constraint types.

The reason for the two differing approaches touches briefly on the properties of *bitwise logic*. Because this subject has not been touched upon elsewhere in the book, let's take a brief look at it here.

Consider the following piece of code:

```php
$var3 = ($var1 && $var2);
```

The conditional statement here clearly requires that $var1 is true (either literally, or as some nonzero or non-empty value), and that $var2 is true (employing traditional use of the && operator to express Boolean logic). If both are true, $var3 will also be true. This if fairly basic, but there is a second form of comparison logic that uses the same basic operators, AND and OR.

Consider the following:

```php
$var3 = ($var1 & $var2);
```

Note the *single* ampersand. This indicates that you want to perform bitwise (rather than Boolean) logic to effect the comparison. What then takes place (assuming that $var1 and $var2 are integers) is that the corresponding binary bits of each value are subject to the traditional Boolean comparison (with 1 meaning true and 0 meaning false). If $var1 is 34 and $var2 is 11, then the following applies:

```
34       =       00100010
11       =       00001011
34 & 11 =        00000010     =     2
```

Accordingly, the bitwise logic of 34 and 11 yields 2, because it is only in the 2 column where both bits are 1 in each number.

What does this have to do with constants? Put simply, it enables you to combine constants to form a single value (which consists of the arithmetic sum of its constituent constants), and then easily determine later what those constituent constants are.

If each constant represents the incrementing decimal value of a single bit of a binary number (essentially, a power of 2), then when summed together, the resulting binary number will have bits set to 1 representing those constants that have been included in that sum:

```
CONST_A =        1       =        00000001
CONST B =        2       =        00000010
CONST C =        4       =        00000100
CONST D =        8       =        00001000
CONST E =        16      =        00010000
```

For example, say that you want to define a parameter consisting of constants B, D, and E combined (whatever that might mean). Simply add the values 2, 8, and 16 together to get a value of 26. Take a look at what 26 looks like in binary, next to its constituent components:

```
CONST B =        2       =        00000010
CONST D =        8       =        00001000
CONST E =        16      =        00010000
CONST_B+D+E =    26      =        00011010
```

Notice that you can clearly recognize that the constituent constants of the combination are B, D, and E; but how do you test for this in code?

Enter and run the following code from the command line (rather than in a Web browser). Normally, you'd just type **php** at a command prompt to do this, but if the PHP executable isn't in your path, you'll need to hunt it down first — try /usr/local/php/bin on UNIX:

```php
<?php
define('CONST_A', 1);
define('CONST_B', 2);
define('CONST_C', 4);
define('CONST_D', 8);
define('CONST_E', 16);

$myCombinedConstant = CONST_B + CONST_D + CONST_E;

if ($myCombinedConstant & CONST_A) {
 print "Combined constant contains A\n";
};
```

```
if ($myCombinedConstant & CONST_B) {
 print "Combined constant contains B\n";
};
if ($myCombinedConstant & CONST_C) {
 print "Combined constant contains C\n";
};
if ($myCombinedConstant & CONST_D) {
 print "Combined constant contains D\n";
};
if ($myCombinedConstant & CONST_E) {
 print "Combined constant contains E\n";
};
?>
```

Press Ctrl+D (UNIX) or Ctrl+Z (Windows) to finish typing your script. You will see output similar to the following:

```
Combined constant contains B
Combined constant contains D
Combined constant contains E
```

As you have probably deduced, the test to determine whether a combined constant contains a particular original constant is simply to perform a bitwise AND against that original constant. This will produce a nonzero (that is, true) value only if the bit in question is set both in the original constant and in the combined constant you are testing.

Note how this tactic is adopted in the constants for expressing request methods, but not in the constants used to express constraint types. This is because the code might allow the combination of request methods as a parameter for a method at some stage in the future. However, the nature of constraint types means that one constraint object has one constraint type. To combine constraints, therefore, their objects must be combined (not the constants behind them). Accordingly, note how a linear (1, 2, 3, 4, 5) numbering system has been adopted for these constants, because they will never be added together in the way described in this section.

The Request Class

The request object itself represents the request made by the user in order to generate the page. Those of you who have ever worked in .NET may be familiar with using a pre-instantiated object to access parameters, but this Request class is somewhat more sophisticated.

Unlike .NET, you must instantiate the request object yourself, but you will notice that the constructor written requires no parameters. It examines the existing (and globally accessible) $_REQUEST, $_COOKIE, $_POST, and $_GET hashes itself quite successfully in order to populate its various member variables.

You could start to make use of the request object right away. By using the various methods supplied to retrieve parameters, you could build your application. Doing this, however, disregards the tremendously useful syntax validation methods provided by the Constraint class and its sister ConstraintFailure class.

Examine the following source code, called `request.phpm`, in detail:

```
<?
require_once("constants.phpm");
require_once("constraint.phpm");
require_once("constraintfailure.phpm");
class request {
  private $_arGetVars;
  private $_arPostVars;
  private $_arCookieVars;
  private $_arRequestVars;
  private $_objOriginalRequestObject;

  private $_blIsRedirectFollowingConstraintFailure;

  private $_blRedirectOnConstraintFailure;
  private $_strConstraintFailureRedirectTargetURL;
  private $_strConstraintFailureDefaultRedirectTargetURL;

  private $_arObjParameterMethodConstraintHash;
  private $_arObjConstraintFailure;
  private $_hasRunConstraintTests;

  function __construct($check_for_cookie = true) {
    // Import variables
    global $_REQUEST;
    global $_GET;
    global $_POST;
    global $_COOKIE;
    $this->_arGetVars = $_GET;
    $this->_arPostVars = $_POST;
    $this->_arCookieVars = $_COOKIE;
    $this->_arRequestVars = $_REQUEST;
    if ($check_for_cookie) {
      if ($this->_arCookieVars["phprqcOriginalRequestObject"]) {
        $cookieVal = $this->_arRequestVars["phprqcOriginalRequestObject"];
        $this->_blIsRedirectFollowingConstraintFailure = true;
        if (strlen($cookieVal) > 0) {
          $strResult = setcookie ("phprqcOriginalRequestObject", "",
                    time() - 3600, "/");
          $origObj = unserialize(stripslashes($cookieVal));
          $this->_objOriginalRequestObject = &$origObj;
          $this->_arRequestVars["phprqcOriginalRequestObject"] = "";
          $this->_arGetVars["phprqcOriginalRequestObject"] = "";
          $this->_arPostVars["phprqcOriginalRequestObject"] = "";
        };
        $this->_blIsRedirectOnConstraintFailure  = true;
      } else {
        $this->_blIsRedirectOnConstraintFailure  = false;
      };
    } else {
```

```
      $this->_blIsRedirectOnConstraintFailure  = false;
      };
   $this->_arObjParameterMethodConstraintHash = Array();
   $this->_arObjConstraintFailure = Array();
   $this->_blHasRunConstraintTests = false;
}

function IsRedirectFollowingConstraintFailure() {
 return($this->_blIsRedirectOnConstraintFailure);
}

function GetOriginalRequestObjectFollowingConstraintFailure() {
   if ($this->_blIsRedirectOnConstraintFailure) {
     return($this->_objOriginalRequestObject);
   };
}

function SetRedirectOnConstraintFailure($blTrueOrFalse) {
   $this->_blRedirectOnConstraintFailure  = $blTrueOrFalse;
}

function SetConstraintFailureRedirectTargetURL($strURL) {
   $this->_strConstraintFailureRedirectTargetURL = $strURL;
}

function SetConstraintFailureDefaultRedirectTargetURL($strURL) {
   $this->_strConstraintFailureDefaultRedirectTargetURL = $strURL;
}
   function GetParameterValue($strParameter) {
   return($this->_arRequestVars[$strParameter]);
}

function GetParameters() {
   return($this->_arRequestVars);
}

function GetCookies() {
   return($this->_arCookieVars);
}

function GetPostVariables() {
   return($this->_arPostVariables);
}

function GetGetVariables() {
   return($this->_arGetVariables);
}

function AddConstraint($strParameter, $intMethod, $objConstraint) {
   $newHash["PARAMETER"] = $strParameter;
   $newHash["METHOD"] = $intMethod;
```

```
      $newHash["CONSTRAINT"] = $objConstraint;
      $this->_arObjParameterMethodConstraintHash[] = $newHash;
}

function TestConstraints() {
  $this->_blHasRunConstraintTests = true;
  $anyFail = false;
  for ($i=0; $i<=sizeof($this->_arObjParameterMethodConstraintHash) -1; $i++) {
    $strThisParameter =
                $this->_arObjParameterMethodConstraintHash[$i] ["PARAMETER"];
    $intThisMethod = $this->_arObjParameterMethodConstraintHash[$i]["METHOD"];
    $objThisConstraint =
                $this->_arObjParameterMethodConstraintHash[$i] ["CONSTRAINT"];
    $varActualValue = "";
    if ($intThisMethod == VERB_METHOD_COOKIE) {
      $varActualValue = $this->_arCookieVars[$strThisParameter];
    };
    if ($intThisMethod == VERB_METHOD_GET) {
      $varActualValue = $this->_arGetVars[$strThisParameter];
    };
    if ($intThisMethod == VERB_METHOD_POST) {
      $varActualValue = $this->_arPostVars[$strThisParameter];
    };
    $intConstraintType = $objThisConstraint->GetConstraintType();
    $strConstraintOperand = $objThisConstraint->GetConstraintOperand();
    $thisFail = false;
    $objFailureObject = new constraintfailure($strThisParameter,
                        $intThisMethod, $objThisConstraint);
    switch ($intConstraintType) {
      case CT_MINLENGTH:
        if (strlen((string)$varActualValue) < (integer) $strConstraintOperand) {
          $thisFail = true;
        };
        break;
      case CT_MAXLENGTH:
        if (strlen((string)$varActualValue) > (integer) $strConstraintOperand) {
          $thisFail = true;
        };
        break;
      case CT_PERMITTEDCHARACTERS:
        for ($j=0; $j<=strlen($varActualValue)-1; $j++) {
            $thisChar = substr($varActualValue, $j, 1);
            if (strpos($strConstraintOperand, $thisChar) === false) {
              $thisFail = true;
            };
        };
        break;
      case CT_NONPERMITTEDCHARACTERS:
        for ($j=0; $j<=strlen($varActualValue)-1; $j++) {
            $thisChar = substr($varActualValue, $j, 1);
            if (!(strpos($strConstraintOperand, $thisChar) === false)) {
```

```
              $thisFail = true;
          };
        };
      break;
  case CT_LESSTHAN:
      if ($varActualValue >= $strConstraintOperand) {
        $thisFail = true;
      };
      break;
  case CT_MORETHAN:
      if ($varActualValue <= $strConstraintOperand) {
        $thisFail = true;
      };
      break;
  case CT_EQUALTO:
      if ($varActualValue != $strConstraintOperand) {
        $thisFail = true;
      };
      break;
  case CT_NOTEQUALTO:
      if ($varActualValue == $strConstraintOperand) {
        $thisFail = true;
      };
      break;
   case CT_MUSTMATCHREGEXP:
      if (!(preg_match($strConstraintOperand, $varActualValue))) {
        $thisFail = true;
      };
      break;
   case CT_MUSTNOTMATCHREGEXP:
      if (preg_match($strConstraintOperand, $varActualValue)) {
        $thisFail = true;
      };
      break;
  };
  if ($thisFail) {
    $anyFail = true;
    $this->_arObjConstraintFailure[] = $objFailureObject;
  };
};
if ($anyFail) {
  if ($this->_blRedirectOnConstraintFailure) {
      $targetURL = $_ENV["HTTP_REFERER"];
      if (!$targetURL) {
        $targetURL = $this->_strConstraintFailureDefaultRedirectTargetURL;
      };
      if ($this->_strConstraintFailureRedirectTargetURL) {
        $targetURL = $this->_strConstraintFailureRedirectTargetURL;
      };
      if ($targetURL) {
        $objToSerialize = $this;
        $strSerialization = serialize($objToSerialize);
        $strResult = setcookie ("phprqcOriginalRequestObject",
```

```
                              $strSerialization, time() + 3600, "/");
                  header("Location: $targetURL");
                  exit(0);
              };
          };
      };
      return(!($anyFail));   // Returns TRUE if all tests passed, otherwise returns
                             //   FALSE
  }

      function GetConstraintFailures() {
      if (!$this->_blHasRunConstraintTests) {
        $this->TestConstraints();
      };
      return($this->_arObjConstraintFailure);
    }
  }
  ?>
```

Take a look at each of the member variables shown in Table 13-2. These are all private, and accessor methods are provided to get to or set their useful values. Hungarian notation has been used — that is, a hint is included as to which data type each member variable should contain at the start of the variable's name.

Table 13-2 Member Variables

Member Variable	Role
$_arGetVars	A copy of $_GET, an associative array of HTTP GET variables passed in this request
$_arPostVars	A copy of $_POST, an associative array of HTTP POST variables passed in this request
$_arCookieVars	A copy of $_COOKIE, an associative array of pre-existing cookies passed in this request
$_arRequestVars	A copy of $_REQUEST, an associative array of GET and POST variables, as well as cookies, combined into one. Where GET/POST variables or cookies of the same name exist, precedence is determined by PHP.INI.
$_objOriginalRequestObject	In the event that the user has been redirected back to the original page by the request object as a result of passing parameters that failed constraint tests, this will contain a copy of the original request object supplied.
$_blIsRedirectFollowing ConstraintFailure	A Boolean variable determining whether this request has been created as a result of a redirect following a constraint test failure
$_blRedirectOnConstraint Failure	In the event that a constraint test is failed, should the request object automatically redirect the browser back to the original page, or to some other URL?

(continued)

Table 13-2 *(continued)*

Member Variable	Role
$_strConstraintFailure RedirectTargetURL	In the event that a constraint test is failed and _blRedirect OnConstraintFailure is set to true, this specifies whether the request object should be diverted to a particular URL. If this is left blank, the referring URL shall be used.
$_strConstraintFailure DefaultRedirectTargetURL	In the event that _strConstraintFailure RedirectTargetURL is not set, _blRedirectOn ConstraintFailure is set to true, and no referring URL is available, this specifies the URL to which the browser should be redirected.
$_arObjParameterMethod ConstraintHash	An array of constraints, the indices of which contain three keyed components in a hash: the parameter name on which the constraint applies; the method in which this parameter is expected to be passed (as a constant); and the constraint object expressing the test to be applied.
$_arObjConstraintFailure	An array of constraint failure objects, should any constraints have failed, assuming that the tests have been run
$_blHasRunConstraintTests	A Boolean variable expressing whether the constraint tests have yet been run on this request object

Table 13-3 shows the methods provided by the request object.

Table 13-3 Methods Provided by the Request Object

Method	Role
__construct	Instantiates the request object. Does not take any required parameters. Instead, it consults $_REQUEST, $_POST, $_GET, and $_COOKIE, and populates member variables (see Table 13-2) as appropriate. In addition, the existence of a cookie called phprqcOriginalRequestObject is checked for. Should it exist, another request object is assumed to be passed back as a result of throwback following constraint test failures. The cookie is nullified at this stage to prevent an infinite loop when the original request object is created. Its contents are then unserialized (via the stripslashes PHP function) into a new request object, which is then made available for interrogation through the GetOriginalRequest ObjectFollowingConstraintFailure accessor method (detailed in this table).

Method	Role
`IsRedirectFollowing ConstraintFailure`	If the page being displayed has been automatically loaded following a 302 redirect issued as a result of a constraint test failure, then this method returns `true`.
`GetOriginalRequest ObjectFollowing ConstraintFailure`	If the page being displayed has been automatically loaded following a 302 redirect issued as a result of a constraint test failure, then this method returns the `request` object that existed when that page was called, just before the constraint tests failed.
`SetRedirect OnConstraintFailure`	Accepting `true` or `false` as a parameter, this method enables you to tell the `request` object whether it should perform a 302 redirect upon any constraint tests failing. The target for that redirect is set using the `SetCons traintFailureRedirectTargetURL` and `SetConstraintFailureDefaultRedirectTargetURL` methods.
`SetConstraintFailure RedirectTargetURL`	Sets the target for a 302 redirect following a constraint failure. If one is not set, then either the referring page (which is normally the desired target) is used or, if that is not available, a default URL is used (which is set using the `SetConstraintFailure DefaultRedirectTargetURL` method).
`SetConstraintFailure Default RedirectTargetURL`	In the event that no target URL is set using the preceding accessor method, the referring page is used should a referral become necessary as a result of a constraint test failing. If no referring page is available (for example, as a result of a user visiting from a bookmark), the default URL specified using this method is used instead.
`GetParameterValue`	Returns the value of the specified parameter. This value is pulled directly from `$_REQUEST`, so the precedence of search for GET variables, POST variables, and COOKIE variables depends on PHP's overall configuration.
`GetParameters`	Returns a hash of parameters — essentially, a direct copy of `$_REQUEST`
`GetCookies`	Returns a hash of cookies — essentially, a direct copy of `$_COOKIE`
`GetPostVariables`	Returns a hash of POST variables — essentially, a direct copy of `$_POST`
`GetGetVariables`	Returns a hash of GET variables — essentially, a direct copy of `$_GET`

(continued)

Table 13-3 *(continued)*

Method	Role
AddConstraint	Adds a constraint to this request. A constraint is applied to a single parameter and specifies a condition that must be met in order for that constraint to be considered met. This method takes the name of the parameter, the delivery method (VERB_METHOD_GET, VERB_METHOD_POST, or VERB_METHOD_COOKIE as a constant) and a constraint object (discussed shortly) as its parameters. After a constraint is added, it cannot be removed. More than one constraint may be applied to a single parameter.
TestConstraints	Tests each constraint in turn and makes a note of any that fail by populating the member variable $_arObjConstraintFailure, accessible using GetConstraintFailure. In the event that $_blRedirectOnConstraintFailure is set to true, it redirects automatically to the appropriate URL, having first issued a temporary cookie that is a serialized representation of the current request object.
GetConstraintFailures	When a call to TestConstraints() indicates that one or more constraints fail, this method will return an array of ConstraintFailure objects representing all such failures. This method will need to be accessed from the original request object, accessed using GetOriginalRequestObjectFollowingConstraint Failure (described earlier in this table).

Don't worry if the theory isn't quite clear from Table 13-3. Later in this chapter, you'll find a practical example showing how to employ this class and the rest of the toolkit in the real world. All should become clear then.

Now let's take a look at the Constraint class and its close cousin, the ConstraintFailure class.

The Constraint Class

The Constraint class exists only as an object-oriented encapsulator. It does not concern itself with the code necessary to test whether the constraint is passed. As you have just seen, this is handled by the request object.

Enter the following code in a file called constraint.phpm:

```php
<?php
require_once("constants.phpm");
class constraint {
  private $_intConstraintType;
  private $_strConstraintOperand;
```

```
    function __construct($intConstraintType, $strConstraintOperand) {
      $this->_intConstraintType = $intConstraintType;
      $this->_strConstraintOperand = $strConstraintOperand;
    }

    function GetConstraintType() {
      return($this->_intConstraintType);
    }

    function GetConstraintOperand() {
      return($this->_strConstraintOperand);
    }
  }
?>
```

Note how the constructor takes the constraint type (chosen from one of the constraint types that have been enumerated as constants) as its first parameter, and the operand as its second parameter. The meaning of the operand depends on the type of constraint. Its interpretation is up to the `request` object in its implementation of each type of constraint. For example, for a CT_MAXLENGTH constraint, the operand should contain the maximum length of the parameter. For a CT_PERMITTEDCHARS constraint, the operand should contain a string containing all permitted characters that may exist in the parameter.

To accommodate this flexibility, the operand is a string. However, it will be cast back to its most appropriate native form when the test takes place.

Note that you do not store the name of the parameter being tested in a constraint object. A constraint is simply a condition, and it can be applied to any (or even multiple) parameters using the methods in the `request` object. For that reason, to encapsulate neatly any given failure of a constraint, you must also store the parameter and delivery method that have provoked the failure. This is done using an instance of the `ConstraintFailure` class.

The ConstraintFailure Class

A `ConstraintFailure` object is instantiated whenever a particular constraint fails. Its constructor expects the name of the parameter, the delivery method (VERB_METHOD_GET, VERB_METHOD_POST, or VERB_ METHOD_COOKIE), and the original constraint object that caused the failure.

In normal use, the `GetFailedConstraintObject` method will be used to determine the nature of the constraint that failed through the use of the native `Constraint` class methods described previously.

Take a look at the following code, in a file called `constraintfailure.phpm`:

```
<?php
require_once("constants.phpm");
require_once("constraint.phpm");
class constraintfailure {
  private $_strParameterName;
  private $_intVerbMethod;
  private $_objFailedConstraintObject;
```

```
function __construct($strParameterName, $intVerbMethod,
                     $objFailedConstraintObject) {
  $this->_strParameterName = $strParameterName;
  $this->_intVerbMethod = $intVerbMethod;
  $this->_objFailedConstraintObject = $objFailedConstraintObject;
}

function GetParameterName() {
  return($this->_strParameterName);
}

function GetVerbMethod() {
  return($this->_intVerbMethod);
}

function GetFailedConstraintObject() {
  return($this->_objFailedConstraintObject);
}
};
?>
```

This class neatly encapsulates a failure that has occurred as a result of the user's input to the page not meeting your acceptance criteria.

As shown in the preceding code, it contains the name of the parameter that has failed, the method (GET, POST, or Cookie) in which the parameter was passed, and the constraint (expressed as a constraint object) test that has failed.

Instances of this object can be retrieved from the Request class using the GetConstraintFailures method, provided that the Request class has been instantiated in the context of a 302 redirect following redirection caused by constraint failures.

Using the Toolkit

Now that you've learned a little bit about the basic classes that constitute the toolkit, it's worth looking at how you'd go about implementing this in a real-world application.

You'll also see in this example a practical case of an MVC approach as defined earlier in the chapter — namely, the use of native PHP templating. (The section "True Templating" later in this chapter goes into further detail about how this works.)

Assume that you have a search engine consisting of two pages: a search page in which the terms are entered, and a search terms page in which the results are displayed.

search.php

The initial search controller has the following jobs:

❑   Require all the necessary components.

❑   Define the template file (search.phtml).

❑ Define an associative array ($displayHash) to contain the content to be rendered by the template file (the view).

❑ Check to see whether this page has been reached as a result of a referral following a constraint failure (as opposed to simply being requested by a user for the first time):

   ❑ If so, set part of the $displayHash to indicate this, and retrieve the original failed request object from the current request object (which has been made available through the temporary cookie).

   ❑ Retrieve an array of constraintfailure objects from this retrieved request object.

   ❑ Loop through these constraintfailure objects, populating a newly formed array in $displayHash with the type of failure in each case.

❑ Require the template file for immediate rendering.

The code for search.php (not search.phtml — you'll get to that) is reproduced here:

```php
<?php
require_once("constants.phpm");
require_once("request.phpm");
require_once("constraint.phpm");
require_once("constraintfailure.phpm");

$strTemplateFile = "search.phtml";

$displayHash = Array();

$objRequest = new request();
$blHadProblems = ($objRequest->IsRedirectFollowingConstraintFailure());

$displayHash["HADPROBLEMS"] = $blHadProblems;

if ($blHadProblems) {
  $objFailingRequest =
   $objRequest->GetOriginalRequestObjectFollowingConstraintFailure();
  $arConstraintFailures = $objFailingRequest->GetConstraintFailures();
  $displayHash["PROBLEMS"] = Array();
  for ($i=0; $i<=sizeof($arConstraintFailures)-1; $i++) {
    $objThisConstraintFailure = &$arConstraintFailures[$i];
    $objThisFailingConstraintObject =
        $objThisConstraintFailure->GetFailedConstraintObject();
    $intTypeOfFailure = $objThisFailingConstraintObject->GetConstraintType();
    switch ($intTypeOfFailure) {
    case CT_MINLENGTH:
      $displayHash["PROBLEMS"][] = "Your search term was too short.";
      break;
    case CT_MAXLENGTH:
      $displayHash["PROBLEMS"][] = "Your search term was too long.";
      break;
    case CT_PERMITTEDCHARACTERS:
      $displayHash["PROBLEMS"][] = "Your search term contained characters
      I didn't understand.";
```

```
        break;
      };
    };
  };

  require_once($strTemplateFile);
  exit(0);
  ?>
```

Note the `exit` statement at the end. While it's not strictly necessary, it does prevent you from accidentally writing code after the template has been handed control.

Now let's take a look at the template itself.

search.phtml

The template has the sole responsibility of intelligently rendering the contents of `$displayHash` with appropriate surrounding HTML. Note how you do not need to declare `$displayHash` as global. The act of requiring the template glues it to the end of the original script. The PHP interpreter treats it as a single script at the point of execution.

In this particular template, in addition to rendering the straightforward HTML required to create the search form, you must render any error messages generated as a result of a failed search that has just taken place.

It's worth remarking that the following HTML is very, very simple — not exactly whizzbang semantic XHTML with all the latest CSS. It is hoped that you've realized that this is merely for clarity in these examples. In your own applications, your templates will doubtlessly be considerably bigger and more sophisticated.

Save the following as `search.phtml` (as opposed to `search.php`, which was already created):

```
<html>
<head>
  <title>Ed's Search Page</title>
</head>

<body>
<H1>Ed's Search Page</H1>
<hr>
You can search for types of steak here.
<BR><BR>
<? if ($displayHash["HADPROBLEMS"]) { ?>
  <B>Sorry, there <?=((sizeof($displayHash["PROBLEMS"]) > 1) ? "were problems" :
  "was a problem")?> with your search!</B>
  <? for ($i=0; $i<=sizeof($displayHash["PROBLEMS"])-1; $i++) { ?>
    <?=$displayHash["PROBLEMS"][$i]?>
  <? }; ?>
<? }; ?>
<FORM METHOD="POST" ACTION="searchresults.php">
  <TABLE BORDER="0">
```

```
        <TR>
          <TD>Type of Steak</TD>
          <TD><INPUT TYPE="TEXT" NAME="typeOfSteak"></TD>
        </TR>
      </TABLE><BR>
      <INPUT TYPE="SUBMIT">
    </FORM>

    </body>
    </html>
```

Note how simple the PHP is, including very basic statements such as `if` and `for`. As a rule, if you find yourself writing code of greater complexity in a template file, then it is most likely in the wrong place, and should be in either the controller page (`.php`) or one of the classes (`.phm`).

Later in this chapter, you'll learn about an alternative for using these simple statements in templates, a method that doesn't use PHP at all: *true templating*.

If you fire up `search.php` in your browser, you should see that it successfully renders a standard search form, as shown in Figure 13-2.

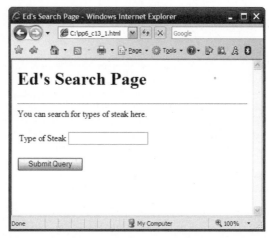

Figure 13-2 Standard search form from search.php

Obviously, the search page needs a target. This is provided using two distinct files: a controller and a template.

searchresults.php

The search results page will be the immediate target of the search page and has the job of determining whether its input is acceptable.

It does *not* have the job of informing the user whether the input is not acceptable. Instead, the user will be diverted via a 302 HTTP redirect *back* to the original search page, which then explains the shortcomings.

327

The conditions that apply in the following example relate to the only search parameter passed to the script — the search string provided by the user. It must contain between 4 and 11 characters, which must be letters, not numbers:

> **Do not try to run this code directly in your Web browser. It expects to be invoked from the search page.**

```php
<?
require_once("constants.phpm");
require_once("request.phpm");
require_once("constraint.phpm");
require_once("constraintfailure.phpm");


$strTemplateFile = "searchresults.phtml";

$displayHash = Array();
session_start();

if ($_POST) {

  $objRequest = new request();
  $objRequest->SetRedirectOnConstraintFailure(true);

  $objConstraint = new constraint(CT_MINLENGTH, "3");
  $objRequest->AddConstraint("typeOfSteak", VERB_METHOD_POST, $objConstraint);
  $objConstraint = new constraint(CT_MAXLENGTH, "12");
  $objRequest->AddConstraint("typeOfSteak", VERB_METHOD_POST, $objConstraint);
  $objConstraint = new constraint(CT_PERMITTEDCHARACTERS,
   "ABCDEFGHIJKLMNOPQRSTUVWXYZabcdefghijklmnopqrstuvwxyz");
  $objRequest->AddConstraint("typeOfSteak", VERB_METHOD_POST, $objConstraint);

  $objRequest->SetConstraintFailureDefaultRedirectTargetURL("/search.php");
  $objRequest->TestConstraints();

  # If we've got this far, tests have been passed - perform the search.
  $displayHash["RESULTS"] = Array();
  $arSteaks = array("fillet", "rump", "sirloin", "burnt");

  for ($i=0; $i<=sizeof($arSteaks)-1; $i++) {
    if (!(strpos(trim(strtolower($arSteaks[$i])),
    strtolower(trim($objRequest- >GetParameterValue("typeOfSteak"))))
        === false)) {
      array_push($displayHash["RESULTS"], $arSteaks[$i]);
    };
  };

  $_SESSION['dh'] = $displayHash;
  header("Location: searchresults.php");
  exit(0);
```

```
    } else {

        $displayHash = $_SESSION['dh'];
        require_once($strTemplateFile);
        exit(0);

    };
    ?>
```

Note that the `$displayHash` template content variable is defined again just as the request object is instantiated again.

First and foremost, the controller tests whether it has been called as a result of an HTTP POST. If it has, then each constraint on input is defined as a new instance of a constraint object. It is then added using `AddConstraint`, specifying the delivery method (POST, in this case) and the parameter name as additional operands.

To negate the need for the referral page to be available, you specify a default URL (the original search page). If you are trying out this example, you will need to adjust the path to this chapter's scripts accordingly.

A single method is then called: `TestConstraints()`. This performs the tests necessary to validate whether all the constraints you have expressed have been met. If one has not, then it is added to the array of constraint failures contained in this `request` object.

At the end of these tests, if *any* one of them has resulted in failure, the `request` object is authorized to force the user back to the search page, as a result of the use of `SetRedirectOnConstraintFailure()`. First, it serializes a snapshot of the `request` object as it stands on this page, and then pushes this as a cookie to the browser. When the user returns to the search page, this cookie will be parsed by the `request` object to determine what went wrong.

If a redirect takes place, then the template is not displayed at all. As a result, users are none the wiser that they have hit the second page at all. This improves the user experience. Users do not feel as if they have "left" the original search page. Hence, they instantly recognize that something is wrong.

Assuming that the tests passed, the search can go ahead. In the example, notice that the search mechanism is pretty simple. In a real-world scenario, external classes would undoubtedly be used to execute the search.

After a search results variable has been populated, it is stored temporarily in the session. A redirect is then issued to reload the page using HTTP GET. Upon reload, the template can be displayed by bringing back the value of the display hash from the session. Notice how, upon reload, the validation and search are not performed, as the `if ($_POST)` conditional evaluates to `false`.

searchresults.phtml

The following search results template is extremely simple. It merely displays the results of the search. There is no provision in the example for displaying a `your search produced no results` message. However, the implementation of such a message would be relatively straightforward.

```
<html>
<head>
  <title>Ed's Search Page</title>
</head>

<body>
<H1>Search Results</H1>
<hr>
Here are the results of your search.
<UL>
<? for ($i=0; $i<=sizeof($displayHash["RESULTS"])-1; $i++) { ?>
  <LI><?=$displayHash["RESULTS"][$i]?></LI>
<? }; ?>
</UL>
<A HREF="search.php">Go back and search for more steaks!</A>
</body>
</html>
```

Try It!

Assuming that you've entered the code for the previous four files, you can open the search page (`search.php`) again (as you did before) and enter some search terms.

First, try an example that should work just fine. Enter **fil** as your search term and click the Submit Query button. This should bring back `fillet` as a search result, as shown in Figure 13-3.

Figure 13-3 Bringing back "fillet" as a search result

Assuming that works fine, it's time to try out the real purpose of the toolkit: handling things when bad input is supplied. Try offering **fi** as a search term. This is only two characters in length, so it should fail, as shown in Figure 13-4.

Figure 13-4 Failing attempt to enter a search term

As you can see, you are immediately redirected back to the search page and an error message is displayed.

The `searchresults.php` ran three constraint tests against your search parameter and failed on one. That one failure caused a bounce back to the search page, but not before a snapshot serialization of the `request` object you had generated had been taken.

That snapshot was issued to your browser as a cookie immediately before you were redirected back to the original page. The search page then detected the presence of that cookie, and knew that you had been referred back to it following a failure as a result. It then proceeded to read the constraint failures that were embedded in that object, and display them to you one at a time.

Try entering a string that is too long (**myfavoritesteak**) or a term that contains invalid characters (such as **11431**) and you will see similar failure messages. Enter something like **my 1st choice**, which violates more than one constraint, and you should be chastised twice.

A Word about PRG

Before moving on, it's worth taking a moment to explore something you implemented in the previous example without even realizing it — a design pattern known as *post-redirect-get*, or *PRG*.

In the original HTTP protocol, HTTP GET was designed to display pages of content or information, and HTTP POST was designed to perform some action (especially one that modified data). Therefore, virtually all <form> implementations would make use of HTTP POST. The only ones that would use GET would be those concerned with simple logic such as pagination. As a rule of thumb, anything that either changed data at the remote host or required considerable processing to take place should have used HTTP POST.

However, both HTTP GET and HTTP POST can send output to the Web browser in just the same way. It's perfectly viable for an HTTP POST to result in output being sent to the Web browser — but what happens if you click Refresh (or press F5) on such a page? Figure 13-5 illustrates just that.

Figure 13-5 Error message when attempting to refresh the page

The dialog shown in Figure 13-5 is a royal pain, but it exists to protect users from themselves. Who is to say what would happen if the page were resubmitted? If this were an "add to cart" page, an item could be added to the shopping cart more than once. If it were a "pay for order" page, the order could be paid for more than once.

Using PRG, this dialog *never* appears. Every HTTP POST (no matter how trivial) results in a subsequent HTTP GET, initiated using a 302 redirect — in practice, something achieved using the header() function in PHP. This tells the browser to request a different page, rather than render any output. You can store whatever output of your page should be temporarily in the session, or even in a client-side cookie in a pinch. Just don't render it to the browser, as sending even a single byte of HTML will make redirection impossible.

This whole process is virtually invisible to the end user, but it means that should the user refresh the page following an HTTP POST, it will, in fact, be the subsequent HTTP GET the user is refreshing, not the POST at all. This GET should be benign. It should simply render output in a matter-of-fact kind of way. The refresh, therefore, is of no great consequence.

For more information about this, use Google to search for "post-redirect-get," or see
`http://en.wikipedia.org/wiki/Post/Redirect/Get`.

The Toolkit in the Wild

By this point in the chapter, you have built a mini toolkit that enables you to easily handle requests and constraints as part of using an MVC design pattern in your projects. You have also learned a simple method for using templates in native PHP.

The built-in constraints in the `request` object you have created here are relatively simple and, admittedly, could be quite easily implemented in raw PHP within your control page. Constraints really come into their own when they become complex, such as when they need to query a data source to determine validity. On occasions such as this, it may make sense to "genericize" your `request` object, and then extend it to form multiple `request` objects (perhaps one per page) that handle a different range of constraints in each case.

Later in this chapter, you'll learn about Smarty — an entirely different way of doing templating.

True Templating

You've now met "native" PHP templating, but what is "true" templating, and how is it different?

Recapping Native PHP Templating

The early parts of this chapter familiarized you with the concept of MVC. By now, you should realize that approaching large PHP projects using some variety of templating makes sense.

So far, all the templating you've looked at has revolved around the principle of populating a single, multidimensional hash of content, and then injecting HTML (or some other markup language) with that content using simple PHP statements such as `if`, `for`, `while`, or others.

However, the very fact that you are required to discipline yourself into only using certain PHP keywords within the templates points to some very clear pitfalls with this approach. Anything that requires self-discipline — rather than enforces hard-and-fast rules — is open to abuse.

The Pitfalls of Native Templating

The first and most obvious problem is that you are using a very powerful language (PHP) to do a very simple job (spitting out content). The problem is not a performance issue, though. It's simply that by using PHP to take care of the content rendering, you are introducing yet another point in your project where things can go wrong.

Think of the common problems you face when writing big classes — typographical errors, misspelling variable names, or accidentally reusing counter variables in heavily nested `for` loops. All these problems are just as constant if you also use PHP for your templating.

The second (and perhaps more serious) problem becomes obvious when you consider larger projects. One of the big advantages of using MVC in PHP projects is that the view (that is, any templates required) can be delegated to developers skilled in the art of design and HTML, but possibly not so skilled with PHP. This enables the relatively expensive software architects and engineers to work on the heavy-duty PHP driving the model of the project, and the less-expensive Web developers to work on the interface.

As producing valid, semantic, and accessible XHTML/CSS fast becomes an art form in and of itself, this not only makes economic and commercial sense, it enables individuals to play to their strengths. Few PHP gurus have an encyclopedic knowledge of the subtle nuances of IE6 Quirks Mode.

However, if you choose to use PHP templating, then the Web developers have no choice but to write in PHP. Admittedly, there's not much PHP they need to know. It's the kind of PHP that could easily go on a cheat sheet. The problem is not so much one of a learning curve, but rather one of danger. PHP, after all, does not restrict what these Web developers may or may not use in their templates. Rather, they must restrict themselves. Infinite loops, dangerous system calls, and other potentially critical mistakes are just a tiny typographical error away.

If there were some way to enable Web developers to render the output of a page using flexible tags as part of an arbitrary language, rather than using PHP, this problem could easily be negated. Smarty provides just such a solution.

True Templating with Smarty Templates

Smarty is a package for PHP that enables developers to easily prepare output for a template, and then leave the template to display it in whatever way it sees fit.

Smarty is unique in that it provides not just simple "dump value" methodology, but also allows loops, conditionals, and the traversing of multidimensional arrays. In a nutshell, it replicates all the traditional simple PHP methods used in native PHP templating, without using PHP at all.

Another big advantage of Smarty is its speed. Believe it or not, it actually works by *creating* native PHP from the template. That native PHP is then cached, such that if the template is not changed with subsequent requests, the template itself does not have to be translated into PHP again. It is simply pulled straight from the cache and executed. After that first initial execution, there is no speed penalty whatsoever.

Installing Smarty

Installing Smarty is straightforward. Unlike many other template engines, however, it is not a traditional PEAR package, so you have to download and install it manually.

Currently, Smarty resides at www.smarty.net.

The following instructions assume you're running on Mac OS X, UNIX, or Linux. If you're running on Windows, instructions are provided at http://smarty.incutio.com/?page=SmartyInstallationWindows. *After you have downloaded it, unpack it:*

```
root@linuxvm:~# tar -xzvf Smarty-2.6.2.tar.gz
Smarty-2.6.2/
Smarty-2.6.2/COPYING.lib
Smarty-2.6.2/.cvsignore
Smarty-2.6.2/BUGS
Smarty-2.6.2/demo/
...
Smarty-2.6.2/misc/smarty_icon.README
Smarty-2.6.2/misc/smarty_icon.gif
root@linuxvm:~#
```

Next, you must shift the libraries provided by Smarty to somewhere PHP can see them. Generally, all you need to do is copy the full contents of the libs/ subfolder into /usr/local/lib/php, like so:

```
root@linuxvm:~/Smarty-2.6.2# cp -r libs/ /usr/local/lib/php
```

Next, you must hook up your application to use Smarty. Immediately beneath the PHP files that will be using Smarty in your application, you must create directories called templates, templates_c, cache, and configs:

```
root@linuxvm:~# cd public_html/tests/prophp6/mvc/
root@linuxvm:~/public_html/tests/prophp6/mvc# mkdir templates_c
root@linuxvm:~/public_html/tests/prophp6/mvc# mkdir configs
root@linuxvm:~/public_html/tests/prophp6/mvc# mkdir templates
root@linuxvm:~/public_html/tests/prophp6/mvc# mkdir cache
```

Mercifully, Smarty is sympathetic to the needs of real-world projects, for which configuration steps such as these might not always be possible (such as when your PHP scripts reside in multiple directories). You can also manually specify where these folders should exist from within your PHP code. You will learn how later in this chapter.

Next, you need to set some permissions on two of these folders: `template_c` and `cache`. Set the ownership of these folders to be that of the username of your Web server. In most cases, this is the `nobody` user, but it may also be `apache` or various others. If you are unsure, you can check by issuing the following:

```
ps axuw | grep httpd | grep -v grep | awk '{print $1}' | tail -1
```

What is important here is that this user, and the group of which that user is a member, can read and write to these folders freely. Set permissions as follows:

```
chown nobody.users ./cache
chown nobody.users ./template_c
chmod 770 ./cache
chmod 770 ./template_c
```

The mode 770 means that the owner of these folders may read, write, and execute the contents, and that no one else may. If this bothers you, and you are unable to become the root on this machine, you may want to use 775 instead, which allows others read and write access. You may, however, rightly deem this to be a security risk.

Using Smarty

A typical Smarty implementation consists of a controller (much as before) ending in `.php`, and a template file representing the view, this time ending in `.tpl`.

smartytest.php

Take a look at the following very simple example:

```
<?
require('Smarty.class.php');

$objSmarty = new Smarty;
$strTemplate = "smartytest.tpl";

$objSmarty->assign("test_variable", "This is the value of my test variable");

$objSmarty->display($strTemplate);
?>
```

You must also enter the template code for this script, which must reside in the folder called `template` that you have created underneath this one.

smartytest.tpl

Take a look at the following code:

```
<html>
<head>
  <title>Untitled</title>
</head>

<body>
  This is my template!<BR>
  The value of the variable is: {$test_variable}

</body>
</html>
```

You've probably guessed that the output from running `smartytest.php` (which then invokes the output `template smartytest.tpl`) is something like the following:

```
This is my template!
The value of the variable is: This is the value of my test variable
```

As you can see, you have assigned your Smarty template object a variable called `test_variable`, the output of which has successfully been rendered by using the syntax `{$test_variable}` in the template itself.

This is simple enough, but how do you go about expressing arrays, displaying content conditionally, and taking advantage of all the functionality traditionally available in the native PHP templating discussed earlier?

Linear Arrays in Smarty

Pushing a linear array to Smarty and then recursing its contents are relatively simple. Consider the following code in your PHP control script:

```
$objSmarty->assign("FirstName",array("John","Mary","James","Henry"));
```

As you can see, you can assign PHP variables to your Smarty template object in exactly the same way as you would assign a normal garden-variety string. To render it, you typically use the Smarty equivalent of a `for` loop, as shown here:

```
{section name=x loop=$FirstName}
  {$FirstName[x]}<BR>
{/section}
```

The output is predictable enough:

```
John
Mary
James
Henry
```

Associative Arrays in Smarty

You can approach associative arrays (hashes) in a very similar manner to how you approach linear arrays. Consider the following control code to supply the Smarty template:

```
$arHash["Name"] = "Ed";
$arHash["Age"] = 27;
$arHash["Location"] = "London";
$objSmarty-assign("Writer", $arHash);
```

Again, the approach for assignment appears to be very similar. The following shows how you can now render the output in your template:

```
The author of this chapter is {$Writer.Name}, {$Writer.Age} years of age,
currently residing in {$Writer.Location}.
```

Notice the simple syntax of {$X.Y}, where X is the name of the Smarty variable, and Y is the key from the hash that has been assigned to it. This yields the following output:

```
The author of this chapter is Ed, 27 years of age, currently residing in London.
```

Conditionals in Smarty

What if you want to display content only if a certain condition is met? This would be of particular interest to you in displaying error messages. You would want to display the error only if an error has definitely occurred.

You assign variables in your controller as follows:

```
$objSmarty->assign("isError", 1);
$objSmarty->assign("ErrorText", "You did not specify a search term.");
```

The following template logic can support this:

```
{if $isError == 1}
    The following error occurred: {$ErrorText}
{/if}
```

As you can see, a conditional expression is very similar to what you would use in PHP to perform the test. This will render only the introductory text, and the error itself, if isError is set to 1:

```
The following error occurred: You did not specify a search term.
```

To prove this to yourself, change the assignment to isError in your controller to 0. The output is not rendered at all.

This is somewhat laborious, though. In native PHP templating, you would probably just check whether an error message has been defined. You can also do that in Smarty:

```
{if $ErrorText}
    The following error occurred: {$ErrorText}
{/if}
```

This completely negates the need to explicitly tell Smarty whether an error exists. It can determine this for itself by looking for a non-blank value in the conditional.

Rewriting search.php with Smarty

Now you can put these skills into practice with a slightly more complex example. Using Smarty, you can quite easily rewrite the search.php and search.phtml pair from the first part of the chapter.

Look at the content you are creating in search.php so that you know what you have to reproduce using Smarty. Currently, by the time it reaches search.phtml, the $displayHash variable may contain the following:

- ❑   HADPROBLEMS — A true/false variable, which, again, you can represent as an ordinary variable in Smarty

- ❑   PROBLEMS — An array of strings, each of which is a problem that has been experienced, only to be echoed if HADPROBLEMS is set to true

Quickly modify search.php so that it looks like the following. The shaded area indicates the code that's been modified or added from the original version:

```
require_once("constants.phpm");
require_once("request.phpm");
require_once("constraint.phpm");
require_once("constraintfailure.phpm");

$strTemplateFile = "s_search.tpl";

require("Smarty.class.php");
$objSmarty = new Smarty;

$objRequest = new request();
$blHadProblems = ($objRequest->IsRedirectFollowingConstraintFailure());

if ($blHadProblems) {
  $objSmarty->assign("HADPROBLEMS", "true");
};

if ($blHadProblems) {
  $objFailingRequest =
        $objRequest->GetOriginalRequestObjectFollowingConstraintFailure();
  $arConstraintFailures = $objFailingRequest->GetConstraintFailures();
  $problemArray = Array();
  for ($i=0; $i<=sizeof($arConstraintFailures)-1; $i++) {
    $objThisConstraintFailure = &$arConstraintFailures[$i];
    $objThisFailingConstraintObject =
        $objThisConstraintFailure->GetFailedConstraintObject();
    $intTypeOfFailure = $objThisFailingConstraintObject->GetConstraintType();
    switch ($intTypeOfFailure) {
      case CT_MINLENGTH:
```

```
            $problemArray[] = "Your search term was too short.";
            break;
        case CT_MAXLENGTH:
            $problemArray[] = "Your search term was too long.";
            break;
        case CT_PERMITTEDCHARACTERS:
            $problemArray[] = "Your search term contained characters I
                            didn't understand.";
            break;
      };
    };
  };
```

```
if ($problemArray) {
  $objSmarty->assign("PROBLEMS", $problemArray);
};
$objSmarty->display($strTemplateFile);
```

Create a corresponding template file in the `templates` subfolder called `s_search.tpl`:

```
<!DOCTYPE HTML PUBLIC "-//W3C//DTD HTML 4.01 Transitional//EN">

<html>
<head>
  <title>Ed's Search Page</title>
</head>

<body>
<H1>Ed's Search Page</H1>
<hr>
You can search for types of steak here.
<BR><BR>
{if $HADPROBLEMS}
 <B>Sorry, there were problems with your search!</B>
  {section name=x loop=$PROBLEMS}
    {$PROBLEMS[x]}
  {/section}
{/if}
<FORM METHOD="GET" ACTION="searchresults.php">
  <TABLE BORDER="0">
    <TR>
      <TD>Type of Steak</TD>
      <TD><INPUT TYPE="TEXT" NAME="typeOfSteak"></TD>
    </TR>
  </TABLE><BR>
  <INPUT TYPE="SUBMIT">
</FORM>
</body>
</html>
```

Run the revised `search.php` and try to generate errors as you did before. You'll notice that the output upon receiving such errors is almost exactly the same, so the template conversion has been a resounding success.

small problem, however. If you generate only one error, you will still receive a message
t "there were problems," rather than "there was a problem," with your search.

.e original .PHTML native PHP template, you accounted for this using the following:

```
<B>Sorry, there
<?=((sizeof($displayHash["PROBLEMS"]) > 1) ? "were problems" : "was a problem")?>
with your search!</B>
```

Thankfully, you can account for this in Smarty, too. All you need to do is measure the size of the array
and adjust the output accordingly, exactly as you do in native PHP:

```
<B>Sorry, there {if $PROBLEMS[1]}were problems{else}was a problem{/if}
with your search!</B>
```

There is some slight cheating going on, however. There is no way in Smarty to measure the size of an
array without calling upon PHP code, so the code simply checks for the existence of a second element in
the array. If it exists, then the user sees the plural text. Otherwise, the user sees the singular text.

If you modify your template to use this new code, you should find that the output of the script is exactly
the same now as it was when you used native PHP templating in the first half of the chapter. You could,
of course, rewrite searchresults.php and searchresults.phtml using the same technique. Why not
try doing that now?

Advanced Smarty

Now that you've familiarized yourself with basic Smarty use, it's worth looking in a little more detail at
some of the more advanced features it offers.

Run-time Configuration

As mentioned at the beginning of this section, you may well find yourself confronted with situations in
which creating subfolders under every single location where .php files reside is undesirable. Thankfully,
Smarty enables you to specify these locations at run-time:

```
$smarty->template_dir = '/web/www.mydomain.com/smarty/guestbook/templates/';
$smarty->compile_dir = '/web/www.mydomain.com/smarty/guestbook/templates_c/';
$smarty->config_dir = '/web/www.mydomain.com/smarty/guestbook/configs/';
$smarty->cache_dir = '/web/www.mydomain.com/smarty/guestbook/cache/';
```

Multidimensional Arrays

Multidimensional arrays may be treated in much the same manner as their single-dimensional
counterparts, whether they are associative, linear, or a mixture:

```
$multiArray = Array(Array("x","o","x"),Array("o","x","x"),
Array("o","o","x")); $objSmarty->assign("TicTacToBoard", $multiArray);
```

Tie this to the following template:

```
<TABLE BORDER="1">
  {section name=y loop=$TicTacToBoard}
    <TR>
      {section name=x loop=$TicTacToBoard[y]}
        <TD>{$TicTacToBoard[y][x]}</TD>
      {/section}
    </TR>
  {/section}
</TABLE>
```

This is the expected, familiar Tic-Tac-Toe board, with X winning down the left-to-right diagonal.

Variable Modifiers

Variable modifiers may be used by template designers to perform very simple modifications to the variables they have received:

```
$smarty->assign('bookTitle', "Professional PHP5");
```

Couple this with the template code:

```
{$bookTitle|replace:"PHP5":"PHP6"}
```

The output is very much as expected.

Functions

Smarty defines a number of functions in its language. It considers some to be built-in — that is, unable to be modified or overwritten. The functions provided in Smarty are really better described as methods, in that they do not generally perform any function on an input, unlike the modifiers you have just met (such as replace, which changes its input before rendering it).

One very useful example is the strip function, which enables you to neatly lay out HTML properly tabulated and spaced, safe in the knowledge that any extraneous white space will be stripped out before it is sent to the browser. This makes the templates very easy to maintain:

```
{strip}
<table border="0">
 <tr>
    <td>
        Here is some content.
    </td>
 </tr>
</table>
{/strip}
```

This is a great deal easier for a human being to read. When the HTML is sent to the browser, however, how it looks behind the scenes is far less important than how it is displayed to the user. The {strip} tag removes any whitespace for you that might disturb the output:

```
<table border="0"><tr><td>Here is some content.</td></tr></table>
```

Capturing Output

Sometimes, rather than simply spit the parsed template output directly to screen, you may want to capture it into a variable. For example, this can be particularly useful should you want to render XML content using Smarty, and then pass it through an XSL stylesheet to actually render it to the Web browser. Alternatively, you may not want to pass the rendered content at all. For example, you may be sending an HTML e-mail. Here, Smarty is very useful indeed, as you may have discovered in Chapter 11:

```
// capture the output
$strOutput = $objSmarty-fetch("index.tpl");
```

Simply assign the rendered template's output HTML to the variable $strOutput, with which you can then do whatever you desire.

Including Other Templates

Smarty even enables you to include other templates, which will be parsed in the normal way. You could use this to add common headers and footers to your pages:

```
{include file="header.tpl"}
```

Further Reading

The functionality of Smarty is enormous and far beyond the scope of this chapter. Having been introduced to some examples of standard usage, however, you should now be well equipped to explore its features further.

The obvious starting point is the Smarty reference site at www.smarty.net/manual/en/ All modifiers, functions, and even obscure configuration parameters are documented here in full. Conveniently, the documentation is divided into two sections that target both programmers (the people doing the PHP) and HTML template developers.

When to Use Smarty vs. Traditional Templating

The decision to use Smarty over traditional native PHP templating should not be taken lightly. Although Smarty is clearly a great tool for simple templating, its functionality is still only a subset of what might be needed in large-scale projects.

Although it can be extended with native PHP through the use of the {php} and {/php} tags, doing so rather defeats the purpose of using safe templates in the first place. Indeed, Smarty's own Web site states that "embedding PHP code into templates is highly discouraged."

The skills and experience of any other developers working with you on the project are likely to be the deciding factor. If you are the sole engineer working on a project, it is almost certainly better to use native templating. Conversely, if the project requires a number of designers and HTML specialists working on the output from your scripts, Smarty templates are a much safer bet, because they allow such individuals to manipulate the display logic of your application to their hearts' content, without touching the PHP code behind it.

A Spot of Modeling Work

So far, this chapter has examined the controller (the bit that handles the user journey through the site and all of the logic associated with it) and the view (the bit at the front end that handles the display of output data and the capture of input data); but you've not yet examined the model in much detail.

This is a conscious decision. The model is the bit that is truly independent of your choice of controller implementation, or your choice of templating system. It doesn't matter; it should never change. Your model should comprise a suite of reusable, modular classes — smart building blocks that you can click in and out of your project as and when you need.

In Chapter 7, you saw how the classes that comprise your application's model can be divided broadly into *utility classes* (which do useful things such as sending e-mail, handling external data providers, and so forth) and *business objects* (which represent useful entities in your application such as orders, customers, products, and so forth).

The difference in nomenclature is revealing: a utility *class*, and a business *object*. As a rule of thumb, a utility class is never instantiated. It is used statically because, by its very definition, there should never be any difference between one instance and another. Conversely, a business object is almost always instantiated (although it may have static methods), as one or more *instances* are usually recorded in the underlying data source. Put another way, your application will typically have many "users," but only one "e-mail sending facility."

Earlier in this chapter, you learned that if you have the separation of MVC just right, you should theoretically be able to drop your business and utility classes into an entirely different application — not even a Web-based application — and they will still work. As it happens, there's a good reason you might want to do that, and it's called *unit testing*.

Introducing Unit Testing

Ensuring that a component does exactly what you want it to do is an essential step in application development. As you have already learned elsewhere in this book, it is vital that components are tested *before* they are integrated within the bigger picture application. Always write the application around the core components. Never write your core components around your application.

For slightly more complex classes (or even hierarchies of several classes), devising a suitable test strategy can appear to be quite tricky. The temptation to resort to spitting out huge chunks of data with `var_dump()` or using the error log can be overwhelming, but you should resist it, because you can save yourself a great deal of time by using a prewritten *unit testing framework*. Not only that, but a coherent, thorough, and professional approach to testing is something you can actively demonstrate to your clients (or your boss), whereas having hundreds of `error_log()` statements is not.

Here's a quick checklist for you. Does the following approach seem familiar?

1. Write the class.

2. Produce a short test script that `requires` the class, instantiates it, calls some methods, and spits out some output.

3. Run the script.

4. Check the output of the script against what you expected (in your head).

5. If the output looks good, move on. If not, adjust the class and repeat Steps 3 and 4 until the output appears to work.

6. Possibly many weeks later, integrate the component into the mother application.

It sounds almost comical, but this kind of process is actually more widespread than you might think. The problem with approaching your component testing this way is that it's neither thorough nor systematic. In other words, not only are you potentially testing only a small subset of your component, you're also taking longer than you really need to. Furthermore, if you do find problems, your short test script won't be of much help when it comes to tracking them down. You'll have to decide whether your test is successful or not every time you test.

Thankfully, there is another way. Revise the component test workflow to look more like this:

1. Design the interface (but not the implementation) of the class.

2. Create a test suite for the (empty) class, and check that it tests okay.

3. Write the implementation of the class.

4. Run the test suite again.

5. Fix any errors that are causing unexpected results and then go back to Step 4.

6. Integrate the component into the other application.

Next, you'll take a look at these steps in more detail to discover exactly what is meant by a "test suite." The concept of the test case is covered a little later in this chapter.

Designing the Interface of Your Class

Let's first recap some object-oriented programming (OOP) edicts. In OOP design, it's often said that the most important part of your object hierarchy is the interface, and the least important part is the implementation.

This might sound odd, but think of it as follows. If you're designing a user class, what's actually going through your head?

"I'll need to have username, first name, last name, and encrypted password properties, and I'll need methods to tell my application which security groups this user belongs to, and a method to work out how long it's been since their last login, and . . ."

You're being smart without even realizing it. You're listing to yourself the methods and member variables of the object. This is the *business analysis* of object modeling. What you're not trying to do is to figure out how long it has been since the user's last login. In fact, there's probably more than one way to do that. It doesn't really matter. Whichever way you go about it won't affect your interface.

In fact, the interfaces of your application's suite of classes is *subjective*. In other words, some analytical skill is required in translating paper specifications into a class hierarchy with methods and member variables. Conversely, making those methods do what they say they will do is *objective*. It either works as expected or it doesn't work. As a PHP professional, you might prefer to have a junior software engineer (if you're fortunate enough to have one working under you) handling this detail, so that you can make the big decisions at the top.

Approaching this in terms of a unit-testing-friendly workflow is simple. On the first draft of your class, *leave all the methods completely blank*. Use nothing but white space between opening and closing braces. You'll look at this in more detail later in this chapter.

Creating a Test Suite for Your Class

With the skeleton class to test, it's not a bad idea to go ahead and create your test suite. Right now, you'll learn about the theory. The specifics of how to implement this with a particular testing framework are covered later in this chapter.

The function of a test suite is to provide a simple, black-box solution for testing your class. When invoked, it hooks directly into the important functionality of your class, performs a series of tests, and then states whether those tests were successful. It is truly an appliance.

The nature of these tests is important to understand. You implement a test suite by extending what is known as the *test case class*. This is provided as part of the unit testing framework you choose to use (in this case, PHPUnit, which is covered in much more detail later in this chapter). You must be careful with certain administrative bits and pieces in the extended class (largely relating to instructing the test unit how to instantiate and destroy the test class); but after that, it's up to you to provide a test method for every actual method in the test class.

The test methods must be named according to the unit testing framework's requirements so that it knows to execute them as part of the test suite's run-time behavior. They are responsible for testing the core functionality of the test class.

Each test method follows the same basic pattern:

1. Decide upon some input parameters for the test class method.
2. Determine (as a human being!) the result expected to be returned from the test class method, based on those input parameters.
3. Call that method (with those input parameters) and trap the result.
4. Assert the result to be equal to the expected result.

You don't need to worry about doing anything else. You should assume that the test suite functionality provided by your unit testing framework knows what to do when that assertion is or isn't true. This is certainly true of PHPUnit, which you'll meet shortly.

By creating your test case class, you have effectively provided the *modus operandi* — that is, the operational inner workings — for your test suite.

At this stage, you would run your black box for the first time and watch it fail spectacularly. It will fail, of course, because you don't have any implementation in your class yet, so by definition any values returned won't be what is expected (or "asserted"). You should, however, at least be able to get your first idea of what the test results will roughly look like when the implementation has been taken care of.

Writing the Implementation of Your Class

Without altering the interface of your class, go about writing your code to make it work. There's no need to test anything as you go; this is what the test suite is for. However, you may want to do a syntax check along the way to ensure that you haven't made any typos. A test suite is really for rooting out logic errors, rather than compilation errors.

In case you've not encountered it before, you can perform a syntax check at the command line by using `php` with the `-1` parameter, followed by the filename of the class or script whose syntax you want to check.

If your class talks to a database, it may not be a bad idea to also check any database SQL queries before you walk away from the implementation. Because PHP isn't closely linked into the database server, rooting out malformed SQL syntax may be easier to do now than after you discover that your test suite fails on one or more methods. In addition, keep in mind that because data in a database can change independently from your code, you'll find it tricky to accurately predict the expected output of methods that do query a database.

Take a look at the following sample query, pulled from a typical user class:

```
$sql = "SELECT group_id FROM user_group WHERE user_id = $user_id";
```

Substitute the `$user_id` for a sensible value and confirm that the query works in the PostgreSQL (or other) console. If it does, you're in business.

Assuming that your PHP syntax and SQL queries check out okay and you've implemented all your methods, you can go ahead and start testing.

The Second Run

Fire up your test suite black box once more. Now that you've implemented your class, you should have more luck with the test results than the last time you ran it. If your class didn't pass all the tests, it's time to retrace your steps using traditional debugging techniques.

After your test suite runs with a 100 percent success rate, you can be fully confident that your class is ready for the production environment, and you can accordingly integrate it into the mother application.

Introduction to PHPUnit

PHPUnit is developed by Sebastian Bergmann and is one of a small number of PHP unit testing frameworks currently available. You might prefer PHPUnit to some of its competitors because it is free, easy to use, and, best of all, available from PEAR.

Perhaps rather confusingly, two packages are readily available for PHP, both of which are named PHPUnit and both of which perform essentially the same task. Indeed, they even share a similar implementation. The implementation examined in this chapter is by Sebastian Bergmann, which is better suited for PHP 6.

The PHPUnit package is effectively a suite of classes, rather than a single class. This chapter focuses on its test case and test suite functionality. There is more to PHPUnit, of course. If you're curious, when you're finished with this chapter, you may want to take a look at www.sebastian-bergmann.de/ PHPUnit/, which goes into more detail.

Those of you with a Java background may have already drawn comparisons to JUnit (www.junit.org), and you would be right to do so; PHPUnit is, in fact, loosely based on JUnit. Much of this chapter's content may, therefore, already be familiar to you. What you may not be familiar with is just how easily this powerful methodology can be put to use in PHP 6.

Installing PHPUnit

A good starting point is to get your PHP setup equipped with PHPUnit. It is not part of the PEAR Foundation Classes, so you need to install it yourself. Even if you have previously installed it, it might not be a bad idea now to check whether you are running the latest version.

Use the standard PEAR syntax to execute an installation of PHPUnit. If you are running the latest version, PEAR will tell you. If not, or you don't have it installed, you will see output similar to the following (on a UNIX-like environment):

```
root@genesis:~# pear install PHPUnit
downloading PHPUnit-0.6.2
...done: 11,551 bytes
install ok: PHPUnit 0.6.2
root@genesis:~ #
```

If you want (or need) to install manually (for example, on a production environment in which you are not blessed with root access to the server), simply visit the PEAR package page at www.phpunit.de/. Download and decompress the archive into an appropriate place. After everything's installed correctly you can continue safely.

Test Cases

This section takes a look at how to create a test case using PHPUnit. Assume that you have a test class saved in a separate file, testclass.phpm. Because you're still looking at the theory of PHPUnit, it doesn't matter too much at this stage what's in that class. Something similar to the following will suffice for now:

```php
<?php
class TestClass {
 private $testVar;

 function myMethod($strParam) {
  $this->testVar = $strParam;
  return('expected result');
 }

};
```

You can now create the test case in a separate PHP file, testcase.phpm. The first two lines of the test case should include both the necessary PHPUnit class and the test class file(s):

```php
require_once("testclass.phpm");
require_once("PHPUnit.php");
```

Assuming that you used PEAR to install PHPUnit, it should be able to find `PHPUnit.php` just fine. If not, and you had to install it manually, then you may have to help PHP out by pointing it to the correct file, as follows:

```
require_once("/home/ed/myphplibs/PHPUnit.php");
```

In this case, PHPUnit is installed in `/home/ed/myphplibs`.

Now take a look at how to extend the `PHPUnit_TestCase` class to form your very own test case with some pseudocode:

```
class MyTestCase extends PHPUnit_TestCase
{
    var $objMyTestClass;

    function __construct($name) {
        $this->PHPUnit_TestCase($name);
    }

    function setUp() {
        $this->objMyTestClass = new TestClass();
    }

    function tearDown() {
        unset($this->objMyTestClass);
    }

    function testMyMethod() {
        $actualResult = $this->objMyTestClass->myMethod('parameter');
        $expectedResult = 'expected result';
        $this->assertTrue($actualResult == $expectedResult);
    }
}
```

You can now go through this step by step. Consider the first line of code:

```
class MyTestCase extends PHPUnit_TestCase
```

Name the class whatever you want. Ensure that it extends `PHPUnit_TestCase`, however.

Next, take a look at this line:

```
var $objMyTestClass;
```

The only member variable your extended test case class needs is a single instance of your test class. However, in more complex situations you may want to use multiple instances of the same class, or even more than one class. However, try to keep the number of classes involved in any given test case to a minimum, for the sake of simplicity. Certainly, you should never group unrelated classes together in a single test case.

Consider this code:

```
function __construct($name) {
    $this-PHPUnit_TestCase($name);
}
```

The constructor for your extended test case class falls here. Its only job is to call its parent constructor. Note the non-optional $name parameter, however, which is used by the test suite class.

Now take a look at the following code:

```
function setUp() {
    $this->objMyTestClass = new TestClass();
}

function tearDown() {
    unset($this->objMyTestClass);
}
```

These two methods are best described as virtual constructors and destructors. These are called before and after the various test functions are executed. Usually, their only job is to instantiate a working instance of your test class into the member variable you defined earlier.

The following code is where the real meat of your test case is defined:

```
function testMyMethod() {
    $actualResult = $this->objMyTestClass->myMethod('parameter');
    $expectedResult = 'expected result';
    $this->assertTrue($actualResult == $expectedResult);
}
```

Here, you declare one method for each method of your test class that you want to test. The method must begin with the word test in order for it to be automatically executed by the test suite. You should name the method test, followed by the name of the real method in your test class. This makes things a great deal clearer if you need to look at the test case again.

The actual functionality of this method is largely up to you. Ultimately, however, you will be doing four things:

1. Declaring (that is, hard-coding) or determining a test parameter to pass into your test class's method

2. Declaring or determining the *expected* result based on that parameter

3. Calling the method with that parameter and capturing the actual result

4. Comparing the actual result to your hypothesis

That comparison should be done using one of a number of assertion methods provided by PHPUnit. It is these assertions that enable the test suite to report test results. Essentially, it is the accuracy of your assertions that will be reported.

Numerous assertion methods are available — assertEquals, assertTrue, assertFalse, assertNotNull, assertNull, assertSame, assertNotSame, assertType, and assertRegExp. They pretty much all do exactly what you'd expect from their name. However, if you're curious and need definitive explanations, check out /usr/local/lib/php/PHPUnit/Assert.php or the file Assert.php in the directory in which you installed PHPUnit.

You may be wondering why having so many assert methods is necessary. Surely all comparisons can be handled using assertEquals and making liberal use of appropriate built-in PHP functions, right? This is true. All the variations are really just a convenience to make your code a little easier to read, and to enable you to avoid using double negatives and so forth. In later versions of PHPUnit, the assertions actually provide assertion-specific details with any failed test (such as showing the two types in question in assertType, and which characters don't actually match when comparing two strings).

The Test Suite

Having developed your test case class, using it in a test suite is actually a relatively simple mechanism. You might name the following testsuite.php:

```php
<?php
require_once 'testcase.php';
require_once 'PHPUnit.php';

$objSuite = new PHPUnit_TestSuite("MyTestCase");
$strResult = PHPUnit::run($objSuite);

print $strResult->toString();
?>
```

Replace MyTestCase with the actual name of your test case class. If you run this from the command line (as opposed to using your Web browser), you'll get output that looks something like this if things worked:

```
TestCase objMyTestClass->myMethod() passed
```

It will look like the following if things didn't work:

```
TestCase objMyTestClass->myMethod() failed: expected true, actual false
```

Note that if you want to run in a Web browser, rather than at the command line, you should use toHTML rather than the toString method on the output string so that carriage returns are converted to <br/> and so forth.

Why Bother?

At first glance, it might be difficult to see the immense advantages arising from using this method of testing over a more quick-and-dirty method involving the server error log (such as the one somewhat contemptuously described earlier). The following sections describe why you should be using unit testing frameworks.

Regression Testing

The vast majority of code you'll ever work on will, at some stage, need to evolve. It may not necessarily be you who works on it, but you can be fairly certain that it won't remain untouched for too long.

For example, you might need to rework an existing method to make it provide exactly the same functionality as it did before but with a big performance increase. The only way to do this is to completely rewrite the method, keeping the interface the same but with an optimized inner algorithm. In this kind of example, your testing suite is immensely useful. Simply run it before and after your new algorithm has been developed, and confirm that you get the same results both times.

A more likely scenario is that your class must be extended with a new method to support some new business requirement. Even then, your testing suite is useful in its unmodified form. You can ensure that your new method does not in any way impact the functionality of any other methods. After verifying this, you can simply extend your test case class to test your new method.

Either way, you can see that using unit testing frameworks for this kind of testing (commonly known as *regression testing*) makes good sense.

Framework Usability

Your test case classes may have wider uses than you think. Other classes you develop with similar or identical interface functionality can be quickly and reliably tested using your existing test suites.

In particular, you may have inherited classes that overwrite the functionality of their parent class. Alternatively, taking advantage of PHP 6's object model, you may have classes that implement abstract interfaces. A good example of this is objects representing entities stored in a database, which will almost certainly have `getProperty` and `setProperty` methods, and so forth, as you saw in Chapter 7. With little or no adaptation, you can use a standard test suite to provide an instant and reliable commentary on the functionality of such generic classes.

Demonstrable Quality Assurance

A professional software development environment can often contain a complex hierarchy of individuals involved on any given project — from the project manager right through to the lead architect, the software engineers, the designers, and others.

In this kind of environment, literally tens of thousands of lines of code can be churned out every day. It is simply impossible for the project's lead architect to test every single component his or her developers produce.

With this kind of structured testing methodology, the management buzzword of *empowerment* becomes an achievable reality. That is to say, engineers can be safely trusted to test their own code, because this methodology encourages a thoroughness that is often absent in other, more haphazard component-testing techniques. Lead architects can easily standardize quality assurance across all component production, and have far greater confidence in his or her team's output as a result.

The formal nature of this process is likely to be viewed favorably by nontechnical individuals with a keen interest in the progress of a project (such as project and account managers).

Reducing the Burden of Functional Testing

It's often said that the least sexy part of the project life cycle is functional testing. Whether this statement is fair or not, it is certainly an additional cost that must be borne and budgeted for.

By requiring the development team to take ownership of the functional testing of its own components, the need for exhaustive and extensive functional testing of the completed application can be greatly reduced. It is not eliminated entirely, however; and as you will learn in Chapter 20, it is still vitally important.

Developing the Model in Isolation

In a typical Web application development project, the most contentious aspect of the build itself is often the look and feel and user journey — in other words, it is often the information architecture ("wireframes"), site map, and page treatments that are signed off last. Because these together form a dependency that holds up the development of any finished HTML, software engineers can often be waiting with little to do, wondering when they can get started.

However, debate over the user journey, page layout, site maps, navigation, or creative implementation shouldn't necessarily mean that decisions over business objects cannot be taken in a separate developmental branch. For example, if you know that user registration is a requirement in the finished application, and you can make educated guesses about which fields will be required during registration, then it is within your power to deduce that a business class (probably a data-bound object, as covered in Chapter 7) called `User` must be built, as well as a utility class called `Registration`.

Moreover, you can probably deduce what member variables and methods these classes should have, too. Develop those methods in isolation within a test suite, test them, and be confident that you can "drop them" into the application once other elements of the project plan have fallen into place.

Summary

In this chapter, you learned about the model-view- controller (MVC) design pattern, and its importance in sound application architecture.

As well as learning the theory behind MVC methodology, you were introduced to two very different ways in which that methodology can be followed. First, you met an MVC toolkit that enables you to implement a `request` and `constraint` object hierarchy in your projects to better enforce the separation between model, view, and controller.

Then you were introduced to the concept of templating, and how and why it proves to be an excellent example of best-practice MVC compliance. You also met post-redirect-get (PRG) and saw why the best implementations of MVC make use of it.

You also looked at Smarty templates in some detail, and saw just how easily you can convert native PHP templates into Smarty templates in just a few minutes, as well as how some of the advanced features of Smarty can provide a valid templating choice for all but the most complex projects.

Finally, you looked at the role of the model in the MVC paradigm, and how unit testing can provide a useful mechanism for developing the model in isolation.

In Chapter 14, you'll look at some ready-made, off-the-shelf toolkits that (among other functionality) try to provide MVC-like architecture out-of-the-box. It's an entirely different approach to "rolling your own" as you did in this chapter, but, as you'll see, it does have its benefits.

14

PHP Application Frameworks

As the name suggests, this book is a professional title, pitched squarely at developers looking to make a career out of writing code in PHP — or hobbyists who want to do it "how the pros do it."

Such titles are available for virtually all Web application development languages — .NET, classic ASP, ColdFusion, JSP, and so forth — because for each and every one of those languages there is a need to differentiate between "how to get started" and "how to do it right."

PHP, however, probably needs books like this more than any other development language. As mentioned numerous times throughout this book, one of PHP's greatest assets is also one of its greatest weaknesses — its simplicity and shallow learning curve. Like a powerful European sports car, it is phenomenally dangerous in the wrong hands. Therefore, throughout this book, we have been at pains to demonstrate best practices across every programming discipline — objects and classes, database abstraction, event-driven programming, logging and debugging, communicating with users, and much more.

This chapter introduces you to something supremely useful: the concept of *application frameworks*, which remove a lot of the hassle for you by forcing you to do things right from the word "go." Make no mistake, the previous 13 chapters were vital to give you the "why" as well as the "how" — but now you know "why" you can make life considerably easier for yourself by letting something else take care of the best practices for you.

Introduction to Frameworks

In simple terms, a *framework* is a pre-prepared set of code that provides you with a predrawn pencil sketch on which to paint your completed application. In some cases, the framework is simply a collection of PHP classes. The onus is then on you, as a developer, to use them properly. In other cases, a more intimate relationship with the application server is achieved, which means that compliance is enforced — rather than requested.

A huge number of frameworks have made it into the marketplace. Virtually all are free. Some are better maintained than others. Some are better supported than others. Crucially, only one has a notional nod of assent from the PHP development community. In each case, though, they attempt to address a number of core objectives — some frameworks implementing more than others.

Application Structure

If you've ever been unfortunate enough to encounter a junior developer's PHP project for maintenance purposes, you no doubt have been unsure exactly where to start. Furthermore, you've no doubt discovered a myriad of files and folders with no obvious place for anything, some code in classes, some not; some HTML held in templates, some written from code; some images in the database, others on disk — it's probably not a pleasant memory, to say the least.

That PHP leaves the structure and layout of an application to the developer is something of a double-edged sword. In the right hands, it allows for enormous flexibility. There is no "scaffolding" required to start a project, as there is in the likes of Ruby on Rails (RoR), and so no constraints are placed from the outset. In the wrong hands (or in the absence of comprehensive architectural documentation), this can understandably lead to confusion.

Many application frameworks attempt to redress this by imposing on the developer a semi-rigid application structure. This can be as simple as a preferred directory hierarchy — perhaps allocating a folder for utility classes, one for templates, and one for business objects. At a more sophisticated level, it can get intimately involved at the HTTP request level, and "route" requests through a set of classes that must conform to a predetermined structure.

This is particularly true in the case of those frameworks that implement model-view-controller (MVC) to its natural conclusion. In such frameworks, an HTTP request to `/admin/edituser.php?id=12345` would not be permitted. Instead, an equivalent request such as `/user/edit/12345` might automatically invoke an "edit" method of a "user" class — a class that must implement a very specific interface.

Such an approach is pretty radical. It disposes entirely with the concept of PHP as a linear scripting language, and instead divides applications into component parts driven by user behavior. As you'll see later in this chapter, this can speed up authoring code and reduce unnecessary duplication — but it can also be a little unduly constraining for advanced developers.

Separation of Code and Display Logic

Even when a PHP framework chooses not to implement the kind of radical MVC methodology discussed in the previous section, virtually all will insist upon a best-practice separation of code and display logic, as endorsed throughout this book.

This can be achieved in a number of different ways. Some will simply look to separate scripts into two sets of PHP code (one for behavioral logic, and another for display logic with intermingling HTML). Others will make use of an off-the-peg templating platform such as Smarty. Others will "roll their own" templating system.

You should only look for a framework that uses a proprietary templating system if you are absolutely certain you are happy sticking with that framework for life, given that individual template portability is likely to be impossible. That's a decision you should make in the context of understanding that certain PHP frameworks are labors of love rather than money, and are not necessarily going to be maintained or supported forever.

Validation

Validation of user input against pre-defined constraints is vital for any application, big or small. Certain requirements are undeniably straightforward to implement yourself — such as checking that an e-mail address is valid. Others are more complex — perhaps guarding against creating a duplicate record in a database table.

Whatever the requirement, a consistent and easily maintainable approach to validating user input is a must. Rather than roll your own, many frameworks provide their own implementation, covering constraint class definitions, erroneous input reporting, fault stacks, and constraint polymorphism.

In a simple project, most will never be used, but that uniform approach provides a degree of scalability and maintainability that simply "hacking something in yourself" just won't do.

Naturally, if you have your own suite of validation classes to which you are heavily wedded, most frameworks will not shirk at their usage in lieu of those that come in the box.

URL Rewriting

There's no doubt that as Web applications have become more sophisticated, so, too, have the URLs that comprise all HTTP GET requests become more bloated, long, and unattractive.

It's not just aesthetic. There are genuine issues with long and complex URLs. Users copying and pasting URLs to friends and colleagues using IM, e-mail, or Facebook often make errors when URLs are too long. Memorability becomes an issue when URLs need to be cited only from recall. Search engines prefer short, human-readable URLs that relate to the content contained therein. In addition, complex "techie" URLs help expose the inner workings of your application — a temptation for hackers.

Therefore, many frameworks provide some mechanism for *URL rewriting* — either static (such that, as a developer, you may specify that, for example, /Home, in fact, represents /home.php) or dynamic (as mentioned in the earlier discussion of MVC).

This is normally achieved through close cooperation with the Web server. It is, after all, the Web server that first intercepts HTTP requests before handing them over to PHP. It is therefore nearly impossible to achieve the effects discussed previously without changes at the server level. Normally, with Apache, this is accomplished with mod_rewrite.

Thankfully, as a developer, you don't have to think about it too much. Most frameworks that provide URL rewriting will either configure your Web server for you or provide simple step-by-step instructions for you to follow. You do need to consider what implications this might have when deploying to your production environment, though — a topic we'll return to later.

Form Persistence

When you first started building Web applications, you probably suffered a brief, mild depression when you realized that while HTML has support for a whole host of Windows-like form controls (text boxes, radio buttons, check boxes, drop-down lists, and so forth), HTTP has no support for persisting the value or state of those controls between requests.

Therefore, even with the most fantastic validation (as discussed earlier), the onus is still on the developer to ensure that the value of those controls is persisted between requests, such that if users are "thrown back" to a form with errors (missing a mandatory field, for example), everything they have entered thus far is retained — exactly as they would expect.

This means that text boxes contain the text that the user entered, radio buttons and check boxes are selected exactly as they were by the user, and drop-down lists are dropped down to (as you might have guessed) whatever option the user chose.

This isn't just important for form validation. In certain Web applications, it may be valuable to retain a value even if a user navigates through to another page. For example, a sophisticated "advanced search" page may contain several form controls. If users want to modify their search terms slightly to generate a whole new set of results, it is rather churlish to expect them to reenter every single criterion. By storing form state data in sessions, a more "Windows-like" experience can be achieved.

It's certainly possible to achieve this effect yourself. Indeed, when you started working with PHP, you probably hacked in some procedural code to achieve exactly this. As you progressed, you probably wrote your own library for regular re-use. (How many of those do you have now? Most likely a few.)

Most frameworks have such functionality available out of the box — indeed, it's one of the features that's more difficult to turn off. Therefore, if you're going to use one of the frameworks discussed in this chapter, it's best to dump your own in favor of the officially sanctioned route.

Object Relation Mapping

Earlier in this book, you were introduced to the concept of Object Relation Mapping (ORM). You will recall that it provides a layer of abstraction when building applications that feature an object model with a suite of "business objects" — classes that represent instances of entities stored in a database.

By using ORM, common database functions (such as creating, reading, updating, and deleting) can be performed without writing any SQL. The ORM layer takes care of it for you. This not only means you wind up writing less code (thus speeding up development and reducing errors), it also adds a degree of portability to other database platforms not normally realistic or achievable.

You have also learned about `DataBoundObject` — an abstract class you can extend to provide a simple business object implementation, which connects seamlessly to an underlying database table. As you might expect, most PHP application frameworks appreciate the benefits of this approach and therefore provide you with something quite similar, an implementation of their own — called something suitably pithy and catchy like `GenericObject`, `DataObject`, or `ActiveRecord`. They're all designed to do much the same thing, although few provide an implementation quite as architecturally correct as `DataBoundObject`, as they do not necessarily take advantage of the full feature set of PHP 6.

As with so much in these frameworks, you aren't duty-bound to make use of their pre-supplied implementation — unless, that is, you are planning to use one of the MVC frameworks in which the model and view are inextricably linked, something you'll learn more about later.

Database Abstraction

In Chapter 6, you were introduced to PHP Data Objects (PDO), and you were coached intensely on why it is a Good Thing. It is hoped that, therefore, you're already fully sold on the concept of database abstraction, and why PDO — the officially PHP-sanctioned mechanism for database abstraction — is the way to go.

It is a pity, then, that a number of PHP frameworks still choose to provide their own abstraction classes. They may have the best of intentions at heart, but by attempting to force authors to go against the generally accepted principles of PHP, they are encouraging poor code. You should take the moral high ground and boycott such homemade abstraction layers. Stick to PDO, and throw anything that comes in the framework in the trash.

Utility Classes

Most (if not all) of the PHP frameworks you'll encounter will include a number of utility classes that don't really seem to fit anywhere. These are classes that perform useful library functions such as encryption, sending e-mail, authenticating users, and so forth — things that (arguably) should have been built into the PHP language in the first place.

You've probably built up your own library of code over time, so you shouldn't necessarily shy away from sticking with it if the idea of throwing it away in favor of someone else's code jars a little. Library code tends to be a deeply personal thing, and working with the unfamiliar library code base of a framework is a little like putting on a pair of someone else's shoes — they may be functional, but they just don't feel right.

Also remember that utility classes provided by frameworks are likely to be afterthoughts at best — or at worst, something thrown in from the framework author's own personal collection.

Use Case Scenario

Before you learn about some framework contenders, let's consider a sample application that might benefit from the framework treatment.

The application that follows has a simple task: enable users to sign up for a company's e-mail newsletter. It must validate first name, last name, and e-mail address; ensure that the record does not already exist in the database; throw errors if any validation errors occur; and thank the user after they are successfully signed up. It's a common PHP application, but consider the following challenges you face:

❏ Validating first name, last name, and e-mail address

❏ Creating a business object that represents a newsletter subscriber

❑ Ensuring that a subscriber does not already exist before accepting the submission

❑ Informing users of errors, and allowing them to correct them

❑ Persisting form data

❑ Using database abstraction to ensure portability

❑ Separating business logic from display logic

All of these challenges should be reasonably straightforward if you've already read the rest of this book in detail — it's certainly all been covered; but you would be forgiven for sighing when you realize just how much work you must do to build what is, after all, a pretty trivial application.

In the sections that follow, you will see examples of three PHP application frameworks. In one, you'll implement a fully complete application that does exactly what has been discussed earlier. In the others, you'll see a short overview so that you can try them out for yourself.

They all attempt to make the headaches cited previously far easier to contend with by employing some of the techniques you met earlier in this chapter. They all have their pros and cons. Later in this chapter, you'll see the kinds of considerations you must take into account when deciding which framework to deploy in your own enterprise project.

Underlying Database

It's worthwhile having a sample database in place when exploring these frameworks, and a sample database table within that database. To continue the example requirement suggested earlier, you can create a single database table that contains details of subscribers to the company's newsletter.

Start up a console on your development server, and create a database called `newsletter`:

```
$ /usr/local/pgsql/bin/createdb newsletter
CREATE DATABASE
```

With that database created, create a user called `newsletter` that can connect to that database. For the purposes of this chapter, use the password `password`. You might want to pick something more secure for a production environment (just a thought). Here's the code:

```
$ /usr/local/pgsql/bin/createuser newsletter -P
Enter password for new role:
Enter it again:
Should the new role be a superuser? n
Should the user be allowed to create databases? n
Should the user be allowed to create more new roles? N
CREATE ROLE
```

Great. Now open the database in the PostgreSQL console and create the table. Here's the SQL syntax you'll need:

```
CREATE TABLE "subscriber" (
    "id" SERIAL PRIMARY KEY NOT NULL,
    "first_name" character varying (128),
```

```
 "last_name" character varying (256),
 "email_address" character varying(256) NOT NULL,
 "date_of_signup" date NOT NULL,
 "time_of_signup" time NOT NULL,
 "remote_addr" character varying(15) NOT NULL
);

GRANT ALL PRIVILEGES ON "subscriber" TO "newsletter";
GRANT ALL PRIVILEGES ON "subscriber_id_seq" TO "newsletter";

CREATE UNIQUE INDEX "em_unq_idx" ON "subscriber"("email_address");
```

That unique index at the end isn't strictly necessary, as you'll be sense-checking to ensure that the current subscriber does not exist as part and parcel of your data input validation; but it's good from a belt-and-braces point of view. Should you ever want to extend your application to allow data manipulation from a third-party source, the uniqueness of your subscriber database can be guaranteed.

An Example Application

With your sample database in place, it's now time to start looking at some individual frameworks. They all seek to achieve much the same goal, but they all approach it slightly differently. Like boxers versus briefs versus going "commando," a lot of it comes down to personal preference.

Let's start by looking at a complete application written in a newcomer PHP framework developed especially for PHP 6 — *Ulysses*.

Introducing Ulysses

Ulysses is an open-source, object-oriented PHP application development framework available free under the BSD (Berkeley) license. This means that regardless of the ultimate goal of your project (altruistic, commercial, or downright Mephistophelean), it's free to download, use, and deploy. Support and documentation is available on a commercial basis.

Installing Ulysses

To download Ulysses, visit the project's Web site at www.ulyssesframework.com. You'll be redirected to the project's home page on SourceForge, from which you can download the latest version.

Move the downloaded .tgz file into /usr/local/lib/php — or wherever your PHP libraries are normally kept. Then, unarchive it using the following standard syntax:

```
tar -xzvf ulysses-3.0.23.tar.gz
```

You should see that a folder /usr/local/lib/php/ulysses is created, resplendent with numerous classes and helper files.

Ulysses is only compatible with the Apache Web server, and you must configure virtual hosts that make use of the framework in a certain fashion so as to enable the "short" URLs you'll meet later. Apache must also be compiled with mod_rewrite support. If you follow the best-practice installation discussed in Appendix D, this will be the case. If not, see either http://httpd.apache.org/docs/1.3/mod/mod_rewrite.html (for Apache 1.3.x) or http://httpd.apache.org/docs/2.0/mod/mod_rewrite.html (for Apache 2.x) for details about how to get it installed.

Ulysses Web applications work on a "one per virtual host" basis — you cannot have multiple Web sites operating on a single host. A virtual host entry will look something like the following. If you are creating a brand-new virtual host, you should place such an entry right at the very tail end of your Apache configuration file (httpd.conf):

```
<VirtualHost>
ServerName newsletter.example.com
ServerAdmin ed@example.com
CustomLog /home/ed/logfile_newsletter common
ErrorLog /home/ed/errlog_ newsletter
DocumentRoot /home/ed/public_html/newsletter
Alias /ulysses/ "/usr/local/lib/php/ulysses/"
RewriteEngine on
RewriteRule ^(\/)([A-Z]{1,})(.*)$ /ulysses/php/controller.php?page=$2$3 [QSA,PT]
RewriteRule        ^/$    /Home [QSA,L,R]
</VirtualHost>
```

Following are the four vital lines:

```
Alias /ulysses/ "/usr/local/lib/php/ulysses/"
RewriteEngine on
RewriteRule ^(\/)([A-Z]{1,})(.*)$ /ulysses/php/controller.php?page=$2$3 [QSA,PT]
RewriteRule        ^/$    /Home [QSA,L,R]
```

The first line maps a virtual directory to the path to the PHP framework. The second enables the Apache URL rewriting engine. The third and final lines tell Apache to redirect any requests that begin with a capital letter to the Ulysses framework's core controller.

This means that requests that look like the following will be redirected to the Ulysses engine:

```
http://www.example.com/Home
```

However, requests that look like the following will not:

```
http://www.example.com/home
```

This means that images, CSS stylesheets, and everything static will not be served through the engine — so long as you don't use capital letters to begin directory names.

The final line makes requests to / (for example, `http://www.example.com/`) direct to the "starting" *servlet* for your application — normally called `Home`.

Working with Ulysses

With Ulysses installed on your Web server, it's available to all of your PHP projects from this point on — you don't have to install it ever again. It's now time to start making use of the code base it has to offer.

Create a project folder for your example application. In the virtual host example cited earlier, you've used `/home/ed/public_html/newsletter` — so just create a folder that matches the virtual host you've created for your application.

Although Ulysses doesn't enforce an especially rigid directory structure, there are a few folders you *must* create:

```
/your/web/root/tpl
/your/web/root/phpm
/your/web/root/phpm/business
/your/web/root/phpm/utility
/your/web/root/phpm/controls
/your/web/root/phpm/custom
/your/web/root/phpm/settings
```

Any other folders you might create (for images, CSS stylesheets, JavaScript, and so forth) are entirely up to you.

However, keep in mind the following:

❑ You must place your page templates (which normally contain HTML) under `tpl`.

❑ You must place your business objects under `phpm/business`, and utility classes under `phpm/utility`.

❑ You must place your application settings under `phpm/settings`.

Keep to these simple rules and you should be fine.

Setting Up

There are a few files you'll need to create under `phpm/settings`. These define the root database for your application (although you can define as many as you want), and the directory location in which the in-built session class will save its sessions.

Create `phpm/settings/constants.phpm` as shown here:

```
<?
    define("BASE_SESSION_PATH", "/tmp");
?>
```

For the purposes of this exercise, you're storing your sessions on disk — something that, if you've been following along in this book from the first page, you know is frowned upon. You can, of course, use a TMPFS or RAM drive instead — a much better bet when you deploy onto production servers. Alternately, you can swap the Ulysses session class for one of your own, which uses databases or `memcache`.

Now you need to tell your application where to find your database. Create `phpm/settings/dbaccess .phpm` as follows:

```
<?
    // Definitions for connecting to a postgreSQL database.
    define("DATABASE_USERNAME", "newsletter");
    define("DATABASE_PASSWORD", "password");
    define("DATABASE_HOSTNAME", "localhost");
    define("DATABASE_BASENAME", "newsletter");
    define("DATABASE_DRIVER", "pgsql");
    define("PDO_DSN", DATABASE_DRIVER . ":dbname=" . DATABASE_BASENAME .
           ";user=" . DATABASE_USERNAME . ";password=" . DATABASE_PASSWORD .
           ";host=" . DATABASE_HOSTNAME);
?>
```

If you've deviated from the database name, username, or password suggested earlier in this chapter, this is where you need to change it. Of course, being PDO, you could just as easily specify a MySQL database here.

Finally, you need to tell Ulysses to include these database settings, so create `phpm/requires.phpm` as shown here. (Ulysses will automatically load this class for every page.)

```
<?
require("$appDir/phpm/settings/dbaccess.phpm");
?>
```

Don't worry that you haven't defined the variable `$appDir` — you don't need to, as Ulysses will figure it out for you.

Business Objects

Only one business object is required in this hypothetical application — one that represents a subscriber in your newsletter subscription database. Ulysses prefers that you use `DataBoundObject` as your "active record" pattern class — but, in practice, you can use whatever you wish. `DataBoundObject` is, however, included out-of-the-box.

You can save the following code as `phpm/business/subscriber.phpm`:

```
<?php

class Subscriber extends DataBoundObject {

    protected $FirstName;
    protected $LastName;
    protected $EmailAddress;
```

```
        protected $DateOfSignup;
        protected $TimeOfSignup;
        protected $RemoteAddr;

        protected function DefineTableName() {
                return("subscriber");
        }

        protected function DefineRelationMap() {
                return(array(
                        "id" = > "ID",
                        "first_name" = > "FirstName",
                        "last_name" = > "LastName",
                        "email_address" = > "EmailAddress",
                        "date_of_signup" = > "DateOfSignup",
                        "time_of_signup" = > "TimeOfSignup",
                        "remote_addr" = > "RemoteAddr"));
        }


}
?>
```

If you've read Chapter 7, this code should look pretty straightforward — you've created a business object called `Subscriber` that is allied to the table `subscriber` in your database, and you have mapped the necessary columns out.

There's a method missing, though. One central requirement of this application is "no duplicates" — that is, someone should only be able to sign up once. Therefore, you should add a standard static method that will check for the existence of a specified e-mail address:

```
static function checkExists($strEmail) {
     $strEmail = strtolower($strEmail);
     $strSQL = "SELECT \"id\" FROM \"subscriber\" WHERE
                lower(\"email_address\") = :email";
     $objPDO = PDOFactory::GetPDO();
     $objStatement = $objPDO->prepare($strSQL);
     $objStatement->bindParam(':email', $strEmail, PDO::PARAM_STR);
     $objStatement->execute();
     $arRow = $objStatement->fetch(PDO::FETCH_ASSOC);
     $id = $arRow["id"];
     return ($id > 0);
}
```

Add this method to your class and save it. You'll call this method whenever your user enters an e-mail address, to ensure that it does not already exist. If it does, then this method will return `true` and your application will decline to save the record (and inform the user as such).

You must also make Ulysses aware of your `subscriber` class, so modify `phpm/requires.phpm` and add the following line:

```
require("$appDir/phpm/business/subscriber.phpm");
```

In so doing, the business class will be loaded with every HTTP request made to the Ulysses engine.

Servlets

In the Ulysses framework, HTTP GET and POST requests are made to *servlets*. If you are familiar with Java, then this is already a well-known phenomenon to you. It is a class with two mandatory abstract methods: one to handle GET requests, and another to handle POST requests.

A request on your Web server made to www.example.com/Home will, in fact, look for a servlet called HomeServlet. A request made to www.example.com/Signup will look for a servlet called SignupServlet — and so on.

Each servlet is trained to automatically seek out a matching page template for that servlet when called using HTTP GET. The expected behavior of any servlet invoked using HTTP POST is to redirect the user to another servlet via HTTP GET — a best-practice model discussed earlier in this book called Post-Redirect-Get (PRG).

You can create your first servlet now. Create phpm/servlets/homeservlet.phpm as shown here:

```
<?

    class HomeServlet Extends Servlet {

        public function __construct($objSmarty, $objSession, $queryStringParms,
                                    $strPageIdentifier) {


            parent::__construct($objSmarty, $objSession, $queryStringParms,
                                $strPageIdentifier);
        }

        public function _doGet($objSmarty, $objSession, $queryStringParms) {


        }

        public function _doPost($objSmarty, $objSession, $queryStringParms) {


        }

    }
?>
```

Not much to it, is there? This is what's known as a *blank servlet* — a servlet that does nothing other than try to load the corresponding page template and display it — provided it is called using HTTP GET. If HTTP POST is used, the Ulysses engine will automatically cause the browser to request the page again using HTTP GET.

You can now create a dummy template to go with it. Create the following template and save it as `tpl/home.tpl`. Note the capitalization — templates must always begin with a lowercase letter, and the corresponding class with an uppercase letter:

```
<?xml version="1.0" encoding="utf-8"?>
<!DOCTYPE html PUBLIC "-//W3C//DTD XHTML 1.0 Strict//EN"
     "http://www.w3.org/TR/xhtml1/DTD/xhtml1-strict.dtd">
<html xmlns= "http://www.w3.org/1999/xhtml"  lang= "en"  xml:lang= "en">
     <head>
     </head>
     <body>
          <h1>Home Page</h1>
     </body>
</html>
```

With the servlet and template created, you should now be able to request the URL /Home (note the capital letter) on your virtual host, and see exactly what you would expect — an empty page, but for the heading "Home Page."

This isn't very exciting, so let's change that. In Ulysses, you add elements to a page using *controls* — a bit like the controls you might have used in Visual Basic. Controls are used for input fields such as text boxes and radio buttons, but also for labels that display dynamic information. Controls must be declared in both the servlet and the template — in the template so the Ulysses engine knows where to combine them with your HTML, and in the servlet so they can be declared as classes.

That all page controls are classes might seem extreme at first, but when you consider that classes can be overridden and extended, it starts to make sense. Don't like the text box class that comes in the box? Just extend it and override whatever methods you like.

Modify the Home Page servlet you just created (`servlets/homeservlet.phpm`) so it looks like the following. (You're putting the additional code in the constructor and the member variable declaration space.)

```
<?

    class HomeServlet Extends Servlet {

        public $objTitle;
        public $objFirstName;
        public $objLastName;
        public $objEmail;
        public $objStatusLabel;
        public $objSuccessLabel;

        public $objFirstNameLabel;
        public $objLastNameLabel;
        public $objEmailLabel;

        public function __construct($objSmarty, $objSession, $queryStringParms,
                             $strPageIdentifier) {
```

```
            $this->objTitle = new Title("Email Bulletin Signup", "default");
            $this->objFirstName = new TextBox("firstname");
            $this->objLastName = new TextBox("lastname");
            $this->objEmail = new TextBox("email");

            $this->objStatusLabel = new Label("status");
            $this->objSuccessLabel = new Label("success");

            $this->objFirstNameLabel = new Label("firstnamelabel", "First
                                                Name");
            $this->objLastNameLabel = new Label("lastnamelabel", "Last Name");
            $this->objEmailLabel = new Label("emaillabel", "Email Address *");

            parent::__construct($objSmarty, $objSession, $queryStringParms,
                                $strPageIdentifier);
        }

        public function _doGet($objSmarty, $objSession, $queryStringParms) {


        }

        public function _doPost($objSmarty, $objSession, $queryStringParms) {


        }

    }
? >
```

You must also modify the ultra-simple template you created. Do that now, replacing the HTML with the following:

```
<?xml version="1.0" encoding="utf-8"?>
<!DOCTYPE html PUBLIC "-//W3C//DTD XHTML 1.0 Strict//EN"
    "http://www.w3.org/TR/xhtml1/DTD/xhtml1-strict.dtd">
<html xmlns= "http://www.w3.org/1999/xhtml" lang="en" xml:lang="en">
    <head>
        <tpl:title id="default" />
        <style type="text/css">
            .erroneous { color: red; }
        </style>
    </head>
    <body>
        <h1>Signup</h1>
            <tpl:if $success neq "">
                <div id="submission">
                    <p class="successText">
                        <tpl:label id="success" />
                    </p>
```

```
                        <p class="summaryText">
                            You can unsubscribe
                            at any time by using the
                            link at the top of the emails
                            we'll send you.
                        </p>
                        <p class="summaryText">
                            Why not visit our company web site?
                            <a href="http://www.example.com">Click here</a>
                            to go there now.
                        </p>
                    </div>
                <tpl:else>
                    <p>
                        Hello; we'd very much like for you to sign up to our
                        email newsletter.
                    </p>
                    <p>
                        We won't sell your email address and it's easy to
                        unsubscribe (just click on the link at the top of one
                        of our emails).
                    </p>
                    <form method="post" action="/Signup">
                        <label for="firstname"><tpl:label id=
                            "firstnamelabel" /></label>
                        <tpl:textbox id="firstname" /><br />
                        <label for="lastname"><tpl:label id=
                            "lastnamelabel" /></label>
                        <tpl:textbox id="lastname" /><br />

                        <label for="email"><tpl:label id="emaillabel" /></label>
                        <tpl:textbox id="email" /><br />
                        <input type="submit" value="Sign Up" />
                        <tpl:if $status neq "">
                            <p class="errorText">
                                <tpl:label id="status" />
                            </p>
                        </tpl:if>
                        <br /><br />
                        <i>* Required Field</i>
                    </form>
                </tpl:if>

        </body>
    </html>
```

Fire up a Web browser and point it to /Home on your virtual host. You should see something that looks like Figure 14-1.

OK, it's not that pretty, but it's more or less what you'd expect from a newsletter signup page.

Figure 14-1 Sample newsletter signup page

If you look again at the servlet, it should be reasonably easy to figure out what's going on behind the scenes:

```
$this->objTitle = new Title("Email Bulletin Signup", "default");
$this->objFirstName = new TextBox("firstname");
$this->objLastName = new TextBox("lastname");
$this->objEmail = new TextBox("email");
$this->objStatusLabel = new Label("status");
$this->objSuccessLabel = new Label("success");
$this->objFirstNameLabel = new Label("firstnamelabel", "First Name");
$this->objLastNameLabel = new Label("lastnamelabel", "Last Name");
$this->objEmailLabel = new Label("emaillabel", "Email Address *");
```

Each of these lines represents the declaration of a *control* on the page. The syntax for declaring a title control (which emulates an HTML title tag) is simple — title text first, followed by an identifier:

```
$this->objTitle = new Title("Email Bulletin Signup", "default");
```

The corresponding entry in the template is simple, too:

```
<tpl:title id="default" />
```

The Ulysses framework, when parsing the template, will look for an instance of the Title class declared in the corresponding servlet, extract its textual value, and render the necessary HTML title tag:

```
<title>Email Bulletin Signup</title>
```

Other controls work in a similar fashion. Labels and text boxes are declared in this example. Notice how labels do not necessarily have to have an initial value — which is useful if you are using labels to (maybe) display error messages on a conditional basis. The `status` label and `success` label work exactly this way — and conditional syntax in the template ensures they are only displayed if they are nonblank:

```
<tpl:if $status neq "">
    <p class="errorText">
        <tpl:label id="status" />
    </p>
</tpl:if>
```

This template syntax may look familiar to you. Indeed, it should — it's just the Smarty template engine in disguise, something you met earlier in this book.

Processing User Input

Should you try to submit the data capture form as it stands, you'll meet a 404 error — for the simple reason that the target of the form does not exist. Review the template:

```
<form method="post" action="/Signup">
```

As you can see, the form is attempting to post to `/Signup`, which implies that a servlet called `SignupServlet` must be created, and its `_doPost()` method populated.

This servlet serves two functions: validating user input and, if it passes, saving the entry into the database. It only has one ultimate course of action: passing control back to the original submitting servlet. In so doing, it can "talk" to the servlet it is about to pass control back to, setting values of page controls such as labels and text boxes.

The following code comprises `signupservlet.phpm` in `phpm/servlets`. There's no corresponding template, as this servlet has no GET method:

```
<?

    class SignupServlet Extends Servlet {

        public function __construct($objSmarty, $objSession, $queryStringParms,
                               $strPageIdentifier) {

        }

        public function _doGet($objSmarty, $objSession, $queryStringParms) {
            header("Location: /Home");
            exit(0);
        }

        public function _doPost($objSmarty, $objSession, $queryStringParms) {
            $objServlet = Servlet::GetReferringServlet();

            # Validate
```

```
$strFN = $objServlet->objFirstName->GetValue();
$strLN = $objServlet->objLastName->GetValue();
$strEM = $objServlet->objEmail->GetValue();

$objServlet->objEmailLabel->strCSSClass = "";

If (strlen($strEM)<1) {
    $objServlet->objEmailLabel->strCSSClass = "erroneous";
};

try {
    If (strlen($strEM)<1) {
        throw new Exception("Sorry, you didn't fill in all
        required fields. Please try again.");
    };
    if (Subscriber::checkExists($strEM)==true) {
        $objServlet->objEmailLabel->strCSSClass = "erroneous";
        throw new Exception("Sorry, a subscriber by this
                    address already exists. Please try again.");
    };
    if (preg_match('/^[a-z0-9!#$%&*+-=?^_`{|}~]+
                    (\.[a-z0-9!#$%&*+-=?^_`{|}~]
                    +)*@([-a-z0-9]+\.)+([a-z]{2,
                    6})$/ix', $strEM) <= 0) {
        $objServlet->objEmailLabel->strCSSClass = "erroneous";
        throw new Exception("Sorry, that email address isn't
                        valid. Please try again.");
    };
} catch (Exception $e) {
    $objServlet->objStatusLabel->SetCaption($e->getMessage());
    $objServlet->redirectTo();
};

# TODO - Save here

    }

}
?>
```

You'll notice there's a TODO here. If all validation is successful, you want to save the record to the database. You'll fill that bit in shortly. For now, it's omitted for clarity.

Persistence

The first thing you'll notice is that there's no explicit code to handle the persistence of user input controls such as text boxes. Great news — it's not needed. The Ulysses framework takes care of it for you. As soon as you submit a page, its entire contents (or *state*) is captured and held in the session. If the user returns to that page for any reason, the form will appear in exactly the state it was submitted.

This holds equally true for non-user modifiable controls — labels, for example. If the value (that is, content) of a label is modified either in the servlet itself or in a foreign servlet (as is perfectly permissible), then that value is retained for the remainder of that user's session.

During application development, you may find this frustrating from time to time. You may want to "reset" a page to its natural state, and not have your test input cluttering up text boxes. What's the easiest way to do this? Simply flush your browser's cookies. Your session will be lost, a new one generated, and the page reset to its "natural" state.

Validation

A few checks are performed on user input during the signup process. The only non-optional field is an e-mail address; first and last name are considered optional. For that reason, all checks relate to the e-mail address field — is it present, is it valid, and, most important of all, has it already been submitted?

Only if all three checks are passed will the user's input be saved. Otherwise, the user is admonished suitably and asked to correct it.

The first thing you'll notice is that the value of the user input isn't retrieved using $_POST. Instead, Ulysses gives you access to a foreign servlet's controls, as shown here:

```
$objServlet = Servlet::GetReferringServlet();
$strFN = $objServlet->objFirstName->GetValue();
$strLN = $objServlet->objLastName->GetValue();
$strEM = $objServlet->objEmail->GetValue();
```

This is useful, because there may well be times when you don't want raw POST data. Since you can access any method the page control exposes, you are not just limited to GetValue(). Indeed, that method can be overloaded, meaning the manner in which its value is returned can be refined within the control class itself — and not within your servlet.

Ulysses does not provide any special validation routines. You can either roll your own or use one of the many available PEAR classes to do the trick. In this case, the validation is so simple that native PHP code is used to check that the e-mail address is valid, that it has been provided, and that it is not already in the database.

Should any of those checks fail, an exception is thrown. When it is caught, the status label of the original servlet is set to an error message passed to the exception. Its redirectTo() method is then invoked, which throws the user back to the home page:

```
} catch (Exception $e) {
            $objServlet->objStatusLabel->SetCaption($e->getMessage());
            $objServlet->redirectTo();
        };
```

When the home page reloads, the updated status label indicates to the user that there is a problem, and the user is invited to correct the submission.

Notice how CSS classes are used to highlight incorrectly filled fields:

```
$objServlet->objEmailLabel->strCSSClass = "erroneous";
```

This enables the e-mail address label to be highlighted in red, which shows the user at a glance where the error lies.

A Quick Check

Before proceeding any further, prove to yourself that the code works by attempting to submit the form with an empty e-mail address field. You should see something similar to Figure 14-2.

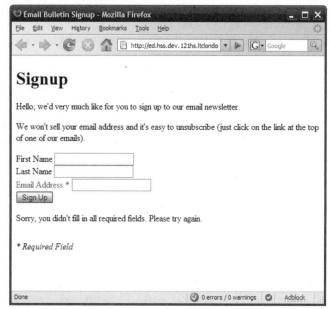

Figure 14-2 Result of submitting a form without an e-mail address

When viewed on your screen, the "Email Address" field is highlighted in red, and a message admonishing the user is presented.

Click Refresh in your browser, and you'll see that the page state is still retained — and, importantly, there's no resubmission of the form.

Saving Input

Remember the earlier block of servlet code where you saw a comment saying TODO? That was where you were going to save the subscriber if the submission was successful (that is, all validation checks were passed).

You can put that code in now by substituting that comment with the following. This code will only ever be reached if no exceptions are invoked that cause premature termination of the servlet:

```
$objSubscriber = new Subscriber(PDOFactory::GetPDO())
$objSubscriber->setDateOfSignup(date("Y-m-d"));
$objSubscriber->setTimeOfSignup(date("H:i:s"));
$objSubscriber->setRemoteAddr($_SERVER["REMOTE_ADDR"]);
$objSubscriber->setEmailAddress($strEM);
$objSubscriber->setFirstName($strFN);
$objSubscriber->setLastName($strLN);
$objSubscriber->Save();
$subID = $objSubscriber->getID();
if ($subID <= 1) {
        $objServlet->objStatusLabel->SetCaption("Sorry, a technical
                                        fault meant we couldn't save
                                        your details. Please try again
                                        in a minute or two.");
        $objServlet->redirectTo();
} else {
        $objServlet->objStatusLabel->SetCaption("");
        $objServlet->objSuccessLabel->SetCaption("Thank you,
                        your details have been saved. Your
                        subscriber ID is " .
                        sprintf("%08d", $subID) . ".");
        $objServlet->redirectTo();
};
```

If you read Chapter 7, the preceding code should be pretty straightforward to follow. You are creating a new instance of the `Subscriber` class, setting its properties, and saving it. Note that you are using PDOFactory to retrieve an instance of the PDO object. PDOFactory is included in the Ulysses framework, so you don't need to explicitly `include()` or `require()` it in your code. When called with no parameters, the Ulysses-provided variant of PDOFactory will use the database settings you defined earlier in phpm/settings/dbaccess.phpm, so now would be a good time to double check that you have them entered correctly.

Having saved it, the code checks to ensure that a valid entry was created in the database by testing its ID. One of two possible routes is as follows. If it is unsuccessful (that is, not saved), then the origin servlet's status is set to an error message, and the redirection performed. If it is successful (that is, saved), then the origin servlet's status is made blank (that is, no error), and the `success text` label set to a congratulatory message.

Heading Home

Finally, you can prove to yourself that all is working correctly by filling out the form with no mistakes and submitting it.

You should see something similar to Figure 14-3.

You may want to check the underlying PostgreSQL database just to be sure the record went in successfully, and that the ID in the database matches the one displayed on the screen (52 in Figure 14-3).

A Quick Summary

Well, there it is — the Ulysses framework in a nutshell. Cast your mind back to earlier in the chapter where you considered the key features of most frameworks. How well does Ulysses fit the brief in each case?

Figure 14-3 Result of submitting a correct form

❑ *Application structure* — Ulysses uses a servlet metaphor, not dissimilar to Java servlets. In so doing, it consigns the original concept of a PHP "script" to the trash can — and enforces a rigid structure in the process. There is some mandatory directory organization for things such as utility classes and business objectives, but not to the restrictive extent required by some other frameworks.

❑ *Separation of code and display logic* — Each servlet in a Ulysses application has a corresponding template. In fact, such templates are based loosely on the Smarty platform. Because templates are built by placing controls on a page, this template paradigm is rigorously enforced. Indeed, any attempt to place HTML code inside a servlet will cause a parser error.

❑ *Validation* — This is one area where Ulysses is weak. There's no built-in system for validation — you are instead encouraged to roll your own or make use of PEAR. Having said that, the page control metaphor makes validation exceptionally easy, and the presentation of errors to the user is made with considerably less hassle by virtue of the servlet metaphor.

❑ *URL rewriting* — Not only is URL rewriting built into Ulysses, unlike many other frameworks it is non-optional and completely transparent. This ensures a degree of security. There is no scope for users to attempt to invoke the controller PHP script themselves, and many cross-site-scripting (XSS) vulnerabilities are rendered null and void.

❑ *Form persistence* — This is Ulysses' sweet spot: it's completely automatic. Every page servlet that features a form submitting to another servlet will have its state saved automatically at the time of submission. This means the value of every text box, label, check box, radio button, drop-down list — indeed, any control whatsoever — will be saved into the user session. Even if the user then navigates to another page and then back again to the form entry page, that state will be retained transparently.

❑ *Object Relation Mapping* — Ulysses reproduces verbatim the `DataBoundObject` class you met earlier in this book — and it's included as part of the archive you downloaded earlier. Having said that, you are free to use your own. Unlike many frameworks, business objects are not tied inextricably to page logic, so should you prefer to use an active record class from PEAR, you can do so easily.

❑ *Database abstraction* — As a PHP 6–specific framework, Ulysses does not itself feature any database abstraction layers. PHP 6 best practice is to use PDO, and that's exactly what you're expected to do. If, for some reason, you prefer to use another layer, or indeed no layer at all, that's fine, too — again, Ulysses doesn't get too heavily involved in database access.

❑ *Utility classes* — Finally, how does Ulysses fare on the provision of utility or "helper" classes? Not well, but that's by design. This is an exceptionally lightweight framework at just 18KB, and, as such, authors are encouraged to either write their own or make use of the PEAR repository.

Some Other Contenders

You've now met the Ulysses framework in detail, and built a sample application that showcases some of its neat features. Indeed, it's the favorite framework of the authors of this book — the one we use every day ourselves. It does some things very well indeed, but there may be times you find it a little lightweight, given the amount of code you'll still end up writing. That "lightweightedness" gives you enormous flexibility — but some may prefer true "point and shoot" coding.

In addition, although Ulysses is downloadable free of charge, free documentation is non-existent. It is only provided to commercial customers, along with telephone and e-mail support — meaning you have to pay for it.

Finally, although it is in heavy use around the world, Ulysses does not have the official seal of approval from anybody in the official PHP community itself — meaning that just occasionally, client IT departments may raise an eyebrow at its selection.

With those three factors in mind, it's only fair to look at a couple of other frameworks. You're not about to meet anything containing the same depth of detail you just did when checking out Ulysses, but in both of the following cases, you are invited to recreate the sample newsletter signup application as an exercise. This should give you a feel for which you prefer.

Of course, there are literally hundreds of other frameworks out there. An excellent online resource, `www.phpframeworks.com`, maintains an up-to-date database of the most common. If you have time on your hands, feel free to experiment.

Prado

The Prado Framework (`www.pradosoft.com`) is designed for PHP 5, and is not (as of this writing) available for PHP 6. It should, however, be completely backwardly compatible.

It is a component-based and event-driven framework with some similarities to Ulysses, and is one of the most popular frameworks used by large digital advertising agencies in their own development. For that reason, it is one of the most common to feature on the resumes of hungry young software engineers.

Prado makes use of a "scaffolding" application, something that may be familiar to you if you have ever encountered Ruby on Rails. This application creates a skeleton application in a directory of your choice, the foundation on which you can build your own project. It includes a single controller — `index.php` — generated in the root directory of your application, which is used to render every page.

Just as Ulysses has the concept of servlets, so, too, does Prado have its own metaphor for requests — *pages*. Each page consists of a `.page` file (which is its HTML template) and a `.php` file (which contains the page logic itself).

Prado page templates make use of page components — buttons, labels, text boxes, and so forth. Unlike Ulysses, however, these components are event-driven. That is, an event is wired up to each one to handle events such as `onClick` — much like a Visual Basic application. This wiring up takes place in the template, but the actual event code is placed in the code-behind file (that is, the corresponding `.php` class for that page).

Much like Ulysses, the state of controls can be modified from within events, allowing for a continuation of the Visual Basic–style rapid application development metaphor. It's taken to an even more extreme degree in Prado. Even textual links on a page can be given an `onClick` event, just as with ASP.NET. The old models of `GET` and `POST` are more or less killed off.

The slight downside to this approach is that the Web just isn't designed for event-driven programming. As a result, many of the events Prado can "listen for" are (just as in .NET) heavily dependent on the use of JavaScript. That can impact your site's accessibility for people with disabilities, and can have implications on search engine optimization and bookmarking — just something to be aware of.

Having said that, Prado is immensely powerful, simple, and easy to learn. It's also one of the most rapid ways to build an application. It's not quite as lightweight as Ulysses, and doesn't feature such sophisticated page-state management techniques, but it is arguably more widely used — an important consideration when choosing a framework.

A short "hello world" demonstration movie can be found at `www.pradosoft.com/docs/movies/ HelloWorld.mov` (QuickTime format), and is well worth a watch.

Zend Framework

The Zend Framework (`http://framework.zend.com/`) is about the closest thing that PHP has to an officially sanctioned framework. That's because it's from Zend, the folks who write the engine at the heart of PHP. The people who put the framework together also put PHP together — so they know what they're talking about.

The Zend Framework is what may be called a "traditional" MVC framework. If you've ever used Java, you may well have used Struts. It's no coincidence that the Zend Framework has distinct similarities with Struts. It's been designed with easy adoption in mind, meaning that those who have used such traditional MVC frameworks in the past should pick it up with no problems. Conversely, those who are familiar only with Ulysses or Prado will find it more challenging, as it is not event-driven, and does not sport a simple "page and page component" model.

In the Zend Framework, a single *front controller* (actually comprised of two files: a master index page and a boot strapper) handles all HTTP requests — no exceptions. As part of its logic, it inspects the URL and attempts to pass off control to a further *page controller*. An application, therefore, comprises several page controllers, all of which handle distinct pieces of site functionality. That accounts for the "controller" part of the MVC paradigm.

Templates in the Zend Framework are actually just PHP files — albeit with the `.phtml` extension to avoid confusion. The full suite of PHP functionality is, therefore, available to you in such templates — a loaded gun that must be treated with extreme care in the name of following best practices. That's the "view" in the MVC paradigm.

The "model" is where it gets controversial — you are more or less compelled to use Zend's built-in functionality for mapping classes to database tables. It's nothing like the ORM that you met earlier in this book, and it certainly may not be to your taste.

The Zend Framework is something of a behemoth — a wealth of functionality for validation, persistence, ORM, and a lot more. It's fair to say that it's enterprise-grade — plenty of big applications out there are using it — and because it's from Zend it will be around more or less forever, and well maintained in the process.

There are two big downsides. First, it's Zend's way or the highway. Unlike Ulysses and Prado, it's very difficult to escape the officially sanctioned Zend Framework route — so using your own ORM class, for example, is a definite no-no. Second, don't think you're going to save precious hours not writing code — you won't. Zend applications are some of the biggest on a KLOC metric (thousands of lines of code). The Zend Framework is more about enforcing a "way of doing things" than providing you with helpful shortcuts to instant application gratification.

It's definitely an acquired taste, so the best suggestion, as always, is to try it out for yourself. The quick-start guide at `http://framework.zend.com/docs/quickstart` should provide you with everything you need to recreate the newsletter application you met earlier in this chapter. Grab a strong coffee and get going.

Deployment Considerations

Keep in mind that most PHP frameworks (including all those met in this chapter) often have reasonably in-depth server integration requirements. This means that they may require installation into a root-owned directory (such as `/usr/local/lib/php`), changes to Apache or global PHP configuration, or installation of PEAR or PECL dependencies.

That pretty much rules out using a framework on a shared hosting environment; but with virtual dedicated server prices starting at $20 per month, that probably won't be much of an issue.

Consider two things, though. First (and foremost), are the joys of version management. The more industrious framework authors keep theirs up to date and, in so doing, generally release a new version every few weeks — sometimes with new features, yes, but typically with bug fixes. You'll obviously want to stay current, but what if a new version of the framework "breaks" your code? Consider, too, how you would cope if your development environment ran a different version than your production environment — would you perhaps encounter the dreaded "works on my machine" scenario? What if you had a new version of your application to deploy that used a newer version of the framework; which would you deploy to production first? The new framework version, or your new code? Most likely, you'd have to take the whole site down for a few moments while you did both.

For larger projects, also consider that you may well not have full control of the production environment. This is especially true when deploying to production environments run by big corporations, whose IT departments generally want to retain control of the hosting of all Web applications. You may have encountered this tricky state of affairs before — perhaps you develop on Linux, and your client uses Solaris servers. Using a PHP framework adds a whole new dimension. You'll have to brief your client well in advance regarding your requirements for the installation of your chosen framework, Apache, and PHP configuration changes, and PEAR class installation. It's all doable, of course — it's just something else to add to your to-do list.

Having said all that, your client's IT department will probably breathe a sigh of relief to hear you're using an industry-accepted framework. It will make your application easier for them to maintain should they ever inherit it.

Summary

In this crucial chapter, you were introduced to the concept of a Web application development framework — specifically, those that provide an out-of-the-box toolkit for developing PHP applications using some of the best-practice methodologies discussed in this book.

You were introduced to the facilities provided by frameworks — enforced structures, database abstraction, form validation, MVC routing, and ORM. Furthermore, you learned about the benefits of using a framework rather than rolling your own, especially for bigger projects. You then met several off-the-shelf frameworks, all of them free, and learned how you'd implement a simple Web application in one. In so doing, you saw the pros and cons of each, most likely drawing the conclusion that "none of them is perfect."

Still, each one is better than trying to reinvent the wheel. Therefore, with that in mind, you should consider their deployment in any medium to large-scale PHP application — especially one with a large, dispersed development team.

In Chapter 15, you'll start getting your hands dirty — and it's about time, too. You'll be putting the last 14 chapters of theory to work in the most compelling way possible — a real, live project. Welcome, then, to the wonderful world of widgets.

Part III

A Real-World Case Study

15

Project Overview

In the previous two parts of this book, you learned about the fundamentals of architecting and building enterprise-grade Web applications in PHP.

You started out in the first chapter by acquainting yourself fully with object-oriented programming (OOP), and learned not only why it's the right approach for large-scale projects, but also how PHP 6 provides a relatively robust implementation for you to work with. You then moved on to databases, learning about how PDO provides one layer of database abstraction, and ORM yet another. Finally, you learned the principles of effective software architecture, including how best to implement session management and model-view-controller (MVC) project layout.

Along the way, it is hoped that you noticed that the chapters were littered with short examples demonstrating the concepts being discussed. If you didn't try those examples out then, you are strongly advised to do so right now. You'll find that things sink in a lot better that way when it is time to write the software.

Don't kid yourself — writing software is difficult. If it were easy, then you wouldn't be bothering to read this book, and we'd all be enslaved by machines by now — so thank your blessings that it's not a trivial task.

Why should software development be difficult? It requires no purchase of paint or canvas, and it binds you by few physical constraints. It should be the ultimate blank slate. Yet, one of your biggest impediments is that of logically painting yourself into a corner. In essence, your own mind is one of your biggest enemies.

Another constraint is time. Although few things are technically beyond your means, as a mortal you cannot possibly physically create something as powerful and flexible as the entirety of the GNU/Linux operating system in just two weeks.

In addition, for whom is this software being written? Yourself? Your friends? A rather common scenario is writing custom software for a client. The fantasy client used as an example in this chapter is called "Widget World." The type of scenario it presents is very common, because the majority of software is not written for consumers, but rather to meet the specifications of businesses, governments, and other groups.

This chapter assumes that you're an average developer, working on an average project at an average company with average clients. For simplicity's sake, however, this example project has some perhaps uncommon traits:

❑ You are developing a new product. (A much more common scenario would call on you to modify a currently existing system.)

❑ You are working alone (because you are reading this text alone). In the real world, you would most likely be working closely with, or interfacing with, other developers.

Widget World

Widget World designs, produces, and sells widgets. It has a dedicated, distributed sales staff that scours the globe attending the latest widget conventions and approaching widget-friendly businesses. Widget World engages in old-fashioned cold-calling, and creates a grassroots suburban Widget Ware sales-party network.

Widget World is also the victim of its own success. Like many businesses, it has not planned for double-digit growth, and it is failing to keep its sales force supplied with information about sales opportunities and the latest in widget technology. Nor is it managing to obtain quick and timely feedback from the sales staff in order to capitalize on trends in widget fashion.

Widget World cannot hire enough summer interns to work the phones and fax machines to keep the widgets flowing. The Widget Master is well aware that Widget World needs to be more efficient. Therefore, after looking at commercial offerings, the Widget Master has decided to commission the writing of specialized software called the Widget World Sales Force Automation Tool (WW-SFAT).

Although the Widget Master holds the purse strings, she utilizes the Widget marketing department to forecast the latest trends, which in turn helps plan the road map of Widget World.

The Widget marketers depend upon the regional Widget sales managers (both Eastern and Western) to keep them supplied with up-to-date information. Widget marketers also let the managers know about the pricing of widgets in reference to their competitors.

The regional Widget sales managers reward and motivate their widget sales personnel by supplying them with timely information regarding widget hot spots. They also set quotas, cut bonus checks, and ensure that all salespeople are doing their best to put a Widget on every desktop.

The WW-SFAT manager is a newly created position with input from both Widget marketing and regional Widget managers. The WW-SFAT manager is charged with creating a process, as well as accompanying software, to solve the problem of automating the streamlining of the Widget World sales force's daily operating procedures.

The WW-SFAT manager is also given the significant (and crucial) power of "stopping the buck" — whatever the WW-SFAT manager decides goes. This power is critical to the success of the project, because it limits the number of meetings and documentation required. The WW-SFAT manager is also dedicated to working closely with you on this project. Because you know nothing of widgets or sales, and you are charged with streamlining the Widget World sales force's existing paper-based phone and fax system of tracking salespeople and contacts, you have a million questions. Figure 15-1 shows the current tracking form in use.

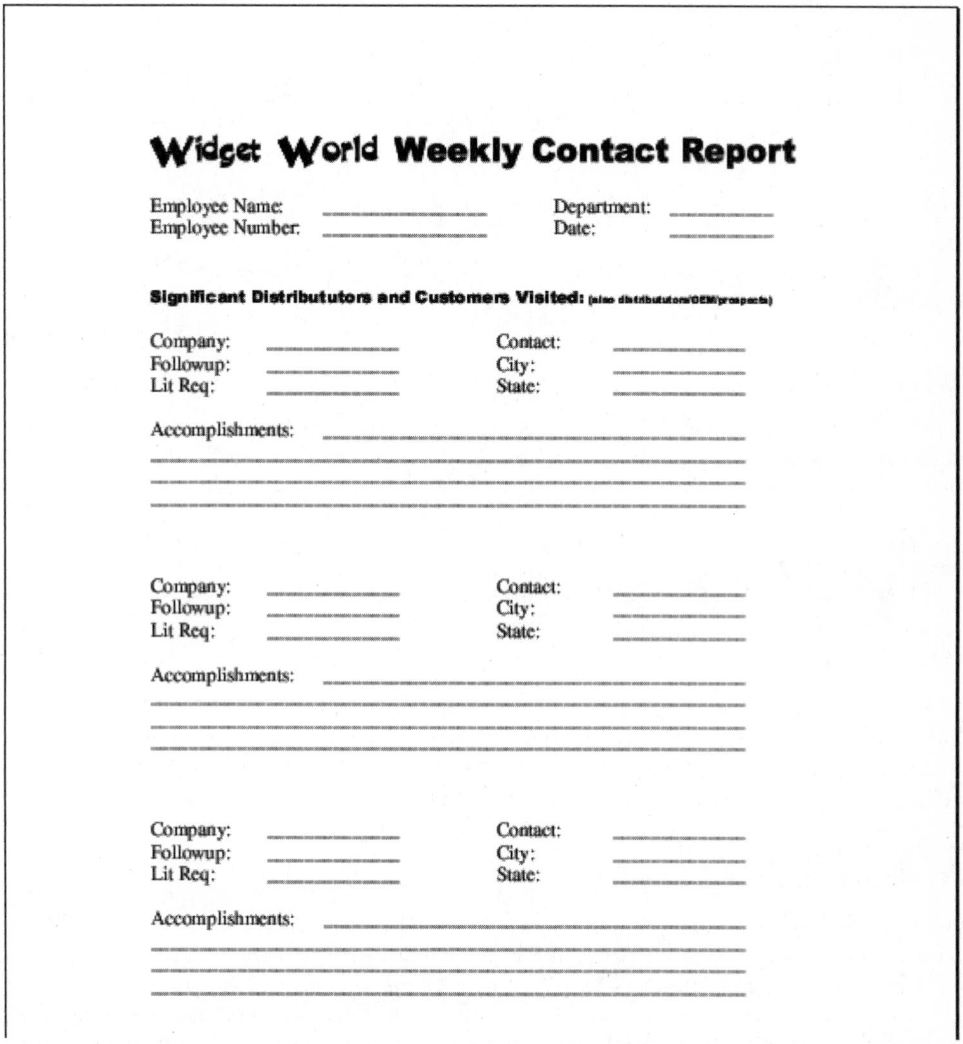

Widget World Weekly Contact Report

Employee Name: ______ Department: ______
Employee Number: ______ Date: ______

Significant Distribututors and Customers Visited: (also distribututors/OEM/prospects)

Company: ______ Contact: ______
Followup: ______ City: ______
Lit Req: ______ State: ______

Accomplishments: ______

Company: ______ Contact: ______
Followup: ______ City: ______
Lit Req: ______ State: ______

Accomplishments: ______

Company: ______ Contact: ______
Followup: ______ City: ______
Lit Req: ______ State: ______

Accomplishments: ______

Figure 15-1: Current Widget World tracking form

Here are a few questions that might occur to you:

- ❏ "Do you want to see the time in 12- or 24-hour format?"

- ❏ "Do different time zones matter?"

- ❏ "By what date should X's report be submitted?"

- ❏ "What happens if X's report is *not* in by the required date?"

- ❏ "How are expenses reimbursed?"

- ❏ "How often does the federal mileage reimbursement change?"

- ❏ "Does the federal mileage reimbursement need to be historical? Retroactive?"

The Widget World Landscape

The following discussion details the makeup of the Widget World landscape. These include the technical, financial, and political layers, as well as your role in them.

The Technical Layer

If you've been paying close attention, you'll notice that information needs to flow from the Widget sales personnel up the chain to the Widget Master, and back down again. In this case, information flow is definitely a two-way street:

- ❏ Widget marketing needs the sales information summarized by region.

- ❏ Widget sales managers need to track various aspects of their personnel.

The Financial Layer

This project should save Widget World money by making the staff more efficient, which is ultimately why the Widget Master is willing to invest money in the project. However, it's currently a toss-up as to what would save money quicker — supplying the Widget World sales staff members with more information or receiving more information back from them.

The Political Layer

One of the Widget regional managers secretly distrusts Widget marketing. He thinks that the Widget marketing department will use his supplied information as a tool to retire him early. The Widget sales staff welcomes the use of hard numbers to show how hard it's working — it keeps the regional managers honest and indicates who's getting promoted based on nepotism instead of on the basis of performance. Widget marketers want to have press releases with nice-looking graphs that they can show to their golf buddies.

You

You landed this job by responding to an ad in your local paper that said "Widget World Needs a Sales Force Automation Tool Developer." You were contacted by the WW-SFAT manager, passed the Widget World technical examination (in part because of your dedicated study of *Professional PHP 6!*), and arrived at your job eager to start your new career in software development.

It happens to be 8:00 A.M. on Monday, and you'll never be this naive again.

Is It Really About Technology?

WW-SFAT requirements appear to consist vaguely of the following:

- ❑ Sales contact reports
- ❑ Sales lead reports
- ❑ Sales contact management lists distributed by e-mail, BlackBerry, fax, and Web reports
- ❑ Widget production feed based upon sales performance
- ❑ Widget marketing reports and full-color, glossy, ready-to-print graphs
- ❑ Widget accounting reports
- ❑ Training

It's really the embodiment of a common scenario: a typical project using best-of-breed development techniques to keep the customer happy. However, even though the "customer" may appear to be just like the WW-SFAT manager, the customer doesn't live in a vacuum. All the actors here have a vested interest in the outcome of their portion of the project.

The Development Approach

You'll begin to utilize some development practices typified by extreme programming (XP). Don't let the name fool you. XP is a collection of agile development methodologies, and the following list of practices were best characterized by Kent Beck and Cynthia Andres in *Extreme Programming Explained: Embrace Change, Second Edition* (Addison-Wesley, 2004):

- ❑ *Planning* — Determine the scope of the project by combining business priorities and technical estimates, continually updated.

- ❑ *Small releases* — Get the system used to the people who will be using it, and release new versions on a very short schedule.

❏ *Simple Design* — Keep the design as simple as possible at all times. Complexity is removed on an ongoing basis.

❏ *Testing* — Developers continually write unit tests to ensure that the system runs flawlessly at all times. Customers write tests to demonstrate that features work as required.

❏ *Refactoring* — Restructure the code without modifying the behavior to keep it easy to read, to remove duplication, or to simplify it.

❏ *On-site customer* — The WW-SFAT manager is half your team, and is available at all times to answer business-related questions.

These practices enable you to manage the complexity and scope of both the project and the software that you are developing. A typical system flows similarly to the curve shown in Figure 15-2. By managing complexity from many different angles, you can make the curve drastically different, as shown in Figure 15-3.

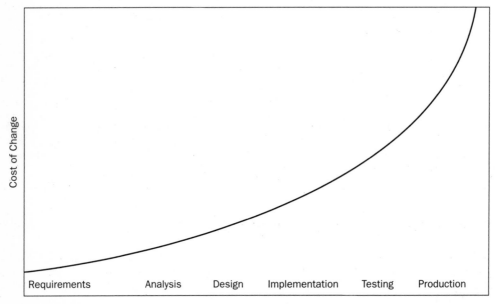

Figure 15-2: Typical system flow

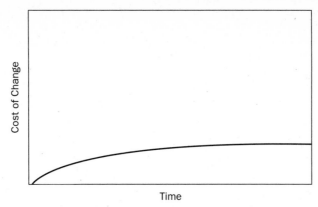

Figure 15-3: Changing the curve by managing complexity

Creating features as you need them is a great way to manage the complexity of your system. The cost of adding features later is not significantly higher than it is now (whenever "now" would be in the process), which means that you aren't forced to guess about what you think you'll require in the future, and you can avoid building features that won't be used for some time to come.

Think of it like this: Using the traditional approach to complexity, if the cost to you (in time) is $5.00 to add a feature now, but later that same feature would cost you $100.00, it would be safer to add it now; but if you can manage to set it up such that the cost to add the same feature now is $5.00 and the cost to add it later is $6.00, then you gain little by adding it now. Omit it for now; your system stays simpler, and you end up only with features that are used from the outset.

What This Means to You

Consider the traditional waterfall approach first documented by Dr. Winston W. Royce (see "Managing the Development of Large Software Systems: Concepts and Techniques," Proceedings of IEEE WESCON, August 1970). Figure 15-4 represents this concept, which calls for the following:

- ❑ Two weeks of gathering requirements
- ❑ Two weeks of analyzing and debating them
- ❑ Two weeks of designing the system
- ❑ Eight weeks of coding it
- ❑ Four weeks of quality assurance (QA) and other testing

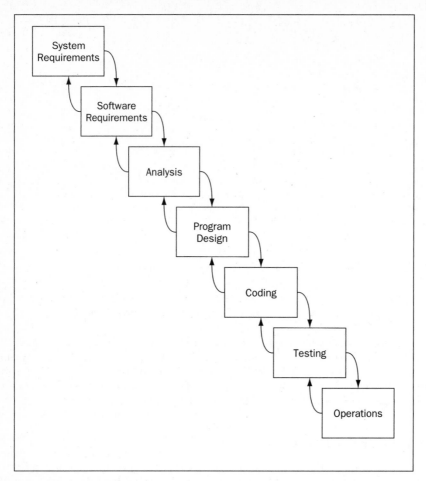

Figure 15-4: Waterfall approach

Although it's very regimented, the waterfall model tends to be implemented as a shotgun approach, and it has a couple of weaknesses:

❑   It lacks flexibility and assumes that design will be done correctly the first time. With a span of weeks between phases, little or no time is available for a feedback loop — and, of course, hindsight is 20–20.

❑   It is hard to predict needed features because requirements are more than likely to change.

This certainly sounds almost like a setup for failure, which is why you're going to follow Kent Beck's principles (listed previously) in order to create a small, flexible system that is thoroughly tested as you write the code. You will work closely with your WW-SFAT manager and get all required questions answered. Your WW-SFAT manager has a wide breadth of Widget World business experience and will use the system on a daily basis.

This also means that you'll fix problems that you see and remove functionality that is no longer required. You'll stick to the "once and only once" rule, which means that you'll consolidate duplicate logic, and you'll be ruthless about it. Refactoring mercilessly keeps your entire system lean and powerful.

Finally, you'll have your unit tests. By testing every piece of functionality that you create, you'll always have a fully tested system. A fully tested system is very powerful because it makes you keenly aware of breakages and symptoms that are caused by secondary or tertiary bugs. A fully tested system lets you know instantly when something went wrong.

Having the safety net of a well-written test suite enables you to indulge in modifying features drastically. The test suite does not shackle you unnecessarily, but rather allows you to be a bolder developer by letting you take your system in different directions as (and when) business needs change.

This is really just a 10-minute introduction to XP, which is one of the more agile development methodologies. It's okay if you don't quite buy everything that you've just read, because you'll explore in the next few chapters how this methodology truly pays off. Soon, you'll realize that by using the practices described here, you'll not only be shipping software that is small, fast, and flexible, but also adapting a process that enables your client to be actively involved in the development process.

The Technology

Although you've been warned about not building too much up front, these are some of the technological features that you'll be touching upon:

❑   *Unified Modeling Language (UML)* — Where appropriate, the design snapshots (class and sequence diagrams) will be shown in UML. A quick cheat-sheet is available.

❑   *Design patterns* — This includes how to effectively use them and spot them in your code.

❑   *Collections and iterators* — Where they make sense and where they don't

❑   *Dispatchers* — Just to get a taste of event-driven programming

❑   *Simple Object Access Protocol (SOAP)* — This will be used for one of the data feeds.

Summary

Now that you understand the background of Widget World and its business needs, you can soon get to work utilizing the development techniques that were briefly outlined here.

Rather than follow the regimented waterfall development approach, you can use a more flexible approach that highlights quick releases, simple design, a well-tested code-base, a dedication to continuous code improvement, and a means of having continuous feedback with access to the customer.

By utilizing this approach, you can produce an application that is capable of delivering business value in the first release, measurable in days and weeks, rather than in months and years.

So, what's next? You could go ahead and put a project plan together — all the hard work that will ensure your project is delivered on time, on budget, and to a high standard — but it's far better to get an understanding of what makes a project a true success before you throw yourself in at the deep end.

In Chapter 16, you'll start learning just that — a series of techniques that together are usually called *project management* methodologies. You'll have just one chapter of theory before getting back to planning the tool itself. Only then can you get your favorite editor out and actually build the tool.

16

Project Management

Many traditional Web project leads come from a project management background. They entered the industry having left university or college as a "junior producer" and rose through the ranks to be finally given the freedom and latitude to run their own projects. But while many excellent project management professionals do indeed follow such a path, in recent years there has been a trend toward software development professionals *sidestepping* — that is, laying down their development tools in favor of a chance to run a team of former colleagues and play a crucial role in the success (or failure) of the project.

Indeed, such a development is quite welcome, if truth be told. If you've ever found yourself frustrated as a software developer with your project lead, chances are good it's been because they "just don't get it." In practice, no matter how talented project managers are, if they have no experience writing code, then they often find it difficult to appreciate your point of view.

Even if you are never confronted with your own project to manage, you will find it immensely useful to understand what the project manager (who is running the show) must contend with on a daily basis. It will make you stronger as a software architect and as an individual to understand and be sympathetic to the skills required to run a successful development project from start to finish.

Moreover, in the event that you do find yourself in charge of a team of bright-eyed young developers one day, you'll find that the skills gleaned from this chapter and the next will serve you well.

This chapter discusses how to collate business requirements into a coherent brief, and how to respond appropriately with a rock-solid specification and project plan. You'll learn how to identify and select the key personnel who will report to you, as well as how to guide and manage them throughout the project life cycle. You'll also look at a couple of programming paradigms, discover how to evaluate their usefulness for your own project, and look at the two key approaches to tackling the development work on the shop floor. Finally, you'll discover how to effectively manage your working relationship with your clients.

Admittedly, this chapter doesn't have a whole lot to do with the specifics of PHP 6. Nonetheless, the material covered here is very relevant to any PHP project you might work on, even though the techniques demonstrated apply just as much to ASP.NET, Java — any language. They are included in this book nonetheless because they might well revolutionize the way you tackle big projects.

Do Your Homework

Generally, the most common, visible first step for a project occurs when a project manager tells a senior member of his development staff that he has something new for the team to work on, something that often happens as nothing more than an informal chat around the office water cooler or during a smoke break. In practice, of course, the idea behind the project starts much further back. Tracing the roots of any given project is essential. A project management methodology can be successful only if it is applied from the very beginning of the project.

Before you take steps to receive the formal brief for the project, there are a few key questions to ask — your homework, if you will. These questions taken together will form the foundation of the strategy you adapt when receiving the formal brief. The first question to ask is, "Why?"

Why Is the Project Happening?

This simple question has an enormous influence on everything you do from here on in because the way in which you approach and build your project (from start to finish) should be determined by its intended function.

Typical scenarios underlying the need for a new Web site or application might include the following:

❑ Starting a new business for which "the business is the application"

❑ Replacing an existing application that is failing or no longer adequate

❑ Taking over where an existing supplier has failed to deliver either on time, on budget, or what is required (or, in some cases, all three)

There are, of course, other reasons that may require a new project to be taken on, and not all of them are as critical as the three listed here. For example, you may simply find yourself having to implement the pet project of a VP or executive. Whatever it is, determining the *raison d'être* of the project is a number-one priority.

Who Is the Project For?

This is sometimes not as easy a question to answer as you might think. At the simplest level, the project is for another department within your own company or organization, a new customer, or an existing customer. Remember that you must identify the recipient of the project in the sense of who has actually commissioned the work. If a man goes to the store to buy his wife nail polish, he's not the real customer — he's simply carrying out the real customer's request.

Similarly, your client may be commissioning this work only to satisfy some requirement of a third party to whom he or she is responsible. These ultimate end users of the product are known as *domain experts,* and you ignore them at your peril.

The end users for your product will often be the most hands-on people in your client's organization, and as such their needs for the project will often be immensely different from the requisitioning individual who approaches you as a potential supplier.

Identifying Roles and Agenda

By way of example, say that you are the chief technical officer (CTO) of a medium-size organization, and that you have been commissioned by the human resources (HR) director to build a new intranet for your whole company. You have both permanent and contract staff at your disposal. What do you think the various agendas of each role (you, the client, and the domain experts) are?

To take a slightly cynical perspective on things, the scenario most likely looks something like this:

❑   You (as a developer) want to deliver a high-quality, effective, efficient, and satisfactory solution as quickly as possible, and with as little investment as possible, so that you look good to your client, your peers, and your boss.

❑   The HR director wants you to deliver a high-quality, effective, efficient, and satisfactory solution that makes him or her look good.

❑   Daily users of the intranet (the domain experts) want you to deliver a high-quality, effective, efficient, and satisfactory solution that does what they want it to do.

Notice that the only really selfless agenda here is held by the domain experts. The secret is to ensure that all three agenda are met. The first two are incredibly easy to meet; the latter is the most difficult. But by concentrating on the third, the first two will generally drop into place by default.

Therefore, this is your sweet spot: *look after the domain expert*. Everything you design or build, and every decision you take in the process, should have the domain expert firmly in mind. Sure, *you* may use Pico to edit text files, or Google Chrome to browse the Web, but does your user? Probably not. Rather than take the moral high ground ("well, they *should* be using Pico"), you should deliver what it is they actually want and need.

Realizing the difference between "being right" and "doing right" is what defines the gap between a bedroom coder and a software development professional.

Manipulating Roles to Your Advantage

Consider this: Your client is merely a conduit to the domain experts on a project, no matter what else he or she might tell you. Although it is a lot easier for your client to express immense pleasure with what you've built at the point of delivery and walk away, if the domain experts don't like it, the axe will fall on the client's head — and so, in turn, will it fall on yours some days, weeks, or months later. It is very much in the client's interest to represent the needs of the domain experts from the outset.

A good client will be able to sympathize with the true needs and requirements of his or her domain experts and to assemble them into a single, harmonious voice for you to listen to. However, in practice, you will need to prod, probe, and cajole your client into representing the realistic and reasonable requirements of his or her domain experts properly.

If you feel that your client is not representing his or her domain experts sufficiently, it is vitally important that you suggest that he or she reimplement the consultative process. This can be accomplished through the following:

❑ A brainstorming session

❑ An anonymous suggestion box approach

❑ Appointing a working party to represent the needs of the domain experts, and involving them in the project process

It is vitally important that if the roles aren't clearly carved out from the start, you must help carve them out. That way, when you do receive the formal brief for the project, you'll be able to respond to it, safe in the knowledge that what you're responding to is, in fact, what is really required.

What Is the History of the Project?

It is also vitally important to establish whether this project has any baggage attached to it. A fresh project is always exciting, but it may not actually be as fresh on the inside as it appears on the outside. Having a good handle on the history of the project enables you to tweak certain aspects of your approach accordingly.

Generally speaking, a project has serious baggage only if another attempt has been made to get it off the ground previously — *a false start*. If you know this to be the case, then you should immediately make yourself aware of the following potential baggage, no matter how long ago that previous attempt was made:

❑ *Departed staff* — If this project was previously handled by a member of staff who has since resigned, been fired, or been moved to other duties in the organization, beware. It is almost inevitable that the client considers the former staff member to have failed in his or her appointed task. The trick here is to gain a good idea of the strengths and weaknesses of the new representative that the client puts forward to work with you. This is addressed a bit more later in this chapter.

❑ *Departed supplier* — If you are undertaking the project as a replacement for another supplier (either commercial or internal), it is worth sizing up the reasons why the client dropped that supplier in the first place; or, indeed, why the supplier dropped the client — it does happen from time to time. If necessary, dig around with other former clients of that supplier to examine their experiences, and shape your approach according to any useful information you acquire. The client will want to trust you from the outset, so give him or her good reason to.

❑ *Difficulties working with in-house staff* — If a project has been outsourced by a company to you, you may experience difficulties working with the client company's IT department. Sometimes this situation can arise even when no attempt to start the project has ever been made internally, but there has been an expectation that one should have been made. The best advice is to get that IT department involved from the start. Give that department a call while you're writing the technical specification — it will be caught well and truly off guard and may even prove to be a great help as a result.

What Are the Anticipated Prerequisites of the Project?

You should be aware of these as early in the project life cycle as possible, because they may even influence your decision as to whether you wish to proceed. Some typical prerequisites might include the following:

❑ *Platform* — Does the client require the project to be built in ASP.NET, J2EE, or some other development language not overly familiar to you as a PHP professional? There may be sound commercial reasons for this, and this is the most common reason for determining PHP is inappropriate for a given piece of work

❑ *Deployment* — Does the client need this application to be deployed onto existing servers? If so, is the client happy for you to reconfigure those servers if necessary?

❑ *Timescales* — Does the client have any specific expectations about delivery from the outset, possibly to meet some internal target or deadline?

❑ *Budget* — Does the client have a specific budget? Is it realistic?

It is very important to get these prerequisites established before you embark upon the process of receiving the brief. After all, if you can't fulfill the prerequisites, there's little point in moving to the next step.

Receiving the Formal Brief

Having done your homework, you should receive the formal brief. The most important part of any brief is to get it in writing. By this stage, you've probably already received a fair bit of information about the project, but getting the brief in writing ensures that you and your team are able to respond to it in the most effective manner possible.

If your client is only prepared to brief you in person, rather than provide any kind of written documentation, be sure to take detailed notes, and then *write them up*.

Quite rarely, however, will the initial brief be in a satisfactory form — whether verbal or written. As a result, it's often up to you to turn the client's wishes into a coherent brief in a format you can all work with. Rather than make this a separate document in its own right, it is often best to incorporate this as part of your pitch, which is examined later.

Getting a client to articulate his or her requirements is one of the toughest things you'll ever have to do as a project manager. Worse still, clients rarely differentiate between incorrect assumptions you've made based on the absence of information and assumptions you've made that are simply plain wrong. The way around this problem is to ensure that all the assumptions and guesses you're making in your pitch are based on the best and most exhaustive information available to you. Therefore, you must be thorough in extracting the minutiae of the client's business requirements at this early stage.

> *Whenever possible, try to glean a phone conversation or, ideally, a meeting with the client, before writing the brief and responding to it.*

If you are fortunate enough to get a phone conversation or meeting with the client from which you construct the formal brief, it's important that you ask the right questions. You must focus on a number of key areas that are covered here. After you have covered these, you will be in a position to write your brief.

Business Requirements

Establish exactly what the broad requirements of the system or application you are building are at this stage. Focus on asking questions about the goals of the domain experts, rather than the anticipated solution the client has in mind.

It doesn't matter if the solution you recommend is nothing like what the client is expecting, as long as you can precisely map your decisions to the goals of the domain experts on a "cause-and-effect" basis. These mappings form the basis of your overall solution's rationale and are a key component of your pitch.

Ask leading questions. Try to listen rather than talk. The unprompted musings of the client can be immensely useful in optimizing your proposal to best suit his or her needs, even at a subconscious level. Try to effect a strong mix of commercial and logistical probing. For example, the following generic questions may be useful:

- ❑ What other solutions have you looked at?
- ❑ Why have you rejected them?
- ❑ Who will the end users of this system be?
- ❑ How are you currently handling this process without a system in place?
- ❑ What benefits do you think the system might bring?
- ❑ What kind of return on investment are you looking for?
- ❑ How will you measure that return?
- ❑ What are the three most important requirements you have of a supplier who wants to provide this solution to you?
- ❑ How many other suppliers have you looked at?
- ❑ How satisfied have you been with the proposals you have received to date?
- ❑ Do you have a time frame for choosing a supplier, and what is driving this time frame?
- ❑ What people are likely to be involved in the decision-making process, and what are their roles?
- ❑ What are the biggest concerns you have about this project moving forward?
- ❑ Have other suppliers addressed those concerns to your satisfaction?

Again, don't be afraid to let the client do most of the talking. Try to avoid letting individual points drop as you scribble down notes. Instead, ask probing questions to extract that "extra ten percent" from the client.

Here's an example dialogue between supplier and client:

> *Supplier:* Do you have a time frame for choosing a supplier?
>
> *Client:* Absolutely. We'll have made our decision by the thirtieth.
>
> *Supplier:* The thirtieth of this month? Really. You guys are keen to get this off the ground, then?
>
> *Client:* Definitely. We have a big advertising campaign starting next month.
>
> *Supplier:* Oh, right. Is this system likely to be a big part of that advertising campaign?
>
> *Client:* Yes. If we have the build under way by then, it will definitely be a big selling point.

Compare the same dialogue without the additional probing:

> *Supplier:* Do you have a time frame for choosing a supplier?
>
> *Client:* Absolutely. We'll have made our decision by the thirtieth.
>
> *Supplier:* Great, thanks.

Notice the extra information gleaned from the probing:

> The client has an advertising campaign taking place next month.
>
> The client would like to be able to show the unfinished system to prospective clients as part of his or her sales pitch.

This information is no secret, and the client isn't holding back deliberately — it just hasn't occurred to him or her to mention it. But, make no mistake about it — this extra information should be very useful to you indeed.

The moral of the story is don't be afraid to take an interest in what your client is saying, and ask the extra questions that might get you that extra nugget of information. It might just give you an edge over your competition.

Scope

After you have established the broader business requirements of the system and worked out exactly what problem or need the client is trying to solve or fulfill, it's worth probing the client some more about the scope of requirements. Let's be clear about what is meant by the term *scope* here. By establishing scope, you are looking at how *far* you are going to go to solve that problem or fulfill that need.

People often speak of *scope-creep* or *feature-creep*, but in practice it's a misused phrase. It actually refers to the magnitude of what's required growing in the middle of the project without regard to commercial impact. It does *not* refer to requirements themselves changing. There's no phrase for that; that's just poor planning.

By establishing the scope now, you can prevent scope creep from happening as much as possible. The specifications you produce enable you to enforce this chosen scope by mapping it to the specific components of functionality that will be included in the build process.

Scope is almost always artificially throttled by time and money, but it can be a useful exercise to help manage expectations even at this early stage by drawing phase boundaries. Nine times out of ten, suggesting a two-phase approach to the client can help you immensely, because the client will instantly illustrate for you the kind of functionality that might drop into a second phase of development and the kind of functionality that is required now. Commit to just the latter of these, and you have your initial scope well and truly defined.

If the client is reluctant to look at dividing the project into phases, then a more direct approach is needed. Explain to the client that the only limitations to meeting his or her requirements are those of time and money, and that understanding what the absolutely essential components of the project are now can make his or her life easier, as he or she will be able to interpret proposals on delivery time and cost on a more equal footing. If no other suppliers are pitching for the work, explain to the client that establishing scope now will save huge amounts of time later, and enable the project to progress more quickly with fewer revisions to specifications.

It's important to discuss scope in the context of time and budget. Rather than ever say no to your clients, you can tell them when their requirements are likely to stretch the time line or cost them more than they have budgeted for. Let's look at those now.

Timelines

Establishing timelines is about much more than just figuring out when the client needs the system to be delivered. It's vitally important to set milestones and agree to them with the client, even at this early stage. You should try to gauge milestones for the following:

- ❏ The date by which the proposal is required
- ❏ The date by which a decision will be made on a chosen supplier (if appropriate)
- ❏ The date by which any written specifications are required from the supplier
- ❏ The date by which any written specifications will be signed off by the client or, if amendments will be required, those amendments will be tabled
- ❏ The date by which the specification process (including all amendments) must be finished
- ❏ The date by which any designs produced by the supplier must be put forward for initial approval
- ❏ The date by which any designs (including all amendments) must be finished
- ❏ The date by which the build must commence
- ❏ The date by which the build must be completed to beta standard
- ❏ The date by which the build must be completed to finished standard
- ❏ The date by which testing must take place
- ❏ The date by which the handover of the finished product must take place

Of course, asking for all these dates from clients can overwhelm or even irritate them. To avoid this, pick what you consider to be the key milestones and fill in the blanks yourself. You can even have a positive effect on the client's view of your processes at this early stage by announcing where the dates will fit together. Consider the following snippet of dialogue:

> *Supplier:* When do you need the completed system to be handed over?
>
> *Client:* We need to be up and running with the staff by the first of June.
>
> *Supplier:* In that case, we should aim to have the system handed over to you by May 22, to allow a few days for any last-minute tweaks and changes that might need to be taken care of.

Don't forget to note all milestones carefully throughout the briefing process and, when necessary, guide the client away from any unrealistic expectations, as shown in the following example:

> *Supplier:* When do you need the completed system to be handed over?
>
> *Client:* We need to be up and running with the staff by the first of May.
>
> *Supplier:* I think that, given the kind of scope we've agreed on, that is going to be a difficult date to meet. I would suggest a delivery date of May 22 is probably closer to the mark, which should have you up and running shortly afterward. I think we have two options. We can either reduce the scope of the system at this stage, or we have to look at a slightly later delivery date.
>
> *Client:* Well, in all honesty, we could live with the May 22. We'd rather get it right first time.

Notice how passive language is used to explain to the client that his or her date is unrealistic. You do not "tell" the client, because he or she may well think you are attempting a "we know best" tactic, which might offend. Rather, you "suggest," and in many cases (as in the preceding example) you'll often find that there is a little more room for maneuver than originally stated.

Always be sure to point out unrealistic dates; never let them slip through unchecked. The client will expect anything unattainable to be pointed out now. If it is not mentioned until your written proposal comes through, you risk alienating the client, especially if they have already told others involved in the project of the anticipated dates. Essentially, anything not contradicted will be taken as tacit agreement, so beware.

It is hoped that you know your own estimating skills. If you frequently go over your initial estimate in practice, work out by how much, and then use this as your contingency margin. If you're following the techniques in this book, you'll deliver quicker than your competitors anyway, so there's no harm in adding 20 percent contingency to protect yourself, especially if your contract calls for ever-terrifying penalty clauses for late delivery.

Budget

Budget can be a thorny issue. Even if you are delivering a solution internally, you still have your direct costs to think about. Many larger companies bill each other's cost centers for internal activity, so budgeting and negotiations can be just as intense for internal work as they are for an external commission.

Don't ask the budget question too early. It is immensely off-putting. Clients expect to be asked about it, but they may quickly judge what they deem to be your own priorities as a supplier based on the order in which you ask questions. The right time is probably close to when the subject of scope is raised, because you have already established that scope is more than likely going to be limited by time and money. Keep in mind that your client may ask about your rate card (that is, the rates at which your personnel are charged out) before overall project budgets are broached. You shouldn't shy away from answering this question. It is hoped that you're proud of your charge-out rate; you know it's good value, and you know it reflects your seniority.

A good way to phrase the overall budget question would be as follows: "When I've looked at implementing similar solutions to this for companies like Acme in the past, they have typically been expecting to invest between $35,000 and $65,000. Does that sound like the kind of ballpark you had in mind for this project?"

First of all, note that you haven't asked what the budget is. Rather, you have suggested the following:

❑   You have worked on similar projects in the past — *positive*

❑   You have worked with companies like Acme in the past — *positive*

❑   These companies have invested anywhere between $35,000 and $65,000 — *neutral*

The emphasis on the positives in your interrogation means that any negative thoughts associated with determining budget will not kick in quite as automatically as they would if you were to ask the question directly.

Second, note that you have offered a ballpark range. This range is, in fact, quite broad. Always do this; to be too specific at this stage suggests arrogance with respect to an understanding of the client's requirements, which you don't have yet. By suggesting a broad price range, you suggest subconsciously to the client that you still have yet to zero in on exactly what is required. Ensure that the minimum you suggest is the absolute minimum you're prepared to do the work for, and that the maximum is about 40 to 50 percent more than that figure. That way, if the client agrees, you know for sure that you will have a profitable job on your hands. By how much remains to be seen, true; but you've negated the chances of a loss-maker.

Finally, note the phrase "they have typically been expecting to invest." This is used in preference to "we have typically quoted them" for a good reason — namely, you are suggesting that these companies actually anticipated spending this amount *before* they spoke to you, *not* that this is the amount you quoted them.

Of course, this does not answer the eternal question of "What is your budget?" What it does, generally speaking, is implant a firm idea in the head of the client as to what the project is actually worth in market terms.

Upon becoming aware of this knowledge, if the client realizes that there simply isn't the budget to proceed, he or she will usually tell you. This obviously isn't a good thing in itself, but it does enable you to judge very quickly whether the time you spent receiving the brief is time well spent.

Consider the following two approaches. In both dialogues, the supplier needs to charge around $15,000 just to break even on the application. The client's budget is only $5,000. Here is the first scenario:

> *Supplier:* Did you have a budget in mind?

> *Client:* I'd rather not give you a budget. When we've done that with suppliers in the past, they've simply come back and quoted what I told them my budget was. I'd rather you just come up with a quote and I'll tell you whether it's doable or not.

> *Supplier:* OK, no problem.

Contrast that with the following:

> *Supplier:* John, I wanted to broach with you the issue of budget. When I've looked at implementing similar solutions like this in the past, clients have typically been expecting to invest between $15,000 and $22,000. Does that sound like the kind of ballpark you had in mind for this project?"

> *Client:* Oh . . . no, it really isn't. I'm afraid the maximum we can afford to part with is $5,000, maybe $7,000 at a push.

> *Supplier:* Okay, John. In that case, I'm afraid I don't think we're going to be able to do business on this occasion unless you're prepared to narrow down the scope of work considerably. You might find that a smaller local supplier is a better bet.

In neither situation does the supplier get the business; but in the second situation, the supplier knows immediately that there's no sale in sight, whereas in the first situation, days would be lost creating a comprehensive pitch, only to be turned down later.

Note also that you suggest an alternative for the client — that he or she might want to approach a smaller local supplier. It can grate a little bit, sending business elsewhere — but it's a refreshing approach. Your prospective client will appreciate your honesty, and you might get one or two unexpected benefits: You might be bought a beer by that other supplier, and the lost client might even recommend you to somebody in the future — "Hey, these guys I spoke to a few months ago were too expensive for us, but they might be right for you."

Don't be embarrassed to ask about money; it's the lifeblood of any business. Confront the issue honestly and pick your language and your timing carefully.

Commercial Terms

It's not a bad idea to talk about commercial terms, even at this early stage. If you've established that the client is happy to pay approximately $50,000 to have his or her project developed to completion, this is certainly a good start — but certain technicalities that often don't get mentioned can pour cold water on this head start very quickly.

Payment terms do matter, especially if you're a small supplier. If your project won't involve any direct costs (such as hardware, software, media costs, and so on), then it's just a question of cash flow — you have to do a piece of work and then wait to be paid. If you're going to be purchasing external goods or services, then you should ensure that you're not parting with the cash sooner than you will be getting paid by your client. Otherwise, you're basically acting as a lender to your client.

As with budgetary concerns, it's far better to get the issue of commercial terms out of the way early. That way, if they prove to be stumbling blocks, you can be aware of them now and back out if necessary. The following questions are probably more relevant to smaller businesses rather than enormous technology agencies, but they are still worth asking if you have any payment-related concerns:

- ❏ "We normally like to ask our clients for an up-front percentage contribution so that we can cover any incidental costs during the build process. Would this be a problem?"

- ❏ "Because we're a small company, we have to be quite firm with our payment terms. All our invoices are strictly 30 days. Do you think this would be all right with your accounts payable guys?"

Again, phrasing is very important here. For example, using the friendly interrogative statement "Would this be a problem?" is highly recommended. You are far more likely to solicit a sympathetic "Oh, no, I wouldn't think so" response, rather than something more aggressive or perfunctory.

Another stock phrase is "Do you think this would be something that could prevent us from doing business together?" It sounds incredibly emotive, but it suggests "no" as an appropriate answer in its tone, and so is much more likely to solicit that kind of answer. Positive responses are useful not just because they're what you want to hear, but also because they're what the client wants to say.

> Research suggests that a meeting in which parties have used positive words and body gestures leaves a far better impression than one littered with "no" and shakes of the head.

By leaving your clients with a positive impression of the meeting, you're leaving them with a positive impression of you as an individual.

It's also worth being up front with your client about markup. If you're buying in external goods or services, you may well charge them forward to your client at a small markup to cover your administrative costs — probably a flat percentage (15 percent is typical). Ensure that your client knows you are doing this. Again, being honest will engender an atmosphere of trust and respect.

Future Plans

As far as is reasonably possible, you should endeavor to press clients for their future plans for the system. You may well have determined what is "in scope," but it is equally important to know what is both "out of scope" and likely to become a requirement in the future.

As a software architect, you may be more than familiar with the concept of "coding yourself into a corner." The best project managers are aware of these concepts, too, which is yet another reason why many of the best project managers tend to have backgrounds in architecture (something that was posited at the very beginning of the chapter).

With that in mind, determine as early as possible what is likely to become a requirement at a later date, even if it is conceivable (or likely) that another supplier will be taking on the work. Showing interest in what is clearly not going to be paid for or carried out at this stage demonstrates a commitment to avoiding "hit and run" programming and demonstrates that you are the kind of supplier with whom the client can forge a long-term relationship.

Look and Feel

There is no excuse these days for even the simplest or most functional of Web applications not to look good. Design must be an integral part of your process, not just an afterthought, and this should be emphasized to the client whenever possible.

Determine at this stage whether any requirements or specific requests exist on the part of the client with respect to the look and feel of what is being produced. For example, is there an expectation that a particular corporate branding will be followed? Does the system need to closely resemble an existing system? How likely is it that the branding will change, and how often?

Technology

There's a good chance that the individual you are dealing with from the client company is not a technical person. For most projects, this is understandable because the commercial or functional goals of the required system (for which you are receiving the brief) are unlikely to be technical in nature. Even with this in mind, it is an immensely good idea at this stage to ask probing questions about technology.

Essentially, you must gauge how much free rein you have regarding making these decisions. At the very least, in your written proposal you need to outline the platform and infrastructure choices you have made and be able to justify them if necessary. Aim to ask the kinds of questions that will determine whether the client is happy for you to code with PHP, what deployment issues there may be, and what security issues might need to be addressed.

If any restrictions you discover appear to be onerous, then this may be another red flag — a sign that you need to cut your losses and pull out. As a PHP professional, if the client insists on ASP.NET and SQL Server, then you would be wise to think about declining the work or, alternatively, trying to understand why the client has decided that. Maybe you could convince the client that PHP is the way to go — but only if there's no underlying commercial reason adhering them to that alternate platform.

Either way, it is a conversation you must have early to prevent any fruitless pitching. It is another sign of a true professional that you know when to walk away. If your client is wired up to the hilt with Microsoft-based hardware and software with a suite of incumbent .NET applications, why would you try to pitch a PHP-based solution?

Support

If there is one issue you should always try to raise with the client, it's the issue of after-production support. It may not have even crossed a client's mind, but it's extremely useful to establish what the client's expectations are and how they jibe with your own.

Determining who will create user-orientated documentation (if required), who is to provide support after the system is deployed, and what kind of service the client expects during handover are all important issues to address. If the client appears at a loss, attempt to suggest suitable answers to your own questions, and gain the client's tacit approval for inclusion in your pitch.

Bizarrely, many clients unused to contracting Web development professionals seem to labor under the delusion that they can expect lifetime after-sales support and maintenance without additional charge. It's worth ensuring that this isn't the case on your project, and if it is, setting the client straight.

What Now?

Now that you have a formal brief and have talked at length with your client about time, budget, design, technology, and support, it's time to proceed with winning the business. If you're in the fortunate position of developing a project for another department in your own organization, you can probably skip the next section, as it probably won't be a pitch situation in the first place.

However, if you need to actually convince the client of your worthiness as a supplier and provide a fully costed proposal in the process, read on.

Constructing the Pitch

The pitch itself can take many forms. It can be a presentation, a mock-up, a sample system, or even a demo of a similar solution you've worked on in the past. Regardless of the scenario, a written component is typically part of every pitch, and that is what this section addresses.

The first question, of course, is whether you need a pitch at all — or whether a mere quotation will suffice.

Pitches Versus Quotes

It goes without saying that you must provide (at the very least) a quote for the work you've been briefed about. When to expand that quote into a full-fledged pitch, however, can be a tricky decision.

Consider the last time that you, as a consumer, were actively "sold to." It was probably the last time you bought a car, a high-end TV or home entertainment system, or a new kitchen. You expect to be pitched when you are looking at $400 televisions, so why is it that when you go to the store to buy $400 worth of groceries for the family during the holiday season, you aren't pitched to in the supermarket?

The difference is pretty clear. The television is a long-term expense; the groceries will be gone in a few weeks. Think along the same lines with the work you're quoting. Try not to get too hung up on the cash value. Consider instead what the work you're proposing means to the client. If it will have a long-term impact, then you need to sell it, so you need to produce a pitch. If it's simply a short-term requirement — a consumable — then, more than likely, all you need is a quote.

Examples of work that may require only a quote would include specific changes to an existing application (provided that they are relatively simple) or the installation and configuration of PHP, Linux, MySQL, and Apache on a rack of servers. In both cases, there isn't a great deal to say — so don't say it.

If you are providing only a quote, it may be useful to have a few pages of stock library material (call it "propaganda") about your business — perhaps outlining some of your key skills, experience, past clients, and so on. This can be handed over with your quote in case anyone at the client company needs to see some traditional sales material.

For the rest of this section, let's assume that you've gone the whole hog and opted for a pitch, rather than a quote.

Pitches Versus Specifications

If you're serious about winning the business, plan to put some serious effort into your pitch. This is not a bad thing in itself, but you do need to be very careful not to fall into a very serious trap — that is, actually producing a specification, rather than a pitch.

You'll meet up with specifications later. Essentially, they are detailed blueprints for the system you will be building. At the pitch stage, however, you want to be careful not to get into that level of detail. Not only will you be doing more work than necessary, you may be giving away free advice if you don't eventually win the pitch.

Think carefully about what you are trying to accomplish with your pitch. You are trying to convince the client company of the following:

- ❑ You have fully understood the client's brief.

- ❑ You have devised an efficient, effective, and innovative response to the client's brief.

- ❑ You are able to deliver the solution you are recommending within the client's required time frame.

- ❑ You are able to deliver the solution at price X and have arrived at that price in a methodical manner.

- ❑ You are the kind of supplier with whom the client should do business.

Going into intense detail on the functionality or technology behind the system does not contribute to accomplishing these aims and, therefore, should be omitted.

Sometimes, a degree of upward management of the client is required to justify the absence of full functionality in the pitch document. Be totally candid. Explain to the client that you have adopted a rigorous specification process to ensure that the system is delivered exactly to the client's requirements. At this stage, you are a high-quality solution provider who has fully understood the requirements (rather than the specifics) of the system. If the client accepts these assertions, then he or she must, by inference, accept that you are able to fully provide the required system.

If you're still pressed for more detail, proceed with caution. Don't sell yourself short by giving away free advice at the drop of a hat.

Who to Involve When Pitching

By now, you probably have a good idea of who you want to involve in the project if you win the business. You'll learn more about this later in the chapter; but for now, it's worth considering who you should be involving in putting together the pitch. Because the pitch is your responsibility, ultimately any editorial decisions about its content lie with you.

That said, be aware that there is an element of creativity involved in the pitch process! You must clearly demonstrate an edge over other suppliers competing for the business, as well as the competence to deliver the required solution within the budgetary constraints of your client. With this in mind, it's definitely worthwhile to get people who may be able to contribute to the creative process involved at this early stage.

Because you are not getting bogged down in specifics, however, it is not necessary to have more than maybe one senior technologist and one senior creative on board, assuming that you have such people at your disposal. How the three of you arrive at the content of the pitch is very much up to you. Producing the entire document in a brainstorming environment, with the project manager in the driving seat, has proven to be a lot more effective than simply dividing the pitch into assignable chunks and gluing it together later.

When to Go the Extra Mile

Some clients will really make you work to win the business. In many cases, it's well worth it. At other times, it can be too much of a risk. Knowing when and when not to go the extra mile is an essential skill. Don't think of this as being lazy; your time may be far better served chasing down other potential business leads rather than pouring effort into an unlikely candidate.

The extra steps sometimes requested by clients may include on-site presentations, demonstrations of similar systems you have developed in the past, and even references and testimonials from previous clients. Some will ask for proof of financial standing, too (such as accounts, bank statements, and copies of tax returns). The questions you should ask yourself at this point are the following:

- ❑ How likely are you to win the business?
- ❑ What are the costs involved in taking these extra steps?
- ❑ What are other suppliers doing?

If you're getting strong signals from the client that you are close to closing the deal, you should most certainly consider proceeding. If, however, the client isn't making the right noises, the decision may already be tilting in someone else's favor, in which case you should decline the invitation to provide more information.

Always assess the cash cost (travel, consumables) and effective costs (time expressed as potential lost revenue) of taking these extra steps. As a rule, if the costs appear to be approaching anything more than 5 percent of the value of the project, definitely consider taking a step back.

If you can, try to dig around to see what other suppliers are up to. Having a friendly insider at the client can be hugely useful here. A receptionist, for example, is clearly not a decision maker, but probably keeps his or her ear quite close to the ground. Try to glean what knowledge you can; if your competitors are going the extra mile, then so should you.

When to Say No

Curiously, few professionals consider when it is appropriate to decline to pitch on a particular piece of business, and yet it is just as important to know when to walk away as it is to know when to grab a brief with both hands and give it everything you have.

Aside from the obvious (such as lacking the necessary skills or personnel, or the client lacking the necessary budget), you should always keep a close eye out for the following:

- ❑ *"Just curious" briefs* — The client has no real authority to commission you to carry out the project, but has read about it in a trade journal and is curious to know how much it would cost. Typical warning signs include being briefed by a junior-level member of staff who makes frequent references to needing to talk to the boss.

- ❑ *"Driving down a quote" briefs* — The client has already picked a supplier, but wants to drive that supplier's quote down by obtaining quotes from other suppliers to use as leverage.

❑ *Pet projects* — Typically, the brief is given by a relatively senior player in the company, but no one else seems to be involved or have any interest. Although the money can certainly be there for such projects, if that senior player disappears, it's quite likely that your project will, too.

Always keep the dollar in mind. If the project seems like more trouble than it's worth, then don't be afraid to take a step backward. The client may even respect you for it.

Structuring the Pitch

The written aspect of your pitch can follow almost any structure you wish, as long as it is consistent from pitch to pitch. This is particularly important if you are likely to be producing multiple proposals for a single client; consistency from document to document is crucial.

A few key points are worth following:

❑ *Present an introduction* — Always date the pitch, title it with the name of the client (not your name), and add the line "prepared for X," where X is the name of your principal contact at the company — it's an instant points-winner.

❑ *Always reproduce the brief's key points as your first section* — If the client has provided a written brief, do not reproduce it verbatim, but summarize it in approximately half a page. Many clients will make their decision based on just the first page of your proposal, and the price — so use the space wisely.

❑ *Propose your solution* — Include simple Visio diagrams or illustrations, if necessary, and describe your solution in full in not more than two or three pages. Again, don't get bogged down in detail. This is a ten-mile-high, top-down overview of the system — your own creative interpretation of the brief you have just described. Provide bulleted points of "neat features" and ideas you have, rather than simply list components.

❑ *Always provide a clear "investment summary"* — Call it this, rather than a quote. *Investment* has a much more positive connotation, suggesting long-term benefits to the client. Of course, don't try to hide the price from the client. Show clearly how you have arrived at the price, and include details about any commercial terms you are proposing.

❑ If you have quoted for this client before, ensure that your quote is consistent with previous quotes. For example, if you have worked at a flat rate of $800 per day on previous quotations, don't be tempted to use a daily rate of more than $800 per day on this occasion without being fully prepared to justify it when the client picks it up.

❑ *Go into some detail* — Talk about your process (if you have one), your company, and its history and background. Name-drop previous satisfied clients if possible, especially if they're well-known names.

❑ *Be candid about dates* — Explain to the client both how long it will take you to do the work, when you expect to hand over, and when you expect the client to be able to start using the system. Emphasize that you are fastidious when it comes to keeping deadlines. Provide a simple GANTT chart, if necessary, showing any dependencies — particularly those for which you need the client's involvement.

❑ *Set objectives and expectations* — Include a "what-to-do-next" line advising the client how to contact you with questions, and how to proceed if client wants to get started right away.

If you had a face-to-face meeting or telephone call when receiving the brief, try to refer to some of the leading questions you asked and the answers provided. Remind the client of these answers, and show how you have used them to drive the decisions you have made thus far. For example, "You told us when we met that you required the system to be accessible as an XML Web service. We have, therefore, included in our proposed solution the capability to . . . ."

If you're sending the document electronically, try to use PDFs, rather than MS Word documents or any other proprietary format. In addition, always follow up with a phone call to check whether the client has received the document, but resist the temptation to chase the client at this point. Let at least a week go by before any follow-up phone call.

Most important, if you've promised the client the pitch document by a certain time and date, don't miss the deadline. First impressions count, and you get to make only one.

Remember that you won't win them all, no matter how good you are.

Unless your strike rate is proving disastrous, however, don't dwell on any missed pitches. Move on, and try to get some friendly feedback from the client as to what you could do to improve your approach next time around.

Assuming you get the go-ahead from the client, you will have to assemble a project team pretty quickly. Let's look at that now.

Choosing Your People

Before you can get started moving the project forward, you must assemble a team to work on delivery. Set aside a full day for this process if possible — and make it clear to the client what you're doing. How big this team ends up being is obviously governed by the resources available to you and the requirements of the project. This section looks at the different roles in the project and how they all fit together.

Project Manager

If you're reading this chapter, this is a role that you will probably occupy. The project manager (sometimes called a *producer,* depending on locality) has responsibility for the day-to-day running of the project, from the pitch right through to delivery and handover. Generally speaking, the project manager works directly with the senior members of the build team and, if no account manager is handling the relationship with the client, with the client directly.

The project manager sets internal deadlines and objectives that are compatible with the broader goals for delivery of the project, manages progress, and identifies and resolves any conflicts or difficulties encountered by the build team throughout the process.

It is not a technical role in itself, but having a thorough understanding of the work undertaken by software architects, software engineers, and others is all but essential to be an effective project manager. The ideal project manager, therefore, is an approachable, technically aware, highly organized and efficient individual, with a proven track record in delivering projects on time and within budget.

Any given project should need only one project manager unless a specific requirement to the contrary exists.

Account Manager

If available, an account manager is a valuable addition to your project team. The account manager provides the sole point of contact between you (the supplier) and your client. All communications in either direction are channeled through the account manager.

Should the client have a particular request for the build team, the client would put it to the account manager, who would, in turn, pass the request on to the project manager. The project manager would then handle the request internally, working with the build team as appropriate.

The account manager does not get involved in the day-to-day running of the project itself, but is instead concerned with managing the relationship between client and supplier. However, it is important that the account manager and project manager communicate on a regular basis so that the account manager can keep the project manager abreast of the expectations of and feedback from the client, and the project manager can make the account manager aware of the progress and attainment (or otherwise) of key project milestones.

An account manager is not essential but often provides a closer, more fruitful relationship with the client, because this role does not have the team-focused responsibilities of that of the project manager. By the same token, however, this can sometimes lead to account managers being rather too quick to agree to demands of clients, because the burden of the actual implementation of such demands does not fall on the account manager's shoulders.

The ideal account manager is a gregarious and warm individual — the kind of person who can easily strike up and maintain a rapport with everyone he or she meets. In addition, the account manager must be sympathetic to limitations regarding what can and cannot be accomplished by the rest of the project team and be able to communicate these limitations to the client when necessary.

As with the project manager, only one account manager should be assigned to any given project.

Lead Architect

The lead architect for the project is the technical decision maker for the entire project life cycle. It is his or her responsibility to translate the immediate requirements of the project (on a day-to-day basis) into decisions about how those requirements should be realized through technology.

The lead architect on any given project will always be a software architect, rather than an engineer, and hence considerably more experienced. However, the lead architect must also have some degree of project management experience to ensure that his or her decisions are client-led. The lead architect should also possess exceptional team-management abilities, because more junior technologists will report directly to him or her.

In addition to possessing thorough competence as a software architect, the lead architect must have a thorough understanding of systems and networks, such that he or she may suitably devise any deployment infrastructures that the project may require.

Typical software architecture duties undertaken by the lead architect include creation or ratification (or both) of the database schema and object model for the project, maintaining coding standards, and holding regular code reviews.

Given the scope of this position's duties, only one lead architect should be assigned to any given project.

Software Architects and Engineers

Any given project requires a number of software architects and engineers to work on the back-end technology behind the application (in the case of this book, PHP). The difference between the two roles is one of seniority.

A *software architect* has a degree of autonomy (within the confines and standards set by the lead architect) to make decisions about architecture, layout, structure, infrastructure, and coding standards. By contrast, a *software engineer* must follow the edicts and standards set forth by the software architect.

If resources do not allow for the use of client-side developers (see the next section), software engineers may also be assigned the task of developing templates and HTML for use on the site.

Of course, there need be no limit to the number of architects and engineers that can be assigned to a project.

Client-Side Developers

The responsibility of client-side developers is solely to produce the HTML, CSS, and JavaScript that provide the user interface to the application being developed. Generally, they will work in a template-driven environment — for example, using Smarty Templates. There is not generally any requirement for them to know PHP or any other server-side scripting language.

They work with the senior designers and studio artists on any given project to receive the designs for preparation in HTML, but will report directly to the lead architect.

There is no limit to the number of client-side developers who may be deployed on any given project.

Information Architects

On all but the very simplest applications, you'll want some dedicated resource to take care of the all-important *information architecture* of your build — that is, the design and production of wireframes in Visio or some similar package. These wireframes can form part of the functional specification process, and can be used as a starting point for designers who want to produce creative treatments for the project.

Information architects are something of a specialist breed. They are an odd hybrid of technical, commercial, and creative. It is not really a technique to teach or learn, but rather a skill with which its best practitioners have a natural affinity.

Senior Designers

The design process is headed up by senior designers, who are responsible for the overall conceptual design of the application being produced. These are the team members who will produce initial designs for approval by the client and make broader decisions regarding fonts, colors, and imagery. They work with the lead architect in making such decisions to ensure that the concepts being created are within the technical constraints of the project.

Usually, a project has no more than two senior designers, one of whom typically assumes a leading role.

Studio Artists

Senior designers have a more junior resource at their disposal, too — that of studio artists. Not assigned creative concepts per se, studio artists are still skilled in Photoshop, Illustrator, and other design packages and typically respond systematically to requests for particular components. For example, the production of a navigation bar with a certain set of captions would normally fall under the responsibility of a studio artist.

Studio artists typically work only with existing templates, styles, and colors specified by the senior designers on a project.

Any number of studio artists may be deployed on a given project.

Doubling Up of Roles

Resourcing can often be a challenge, even for the biggest of agencies. With this in mind, the following pointers may be helpful, should you be forced to double up roles:

❑ Project managers often make effective account managers, provided that they are client-facing by nature. They can also, in a pinch, undertake basic information architecture.

❑ The lead architect can obviously perform all the roles normally performed by software architects and software engineers.

❑ Software engineers usually can do the development work assigned to client-side developers.

❑ Senior designers can, of course, perform all the duties normally assigned to more junior studio artists.

Working Practices

To the extent possible, it's a very good idea to have your project team work in one room together. That way, the often talked about and largely theoretical concept of synergy becomes one step closer — that is to say, that extra competitive edge derived from having a workforce whose strength is greater than the sum of its individuals. Perhaps more important, having your whole team under one roof makes your job as project manager that much easier.

Your Client's Role

It is just as important for your client to define distinct roles for the project and assign personnel to those roles as it is for you to have your own team structured correctly. This is obviously something over which you have considerably less control than you have over the allocation of roles in your own project team.

If at all possible, however, you should ensure that your client assigns a relationship manager to act as your first point of contact with the client — to handle, raise, and address any queries regarding the project, as well as any commercial queries. The client should also assign an internal project manager should the client be required to provide any regular input into the project — typically, providing content. This individual is responsible for managing or carrying out any work at the client's end needed to provide you with this content.

Summary

In this chapter, you learned (in some detail) the basics of successful management of a software application project. You learned the importance of receiving a brief, including the key questions you should be asking to gain a competitive edge over other suppliers, as well as how to respond to that brief, including how and when to construct a suitable proposal.

In Chapter 17, you'll learn about different software development processes and methodologies, how they apply to your team, and how to determine which is best for you.

17

Project Planning

In truth, you'll rarely develop big sites on your own. As your development career progresses, you'll find yourself taking a more senior role in ever-bigger projects. Yet, developing complex, dynamic PHP-based Web sites and applications alongside a team of technical and business professionals is not a simple prospect. You'll be faced with many challenges, some of which won't be entirely technical in nature.

The business-planning framework that you choose to work with will certainly affect the direction in which your software project grows. Choosing a process that offers a strict (yet comfortable) structure will place limits on how dynamically your project can change, but conversely reward you with a paper trail and a detailed road map to follow. Taking a more dynamic approach to planning may, however, mitigate the risk associated with technical or business unknowns.

The decision regarding which approach to system planning best fits your project is not one to take lightly, and you should be familiar with all planning options before making that decision, regardless of your personal or professional preferences.

Choosing a Process

Now that you have your project team together, no doubt you're eager to get started delivering the solution that your client is so eagerly awaiting. Before you begin, however, you must determine which process to adapt for building the finished product.

The internationally renowned Project Management Institute (PMI) advocates a number of standards and practices in the field of project management. This includes training and accreditation, and the definition and documentation of a number of formal approaches to project planning and execution.

See www.pmi.org *for more information about PMI.*

There are a few to choose from, but the two most fundamental processes are known as the *waterfall process* and the *spiral process*. Both of these processes have the same basic stages (or phases) and elements in common. The difference lies in the order and manner in which they are approached. Both processes share the following four consecutive phases:

1. Specification

2. Design

3. Build

4. Test

The Waterfall Process

In the waterfall process, the entire project is treated as a single solution to be delivered in its entirety — it's only done when it's done, in effect. Figure 17-1 shows the approximate process that is followed.

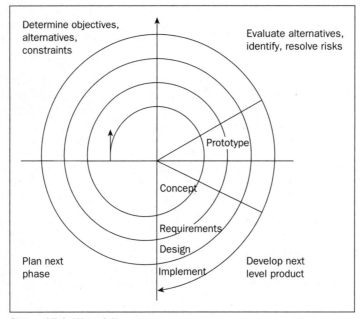

Figure 17-1: Waterfall process

The most important principle of the waterfall process is that none of the project phases may begin until its predecessor has been completed in full. For example, the written specification for the entire project must be completed and approved in full before the design and architecture phase for the project is completed. Only then can the build process of the project be completed and approved. Finally, the test phase of the project may take place.

This traditional process is fine in principle but it has some latent problems in practice. For example, if an error is made during a particular phase that is not detected until later, that phase and all phases following it may need to be repeated, which is immensely time-consuming and expensive. An error at the specification stage not picked up by the client until delivery will require respecification, redesign, rebuild, and retesting.

Another potential problem can arise because the solution is built in one fell swoop, making it very difficult to offer the client anything partly finished to play with early on in the development process. If the client wants to provide early demos, or just needs reassurance as to progress, these can be very difficult to accomplish until very late in the project life cycle.

The Spiral Process

The spiral process has the same core components as those of the waterfall process: specification, design and architecture, build, and test. However, rather than approach the entire solution as a single entity to which these four steps are applied, the system is divided into individual components, and the process is then applied to each component.

A component may be either a discrete piece of functionality, or a partial evolution (or layer) of a piece of functionality. For each component, the four phases are applied: specification of that component, followed by the design and architecture of that component, followed by the build of that component, followed by testing of that component — all in isolation.

The process is called the spiral because you follow the path of a spiral — progressing down the path but passing the same four compass points (each of the four phases) again and again, as shown in Figure 17-2.

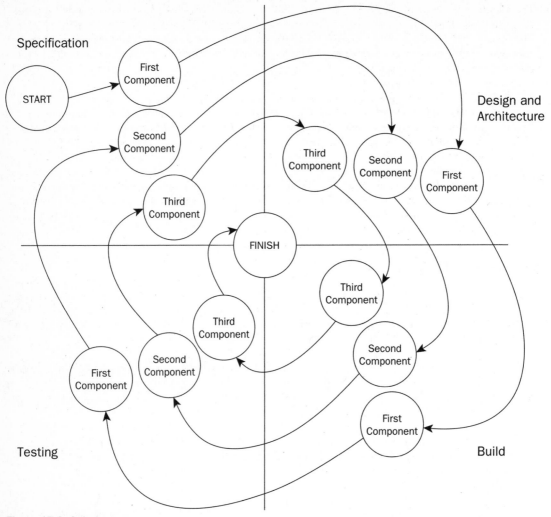

Figure 17-2: Spiral process

The big advantage of this process is that if an error is spotted at any stage during the four phases, then the steps backward that must be retaken are much smaller because you are dealing with only one discrete component, rather than the entire application. In addition, the client is able to play with the first components of your application much sooner, which can have huge political benefits.

Note that the testing phase in the waterfall process deviates slightly from the spiral process in that the tests applied with each new component should ideally include all the previous tests from previous components, too. This is to ensure that no new piece of functionality is causing a previously tested and signed-off piece of functionality to fail — a process known as *regression testing*.

Making the Decision

This chapter does not advocate either process over the other. Later in this book, you'll see one of the processes again in the context of the planned Widget World sales force automation application, but for now, let's leave the door wide open. Which method you choose depends very much on the project at hand.

Although the spiral process certainly has huge advantages from a change-request and exception-handling perspective, the additional paperwork and administrative involvement has a cost to it, too, which must be weighed equally.

Your own experience will give you a feel for both processes. In many cases, the decision comes down to personal preference as much as anything else. If you're the project lead, you'll doubtlessly be given latitude to exercise your discretion in choosing an approach. Whichever way you go, there are common steps and a best practice for each one, so let's take a look at those next.

Common Process Practices

As mentioned previously, both the waterfall and spiral approaches are consistent in their insistence that all development must have a specification phase, followed by a design phase, followed by a build phase, followed by a testing phase.

The difference lies in how much specification, design, build, and testing is done with each iteration, and the size of the chunks in which it is done. Moreover, the words *specification*, *design*, *build*, and *test* are very much open to interpretation in and of themselves. Let's examine a little more closely now how you might implement each phase, regardless of whether you have chosen a waterfall or spiral approach for your project.

For the purposes of this example and to maintain clarity of language, let's assume that you have adopted a waterfall approach for your project. Hence, this examination describes the phases in application to an entire project, rather than an individual component. However, if a spiral approach has been adopted, you can apply exactly the same methodology to each component in your spiral.

Specification Phase

In many respects, the specification phase is the most difficult part of any project, often much trickier than the build process itself. This is particularly true if you are assigned to build a slightly mundane system (a front end to a simple database, for example). The task of development is not particularly challenging; it is the task of getting it right for the client the first time that's difficult.

This phase is about ensuring that you know what you're planning to build and, more important, that the client knows what it is you're planning to build — and that it matches the client's original business requirements as closely as possible. The easiest approach to adopt here is to produce paper specifications for the project — both a functional specification and a technical specification.

Functional Specification

The *functional specification* for a project describes in detail the functionality of the system at a predesign level. It should be written in plain English, and not place too much emphasis on (or provide a rationale behind) technology-led decisions. As a rule, roughly follow your pitch document (if you wrote one) and reproduce the brief in some detail here. It provides an excellent starting point for seeking affirmation from the client that the terms of reference for the project remain the same.

This is where the similarities with your pitch end, however. All the detail that you were implored not to include in your pitch document should be included here. Remove any ambiguity from areas you would rather not repeat in case you get it wrong. Getting the level of detail right is a fine balancing act. Too much, and the document becomes unreadable; too little, and there is too much scope for interpretation or later disagreement over functionality.

With this in mind, try to be clear in any areas you think could be open to interpretation. For example, if you use the phrase "users will be able to upload photographs to associate with their profile," the client is unlikely to latch on to the fact that you have omitted the number of photographs or what format they may be in. In this case, when a scenario crops up whereby a user wants to upload 800 .pcx files but your application cannot support it, you may be in trouble. Instead, try to use phrases such as "users will be able to upload a maximum of eight photographs in JPEG format to associate with their profile."

By the same token, however, mind-numbing detail should be avoided, because huge amounts of information can overwhelm, frustrate, or irritate even the most patient of clients. If you find yourself using a sentence such as "The page will have a Home button that, when clicked, will take the user to the home page," you're guilty. Furthermore, just as overly technical information can be daunting, overly simplistic information can seem condescending.

The litmus test for whether a specification is on the money is whether you could give it to five different teams of competent development and design staff, and, in each of the five cases, have roughly the same thing built. At the same time, though, you should leave open to interpretation any decisions that may best be left to a later phase or to others on the project. For example, sentences such as "The page will have a Home button positioned 124 pixels from the left side of the screen," should be avoided, because this decision should be left to a senior designer during the design phase.

In your functional specification, try to lay out the document as clearly and consistently as possible. The following is a suggested layout from start to finish:

❑ Replication of the client's original brief (or your Scope of Work document, if you produced one). Try to limit this to not more than half a page, and ensure that it is in your own words.

❑ An explanation regarding what this document provides, what is expected of the client, and what other documents you will deliver as part of the specification process. At this stage, be clear that this is a document you expect the client to physically sign off on before you move forward.

❑ Explain (in not more than half a page) a top-line summary of your proposed solution, and list the components it is likely to entail.

❑ For each component, provide a detailed explanation of its functionality, including typical usage walk-throughs for "dummy" users.

❑ Provide diagrams if you genuinely feel it will improve clarity; otherwise, avoid them. No matter how hard you stress that they are only diagrams, clients invariably interpret them as completed designs, with predictable consequences. The same pitfall is equally true with "wireframes" (sometimes called information architecture), which you will meet later in this chapter.

❑ Complete the document with an explanation of what the client must do next if he or she wants to ask questions or make changes, or wants to sign off on the document. Explain the next stages after the document has been signed off on, and gently advise that previously agreed on delivery milestones are all subject to timely agreement to this document.

In practice, you will likely require at least two or three iterations of the specification before the client is happy. Indeed, you should be wary of any client who immediately signs off on an initial specification. Nine times out of ten, this implies that the client hasn't read it.

Technical Specification

Whereas the functional specification describes *what* you plan to do, the *technical specification* describes *how* you plan to do it. The level of detail you need to include here varies dramatically from client to client. Generally, if the client has an IT department taking a keen interest in the project, then you will need to provide an exhaustive level of detail, right down to your coding practices. Otherwise, you can usually get away with providing the following:

❑ Suggested language for build (with rationale and explanations), as well as comparisons and rejections of other, rival languages

❑ Suggested database platform (with rationale and explanations), as well as comparisons and rejections of other database platforms

❑ Suggested operating system for Web and database servers — again, with comparisons to other platforms and reasons for their rejection

❑ An explanation of the hosting and deployment plans for the project (if any), including detail on bandwidth requirements, and so on, where appropriate.

❑ An explanation as to what this document provides, what is expected of the client, and what other documents you will deliver as part of the specification process. Be clear that this technical specification relates directly to the functionality the client has already signed off on in the functional specification.

If you have chosen to adopt a spiral process for your project, it is not necessary to provide a technical specification for every traversal of your spiral. Instead, provide a single technical specification at the beginning of the project, and explain to the client that this specification relates to the implementation of all individual components to follow.

With many clients (especially those not equipped with their own technology department), this document may prove to be quite alien. If so, you have two options:

❑ Go to great lengths to explain the document in detail with the client to ensure that the client is happy with the decisions you've made.

❑ Let the client sign it blindly (which the client may be more than happy to do).

Sometimes, the latter decision is easiest. After all, most clients believe that they are paying you to tell them what is technically sound, not to ask their permission.

Design Phase

The word *design* may prove to be misleading here. It relates both to graphic design and to software design; but of course the two are very different disciplines, and you should be aware of the distinction. Still, it is almost inevitable that the client will want to see some individual graphic designs for the key components of the project as soon as possible.

It is absolutely fine for the senior designer on a project to take responsibility for and produce these designs, as long as it is done closely in consultation with the lead architect to ensure the technical feasibility of what is being proposed. Skilled senior designers will be aware of technical limitations, and therefore require less guidance when designing for the Web.

Again, expect to produce a few iterations of the designs before you get them exactly right. This can be immensely tricky. Clients have their own unique vision of what is wanted, and they may struggle to articulate it to you as the supplier. Sometimes clients only know that what you have produced is not what they want, and they will not hesitate to make this clear to you.

When presenting designs to a client, sometimes it is useful to have the senior designer present the designs, possibly even using a laptop loaded with graphics and RAD software so that suggested changes can be made in front of the client. A reaction such as "That's it, that's how I want it," can be most gratifying, as well as commercially useful.

Creative Specification

With the key designs signed off on, it is a very useful exercise to produce what is known as a *creative specification*, or *style guide*. This document is not normally presented to the client for inspection, although, if the client is very protective of branding or has in-house graphics staff, it may not be a bad idea.

The traditional purpose of this document is to communicate the artistic vision of the senior designer to more junior studio artists and to ensure that any future design work carried out on the project is also consistent with that vision.

The style guide includes details of fonts, colors, layout, logos, backgrounds — all the components that make up the broader artistic vision. This guide ensures that if a request is made, such as "produce a button that says Add to Basket," the result looks exactly like the senior designer would want.

Information Architecture

Possibly the most controversial component of the design phase is that of information architecture, sometimes called *page maps*. Essentially a wireframe, black-and-white model of a given page in the user's Web browser, it attempts to articulate the user interface (UI) without communicating any facets of the design. It enables the general UI to be approved separately from the graphic design, when commercial or political pressures mean this could be useful, or when no specific graphic design has been produced for this page.

In addition, it can be given to the development team, along with the creative specification, such that they can directly commission studio artists and client-side developers to produce designs and HTML code needed to deliver some particular component. In practice, however, wireframes have two major pitfalls.

First, it is often difficult for clients to separate the concepts of UI and design. This can mean that presenting completed information architecture to a client can be a tiresome and stress-inducing task, because the client perceives your wireframe diagrams as the finished look and feel, and balks at the prospect. As a result, feedback will often not relate to the user interface at all — for example, your client may ask you to "make that button a bit bigger." Obviously, you must make it clear exactly what you are presenting from the outset, but even with that in mind, it can be a hugely frustrating process trying to coach clients unfamiliar with the process in order to eke out vital feedback on the UI.

Second, the personnel remit for actually producing information architecture is hard to define. Graphic designers are rarely experts at producing "interfaces" per se and are often loathe to using Visio and other packages required to produce these deliverables. Project managers are usually far too busy. As a result, the task often falls on the shoulders of the lead architect. Given that the role of imparting a vision for the production of particular components to software architects and engineers is at the heart of the remit of the lead architect anyway, the arguments for documenting this vision are weakened.

Software Architecture: Ten-Point Plan

Again, another piece of documentation that you may or may not want to present to the client for approval is the *software architecture plan*. This is often called a *ten-point plan*, because it is generally a series of short, punchy bulleted points outlining the best approach to the actual project or component in hand, instead of being a prose-heavy document.

The production of this document is very much the remit of the lead architect, who normally produces it well after the technical specification has been approved and signed off on. As such, it doesn't concern itself with technology options, hardware, hosting, and so forth. Rather, it concentrates on issues such as database schema, object models, and implementation of design patterns such as MVC.

The lead architect communicates the document to his or her software architects, who in turn interpret it as they see fit. In theory, the "architectural vision" should cascade down to software engineers working beneath them, too.

Whether you choose to show this document to your client depends on the ability and capabilities of technical personnel provided by your client. If your client has no one sufficiently technical (for example, if they have general IT practitioners, but no development function), then feedback is unlikely to be forthcoming. If they do sometimes undertake their own development work, then it would be advisable to see the buy-in of those developers at a senior level, too. (Your client should be able to make the necessary introductions.)

Keep in mind, however, that no matter how robust your software architecture is, a risk of "not invented here" syndrome exists. You may well find your clients' developers picking holes in your approach on a point of principle. Such people are best humored (to a point), but don't be afraid to let your clients know if they are starting to affect delivery dates. You'll be amazed how quickly they are motivated to back down.

Build Phase

With all design parameters agreed upon, the build process itself can commence. There is no written documentation to accompany this phase, but a few points are worth keeping in mind:

❑ Always maintain both development servers and a staging server, as well as the production server. These do not necessarily have to be separate physical servers, but it is vitally important that you can release partly completed stages of development to the client in order to document the progress you are making. You may also decide to expose a "bleeding" server, on which the client can check progress at any time — with the proviso in place that what the client sees is a work in progress, and might not necessarily work perfectly.

❑ Try to adapt a programming methodology, if one is appropriate to your project. These are discussed in more detail later in this chapter in the section "Programming Methodologies and Practices."

❑ It is the responsibility of the lead architect to manage the build process and ensure that his or her team delivers all components on time, and at the required standard, so that the entire system can be delivered to the project manager as a completed package, rather than piecemeal.

❑ Always maintain fastidious version control. Elsewhere in this book, you'll learn about Subversion, a free solution to this often problematic issue.

Testing Phase

Having built the solution, it is vital for you to conduct suitable testing — both to assure yourself of the quality of what you have produced, and to reassure the client that he or she doesn't have to perform exhaustive testing.

The testing you conduct should always be accompanied with written reports detailing your findings. For obvious reasons, don't release these reports until you are 100 percent happy that the testing has been a complete success.

Functional Testing

Functional testing ensures that the product works exactly as expected, both that it fulfills the specification exactly and that it is free from errors or malfunction. Be systematic. Test each area of functionality relentlessly, using a number of different data sets and/or input parameters. Record your findings systematically, so that you can, in effect, demonstrate a "checked off" status in the box next to each distinct feature.

Of course, always stress to your development team that it is vital to "test as they go" as far as possible, and never turn in code they know to be seriously buggy. You might consider using a bug-tracking system such as Mantis (www.mantisbt.org) to maintain a centralized repository of bugs as each is discovered, assign the bugs to developers, and annotate them appropriately.

Load Testing

If the application you are building is likely to be a high-traffic one either now or at some point in the future, it makes sense to know how much it can take before it falls over.

Load testing can be conducted only if you can deploy the application onto a realistic environment, usually the production server. There is no point in testing your application on your Xeon-driven Linux development server if you know you'll be forced to deploy onto a Sun box running Solaris. A number of packages are available, the most popular of which is probably LoadRunner (visit `https://h10078.www1.hp.com/cda/hpms/display/main/hpms_content.jsp?zn=bto&cp=1-11-126-17%5E8_4000_100&jumpid=reg_R1002_USEN` for more information). Similar results, however, can be achieved using a suite of custom-built test scripts.

The key to load testing is to never be afraid to turn the volume up as high as it will go until the speakers explode. Simply knowing that the client's traffic expectations can be handled is good, but knowing exactly how much more they can handle beyond that is even better. The client will be gratified if you can provide an exact figure, such as "the site will handle 1,000 simultaneous users without any problems."

Handover

Having produced a thoroughly documented, well-designed, fully tested piece of software, it is vital to arrange a proper handover meeting with the client. This is the client's final sign-off — either for the whole project or for this component, depending on which process (described earlier in the chapter) you decided to adapt.

During the handover process, you should ensure that the client is fully comfortable with the inner workings of the finished product. An element of training may be required as a result. In addition, remember what you're there to do — hand over the project. Presenting the client with a DVD containing a copy of the source code can have a symbolism that is hard to measure.

It is almost inevitable that small change requests will crop up during the handover process. Later in this chapter, you will learn how to handle them.

Programming Methodologies and Practices

Let's look briefly at the build process itself. There are a couple of best-practice methodologies you may want to adapt during the build process, regardless of the overall project process you have chosen.

Test-Driven Development

In Chapter 13, you briefly met PHPUnit, and you learned how to use it to build unit testing frameworks. This knowledge can only be applied, of course, if you have built your application in a unit-driven fashion.

Test-driven development requires that you write the test before the code. The act of writing the test for the class in which you intend to code forces you to think about exactly how you plan to use a particular class, what it needs to do, and what its interface should be. PHPUnit (available through PEAR at `http://pear.php.net`) is a good framework for testing.

You want to confirm that your unit test works before attempting to write the class itself. This may require using a dummy class with the same interface as that of your real class to make the test run and naturally fail.

After being constructed, the unit tests for that class will probe the interface of your PHP class and analyze in detail the data that is returned. As a developer, your responsibility is to code the class in order to satisfy your unit tests.

Try to keep your unit tests as generic as possible. If you have numerous classes with similar interfaces, you can combine your unit tests into a single PHPUnit instance.

Using unit testing has numerous advantages, which are explored in more detail later in this book when you start to build the `discovernewbands.com` portal. Whether it's right for your project is, once again, a judgment call. It is a testing methodology arguably much better suited to larger projects with more distinct components than to simple traditional "database applications."

Extreme Programming

The concept of *extreme programming (XP)* is perhaps the truest example of a programming paradigm. It is a paradigm in the sense that it is perhaps more ambitious than it is practical in every development case and is not without its share of critics. However, as a working model, it has many facets from which to pick and choose as required.

It's just one example of what are sometimes called *agile development methodologies* — a suite of variably unorthodox approaches that claim to be better suited to twenty-first-century application development.

Understanding XP

The effectiveness of XP is realized through a number of distinct working practices. They are too numerous to list in full, but let's look at a few in detail.

The main goal of XP is to deliver quality software driven by the needs of the client. It achieves this goal by managing complexity. As a system grows increasingly complex, the cost to add and modify features increases. Conversely, if the system does not get unnecessarily complex, then the cost of adding features later is roughly the same as adding features now.

This is a very powerful weapon, because traditional methodologies tend to follow the curve whereby the software modification cost increases exponentially as more time is spent with all the phases of development.

For example, it is more cost effective to add features in the requirements phase than during implementation, when it costs significantly more; but suppose your project development followed a curve whereby the costs of change grow more slowly and level off more quickly. If you had the freedom to add, remove, and modify features whenever you'd like, then there would be pressure or reason to try to predetermine the entire feature set during the initial phases of the project.

As clearly outlined by Kent Beck and Cynthia Andres in *Extreme Programming Explained, Embrace Change, Second Edition* (Addison-Wesley, 2004), the act of XP is that of following a set of practices:

❑ *Planning* — Determine the scope of the project by combining business priorities and technical estimates, continually updated.

❑ *Small releases* — Get the system to the people who will be using it, and release new versions on a very short schedule.

❑ *Simple Design* — Keep the design as simple as possible at all times. Complexity is removed on an ongoing basis.

❑ *Testing* — Developers continually write unit tests to ensure that the system runs flawlessly at all times. Customers write tests to demonstrate that features work as required.

❑ *Refactoring* — Restructure the code without modifying the behavior in order to keep it easy to read, to remove duplication, or to simplify it.

❑ *On-site customer* — The client should always be available to answer questions at all times throughout the development process.

The client, always being available throughout the build process, is in effect made *part of* the development process, instead of simply driving it forward through his or her requirements. If at all possible, this is best accomplished by having the client (preferably some reasonably technical representative with domain expertise) on site at key stages during the development process.

Don't worry about clients unnecessarily harassing your team. As long as they are suitably involved, your team will upward-manage the clients. This tenet of XP is particularly important in the attainment of elevated customer satisfaction. There can be no cries of "this isn't what I wanted" if the customer has been involved from day one.

By creating unit tests for your classes before the classes themselves, you save time if your code doesn't work the first time. Across a larger project with a number of distinct classes, this time savings can easily amount to days.

Using unit testing brings with it other benefits. First, psychologically, it conditions software architects and engineers to consider more fully and thoroughly the requirements of a given component, meaning that the finished product is often a closer fit to the true requirements than a non-unit-driven approach would have permitted. In addition, there is a positive, direct impact on coding style that is highly beneficial to all those involved in the development process.

Second, it ensures that coding standards are determined early on in the project, and that the entirety of the development team sticks to them. There is no "code ownership," so any developer is allowed to modify any piece of code, as long as the unit tests continue to work.

Perhaps the most famous aspect of XP is that it permits two software engineers (or perhaps a software architect and an engineer) to code at a single workstation simultaneously. Generally, the best configuration is for both individuals to sit side by side, but with one driving (that is, controlling keyboard and mouse) and another guiding the code-authoring process. With two people actively involved in the development of each piece of code, the business and technical expertise is not stuck inside any single developer's head, which allows for a more even distribution of information and avoids having the project be dependent on any specific developer. Besides, the old cliché is true: Two heads are almost always better than one; and pair programming doesn't just affect the quality of code, it also reduces the number of bugs.

The most controversial of XP's tenets is that overtime (that is, working programmers until they collapse) is frowned upon, even "banned." The argument is that when a project is properly specified, budgeted, and managed, there should be no need for overtime in the first place; and when overtime is generally needed, the project is doomed to late completion anyway.

When to Use XP

XP is most at home when the project in question has a high element of risk attached to it. Perhaps there is a tight deadline to be met. Maybe some unknown quantity or dynamic requirement means that the proposed solution is not cast-iron guaranteed to meet the eventual needs of the client. Conceivably, the solution being proposed is so cutting-edge that it carries the risk of simply not working.

The actual development team should be small — not fewer than two, and not more than 10 or 11 — and all members of the project team (not just the development team) are free to take ownership of the build process.

The desired results of XP are as follows:

- ❏ The productivity of those in the development team is greatly increased.
- ❏ Client satisfaction is more easily attained.
- ❏ High standards of quality are attained and maintained.
- ❏ The client's requirements are met more precisely.
- ❏ Deadlines are met with greater accuracy and consistency.

There is a huge amount of debate among the programming community over both the relative success and the feasibility of XP. Often, enormous commercial pressures mean that it is simply an impossible paradigm to follow. As with any paradigm, however, it is simply a model — something to aim for. You can find a great deal more detail on the practices and recommendations of XP at http://www.extremeprogramming.org/.

Change Management

In almost every project of any scale, change requests will be made by the client. Managing these changes is enormously important. Not only must you assess the commercial impact of any changes you make, but you must also understand the enormous disruption that can occur through major changes to a well-entrenched software or systems architecture.

This section looks at some of the most common varieties of change requested by clients, and the best way to handle each of them.

Specification Revisions

These are not only inevitable, but should be actively encouraged. Your client will want to make changes to the specification you have produced, because it is almost certain that you will not quite have managed to hit the nail on the head first time around.

Collate any change requests together into 48-hour periods. Use a change management package such as Microsoft Project or BaseCamp (http://www.basecamphq.com) if necessary. Every 48 hours, incorporate the previous two days' changes into a new release of the specification, and offer it back to the client.

Be sure to make the client aware of any requests that will (for one reason or another) prove unfeasible as soon as they are put forward. This is why it's vital that work-in-progress meetings with clients are attended by somebody with practical knowledge of application development; simply sending "suits" is counterproductive.

Specification Changes That Arise After Sign-Off

If the client requests changes after signing off on the specification, you may have a problem on your hands. First, don't panic. You have the moral high ground. The client's signature on your specification is an affirmation that he or she was 100 percent happy with what has been produced. Should you feel the need to bill the client for the change, you are, strictly speaking, within your rights to do so.

Before you make a decision, however, consult the rest of your team. Try to determine how far into the design and/or build phases your team has progressed. Try to quantify, in terms of work hours, the kind of disruption that is involved in rewinding the process back to the specification stage so that the requested change can be made.

If you can put a price tag on the work, make a judgment call as to whether it is worth passing this cost on to the client. It is normally considered to be in the interest of good client relations to show some grace and flexibility in these situations, unless they become a regular occurrence.

If you decide to proceed with the change, be sure to make it very clear to the client the time impact it will have, and come to an agreement concerning any revised milestones that the change may necessitate. Ensure that your project team concurs, and that the new timelines include a contingency margin.

Disputes Arising from Differences in Interpretation

Sometimes, a client can query the interpretation of a specification and request changes as a result. These queries are always difficult to manage. After all, you cannot accuse the client outright of simply being wrong. The best approach with these situations is to do your best to avoid them altogether in the first place by being as fastidious and specific as possible in your specification, avoiding ambiguity wherever possible.

When ambiguity does crop up, however, be prepared to negotiate with the client. Listen carefully to the client's concerns, and endeavor to understand his or her point of view. Discuss with your team the time required to make the changes in question, and then put them to a simple commercial test: *In terms of cold, hard cash, is it worth arguing the point?*

Bugs Reported by the Client

Be careful to determine whether the client is concerned about a bug or a change to the system. At this stage, any post-handover changes requested by the client are almost certainly outside the scope of the specification, and as such should be considered additional, billable work.

Always respond to bugs reported by the client as a priority, even if they appear to be nonbugs (for example, the client has made an error). Use a bug-tracking system such as Mantis to keep track of all bugs reported, and give clients access so that they may report their own. Encourage clients to use this system in preference to immediately calling you about it.

Clients are generally sympathetic to bugs; most people these days are enlightened enough to accept that "these things happen." Responding quickly, efficiently, and systematically (even after the system has gone live) can mean the difference between being on the receiving end of sympathy versus angry telephone calls.

Summary

You now know the value of ensuring that a tight methodology is maintained even after you've won the business, right through to the completion of the project. You've met the various people who might play a part in your project and have looked at two different methodologies for running the show itself. You've also examined a couple of theoretical paradigms, which you might want to apply during the build process itself.

Finally, this chapter provided a brief overview of change management and how to best deal with the situations that can arise as a result.

In Chapter 18, you'll look at how to plan a suitable hardware and systems infrastructure for your project.

18

Systems Architecture

Having now read through a few hundred pages of software architecture details, you may be tempted to immediately head out and start building your latest project. You've planned the system, chosen your people, selected an appropriate methodology, and gleaned specifications detailing the business requirements and the feature set. However, the final consideration to be made — the systems architecture — should not be undertaken lightly.

This chapter familiarizes you with the basis of systems architecture — what it is, why it's important, and how to effectively undertake a systems design most appropriate for your project, based on the decisions you've already made about the architecture of the application itself.

What Is Systems Architecture?

At its simplest, systems architecture refers to the infrastructure supporting the application you're planning to build. In general, this refers to the following:

❑ The nature of the hardware on which your application will be deployed

❑ The specific manner in which the server (or servers) will be configured, connected, and secured

❑ The use of specialized appliances such as firewalls, load balancers, switches, and routers

❑ The physical location of this equipment, and the provisioning of electricity and Internet connectivity

As you might have guessed, this is a big topic. The discussion over the next few pages merely scratches the surface, but it is hoped that it provides enough detail to get you thinking about the systems requirements, and to encourage you to explore additional resources to learn more.

Why Is It Important?

Getting the right infrastructure for your application is vitally important. As an application developer, you may have just one development server in your studio. This may double up as both a Web server and a database server, maybe running both MySQL and PostgreSQL. If you develop in more than just PHP, you may have other application servers and programming language environments (for example, J2EE, Python, Ruby, and so on). This machine probably lives in a server closet in your office, along with your company's other infrastructure. In some cases, this environment may very well match that of a simple shared-hosting environment onto which smaller applications will be deployed. However, enterprise-class applications generally require more fault tolerance, performance capabilities, and security than a single server can provide.

One of the authors of this book recently deployed an application moving more than 2 TB of data per month through a popular and heavily advertised Web application for a major packaged goods manufacturer. The $20 per month shared hosting environment typical of smaller home-grown applications would quickly topple under the demands of this sort of load. However, through careful planning, a thorough understanding of the media buy (the amount and nature of the advertising planned for the site), a careful analysis of the application performance parameters, and knowledge of systems architecture principles, a hosting arrangement was designed that was able to quickly scale to that level of throughput with no interruptions.

Later in this book, you'll learn more about the principles of *quality assurance (QA)*, which are also critical to avoiding unplanned interruptions. You can save yourself a lot of time and trouble now by designing an effective systems architecture to complement and support the software architecture you've already developed.

What Needs to Be Done?

Your systems architecture is effectively a battle plan for your live environment. You may well wish to draw up a separate document to support it, or incorporate the plan in your existing technical specification. In either case, obtaining buy-in from key stakeholders is essential, because the costs can be substantial. Failure to coordinate between marketing activities and technology expectations are a frequent source of problems and unplanned outages.

Carefully informed assumptions about the expected load and planned spikes in traffic form the heart of your systems architecture. As it is developed between you and your client, this knowledge can be translated into effective systems decisions.

Following are the key decisions to be made:

❑ *Hosting* — Where is the application to be physically housed? Is it a suitable environment (that is, air conditioned and equipped with uninterruptible power supplies)? If it is part of an existing corporate data center, have reasonable provisions been made for the additional demands on bandwidth, and have security considerations been taken into account?

❑ *Internet connectivity* — What kind of link to the Internet is required? Who will provide it? How much is it likely to cost? What sort of redundancy is built in, in case of an outage from the ISP?

❑ *Servers* — How many servers are required to support the application, and what are their specifications?

❑   *Network* — What kind of topology is best to support those servers?

❑   *Redundancy and resilience* — What kind of guaranteed availability is required? Can there be a single point of failure?

❑   *Maintenance* — Who will be responsible for maintaining each server and its software?

❑   *Security* — How will the infrastructure be secured from the outside world?

Each of these decisions is examined in more detail later in this chapter; but first, let's face it, the rhetorical questions just posed will rarely be questions you can put directly to your client.

Although you may be confronted from time to time with projects for which the client takes full ownership of systems architecture and simply wants you to build the application (in which case, you can skip to the next chapter), it is far more likely that you're expected to make the big decisions based on what the client has told you, or based on the answers to questions you've asked.

It is far more likely, therefore, that you're the one who will have to ask the questions. These questions should be designed to fill a veritable stockpile of information, which you can then use to design your environment. In the next section, you'll look at what questions you should ask.

Determining Business Requirements

As part of the initial discovery phase, it is essential that you determine client hosting requirements as early as possible. Following are several key considerations:

❑   *Who is responsible for hosting the application?* — Some clients have an existing IT department that is well versed in setting up Web application environments. Many do not, in which case the responsibility will likely fall to you and your team.

❑   *Is there existing infrastructure that should be or can be leveraged?* — There is no point in creating unnecessary infrastructure if a perfectly good environment already exists. If it either does not exist or is not perfectly good, then the investment is justified.

❑   *Are there other systems with which this application must communicate?* — For example, if authentication and authorization must happen against a client's Windows Active Directory (AD) system, then the hosting must be arranged in a manner to allow PHP to get past any security barriers to communicate with the AD systems. For example, if an application must present billing data from a mainframe, how will that information be made available to PHP?

❑   *What is the planned traffic level?* — This is often a difficult question to answer, but there are a few ways to get to a reasonable number other than blind guessing, or coming up with overly optimistic "hoped for" numbers. For example, you can look at the media buy. If there will be 100 million standard banner ad impressions over three months, you can assume an average click-through rate of 0.1 percent. This would result in an expected traffic volume of 33,000 visitors per month (on average), or about one thousand visitors per day. This is an effective way to determine traffic levels for a marketing-oriented site. For a more transactional model (for example, an application designed to process insurance claims information), you can determine expected traffic levels by looking at historical data on the typical number of claims processed per day.

❑ *What is the budget?* — Complex managed-hosting platforms can cost thousands of dollars per month, and require 12-month (or longer) contract commitments. If this is what the application requires to handle the expected traffic volume, is the cash available to pay for it?

❑ *Are there any particularly complex security considerations or regulatory requirements?* — A Web site that collects e-mail addresses for marketing purposes requires reasonable security. However, an application that collects social security numbers and credit card details requires an entirely different configuration and further consideration. If the application is for a heavily regulated industry (such as banking), there may be additional regulatory requirements.

❑ *What are the storage requirements?* — If this is a primarily read-only application, you can examine the PHP, database, images, and other assets to immediately determine storage requirements. However, for anything with user inputs, you must carefully plan the storage considerations. Again, keep in mind any regulatory requirements that may necessitate keeping far more information (especially in regard to application logs, e-mails, and backups) than you might have otherwise planned for. Growth in the number of application users should be mapped to an average storage requirement per user.

❑ *Finally, what are the backup requirements?* — If the application is primarily read-only, and the data, source code, and other assets are otherwise backed up elsewhere (for example, in a subversion repository), a far simpler backup strategy is required than for a heavily transactional Web site (such as an e-commerce application), or a write-heavy application (such as a wiki or popular blog).

These business requirements directly translate into systems architecture considerations, which you can now begin to examine.

Determining Hardware Requirements

There are several pieces of hardware to consider, each with an important role. In smaller installations, a single piece of hardware may perform multiple functions that in a larger architecture may be handled by a dedicated appliance.

Web Servers

As the front line of user activity, this is where the execution of the PHP code will take place, along with the serving of HTML, images, and other assets. These machines will be running Apache or another HTTP daemon, and they represent the first place to consider some redundancy, in the form of multiple load-balanced machines. RAID 1 (mirrored) hard drives should also be considered to protect against catastrophic hardware failure (which happens to hard drives more often than you might think).

Database Servers

A dedicated machine or array of machines to handle database transactions is strongly recommended for reasonably well-trafficked Web sites. By offloading the heavy data-crunching to separate hardware, you enable slow queries to proceed without interrupting the performance of more routine front-end application functionality. RAID 5 hard disks are strongly recommended here, as is some redundancy in the form of multiple, clustered database machines. Both PostgreSQL and MySQL now have fairly robust clustering support, as well as abundant documentation on how to best implement it.

Load Balancing

Wherever more than one machine is handling the same function, something must determine to which physical machine the requests are directed. There are three ways to implement load balancing:

- ❑ DNS-based load balancing
- ❑ Software-based load balancing
- ❑ Dedicated load balancing

DNS-Based Load Balancing

DNS-based load balancing involves making DNS records for a single hostname that points to more than one IP address. For example, normally, you might have a DNS entry that looks like this:

```
$ORIGIN example.com.
www                      IN    A     192.168.111.222
```

You could instead specify a pool of addresses for that same record, as shown here:

```
$ORIGIN example.com.
www                      IN    A     192.168.111.222
www                      IN    A     192.168.111.223
www                      IN    A     192.168.111.224
```

When clients attempt to resolve the address of your Web server, their computers will be presented with an address at random from the pool of addresses you have specified. Accordingly, different clients will use different Web servers. This method is very easy to implement.

The downside to this approach is twofold. First, many operating systems (Windows in particular) cache the IP address after performing a name lookup. This means that subsequent requests to the same hostname will continue to send traffic to that machine, regardless of how much additional load is already on that box. Second, if that machine should go down, then the Web site appears to the user to be broken, because the user's operating system will not attempt another name resolution.

Software-Based Load Balancing

The second method is to use software-based load balancing on the Web servers themselves. In a system with two Web servers, a common IP address is shared on a virtual network interface between them. (This is the IP address to which the www hostname will resolve.) The software allows the servers to negotiate among themselves which machine will handle the next incoming request. This is fairly simple to set up for two machines, but when there are more than two servers, it starts to get a little hairy.

Dedicated Load Balancing

The third method is to use a dedicated load-balancer. This can be either commodity hardware running Linux and an open-source load-balancing application, or a dedicated commercial appliance. This machine is assigned the public IP address, and the Web servers are assigned private, nonroutable IP addresses on an internal network shared by the Web servers and the load balancer. The load balancer handles the incoming request and forwards it to the machine best able to handle it.

Possible load balancing methods include the following:

- *Round-robin* — Directs each request to the next machine in the list of available machines

- *Session-based* — Directs all requests in a particular session to the same machine. (A given user will have all of his or her activity handled by a single physical machine.)

- *Methods* — These can examine the number of connections to each machine, directing the request to the machine with the smallest load.

The load balancer will automatically remove a machine from the pool if it should become unavailable (for example, in the event of a crash). Where a dedicated load balancer is used, always consider using a redundant pair. You can have 20 Web servers, but if even one load balancer fails, no one will be able to reach those Web servers, and the application is down.

Firewall

Intrusion prevention and detection is the topic of countless books, and is not covered in depth here. While each machine is capable of running its own firewall software, a dedicated appliance has the benefits of a single point of administration, and offloads the CPU burden for packet analysis to a machine not otherwise involved with application processing. As with load balancers, it would behoove the application architect to consider using a redundant pair of firewalls in case one fails.

Understanding the Physical Environment and Connectivity

The physical location of the servers is an important consideration for performance, security, and reliability. Without a doubt, the best approach here is a dedicated data center. The sole purpose of such a facility is to provide a secure, air-conditioned, controlled environment for servers and other equipment, and the provision of bandwidth and IP addresses.

Because these facilities house servers designed solely for remote access, they are often rather inhospitable environments for human beings. The use of carcinogenic fire retardants has been outlawed in most states and countries, but the intense air conditioning can provide even the fittest and healthiest software architect with a wheeze upon exit. However, this environment is perfect for servers.

There are two types of data centers: carrier-specific and carrier-neutral. A *carrier-specific* data center is typically owned by the ISP providing bandwidth and connectivity. Therefore, only that particular ISP is available for connectivity. A *carrier-neutral* center concerns itself only with housing equipment, and enables you to connect with any number of ISPs providing connectivity there.

Both have their advantages and disadvantages. Carrier-specific centers tend to have a more integrated support and billing approach, which can certainly cut down on the hassle. With a carrier-neutral center, however, should one ISP prove unreliable or inappropriate (or you just fancy a change), you can move your equipment without physically moving it at all. Either way, you will typically be presented with a product that consists of a certain amount of rack space, a suite of IP addresses (or, in some cases, a range of addresses and a single IP on their network, requiring you to fit a router of your own), and a handoff — a physical Ethernet link into your ISP's network. Your ISP will, of course, give you a decent helping of support and assistance in getting up and running, but it's important that you order the right product in the first place.

Your ISP will sell you either a quantity of bandwidth measured as a committed information rate (CIR), in megabits, or a quantity of monthly transfer, measured in gigabytes.

Calculating CIR

A CIR will almost always be the more expensive option, but it is essential for bigger sites. It enables you to push as much traffic as possible within a given bandwidth. To calculate a CIR, consider the number of simultaneous sessions your application is likely to support.

Suppose, for example, that your Webmail Web application must support a total of 1,000 simultaneous sessions. This represents 1,000 people all using the application at any given point in time. It does not represent 1,000 simultaneous connections. The distinction is important. When using any given application, each session consists of a flurry of HTTP requests (page plus images), followed by a pause while content is read, followed by another flurry of HTTP requests, and so on. With this in mind, connectivity is being made only a given percentage of the time.

It is also important to understand the likely *dwell time* on each page. This is something only user testing can determine accurately, but you could estimate it to be something like 30 seconds for a typical Web page on a consumer Web site, or 60 seconds on a Web application (such as a Webmail application).

If you assume that each page takes approximately 10 seconds to load, then on a Web application, there will be a *pattern per session* of 10 seconds of traffic, followed by 60 seconds of no traffic, followed by 10 seconds of traffic, and so on.

With one quick and slightly crude calculation (that is, 10 seconds divided by 60 seconds), you can see that at any given moment in time, there is about a 15 percent possibility that any given session is transferring data. The number of simultaneous connections is, therefore, likely to be equal to 15 percent of your simultaneous sessions for a Web application, or 2 percent for a Web site.

In the preceding example of 1,000 simultaneous sessions, you can tell that this represents 150 simultaneous connections; but with some users on 6 Mb cable modem connections, and others on 56 KB dial-ups, how do you know what bandwidth requirement this represents?

This is where the data mined from your client comes in handy. The client may well have some figures on his or her projected demographic. People in offices, for example, are all likely to have T1 or T3 lines, but these are likely to be shared among other people in each office. For home users, you can use national figures on broadband penetration to figure out the likely percentage on broadband, as well as the likely percentage on dial-up. Even better, if you have access to server logs for similar past projects, dig them out and do the math yourself.

Calculating Monthly Transfer

Another option available to you is a monthly transfer limit, an "all you can eat" of the ISP's bandwidth within that limit. Depending on the type of site involved, this may work out to be less expensive. For example, if you have a huge surge of users at 6:00 P.M., but a lot of dead time elsewhere, this option could be appropriate for you.

To calculate your monthly transfer requirement, simply multiply the number of monthly user sessions you expect to receive by the amount of data each will transfer.

For example, if a typical session consists of 10 requests, and each request has an average page weight of 50 KB, each user session will consume about a half-megabyte of transfer. If 5,000 regular users each use the system once a day, this represents 5,000 sessions per day, or 2.5 GB of transfer. During a month, this works out to 75 GB.

Rack Space Considerations

How much rack space you require is obviously determined by the number of servers you'll be using. Keep in mind, though, that any network appliances (such as switches and routers) also take up space.

In planning for future expansion, you may wish to allow a certain amount of free rack space beyond your immediate requirements. If you buy only five units in a shared rack, for example, it is almost inevitable that space on either side of you will be sold by your ISP more or less right away, and that future equipment may have to be sited elsewhere as a result.

Network Considerations

Hooking all this equipment up might seem to be the simple part, but a bit of planning in this department can save you grief and heartache later.

Consider the traffic going across each interface and try to plan around that. For example, a database-heavy Web application will have enormous amounts of traffic going to and from the database server, traffic that is completely unrelated to the Web request being made by the client Web browser. With this in mind, you should consider having a separate interface on each Web server linking into the database server.

Such a configuration is common. You have a core switch into which all your Web servers link, and into which your firewall's internal interface will link, too. Your database switch is linked to the secondary NIC of each Web server, and to the NIC of each database server you use.

As a result, traffic between Web servers and database servers doesn't interfere with true Web traffic — a performance increase. If you are using a high-end switch, you can even use a virtual local area network (VLAN) to separate, say, 24 ports into two virtual switches of 12 ports each — one for the Web servers and firewall, as well as one for the database servers and secondary Web server NICs.

A side-effect of this configuration is yet another layer of protection for your databases. With no exposed interface to the Internet, they are yet another step away from being compromised.

Storage Considerations

With a large application requiring the storage of large amounts of data, the onboard hard disks in a rack-mountable server may be insufficient. Storage area networks (SANs) are frequently available from the better-managed hosting providers, and often allow for a nearly limitless (and expandable) amount of hard disk space, which is ideal for storage-intensive applications that must quickly scale.

Other storage solutions include drive enclosures, which in their more sophisticated forms enable multiple servers to connect to the same drive array. There are also Web-services-based solutions (such as Amazon's S3) that use a third party to store data and provide an API for upload and retrieval.

Managing Maintenance

Managed hosting providers will perform basic maintenance on your servers (including kernel patches, software installation, and updates), and provide support with general systems administration. Whether you opt for this solution or decide to take care of these tasks yourself depends on both you and your relationship with your client.

If you do decide to bear the burden, then you should devise a weekly action plan for server maintenance. This should be a list of tasks to perform weekly to ensure that your servers are clean, efficient, and up-to-date. Tasks for your action plan should include the following:

❑ *Kernel version* — Is each server running the latest version?

❑ *Apache and PHP versions* — Is each server running the latest version?

❑ *PHP dependencies* — Are `libxml`, `libxslt`, and `expat` all up-to-date?

❑ *Disk space* — Does each server have enough space on each partition? Are any log files growing out of control and in need of trimming? Apache, in particular, will not allow you to exceed 2 GB in size for any given log file, and will crash quite spectacularly if you do.

Summary

In this chapter, you learned about the importance of a robust systems architecture for your application. With a definition of systems architecture in hand, you then learned about the right questions to ask your client to determine, in plain English, the exact system requirements.

Next, you learned how to take that information and translate it into justifiable technical decisions. This way, when your project goes live, you won't encounter nasty surprises.

How you present this information is largely up to you. A three- or four-page guide for your client's reference might be enough, or you may wish to incorporate it into your technical specification. The important thing is to do the planning immediately, well ahead of application development. Load testing later on will ensure that your theories are correct. It's better to have slightly wrong predictions now than to have no predictions at all.

Following the project management methodologies and design patterns you have learned so far, Chapter 19 explores how you can use the toolkit components and your newfound knowledge to put together a sales force automation project.

19

Building the Application

Now that you understand how the technology works, this is your chance to put it together as a cohesive whole. This chapter is about developing software from the ground up, and because it is a small project you'll be utilizing many of the techniques of extreme programming (XP).

With all the fanfare and drama of starting on a new important project, it's easy to mentally jump ahead and begin thinking about *how* to do things when you should be trying your best to consider *what* should be done.

Therefore, put your computer away. Forget about your logins, passwords, databases, and, just for now, you won't need PHP either. Instead, you'll be using a technology that humans have spent the last few millennia refining — paper.

Yes, paper is technology. It's ubiquitous, inexpensive, readable even if wet, and requires no batteries (unless you're in the dark). The same media type supports both write-only, rewriteable, and color and black-and-white inks. When paper is cut into small index-size cards, it can be used quite nicely for representing your PHP classes. Not only are these cards moveable, they can be mounted on a wall, traded, stapled, clipped, sorted, and stored.

In short, your design and development process depends just as much on social interaction, wits, and thousand-year-old technology as it does on computer hardware and software.

Starting the Project: Monday

You arrive at work well rested and happy. Although the Widget World IT department is busily setting up your computer for your first day of work, fortunately, your office-supply closet contains what you need for today's work:

❏ Pens

❏ 3 × 5 index cards

❏ 4 × 6 index cards

Bridget (the Widget World sales force automation tool manager) sits near you and is ready to work with you on your first day. Bridget mentions that because Edwina (the Widget World eastern regional sales manager) is in the office today, she has scheduled a meeting. Harold is a salesperson who happens to be working in the office because of conflicts; he will be available for the next two weeks. Wade (the Widget World accountant) is also there, and he is available for you 100 percent between 9:30 A.M. and lunchtime, every day (if needed).

Off to the meeting, and don't forget your cards.

Getting an Earful

At the beginning of the meeting, after everyone has been introduced, you explain that you're here to collect *stories* about what they would like from the new system, and how they'd like to use the new system.

Using your thousand-year-old technology of pen and paper, document the stories. Put each one on a separate card and insist that Wendy, Wade, and Edwina all partake in the fun. Of course, they may have questions about what is and is not technically possible, who must sign off on what, and how the workflow goes.

Keep in mind that each story (or feature) should be broken down so that each is about the same size. In the context of this exercise, *size* means the amount of effort that it would take for you to implement the story. This is probably the most difficult part as you (the developer) keep everything in perspective.

Determining the correct size for each story as a unit of time is not a trivial task. Try to keep the unit of time from around a minimum of half a day to a maximum of up to a week or two. Again, each story should be roughly the same size. The story size and time estimates will be used later to help you determine the amount of work you're doing, and how to better estimate future tasks.

For example, if one of the features is "build a rocket ship," break it down into smaller, more manageable chunks, such as "the escape pod should be launched within 10 seconds after the escape hatch is closed."

Your nearly all-day session results in the following stories. Documenting the person who suggested it (or insisted on it) is not mandatory, but a method of doing so is displayed here to give you an idea of how the process is often worked out. Beginning with physical forms (see Figure 19-1) is often a good starting point because it fits with the current workflow and structure:

❑   *Story 1* — Edwina: "We track the salesperson's contacts using this faxable form, which is how we determine where to send them next depending on the feedback. Having access to this information in some sort of electronic format would be great."

❑   *Story 2* — Wade: "Collecting all the daily travel expenses and receipts of the salespeople is time-consuming and error-prone. We'd like to collect them on a weekly basis, subtotaled by date and category."

❑   *Story 3* — Harold: "Sometimes I need to explain a certain expense. For example, I put $30 under "postage" for a special FedEx delivery. I'd like a way to add comments at the bottom of the expense report."

❑   *Story 4* — Wade and Harold: "The expense report should subtotal the items in a manner similar to a spreadsheet."

❑   *Story 5* — Wade: "I'd like to be notified, with a summary, when an expense report is submitted."

❑   *Story 6* — Edwina: "I'd like to be notified, with a summary, when a contact report is submitted."

❑   *Story 7* — Harold: "I'd like each salesperson to receive the same notifications, just so they have the option of double-checking."

❑ *Story 8* — Edwina: "The mailroom needs to be notified when a contact report contains a literature request."

❑ *Story 9* — Edwina and Harold: "Each salesperson needs to have his or her own private login."

❑ *Story 10* — Wade: "I don't authorize the cash advances but I still need to track them. Add "Less Cash Advance" to the expense report."

❑ *Story 11* — Harold: "The cash advances come from multiple sources, so allow the salespeople to control the amount. Don't automatically debit it from a special account; just allow it to be entered in the expense report."

❑ *Story 12* — Wade: "Store the amount of the cash advance so that I can track the total amount per salesperson."

❑ *Story 13* — Wade: "I'd like to be able to get the data from the expense reports in order to feed it into my special spreadsheets."

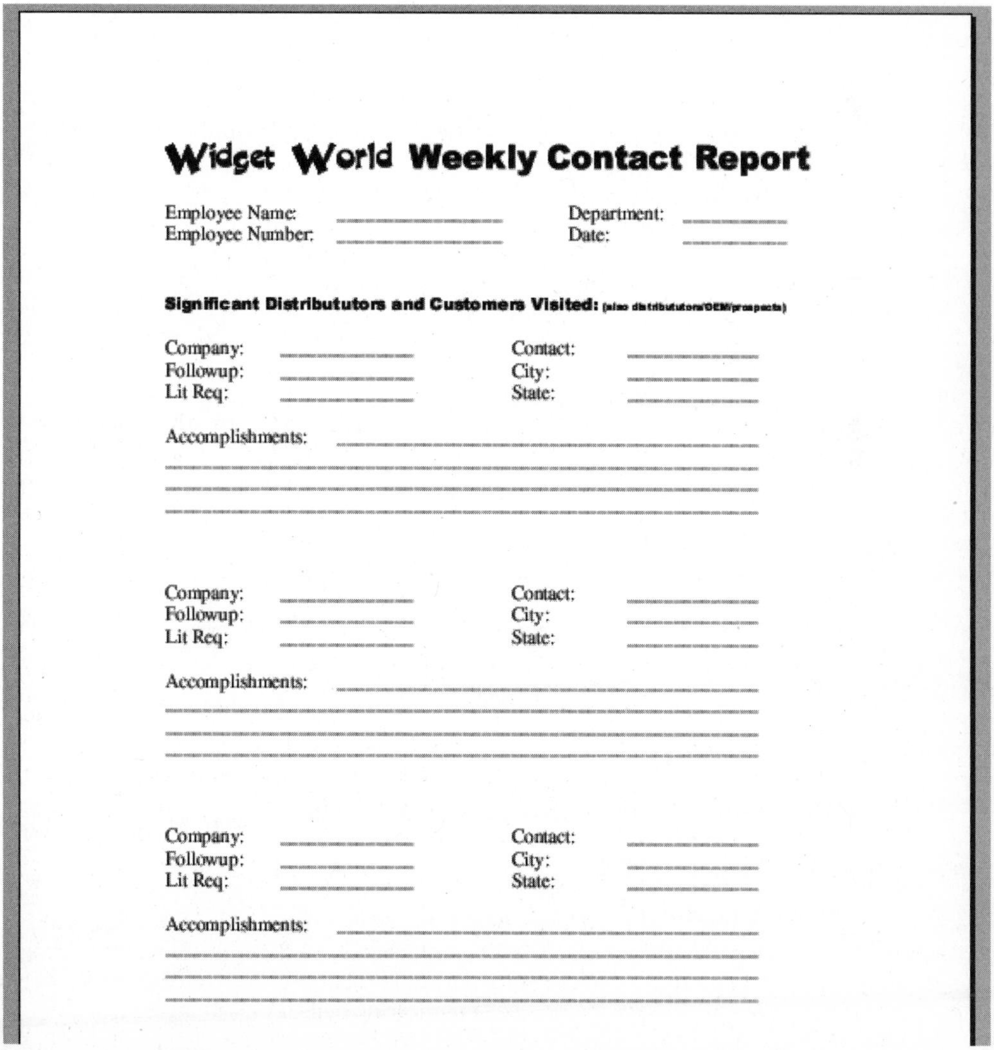

Figure 19-1: Faxable form

At this point, you have a plan for implementing the first revision of the software that Widget World needs in order for its sales force to be more productive.

This should round out your first day at work. The client stories that you collected today are the seeds of a plan that is based on the needs of your clients. Of course, you're not going to start writing the software yet, because your plan is not yet complete.

Story Weight Estimation

Now that your story sizes are roughly in the same ballpark in relation to each other, you can sit down and try to estimate how much effort it will take to implement each one. This is done by assigning a numerical value to each story. A simple project might have only three values:

- ❑ 1 (light)
- ❑ 2 (medium)
- ❑ 3 (heavy)

Another option is to take a stab at guessing the relative weight of each story implementation by the number of perfect-engineering time units that it would take to implement it. A *perfect-engineering time unit* is the number of hours, days, or weeks that you envision a task taking if absolutely nothing goes wrong, and your performance is stellar.

For example, consider Story 9: "Each salesperson needs to have his or her own private login." Think about that for a moment: "Private login" means that you shouldn't be dependent on something like Apache's built-in security, but it could run the gambit from PHP sessions to URL rewriting, including something in between the two.

However, let's face it: Sessions are not that difficult to do correctly if done early. Therefore, if you were using the simple point scale, it would be rated as a "1 (light)." If your points are based on "perfect engineering half-days," it would probably still be rated as a "1." However, if your points are based on "perfect engineering weeks," and the particular story would be complete in a matter of hours, it's an indication that this particular story needs to be more uniform in size with your other stories, which are presumably based on "perfect engineering weeks" rather than days or half-days.

Let's walk through a few more stories. Consider Story 13: "I'd like to be able to get the data from the expense reports in order to feed it into my special spreadsheets." Wade needs access to the expense-report data in a format that is importable by spreadsheet software.

Although the point system is based on "perfect engineering half-days," the word "perfect" here is deliberately given some often all-too-necessary wiggle room in its exact meaning. For example, this story was submitted by Wade, the Widget World accountant, and it may very well apply only to his role as an accountant. This means that, in addition to using a login screen, you'll need to classify the users of the system into Wade and not-Wade — that is, accountant and user. Write that information directly on the card.

Spreadsheets can readily import data from files using comma-separated values (CSV files), which technically isn't challenging because it's simply a different view of the data set. Therefore, adding a user classification system and outputting a data set as CSV would probably collectively rate as about one perfect engineering day, or in your system of perfect engineering half-days, 2 points.

Take a look at Story 5. Wade needs to be "notified, with a summary, when an expense report is submitted." This is directly dependent upon the expense report described in Story 2, which includes "collecting all the travel expenses and receipts." Write that dependency on the card, and estimate the story as being "slightly easier than Story 2." Estimate the value after estimating Story 2.

Now, consider Story 6. Edwina needs to be "notified, with a summary, when a contact report is submitted." Note that the functionality is similar to that of Story 5, so write it on each card.

Next, work through each story, estimating how long it will take, writing required features on each, and noting dependencies between them. Feel free to break stories up if they are too big; conversely, consolidate them if they are too small.

Here is the list you now have:

❑ Story 1: "Track the salesperson's contacts using this faxable form."

   ❑ Basic employee information: 1 point

   ❑ Each distributor/customer can be unique

   ❑ One-to-many relationship between salesperson and customer: 1 point

Putting it all together (making sure that the Web form works and so on) would be another point, for a total of 3 points, or two perfect-engineering days.

❑ Story 2: "Collect the daily travel expenses and receipts of each salesperson on a weekly basis, subtotaled by day and category."

   ❑ This is the Travel Expense Report

   ❑ One-to-many relationship between salesperson and customer

   ❑ It should look sort of like a spreadsheet. This is a nontrivial request: *4 points*

   ❑ Broken down by category: *1 point*

   ❑ Getting everything right: *2 points*

   ❑ *7 points total*

❑ Story 3: "Comments at the bottom of the expense report."

   ❑ Should probably be rolled into Story 2

   ❑ That makes the relationship more interesting — rather than just being an employee-to-daily expense, you're now charged with an employee-to-daily expense and employee-to-weekly comments of daily expenses, as shown in Figure 19-2: *2 points total*

   ❑ Keep as a separate story, but note that it's dependent upon Story 2

   ❑ *2 points total*

sales person					Week starting: 5 Jan 2004		
	sun	mon	tue	wed	thr	fri	sat
breakfast	1						
lunch	2						
dinner	3						
sub total	6						
Sales person comments: Blah blah...							

Figure 19-2: Comments at bottom of expense report

❑ Story 4: "The expense report should subtotal the items in a manner similar to a spreadsheet."

    ❑ Although just front-end work, it'll be time-consuming: *4 points*

    ❑ *4 points total*

❑ Story 5: "Notify accountant, with a summary, when an expense report is submitted."

    ❑ Via e-mail

    ❑ E-mail configuration, management, and so on: *1 point*

    ❑ Dependent upon Story 2: *1 point*

    ❑ *2 points total*

❑ Story 6: "Notify sales manager, with a summary, when a contact report is submitted."

    ❑ Each sales manager has multiple salespeople.

    ❑ One-to-many relationship: *2 points*

    ❑ Dependent upon Story 5 but easy: *1 point*

    ❑ *3 points total*

❑ Story 7: "Notify salespeople with expense-report details."

    ❑ If dependent upon Story 2: *2 points*

    ❑ If dependent upon Story 5: *1 point*

    ❑ *1 or 2 total points*

❑ Story 8: "The mailroom needs to be notified when a contact report contains a literature request."

    ❑ Conditional notification: *1 point*

    ❑ If dependent upon Story 2 or Story 5: *1 or 2 points*

    ❑ *2 or 3 total points*

❑ Story 9: "Each salesperson needs to have his or her own private login."

    ❑ Authentication: *2 points*

    ❑ Authorization: *2 points*

    ❑ *4 points total*

❑ Story 10: "Add 'Less Cash Advance' to the expense report."

   ❑ Same problem as Story 3 (comments on expense report).

   ❑ Dependent on Story 2.

   ❑ Not debited, so no account tracking needed

   ❑ Persisted, not calculated: *2 points*

   ❑ *2 points total*

❑ Story 11: "Allow the salespeople to control the amount of cash advances. Don't automatically debit it from a special account; just allow it to be entered in the expense report."

   ❑ Dependent on Story 10.

   ❑ This story is not really a story. It is a critique of the current system. Remove this story and add note: "Not debited" on Story 10.

   ❑ *0 points*

❑ Story 12: "Store the amount of the cash advance so that I can track the total amount per salesperson."

   ❑ Dependent on Story 10.

   ❑ This story is trivial. Add note: persisted.

   ❑ *0 points*

❑ Story 13: "Export expense report data for spreadsheets."

   ❑ Accountant only: *1 point*

   ❑ Work: *2 points*

   ❑ *3 points total*

You've now broken the stories down and made your first pass at estimation. This step may take several iterations and require going back to ask the clients such questions as the following:

❑ Can the notifications be done utilizing e-mail?

❑ Are there three types of users: managers, salespeople, and accountants?

❑ Can the accountant accept CSV for the expense report export?

❑ How does the accountant want to specify the export? (It could be done by employee, by employee and date, or something different such as by sales manager.)

After all the questions are answered, however, you still aren't out of the woods. After all, you don't actually know whether the system supports outgoing e-mail; and even if it does, do you know how to do it in PHP?

Refining Your Estimation

Talk with your clients and get the answers to your new questions. It's important that they be available because you don't want these issues to hold up your work. In addition, each of your clients (Wendy, the project manager; Wade, the accountant; Edwina, the sales manager; and Harold, the salesperson) will be using the system in some respect, so it's really their project and you're the one who makes it go.

Meanwhile, your client questions have been answered:

- ❏ *Q:* Can the notifications be done utilizing e-mail?

- ❏ *A:* Yes, and any summaries associated with the e-mail should be included as attachments.

- ❏ *Q:* Are there indeed three types of users: managers, salespeople, and accountants?

- ❏ *A:* Yes.

- ❏ *Q:* Can the accountant accept CSV for the expense report export?

- ❏ *A:* Yes, he does it all the time.

- ❏ *Q:* How does the accountant want to specify the export: by employee, by employee and date, or by something different, such as sales manager?

- ❏ *A:* Just by employees and date.

That leaves you with only the technical questions:

- ❏ How do you e-mail something using PHP?

- ❏ What about e-mail attachments?

The Spike

Of course, the last two questions are rhetorical technical questions. Your clients do not have the answers to your technical questions — that's your area. At this point, you don't have enough information to make a complete estimate.

It's time to do some homework, called a *spike*. Although the work may seem tangential, it is required in order to determine whether your line of thought will pay off or, in this case, answer a technical question.

Set aside some time to determine the *if* or *how* questions that invariably show up. These things may take some time, possibly a day or two, but in this case the answer is arrived at in short order. A walk through the PHP API reveals the following:

```
mail("wade@widgetworld.com", "Email Spike Test", "One\nTwo\nThree");
```

Yes, PHP can send e-mail in an easy fashion, so now you must test it or talk to the administrator in order to get it working.

As for e-mail attachments — those are not so easy. PHP does not support attaching e-mail as an easy-to-use function, but that's because the MIME e-mail definition is well documented in RFCs such as RFC 822 (message headers), 2045 (MIME), and 2046 (MIME types). Therefore, a lot of reading and a little bit of coding result in this tidbit:

```
$mime_boundary = "<<<-==+X[".md5(time())."]";
$headers .= "MIME-Version: 1.0\r\n";
$headers .= "Content-Type: multipart/mixed;\r\n";
$headers .= " boundary=\"".$mime_boundary."\"";
$message .= "This is a multi-part message in MIME format.\r\n";
$message .= "\r\n";
$message .= "-".$mime_boundary."\r\n";
$message .= "Content-Type: text/plain; charset=\"iso-8859-1\"\r\n";
$message .= "Content-Transfer-Encoding: 7bit\r\n";
$message .= "\r\n";
```

The preceding code adheres to the aforementioned RFCs, which define the MIME mail headers (the lines defined in $headers) and the message content before the message is finally put together and passed off to your Message Transfer Agent (MTA). Reading through RFCs can be tortuous work, so be sure to test it on a real mail system, using the same mail clients that your customers use, and get it working without error.

This will easily burn off at least one point.

Estimation Tips

Now that all your remaining technical questions have been laid to rest, you can confidently go ahead and fill in your story estimates:

- ❑ Story 1: Customer Contact Report, *3 points*
- ❑ Story 2: Travel Expense Report, *7 points*
- ❑ Story 3: Expense Report Comments, *2 points*
- ❑ Story 4: Expense Report as Spreadsheet, *4 points*
- ❑ Story 5: Accountant Notification, *3 points*
- ❑ Story 6: Sales Manager Notification, *3 points*
- ❑ Story 7: Sales Person Notification, *1 point*
- ❑ Story 8: Mail Room Notification, *2 points*
- ❑ Story 9: Authentication and Authorization, *4 points*
- ❑ Story 10: Persisted Expense Report Cash Advance, *2 points*
- ❑ Story 11: *0 points*
- ❑ Story 12: *0 points*
- ❑ Story 13: Expense Report Export, *3 points*
- ❑ *Total points: 34*

Don't fall into the trap of assuming that 34 points is only 17 perfect engineering days, because the keyword here is "perfect." You'll have meetings to attend, there will be fast and slow days, not to mention having to deal with changes in the plans, and many more human and otherwise imperfect items.

Plus, this is really only your first estimate. After each story has been completed, you'll write down exactly how much real time it took, and after a week or two, your estimates will grow more precise, as will your point-to-time estimates.

For now, you're happy.

Release Planning

After speaking more with Wendy, Wade, Edwina, and Harold, you realize that the first "release" of this project falls into three distinct segments. (You can think of them as buckets.) All parties agree that the segments need to be released, roughly, in this order:

- ❑ Customer Contact Report
    - ❑ Story 9: Authentication and Authorization, *4 points*
    - ❑ Story 1: Customer Contact Report, *3 points*
    - ❑ Story 6: Sales Manager Notification, *3 points*
    - ❑ Story 8: Mail Room Notification, *2 points*
- ❑ Travel Expense Report
    - ❑ Story 2: Travel Expense Report, *7 points*
    - ❑ Story 3: Expense Report Comments, *2 points*
    - ❑ Story 10: Persisted Expense Report Cash Advance, *2 points*
    - ❑ Story 4: Expense Report as Spreadsheet, *4 points*
- ❑ Travel Expense Services
    - ❑ Story 5: Accountant Notification, *3 points*
    - ❑ Story 7: Sales Person Notification, *1 point*
    - ❑ Story 13: Expense Report Export, *3 points*

The decision they put forth is that the Customer Contact Report is needed in a more timely manner than the Travel Expense Report. The Customer Contact Report is also a much "simpler" input form with less interaction than the Travel Expense Report, yet the Customer Contact Report would also represent nearly an end-to-end test of the system as a whole.

Each of the buckets in which the stories fall is called an *iteration*, and in this case each one should take no longer than three weeks to complete. For now, this is the overall plan, and the end of each iteration should produce something that your client can use.

Therefore, your first goal is to create the Customer Contact Report, complete with logins and notifications for the salespeople. After you complete the first iteration, you'll see how well your estimates worked out in several respects:

❑   In relation to each other

❑   In relation to your original estimates

❑   In relation to time or your points per week

The end of each iteration is when you take a step back and measure the progress, get feedback from the client, and adjust the plan in accordance with the evolving needs and goals of your client. Don't sweat it too much; this process is designed to be flexible and responsive to the needs of both you and your clients.

Thus far, you have learned how to divide your problem space into user-defined stories, and how stories can be created and broken out into more stories or consolidated into fewer stories of roughly the same size. Story estimation is an ongoing process, and feedback (such as a tangential spike) will help to solve technical issues.

It is important to work with your clients to determine what is most important to them, and to give them honest feedback regarding the difficulty of each requested feature. This enables you to make better and more timely estimates. It enables your clients to see the system in action, and to make informed decisions regarding the current state of the system.

Starting the Work

Now, you and your clients understand exactly what will be implemented in the first iteration, or the Customer Contact Report:

❑   Story 9: Authentication and Authorization, *4 points*

❑   Story 1: Customer Contact Report, *3 points*

❑   Story 6: Sales Manager Notification, *3 points*

❑   Story 8: Mail Room Notification, *2 points*

Outlining the Details of Story 9

"Each salesperson needs to have his or her own private login."

This presumes, for one thing, that a "salesperson" exists as a logical entity (not necessarily a PHP class, yet), so let's outline its needs.

There exists the need for basic human-readable user information:

```
First Name
Last Name
```

Yes, you *are* a number as well as a name:

```
Employee ID
```

Because the user must log in to the system, let's allow him or her to choose both a login name and a password:

```
Login Name
Login Password
```

You also need to know the role in which the person accesses the system. Although a person's role may be related to a job title, titles tend to be ephemeral. In addition, you must determine only one of three roles: salesperson, accountant, or sales manager.

```
Company Role
```

This raises some good questions. Can someone be in more than one role at a time? Can someone both be an accountant and a sales manager? What about a salesperson and a sales manager? Wendy answers your questions by saying, "Probably not; Wade and Edwina's responsibilities don't overlap." Popping your head into Wade's tidy cubicle confirms your hypothesis, as does a phone call to Edwina. Roles, therefore, are exclusive.

Because you are taking care of authentication, let's decide how to use the system.

Writing Tests

Ask yourself a few questions:

- ❑ How do you want to enable login?
- ❑ For what purpose should the login be used? Should it be simple authentication?
- ❑ Who should use the login feature?

You know what the user consists of:

```
Employee ID
First Name
Last Name
Company Role
```

You also know what is required for authentication:

```
Login Name
Login Password
```

Recall from Chapter 12 the HTTPSession class. Don't go looking for it just yet; you won't need it right now — but this is a plausible choice to use with two yet-to-be-defined classes, WidgetSession and WidgetUser:

```php
<?php
$session = new WidgetSession(); // inherited from HTTPSession
$session->impress();
// authentication
$session->login("ed","12345");
if ($session->isLoggedIn() == false) exit;
$user = $session->getUser(); // returns WidgetUser
print $user->first_name;
print $user->last_name;
print $user->email;
// authorization
print $user->role;
print $user->isSalesPerson();
print $user->isSalesManager();
print $user->isAccountant();
?>
```

Keep in mind that the preceding code snippet is only "a plausible scenario." It's not yet a formalized test or running code. It is what exists solely in your mind regarding the use of new classes. When you are happy with this "what-if" scenario, you formalize its use in a test. Let's continue and write some tests!

PHPUnit

The idea here is to write the test to simulate the way in which you plan on using the software associated with your current story. It's called *test-driven development,* and, in addition to its development strengths, you end up with a great suite of tests. You met it first in Chapter 13 when you looked at application architecture. It is hoped that you still have PHPUnit installed.

> Testing the application in the same manner in which you will be using it forces you to look at the function or object and nail down the arguments and other elements. This avoids creating functionality that isn't used, or is used in the wrong places.

Far from "tying you down," having a testing suite provides you with a great degree of freedom, because you know instantly whether you happened to break distant parts of the system by adding new features or modifying existing code.

Here are some new tests that are designed to reflect the common usage scenario. Save the following as test.widgetsession.php:

```php
<?php

require_once ("widgetsession.phpm");
require_once ("lib/phpunit/phpunit.php");

class TestWidgetSession extends TestCase {

    private $_session;
    function setUp() {
        $dsn = array ('phptype'  => "pgsql", hostspec' => "localhost",
```

```
                                'database' => "widgetworld",
                                'username' => "wuser",
                                'password' => "foobar");
            $this->_session = new WidgetSession($dsn, true);
        }

        function testValidLogin() {
            $this->_session->login("ed","12345");
            $this->assertEquals(true, $this->_session->isLoggedIn());
        }

        function testInvalidLogin() {
            $this->_session->login("ed","54321"); // fail
            $this->assertEquals(false, $this->_session->isLoggedIn());
        }

        function testUser() {
            $user = $this->_session->getUser();
            $this->assertEquals("Lecky-Thompson", $user->last_name);
            $this->assertEquals("Ed", $user->first_name);
            $this->assertEquals("ed@lecky-thompson.com", $user->email);
        }

        function testAuthorization () {
            $user = $this->_session->getUser();
            $this->assertEquals("Sales Person", $user->role);
            $this->assertEquals(true, $user->isSalesPerson());
            $this->assertEquals(false, $user->isSalesManager());
            $this->assertEquals(false, $user->isAccountant());
        }
}
$suite = new TestSuite;
$suite->addTest(new TestWidgetSession("testValidLogin"));
$suite->addTest(new TestWidgetSession("testInvalidLogin"));
$suite->addTest(new TestWidgetSession("testUser"));
$suite->addTest(new TestWidgetSession("testAuthorization"));
$testRunner = new TestRunner();
$testRunner->run( $suite );
?>
```

However, when the preceding is run, you get the following error:

```
Class 'WidgetSession' not found in test.widgetsession.php on line 16
```

For now, let's mock up appropriate dummy `WidgetSession` and `WidgetUser` classes so that the tests can at least run. Incorporate the following code at the top of the previous listing for `test.widgetsession.php`:

```
class WidgetSession {

    public function __construct ($one, $two) {}
    public function login() {}
    public function isLoggedIn()      { return null; }
    public function getUser() {
        return new WidgetUser();
    }
}

class WidgetUser {
    public $first_name = "";
    public $last_name = "";
    public $email = "";

    public function isSalesPerson()  { return null; }
    public function isSalesManager() { return null; }
    public function isAccountant()   { return null; }
}
```

Now run the tests again in `test.widgetsession.php`. Here is the corresponding output from PHPUnit:

```
TestWidgetSession - testValidLogin FAIL
TestWidgetSession - testInvalidLogin FAIL
TestWidgetSession - testUser FAIL
TestWidgetSession - testAuthorization FAIL
4 tests run.
9 failures.
0 errors.
Failures
    1. testValidLogin
            true    type:boolean
            null    type:NULL
    2. testInvalidLogin
            false    type:boolean
            null    type:NULL
    3. testUser
            Lecky-Thompson  type:string
            type:string
    4. testUser
            Ed    type:string
            type:string
    5. testUser
            ed@lecky-thompson.com  type:string
            type:string
    6. testAuthorization
            Sales Person  type:string
            type:string
    7. testAuthorization
            true    type:boolean
            null    type:NULL
```

```
8. testAuthorization
       false   type:boolean
       null    type:NULL
9. testAuthorization
       false    type:boolean
       null     type:NULL
```

At this point of the development process, every one of your tests should run without syntax error but fail. This is because you haven't yet implemented any of the functionality for which the tests are designed! So, yes, the first time you run the tests, you should be happy that they all fail. Remember that the tests are based on the common usage scenario, and that you should be testing all the features required by the scenario.

It is now your responsibility to implement the actual code that is required to pass the tests. The login and session process can be fixed quite easily, because that behavior is found in HTTPSession.

Take care of the low-hanging fruit in regard to the WidgetSession. Because WidgetSession is adding functionality to HTTPSession, it makes sense to extend HTTPSession. Therefore, start with your spoofed WidgetSession class and extend HTTPSession in test.widgetsession.php so that it now contains working code:

```
require("httpsession.phpm");
class WidgetSession extends HTTPSession {

    public function getUser() {
        return new WidgetUser();
    }
}
```

Now rerun the test.widgetsession.php tests:

```
TestWidgetSession - testValidLogin ok
TestWidgetSession - testInvalidLogin ok
TestWidgetSession - testUser FAIL
TestWidgetSession - testAuthorization FAIL
4 tests run.
7 failures.
0 errors.
```

By utilizing the functionality inherent in HTTPSession, you've already passed half the tests.

Still editing test.widgetsession.php, start work on the WidgetUser objects by first overriding HTTPSession's getUserObject() function to return a WidgetUser class. Modify the declaration of WidgetSession as shown here:

```
class WidgetSession extends HTTPSession {

    public function getUserObject() {
        $uid = $this->GetUserID(); // calling up from HTTPSession
        if ($uid == false) return null;
        // pull ourselves out of the database
```

```
            $stmt = "select * FROM \"user\" WHERE id = ".$uid;
            $result = $this->getDatabaseHandle()->query($stmt);
            return new WidgetUser($result->fetchRow());
        }
    }
```

Your `WidgetUser` class must hold its state. However, the `WidgetUser` class is getting pumped out from a database, which can return data in an associative array. Therefore, just store `WidgetUser`'s state in an associative array.

Of course, `__set` and `__get` both need to be redefined. Still editing `test.widgetsession.php`:

```
class WidgetUser {
    protected $contentBase = array();

    function __construct($initdict) {
        $this->contentBase = $initdict; // copy
    }

    function __get ($key) {
        if (array_key_exists ($key, $this->contentBase)) {
            return $this->contentBase[$key];
        }
        return null;
    }

    function __set ($key, $value) {
        if (array_key_exists ($key, $this->contentBase)) {
            $this->contentBase[$key]=$value;
        }
    }.

    public function isSalesPerson()    { return null; }
    public function isSalesManager()   { return null; }
    public function isAccountant()     { return null; }
}
```

Once again, rerunning `test.widgetsession.php` results in most of the user tests passing, with one notable exception:

```
1. testUser
   ed@lecky-thompson.com    type:string
   null    type:NULL
```

Hmmm, let's look closer at the PostgreSQL version of the user table that was defined in Chapter 12:

```
CREATE TABLE "user" (    id serial PRIMARY KEY,
  username varchar(32) default NULL,
  md5_pw varchar(32) default NULL,
  first_name varchar(64) default NULL,
  last_name varchar(64) default NULL
);
```

You can see that the user table is missing e-mail, so you must add it to make the table look like this:

```
CREATE TABLE "user" (
   id serial PRIMARY KEY,
   username varchar(32) default NULL,
   md5_pw varchar(32) default NULL,
   first_name varchar(64) default NULL,
   last_name varchar(64) default NULL,
   email varchar(255) default NULL
);
```

You can use the syntax `ALTER TABLE "user" ADD "email" varchar(255)` to achieve this.

Run the `test.widgetsession.php` tests:

```
TestWidgetSession - testValidLogin ok
TestWidgetSession - testInvalidLogin ok
TestWidgetSession - testUser ok
TestWidgetSession - testAuthorization FAIL
4 tests run.
4 failures.
```

Zero errors.

Now that the `testUser` passes, pay attention to the `testAuthorization`. Because "role" is not included in the database yet, add that as well. (The default value of `'s'` is short for "salesperson.")

```
ALTER TABLE "user" ADD "role" char(1) default 's';
```

The table will now look like this:

```
CREATE TABLE "user" (
   id serial PRIMARY KEY,
   username varchar(32) default NULL,
   md5_pw varchar(32) default NULL,
   first_name varchar(64) default NULL,
   last_name varchar(64) default NULL,
   email varchar(255) default NULL,
   role char(1) NOT NULL default 's'
);
```

Putting some state-retrieval accessor methods into `WidgetUser` solves most of the remaining issues. You're still editing the class `WidgetUser`, currently temporarily homed in `test.widgetsession.php`:

```php
public function isSalesPerson() {
    if ($this->role == "s") return true;
    return false;
}

public function isSalesManager() {
    if ($this->role == "m") return true;
    return false;
}
```

```
public function isAccountant()    {
    if ($this->role == "a") return true;
    return false;
}
```

However, the test still fails on "role" because it expects a human-readable string, and instead is limited to the single digits of s, m, and a:

```
1. testAuthorization
   Sales Person     type:string
   s     type:string
```

Recall from earlier what is being tested for:

```
function testAuthorization () {
    $user = $this->_session->getUser();
$this->assertEquals("Sales Person", $user->role);

    $this->assertEquals(true, $user->isSalesPerson());
    $this->assertEquals(false, $user->isSalesManager());
    $this->assertEquals(false, $user->isAccountant());
}
```

Note that because of the nature of the next problem, when $user->role is called, the expectation is to get "Sales Person." Keep in mind that that role is directly from the database, so either change the database or change your software instead.

How about this idea: Because you'd like to continue to directly access $user->role in the __get function, you can determine which role is being queried for and dispatch it to a getRole() function.

Here it is:

```
class WidgetUser {
    protected $contentBase = array();
    protected $dispatchFunctions = array ("role" => "getrole");

    function __construct($initdict) {
        $this->contentBase = $initdict; // copy
    }

    function __get ($key) {
        // dispatch by function first
        if (array_key_exists ($key, $this->dispatchFunctions)) {
            $funcname = $this->dispatchFunctions[$key];
            return $this->$funcname();
        }

        // otherwise return based on state
        if (array_key_exists ($key, $this->contentBase)) {
            return $this->contentBase[$key];
        }
```

```
            return null;
    }

    function __set ($key, $value) {
        if (array_key_exists ($key, $this->contentBase)) {
            $this->contentBase[$key]=$value;
        }

    }

    public function getRole() {
        switch ($this->contentBase["role"]) {
            case "s": return ("Sales Person");
            case "m": return ("Sales Manager");
            case "a": return ("Accountant");
            default: return ("");
        }
    }

    public function isSalesPerson()  {
        if ($this->contentBase["role"] == "s") return true;
        return false;
    }

    public function isSalesManager() {
        if ($this->contentBase["role"] == "m") return true;
        return false;
    }
    public function isAccountant()   {

        if ($this->contentBase["role"] == "a") return true;
        return false;
    }
}
```

Note that isSalesPerson(), isSalesManager(), and isAccountant() all access contentBase, rather than call $this-role. Otherwise, it would be dispatched through the getRole() function, which returns human-readable results such as "Sales Manager." It is not a good idea to try to return Boolean values based on human-readable results because they could change on a whim.

Creating the Login Screen

Now that your WidgetUser and WidgetSession objects are working, it's time to use them with a real login.

Although the login screen is not terribly complicated, you'll continue to use Smarty as the templating system, simply for its convenience.

Here's your initial `index.php` file:

```php
<?php
require_once ("Smarty.class.php"); require_once ("widgetsession.phpm");
$session = new WidgetSession(array ('phptype'  => "pgsql",
                                    'hostspec' => "localhost",
                                    'database' => "widgetworld",
                                    'username' => "wuser",
                                    'password' => "foobar"));
$session->Impress();
$smarty = new Smarty;
if ($_REQUEST["action"] == "login") {
    $session->login($_REQUEST["login_name"],$_REQUEST["login_pass"]);
    if ($session->isLoggedIn()) {
        $smarty->assign_by_ref("user", $session->getUserObject());
        $smarty->display ("main.tpl");
        exit;
    } else {
        $smarty->assign('error', "Invalid login, try again.");
        $smarty->display ("login.tpl");
        exit;
    }
} else {
    if ($session->isLoggedIn() == true) {
        $smarty->assign_by_ref("user", $session->getUserObject());
        $smarty->display ("main.tpl");
        exit;
    }
}
$smarty->display ("login.tpl");
?>
```

The logic for the screen is as follows. If the action variable of the form is `login`, it indicates that a login attempt is trying to be made, so an attempt to log in is made by calling `$session-login()`. A positive result is dealt with by rendering the main menu. A negative result causes an error variable to be set, and the login screen is again presented to the user.

Of course, if you're not trying to log in, `$session-isLoggedIn()` is checked to confirm the login status with the session. If the user is logged in, the main menu screen is displayed. Otherwise, the login screen is again redisplayed.

The two screens, `login` and `main`, along with the header and footer, are all simple.

Following is the code for `login.tpl`:

```
{include file="header.tpl" title="Widget World Login"}
<h3>Please Login:</h3> <p>
{section name=one loop=$error}{sectionelse}
  <font color="#FF0000">{$error}</font><p>
{/section}
<form action="index.php" method="post">
 <table border="0">
```

```
  <tr>
    <td width="20"></td>
    <td>User:</td>
    <td><input name="login_name" type="text" size="20" maxsize="50"></td>
  </tr>
  <tr>
    <td width="20"></td>
    <td>Password:</td>
    <td><input name="login_pass" type="password" size="20" maxsize="50"></td>
  </tr>
  <tr>
    <td width="20"></td>
    <td></td>
    <td><input type="submit" value=" Login "></td>
  </tr>
 </table>
 <input type="hidden" name="action" value="login">
</form>
{include file="footer.tpl"}
```

Following is the code for header.tpl:

```
<!DOCTYPE HTML PUBLIC "-//W3C//DTD HTML 4.01 Transitional//EN">
<html>
<head>
<meta HTTP-EQUIV="content-type" CONTENT="text/html; charset=ISO-8859-1">
<title>{$title|default:"no title"}</title>
</head>
<h1>Widget World</h1>
<hr><p>
```

Following is the code for footer.tpl:

```
<br/><br/>
<hr/>
For Widget World use only - testing environment.
</body>
</html>
```

Following is the code for main.tpl:

```
{include file="header.tpl" title="Widget World Menu"}
Welcome {$user->first_name} the {$user->role}!
<table border="0" cellspacing="8" cellpadding="8">
{strip}
{section name=security show=$user->isAccountant()}
  <tr><td><h3>Accountant functionality goes here.</h3></td></tr>
{/section}
  <tr>
    <td valign="top">
```

```
        <h3><a href="travel-expenses.php">New Travel Expenses</a></h3>
    </td>
  </tr>
  <tr>
    <td valign="top">
      <h3><a href="customer-contacts.php">New Customer Contacts</a></h3>
    </td>
  </tr>
{/strip}
</table>
{include file="footer.tpl"}
```

Figure 19-3 shows what this looks like. After you are logged in, you get the menu shown in Figure 19-4. If you change ed to be an accountant by changing his role to be a, then ed would have a slightly different view, as displayed in Figure 19-5.

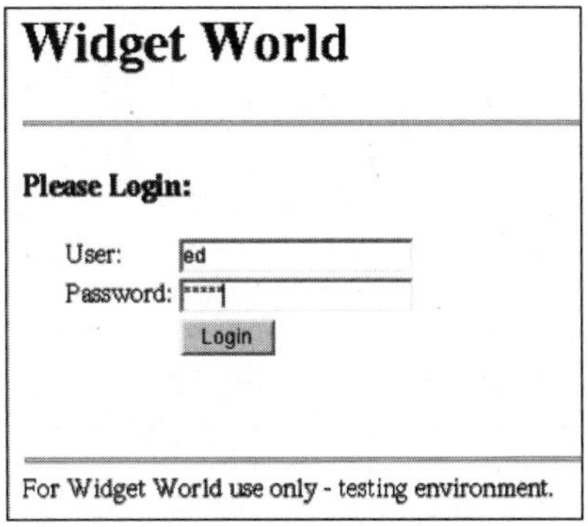

Figure 19-3: Login screen

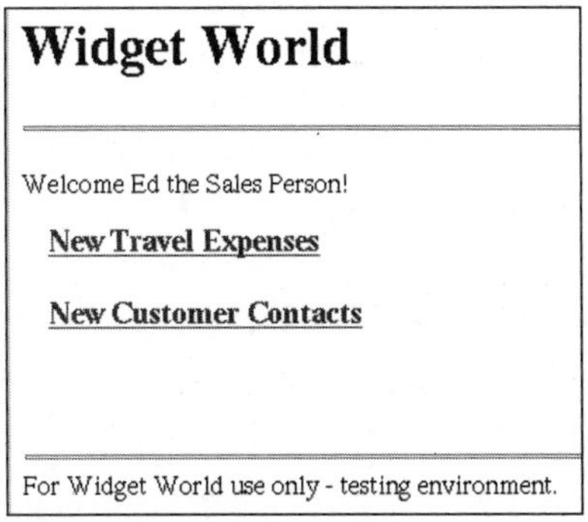

Figure 19-4: Main menu

Figure 19-5: View for Ed

Congratulations! Your first story is now complete. You have done a lot of work with PHP sessions, database lookups, PEAR::DB, and PHPUnit to accomplish the functionality required to determine who is logging in and what that user should be able to do, which is not at all a trivial feat.

Take a nice little break, and enjoy munching on a biscuit; there is a lot more work coming up.

The Next Story

Your previous story (Story 9: "Authentication and Authorization") was worth 4 points. Write down how long in days or half days it took you to accomplish this 4-point task.

Recall that this iteration of the Customer Contact Report is comprised of the following:

- ❑ Story 9: Authentication and Authorization, *4 points* (done)
- ❑ Story 1: Customer Contact Report, *3 points*
- ❑ Story 6: Sales Manager Notification, *3 points*
- ❑ Story 8: Mail Room Notification, *2 points*

Time to get back to work.

Customer Contact Requirements

Recall from earlier in this chapter (refer to Figure 19-1) what the Weekly Contact Report requires. The data requirements for this look something like the following:

```
CREATE TABLE contact_visits (
    emp_id integer NOT NULL,
    week_start date NOT NULL,
    seq integer NOT NULL,
    company_name varchar(40) default NULL,
    contact_name varchar(40) default NULL,
    city varchar(40) default NULL,
    state varchar(40) default NULL,
```

```
      accomplishments text,
      followup text,
      literature_request text
);
CREATE UNIQUE INDEX cv_pk on contact_visits (emp_id,week_start,seq);
CREATE INDEX cv_emp_id ON contact_visits (emp_id);
CREATE INDEX cv_week_start ON contact_visits (week_start);
CREATE INDEX cv_seq ON contact_visits (seq);
```

The data is per week, is associated with the employee, and is unique when completed with the SEQuence column. There may be a lot.

Note that `state` is 40 characters long in order to accommodate non-U.S. states, as well as provinces in Canada and Mexico. Also note that the Customer Contact Report contains the employee's department, which currently doesn't exist in the `user` table. Go ahead and add it:

```
CREATE TABLE "user" (
   id serial PRIMARY KEY,
   username varchar(32) default NULL,
   md5_pw varchar(32) default NULL,
   first_name varchar(64) default NULL,
   last_name varchar(64) default NULL,
   email varchar(255) default NULL,
   role char(1) NOT NULL default 's',
   department varchar(40) NOT NULL default 's'
);
```

Customer Contact Tests

Think about how you intend to use the customer contacts. From this input screen, nearly all the form data is provided to you via the Web server, which means that when you prepare to persist it, you'll need the employee ID available from `WidgetSession`.

In addition, consider what minimum information you'll require before dumping into the table: `id`, `week_start`, and `sequence` with this PHPUnit test:

```
function testValidContactVisit() {
    $cv = new ContactVisit (
        array ('emp_id'             => "1",
               'seq'                => "1",
               'week_start'         => "1980-01-01",
               'company_name'       => "test one",
               'contact_name'       => "Big One",
               'city'               => "Columbus",
               'state'              => "OH",
               'accomplishments'    => "phone call",
               'followup'           => "",
               'literature_request' => ""));
    $this->assertEquals(true, $cv->isValid(), "valid log");
}
```

This testing is the minimum information required by `ContactVisit`. Thus, if `emp_id`, `seq`, and `week_start` contain any values, then `isValid()` will return `true`. Conversely, the opposite should also be tested:

```
function testInvalidContactVisit() {
    $cv = new ContactVisit (
        array ('emp_id'             => "1",
               'week_start'         => "", // date required
               'company_name'       => "test one",
               'contact_name'       => "Big One",
               'city'               => "Columbus",
               'state'              => "OH",
               'accomplishments'    => "phone call",
               'followup'           => "",
               'literature_request' => ""));
    $this->assertEquals(false, $cv->isValid(), "invalid visit");
}
```

Because the visits each require a unique sequence value, they might as well determine their order themselves:

```
function testSequence() {
    $cv1 = new ContactVisit(array());
    $this->assertEquals(1, $cv1->seq);
    $cv2 = new ContactVisit(array());
    $this->assertEquals(2, $cv2->seq);
}
```

Note that by creating `ContactVisits`, the sequence (seq) of each new `ContactVisit` is automatically incremented, which eliminates the need to require the container to assign each one a unique sequence number.

Persistence is still in a state of flux, but this will certainly work:

```
function testPersistence() {
    $this->_session->getDatabaseHandle()->query("delete FROM
        contact_visits WHERE emp_id = 1 and week_start = '1980-01-01'");
    // remove multiples
    $cv = new ContactVisit (
        array ('emp_id'             => "1",
               'week_start'         => "1980-01-01",
               'seq'                => 1,
               'company_name'       => "test one",
               'contact_name'       => "Big One",
               'city'               => "Columbus",
               'state'              => "OH",
               'accomplishments'    => "phone call",
               'followup'           => "",
               'literature_request' => ""));
    $result = $this->_session->getDatabaseHandle()->query("select * FROM
            contact_visits WHERE emp_id = 1 and week_start = '1980-01-01'");
    $this->assertEquals(0, $result->numRows());
```

```
        $cv->persist();
        $result = $this->_session->getDatabaseHandle()->query("select * FROM
                contact_visits WHERE emp_id = 1 and week_start = '1980-01-01'");
        $this->assertEquals(1, $result->numRows());
    }
```

Note that `week_start`'s value of New Year's Day, 1980, was chosen for a reason:

❑   It is not the start of a normal week, which, for Americans, is normally Sunday.

❑   It stands out in your mind, so if something goes horribly wrong and it ends up in the production database, it's easily recognized as not being a real contact.

Before running the tests, don't forget to stub out `ContactVisit` to ensure that the tests successfully FAIL (yet syntactically execute) before correctly satisfying the tests. Here are the contents of `contact.phpm`:

```
class ContactVisit {

    function __construct ($results) { }
    public function isValid() { return null; }
    public function persist() { }
    public function getSequence() { return null; }
}
```

Satisfying the Tests

Because the visits are going to be in sequence, utilize a static variable so that the sequence count is shared across all instances of the class. Incrementing it in the constructor also ensures that all your bases are covered without requiring any more plumbing. Implement the constructor of `ContactVisit` in `contact.phpm`:

```
class ContactVisit {

    function __construct ($results, $dbh = null) {

        static $sequence = 0;

        $this->dbh = $dbh;

        $this->contentBase = $results; // copy

        $sequence = $sequence + 1; // increment across class

        $this->contentBase["seq"] = $sequence;

    }

public function isValid() { return null; }
    public function persist() { }
    public function getSequence() { return null; }
}
```

In addition, note that `ContactVisit` must store a reference to the database. This is in addition to the normal data (company name, city, state, and so on), so return `ContactVisit`'s state in the last `return` of `ContactVisit`'s `__get()` function. Here it is in `contact.phpm`:

```
function __get ($key) {
    if (array_key_exists ($key, $this->contentBase)) {
        return $this->contentBase[$key];
    }
    return $this->$key;
}
```

Put it all together, add some functions for generating its required SQL, and you're set. The file `contact.phpm` is as follows:

```
class ContactVisit {
protected $contentBase = array();
protected $dbh = null; // database handle
    function __get ($key) {
        if (array_key_exists ($key, $this->contentBase)) {
            return $this->contentBase[$key];
        }
        return $this->$key;
    }
    function __construct ($results, $dbh = null) {
        static $sequence = 0;
        $this->dbh = $dbh;
        $this->contentBase = $results; // copy
        $sequence = $sequence + 1; // increment across class
        $this->contentBase["seq"] = $sequence;
    }
private function isEmpty($key) {
if (array_key_exists($key, $this->contentBase) == false) return true;
if ($this->contentBase[$key] == null) return true;
if ($this->contentBase[$key] == "") return true;
return false;
}
public function isValid() {
if ($this->isEmpty("emp_id") == true) return false;
if ($this->isEmpty("week_start") == true) return false;
if ($this->isEmpty("company_name") == true) return false;
return true;
}
private function implodeQuoted (&$values, $delimiter) {
$sql = "";
$flagIsFirst = true;
foreach ($values as $value) {
if ($flagIsFirst) {
$flagIsFirst = false;
} else {
$sql .= $delimiter;
}
```

```
if (gettype ($value) == "string") {
$sql .= "'".$value."'";
} else {
$sql .= $value;
}
}
return $sql;
}
private function generateSqlInsert ($tableName, &$metas, &$values) {
return "insert into ".$tableName.
"        ( ".implode           ($metas,   ", ")." ) ".
" values ( ".$this->implodeQuoted ($values, ", ")." ) ";
}

public function persist() {
if ($this->isValid() == false) return false;
$sql = $this->generateSqlInsert ("contact_visits",
array ( "emp_id",
"week_start",
"seq",
"company_name",
"contact_name",                             "city",
                                            "state",
                                            "accomplishments",
                                            "followup",
                                            "literature_request" ),
                         array ( $this->emp_id,
                                 $this->week_start,
                                 $this->seq,
                                 $this->company_name,
                                 $this->contact_name,
                                 $this->city,
                                 $this->state,
                                 $this->accomplishments,
                                 $this->followup,
                                 $this->literature_request ));
        if (DB::isError ($this->dbh->query($sql))) return false;
        return true;
    }
}
```

Briefly, the methods implemented are as follows:

❑   isValid() satisfies both of your validity tests. isValid() relies upon isEmpty(), which is simply a convenience function.

❑   persist() satisfies your persistence test. persist() calls generateSqlInsert(), which generates a SQL INSERT statement based on the table name, table meta-information, and the values you'd like to insert. generateSqlInsert(), in turn, calls implodeQuoted(), which adds SQL quotes to values that are strings.

Both implodeQuoted() and generateSqlInsert() insist that the arrays are passed by reference, rather than by value. Of course, the default behavior of PHP 6 is to pass objects by reference, but arrays are passed by value in the default case.

Creating the Screen

Consider the following form, called `customer-contacts.tpl`:

```
{include file="header.tpl" title="Widget World - Customer Contact"}
<h3>Customer Contact Report</h3>
<form action="customer-contacts.php" method="post">
 <table border="0" width="100%">
 <tr>
  <td><b>Employee Name:</b></td><td>{$user->first_name} {$user->last_name}</td>
  <td><b>Department:</b></td><td>{$user->department}</td>
 </tr>
 <tr>
  <td><b>Number:</b></td><td>{$user->id}</td><td><b>Start Week:</b></td>
  <td><SELECT NAME="week_start">
        {html_options values=$start_weeks output=$start_weeks
         selected=$current_start_week}
      </SELECT>
  </td>
 </tr>
</table>
<br><br>
<hr>
<p><font size="+1">
    <b>Significant Distributors and Customers Visited:</b>
    </font>
    <br>
    (also distributors/OEM/prospects)<p>
<table border="0">
{section name=idx loop=$max_weekly_contacts}{strip}
<tr>
  <td width="20"></td>
  <td><b>Company</b></td>
  <td><b>Contact</b></td>
  <td><b>City</b></td>
  <td><b>State</b></td>
  <td><b>FollowUp</b></td>
  <td><b>Literature Request</b></td>
</tr>
<tr>
  <td width="20"></td>
  <td><input name="company_name_{$smarty.section.idx.index}"
      size="20" maxlength="50"></td>
  <td><input name="contact_name_{$smarty.section.idx.index}"
      size="20" maxlength="50"></td>
  <td><input name="city_{$smarty.section.idx.index}"
      size="20" maxlength="50"></td>
  <td><input name="state_{$smarty.section.idx.index}"
      size="10" maxlength="50"></td>
  <td><input name="followup_{$smarty.section.idx.index}"
      size="20" maxlength="2000"></td>
  <td><input name="literature_request_{$smarty.section.idx.index}"
      size="20" maxlength="2000"></td>
</tr>
```

```
<tr>
 <td width="20"></td>
 <td colspan="7"><b>Accomplishments:</b></td>
</tr>
<tr>
 <td width="20"></td>
 <td colspan="7">
   <TEXTAREA NAME="accomplishments_{$smarty.section.idx.index}"
     ROWS=4 COLS=95></TEXTAREA><br><br>
 </td>
</tr>
{/strip}{/section}
</table>
<br><hr>
<input type="hidden" name="action" value="persist_contact">
<br><br>
<center>
<input type="submit" name="submit" value=" Save "
          onclick="return checkInputs(this.form);">
</center>
</form>
{include file="footer.tpl"}
```

Note that the main loop, {section name=idx} loop=$max_weekly_contacts}, iterates and creates unique names of inputs: company_name_{$smarty.section.idx.index}}, which are then operated on.

Smarty offers the handy feature of populating drop-down boxes based on an array of dates for the current week:

```
<SELECT NAME="week_start">
  {html_options values=$start_weeks
  output=$start_weeks selected=$current_start_week}
</SELECT>
```

You may have noticed that the input screen is rather Spartan in appearance because it uses regular HTML, rather than something stricter with better cross-platform browser compatibility (such as XHTML and CSS). This is because, at this point in the process, you're more interested in getting the system to work than appearance, because the definition may change slightly in the near future. Later in the process, the display can be spruced up.

Feeding the Beast

Even though ContactVisits know how to persist themselves, it takes a surprising amount of work to gather together several weeks' worth of drop-down information, and then save all contacts to the database. Here is the required functionality, simply placed in functions in customer-contacts.php:

```
<?php
require_once ("Smarty.class.php");
require_once ("widgetsession.phpm");
$session = new WidgetSession(array ('phptype'  => "pgsql",
                                    'hostspec' => "localhost",
```

```php
                                  'database' => "widgetworld",
                                  'username' => "uwuser",
                                  'password' => "foobar"));
$session->Impress();
$smarty = new Smarty;
$GLOBALS["max-weekly-contacts"] = 5;

function getStartDateOffset ($i) {
    if ($i < 0) $i = 5;
    $dates = array("Sunday" => 0, "Monday" => -1, "Tuesday" => -2,
                   "Wednesday" => -3, "Thursday" => -4, "Friday" => -5,
                   "Saturday" => -6);
    return date("Y-m-d", mktime (0,0,0,date("m"),
          date("d")+$dates[date("l")]-(($i-5)*7),date("Y")));
}
function getCurrentStartWeek () {
    if (strlen($_REQUEST["week_start"]) >= 8) return $_REQUEST["week_start"];
    return getStartDateOffset(-1); // this sunday
}
function getStartWeeks () {
    $sudayArray = array();
    for ($i=20; $i > 0; $i-) {
        array_push($sudayArray, getStartDateOffset($i));
    }
    return ($sudayArray);
}
function persistContactVisits (&$dbh, $emp_id) {
    $dbh->query("delete from contact_visits where emp_id
                = ".$emp_id." and week_start = '".getCurrentStartWeek()."'");
    $seq = 0;
    for ($i = 0; $i < $GLOBALS["max-weekly-contacts"]; $i++) {
        $cv = new ContactVisit (
            array ("emp_id"            => $emp_id,
                   "week_start"        => getCurrentStartWeek(),
                   "company_name"      => $_REQUEST["company_name_".$i],
                   "contact_name"      => $_REQUEST["contact_name_".$i],
                   "city"              => $_REQUEST["city_".$i],
                   "state"             => $_REQUEST["state_".$i],
                   "accomplishments"   => $_REQUEST["accomplishments_".$i],
                   "followup"          => $_REQUEST["followup_".$i],
                   "literature_request"=> $_REQUEST["literature_request_".$i]),
            $dbh);
        $cv->persist();
    }
}
$user = $session->getUserObject();
// display
```

```
if ($_REQUEST["action"] != "persist_contact") {
    $smarty->assign_by_ref ("user", $user);
    $smarty->assign('start_weeks', getStartWeeks());
    $smarty->assign('current_start_week', getCurrentStartWeek());
    $smarty->assign("max_weekly_contacts", $GLOBALS["max-weekly-contacts"]);
    $smarty->display('customer-contacts.tpl');
    exit();
}
// persist contact visits
require_once ("contact.phpm");
persistContactVisits ($session->getDatabaseHandle(), $user->id);
$smarty->display('thankyou.tpl');
?>
```

The interesting features of this begin with `getStartDateOffset()`, which populates the Date drop-down by returning the day of the start week based on an integer offset passed in:

```
function getStartDateOffset ($i) {
    if ($i < 0) $i = 5;
    $dates = array("Sunday" => 0, "Monday" => -1, "Tuesday" => -2,
                   "Wednesday" => -3, "Thursday" => -4, "Friday" => -5,
                   "Saturday" => -6);
    return date("Y-m-d", mktime (0,0,0,date("m"),
           date("d")+$dates[date("l")]-(($i-5)*7),date("Y")));
}
```

It works by associating the weekday (say, Tuesday), retrieved by the use of `date("l")` to access the `$dates` array, which returns an integer representing the number of days away from the target day of Sunday. When you know the date of the closest Sunday, the Sunday+week offset is calculated by multiplying the closest Sunday date by 7, and then adding those days to the current Sunday. Thus, regardless of the current day of the week, a Sunday +/− $i weeks is returned.

However, because `getStartWeeks()` returns an array of 20 Sundays by counting from 20 to 0, `getStarteDateOffset()` also automatically adds 5 weeks to the default. As a result, the drop-down selection box for Week has 15 past weeks, the current Sunday, and 4 weeks in the future.

The heavy lifting is done by `persistContactVisits()`, which removes the old contacts, creates new `ContactVisits`, and calls `persist()` on each one in order to save the results in the database.

Figure 19-6 shows the features in action.

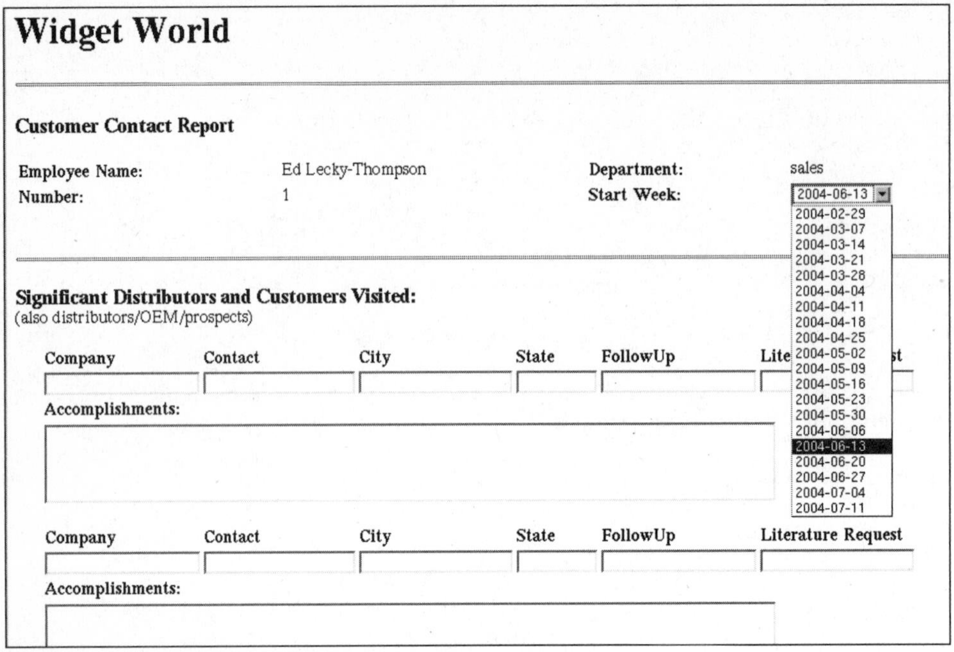

Widget World

Customer Contact Report

Employee Name:	Ed Lecky-Thompson	Department:	sales
Number:	1	Start Week:	2004-06-13 ▾

2004-02-29
2004-03-07
2004-03-14
2004-03-21
2004-03-28
2004-04-04
2004-04-11
2004-04-18
2004-04-25
2004-05-02
2004-05-09
2004-05-16
2004-05-23
2004-05-30
2004-06-06
2004-06-13
2004-06-20
2004-06-27
2004-07-04
2004-07-11

Significant Distributors and Customers Visited:
(also distributors/OEM/prospects)

Company	Contact	City	State	FollowUp	Lite[...]st

Accomplishments:

Company	Contact	City	State	FollowUp	Literature Request

Accomplishments:

Figure 19-6: Drop-down list in the Customer Contact Report

Now, with two stories under your belt, you can take a decadent 10-minute break before heading off to get Wendy, Wade, Edwina, and Harold using the application. You'll need the rest.

Re-estimating

The good news is that Wendy, Wade, Harold, and Edwina love the application; but they are only human, and they have brought up some quite reasonable requests:

❑ Include a Logout button.

❑ Don't allow access to `customer-contacts.php` without first logging in.

❑ Changing the week should bring up a previously saved week.

❑ In the Customer Contact screen, also track the following: number of shop calls, number of engineer calls, number of distributor calls, approximate mileage, territory worked, and territory comments on a *per week* basis.

❑ The number of contacts may occasionally change. Can that be configurable?

Doing some quick estimates, you figure the new tasks as follows:

❑ Include a Logout button: *1/2 point*

❑ Don't allow access to `customer-contacts.php` without first logging in: (bug) *1/2 point*

- ❑ Changing the week should bring up a previously saved week: *1 point*

- ❑ In the Customer Contact screen, also track number of shop calls, number of engineer calls, number of distributor calls, approximate mileage, territory worked, and territory comments on a *per week* basis: *1 point*

- ❑ Configure the number of contacts, which may occasionally change: *1/2 point*

The original plan was as follows:

- ❑ Story 9: Authentication and Authorization, *4 points* (done)

- ❑ Story 1: Customer Contact Report, *3 points* (mostly done)

- ❑ Story 6: Sales Manager Notification, *3 points*

- ❑ Story 8: Mail Room Notification, *2 points*

Considering that the half-pointers don't really count but the new ones do, you discuss it with your clients and determine that they'd prefer it in this order:

- ❑ Story 9: Authentication and Authorization, *4 points* (done)

- ❑ Story 1: Customer Contact Report, *3 points* (mostly done)

- ❑ Story 14: Changing the week recalls a previous week: (new)

- ❑ Story 15: Per-week items on the customer contact report: (new)

They'd also prefer to get the spreadsheet in the next iteration before requiring the notifications, so these can be dropped for now:

- ❑ Story 6: Sales Manager Notification, *3 points*

- ❑ Story 8: Mail Room Notification, *2 points*

Back to work.

Cleaning Up

Before taking off and completing your new stories, consider the state of your current corps of code. Yes, some bits are a bit ugly, but it's completely functional. Some bits are obviously copied and pasted from other places, but it works. It does, however, include a great testing suite.

Don't kick yourself for a few warts on a fully tested, working product. It happens, and it's called *code debt*. Just as in real life, when you're in a hurry or circumstances require, you can go beyond your means monetarily by going into debt.

Now that you have a bit of time to clean things up, it's time to work off the debt. It's easy, although it's best if you follow good development guidelines as you code in order to be as productive as you can without going into debt.

To what is this referring? Take a look at your current working files:

```
index.php
customer-contacts.php
contact.phpm
test.contact.php
widgetsession.phpm
test.widgetsession.php
templates/customer-contacts.tpl
templates/footer.tpl
templates/header.tpl
templates/login.tpl
templates/main.tpl
templates/thankyou.tpl
```

Now ask yourself the following: Are all these files required in the root directory? What if you keep only client "landing points" in there?

Follow that lead and get rid of those PHP-module (.phpm) files and tests. These are certainly things that a regular Web browser shouldn't accidentally land on. Move them into the following hierarchy:

```
index.php
customer-contacts.php
lib/contact.phpm
lib/test.contact.php
lib/widgetsession.phpm
lib/test.widgetsession.php
templates/customer-contacts.tpl
templates/footer.tpl
templates/header.tpl
templates/login.tpl
templates/main.tpl
templates/thankyou.tpl
```

This is now much better because your root directory has only two files, and they're both landed upon by the Web browser. You also might consider moving your testing files (test.*) into another separate directory. However, creating a directory doesn't pay off if it contains only one or two files; do it when you have at least four testing files to drop in.

After you've moved the files, go through them and ensure that you update your includes and requires, and ensure that your tests continue to run. Cleaning house is slightly less fun, but you end up with the same nice feeling afterward.

Refactoring Code

Keep some basic tasks in mind when developing your code:

- ❑ Keep it simple.

- ❑ Don't create things you won't use.

- ❑ Remove duplication (an idea also known as *once and only once*).

- ❑ Remove unused functionality, including classes and functions.

The last item is especially difficult to attain because writing code is hard, so why throw away "good work"? For the same reason that you prune your plants: Getting rid of the dead wood leads to a healthier overall system.

Besides, your code *is* in a source code repository, right? Use CVS, Subversion, SourceSafe, or whatever you have at hand, but put all your files into your source code repository.

Just keep the coding guidelines in mind when knocking out your simple half-point tasks (such as the Logout button) because the `footer.tpl` is used everywhere:

```
<br><br>
<a href="index.php?action=logout">Logout</a><br>
<hr>
For Widget World use only - testing environment.
</body>
</html>
```

Now, before you modify the index, look at the copy-and-paste at the top of `customer-contacts.php` and `index.php`. Both of those files start with the following:

```
require_once ("Smarty.class.php"); require_once ("widgetsession.phpm");
$session = new WidgetSession(array ('phptype'  => "pgsql",
                                    'hostspec' => "localhost",
                                    'database' => "widgetworld",
                                    'username' => "wuser",
                                    'password' => "foobar"));
$session->Impress();
$smarty = new Smarty;
```

It violates the "once and only once" rule, so remove it — just cut it out and put it in another file. For now, put it in `lib/common.php`.

In addition, you really shouldn't have logins and passwords in your Web space, so pull the content out and put it another file that is accessible by PHP, but well outside the Web root where Apache can serve it up to the curious and/or malicious.

Remember that because we're dealing with settings (per request), add a setting for the maximum weekly contacts. All this should be placed in a new file `../../../../settings.php`, located inconveniently outside of the Web root so that someone cannot use your own Web server to read the configuration file and consequently gain access to your database:

```
<?php
/*
 * database setup
 */
$GLOBALS["db-type"]     = "pgsql";
$GLOBALS["db-hostname"] = "localhost";
$GLOBALS["db-username"] = "wuser";
$GLOBALS["db-password"] = "foobar";
$GLOBALS["db-name"]     = "widgetworld";
/*
```

```
 * 3rd party environment
 */
$GLOBALS["smarty-path"] = "/usr/lib/php/smarty/";
/*
 * system settings
 */
$GLOBALS["max-weekly-contacts"] = 5;
?>
```

Your `lib/common.php` file should contain the following:

```
<?php
require_once ("../../../../settings.php");
require_once ("./lib/widgetsession.phpm");
require_once ($GLOBALS["smarty-path"].'Smarty.class.php'); $smarty = new Smarty;
$session = new WidgetSession(array ('phptype'  => $GLOBALS["db-type"],
                                    'hostspec' => $GLOBALS["db-hostname"],
                                    'database' => $GLOBALS["db-name"],
                                    'username' => $GLOBALS["db-username"],
                                    'password' => $GLOBALS["db-password"]));
$session->Impress();
?>
```

While you're at it, you might as well require a login for every page other than `index.php`, which is currently the only page utilizing the login feature. Append this to your `common.php`:

```
/*
 * require login
 */
$scriptname = end(explode("/", $_SERVER["REQUEST_URI"]));
if ($scriptname <> "index.php") {
    if ($session->isLoggedIn() == false) {
        Header ("Location: index.php");
    }
}
```

Now turn your attention to `index.php`, which, after you've added the logic to handle the logout, looks like this (yes, it handles *all* cases):

```
<?php
require_once ("lib/common.php");
if (array_key_exists("action", $_REQUEST)) {
    switch ($_REQUEST["action"]) {
        case "login":
            $session->login($_REQUEST["login_name"],$_REQUEST["login_pass"]);
            if ($session->isLoggedIn()) {
                $smarty->assign_by_ref("user", $session->getUserObject());
                $smarty->display ("main.tpl");
                exit;
            } else {
                $smarty->assign('error', "Invalid login, try again.");
```

```
                    $smarty->display ("login.tpl");
                    exit;
                }
            break;
        case "logout":
            $session->logout();
            $smarty->display ("login.tpl");
            exit;
            break;
        default:
            $smarty->display ("login.tpl");
            exit;
    }
} else {
    if ($session->isLoggedIn() == true) {
        $smarty->assign_by_ref("user", $session->getUserObject());
        $smarty->display ("main.tpl");
        exit;
    }
}
$smarty->display ("login.tpl");
?>
```

When you're trying to log in, you either succeed and go to main.tpl, or fail and go back to the login.tpl. When logging out, you want to log out and go to login.tpl. If there is no action assigned, then you check the login status with $session->isLoggedIn(). Finally, the last line displays login.tpl, even though it's a logical impossibility (currently) for your code to ever reach that point in execution. It may be in the future, however, so it's wise to use this as a "catch-all" in case you ever slip up.

Even though the preceding code technically works, something just isn't quite right about it. The code needs to determine which screen to display, but it is dependent on both the login status and the request variables that represent state. The code ends up looking too verbose, so you should take a few minutes to see what can be done to make it a bit more readable — in other words, it's time to *refactor*.

Refactoring is an ongoing process that may at first seem to be a subjective process, but you'll still objectively end up with a better-looking code base because of it. There is a technique for refactoring out similarities by creating similarities. It seems a little weird at first, but if your code smells as though it is a candidate for the removal of duplication (also known as a *"Once and Only Once" refactoring*), then this technique is probably worth looking into.

Examine the code and consider how you can logically create similarities with what is already there. For example, the following continues to be perfectly legal PHP — it passes the tests and continues to work on the browser side:

```
<?php
require_once ("lib/common.php");
if (array_key_exists("action", $_REQUEST)) {
    switch ($_REQUEST["action"]) {
        case "login":
$session->login($_REQUEST["login_name"],$_REQUEST["login_pass"]);
if ($session->isLoggedIn()) {
```

```php
$smarty->assign_by_ref("user", $session->getUserObject());
                $smarty->display ("main.tpl");
                exit;
            } else {
                if (array_key_exists("login_name", $_REQUEST)) {
                    $smarty->assign('error', "Invalid login, try again.");
                }
                $smarty->display ("login.tpl");
                exit;
            }
            break;
        case "logout":
            $session->logout();
            if ($session->isLoggedIn()) {
                $smarty->assign_by_ref("user", $session->getUserObject());
                $smarty->display ("main.tpl");
                exit;
            } else {
                if (array_key_exists("login_name", $_REQUEST)) {
                    $smarty->assign('error', "Invalid login, try again.");
                }
                $smarty->display ("login.tpl");
                exit;
            }
            exit;
            break;
        default:
            if ($session->isLoggedIn()) {
                $smarty->assign_by_ref("user", $session->getUserObject());
                $smarty->display ("main.tpl");
                exit;
            } else {
                if (array_key_exists("login_name", $_REQUEST)) {
                    $smarty->assign('error', "Invalid login, try again.");
                }
$smarty->display ("login.tpl");

                exit;

            }
            exit;
    }
} else {
    if ($session->isLoggedIn()) {
        $smarty->assign_by_ref("user", $session->getUserObject());
        $smarty->display ("main.tpl");
        exit;
    } else {
        if (array_key_exists("login_name", $_REQUEST)) {
            $smarty->assign('error', "Invalid login, try again.");
        }
```

```
        $smarty->display ("login.tpl");
        exit;
    }
}
$smarty->display ("login.tpl");
?>
```

What you just did was intentionally create similarities by adding the highlighted conditional within your current logical structure. It's copy-and-paste programming at its worst, but for a good reason.

Next, copy the similarities verbatim and create a function passing in any local state that is required. This particular refactoring is called "Extract Method," and is described by Martin Fowler in *Refactoring* (Addison-Wesley, 1999):

```
function displaySmartyPage (&$smarty, {&$session, $pageToDisplay) {
    if ($session->isLoggedIn()) {
        $smarty->assign_by_ref("user", $session->getUserObject());
        $smarty->display ($pageToDisplay);
        exit;
    } else {
        if (array_key_exists("login_name", $_REQUEST)) {
            $smarty->assign('error', "Invalid login, try again.");
        }
        $smarty->display ("login.tpl");
        exit;
    } }
```

With the new function `displaySmartyPage()` at your disposal, what remains with `index.php` is the following:

```
if (array_key_exists("action", $_REQUEST)) {
    switch ($_REQUEST["action"]) {
        case "login":
            $session->login($_REQUEST["login_name"],$_REQUEST["login_pass"]);

            displaySmartyPage ($smarty, $session, "main.tpl");
            break;

        case "logout":
            $session->logout();

            displaySmartyPage ($smarty, $session, "main.tpl");
            break;
        default:

            displaySmartyPage ($smarty, $session, "main.tpl");
    }
} else {

    displaySmartyPage ($smarty, $session, "main.tpl");
}

displaySmartyPage ($smarty, $session, "main.tpl");
```

Now that the code is clearer to read, it's obvious that your logic can be refactored to the following:

```php
if (array_key_exists("action", $_REQUEST)) {
    switch ($_REQUEST["action"]) {
        case "login":
            $session->login($_REQUEST["login_name"],$_REQUEST["login_pass"]);
            break;
        case "logout":
            $session->logout();
            break;
    }
}
displaySmartyPage ($smarty, $session, "main.tpl");
```

Because the displaySmartyPage() function is being called only once, you probably can now see why you refactored out the code into the displaySmartyPage() function.

Now that the displaySmartyPage() function code is unnecessary, you reverse your previous refactoring of "Extract Method" and refactor it back using the "Inline Method" technique (also described in Martin Fowler's *Refactoring*). It's exactly the opposite:

```php
<?php
require_once ("lib/common.php");
if (array_key_exists("action", $_REQUEST)) {
    switch ($_REQUEST["action"]) {
        case "login":
            $session->login($_REQUEST["login_name"],$_REQUEST["login_pass"]);
            break;
        case "logout":
            $session->logout();
            break;
    }
}
if ($session->isLoggedIn()) {
    $smarty->assign_by_ref("user", $session->getUserObject());

$smarty->display ("main.tpl");
} else {
    if (array_key_exists("login_name", $_REQUEST)) {
        $smarty->assign('error', "Invalid login, try again.");
    }
    $smarty->display ("login.tpl");
}
?>
```

With just a little bit of effort, you significantly reduced the complexity, removed extraneous Smarty calls, and reduced the total line count by more than one third.

As you've seen, reducing complexity can lead to some surprising savings, and the code is easier to read and understand. Of course, you should try to stay out of code debt by exercising the "once and only once" rule. Given a choice, keep the solution simple, and don't be afraid to remove unneeded functionality.

Finishing the Iteration

Keeping in mind your newfound skills in refactoring, tackle the remaining stories with an eye toward removing duplication and making the code simpler.

Story 14: Changing the Week Recalls a Previous Week

Recalling state is not difficult because the `ContactVisit` state practically begs it. You quickly get halfway there by adding the following function to `customer-contacts.php`:

```
function gatherContactVisits ($dbh, $emp_id) {
    $result = $dbh->query ("select * from contact_visits where
                            emp_id = ".$emp_id." and week_start =
                            '".getCurrentStartWeek()."' order by seq");
    if (DB::isError($result)) {
        return array();
    }
    $visits = array();
    while ($row =& $result->fetchRow()) {
        array_push ($visits, new ContactVisit($row));
    }
    return $visits;
}
```

You should be lazy about calling the `gatherContactVisits()` function because the act of recalling `ContactVisits()` from the database might not be required each time (for example, when `ContactVisits()` are being saved).

Now, assign the contact visit data by reference to `ContactVisits` and recall it for display like so in `customer-contacts.tpl`:

```
<input name="company_name_{$smarty.section.idx.index}" size="20"
       maxlength="50" value="{$contactVisits[idx]->company_name}">
```

You have everything except for the reload if the week is changed in the drop-down. Here is a cute trick: Drop-downs don't normally cause submits to happen, but in this case you need to force it.

In order to force a submit, you create a hidden form with the `week_start` value defined in it. When the date is changed, call the JavaScript function `reload`, which, in turn, populates the `week_start` with whatever was selected. Then, "submit" it with a new action:

```
{literal}
<SCRIPT TYPE="text/javascript">
<!-
function reload () {
    window.document.forms[0].week_start.value =
                    window.document.forms[1].week_start.value // hidden form
    window.document.forms[0].submit(); // hidden form
}
```

```
// ->
</SCRIPT>
{/literal}
<h3>Customer Contact Report</h3>
<form action="customer-contacts.php" method="post">
<input type="hidden" name="action" value="reload_contact">
<input type="hidden" name="week_start" value="">
</form>
<form action="customer-contacts.php" method="post">
<table border="0" width="100%">
<tr>
<td><b>Employee Name:</b></td><td>{$user->first_name} {$user->last_name}</td>
<td><b>Department:</b></td><td>{$user->department}</td>
</tr>
<tr>
<td><b>Number:</b></td><td>{$user->id}</td>
<td><b>Start Week:</b></td><td>
<td>
   <SELECT NAME="week_start" onchange="reload()">
   {html_options values=$start_weeks output=$start_weeks
    selected=$current_start_week}
   </SELECT>
</td>
</tr>
</table>
<br><br><hr>
```

Story 15: Per-Week Items on the Customer Contact Report

The elements of concern are number of shop calls, number of engineer calls, number of distributor calls, approximate mileage, territory worked, and territory comments. All these occur on a per-week basis.

Realize that you're looking at a many-to-one ratio of contact visits to the new structure, Contact:

```
CREATE TABLE contact (
   emp_id integer NOT NULL default '0',
   week_start date NOT NULL,
   shop_calls integer default NULL,
   distributor_calls integer default NULL,
   engineer_calls integer default NULL,
   mileage decimal(9,2) default NULL,
   territory_worked varchar(60) default NULL,
   territory_comments text
);
CREATE UNIQUE INDEX co_pk on contact (emp_id,week_start);
CREATE INDEX co_emp_id ON contact (emp_id);
CREATE INDEX co_week_start ON contact (week_start);
```

Not a problem, because `Contact` is used in much the same way as `ContactVisits`. Create a test for contact persistence:

```
function testContactPersistence() {
    $this->_session->getDatabaseHandle()->query("delete FROM contact WHERE
        emp_id = 1 and week_start = '1980-01-01'"); // remove multiples
    $c = new Contact (
        array ("emp_id"             => "1",
                "week_start"        => "1980-01-01",
                "shop_calls"        => 2,
                "distributor_calls" => 3,
                "engineer_calls"    => 4,
                "mileage"           => 50,
                "territory_worked"  => "Central Ohio",
                "territory_comments" => "Buckeyes are great. " ),
        $this->_session->getDatabaseHandle());
    $result = $this->_session->getDatabaseHandle()->query("select * FROM
            contact WHERE emp_id = 1 and week_start = '1980-01-01'");
    $this->assertEquals(0, $result->numRows());
    $c->persist();
    $result = $this->_session->getDatabaseHandle()->query("select * FROM
            contact WHERE emp_id = 1 and week_start = '1980-01-01'");
    $this->assertEquals(1, $result->numRows());        }
```

`Contact` also shares the same scope as `ContactVisits`. This is a big hint, because the two classes do pretty much the same thing and share the same scope. They're typically an easy refactoring target. Looking deeper into the classes, you see that your hunch is correct, and that the new `Contact` class, and the existing `ContactVisit` and `WidgetUser` classes, contain common functionality.

As you may recall from earlier, the footprint of `ContactVisit` and `WidgetUser` is as follows:

```
class ContactVisit {
    protected $contentBase = array();
    protected $dbh = null; // database handle
    function __get ($key) {}
    function __construct ($results, $dbh = null) {}
    private function isEmpty($key) {}
    public function isValid() {}
    private function implodeQuoted () {}
    private function generateSqlInsert ($tableName, &$metas, &$values) {}
    public function persist() {}
}

class WidgetUser {

    protected $contentBase = array();

    protected $dispatchFunctions = array ("role" => "getrole");
    function __construct($initdict) {}

    function __get ($key) {}
```

```
    function __set ($key, $value) {}
    public function getRole() {}
    public function isSalesPerson()  {}
    public function isSalesManager() {}
    public function isAccountant()   {}
}
```

This is a great use of "Extract Class" (see *Refactoring*) refactoring in order to consolidate the code. The consolidation moves a lot of persistence functionality up into a new class called `PersistableObject`:

```
class PersistableObject {
    protected $contentBase = array();
    protected $dbh = null; // database handle
    protected $dispatchFunctions = array ("role" => "getrole");

    function __get ($key) {
        // dispatch by function first
        if (array_key_exists ($key, $this->dispatchFunctions)) {
            $funcname = $this->dispatchFunctions[$key];
            return $this->$funcname();
        }
        // then state
        if (array_key_exists ($key, $this->contentBase)) {
            return $this->contentBase[$key];
        }
        // then self
        return $this->$key;
    }
    function __construct ($results, $dbh = null) {
        $this->dbh = $dbh;
        if ($results <> null) {
            $this->contentBase = $results; // copy
        }
    }
    public function implodeQuoted (&$values, $delimiter) {
        $sql = "";
        $flagIsFirst = true;
        foreach ($values as $value) {
            if ($flagIsFirst) {
                $flagIsFirst = false;
            } else {
                $sql .= $delimiter;
            }
            if (gettype ($value) == "string") {
                $sql .= "'".$value."'";
            } else {
                $sql .= $value;
            }
        }
```

```
        }
        return $sql;
    }
    public function generateSqlInsert ($tableName, {&$metas, &$values) {
        return " insert into ".$tableName.
            "         ( ".implode              ($metas, ", ").") ".
            " values ( ".$this->implodeQuoted ($values, ", ").") ";
    }
    public function generateSqlUpdate ($tableName, {&$metas, &$values) {
        $sql = " update ".$tableName." set ";
        for ($i=0; $i<count($metas); $i++) {
            $sql .= $metas[$i]." = ".$vaules[$i].", ";
        }
        return $sql;
    }
    public function generateSqlDelete ($tableName) {
        return " delete from \"".$tableName."\" where ".$this->getSqlWhere();
    }
    // note: should be implemented by concrete classes
    public function getSqlWhere() {

        return "";
    }
    public function isValid() {
        return true;
    }
    public function persistWork ($tablename, $meta) {
        if ($this->isValid() == false) return false;
        $values = array();
        foreach ($meta as $mvalue) {
            array_push ($values, $this->$mvalue);
        }
        if (strlen($this->getSqlWhere()) > 0) {
            $sql = $this->generateSqlDelete ($tablename);
            $this->dbh->query($sql);
        }
        $sql = $this->generateSqlInsert ($tablename, $meta, $values);
        if (DB::isError ($this->dbh->query($sql))) return false;
        return true;
    } }
```

You may have noticed that the addition of generateSqlUpdate and generateSqlDelete enables PersistableObject to respectively update and delete itself in the database. Of course, both of these functions require a SQL WHERE clause so that not every record in the table is updated or deleted. This is why child classes (such as ContactVisit) have the responsibility of defining what makes them unique; they do this by implementing the getSqlWhere function.

Moving the persistence functions (implodeQuoted, generateSqlInsert, isValid, persistWork) and persistence state (contentBase, dispatchFunctions) into PersistableObject enables Contact, ContactVisit, and WidgetUser to be implemented in a much shorter form:

```php
class Contact extends PersistableObject {
    function __construct ($results, $dbh = null) {
        parent::__construct ($results, $dbh);
    }

    public function persist() {
        return $this->persistWork ("contact",
                        array ( "emp_id",
                                "week_start",
                                "shop_calls",
                                "distributor_calls",
                                "engineer_calls",
                                "mileage",
                                "territory_worked",
                                "territory_comments"));
    }

    public function getSqlWhere() {
        return " emp_id = ".$this->emp_id." and
        week_start = '".$this->week_start."'";
    }
}

class ContactVisit extends PersistableObject {

    function __construct ($results, $dbh = null) {
        parent::__construct ($results, $dbh);
        static $sequence = 0;
        $sequence = $sequence + 1; // increment across class
        $this->contentBase["seq"] = $sequence;
    }

    private function isEmpty($key) {
        if (array_key_exists($key, $this->contentBase) == false) return true;
        if ($this->contentBase[$key] == null) return true;
        if ($this->contentBase[$key] == "") return true;
        return false;
    }
    public function isValid() {
        if ($this->isEmpty("emp_id") == true) return false;
        if ($this->isEmpty("week_start") == true) return false;
        if ($this->isEmpty("company_name") == true) return false;
        return true;
    }

    public function persist() {
        return $this->persistWork ("contact_visits",
                        array ( "emp_id",
                                "week_start",
                                "seq",
```

```
                                        "company_name",
                                        "contact_name",
                                        "city",
                                        "state",
                                        "accomplishments",
                                        "followup",
                                        "literature_request" ));
        }

    }
    class WidgetUser extends PersistableObject {
        function __construct($initdict) {
            parent::__construct ($initdict);
            $this->dispatchFunctions = array ("role" => "getrole");
            $this->contentBase = $initdict; // copy
        }
        public function getRole() {
            switch ($this->contentBase["role"]) {
                case "s": return ("Sales Person");
                case "m": return ("Sales Manager");
                case "a": return ("Accountant");
                default: return ("");
            }
        }
        public function isSalesPerson() {
            if ($this->contentBase["role"] == "s") return true;
            return false;
        }
        public function isSalesManager() {
            if ($this->contentBase["role"] == "m") return true;
            return false;
        }
        public function isAccountant() {
            if ($this->contentBase["role"] == "a") return true;
            return false;
        }
    }
```

Boy, it sure is great to have all those unit tests to indicate when something goes wrong. One obstacle you'll face is deciding how your target classes are used and how they differ from one another. For example, Contact and ContactVisit are subtly different in that you persist only valid ContactVisits, but there is always a possibly empty (but still instantiated) Contact.

In addition, notice that Contact implements the getSqlWhere function so that it can be deleted and updated. However, remember that ContactVisit is deleted before insertions take place, and WidgetUser is only persisted to the database, thus not requiring it to implement the getSqlWhere function.

However, the differences between Contact and ContactVisits have less to do with the classes themselves than with the business rules and the environment in which they exist. Therefore, even though your classes are starting to consolidate and share code, their respective unit tests should continue to test individual class diversity.

Now `customer-contacts.tpl` needs a new section in order to display the new `Contact` information:

```
<table border="0">
<tr>
<td>Number of Shop Calls:</td>
<td><input name="shop_calls" size="7" maxlength="17"
    value="{$contact->shop_calls}"></td>
<td width="20"></td>
<td>Number of Engineer Calls:</td>
<td><input name="engineer_calls" size="7" maxlength="17"
    value="{$contact->engineer_calls}">
</td>
</tr>
<tr>
<td>Number of Distributor Calls:</td>
<td><input name="distributor_calls" size="7" maxlength="17"
        value="{$contact->distributor_calls}"></td>
<td width="20"></td>
<td>Approximate Mileage:</td>
<td><input name="mileage" size="7" maxlength="17"
        value="{$contact->mileage}"></td>
</tr>
<tr>
<td>Territory Worked:</td>
<td colspan="2"><input name="territory_worked"
        value="{$contact->territory_worked}"></td>
</tr>
<tr>
<td colspan="7">
   Territory Comments:<br>
   <TEXTAREA NAME="territory_comments" ROWS=4 COLS=95>
   {$contact->territory_comments}
   </TEXTAREA>
</td>
</tr>
</table>
```

Add these new support functions to `customer-contacts.php` in order to read and save the `Contact` information:

```
function persistContact (&$dbh, $emp_id) {
    $c = new Contact (
        array ("emp_id"              => $emp_id,
               "week_start"          => getCurrentStartWeek(),
               "shop_calls"          => $_REQUEST["shop_calls"],
               "distributor_calls"   => $_REQUEST["distributor_calls"],
               "engineer_calls"      => $_REQUEST["engineer_calls"],
               "mileage"             => $_REQUEST["mileage"],
               "territory_worked"    => $_REQUEST["territory_worked"],
               "territory_comments"  => $_REQUEST["territory_comments"]),
        $dbh);
    $c->persist();
}
function gatherContact (&$dbh, $emp_id) {
```

```
        $result = $dbh->query ("select * from contact where
                emp_id = ".$emp_id." and week_start =
                '".getCurrentStartWeek()."'");
        if (DB::isError($result)) return array();
        return new Contact ($result->fetchRow());
}
$user = $session->getUserObject();
// display
if ($_REQUEST["action"] != "persist_contact") {
    $smarty->assign_by_ref ("user", $user);
    $smarty->assign_by_ref ("contact", gatherContact(
        $session->getDatabaseHandle(), $user->id));
    $smarty->assign_by_ref ("contactVisits", gatherContactVisits(
        $session->getDatabaseHandle(), $user->id));
    $smarty->assign('start_weeks', getStartWeeks());
    $smarty->assign('current_start_week', getCurrentStartWeek());
    $smarty->assign("max_weekly_contacts", $GLOBALS["max-weekly-contacts"]);
    $smarty->display('customer-contacts.tpl');
    exit;
}
// persist contact visits
require_once ("lib/contact.phpm");
persistContact ($session->getDatabaseHandle(), $user->id);
persistContactVisits ($session->getDatabaseHandle(), $user->id);
```

Figure 19-7 shows the results of your hard work.

Widget World

Customer Contact Report

Employee Name:	Ed Lecky-Thompson	Department:	sales
Number:	1	Start Week:	2004-06-13 ▾

Significant Distributors and Customers Visited:
(also distributors/OEM/prospects)

Company	Contact	City	State	FollowUp	Literature Request
c	c	c	c	c	c

Accomplishments:

```
c
```

Number of Shop Calls:	1	Number of Engineer Calls:	2
Number of Distributor Calls:	3	Approximate Mileage:	4.00
Territory Worked:	50		

Territory Comments:

```
six
```

Figure 19-7: Adding per-week items to the Customer Contact Report

The speed at which the last story was accomplished indicates that if you keep your code base clean by not going into code debt, your forward momentum will not necessarily fall by the wayside.

Strive for refactoring, which in a way is never complete. Some sections could still have a critical eye applied to them, notably those with striking similarities to the support functions for `Contact` and `ContactVisits`. That the support functions exist at all (as opposed to having the objects take care of everything themselves) is an indication of just how much greater consolidation can often be achieved through the use of shared scope.

Regardless, that is still something that could go in a different direction, and you have to remember that in order for a particular refactoring to be successful, the resulting code should be easier to read and understand. If you find yourself spending more time writing excessive support plumbing or a framework, then take that as an indication that maybe you should stop for a moment. Although large refactorings are sometimes needed, they should definitely be the exception.

Travel Expense Report

The outstanding road map that you have now is as follows:

- ❏ Travel Expense Report
    - ❏ Story 2: Travel Expense Report, *7 points*
    - ❏ Story 3: Expense Report Comments, *2 points*
    - ❏ Story 10: Persisted Expense Report Cash Advance, *2 points*
    - ❏ Story 4: Expense Report as Spreadsheet, *4 points*
- ❏ Travel Expense Services
    - ❏ Story 5: Accountant Notification, *3 points*
    - ❏ Story 7: Sales Person Notification, *1 point*
    - ❏ Story 13: Expense Report Export, *3 points*
- ❏ Outstanding stories
    - ❏ Story 6: Sales Manager Notification, *3 points*
    - ❏ Story 8: Mail Room Notification, *2 points*

By its sheer number of points, the Travel Expense Report will not be a quick knockout.

As shown previously in Figure 19-2, the Travel Expense Report is pretty slim regarding details. Time to get to work talking. From conversations with Wendy and Edwina, you learn that what they really want is something that looks more like Figure 19-8.

Employee Name:	XXXXX XXXXXXX			Department:		XXXXXX		
Number:	X			Starting Week:		YYYY-MM-DD (drop down)		
Territory Worked:	XXXXXXXXXXXX							

	Sun	Mon	Tue	Wed	Thr	Fri	Sat	Total
Lodging								
Lodging and Hotel	1	1	1	1	1	1	1	7
Other	1	1	1	1	1	1	1	7
Tips	1	1	1	1	1	1	1	7
Lodging Total	3	3	3	3	3	3	3	21
Meals								
Breakfast	1	1	1	1	1	1	1	7
Lunch & Snacks	1	1	1	1	1	1	1	7
Dinner	1	1	1	1	1	1	1	7
Tips	1	1	1	1	1	1	1	7
Entertainment	1	1	1	1	1	1	1	7
Meals Total	6	6	6	6	6	6	6	42
Transportation								
Airfare	1	1	1	1	1	1	1	7
Auto Rental	1	1	1	1	1	1	1	7
Auto Maint./Gas	1	1	1	1	1	1	1	7
Tolls / Parking	1	1	1	1	1	1	1	7
Trans. Sub Total	4	4	4	4	4	4	4	28
Num miles traveled	1	1	1	1	1	1	1	7
Miles at XXX / mile	1	1	1	1	1	1	1	7
Trans. Total	6	6	6	6	6	6	6	42
Misc								
Gifts	1	1	1	1	1	1	1	7
Telephone & Fax	1	1	1	1	1	1	1	7
Supplies	1	1	1	1	1	1	1	7
Postage	1	1	1	1	1	1	1	7
Other	1	1	1	1	1	1	1	7
Misc Total	5	5	5	5	5	5	5	35

Comments:				Subtotal	147
XXXXXXXXXXXXXXXXXXXXXXXXXXXXXXXXXX				Less Cash Advance	47
XXXXXXXXXXXXXXXXXXXXXXXXXXXXXXXXXX				Due Employee	100
XXXXXXXXXXXXXXXXXXXXXXXXXXXXXXXXXX				Due Company	

Figure 19-8: Desired Travel Expense Report

Although it takes the better part of the day to order and modify the categories (Lodging, Meals, and so on), what you now have is a close approximation to the appearance of the original Widget World faxable form. Of course, now that your clients realize that things can change, they just may — because even though a certain amount of flexibility and unknowns plague just about any project, you're going to roll with the punches and not overengineer every "just in case" feature that comes to mind.

One more thing: The *XXX* in "Miles at *XXX*/mile" heading is a dollar amount based on Federal tax law. Thankfully, it is a constant, so you don't need to track it for every state/province, and you need to deal with only one country. However, the rate typically changes from year to year, so you need to record the amount at the time of submission.

The all-important cash advance also needs to be part of the calculation; and if the advance is enough, it might spill over into money owed to the company, represented by "Due Employee" and its Boolean counterpart "Due Company."

Ignoring for now the complexity, just start with the simple bits. The core of this sheet is a dollar amount associated with a date and a descriptor.

A quick scribble results in the following data item:

```
CREATE TABLE travel_expense_item (
    emp_id          integer       NOT NULL,
    expense_date    date          NOT NULL,
    description     varchar(40)   NOT NULL,
    amount          decimal(9,2)  NOT NULL );
```

Add the weekly information that needs to be captured:

```
CREATE TABLE travel_expense_week (
    emp_id            integer NOT NULL,
    week_start        date    NOT NULL,
    comments          text,
    territory_worked  varchar(60),
    cash_advance      decimal(9,2),
    mileage_rate      decimal(3,2) NOT NULL );
```

As a technical note, you still need to add defaults, indexes, and so on to the database; and on the business side, note that you're tracking the `cash_advance` and `mileage_rate`. With each travel expense submitted on a weekly basis, the weekly subtotals sections of the form can be easily calculated, so storage of the subtotals is not required.

Travel Expense Item

Let's get to work on the tests. The simple case is just validating the minimum required information, like this:

```
function testValidTravelExpenseItem() {
    $tvi = new TravelExpenseItem (
        array ('emp_id'            => "1",
               'expense_date'      => "1980-01-01",
               'description'       => "one",
               'amount'            => "1.0" ));
    $this->assertEquals(true, $tvi->isValid(), "valid expense");
}
    function testInvalidTravelExpenseItem() {
    $tvi = new TravelExpenseItem (
        array ('emp_id'            => "1",
'expense_date' => "", // date required
               'description'       => "one",
               'amount'            => "1.0" ));
    $this->assertEquals(false, $tvi->isValid(), "valid expense");
}
```

What else does it need to do? If given an array, it can populate itself, so the travel expense item needs to persist itself accordingly. Add another test to the travel expense item:

```
function testTravelExpenseItemPersistence() {
    $this->_session->getDatabaseHandle()->query("delete FROM
            travel_expense_item WHERE emp_id = 1 and expense_date
            = '1980-01-01'"); // remove multiples
    $tvi = new TravelExpenseItem (
        array ('emp_id'      => "1",
               'expense_date' => "1980-01-01",
               'description'  => "one",
               'amount'       => "1.0" ),
        $this->_session->getDatabaseHandle());
    $result = $this->_session->getDatabaseHandle()->query("select * FROM
            travel_expense_item WHERE emp_id = 1 and
            expense_date = '1980-01-01'");
    $this->assertEquals(0, $result->numRows());
    $tvi->persist();
```

```
$result = $this->_session->getDatabaseHandle()->query("select * FROM
         travel_expense_item WHERE emp_id = 1 and
         expense_date = '1980-01-01'");
$this->assertEquals(1, $result->numRows());          }
```

Remember to connect to your testing database when running these tests. The last thing you want is to accidentally torch production data with an errant DELETE statement.

Stub out your travel expense item in the new file, lib/expense.phpm:

```
class TravelExpenseItem {
    public function isValid() { }

    public function persist() { }
}
```

Ensure that the tests run (and fail), and then get to work satisfying them.

Using ContactVisit as a template, it's surprisingly easy:

```
class TravelExpenseItem extends PersistableObject {
    function __construct ($results, $dbh = null) {
        parent::__construct ($results, $dbh);
    }
    private function isEmpty($key) {
        if (array_key_exists($key, $this->contentBase) == false) return true;
        if ($this->contentBase[$key] == null) return true;
        if ($this->contentBase[$key] == "") return true;
        return false;
    }

    public function isValid() {
        if ($this->isEmpty("emp_id") == true) return false;
        if ($this->isEmpty("expense_date") == true) return false;
        if ($this->isEmpty("description") == true) return false;
        if ($this->isEmpty("amount") == true) return false;
        return true;
    }

    public function persist() {
        return $this->persistWork (
            "travel_expense_item",
            array ( "emp_id",
                    "expense_date",
                    "description",
                    "amount" ));
    }

    public function getSqlWhere() {
        return " emp_id = ".$this->emp_id." and expense_date =
        '".$this->expense_date."' and description =
        '".$this->description."'";
    }
}
```

Recall the definition of `ContactVisit`:

```
class ContactVisit extends PersistableObject {
    function __construct ($results, $dbh = null) {}
    private function isEmpty($key) {}
    public function isValid() {}
    public function persist() {}
}
```

Of course, the function `isEmpty()` is now redundant between the two classes, which share a common parent. What does that say to you? It screams "move `IsEmpty()` up into `PersistableObject`"! Don't forget to make `isEmpty()` protected; otherwise, subclasses can't call it.

When you're finished with that, ensure that the `ContactVisit` test continues to pass. The respective classes should now look like this:

```
class PersistableObject {
    protected $contentBase = array();
    protected $dbh = null; // database handle
    protected $dispatchFunctions = array ("role" => "getrole");
    function __get ($key) {}
    function __construct ($results, $dbh = null) {}
    public function implodeQuoted (&$values, $delimiter) {}
    public function generateSqlInsert ($tableName, {&$metas, &$values) {}
    public function generateSqlUpdate ($tableName, {&$metas, &$values) {}
    public function generateSqlDelete ($tableName) {}
    public function getSqlWhere() {}
    public function isValid() {}
    protected function isEmpty($key) {}
    public function persistWork ($tablename, $meta) {} }
class ContactVisit extends PersistableObject {
    function __construct ($results, $dbh = null) {}
    public function isValid() {}
    public function persist() {}
}
class TravelExpenseItem extends PersistableObject {
    function __construct ($results, $dbh = null) {}
    public function isValid() {}
    public function persist() {}
    public function getSqlWhere() {}
}
```

Now go eat a cookie before taking on the Travel Expense Week class.

Travel Expense Week

By now, you can easily knock out the simple test cases for travel expense week. Save these additional methods into `test.widgetsession.php`:

```
function testValidTravelExpenseWeek() {
    $tvi = new TravelExpenseWeek (
        array ('emp_id'        => "1",
               'week_start'    => "1980-01-01",
               'comments'      => "comment",
```

```
                    'mileage_rate'      => "0.31",
                    'territory_worked' => "Midwest" ));
        $this->assertEquals(true, $tvi->isValid(), "valid expense");
}

function testInvalidTravelExpenseWeek() {
    $tvi = new TravelExpenseWeek (
        array ('emp_id'          => "1",
                'week_start'       => "", // date required
                'comments'         => "comment",
                'mileage_rate'     => "0.31",
                'territory_worked' => "Midwest" ));
        $this->assertEquals(false, $tvi->isValid(), "valid expense");
}

function testTravelExpenseWeekPersistence() {
    $this->_session->getDatabaseHandle()->query("delete FROM
            travel_expense_week WHERE emp_id = 1 and week_start
            = '1980-01-01'"); // remove multiples
    $tvi = new TravelExpenseWeek (
        array ('emp_id'          => "1",
                'week_start'       => "1980-01-01",
                'comments' => "comment",
                'territory_worked' => "Midwest",
                'mileage_rate'     => "0.31",
                'cash_advance'     => "0"),
        $this->_session->getDatabaseHandle());
    $result = $this->_session->getDatabaseHandle()->query("select *
            FROM travel_expense_week WHERE emp_id = 1 and
            week_start = '1980-01-01'");
    $this->assertEquals(0, $result->numRows(), "pre check");
    $tvi->persist();
    $result = $this->_session->getDatabaseHandle()->query("select *
            FROM travel_expense_week WHERE emp_id = 1 and
            week_start = '1980-01-01'");
    $this->assertEquals(1, $result->numRows(), "persist");        }
```

In addition, consider the fact that something must be in charge of the life cycle of all your TravelExpenseItems. TravelExpenseWeek? TraveExpenseItem? Does one of those two options sound as though it would make a good container?

An (extremely explicit) test of TravelExpenseWeek as a container would look like the following:

```
function testTravelExpenseWeekContainerRead() {
    // clear out the test database
    $this->_session->getDatabaseHandle()->query("delete FROM
                travel_expense_item WHERE emp_id = 1 and
                expense_date >= '1980-01-06' and expense_date
                <= '2001-09-15'");
    $dbh = $this->_session->getDatabaseHandle();
    // monday
    $item1 = new TravelExpenseItem (
```

```
            array ('emp_id' => "1", 'expense_date' => "1980-01-06",
                'description' => "lodging_and_hotel", 'amount' => "1.1"),
            $dbh);


    $item2 = new TravelExpenseItem (
        array ('emp_id' => "1", 'expense_date' => "1980-01-06",
                'description' => "meals_breakfast", 'amount' => "2.2" ),
            $dbh);
    $item3 = new TravelExpenseItem (
        array ('emp_id' => "1", 'expense_date' => "1980-01-06",
                'description' => "misc_supplies", 'amount' => "3.3" ),
            $dbh);
    // tuesday
    $item4 = new TravelExpenseItem (
        array ('emp_id' => "1", 'expense_date' => "2001-09-10",
                'description' => "lodging_and_hotel", 'amount' => "4.4" ),
            $dbh);
    $item5 = new TravelExpenseItem (
        array ('emp_id' => "1", 'expense_date' => "2001-09-10",
                'description' => "meals_breakfast", 'amount' => "5.5" ),
            $dbh);
    $item6 = new TravelExpenseItem (
        array ('emp_id' => "1", 'expense_date' => "2001-09-10",
                'description' => "misc_supplies", 'amount' => "6.6" ),
            $dbh);
    // wednesday
    $item7 = new TravelExpenseItem (
        array ('emp_id' => "1", 'expense_date' => "1980-01-01",
                'description' => "lodging_and_hotel", 'amount' => "7.7" ),
            $dbh);
    $item8 = new TravelExpenseItem (
        array ('emp_id' => "1", 'expense_date' => "1980-01-01",
                'description' => "meals_breakfast", 'amount' => "8.8" ),
            $dbh);
    $item9 = new TravelExpenseItem (
        array ('emp_id' => "1", 'expense_date' => "1980-01-01",
                'description' => "misc_supplies", 'amount' => "9.9" ),

            $dbh);
```

The TravelExpenseItems populate the first three days of the week, and each represents a different type of item: meals_breakfast, misc_supplies, and lodging_and_hotel:

```
$item1->persist();
$item2->persist();
$item3->persist();
$item4->persist();
$item5->persist();
$item6->persist();
$item7->persist();
```

```
$item8->persist();
$item9->persist();
$week = new TravelExpenseWeek (
    array ('emp_id'      => "1",
           'week_start' => "1980-01-06"),
    $this->_session->getDatabaseHandle());
$week->readWeek();
// monday
$this->assertEquals(1.1, (float) $week->getExpenseAmount(0, 'lodging_and_hotel'));
$this->assertEquals(2.2, (float) $week->getExpenseAmount(0, 'meals_breakfast'));
$this->assertEquals(3.3, (float) $week->getExpenseAmount(0, 'misc_supplies'));
// tuesday
$this->assertEquals(4.4, (float) $week->getExpenseAmount(1, 'lodging_and_hotel'));
$this->assertEquals(5.5, (float) $week->getExpenseAmount(1, 'meals_breakfast'));
$this->assertEquals(6.6, (float) $week->getExpenseAmount(1, 'misc_supplies'));
// wednesday
$this->assertEquals(7.7, (float) $week->getExpenseAmount(2, 'lodging_and_hotel'));
$this->assertEquals(8.8, (float) $week->getExpenseAmount(2, 'meals_breakfast'));
$this->assertEquals(9.9, (float) $week->getExpenseAmount(2, 'misc_supplies')); }
```

After the `TravelExpenseItems` have been persisted, this test shows that the new `TravelExpenseWeek` class will be able to retrieve a week of `TraveExpenseItems`, given the employee ID and starting week.

This is an important test in other respects, because here is where you are defining the interface of your Web page. Recall that `TravelExpenseItem` is day-based, whereas the Web page is week-based, necessitating `TravelExpenseWeek`. Thus, the capability to iterate over the `TravelExpenseItems` in a weekly manner should be paramount.

Note that because `TravelExpenseWeek` knows which day is the first of the week (for Americans, Sunday), you don't need to explicitly spell out your target day. Instead, you can use an offset. Use 0 for Sunday, 1 for Monday, and so on.

The Spike

Before continuing, consider how you'll display what you need to show on the screen. Go back and eyeball Figure 19-8 again. Note that something will have to take care of the subtotaling, not to mention the order. Something must associate human names with what exists in the database.

In addition, remember that "something" ultimately stops with you, and that anything that makes your life easier can't be a bad thing. Clearly, hard-coding the HTML will be a maintenance nightmare.

To avoid a hard-coded HTML maintenance nightmare, consider using a data structure like the following, which can be used to generate what you need to display, as well as map it to your data fields:

```
array(
    array('name' => 'Lodging', 'code' => 'lodging', 'data' =>
                    array('Lodging &amp; Hotel','Other','Tips'),
     'persist' => array('lodging_and_hotel', 'lodging_other',
                    'lodging_tips')),
    array('name' => 'Meals', 'code' => 'meals', 'data' =>
                    array('Breakfast', 'Lunch &amp; Snacks',
                    'Dinner', 'Tips', 'Entertainment'),
```

```
                        'persist' => array('meals_breakfast', 'meals_lunch',
                                            'meals_dinner', 'meals_tips',
                                            'meals_entertainment')),
        array('name' => 'Transportation', 'code' => 'trans', 'data' =>
                        array('Airfare', 'Auto Rental', 'Auto Maint./Gas',
                              'Local Transportation', 'Tolls/Parking'),
                              'persist' => array ('trans_airfare',
                              'trans_auto_rental', 'trans_auto_maint', 'trans_local',
                              'trans_tolls', 'trans_miles_traveled')),
        array('name' => 'Miscellaneous', 'code' => 'misc', 'data' =>
                        array('Gifts', 'Telephone &amp; Fax', 'Supplies',
                              'Postage', 'Other'),
                              'persist' => array('misc_gifts','misc_phone',
                               'misc_supplies', 'misc_postage', 'misc_other')));
```

The first level is an array of sections, which means that each section gets a subtotal and each section contains line items.

Each section has a `data` array (simply the human-viewable description), as well as its computerized counterpart `persist` (which will presumably be the name of each item in the database). The `code` item in the associated array exists in order to automate the creation of semi-meaningful JavaScript variables that must be calculated per section (for example, one for Meals, Lodging, and Transportation). This data structure will be some of the glue that holds the HTML, JavaScript math, database, and PHP objects together; it's your road map.

More Travel Expense Week Tests

Going from PHP's Travel Expense form response to the database is an important step. This is where you'll be defining what you expect to receive from the page. Remember that you need a way to take the entire response and easily create `TravelExpenseItems` from that. Sounds like a good job for the `TravelExpenseWeek` container.

Recall that the naming convention for determining the unique values of each individual cell is `lodging_sun_0`, which represents "section" + "day" + "line item." Because there is a nearly infinite number of ways to describe the same column/row, vertical/horizontal, spreadsheet-cell relationship, this naming convention is quite adequate.

Additionally, you can easily determine which horizontal row you happen to be working with as a result of its section offset (the "0" in `lodging_sun_0`). Day and line item are different types for a reason: your sanity. Manipulating data in different dimensions is hard enough; tracking which way against which one is more difficult, and remembering what they are based on is asking for trouble. With all things being equal, there is more semantic information contained with `lodging_sun_0` than with `lodging_0_0`.

Here is the test for parsing the request:

```
function testTravelExpenseWeekContainerParseRequest() {
    $response = array ( 'lodging_sun_0' => "1.1",
                        'meals_sun_0'   => "2.2",
                        'misc_sun_2'    => "3.3",
```

```
                          'lodging_mon_0'  => "4.4",
                          'meals_mon_0'    => "5.5",
                          'misc_mon_2'     => "6.6",
                          'lodging_tue_0'  => "7.7",
                          'meals_tue_0'    => "8.8",
                          'misc_tue_2'     => "9.9" );

    $week = new TravelExpenseWeek (
                    array ('emp_id'     => "1",
                          'week_start' => "1980-01-06"));
    $week->parse($response);
    $this->assertEquals(1.1, $week->getExpenseAmount(0, 'lodging_and_hotel'));
    $this->assertEquals(2.2, $week->getExpenseAmount(0, 'meals_breakfast'));
    $this->assertEquals(3.3, $week->getExpenseAmount(0, 'misc_supplies'));
    $this->assertEquals(4.4, $week->getExpenseAmount(1, 'lodging_and_hotel'));
    $this->assertEquals(5.5, $week->getExpenseAmount(1, 'meals_breakfast'));
    $this->assertEquals(6.6, $week->getExpenseAmount(1, 'misc_supplies'));
    $this->assertEquals(7.7, $week->getExpenseAmount(2, 'lodging_and_hotel'));
    $this->assertEquals(8.8, $week->getExpenseAmount(2, 'meals_breakfast'));
    $this->assertEquals(9.9, $week->getExpenseAmount(2, 'misc_supplies')); }
```

The $response array is simulating what you'll receive from your form input, and remember that the $response values and the persist meta-values are reflected in your road-map data structure.

Create one more test for persisting the container. It is very similar to the travel expense items test:

```
function testTravelExpenseWeekContainerWrite() {
    $this->_session->getDatabaseHandle()->query("delete FROM
                    travel_expense_item WHERE emp_id = 1 and
                    expense_date >= '1980-01-06' and expense_date
                    <= '2001-09-15'");
    $response = array (
                    'lodging_sun_0'=>"1.1",'meals_sun_0'=>"2.2",'misc_sun_2'=>"3.3",
                    'lodging_mon_0'=>"4.4",'meals_mon_0'=>"5.5",'misc_mon_2'=>"6.6",
                    'lodging_tue_0'=>"7.7",'meals_tue_0'=>"8.8",'misc_tue_2'=>"9.9" );
    $week = new TravelExpenseWeek (
            array ('emp_id'           => "1",
                    'week_start'       => "1980-01-06",
                    'territory_worked' => "Midwest",
                    'comments'         => "comment",
                    'cash_advance'     => "0",
                    'mileage_rate'     => "0.31"),
                $this->_session->getDatabaseHandle());
    $week->parse($response);
    $this->assertEquals(true, $week->persist());
    $week = new TravelExpenseWeek (
            array ('emp_id'           => "1",
                    'week_start'       => "1980-01-06",
                    'territory_worked' => "Midwest",
                    'comments'         => "comment",
                    'cash_advance'     => "0",
                    'mileage_rate'     => "0.31"),
```

```
                    $this->_session->getDatabaseHandle());
            $week->readWeek();
            $this->assertEquals(1.1, (float)
                            $week->getExpenseAmount(0, 'lodging_and_hotel'));
            $this->assertEquals(2.2, (float)
                            $week->getExpenseAmount(0, 'meals_breakfast'));
            $this->assertEquals(3.3, (float)
                            $week->getExpenseAmount(0, 'misc_supplies'));
            $this->assertEquals(4.4, (float)
                            $week->getExpenseAmount(1, 'lodging_and_hotel'));
            $this->assertEquals(5.5, (float)
                            $week->getExpenseAmount(1, 'meals_breakfast'));
            $this->assertEquals(6.6, (float)
                            $week->getExpenseAmount(1, 'misc_supplies'));
            $this->assertEquals(7.7, (float)
                            $week->getExpenseAmount(2, 'lodging_and_hotel'));
            $this->assertEquals(8.8, (float)
                            $week->getExpenseAmount(2, 'meals_breakfast'));
            $this->assertEquals(9.9, (float)
                            $week->getExpenseAmount(2, 'misc_supplies')); }
```

In this test, to be added as an additional method into `test.widgetsession.php`, `TravelExpenseWeek` parses the `$response`, persists the `TravelExpenseItems` in `$week-persist()`, rereads them from the database `$week-readWeek()`, and finally validates what was read.

Note that these tests make heavy use of copy-and-paste programming. Keeping things tidy is a general rule, so if a majority of the tests require the same setup, put them in the setup but don't prematurely refactor your tests. Your tests are typically the first place where changes will get made, so they should be easy to read and modify.

Satisfying the Travel Expense Week Tests

Satisfying `TravelExpenseWeek`'s validity and persistence tests should be predictably easy by now:

```
class TravelExpenseWeek extends PersistableObject {
    public $items = array();

    function __construct ($results, $dbh = null) {
        parent::__construct ($results, $dbh);
    }

    public function isValid() {
        if ($this->isEmpty("emp_id") == true) return false;
        if ($this->isEmpty("week_start") == true) return false;
        if ($this->isEmpty("territory_worked") == true) return false;
        if ($this->isEmpty("mileage_rate") == true) return false;
        return true;
    }

    public function persist() {
        return $this->persistWork ("travel_expense_week",
                                array ( "emp_id",
```

```
                                    "week_start",
                                    "comments",
                                    "territory_worked",
                                    "cash_advance",
                                    "mileage_rate"));
    }

    public function getSqlWhere() {
    return " emp_id = ".$this->emp_id." and week_start
        = '".$this->week_start."'";
    }

    public function parse(&$request) { }
    public function readWeek() { }
    public function getExpenseAmount($offset, $description) { }
}
```

The functions parse, readWeek, and getExpenseAmount are required by the
TravelExpenseWeekContainerParseRequest and TravelExpenseWeekContainerWrite tests; thus,
they are simply syntactic stubs.

Satisfying the Parse Request Test

The TravelExpenseWeekContainerParseRequest test may be a bit tricky because it involves data
manipulation. Your first order of business is to take care of the dependencies, which is part of the meta-
array road map that you were thinking about earlier. Adding this function to the TravelExpenseWeek
class in lib/expense.phpm will take care of the job:

```
public function getExpensesMetaArray () {
    return array(
        array('name' => 'Lodging', 'code' => 'lodging', 'data' =>
            array('Lodging &amp; Hotel','Other','Tips'), 'persist' =>
                array('lodging_and_hotel', 'lodging_laundry',
                        'lodging_tips')),
        array('name' => 'Meals', 'code' => 'meals', 'data' =>
            array('Breakfast', 'Lunch &amp; Snacks',
                'Dinner', 'Tips', 'Entertainment'), 'persist' =>
                array('meals_breakfast', 'meals_lunch',
                    'meals_dinner', 'meals_tips',
                    'meals_entertainment')),
        array('name' => 'Transportation', 'code' => 'trans', 'data' =>
            array('Airfare', 'Auto Rental', 'Auto Maint./Gas',
                        'Local Transportation',
                        'Tolls/Parking'), 'persist' =>
                array ('trans_airfare', 'trans_auto_rental',
                    'trans_auto_maint', 'trans_local',
                    'trans_tolls', 'trans_miles_traveled')),
        array('name' => 'Miscellaneous', 'code' => 'misc', 'data' =>
            array('Gifts', 'Telephone &amp; Fax', 'Supplies',
                        'Postage', 'Other'), 'persist' =>
                array('misc_gifts','misc_phone',
                    'misc_supplies', 'misc_postage',
                    'misc_other')));
    }
```

Along with the meta-array, you also need a way to retrieve each `TravelExpenseItem`. Recall from your `TravelExpenseWeekContainerParseRequest` test that your tests require the `TravelExpenseWeek-getExpenseAmount()` function:

```
$this->assertEquals(8.8, $week->getExpenseAmount(2, 'meals_breakfast'));
```

For now, the function is simply implemented by iterating through `TravelExpenseWeek->item`. Make a note to yourself about the ugliness by adding this to the `TravelExpenseWeek` in `lib/expensepace*.phpm`:

```php
/**
 * todo: put into an associative array
 */
public function getExpenseAmount($offset, $description) {
    $targetDate = $this->addDays($this->week_start, $offset);
    foreach ($this->items as $item) {
        if ($item->expense_date == $targetDate &&
                $item->description == $description) {
            return $item->amount;
        }
    }
    return "";
}
```

Note that you're calling an `addDays()` function with an offset to get the current string-based representation of the date.

Better make an `addDays()` method, and then a quick three-minute hack for adding the number of seconds in a day (86400 is 60*60*24). `TravelExpenseWeek` now contains the following:

```php
/**
 * todo: will this fail on daylight savings time?
 */
public function addDays($start, $days) {
    return date("Y-m-d", strtotime($start)+$days*86400);
}
```

This may come with a catch, however. During the jump to and from Daylight Saving Time in America, there is a difference of one hour's worth of seconds for that particular day. How does PHP return the day? Is it local time or GMT? You'd better figure it out, or in a mere six months you'll be flipping burgers at your local fast-food chain. For now, note the ugliness and continue satisfying your `TravelExpenseWeekContainerParseRequest` test.

The killer function of the `TravelExpenseWeek` object is parsing the PHP's travel expense form response in order to create individual `TravelExpenseItems`, or an associative array of the data.

Recall that you are mapping the following data structure:

```
array('name' => 'Lodging', 'code' => 'lodging', 'data' =>
            array('Lodging &amp; Hotel','Other','Tips'), 'persist' =>
                array('lodging_and_hotel', 'lodging_laundry',
                        'lodging_tips'))
```

In addition, the following naming convention is contained in PHP's response object:

```
lodging_sun_0
```

After you've figured that out, it's just a matter of creating `TravelExpenseItems` and storing them in the `TravelExpenseWeeks->items` array. Add the parse function to `TravelExpenseWeek` in `lib/expense.phpm`:

```
/**
 * This function bridges the gap between the day-based DB and the
 * week-based view
 */
public function getWeekArray() {
    return array ('sun', 'mon', 'tue', 'wed', 'thr', 'fri', 'sat');
}
public function parse (&$request) {
    // section loop
    foreach ($this->getExpensesMetaArray() as $sectionlist) {
        // row loop
        for ($i=0; $i < count ($sectionlist['persist']); $i++) {
            $daynum = 0;
            // day loop
            foreach ($this->getWeekArray() as $day) {
                $index = $sectionlist['code']."_".$day."_".$i;
                if (array_key_exists($index, $request) and
                    $request[$index] <> null and
                    $request[$index] <> "") {
                    // create new item and store in $this->items
                    array_push (
                        $this->items,
                        new TravelExpenseItem (
                            array ('emp_id' => $this->emp_id,
                                   'expense_date' =>
                                   $this->addDays($this->week_start,
                                                  $daynum),
                                   'description' =>
                                              $sectionlist['persist'][$i],
                                   'amount' => (float) $request[$index]),
                            $this->dbh));
                }
                $daynum++;
            }
        }
    }
}
```

Together, these five functions constitute the majority of the functionality implemented in `TravelExpenseWeek`. The class takes on the not so trivial task of modifying a Web-based data structure with a database-centric one.

Satisfying the Travel Expense Week Container Read and Write Tests

Given the minimum amount of data, the employee ID, and the starting week, your test should populate the `TravelExpenseWeek` with `TravelExpenseItems` to and from the database. Recall that the test roughly does the following:

```
$week = new TravelExpenseWeek (
    array ('emp_id'          => "1",
           'week_start'      => "1980-01-061980-01-06",
           'territory_worked' => "Midwest",
           'comments'        => "comment",
           'cash_advance'    => "0",
           'mileage_rate'    => "0.31"),
    $this->_session->getDatabaseHandle());
$week->readWeek();
```

This should do the job nicely. Add the `readWeek()` function to `TravelExpenseWeek` in `lib/expense.phpm`:

```
public function readWeek() {
    $sql = "select * from travel_expense_week where";
    $sql .= " emp_id = ".$this->emp_id." and ";
    $sql .= " week_start = '".$this->week_start."'";
    $result = $this->dbh->query($sql);
    if (DB::isError($result) <> true and $result->numRows() > 0) {
        $row = $result->fetchRow();
        $this->contentBase['comments'] = $row['comments'];
        $this->contentBase['territory_worked'] = $row['territory_worked'];
        $this->contentBase['cash_advance'] = $row['cash_advance'];
        $this->contentBase['mileage_rate'] = $row['mileage_rate'];
    }
    $sql = "select * from travel_expense_item where";
    $sql .= " emp_id = ".$this->emp_id." and ";
    $sql .= " expense_date >= '".$this->week_start."' and";
    $sql .= " expense_date <= '".$this->addDays($this->week_start, 6)."'";
    $this->items = array();
    $result = $this->dbh->query($sql);
    if (DB::isError($result) or $result->numRows() == 0) return;
    while ($row = $result->fetchRow()) {
        array_push ($this->items, new TravelExpenseItem ($row));
    }
}
```

Note that there are really two halves to this. The first database lookup returns the state of the `TravelExpenseWeek`; the second half returns the associated `TravelExpenseItems`, adding them to the `TraveExpenseWeek->items` array.

However, do you notice a subtle problem? Note how you're lazily passing the entire `$row` to `TravelExpenseItem` in its constructor? Recall that the constructor of `PersistableObject`, (`TravelExpenseItem`'s parent) is as follows:

```
function __construct ($results, $dbh = null) {
    $this->dbh = $dbh;
    if ($results <> null) {
        $this->contentBase = $results; // copy
    }
}
```

Thus, does `TravelExpenseItem` blindly store whatever you give it, regardless of *what* data it is? Hmmm, this is definitely wasteful, and although the database contains nothing that isn't found in the `TravelExpenseItem`, the object gets its behavior from `PersistableObject`, of which `TravelExpenseWeek`, `Contact`, and `ContactVisit` are all children. Passing any of those objects PHP's `$_REQUEST` would result in a criminal waste of resources.

To change `PersistableObject`'s default behavior from "store everything" to "store what you expect to find," take a step back and create a new test, one that tests the undesired behavior. Because `TravelExpenseItem` is simple, it's an ideal candidate:

```
function testIgnoreExtra() {
$response = array ('emp_id'       => "1",
                   'expense_date' => "1980-01-01",
                   'description'  => "one",
                   'amount'       => "1.0",
                   'extra'        => "extra bits");
$tvi = new TravelExpenseItem($response);
$this->assertEquals(null, $tvi->extra);
}
```

Sure enough, this test fails. It also means that `TravelExpenseWeek` (which is expected to parse out PHP's `$_RESPONSE` object) will be hugely bloated if you do something silly such as pass in the response during construction.

One way to get around the problem is to know ahead of time what is required by the object in order to ignore anything else. Therefore, rather than have the `TravelExpenseItem->persist()` function look like

```
public function persist() {
    return $this->persistWork (
    "travel_expense_item",
     array ( "emp_id",
             "expense_date",
             "description",
             "amount"));
}
```

the `persist` function would be made more concise by passing in some internal state:

```
public function persist() {      return $this->persistWork (
    $this->contentMetaTable,
        $this->contentMetaOnly);
}
```

507

Put it all together and you end up with the rewritten class. It's not that different. Things are just moved around a bit:

```
class TravelExpenseItem extends PersistableObject {
    protected $contentMetaTable = null;
    protected $contentMetaOnly = null;
    function __construct ($results, $dbh = null) {
        $this->contentMetaTable = "travel_expense_item";
        $this->contentMetaOnly = array ( "emp_id",
                                         "expense_date",
                                         "description",
                                         "amount");
        $content = array();
        foreach ($this->contentMetaOnly as $key) {
            if (array_key_exists($key, $results))
                $content[$key] = $results[$key];
        }
        parent::__construct ($content, $dbh);
    }
    public function isValid() {
        if ($this->isEmpty("emp_id") == true) return false;
        if ($this->isEmpty("expense_date") == true) return false;
        if ($this->isEmpty("description") == true) return false;
        if ($this->isEmpty("amount") == true) return false;
        return true;
    }
    public function getSqlWhere() {
        return " emp_id = ".$this->emp_id." and expense_date
        ='".$this->expense_date."' and description = '".$this->description."'";
    }
        public function persist() {
            return $this->persistWork (
                $this->contentMetaTable,
                $this->contentMetaOnly);
    }
}
```

In this case, you check whether what is being passed in via the constructor is what you're looking for. Repair the last remaining `TravelExpenseWeek` test and then refactor.

The `TravelExpenseWeek` write takes significantly less work, considering that each `TravelExpenseItem` already knows how to persist itself. All you need to do is call the `persist()` function of each one.

Simply add the small loop at the end of your persistence function of `TravelExpenseWeek` in `lib/expense.phpm`:

```
public function persist() {
    $this->persistWork ("travel_expense_week",
                        array("emp_id",
                              "week_start",
                              "comments",
                              "territory_worked",
```

```
                                    "cash_advance",
                                    "mileage_rate"));
        // persist each item to the database
        foreach ($this->items as $item) {
            $item->persist();
        }
        return true;
    }
```

Congratulations! All your unit tests now pass. Now it's time to add some remaining features, including a quick refactoring.

A Quick Refactoring

Satisfying all of your unit tests is an important matter, because during the next refactoring they'll tell you if you have accidentally broken a seemingly unrelated section of code.

Now that `TravelExpenseItem` and `TravelExpenseWeek` have more similar structures, but with varying degrees of error checking, move that functionality up into the `PersistableObject`.

Essentially, you want to add this to `PersistableObject`:

```
protected $contentMetaTable = null;
protected $contentMetaOnly = null;
public function persist() {      return $this->persistWork (
        $this->contentMetaTable,
        $this->contentMetaOnly);
}
```

There is also the same loop in both constructors that can be moved up:

```
foreach ($this->content as $key) {
    if (array_key_exists($key, $results))
        $this->content[$key] = $results[$key];
}
```

Here's a snapshot of the resulting object:

```
class PersistableObject {
    protected $contentBase = array();
    protected $contentMetaTable = null;
    protected $contentMetaOnly = null;
    protected $dbh = null; // database handle
    protected $dispatchFunctions = array ("role" => "getrole");
    function __get ($key) {
        // content removed for brevity
    }
```

```
        function __construct ($results, $dbh = null) {
            $this->dbh = $dbh;
            if ($this->contentMetaOnly <> null) {
                foreach ($this->contentMetaOnly as $key) {
                    if (array_key_exists($key, $results)) {
                        $this->contentBase[$key] = $results[$key];
                    }
                }
            } elseif ($results <> null) {
                $this->contentBase = $results; // copy
            }
        }
        public function implodeQuoted (&$values, $delimiter) {
            // content removed for brevity
        }
        public function generateSqlInsert ($tableName, $metas, $values) {
            // content removed for brevity
        }
        public function generateSqlInsert ($tableName, $metas, $values) {
            // content removed for brevity
        }
        public function generateSqlUpdate ($tableName, $metas, $values) {
            // content removed for brevity
        }
        public function generateSqlDelete ($tableName) {
            // content removed for brevity
        }
        public function getSqlWhere() {
            // content removed for brevity
        }
        protected function isEmpty($key) {
            // content removed for brevity
        }
        public function isValid() {
            // content removed for brevity
        }
        public function persistWork ($tablename, $meta) {
            // content removed for brevity
        }


        public function persist() {
            return $this->persistWork (
                $this->contentMetaTable,
                $this->contentMetaOnly);
        }
    }
```

The constructor is responsible for determining whether data is "keepable." Also note that the behavior is backwardly compatible because if the contentMetaOnly array is null, then PersistableObject simply copies the $results into its contentBase.

Now your `TravelExpenseItem` can be squeezed down ever smaller:

```
class TravelExpenseItem extends PersistableObject {
    function __construct ($results, $dbh = null) {
        $this->contentMetaTable = "travel_expense_item";
        $this->contentMetaOnly = array ( "emp_id",
                                          "expense_date",
                                          "description",
                                          "amount");
        parent::__construct ($results, $dbh);
    }
    public function isValid() {
        if ($this->isEmpty("emp_id") == true) return false;
        if ($this->isEmpty("expense_date") == true) return false;
        if ($this->isEmpty("description") == true) return false;
        if ($this->isEmpty("amount") == true) return false;
        return true;
    }
    public function getSqlWhere() {
        return " emp_id = ".$this->emp_id." and expense_date =
            '".$this->expense_date."' and description = '".$this->description."'";
    }
}
```

Do you see how the `TravelExpenseItem`'s constructor sets up its `PersistableObject` state and then passes the arguments up to `PersistableObject`?

Therefore, although you are charged with making an explicit call to the constructor, it gives you the freedom to preliminarily set state in the parent object, `PersistableObject`.

Now make the same modifications to `TravelExpenseWeek`:

```
class TravelExpenseWeek extends PersistableObject {
    public $items = array();

    function __construct ($results, $dbh = null) {
        $this->contentMetaTable = "travel_expense_week";
        $this->contentMetaOnly = array ( "emp_id",
                                         "week_start",
                                         "comments",
                                         "territory_worked",
                                         "cash_advance",
                                         "mileage_rate");
        parent::__construct ($results, $dbh);
    }

    public function isValid() {

        // content removed for brevity
    }
```

```
    public function persist() {
        if (parent::persist() == false) return false;
// persist each item to the database
        foreach ($this->items as $item) {
            if ($item->persist() == false) return false;
        }
        return true;
    }
    public function getSqlWhere() {
        return " emp_id = ".$this->emp_id." and week_start =
        '".$this->week_start."'";
    }
    public function getExpensesMetaArray () {
        // content removed for brevity
    }
    public function getWeekArray() {
        // content removed for brevity
    }
    public function addDays($start, $days) {
        // content removed for brevity
    }
    public function parse (&$request) {
        // content removed for brevity
    }
    public function readWeek() {
        // content removed for brevity
    }
    public function getExpenseAmount($offset, $description) {
        // content removed for brevity
    }
}
```

Note that TravelExpenseWeek overrides the PersistableObject->persist()function. However, it
first calls PersistableObject->persist()and then persists every TraveExpenseItem that it is
holding. Remember that because the logic behind an insert/update/delete is in PersistableObject->
persistWork(), it continues to work, and all you need to do is remember to implement the
getSqlWhere function in your concrete classes such as TravelExpenseWeek. The tests are still passing?
Good job, but not so fast, considering that a cash advance is not required (as shown in the validity test):

```
function testValidTravelExpenseWeek() {
    $tvi = new TravelExpenseWeek (
        array ('emp_id'          => "1",
               'week_start'      => "1980-01-01",
               'comments'        => "comment",
               'mileage_rate'    => "0.31",
               'territory_worked' => "Midwest" ));
    $this->assertEquals(true, $tvi->isValid(), "valid expense");
}
```

However, every other test sets cash_advance to zero. What happens if you remove cash_advance from the test? It breaks! This is because PersistableObject blindly creates SQL based on every field of the database record.

Modify the persistence test to reflect that neither cash_advance nor comments is required:

```
function testTravelExpenseWeekPersistence() {
    $this->_session->getDatabaseHandle()->query("delete FROM
                        travel_expense_week WHERE emp_id = 1 and
                        week_start = '1980-01-01'"); // remove multiples
    $tvi = new TravelExpenseWeek (
        array ('emp_id'           => "1",
               'week_start'        => "1980-01-01",
               'territory_worked' => "Midwest",
               'mileage_rate'      => "0.31"),
        $this->_session->getDatabaseHandle());
    $result = $this->_session->getDatabaseHandle()->query("select *
               FROM travel_expense_week WHERE emp_id = 1 and week_start
               = '1980-01-01'");
    $this->assertEquals(0, $result->numRows(), "pre check");
    $this->assertEquals(true, $tvi->persist(), "save");
    $result = $this->_session->getDatabaseHandle()->query("select *
               FROM travel_expense_week WHERE emp_id = 1 and week_start
               = '1980-01-01'");
    $this->assertEquals(1, $result->numRows(), "persisted ok");
    $row = $result->fetchRow();
    $this->assertEquals(0.0, (float) $row['cash_advance'],
        "cash advance default");
}
```

The default values of cash_advance are an easy fix, too. Just modify the constructor of TravelExpenseWeek to set the default of zero and an empty string:

```
class TravelExpenseWeek extends PersistableObject {
    function __construct ($results, $dbh = null) {
        $this->contentMetaTable = "travel_expense_week";
        $this->contentMetaOnly = array ( "emp_id",
                                         "week_start",
                                          "comments",
                                         "territory_worked",
                                         "cash_advance",
                                         "mileage_rate");
        $this->contentBase['comments'] = "";
        $this->contentBase['cash_advance'] = "0.0";
        parent::__construct ($results, $dbh);
    }
```

The tests are again passing, which means that you're done now, right? Doing a quick "grep to-do" uncovers this nagging problem:

```
/**

* todo: will this fail on daylight savings time?
*/
public function addDays($start, $days) {
    return date("Y-m-d", strtotime($start)+$days*86400);
}
```

Looking at it again, you decide there may indeed be an issue. Daylight Saving Time ends on the last Sunday in October in most places in the United States, which means that the clocks are set back, and there are more than 86,400 seconds during that day. Write up a test to confirm that it fails:

```
function testDaylightSavingTime() {
    $tvw = new TravelExpenseWeek (array());
    $this->assertEquals("2004-10-30", $tvw->addDays("2004-10-29", 1));
    $this->assertEquals("2004-10-31", $tvw->addDays("2004-10-29", 2));
    $this->assertEquals("2004-11-01", $tvw->addDays("2004-10-29", 3), "no DST");
}
```

Sure enough, there is a problem. Adding three days to October 29 should land in November, rather than October 31, twice. Reading up on your functions, strtotime() can do the date math for you by accepting date offsets. Recode the addDays() function of PersistableObject without the presumption of seconds per day:

```
public function addDays($start, $days) {
    return date("Y-m-d", strtotime($start." +".$days." days"));
}
```

Because your remaining "to-do" of modifying the getExpenseAmount function is really an optimization, it can wait until later. There is no need for pre-optimization, and it's important that you keep the momentum going.

Although that was indeed a lot of work, you now have reasonably well-written, persistable objects that are completely backwardly compatible. Your system is growing in stages, and you'll update Contact and ContactVisit the next time you touch them. Now it's time to turn to finish the current task of the Travel Expense Report.

The Finalized Travel Expense Report

After a few hours of work, you have what is shown in Figure 19-9.

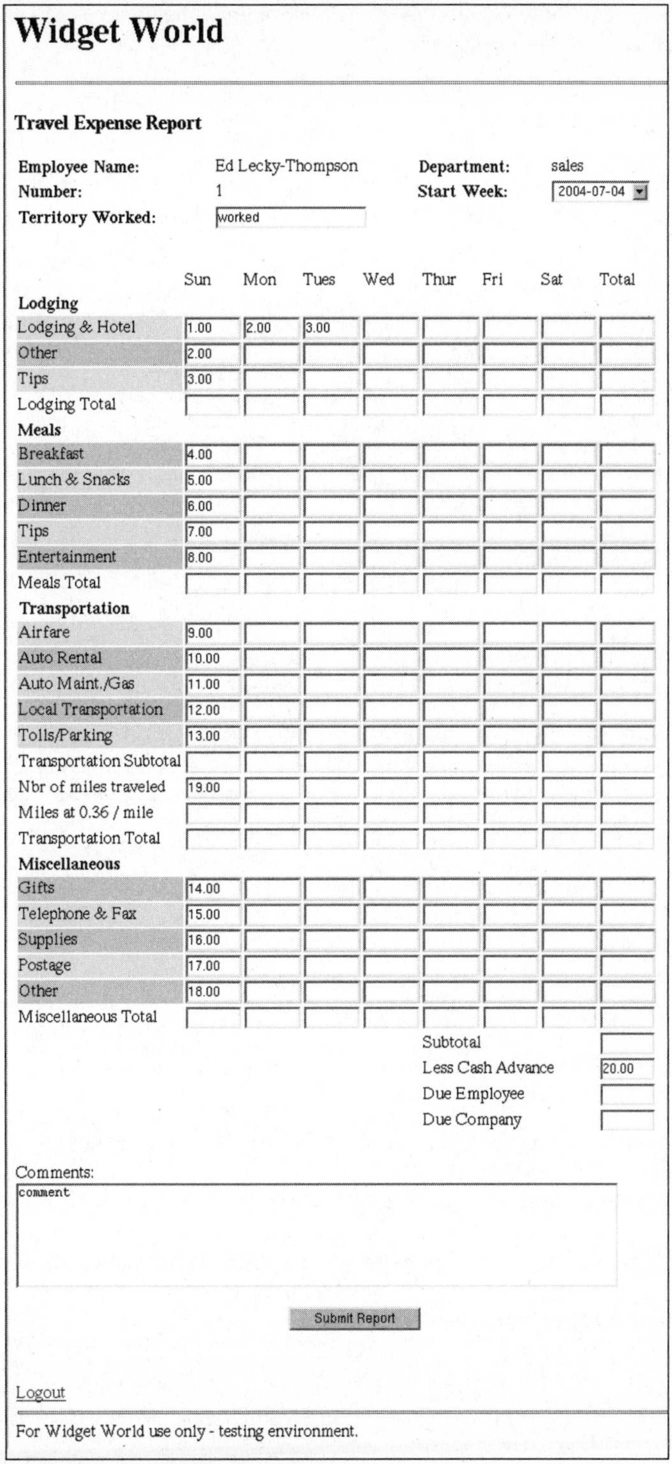

Widget World

Travel Expense Report

Employee Name:	Ed Lecky-Thompson	**Department:**	sales
Number:	1	**Start Week:**	2004-07-04 ▾
Territory Worked:	worked		

	Sun	Mon	Tues	Wed	Thur	Fri	Sat	Total
Lodging								
Lodging & Hotel	1.00	2.00	3.00					
Other	2.00							
Tips	3.00							
Lodging Total								
Meals								
Breakfast	4.00							
Lunch & Snacks	5.00							
Dinner	6.00							
Tips	7.00							
Entertainment	8.00							
Meals Total								
Transportation								
Airfare	9.00							
Auto Rental	10.00							
Auto Maint./Gas	11.00							
Local Transportation	12.00							
Tolls/Parking	13.00							
Transportation Subtotal								
Nbr of miles traveled	19.00							
Miles at 0.36 / mile								
Transportation Total								
Miscellaneous								
Gifts	14.00							
Telephone & Fax	15.00							
Supplies	16.00							
Postage	17.00							
Other	18.00							
Miscellaneous Total								

Subtotal	
Less Cash Advance	20.00
Due Employee	
Due Company	

Comments:

comment

Submit Report

Logout

For Widget World use only - testing environment.

Figure 19-9: Finished Travel Expense form

It's a first pass, so start with how to feed the Smarty template in the file `travel-expenses.php`, which is the user's landing point if coming in from the main menu:

```php
<?php
require_once ("lib/common.php");
require_once ("lib/expense.phpm");
// is the user logged in?
if (!$session->isLoggedIn()) {
    redirect ("index.php");
}
$user = $session->getUserObject();
$week = new TravelExpenseWeek (
    array ('emp_id'           => $user->id,
           'week_start'       => getCurrentStartWeek(),
           'territory_worked' => $_REQUEST["territory_worked"],
           'comments'         => $_REQUEST["comments"],
           'cash_advance'     => $_REQUEST["cash_advance"],
           'mileage_rate'     => $GLOBALS["expense-mileage-travelrate"]),
        $session->getDatabaseHandle());
// display

if ($_REQUEST["action"] != "persist_expense") {

    $week->readWeek();
    $smarty->assign_by_ref ("user",          $user);
    $smarty->assign_by_ref ("week",          $week);
    $smarty->assign('start_weeks',           getStartWeeks());
    $smarty->assign('current_start_week',    getCurrentStartWeek());
    $smarty->assign_by_ref ('expenses',      $week->getExpensesMetaArray());
    $smarty->assign('travelrate',            $GLOBALS["expense-mileage-travelrate"]);
    $smarty->display('travel-expenses.tpl');
    exit();
}

// gather and persist week

$week->parse($_REQUEST);

$week->persist();
print "saved, thanks";
?>
```

Being the user-accessible landing spot, this script has two modes of operation: one is displaying the travel expenses by reading them from the database (`readWeek`), and the other is saving the form data (`persist`) based on whether the action is set to `persist_expense`.

As usual, your very interesting `getExpensesMetaArray()` is the cornerstone of the screen, and is passed in as the Smarty variable `expenses`. Note that all heavyweight objects are passed to Smarty by reference, so copies aren't automatically created.

Now for the basic Smarty template that displays the travel expense page, which is in `templates/` `travel-expenses.tpl`:

```
{include file="header.tpl" title="Widget World - Travel Expenses"}
{literal}
<SCRIPT TYPE="text/javascript">
<!-
function reloadCalc () {
    window.document.forms[0].week_start.value =
      window.document.forms[1].week_start.value // hidden form
      window.document.forms[0].submit(); // hidden form }
// ->
</SCRIPT>
{/literal}
<h3>Travel Expense Report</h3>
<form method="post">
<input type="hidden" name="action" value="reload_expense">
<input type="hidden" name="week_start" value="">
</form>
<form id="calc" name="calc" action="travel-expenses.php" method="post">
<table border="0" width="100%">
<tr>
<td><b>Employee Name:</b></td>
<td>{$user->first_name} {$user->last_name}</td> <td><b>Department:</b></td>
<td>{$user->department}</td>
</tr>
<tr>
<td><b>Number:</b></td>
<td>{$user->id}</td> <td><b>Start Week:</b></td>
<td><SELECT NAME="week_start" onchange="reloadCalc()">{html_options
    values=$start_weeks output=$start_weeks selected=$current_start_week}
</SELECT></td>
</tr>
<tr>
<td><b>Territory Worked:</b></td>
<td colspan=3><input name="territory_worked" size=20 maxsize=60 value=
    "{$week->territory_worked}"></td>
</tr>
</table>
<br><br>
```

The first form on the page is similar to that of the Customer Contact Report, in which you utilized a special "hidden" form that was populated (by JavaScript) with the value for your starting week. The form was then automatically submitted when a new week was selected.

The start of the second form simply contains some of the basic information that you are collecting, including the `territory_worked`.

The next section begins the spreadsheet part of the display. Code is simply replicated between Sunday and Saturday. Remember that this screen is your first attempt and you may have to change items; thus, the neglect of a final "week" loop is understandable. For now, it's just a basic input form without error-checking or spreadsheet-like activity:

```
<table border="0">
<tr><td></td><td>Sun</td><td>Mon</td><td>Tues</td><td>Wed</td><td>Thur</td>
<td>Fri</td><td>Sat</td><td>Total</td></tr>
{section name=idx loop=$expenses}{strip}
<tr><td><b>{$expenses[idx].name}</b></td><td></td><td></td><td></td><td></td>
<td></td><td></td><td></td><td></td></tr>
    {section name=idx2 loop=$expenses[idx].data}{strip}
    {assign var="p" value=$expenses[idx].persist[idx2]}
    <tr bgcolor="{cycle values="#eeeee, #dddddd"}">
    <td>{$expenses[idx].data[idx2]}</td>
<td><input name="{$expenses[idx].code}_sun_{$smarty.section.idx2.index}"
type="text" size="7" maxsize="17" value="{$week->getExpenseAmount(0, $p)}"></td>
```

Remember that you're building up HTML output that looks like this:

```
<input name="lodging_sun_0" type="text" size="7" maxsize="17" value="1.00">
```

The two main loops here iterate through your expense array:

```
return array(
    array('name' => 'Lodging', 'code' => 'lodging', 'data' =>
        array('Lodging &amp; Hotel','Other','Tips'), 'persist' =>
            array('lodging_and_hotel', 'lodging_laundry',
                'lodging_tips'))
```

The Smarty variable $p is dynamically created as a convenience in order to ensure that the Smarty code doesn't get too unwieldy: getExpenseAmount(0, $p) is more readable than getExpenseAmount(0, $expenses[idx].persist[idx2]). Finally, the last two lines representing Sunday are copied six more times to represent each day of the week. They are (thankfully) not displayed:

```
<td><input readonly
        name="{$expenses[idx].code}_week_sub_{$smarty.section.idx2.index}"
        type="text" size="7" maxsize="17">
</td>
</tr>
    {/strip}{/section}
```

This works well, but there is always an exception. Your clients have requested that transportation subtotal before accepting the "number of miles traveled," which then totals that section.

Smarty can handle its own conditionals, so put that in next; but the number of miles traveled is not in your expenses meta-array, so it must be accounted for:

```
{if $expenses[idx].code == 'trans'}
        <tr><td>{$expenses[idx].name} Subtotal</td>
            <td><input readonly name="{$expenses[idx].code}_sun_sub"
                type="text" size="7" maxsize="17"></td>
```

Again, the code is duplicated six more times (not displayed) before the subtotal:

```
<td><input readonly name="{$expenses[idx].code}_week_sub" type=
    "text" size="7" maxsize="17"></td></tr>
        <tr><td>Nbr of miles traveled</td>
            <td><input name="mitr_sun" type="text" size="7" maxsize="17"
                value="{$week->getExpenseAmount(0,
                    'trans_miles_traveled')}"></td>
```

The rest of the week is not shown, for brevity:

```
<td><input readonly name="mitr_tot" type="text" size="7"
    maxsize="17"></td></tr>
<tr><td>Miles at {$travelrate} / mile </td><td><input readonly
    name="mitot_sun" type="text" size="7" maxsize="17"></td>
```

Likewise the duplicated mileage (mitrs):

```
<td><input readonly name="mitot_tot" type="text" size="7"
        maxsize="17"></td></tr>
    <tr><td>{$expenses[idx].name} Total</td><td><input readonly
            name="{$expenses[idx].code}_sun_sub2" type="text" size="7"
            maxsize="17"></td>
    {else}
        <tr><td>{$expenses[idx].name} Total</td><td><input readonly
            name="{$expenses[idx].code}_sun_sub" type="text" size="7"
            maxsize="17"></td>
```

This completes the transportation exception and continues with the standard processing. Essentially, it enables you to avoid adding an extra line to the bottom of transportation for mileage.

```
<td><input readonly name="{$expenses[idx].code}_week_sub" type="text"
    size="7" maxsize="17"></td></tr>
    {/if}
{/strip}{/section}
```

The rest of the screen represents the subtotals, amounts due, and weekly comments:

```
<tr><td></td><td></td><td></td><td></td><td></td>
<td colspan="3">Subtotal</td>
<td>
  <input readonly name="subtotal" type="text" size="7" maxsize="17">
</td>
</tr>
<tr><td></td><td></td><td></td><td></td><td></td>
<td colspan="3">Less Cash Advance</td>
<td><input name="cash_advance" type="text" size="7"
    maxsize="17" value="{$week->cash_advance}"></td>
</tr>
<tr><td></td><td></td><td></td><td></td><td></td>
<td colspan="3">Due Employee</td>
<td><input readonly name="totaldueemployee" type="text" size="7"
    maxsize="17"></td></tr>
```

```
<tr><td></td><td></td><td></td><td></td><td></td>
<td colspan="3">Due Company</td>
<td><input readonly name="totalduecompany" type="text" size="7"
    maxsize="17"></td></tr>
</table>
<br><br>
Comments:<br>
<TEXTAREA NAME="comments" COLS=80 ROWS=6>{$week->comments}</TEXTAREA>
<br><br><center>
<input type="submit" name="submit" value=" Submit Report " >
</center>
<input type="hidden" name="action" value="persist_expense">
</form>
{include file="footer.tpl"}
```

Even though the screen lacks even basic error-checking or any spreadsheet-like features, you're still at a very pivotal point in the project. This screen, as is, could technically be used in production.

Unadvisable, yes, but this is the point where you are delivering business value! Get this into the hands of your clients and start getting their feedback.

This big gulp has just taken care of Stories 2, 3, and 10.

The Travel Expense Report As a Spreadsheet

Your clients are enjoying the Travel Expense Report. They're using it and giving you valuable feedback regarding how, what, and why.

Fortunately for you, the only additional functionality they want is to get it to act like a spreadsheet, so what's that going to take?

JavaScript offers one event that you're interested in: onkeyup. It can be applied to your input boxes in order to recalculate on-the-fly when new information is entered.

However, it turns out that simulating a spreadsheet is not as easy as it sounds. Here is the new template/ travel-expenses.tpl:

```
{include file="header.tpl" title="Widget World - Travel Expenses"}
{literal}
<SCRIPT TYPE="text/javascript">
<!- function subtotal(thisForm, totalcell, cellArray) {
    var subtot = 0;
    for (var i=0; i < cellArray.length; i++) {
        if(isNaN(thisForm[cellArray[i]].value))
            thisForm[totalcell].value = 0;
        else
            subtot = Math.round(subtot*100 +
                                thisForm[cellArray[i]].value*100)/100;
    }
    thisForm[totalcell].value = subtot;
    return subtot;
}
```

Starting from the top, the JavaScript function `subtotal()` takes a form, which is a place to put the answer and an array of numbers to add.

Although JavaScript supports decimals, it doesn't support arbitrary precision. Therefore, because you'd like dollars down to the penny (as in $9.99), you must multiply everything by 100. Do the math, round the result, and then divide by 100.

Therefore, by adding 0.01 to 9.98, multiply everything by 100: 1.0 and 998.0. Do the addition: 999.0. Round the result, 999, and divide by 100: 9.99. Yes, it looks as though it'll be a pain.

The next few functions deal with totaling up columns in each section (Lodging, Meals, Transportation, and so on), vertically totaling each amount per day. Finally, `daycalc()` is called by each of the "cells":

```
function subday (thisForm, totalcell, prefix, maxindex) {
    var cellArray = new Array (maxindex);
    for (var i=0; i < maxindex; i++) {
        cellArray[i] = thisForm[prefix+i].name;
    }
    return subtotal(thisForm, totalcell, cellArray);
}
function subweek (thisForm, totalcell, prefix, postfix) {
    return subtotal (thisForm, totalcell,
        new Array (prefix+'sun'+postfix, prefix+'mon'+postfix,
                prefix+'tue'+postfix, prefix+'wed'+postfix,
                prefix+'thr'+postfix, prefix+'fri'+postfix,
                prefix+'sat'+postfix));
}
function daycalc (thisForm, day, code, thisindex, maxindex) {
    subday (thisForm, code+"_"+day+"_sub", code+"_"+day+"_", maxindex);
    subweek(thisForm, code+"_week_sub_"+thisindex, code+"_", '_'+thisindex);
    subday (thisForm, code+"_week_sub", code+"_week_sub_", maxindex);
    totalcalc (thisForm);
    return true;
}
```

The function `daycalc()` is called from each cell that accepts user input in the HTML form in such a manner:

```
onkeyup="return daycalc(this.form, 'sun', 'lodging', '0', 3)"
```

Remember that the screen is generated from your expense meta-array:

```
array('meals_breakfast', 'meals_lunch','meals_dinner', 'meals_tips',
    'meals_entertainment')
```

However, JavaScript has no knowledge of PHP, or Smarty, or whatever else you're using in the back end, so you must be explicit and tell JavaScript which cell you are working with, as well as how many cells need to be subtotaled. These, respectively, are the last two arguments in the `daycalc()` function call: `'0'` is the current row and `'3'` signifies the maximum number of rows that need to be vertically subtotaled in the `subday` function.

The number of miles (an exception) must be calculated separately. The cells for the mileage input are named `mitr_sun`, `mitr_mon`, and so on. Their subtotal (which is the number of miles multiplied by the mileage rate) is represented by `mitot_sun`, `mitot_mon`, and so on. After the horizontal weekly totals are calculated with `subweek`, the total mileage is updated based on the current vertical day. Finally, the grand total of the transportation section is updated:

```
function micalc (thisForm, day, travelrate) {
    var totalcell = 'mitot_'+day;
    var sourcecell = 'mitr_'+day;
    // mileage input and mileage total
    thisForm[totalcell].value = Math.round(
        thisForm[sourcecell].value * 100 * travelrate)/100;
    subweek (thisForm, 'mitr_tot', 'mitr_', ");
    subweek (thisForm, 'mitot_tot', 'mitot_', ");
    // trans total by day
    thisForm["trans_"+day+"_sub2"].value = Math.round(
        (thisForm[totalcell].value * 100) +
        (thisForm["trans_"+day+"_sub"].value * 100))/100;
    // grand total of week
    subweek (thisForm, "trans_week_sub2", "trans_", "_sub2");
    totalcalc (thisForm);
}
```

Next, some basic error-checking:

```
function checkTransInput (thisForm, day) {
    if (thisForm["trans_"+day+"_sub"].value > 0 &&
        thisForm["mitr_"+day].value == "" ) {
        alert( "Please enter your mileage for "+day);
        return false;
    }    return true;
}
function checkInputs(thisForm) {
    if ( checkTransInput (thisForm, "sun") == false) { return false; }
    if ( checkTransInput (thisForm, "mon") == false) { return false; }
    if ( checkTransInput (thisForm, "tue") == false) { return false; }
    if ( checkTransInput (thisForm, "wed") == false) { return false; }
    if ( checkTransInput (thisForm, "thr") == false) { return false; }
    if ( checkTransInput (thisForm, "fri") == false) { return false; }
    if ( checkTransInput (thisForm, "sat") == false) { return false; }
    if (  thisForm["subtotal"].value == 0) {         alert ("Please enter data.");
        return false;      }      if (thisForm["territory_worked"].value == "") {
        alert ("Please enter your territory worked.");
        return false;      }
    return true;
}
```

Now comes the monster function `totalcalc()`, which ensures that the entire form is recalculated:

```
//
// No easy way to pass a php array to JS unless we generate it by hand.

//
function totalcalc (thisForm) {
    var sectionArray = new Array ('lodging', 'meals', 'trans', 'misc');
    var subtotal = 0;
    for (var i=0; i < sectionArray.length; i++) {
        subtotal = subtotal +
            Math.round(thisForm[sectionArray[i]+"_week_sub"].value*100)/100;
    }
    subtotal = subtotal + Math.round(thisForm["mitot_tot"].value*100)/100;
    thisForm["subtotal"].value = subtotal;
    var total = subtotal - Math.round(thisForm["cash_advance"].value*100)/100;
    total = Math.round(total*100)/100;
    if (total >= 0) {
        thisForm["totaldueemployee"].value = total;
        thisForm["totalduecompany"].value = "";
    } else {
        thisForm["totaldueemployee"].value = "";
        thisForm["totalduecompany"].value = Math.round(total * 100)/100 *\q(-1);
    }
}
```

In the event of an error, the `recalculate()` function will be attached to a Recalculate button. This function "touches" every row and every column in order to cause the screen to be initially calculated. Remember that columns are represented by days, and rows are the first layer of your expense meta-array. Although the `recalculate` function is not the epitome of good programming, it is easier to read when it is laid out by brute force, rather than by relying on another layer of looping:

```
// don't knock it; looping is less readable
function recalculate (thisForm, mileage) {
    daycalc(thisForm, 'sun', 'lodging', '0', 3);
```

Monday through Friday are removed for brevity:

```
    daycalc(thisForm, 'sat', 'lodging', '0', 3);
    daycalc(thisForm, 'sat', 'lodging', '1', 3);
    daycalc(thisForm, 'sat', 'lodging', '2', 3);
    daycalc(thisForm, 'sun', 'meals', '0', 5);
```

Monday through Friday are removed for brevity:

```
    daycalc(thisForm, 'sat', 'meals', '0', 5);
    daycalc(thisForm, 'sat', 'meals', '1', 5);
    daycalc(thisForm, 'sat', 'meals', '2', 5);
    daycalc(thisForm, 'sat', 'meals', '3', 5);
    daycalc(thisForm, 'sat', 'meals', '4', 5);
    daycalc(thisForm, 'sun', 'trans', '0', 5);
```

Monday through Friday are removed for brevity:

```
daycalc(thisForm, 'sat', 'trans', '0', 5);
daycalc(thisForm, 'sat', 'trans', '1', 5);
daycalc(thisForm, 'sat', 'trans', '2', 5);
daycalc(thisForm, 'sat', 'trans', '3', 5);
daycalc(thisForm, 'sat', 'trans', '4', 5);
daycalc(thisForm, 'sun', 'misc', '0', 5);
```

Monday through Friday are removed for brevity:

```
daycalc(thisForm, 'sat', 'misc', '0', 5);
daycalc(thisForm, 'sat', 'misc', '1', 5);
daycalc(thisForm, 'sat', 'misc', '2', 5);
daycalc(thisForm, 'sat', 'misc', '3', 5);
daycalc(thisForm, 'sat', 'misc', '4', 5);
micalc(thisForm, 'sun', mileage);
```

Monday through Friday are removed for brevity:

```
micalc(thisForm, 'sat', mileage);
return (totalcalc(thisForm));
}
function reloadCalc () {
    window.document.forms[0].week_start.value =
        window.document.forms[1].week_start.value // hidden form
    window.document.forms[0].submit(); // hidden form }
// ->
</SCRIPT>
{/literal}
```

Now that there is code to calculate the row and column totals, every cell must respond to the `onkeyup` event by calling `daycalc()`. Modify the seven daily inputs in `templates/travel- expenses.tpl`:

```
<input name="{$expenses[idx].code}_sun_{$smarty.section.idx2.index}"
    onkeyup="return daycalc(this.form, 'sun', '{$expenses[idx].code}',
    '{$smarty.section.idx2.index}', {$smarty.section.idx2.total})"
    type="text" size="7" maxsize="17" value="{$week->getExpenseAmount(0, $p)}">
```

The mileage input functions also need to have their `onkeyup` function:

```
<input name="mitr_sun" onkeyup="return micalc(this.form, 'sun',
{$travel_rate})" ...
```

A Recalculate button should be added. It will aid in debugging the JavaScript in the event that everything doesn't work perfectly:

```
<br><br>
<center>
<input type="button" value=" Recalculate " onclick="return recalculate
(this.form, {$travelrate})">
</center>
```

```
<br><br>
Comments:<br><TEXTAREA NAME="comments" COLS=80 ROWS=6>{$week->comments}
</TEXTAREA>
<br><br><center>
```

The main Submit button now checks for basic input errors by running `checkInputs()` from the `onclick` event:

```
<input type="submit" name="submit" value=" Submit Report " onclick=
    "return checkInputs(this.form);">
```

You're almost done.

There are just a few outstanding issues. For example, if the drop-down start week is changed, the form will reload and recalculate itself, but, unfortunately, that event won't be fired when the form initially loads itself.

You must ensure that the form runs your JavaScript `recalculate()` function when the form is loaded. This is accomplished from the `onload` event of the `<body>` tag, but the `<body>` tag is defined in your `header.tpl`, so here is what you do. In your `travel-expenses.php` file, modify the display section:

```
// display
if ($_REQUEST["action"] != "persist_expense") {
    $week->readWeek();
    $smarty->assign_by_ref ("user",          $user);
    $smarty->assign_by_ref ("week",          $week);
    $smarty->assign('start_weeks',           getStartWeeks());
    $smarty->assign('current_start_week',    getCurrentStartWeek());
    $smarty->assign_by_ref ('expenses',      $week->getExpensesMetaArray());
    $smarty->assign('travelrate',            $GLOBALS["expense-mileage-
                                             travelrate"]);
    $smarty->assign('formfunc',
          "recalculate(window.document.forms[1],".
          $GLOBALS["expense-mileage-travelrate"].")");
    $smarty->display('travel-expenses.tpl');
    exit();
}
```

You're assigning a function to the variable `formfunc`. Now change the `header.tpl` so that it reads accordingly:

```
<!DOCTYPE HTML PUBLIC "-//W3C//DTD HTML 4.01 Transitional//EN">
<html>
<head>
<meta HTTP-EQUIV="content-type" CONTENT="text/html; charset=ISO-8859-1">
<title>{$title|default:"no title"}</title>
</head>
<body onload="{$formfunc|default:""}">
<h1>Widget World</h1>
<hr><p>
```

The $formfunc Smarty variable holds the name of a JavaScript function that is executed when the HTML form is loaded, $formfunc. The onload form property is set to $formfunc, or an empty string if $formfunc is not defined. This enables you to selectively recalculate your entire spreadsheet during the loading process. By doing so, daycalc() must be concerned only with its column, row, and the totals, rather than with recalculating every cell during every keystroke.

Anything Else

Feedback from your clients has indicated that the "Number of Miles" doesn't appear to be persisted correctly from the screen. Being the exception to your meta-array, it's not taken care of in the parse() function.

By now you should know the drill. Whip up a test:

```
function testParsingNbrMiles() {
    $this->_session->getDatabaseHandle()->query("delete FROM
                    travel_expense_item WHERE emp_id = 1 and
                    expense_date >= '1980-01-06' and expense_date
                    <= '2001-09-15'");
    $response = array ('mitr_sun' => "1.1",
                        'mitr_mon' => "2.2");
    $week = new TravelExpenseWeek (
        array ('emp_id' => "1",
                'week_start' => "1980-01-06",
                'territory_worked' => "Midwest",
                'comments'         => "comment",
                'cash_advance'     => "0",
                'mileage_rate'     => "0.31"),
            $this->_session->getDatabaseHandle());
    $week->parse($response);
    $this->assertEquals(true, $week->persist());
    $week = new TravelExpenseWeek (
        array ('emp_id'         => "1",
                'week_start' => "1980-01-06",
                'territory_worked' => "Midwest",
                'comments'         => "comment",
                'cash_advance'     => "0",
                'mileage_rate'     => "0.31"),
            $this->_session->getDatabaseHandle());
    $week->readWeek();

    $this->assertEquals(1.1, (float) $week->getExpenseAmount(0,
                    'trans_miles_traveled'));
    $this->assertEquals(2.2, (float) $week->getExpenseAmount(1,
                    'trans_miles_traveled'));       }
```

Make it succeed accordingly with changes to TravelExpenseWeek lib/expense.phpm:

```
private function createByRequest ($description, $daynum,
                                $index, &$request) {
    if (array_key_exists($index, $request) and
        $request[$index] <> null and
```

```
            $request[$index] <> "") {
            array_push (
                $this->items,
                new TravelExpenseItem (
                    array ('emp_id'      => $this->emp_id,
                           'expense_date' =>
                           $this->addDays($this->week_start, $daynum),
                           'description'  => $description,
                           'amount'       => (float) $request[$index]),
                    $this->dbh));
        }
    }
/**
 * This function bridges the gap between the day-based DB and the
 * week-based view
 */
public function parse(&$request) {
    foreach ($this->getExpensesMetaArray() as $sectionlist) {
        for ($i=0; $i < count ($sectionlist['persist']); $i++) {
            $daynum = 0;
            foreach ($this->getWeekArray() as $day) {
                $index = $sectionlist['code']."_".$day."_".$i;
                $this->createByRequest (
                    $sectionlist['persist'][$i], $daynum,
                    $index, $request);
                $daynum++;
            }
        }
    }
    // arg, mitr is an exception
    $daynum = 0;
    foreach ($this->getWeekArray() as $day) {
        $this->createByRequest ("trans_miles_traveled", $daynum,
                                "mitr_".$day, $request);
        $daynum++;
    }
}
```

A new function, `TravelExpenseWeek-createByRequest()`, rids you of code duplication because it is called during normal processing and for the mileage.

All the tests pass, your clients are happy, the screen works. Now you're done with Story 4: "Expense Report As a Spreadsheet," as shown in Figure 19-10.

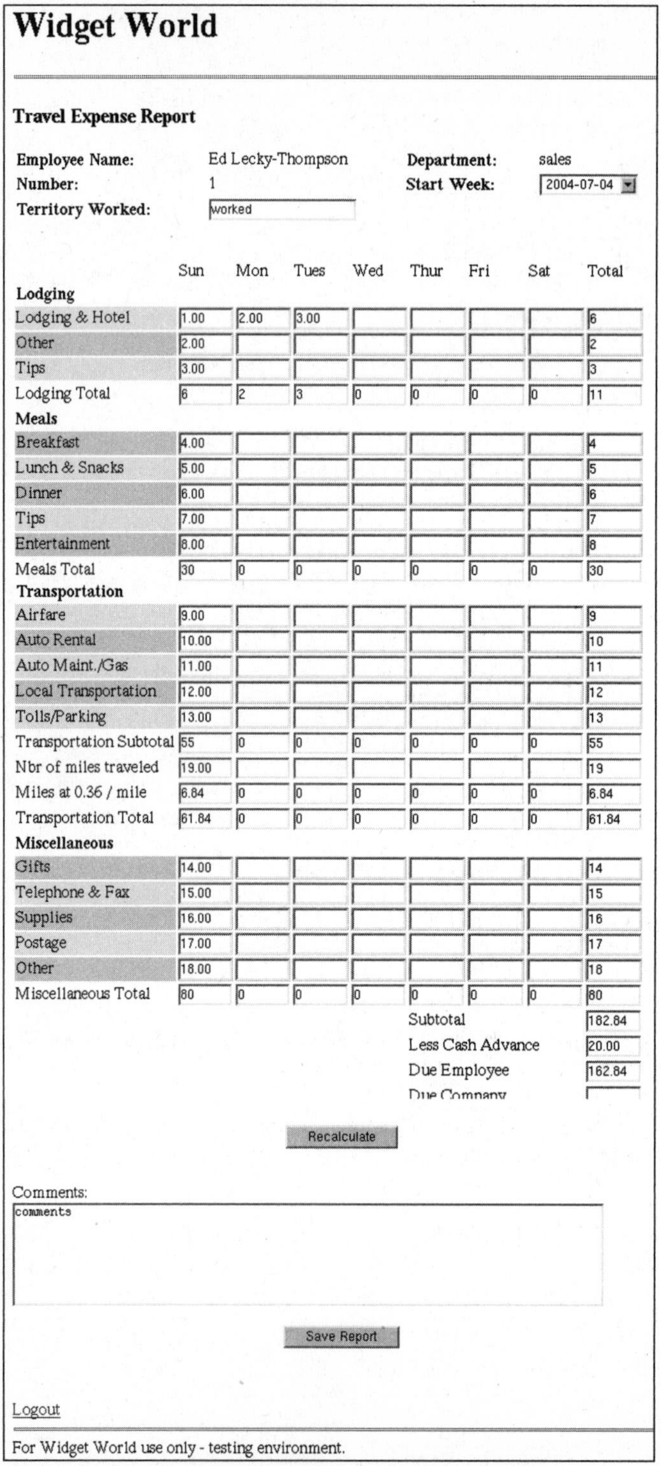

Widget World

Travel Expense Report

Employee Name:	Ed Lecky-Thompson	Department:	sales
Number:	1	Start Week:	2004-07-04 ▾
Territory Worked:	worked		

	Sun	Mon	Tues	Wed	Thur	Fri	Sat	Total
Lodging								
Lodging & Hotel	1.00	2.00	3.00					6
Other	2.00							2
Tips	3.00							3
Lodging Total	6	2	3	0	0	0	0	11
Meals								
Breakfast	4.00							4
Lunch & Snacks	5.00							5
Dinner	6.00							6
Tips	7.00							7
Entertainment	8.00							8
Meals Total	30	0	0	0	0	0	0	30
Transportation								
Airfare	9.00							9
Auto Rental	10.00							10
Auto Maint./Gas	11.00							11
Local Transportation	12.00							12
Tolls/Parking	13.00							13
Transportation Subtotal	55	0	0	0	0	0	0	55
Nbr of miles traveled	19.00							19
Miles at 0.36 / mile	6.84	0	0	0	0	0	0	6.84
Transportation Total	61.84	0	0	0	0	0	0	61.84
Miscellaneous								
Gifts	14.00							14
Telephone & Fax	15.00							15
Supplies	16.00							16
Postage	17.00							17
Other	18.00							18
Miscellaneous Total	80	0	0	0	0	0	0	80

Subtotal	182.84
Less Cash Advance	20.00
Due Employee	162.84
Due Company	

Recalculate

Comments:

comments

Save Report

Logout

For Widget World use only - testing environment.

Figure 19-10: Travel Expense Report as a spreadsheet

Now, rather than "simply working," you have a well-tested system and the beginning of a framework that is capable of evolution.

You've seen how PHP, JavaScript, and browsers do (and do not) interact, how each one is responsible for its layers, and how to move information among all of them. Creating complex spreadsheet-like behavior, although not easy, can be done with relatively little code.

Where do you go from here? Just plod through the rest of the stories? Keep on reading, because there is another important lesson to be learned.

Mock Objects

Sometimes during testing, you must interact with a deterministic object that, for various reasons, you do not have access to in your testing environment. For example, consider the following:

❑   The real object is nondeterministic, such as a real-time stock or weather-feed.

❑   The real object is too slow for your test suites, such as an overloaded transactional production database.

❑   You need to test exceptional situations, such as an intrusion alarm or systems outage.

❑   The real object does not exist. This can be anything from not having access to the required object to necessary intra-object functionality.

Essentially, a *mock object* is an object that feigns enough functionality or required functionality for you to fully test your system.

For example, if you wanted to test for session timeouts, errors, or just malicious cracking, you might import `mock-widgetsession.phpm`, which consists of the following:

```
class MockWidgetSession extends WidgetSession {
    public function getUserObject() {
        return new WidgetUser(
            array (
'id' => 1,
'username' => 'ed',
'md5_pw' => "827ccb0eea8a706c4c34a16891f84e7b",
'first_name' => "Ed",
'last_name' => "Lecky-Thompson",
'email' => "ed@lecky-thompson.com",
'role' => "s",
'department' => "sales"));
    }
}
```

Coding details aside, this `MockWidgetSession` example would enable your testing environment to simulate a login for whatever reason you require.

Smarty can also be used to mock-up HTML screens. Other than displaying the HTML to the screen, you can save the HTML in a variable, and do with it as you please.

For example, Story 6 requires sales manager notification, so you merely need to send an e-mail to the managers when the contacts are saved. Sounds pretty simple, but you're faced with the issue of how intensively you'd like to test, especially as they'd like the content of the e-mail to include the HTML from the input screen.

Getting the screen HTML is not an issue. Essentially, you must test the browser output, which is nice, because up until now you haven't been testing what the browser sees. For end-to-end completeness, the following test will reference the HTML output using a regular expression:

```
function testContactEmail () {
    $u = new WidgetUser(
        array ('id' => 1,
                'username'   => "ed",
                'first_name' => "Ed",
                'last_name'  => "Lecky-Thompson",
                'email'      => "ed@lecky-thompson.com",
                'role'       => "s",
                'department' => "sales"));
    $cv = new ContactVisit (
        array ('emp_id'             => "1",
                'week_start'         => "1980-01-01",
                'company_name'       => "test one",
                'contact_name'       => "Big One",
                'city'               => "Columbus",
                'state'              => "OH",
                'accomplishments'    => "phone call",
                'followup'           => "",
                'literature_request' => ""));
    $c = new Contact (
        array ("emp_id"             => "1",
                "week_start"         => "1980-01-01",
                "shop_calls"         => 2,
                "distributor_calls"  => 3,
                "engineer_calls"     => 4,
                "mileage"            => 50,
                "territory_worked"   => "Central Ohio",
                "territory_comments" => "Buckeyes are great." ),
            $this->_session->getDatabaseHandle());

    list ($email,_$from, $subject, $message, $headers) =
        generateContactEmail($u, $c, array ($cv), false);

    // test screen capture, requires 7bit ascii encoding (read: none)

    $this->assertEquals(1, preg_match ("/Employee Name.............Ed
                    Lecky-Thompson/", $message), "employee name");
    $this->assertEquals(1 preg_match("/company_name_0.
                    ....................test one/", $message),
        "company name");
    $this->assertEquals(1, preg_match  ("/shop_calls.................
                    ...............2/", $message),"shop calls");
    $this->assertEquals(1, preg_match ("/To: ed@lecky-thompson.com/",
                    $headers),"email");
```

```
        // test base64 encoding
        list ($email_from, $subject, $message, $headers) =
                generateContactEmail($u, $c, array ($cv));

        $this->assertEquals(0, preg_match ("/Employee Name......
                        .......Ed Lecky-Thompson/", $message),
                    "employee name");
        $this->assertEquals(1, preg_match ("/To: ed@lecky-thompson.com/",
                        $headers),"email");        }
```

If you're entering the preceding code by hand, be sure that you don't line-break in the middle of the regular expressions; they should be entered on one line.

The `generateContactEmail()` function is designed to return what is required by the PHP `mail()` function: `mail($email_address, $subject, $message, $headers);`.

In this example, you're testing what the browser sees. Instead of testing 100 percent of the HTML output, you're ensuring that the form contains the information you expect. Thus, the simple regular expression of

```
    "/Employee Name.............Ed Lecky-Thompson/"
```

will perfectly match the following generated HTML:

```
<tr><td><b>Employee Name:</b></td><td>Ed Lecky-Thompson</td>
    <td><b>Department:</b></td><td>sales</td></tr>
```

Because the base64 encoding is unreadable by humans, the tests of base64 encoding check only for the existence of the e-mail address in the email header, and not the `Employee Name` because `Employee Name` (being in the message and base64-encoded) can't be normally read.

Here are the functions that might be placed in your `lib/common-functions.phpm`:

```
function mimeifyContent ($content, $mime_boundary,
                        $filename, $flagBase64=true) {
    $message = "";
    $message .= " \r\n";
    $message .= "-".$mime_boundary."\r\n";
    $message .= "Content-Type: text/html;\r\n";
    $message .= " name=\"".$filename.".html\"\r\n";
    // default is 7bit ascii
    if ($flagBase64) {
        $message .= "Content-Transfer-Encoding: base64\r\n";
    }
    $message .= "Content-Disposition: attachment;\r\n";
    $message .= " filename=\"".$filename.".html\"\r\n";
    $message .= "\r\n";
    if ($flagBase64) {          $message .= base64_encode($content);
    } else {
        $message .= $content;
    }
```

```
        $message .= "\r\n";
        return ($message);
    }

    function generateContactEmail &$user, &$contact,
                                  $contactVisits, $flagBase64=true) {
        global $GLOBALS;
        require_once ($GLOBALS["smarty-path"].'Smarty.class.php');
        $smarty = new Smarty;
        $smarty->assign_by_ref ("user", $user);
        $smarty->assign_by_ref ("contact", $contact);
        $smarty->assign_by_ref ("contactVisits", $contactVisits);
        $smarty->assign('start_weeks', getStartWeeks());
        $smarty->assign('current_start_week', $contact->week_start);
        $smarty->assign("max_weekly_contacts", $GLOBALS["max-weekly-contacts"]);
        $email_body = @$smarty->fetch('customer-contacts.tpl');
        $headers = "";
        $headers .= "From: ".$GLOBALS["email-from"]."\n";
        $headers .= "To: ".$user->email."\n";
        if (strlen ($GLOBALS["email-contact-cc"]) > 0)
            $headers .= "Cc: ";
            $headers .= $GLOBALS["email-contact-cc"];
        $headers .= "\n";
        if (strlen ($GLOBALS["email-contact-bcc"]) > 0)
            $headers .= "Bcc: ".$GLOBALS["email-contact-bcc"]."\n";
        $mime_boundary = "<<<-==+X[".md5(time()).")."]";
        $headers .= "MIME-Version: 1.0\r\n";
        $headers .= "Content-Type: multipart/mixed;\r\n";
        $headers .= " boundary=\"".$mime_boundary."\"";
        $message = "";
        $message .= "This is a multi-part message in MIME format.\r\n";
        $message .= "\r\n";
        $message .= "-".$mime_boundary."\r\n";
        $message .= "Content-Type: text/plain; charset=\"iso-8859-1\"\r\n";
        $message .= "Content-Transfer-Encoding: 7bit\r\n";
        $message .= "\r\n";
        $message .= $GLOBALS["email-contact-message"]."\n\n";
        $nextEnding = "\r\n";
        $message.=mimeifyContent($email_body,$mime_boundary,
                                 "customer-contact", $flagBase64);
        $message.="-".$mime_boundary."".$nextEnding;
        $subject = $user->emp_id." ".$user->last_name." : ".$user->email_subject;
        return array ($user->email, $subject, $message, $headers);
    }
```

Note two things here. One, you're calling `$smarty->fetch()` instead of `$smarty->display()`. The `fetch` function places the HTML output into a variable, rather than to the screen, as does the `display` function.

Two, for technical reasons, it's safer to base64-encode HTML output if there is any chance of it using non-7-bit ASCII (e.g., if you're using Unicode or non-English characters). However, base64-encoding the HTML in the e-mail makes it practically untestable, which is why the `$flagBase64` argument exists.

If this function contained the function to physically mail the e-mail instead of simply creating the content, then you would most certainly create and utilize a mock object that simulated the e-mailing API and didn't base64-encode the content.

Summary

With this chapter, the Widget World software development effort is concluding. You would be correct in pointing out that not all the stories and features have been completed, but we have no desire to be historical revisionists of this real-world example or to force you through another 100 redundant pages of the same procedure. By now, you have the tools and know-how to complete it yourself.

Testing is one aspect of software development that has historically been considered little more than "busywork," but you've experienced how test-driven development can help you not only develop your code, but also find bugs and continue to test even when you're working on distant parts of the system.

Refactoring is not just a technical term for "code cleanup." Ideally, it shouldn't even be considered a distinct task from software development. Refactoring is simply a coding priority, much in the same way that developing system objects is a coding priority, too. Plus, you've seen how constant refactoring can help to develop a complex framework without the need for excessive analysis and unused features.

These are just a few of the principles of extreme programming (XP), which is designed to reduce complexity in order to sustain development by keeping your code base nimble and flexible. Although not every project is a candidate for the complete methodology of XP, that does not mean that your methodology, whether it's spiral, waterfall, or RUP, cannot benefit from some of the practices such as testing and constant refactoring. Additionally, because of a lack of peer programmers (for you, the reader), as well as space and focus on code, many aspects of XP haven't formally been examined, such as planning for a release and measuring the project metrics. XP is quite a disciplined approach, and you should learn more about it, because its strengths and rewards are solidly concerned with the subtleties of software development as a team.

Of course, no matter how methodical and diligent your approach during the build process, you can't skip the most important part of any project — *quality assurance*. That's something you'll meet in Chapter 20, as you discover what steps you can take post-build to ensure that your project features the quality levels your clients have a right to expect.

## 20

Quality Assurance
and Testing

The Widget World sales force automation toolkit site is looking pretty good. You're on schedule and on budget, and the client is, thus far, happy with the beta version running on your development environment and staging server. Furthermore, by employing rigorous unit testing throughout the build process in Chapter 19, you can be sure that the individual components that comprise the application all function more or less correctly independently; hence, there shouldn't be any deep-rooted problems in the code itself.

At this point, you might well be tempted to let your guard down. In fact, you have now reached one of the most critical stages in the entire project. The application is more or less complete, and the client is urging you to let them use it. You must resist, however.

Quality assurance (QA) is a term you might be familiar with. Indeed, it is borrowed from traditional manufacturing and engineering processes, and is the kind of procedure you expect to be carried out on your new DVD player or luxury family sedan. Why would you not, therefore, want to apply it to something as complex and crucial as your application?

This chapter introduces you to the QA process in large-scale PHP projects. You'll learn why quality assurance is of great importance, and what it means in terms of your expectations and those of your client. You'll also learn about the kinds of testing you must do in order to be able to confidently give your application a seal of approval, and how to get your team on board to help you when things go wrong.

Introduction to QA

Somewhat understandably, expectations regarding the reliability of the Web and the Internet at large are still pretty low among its everyday users. Chances are good that you've had a client or two call you recently to say that their e-mail was down, and so they might not have received anything you've sent. Maybe you've tried to order something online recently, only to be kicked off while your credit card was being processed. Or maybe your friend's ISP has been down for a couple of days, and no one in tech support seems to be able to tell him when he'll be back online again.

Scenarios like this are all too common. What is truly shocking is that the parties involved typically shrug their shoulders and accept it. Your clients didn't sound surprised when they told you that e-mail was down. You probably didn't even curse under your breath when your online order went wrong. And your friend likely shrugged his shoulders and got out his 3G data card.

This is a phenomenon still more or less unique to the Internet. If you bought a new car and it stalled on the highway just weeks later, you'd be pretty mad at your dealer. If you ordered a mocha latte before work and your barista gave you a cappuccino, you'd be mad and insist on a new cup. And if your DVD player died soon after purchase, you'd take it back.

There are two reasons why people don't get upset when the Internet doesn't work right. First, most people reason that there's something innately complicated about the Internet, and that it must go wrong as a result. This is a non sequitur, of course. Yes, the Internet is complicated, but so is your DVD player. In practice, too, the underlying infrastructure (that is, the servers, routers, and so forth) of the Internet is pretty much rock solid. It's bad programmers who cause things to break with the bad code they write, and the poor decisions they make when developing.

The second and more crucial reason applies to those who have had previous experience with Internet application developers. Frequently, their past experiences with these agencies and individuals have been such that their expectations with present vendors have hit rock bottom. In fact, and unfortunately, there are few other industries in which such an explosion of dangerously underskilled labor has occurred in the past few years. This has manifested itself in both appalling freelance Web "professionals" (who can barely produce valid XHTML, let alone high-quality back-end code), and some truly awful digital agencies (that revel in producing self-indulgent "award-winning" creative work without so much as a nod to how well it works under the hood). Excellence is the exception rather than the rule. In effect, there are literally thousands of vendors who talk the talk, but don't walk the walk.

The more cynical inference from this observation is that because your client's expectations will be low, you should aim low, too, because they're not likely to get mad at you if things go wrong. This approach, however, is not only cynical, it is also not commercially sensible.

Why You Should Aim High

Aiming to have a high-quality product before handing over to the client is not just about keeping the client happy. It's about maintaining your own sanity, too.

It is inevitable that your assembled system will (initially, at least) be functionally defective in some way. This does not necessarily mean that it will malfunction in the traditional sense. It could be slow when real-world data is applied, or have some unforeseen business logic error. A systematic approach to QA prior to handover ensures the following:

❑   Developer time, and hence cost spent on resolving defects, is minimized through a thorough, structured approach.

❑   The team's timely transition onto other projects can be closely adhered to.

❑   Problems encountered during deployment can be isolated as being unrelated to the application itself.

Quite apart from that, however, compare the following two attitudes:

❑ "The client's expectations are low, therefore I can underdeliver without fear of reprisal."

❑ "The client's expectations are low, therefore when I overdeliver I will be seen to excel."

It goes without saying that being seen to excel will quickly set you apart from the competition. The client's previous experience with other suppliers may have been lackluster, and the client's expectations may be low as a result, but keep in mind that client has not used those other suppliers again.

Aiming high means striving for high quality. The difference between striving and achieving starts with knowing what quality means in the first place.

What Is Quality?

There is some confusion over what constitutes *quality* in a software application. Let's return to the analogy of a family sedan. When automotive journalists review a high-quality car, they are not always referring explicitly to reliability or performance per se, but rather to less tangible and quantifiable factors, such as the following:

❑ The durability of the interior

❑ The use of expensive, solid materials (such as brushed chrome)

❑ Purely aesthetic touches (such as blue-illuminated readouts)

❑ The firm resounding noise made when the driver closes the door.

Quality here is not so much a single deciding factor, or even anything positive. Rather, it is a function of all the areas in which something *could* go wrong but doesn't.

This view is supported in the approach often taken when a car is reviewed or inspected for the first time at a trade show. The repeated activation of the cup-holder mechanism, the pressing of switches, the caressing of upholstery — these are the quick-and-dirty litmus tests used to assess quality. Yet, none of these tests tells you anything about the car's handling, gas mileage, reliability, or annual depreciation. So why are they important?

The truth of the matter is that, although you can't judge a book by its cover, you can often judge a car by its interior. A car with a smoothly ejecting cup holder; tactile, chrome-tipped switches; and seamless mechanisms is almost certainly also going to enjoy superb reliability going forward. The highest-quality brands boasting these exterior facets (such as BMW, Audi, or Mercedes) are all consistently rated among the most reliable on the road, too.

This same principle can be applied to your Web applications. Quality is not just about whether the site stays up and does what the functional specification said it would do. It's more about the little things; and, inevitably, when the little things on the surface are right, the big things underneath are right, too.

Enough about cars! What makes a Web application high quality, and how is it measured?

Measurable and Quantifiable Quality

Several core areas of quality must be assessed when conducting QA on your application. Inevitably, the importance you apportion to each one depends very much on the nature of your product and its target audience.

Functional Compliance

At the most simple and basic level, your application should provide functionality exactly as detailed in your project's original functional specification.

This goes beyond simply ensuring that no PHP warnings or errors appear, of course. The behavior of your application must be correct, under an exhaustive set of test conditions. This includes the following:

- ❏ When an Update button is pressed, the database is actually updated.
- ❏ When a welcome e-mail should be sent to a new user, the e-mail is sent and is correct.
- ❏ When a user conducts a search, the data returned is an accurate reflection of the database and the search criteria specified.

Such compliance may seem obvious, but often the most obvious points are overlooked in QA programs.

Real-World Tolerance

Real-world tolerance (RWT) means that your application should be able to cope with environments and conditions closer to its real-world, live operation than those it may run under during development.

This does not just refer to quantities of users or data on the system. It also refers to the requirement that the system be able to cope properly when a user, for example, does not enter data in an expected format. The correct behavior in such a situation should be, of course, to provide the user with an error message. It is hugely important to simulate such conditions, because it is all but inevitable that not only will users themselves do bad things from time to time, but that the data they supply from time to time will be bad, too.

Grace During Failure

There is a temptation when developing to not account for every possible scenario. For example, certain scenarios might seem unlikely. However, this temptation should be resisted. The only thing worse than the failure of a user's credit card to be processed successfully, for example, is failing to inform the user that his or her credit card was not processed successfully.

At any stage at which a failure could occur, however unlikely it may be, your application must cope gracefully. Consider, for example, an unreachable database server. Clearly, this is an undesirable situation, and the application will not function correctly when this occurs. With luck, it is a problem that will be resolved correctly by your system administrators. However, if not accounted for, your application may simply return zero search results on searches, or tell people their login is incorrect. Both of these outcomes arise because your application does not account for the condition of the database being completely inaccessible, and users will be severely misled as a result. Providing a simple "Sorry, the site is unavailable at present" page offers an obvious and immediate workaround.

Load Tolerance

During functional testing, your application will be hit by a combined audience probably not much bigger than your development team — probably less than a dozen simultaneously using the system. In practice, of course, your audience will certainly be much bigger than this, with a requirement for 100, 1,000, maybe even 10,000 simultaneous users to be supported.

You will know the actual figure or estimate from your technical specification, and will have drafted an architecture to suit. What may have worked on paper will not necessary translate to the real world, however. It is vital, of course, that it does.

If the application's response under heavy load is an unacceptable response time or, worse still, outright failure, then clearly the client will not accept the product as satisfactory.

Usability

The latest buzzword in interface architecture these days is that of *usability*. Championed by leading experts such as Jakob Nielsen (see his excellent Web site at www.useit.com), it refers to the inherent intuitiveness and logic of a user interface. It can apply to not only the Web, but also traditional client-side software applications, and even the control panel of a washing machine.

It is typically measured by the ease and speed with which a user new to the application can perform certain tasks. These tasks are expressed as objectives, and no specific instructions on their completion are issued. For example, users of a Web mail application might be asked to compose a new message to foo@example.com. However, they would not be guided to click the Compose button in the top-left corner of the screen, or enter foo@example.com in the recipient box, and so forth.

Observing the user's effectiveness in carrying out these tasks is the cornerstone of usability testing, discussed shortly.

Veneer

Just one step removed from usability is the *veneer* (or finish) of the product. Remember the earlier analogy involving chrome switches and cup holders in the sedan? The veneer of your application is the direct equivalent, and because it is the first real experience users will have of your application, it provides a telling insight into the underlying quality of the application.

What is meant by veneer? Consider the quick-and-dirty examples throughout this book, outside the realm of the larger Widget World project. Each has been constructed to demonstrate a concept, with no other purpose in mind. As a result, they've never looked or felt that great — a bit rough around the edges, perhaps. That's never really mattered, however, because they have merely been demonstrating a technical concept. A finished product should never adapt this approach, of course.

The chrome switches in the driver's cabin are the properly rendered Previous and Next buttons on your pagination. The cup holders' smooth eject mechanism is the manner in which the navigation refreshes updates with each section of your application selected. This is the veneer (or finish) of your application, and, although it is not a showstopper if poorly implemented, it can speak volumes about the overall quality of your application.

Many software architects and engineers are less gifted with designing the aesthetics of a user interface than you might think. As part of your own project-management methodology, it is important to ensure that an experienced senior designer with interface architecture skills is on hand to ensure that the polish on your finished product stays well and truly intact.

When a small change is requested late in the project, it is tempting to cut corners and allow a software engineer to take ownership of the new feature. Do this only if you have a rock-solid style guide in place, as discussed in Chapter 16. Otherwise, you may find your beautiful application blighted by the appearance of a grey, rectangular Submit button on an otherwise lovely interface.

Testing

It goes without saying that the single most effective way to ensure that the core qualities alluded to previously pervade your project and that is to test, test, and test some more.

Testing can take many forms, however. Each of the previous qualities has one or more testing methodologies associated with it. Let's look at them in turn.

Unit Testing

The good news is that you've already done this at least once before — that is, you have if you followed Chapter 13 in detail, where you would have encountered unit testing as part of the build of the Widget World application.

The concepts of unit programming and a testing framework were touched upon earlier in this book, including the theory of why these are good practices to employ in large projects. In Chapter 13, you put that theory into practice in building the application.

Let's recap briefly, however. Unit-driven programming involves constructing your application in neatly packaged, distinct components that have an interface yielding human-predictable results from a given set of a data. A testing framework is then constructed for each component that asserts a series of human-determined theoretical results based on a series of theoretical inputs, and then tests the validity of those assertions by comparing those theoretical results against the actual results derived from the execution of that component's methods.

These frameworks become black boxes that enable you to continuously test the functionality of your components throughout their evolution. You can construct such frameworks, therefore, early in your project, and regression-test your components as they evolve and become more sophisticated to ensure that they still produce the results expected. Put crudely, you can test to ensure that your changes have not broken something that used to work!

Unit testing picks up coding errors. Such errors are typically oversights on the part of the programmer. Unit testing does not pick up any other form of a problem; hence, it is only a part of the testing required to ensure high levels of quality with respect to functional compliance.

As an example, consider a Web mail application. You may have built a user class, a mailbox class, and a message class. All three may pass your unit tests. However, consider the Reply button on a message being viewed. It would instantiate a new message object and copy the sender property of the original message object to the recipient object of the message object. This action may not be performed by any specific method in any class, and hence may not be the subject of any unit test.

If the recipient of the e-mail is not set correctly when Reply is clicked, then this is very clearly a functional error that must be resolved. It is not, however, one that a unit testing framework would pick up in any three of the tests being performed. You can see, therefore, that unit testing is not the ultimate test of functional compliance. In effect, it tests only the "model" in your model-view-controller (MVC) design pattern.

Functional Testing

Functional testing is the other half of ensuring functional compliance quality on your project. It is normally conducted with due deference to the original functional specification of the project.

There are a number of possible approaches to formalizing functional testing. The most important rule to follow is that it is, in fact, formalized in the first place. Merely having a developer perform a quick run-through of key functionality isn't enough on a large-scale project.

One approach to consider is to assemble a team of test personnel, ideally relatively intelligent individuals typical of your target audience, and issue them formal paperwork for completion. Consider assigning each test team member a specific area of the site to test.

The Functional Test Paper

Considering the Web mail example, you might devise a form that looks something like Table 20-1. The "Action" and "Expected Result" columns should be completed by you in your role as project manager. Your test team will complete the "Actual Result" column, which you can then use to score each test as either a FAIL or a PASS.

Table 20-1: Functional Test Form for Web Mail Example

Action	Expected Result	Actual Result	Score
Open the login page by clicking the login link on the navigation.	The login page is displayed, featuring username and password text boxes, and the Submit button.	Expected result	PASS
Enter the login **joet1301f** and the password **ixrsh0z1** and click Login.	The form submits and the page reloads, stating that your login is successful. After five seconds, you are automatically transferred to the home page.	Expected result	PASS
Click the Inbox link in the navigation.	You will be taken to your Inbox. You will see a number of messages listed. For each message, subject, date received, and sender should be listed. The total number of pages comprising this mailbox will be shown. Previous and Next buttons will be visible if more than one page exists	Expected result *except* that no Next button displayed despite showing page 1 of 18	FAIL

It is, of course, extremely important that any FAIL marks are followed up. As project manager, you should assume a role whereby you first double-check any failures yourself. If any are found to be genuine, they can be entered into a fault-management system, the likes of which are discussed later in this chapter.

The actions you place on each functional testing paper will, of course, be derived directly from the functional specification in one form or another. Essentially, you are devising a user journey. Your test team will need to follow the actions sequentially. For example, it is obviously important that any logins take place before any activity dependent on the user being logged in. Advise your test users that if they find themselves unable to execute subsequent actions because of a block failure, they should mark their papers accordingly and move on.

Functional Testing Considerations

You must ensure that each branch of the user journey is covered in testing, at least to the extent that you can be reasonably confident that the system is functionally correct. A branch occurs every time a decision is made. For example, if logins to your system come in three flavors (say, a normal user, super user, and administrator), you need to have three initial branches. If, for each of these logins, a user may choose one of three mailboxes to view, then an additional three branches per initial branch will be created.

It may be helpful to draw all the possible user journeys using a tree diagram of some sort, which you can then translate into the previous testing paperwork.

This method of functional testing is not infallible, but far more effective than simply asking the development team to "test thoroughly." The resulting paperwork also forms a sort of affidavit that can be presented to the client as documented proof that the system has been thoroughly tested prior to handover.

Load Testing

The general principle of load testing is to determine exactly what kind of extreme environmental conditions your application can cope with before it falls over.

The traditional belief is that it is sufficient to simply ascertain whether the application can support the number of simultaneous users specified in the technical specification, and whether the response times under such a usage level are within a reasonable limit.

A more bullish approach is to keep turning up the amp until the speakers blow. Clients much prefer to be told that "your site can, under its present infrastructure, support 530 simultaneous users" than simply "yes, your site supports the 500 simultaneous users you need it to." Knowing that the system has support for only 30 additional users may not be the news that clients want to hear, but it is better that the client hears it sooner rather than later.

The principles of load testing are detailed further in Appendix C, "Performance Tuning PHP."

Usability Testing

Cast your mind back to the sample functional testing worksheet shown in Table 20-1. You allocated tasks to your testers such as "Open the login page by clicking the login link on the navigation."

A similar task in *usability testing* would be simply phrased "Log in to the system." The purpose is quite different, of course; hence, the very different phrasing. Usability testing does not concern itself with whether things work. This is established during functional testing. Rather, it asks how effectively or easily the user can perform the task in question.

Perhaps uniquely in software testing, usability testing rarely involves questions put directly to the test subjects. Instead, observation is the key.

When instructed to, for example, "Log in to the system," the user will be observed (either in person or remotely). It is the user's actions, or behavior, in achieving (or not achieving) the task required (which are only in part quantifiable in figures) that are of interest.

For example, you may want to attempt to answer the following questions:

❑ Where does the user physically look for the login link? Is it where you placed it or somewhere else? (Note that the position of a user's cursor on-screen is often a clue to where the user is looking.)

❑ What sort of delay is there between when the login screen loads and the user starts typing his or her username?

❑ Does the user visit any other pages in error prior to finding the login page?

The answers to these questions will provide you with a good indication of the usability of your application. Admittedly, it can be difficult to quantify such research into figures, however.

Usability testing and the useful metrics it can supply is a huge topic in and of itself, and outside the scope of this chapter. More information on the various approaches available can be found on the excellent site www.useit.com, run by Jakob Nielsen.

Fault Tracking

The testing you carry out using the techniques previously described will inevitably lead to observations, such as the following:

❑ Functional testing has shown that the recipient address is not correctly copied into the new message when replying to an existing message.

❑ Load testing has shown that the system does not respond in a sufficiently timely manner to requests made at 530 simultaneous sessions.

❑ Usability testing has shown that people expect the Previous and Next buttons in the Mailbox view to be at the top of the page, not the bottom.

These observations are relatively useless without the tabulation of corresponding action points. For the issues outlined previously, you might raise action points as follows:

❑ Ensure that when replying to a message, the recipient is automatically set to be the sender of the message being replied to.

❑ When 530 sessions are active, divert additional users to a "service unavailable" page explaining that the server is not able to process their requests at this time.

❑ Move the Previous and Next buttons in the Mailbox view to the top of the page.

These actions are all simple enough for a small project, but on a larger project you may have hundreds, or even thousands, of action points (such as bugs that need fixing and tweaks for fine tuning). How do you keep track?

It's certainly possible to use the well-known default solution of any office worker thrust without warning into the world of project management — that of Microsoft Excel. It certainly gives you a quick-and-dirty mechanism for keeping track of project fault reports and their status, in the form of a color-coded table updated on a regular basis by all participating on the project.

However, its limitations will soon become clear. No Web-based access means that users must be in the same office where that spreadsheet resides on a local file server. No multiple-user access means that only one user can update the spreadsheet at a time. An onus on those using it to check it and update it frequently and regularly (with no prospect of notifications when issues requiring their attention become prescient) means that issues often go unchecked, even when urgent.

That's where a purpose-built solution can provide an effective alternative.

Effective Fault Management Using Mantis

This section takes a look at a fault-management system known as Mantis, a free package currently available from `www.mantisbt.org`.

The purpose of Mantis is to enable you to effectively keep tabs on all faults and defects in your projects, assign them to developers for resolution, and enable developers to pass comments on them where appropriate.

Mantis is a Web-based application written in PHP (what else?) that typically functions as an extranet. Whether you choose to open it up for access to your clients is entirely up to you. When working with smaller clients, this can often be beneficial because it enables them to feel part of the QA process. Mantis supports multiple users, each with his or her own access levels and rights, so you can offer different access to yourself and, say, your developers.

Many other fault-management systems exist, of course. This discussion examines Mantis specifically because it is freely available, easy to use, and written in PHP. This means that you could, in theory, modify and extend it to better suit your needs if so required.

Installing Mantis

Download the Mantis installation archive from its Web site and unpack it in the usual manner:

```
# tar -xzvf mantis-1.1.2.tar.gz
```

This will create a directory called `mantis-1.1.2` containing all the source and configuration files for Mantis. You should have a `VirtualHost` in Apache's `httpd.conf` configuration file pointing to this location as follows:

```
<VirtualHost 192.168.168.2>
        ServerAdmin you@example.com
        ServerName mantis.example.com
        CustomLog /home/production/logfile_mantis common
        ErrorLog /home/production/errlog_mantis
        DocumentRoot /home/production/public_html/mantis-1.1.12
</VirtualHost>
```

If you are using a Web server other than Apache, you should set up a virtual server to support Mantis in the manner in which you are accustomed.

Configuring Mantis for the First Time

Previous versions of Mantis have supported only MySQL. As you have read throughout this book, the authors generally favor PostgreSQL because it provides a genuinely free, open source, and more feature-rich alternative, closer to its commercial enterprise counterparts such as Oracle, at the expense of some loss of performance and, of course, wider support.

Mercifully, in the more recent versions of Mantis, PostgreSQL has been equally well supported. Indeed, it is the use of a database abstraction layer (the likes of which was advocated back in Chapter 6) that has enabled the developers of Mantis to bow to popular demand and add support for PostgreSQL out of the box.

Open your Web browser and point it to the virtual host you set up in the previous section. You should see a screen like the one shown in Figure 20-1 — a "one time run" installation screen. Note that the URL in the browser window has been partially obscured for reasons of security.

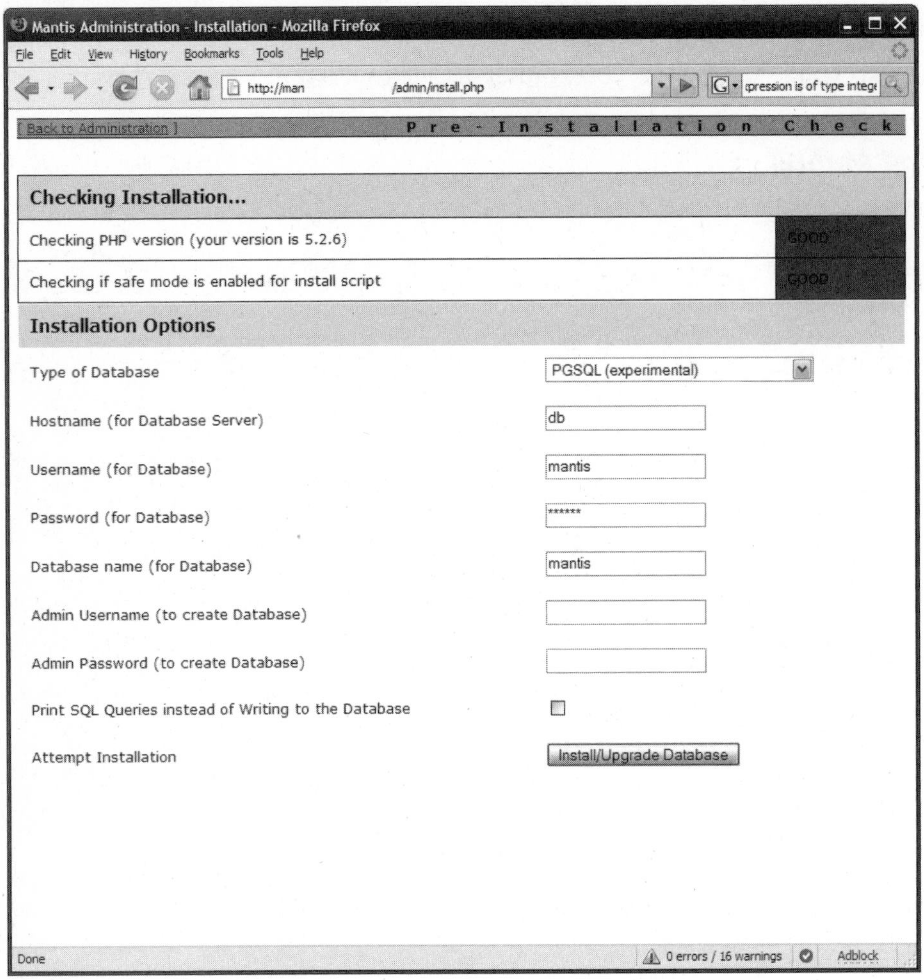

Figure 20-1: Mantis installation

As you can see from Figure 20-1, Mantis wants to know the details for your database. Before you proceed, you must create an empty database in PostgreSQL, as well as a user (with a password) that Mantis can use.

From your shell, use the following syntax to do just that:

```
root@gdmsrv02:~# /usr/local/pgsql/bin/createuser -P mantis
Enter password for new role:
Enter it again:
Shall the new role be a superuser? (y/n) n
Shall the new role be allowed to create databases? (y/n) n
Shall the new role be allowed to create more new roles? (y/n) n
```

Don't forget to make a note of the password you've chosen. Next, create the empty database as follows:

```
root@gdmsrv02:~# /usr/local/pgsql/bin/createdb mantis
```

You can now point the Mantis installation screen (still open in your Web browser, it is hoped) at the database you just made and click Install/Upgrade Database.

The installation screen should tell you that all was successful, and provide a link for you to "continue" to log in to Mantis for the first time.

Logging in As Administrator

Fire up your Web browser and point it at the virtual host you created earlier. You should see a login screen similar to what is shown in Figure 20-2. Again, the full URL has been blanked out for security.

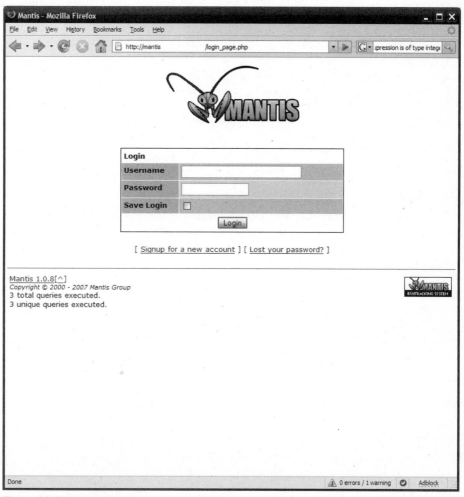

Figure 20-2: Login message

Now, log in as `administrator`. By default, the password has been set in the PostgreSQL database generation script to be `administrator`.

After you've logged in, you should first lock down your Mantis installation. The best way to do this is to create another account, not named `administrator`, with a more secure password that you can use for day-to-day administration. This is particularly important if you are able to access your Mantis installation over the public Internet.

You may also notice that your installation of Mantis implores you at login to delete the `admin` directory from your installation. You should do just that. You won't need that folder anymore, so either delete it or remove it from your Web server's document root entirely. Once it's removed, the nagging message disappears accordingly.

Creating and Editing Users

Everyone who will have access to Mantis (that is, yourself, your development team, and maybe your client's representatives) will require a user account.

To create an account, click the Manage link when logged in as an administrator. "Manage Users" is selected by default, and, accordingly, you will see a list of user accounts on the system. Creating a new account is as simple as clicking Create New Account. Don't forget to set the access level to an appropriate level. Anyone whose only task is to report bugs or defects can be set as a reporter, whereas you want your own account to be administrator.

After you have created all the necessary user accounts (including at least one with administrative privileges), you can completely remove the administrator account.

Once a user is created, you can modify even more properties of that user's account by clicking his or her username. Figure 20-3 shows a typical user editing session in Mantis.

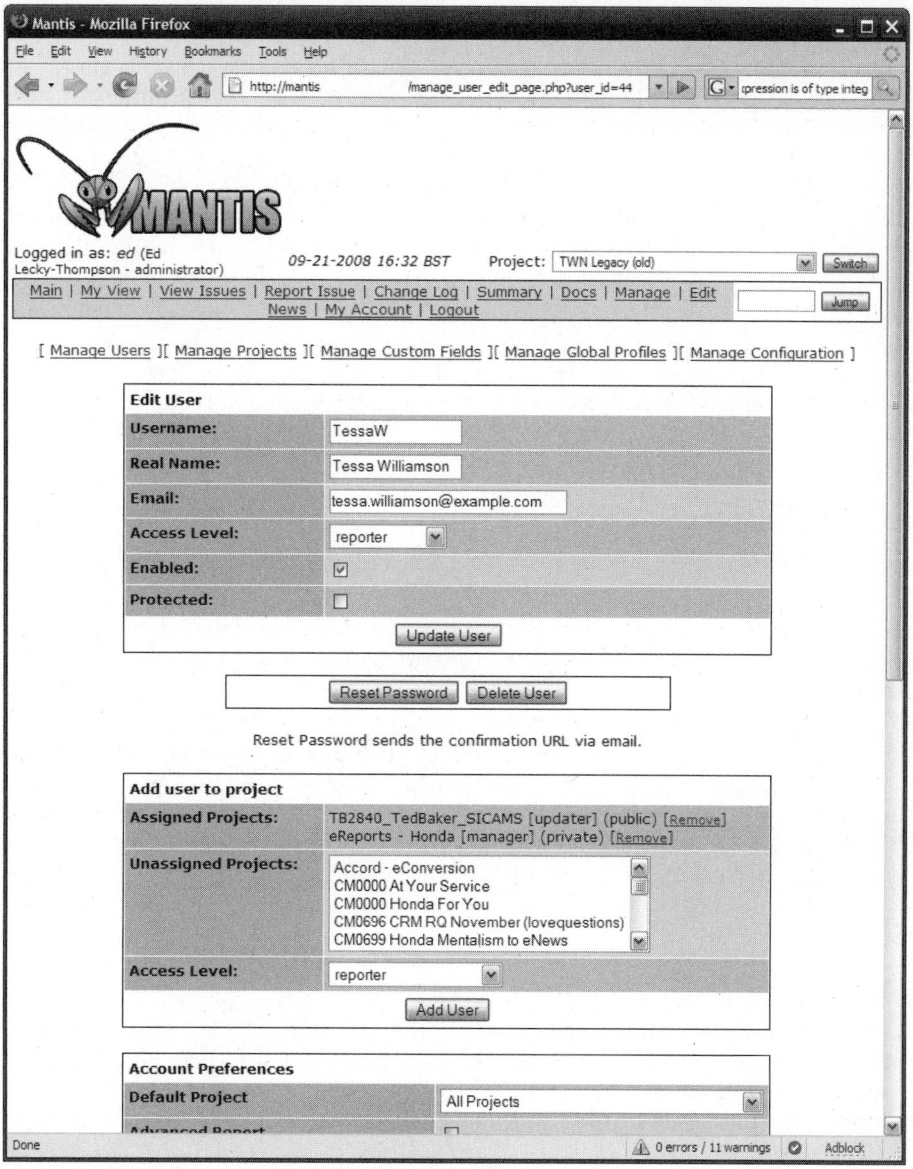

Figure 20-3: Typical user editing session in Mantis

Adding a User to a Project

Crucially, you can use the Edit User screen not only to edit the user's details, but also to add that user to a project. By default, a user does not have access to any projects, which means that even if he or she has reporter status, that user can't report any bugs.

To add the user you are editing to a project, select the project in question (if this is your first time using Mantis, you won't have any yet) and click Add. If a project is marked as public, you can skip this step because all users will have access. This is very rarely desirable, especially if you have clients using the system.

Note that when creating an account, your new users will automatically be sent an e-mail message containing their usernames and passwords, and the URL for accessing this installation of Mantis. If this behavior is not desirable, you can disable it in the Mantis configuration file you were editing a few moments ago.

Creating New Projects

There is no limit to the number of projects that Mantis can support.

To create a new project, select the Manage Projects link toward the top of the screen. A similar view to that shown in Manage Users will be shown, with all current projects displayed. To create a new project, click Create New Project.

Initially, you will be asked to specify a project name, status (which is an arbitrary flag for your own reference), view status (which should be set to private for the reasons discussed previously), description, and an upload file path. The upload file path is the place where any binary files (such as screenshots of the bugs being replicated) attached to bugs lodged in the system will be stored. This must be writable by the Web server, which you may need to effect by manually changing the permissions of that particular folder on your server.

Setting Up Project Bug Categories

After you have created a new project, you can edit its finer details by clicking its name. The most important detail you will want to set is the categories for the project. Each defect entered into the system can be placed in a category, and you will want to define as many as you see fit. Figure 20-4 shows a typical project being managed in this way, with bug categories being added to make the project ready to use.

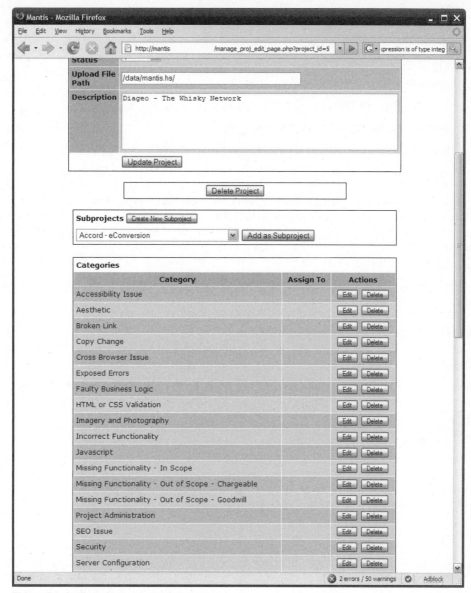

Figure 20-4: Managing a typical project

You may want to have categories similar to the following:

- ❑ Copy/text Change
- ❑ Design and Appearance
- ❑ Usability
- ❑ Functionality: Business Logic

- ❑ Functionality: Desirable (out of scope and chargeable)
- ❑ Functionality: Incorrect
- ❑ Functionality: Malfunction
- ❑ Functionality: Missing (but detailed in specification)
- ❑ Functionality: User Interface
- ❑ Project Management and Administration
- ❑ Database Schema
- ❑ Systems and Infrastructure

After you have created a set of categories, you can easily reuse these on future projects by using the Copy Categories From and Copy Categories To buttons judiciously. These can be found by editing the categories on a project (select Manage ⇨ Manage Projects) and then scrolling to the very bottom of the list of the existing categories you are maintaining. You will probably find that a universal list of categories similar to the preceding will serve you well in any future projects upon which you might embark.

With your project set up, you may need to select it whenever you log into Mantis in the future, especially if you have more than one project on the system. The small drop-down list box in the top-right corner of the screen enables you to flip among projects by name.

Reporting Bugs

Now that you have the project set up, you and your team can start entering bugs that were found. Be sure to translate any faults into more specific tasks, rather than simply announce the problem. For example, "Move the pagination bar from the bottom to the top of the page," is more productive than "The pagination bar is in the wrong place."

To report a bug, simply select Report Bug from the main navigation.

You must select a category for the bug. This list will be generated dynamically from the selection of categories you entered earlier.

Other information you need to enter includes the following:

- ❑ *Reproducibility* — If this is a fault, rather than a simple request, state how frequently the problem can be reproduced. If this is a request for a new feature, select N/A, because there is nothing to reproduce.

- ❑ *Severity* — This list is hard-coded into Mantis and relates to the impact the fault is having on the project. Most of these are self-explanatory. *Feature* refers to a fault at the feature-level and implies that a key feature is either missing or rendered completely unusable by the fault. *Block* means that other testing is being held up as a result of this fault.

- ❑ *Priority* — This indicates a relative severity level for the fault to be attended to by the development team.

- ❑ *Summary* — This is a brief, one-line summary of the fault or, if there is insufficient space, the area in which the fault is developing (for example, "Auto-completion of text fields when replying to e-mails").

❑ *Description* — This provides further detail about the fault.

❑ *Additional Information* — This provides any additional points that may aid the developers in resolving the problem.

❑ *Upload file* — If you wish to associate a binary file with this fault (for example, a screenshot showing the fault in action), you can upload it here. It will be stored in your server in the location you specified when you set up the project.

❑ *Report Stay* — If you check this box, you will be taken back to the "report new bug" screen when the bug is successfully entered. This enables you to batch-enter bugs more easily.

After you have entered a bug, you can view it under View Issues from the main navigation menu. One key point worth noting is that the bug is not yet assigned to anyone. This is the next step.

Assigning Bugs

After bugs have been entered into the system, you will doubtlessly want to use your own Mantis login to assign their resolution to one of your development team.

Select the bug by its number from the list shown under View Issues, and you will see a drop-down list of users next to the button named Assign To. Select the user to whom you wish to assign the bug (which can be yourself) and click the button. The user lucky enough to be given the task of resolving this bug will be sent an e-mail with a direct link to the bug.

You can also bulk-assign bugs from the View Issues screen. This can be useful if you are working on a small project and you want to assign all open bugs to a given user. Place a check mark next to the bugs you want to assign, select Assign in the drop-down list box at the bottom of the list, and click Go. You will be invited to select a user, and the checked bugs will then be assigned to that user in the same way.

Annotating Bugs

Your developers may take issue with a bug you have raised or, alternatively, want to add their own questions or comments. They can do this by viewing the bug, entering text in the relevant text box, and clicking Add Bugnote. The comment will be recorded against the bug, and a copy is sent to the person who raised the bug in the first place. The bug raiser may then want to add his or her own comments (in reply, if necessary), which will in turn be sent to the developer, and so on.

A developer may also want to make use of the resolution status of the bug to indicate his or her progress on the task at hand, or reaction to the bug overall. This includes such flags as "not a bug," "won't fix," "fixed," and so forth. Any changes in status also generate notification e-mails to the bug raiser.

Resolving Bugs

After a developer has fixed a bug, he or she simply marks it as resolved by clicking the Resolved button. This changes both the resolution status and the overall status of the bug to "resolved," firing e-mails to the bug raiser in the process.

If the project administrator agrees that the bug is resolved, he or she may set its overall status to "closed." If he or she disagrees that it is resolved, it can be assigned again, and the resolution status is set to "reopened." The developer will be notified that the bug has been reopened.

Both status flags are of particular use in the View Issues view, in which filters may be applied to see only bugs of a specific status. Color-coding is used to indicate the status of bugs at a glance.

Getting the Most out of Mantis

In addition to being quite straightforward to get started with, Mantis is a hugely powerful package that requires and deserves in-depth attention. A complete discussion of all its features and capabilities is beyond the scope of this chapter, but the Mantis Web site at www.mantisbt.org offers detailed instructions, including a useful FAQ.

Summary

This chapter introduced you to the basics of quality assurance (QA). You first learned what quality really means in application development, and the six core concepts that constitute it.

You then learned how many of those concepts can be tested in the real world to determine and measure quality on any given project, and how best to record the results of those tests.

Finally, you were introduced to Mantis, a powerful bug-tracking and fault-management tool. You learned how to install and configure it, as well as how to use it on a daily basis for your own projects.

By now, you should have a quality product, free from defects. In Chapter 21, you'll learn how to devise an effective deployment strategy for getting that product from your development and staging servers onto a live environment.

21

Deployment

The Sales Force Automation toolkit is now not only fully complete in accordance with the agreed specifications and blueprints, but also fully bug-free, thanks in no small part to some thoroughgoing quality assurance (QA) and testing in Chapter 20.

The process of getting your application uploaded onto a production server might have seemed simple enough when you first started out in Web development, but for a true professional, there is (as always) a best practice to be followed. This best practice is not just posturing. It is vital to ensuring effective version control and QA — two subjects touched upon elsewhere in this book.

In this short chapter, you'll learn about structuring a server environment for a development team and managing the transition of source code between each server as you "go live." You'll also examine how and when to apply each transition to match the immediate commercial objectives of both your team and your client.

Devising Development Environments

When developing a large-scale PHP application, there is generally an inescapable requirement for multiple servers or development environments to play their respective roles throughout the development process.

Of course, ultimately, your completed application (be it a public Web site, or a closed intranet application) will reside on a server somewhere. This server may be in a dedicated data center or simply in the server cupboard of the client company.

This server is universally referred to as the *production* server or, if more than one server is involved (as is often the case in high-traffic/high-availability sites, as discussed in Chapter 23), the *production environment*. It may not even have been purchased when you started the project. As a result, a series of interim environments are required to provide the chronological stepping-stones for the deployment of your application.

The Studio Development Environment

As project lead, you must equip your development team with a local development environment in which to develop. This example assumes that your project is called Widgets. Your local development server will probably sit on your internal network only, with a private IP address of 192.168.1.1 (or similar); and it should not be exposed to the outside world, because the outside world will never need to access it. You may also have devised an internal domain name — maybe `mydevelopmentco.local` — that resolves using only your own internal DNS servers.

You may then establish a virtual server in Apache or your Web server of choice:

```
http://dev.widgets.mydevelopmentco.local
```

The corresponding entry in a UNIX/Linux installation of Apache's `httpd.conf` would be as follows:

```
<VirtualHost 192.168.1.1:80>
 ServerName dev.widgets.mydevelopmentco.local
 ServerAdmin ed@example.com"
 CustomLog /home/widgets/logfile_wid common
 ErrorLog /home/widgets/errlog_wid
 DocumentRoot /home/widgets/public_html/dev/php
</VirtualHost>
```

Obviously, you would amend the IP address, server name, e-mail addresses, and paths to match; and configuration syntax in other Web servers would, of course, be subtly different.

You also must expose the home directory of the user widgets to all of your development team, such that they may easily modify the code using their chosen development environments. In a typical setup, they may be using Windows workstations to modify code. In such a case, the use of Samba (`www.samba.org`) is highly recommended to create a network drive letter from which they can access the source base and amend it directly on the development server.

Modifications that your team then makes to the source base will be visible only at the development URL (`http://dev.widgets.mydevelopmentco.local`) and not on the live site.

If you are using any form of version control methodology, as described in Appendix A, you must provide virtual server instances for each of your developers, too — such as `http://johndoe.dev` `.widgets.mydevelopmentco.local`. More detail on this setup and the role it plays in version control is provided in Appendix A. In such a setup, the master development server mentioned previously still exists, but it is a reflection of the source base as committed to the version control repository, rather than any live in-progress development.

> It can be time-consuming in larger development studio environments to have to create DNS entries for every new project and, when using version control, every new developer, too. If you are using just one physical server for all your projects, then you can simplify this process by using a Wildcard DNS setup. This means that `*.` `mydevelopmentco.local` will automatically resolve to 192.168.1.1. You can find information on how to do this on the Web. Just search for "Wildcard DNS."

The Studio Staging Environment

As a development outfit, you will want a production server of your own — a place for you and your team to host your own ratified, finalized code prior to dispatch to your customer.

If you're using version control, this will be a reflection of your repository, but not necessarily of the very latest versions in all cases. Rather, it will be the latest versions of each file that have been approved for submission to key project stakeholders for approval. In practice, this will represent the versions of each file that have been "tagged" as *release*. You can find more information on tagging in Appendix A, where version control is explored in more detail.

The studio staging environment is generally for internal use only. It is of most use to project managers who want to assess the true progress of a project, as well as for QA and testing, where modifications to the live database cannot be risked.

In the previous example, the studio staging environment might be named as follows:

```
http://studiostaging.widgets.mydevelopmentco.local
```

The corresponding Apache entry may read as follows:

```
<VirtualHost 192.168.1.1:80>
  ServerName dev.widgets.mydevelopmentco.local
  ServerAdmin ed@example.com
  CustomLog /home/widgets/logfile_wid-staging common
  ErrorLog /home/widgets/errlog_wid-staging
  DocumentRoot /home/widgets/public_html/staging/php
</VirtualHost>
```

The Live Staging Environment

The live staging environment provides a test bed for you to demonstrate new functionality to your project stakeholders prior to release in the live production environment.

The staging environment is typically hosted on the same server (or servers) as the production environment, but with a subtly different URL. For example, if your live site were called `http://www.widgets.com`, you might use `http://staging.widgets.com` for your live staging environment.

A typical Apache configuration might read as follows:

```
<VirtualHost 192.168.2.1:80>
  ServerName staging.widgets.com
  ServerAdmin ed@example.com
  CustomLog /home/widgets/logfile_wid-staging common
  ErrorLog /home/widgets/errlog_wid-staging
  DocumentRoot /home/widgets/public_html/staging/php
</VirtualHost>
```

Note the different IP address — indeed, a different subnet — compared with your development server. It's worth using different private address ranges for each cluster of servers for which you are responsible. Because your live staging environment will likely reside in a data center and not on your local network, a second subnet has been introduced: 192.168.2.x instead of 192.168.1.x. Keeping subnets different enables you to configure virtual private network (VPN) access to your remote data center more easily, should you ever wish to do so. It's also a lot less confusing.

If your live production environment uses multiple servers in a load-balanced configuration, you would be wise to run your staging environment off a single server. After all, your staging environment is unlikely to attract the kinds of loads that warrant the use of multiple servers.

It may be prudent to protect your live staging environment with a username and password, because it is, strictly speaking, publicly accessible. It would be potentially disastrous if a member of the general public saw content that was, for example, subject to a press embargo. Imagine the fallout if people could check up on what Apple was about unveil at their latest Worldwide Developer's Conference (WWDC) just by visiting `http://staging.apple.com`!

However, avoid using an `.htaccess` file to accomplish this because that file risks being accidentally replicated onto your production environment during deployment, which would expose your live environment to that same password protection.

Instead, you can add this layer of security directly into your Apache configuration file:

```
<VirtualHost 192.168.2.1:80>
  ServerName staging.widgets.com
  ServerAdmin ed@example.com
  CustomLog /home/widgets/logfile_wid-staging common
  ErrorLog /home/widgets/errlog_wid-staging
  DocumentRoot /home/widgets/public_html/staging/php
  <Directory /home/widgets/public_html/staging/php>
   AuthType Basic
   AuthName Staging
   AuthUserFile /home/widgets/.htpasswd
   Satisfy All
   Require valid-user
  </Directory>
</VirtualHost>
```

The .htpasswd file is created in the normal manner (that is, using `/usr/local/apache/bin/ htpasswd`).

It's important to keep the location of the `.htpasswd` file outside the directory structure of your Web site. In this case, it's three folders up under `/home/widgets`. This ensures that the password file can't be retrieved by a simple HTTP request from a malicious intruder.

As an aside, it's worth remembering that this kind of *basic authentication* (as it is known) is not exactly industrial strength. If you have truly sensitive material on your live staging environment, you should consider using the Apache directives `Allow` and `Deny` to restrict by IP address, too.

The Live Production Environment

Your live production environment provides the environment that the public sees — the live Web site itself. This may not be the general public if this is a closed system, but it is nonetheless the place for fully tested, fully approved, ratified code.

A typical Apache configuration might read as follows:

```
<VirtualHost 192.168.2.1:80>
  ServerName www.widgets.com
  ServerAdmin ed@example.com
  CustomLog /home/widgets/logfile_wid-live common
  ErrorLog /home/widgets/errlog_wid-live
  DocumentRoot /home/widgets/public_html/live/php
</VirtualHost>
```

Development Databases

Assuming that your application is database-driven, you must make a conscious decision about what instance of the database (that is, which physical server and which database on that server) should be used for each of your environments.

This is particularly pertinent considering that certain evolutions of code may require modifications to database schema that, if made against a production database still being driven by an older release of code, would surely cause errors.

With this in mind, consider the following strategy:

❑ Individual development environments (if used) should employ a locally hosted database, specific to that individual. For example, John Doe should use a database called `widgets-johndoe`.

❑ The master development environment should employ a locally hosted database (perhaps simply named `widgets-dev`), not specific to any individual developer, but reflecting the latest database schema required to support the very latest versions from your version control platform.

❑ The studio staging environment should employ a locally hosted database (perhaps simply named `widgets-stg`), not specific to any individual developer, but reflecting the latest database schema required to support the latest release-tagged versions from your version control platform.

❑ The live production environment should, naturally, use the live database server and the live database.

❑ The live staging environment should also use the live database so that when it's being used by the client for testing and approval purposes, it provides an accurate reflection of how the live environment will behave once the changes are deployed.

Of course, with at least four databases in existence at any one time, keeping track of necessary changes to the database schema itself can be tricky.

Version control software is of little use here. Yes, it is possible to maintain a dump of the database structure in your repository, but simply retrieving this dump will not physically update the database schema when it is downloaded. Simply dropping and recreating the database is an option, but this will lose any test data stored therein. It is also difficult to use such a SQL "dump" file to determine differences in database schema when you're working on larger projects.

The best approach, therefore, is one of good communications. Version control can play an important part here. Create a folder called db-changes in your repository. Instructing your developers to add text files containing a series of ALTER statements whenever they make changes to the database schema will mean that any developer performing "get latest versions" will also receive a series of changes to make to his or her own database.

Such files can also be tagged as *release* so that those responsible for maintaining the master development and studio staging environments can ensure that both databases are kept up-to-date to the appropriate degree.

> Telling your application which database to use can result in awkward `switch` statements or, worse, hard-coded values that need changing by hand. There is another way, however. You doubtlessly have a file called `constants.phpm` (or similar) that dictates database IP address, database name, username, password, and so forth. By adapting this to consult the `$_SERVER["HTTP_HOST"]` property, the database IP, name, username, and password can be conditionally and dynamically determined, and the correct database selected automatically, depending on the virtual server being used. That way, everyone can share the same constants file.

The Deployment Workflow

Simply having these development environments does not automatically facilitate best practice deployment strategy. The workflow of source code is important, too.

You may find the diagram shown in Figure 21-1 useful for illustrating the source code flow, from deployment to live.

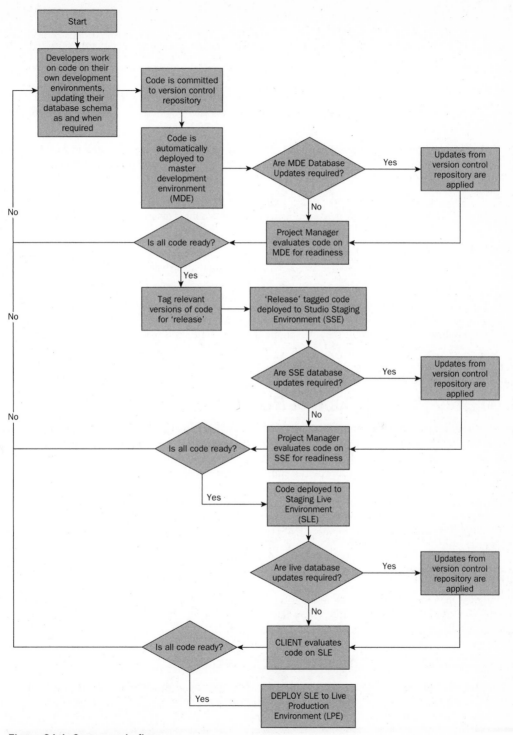

Figure 21-1: Source code flow

Following is the crux of the process:

1.   Individual developers develop against their own development environment, localized to their own database.

2.   This code is deployed to a master development environment. This may happen automatically using a scheduled task, or be initiated by the project manager on a semi-regular basis. Any changes that need to be made to the master environment's database schema are also made at this time.

3.   The code on the master development environment is tested, inspected, and approved by the project manager or, preferably, the project's lead architect. Certain files may be tagged as ready for the studio staging environment and, hence, release.

4.   This code then makes its way either in full or in part to the studio staging environment, where it undergoes a final review before submission to the client. The studio staging environment database is also amended if required.

5.   The code is then deployed to the live staging environment, and the live database is amended to support any schema changes. This is where the client approves or rejects the changes you have made.

6.   Finally, the code makes its way from the live staging environment to the live production environment. There is no need to change the database at this transition, because the same "live" database is used both for the live staging environment and the live production environment.

Let's now look at the technology behind these transitions.

Automated Version Control Repository Extraction

Many larger projects use a technique called *version control*, which is a technique for ensuring that the work done by different developers on a project does not conflict at any stage. It also keeps track of changes made to code as and when they are made, in case something goes wrong during the development process. Appendix A provides more information on version control.

When employing version control on a project, you may find it necessary from time to time to automate the retrieval of the latest versions from the repository. In the previous process, this is required for collating the efforts of your development team to assemble the snapshot master development environment.

Using CVS

Using the Open Source Concurrent Versions System (CVS) program, this can be accomplished using syntax similar to the following. This syntax is for UNIX implementations of CVS. Using the Windows CVS client, the process becomes a simple point and click.

```
cvs -d :pserver:username@cvsserver:/path checkout -r tag module
```

Here, `module` is the project name, `username` is a CVS username with access to that project, and `cvsserver` is the CVS server's hostname. Optionally, you can specify a tag. This may be useful if you want to extract to your studio staging environment.

The tag can be used by the project manager or lead architect to designate different versions of each file on the project as part of a distinct release. For example, a latest stable release of your application might consist of version 1.3 of one file, 1.5 of another, 1.4 of a third, and so on. By tagging each relevant version with a tag such as `lateststable`, those wishing to retrieve a particular release of your application can do so easily.

Such a command may well be committed to your server's `crontab` so that it runs on a scheduled basis. For example, you may have two entries as follows:

❑   Every day at midnight, the contents of the repository (regardless of tag) are extracted to form the master development environment.

❑   Every day at 3:00 A.M., the contents of the repository tagged *release* are extracted to form the studio staging environment.

Using Subversion

Appendix A examines Subversion (sometimes known as SVN, for short) as a somewhat more usable and practical alternative to CVS. In particular, Appendix A demonstrates how tunneling SVN over the SSH protocol can enable the easy deployment of new SVN repositories at the drop of a hat, without worrying about poking holes in firewalls and so forth.

This approach allows for the easy checkout of a given code repository using syntax similar to the following:

```
$ svn checkout svn+ssh://ed@ssh.example.com/home/production/svn/widgets
```

In this example, a project called `widgets` is checked out from a repository, the root of which is located at `/home/production/svn` on the server located at `ssh.example.com`. The checkout is performed as user `ed`. It stands to reason that this user must have file system Read access to the repository in question.

Thankfully, the process of retrieving from a version control repository all those files with a given tag is relatively straightforward.

In Subversion, tags and branches are just copied paths in the repository tree. By convention, tags live under `/tags` and branches live under `/branches`.

```
$ svn copy svn+ssh://ed@hspux01.unix.example.com/home/production/svn/widgets/
    trunk svn+ssh://ed@hspux01.unix.example.com/home/production/svn/hss/
    widgets/release
```

The previous syntax will create a tagged copy of your project based on the current `trunk` version. You can then check it out just like any other repository directory:

```
$ svn checkout svn+ssh://ed@ssh.example.com/home/production/svn/widgets/
    tags/release
```

You can find more about branching and tagging in Subversion at `http://svnbook.red-bean.com/en/1.0/ch04s06.html`.

Using rsync

It is not difficult to see that the most common deployment requirement is to upload the contents of folder A on server B, onto folder C on server D.

This is a simple operation in itself, but when the size of the source base of modern projects is taken into account, the task of shifting hundreds of megabytes across the Internet just to deploy a small change can rightly seem inefficient.

This is where `rsync` comes in. The `rsync` utility is a Linux/Mac OS X/UNIX-only utility, although recently a number of authors have attempted to produce Windows ports. It provides a means to copy the contents of a given folder on a local server to another given folder on a remote server, while copying only the files (or parts of files) that have changed. In other words, it synchronizes the two folders.

However, this is usually a synchronization in only one direction: from A to B. Files that have changed on A since the last deployment to B are copied, but anything that has changed on B in the meantime is not copied back to A. This is not a problem, however, if the pattern of deployment discussed in this chapter is followed rigorously.

The most likely two occasions on which you would use `rsync` are as follows:

❑ For the deployment of the contents of the studio staging environment to the live staging environment

❑ For the deployment of the contents of the live staging environment (after being approved) to the live production environment

`rsync` even works across two folders on the same server. Accordingly, even if your live production environment is the same physical server as your live staging environment, you can still use it to make your deployment. When copying from server to server, `rsync` makes use of the SSH (or, in a pinch, RSH) protocol. Hence, the only firewall rule required in order to allow the copy to take place is for port 22 to be opened for TCP traffic. There is an `rsync`-specific protocol, too, but unless for some reason you cannot use SSH, you will not need to use it.

Basic rsync Usage

You will normally use `rsync` as part of a shell script. For example, you might create a script called `deploy-studio-staging-to-live-staging` and another called `deploy-live-staging-to-live-production`. They all work in much the same way, however, and call `rsync` using syntax as follows:

```
rsync -avrz -e ssh /local/directory/* username@remotehost:/remote/directory
```

The relevant directives are as follows:

❑ The -a flag implements *archive mode,* which provides a useful prepackaged set of settings suitable for the usage described earlier, including causing directory permissions and symbolic links to be left intact when the transfer is initiated.

❑ The -v flag causes verbose output. You will see a detailed list of which files are, in fact, being chosen to be copied.

- ❑ The -r flag causes the copy to take place recursively.

- ❑ The -z flag causes data being transferred to be compressed before transfer. On a same-server copy, this should be omitted.

- ❑ The -e ssh directive tells rsync to use SSH to transfer files, rather than RSH.

- ❑ The source directory is specified as /local/directory/* (the * simply signifying that all files within that directory should be copied).

- ❑ The remote directory is specified as username@remotehost:/remote/directory, but if you're copying to another folder on the same server, the username@remotehost directive should be omitted.

Upon executing an rsync command, you may be prompted for a password. This is the login password associated with the username on the remote server specified, as if you were SSH'ing into that server in the normal fashion.

Let's look at some examples of this syntax at work.

rsync Syntax Examples

Let's first look at how you might deploy the contents of your studio staging environment to your live staging environment at your client's data center. You would use the following syntax:

```
rsync -avrz -e ssh /home/widgets/staging/
    * widgets@staging.widgets.com:/home/widgets/staging
```

If the client then approves the changes on the staging server, you can put them live. In this example, suppose that you put live simply to another folder on the same server. You would use the following syntax:

```
rsync -avr /home/widgets/staging/* /home/widgets/live
```

Note that now you omit the protocol directive, because this is a local-only synchronization. In addition, you do not enable compression because you assume that the speed increase will be minimal.

If your client's live production server were a physically different server, you might use the following syntax:

```
rsync -avrz -e ssh /home/widgets/staging/* widgets@live:/home/widgets/live
```

Alternatively, if your client used load balancing across three servers, you would have to execute the deployment three times, once for each target server:

```
rsync -avrz -e ssh /home/widgets/staging/* widgets@web01:/home/widgets/live
rsync -avrz -e ssh /home/widgets/staging/* widgets@web02:/home/widgets/live
rsync -avrz -e ssh /home/widgets/staging/* widgets@web03:/home/widgets/live
```

Keeping Servers in Sync with rsync

If your live production environment does involve multiple Web servers, there's another phenomenally useful role for `rsync`, too. Many sites involve the use of server-writable `/data` folders. These are containers for large binary files and other data that is perhaps not appropriate for a database such as PostgreSQL or MySQL, or that may, in fact, have been generated as "static assets" out of a relational database. (This is a technique advocated in Chapter 23, which examines how best to support high-traffic and high-availability Web sites.) A good example would be some variety of user-uploaded documents. For example, a user may have uploaded a photograph for a "my profile" page.

In setups with multiple live Web servers, a dilemma arises. How do you make newly uploaded data accessible to all the Web servers in the cluster? One way is to use a centralized file server, much as a centralized database server is used, perhaps exporting its contents via Network File System (NFS). This can be very slow, however, and is additional overhead that must be considered.

The alternative is to use `rsync` between the servers in the cluster on a very frequently scheduled basis, so that when a new binary is uploaded, it is leaked into the other servers in the cluster within just a few minutes (or even seconds).

This approach can be accomplished quite effectively using `rsync`, but the keyboard password prompt discussed previously could prove to be a barrier if you try to schedule any such commands — after all, the `cron` scheduler can't type passwords for you.

Mercifully, there is a workaround. It is the use of what is known as *passwordless SSH* and involves the placement of a key file on both client and server prior to connection. Because `rsync` depends on SSH in an environment with passwordless SSH set up, `rsync` is also passwordless, hence the scheduling of such tasks is made much easier.

Setting up key-driven SSH is slightly challenging and outside the scope of this chapter, but detailed information can be found on the Web. Check out the following excellent "How To" document for all the configuration steps you'll need:

    http://www.cs.toronto.edu/~murray/compnotes/passwordless_ssh.html

Note one caveat, however. If you do adopt this approach, ensure that your application is aware of the fact that binary data may not necessarily be available in the minutes immediately following an upload. For example, if you know that your `cron` job is set to run every five minutes, you should suppress the display of any user profile photograph until five minutes after the upload has completed in favor of displaying a "photo coming soon" message. After the five minutes have elapsed, you can be sure that the photo exists on all the Web servers in the cluster, so you can safely attempt to display the photo normally. To accomplish this, simply add a `time_photo_uploaded` property to the user's database record and measure the time elapsed.

If, for some reason, you simply must allow instant access to such uploaded photographs, consider implementing a system whereby the first time that photograph is requested on a Web server that does not have the photograph (for example, `web01`), that Web server immediately initiates an `rsync` for that file in isolation with other Web servers until it finds one that does (for example, `web04`) and then displays the newly copied photograph to the user. This may sound long-winded, but in practice the user will experience a very short delay while the file is copied; subsequent visitors requesting that photograph from that Web server will be served it in the normal way.

If you do adopt this approach, consider ensuring the uniqueness of filenames of uploaded data so that if they are replaced with a new version, you won't have some servers serving the old version and others serving the new. For example, if your user profile photographs are named using the user's ID from the database table user (for example, /data/userpics/193913.JPG), then consider using a serially numbered suffix, so that the filename becomes 193913_1.JPG, and the next version 193913_2.JPG, and so forth. You would store which serial number was current against the user's record in the database, and, hence, display only the most recent version.

A Word About FTP

Before closing, it's worth taking a quick look at the role of File Transfer Protocol (FTP). It's almost certainly something with which you're pretty familiar already. It's been around for years (longer than the Web itself), and most of the $10-a-month ISPs push it as the principle way to get files to your Web server.

For enterprise or professional-grade development, however, it's a nonstarter. As well as being well-known for the security holes found in FTP server software, and for the rigmarole of enabling the necessary firewall support (FTP is unusual in that in "active" mode the server actually connects *back* into your computer), it also has one major flaw: it's unencrypted.

What this means in practice is that any files you transfer to and from your servers via FTP are potentially at risk of exposure to the outside world — to someone sniffing your wi-fi traffic, to a rogue employee at your ISP, anyone. That code is your intellectual property. It's confidential. Furthermore, letting other people see your code puts you at greater risk of intrusion or attack in the future, as it will be known how your application works under the hood.

In short — *don't do it*. Stick to rsync, which uses Secure Copy Protocol (SCP) or Secure FTP (SFTP). Both of these protocols use SSH as the underlying transport mechanism, which is inherently secure and encrypted. It's not infallible (issues are discovered with SSH from time to time, too), but it's a darn site better than FTP.

Summary

In this brief chapter you learned about the principles of deployment in enterprise-level PHP applications, including the effective structuring of development environments for your team, and managing the transition of source code between each server using repository extraction and rsync.

In Chapter 22, you'll meet some of the most common *content management systems (CMSs)* and *content management frameworks (CMFs)* available for the PHP platform, both free and commercial. You'll learn the pros and cons of each, as well as how to make an informed and educated decision when recommending or specifying a CMS/CMF for your own application.

Part IV

Pushing PHP to Its Limits

## 22

Content Management in the PHP World

Sooner or later, you will get a client who asks you about content management. Back at the turn of the millennium, content management wasn't very well understood, and many marketing departments and business owners were unaware of the benefits of installing such a system.

Today, it's a different story. With the advent of blogs, wikis, and other publishing tools, content management has gone mainstream, and everyone seems to have a good handle on why they're so beneficial. For one thing, business stakeholders immediately grasp the benefits of removing bottlenecks, and of allowing the marketing and content teams to publish information when the business needs it to be "out there."

In this chapter, you'll get an overview of content management — what it is, why companies and organizations benefit from having it, and why these systems are important. Next, you'll get a brief history of content management and a cook's tour of a handful of open-source PHP systems. Finally, the chapter wraps up with a developer's checklist of requirements for content management, just in case you want to write your own system.

What Is Content Management?

The textbook definition of *content management* (the one you'll find at places like `Wikipedia.org`) is "a set of processes and technologies that support the evolutionary life cycle of digital information." That's a pretty cut-and-dried definition, but it gets to the heart of the matter.

When you survey content management from a much higher vantage point (the proverbial "30,000-foot view"), it's easy to pick out the peaks, valleys, slopes, marshes, and towns that constitute the geographic realities of what the term implies.

In no particular order, content management concerns itself with the following:

❑ The *people* who create information published on the Web (that is, content) may be all cooped up in one room or spread across the globe. They may report in to a single chain of command (a marketing department) or be loosely affiliated as a group of volunteer contributors to a site. They may create content in English or in dozens of languages.

❑ The *content* itself may be text, images, movies, rich Internet applications, or audio. Furthermore, content might take any number of forms, such as PDF files, blog posts, forum discussions, white papers, articles, and more.

❑ In the world of content management, *content can be sliced and diced* in a variety of ways. For example, content items may be put into different categories. (These are topic categories, such as content about hobbies, work, religion, politics, and so on.) They may be distinguished by file type or storage medium (such as database, flat file, or XML). Content may also be categorized by locality (that is, U.S. content may be different from U.K. content) and language. It may even be grouped by audience profile (such as basic/beginner, intermediate, advanced wizard, and so on).

❑ Certain *workflow rules* may be applied to content based on any number of factors. For example, content in certain parts of the world may have to be vetted a certain way. Editors and publishers may intrinsically trust certain contributors (such as the ones already on staff) over others (such as freelancers they have never worked with before). Some groups might opt to always put content through various levels of review (such as grammar/spelling/punctuation performed by an editor, fact checking done by a fact checker, final review by a zone editor, final publication by a site manager, and so on). Others might opt to trust the initial contributor to write acceptable content.

❑ There's also a certain set of rules applied to each piece of content *after it has been published*. For example, it may be necessary to automatically review certain types of content (for example, articles or white papers) every 90 days to ensure that it remains relevant and accurate. There's nothing worse than a "best practices" white paper that is woefully behind the curve of industry practices.

Going above and beyond the strict functional requirements of a content management system (CMS), you run into a whole bunch of operational and strategic factors. For example, editors, authors, and publishers of content rarely operate in a vacuum. They must publish their material for a certain audience.

Having an audience and caring what they want necessitates audience analysis. Some organizations go through incredibly rigorous sets of audience analysis tasks to figure out exactly what the audience wants. This includes examining not only what topics are near and dear to their hearts, but also what formats are acceptable, what frequency they find comfortable, and even the tone and slant of such pieces. Other groups take a more heuristic approach, publishing things that they generally know their audience will like because they themselves are members of that audience.

Beyond audience analysis is the needs of the organization. It's easy to forget, but the organization itself (whether profit or nonprofit) and its business partners, vendors, and investors are also stakeholders in the publishing venture. If the company (or its partners or investors, and so on) is trying to achieve a certain objective, then the content published by that organization should support that objective. There's nothing more awkward than a content strategy at odds with a business strategy.

Regardless of strategic direction, most publishing ventures must comply with the overarching organization's policies. It wouldn't do to have a Web site publish material that reveals internal corporate secrets, for example. Imagine the pain and suffering that would befall an organization if its Web site published slanderous, libelous, and otherwise offensive (that is, sexist, racist, or defamatory) content. Even a one-person show, run by a passionate partisan for one position or outlook, would run into eventual problems if all he or she did was publish inflammatory, accusatory pieces that defamed certain individuals.

From an operational standpoint, content deployed on a site via a CMS must be backed up and secured from unlawful deletion. The servers and databases that are used to run the CMS must be maintained, patched, and operated within their own parameters. Any software and operating systems (such as Apache and PHP) must also be maintained, patched, and secured. Most of these functions are handled by IT within an organization, or by an external SaaS (software as a service) or ASP vendor.

To sum it all up, the concerns of content management go way beyond building or installing a CMS. In fact, the technical aspects of content management pale in comparison to the nontechnical side of the house. When considered within the larger bracket of strategic IT (such as general policies for computing or data backups), it might represent only a small piece of an organization's computing needs.

However, you must remember something extremely important: *A CMS is itself a technical response to an organizational need.* That need is very simple: How does the organization quickly, easily, and effectively publish information? Once published, how does it maintain that information?

In short, content management offers one overarching, primary benefit: It helps the organization keep up with the marketplace in terms of information publishing. Once you have your head around that, the rest falls into place.

A Brief History of Content Management

Although you could make an argument for content management that went as far back as the mainframe days, this chapter focuses on *Web* content management, and, as such, the story of content management begins in 1995 with InterLeaf and CNET.

InterLeaf, already an innovative company that created desktop publishing systems, saw a need for publishing information on the World Wide Web, and created Cyberleaf. Cyberleaf was different from other editing products (such as HoTMetaL Pro and Vermeer FrontPage) in that it enabled users to transform documents created in word processing applications into HTML. It also enabled users to manage links between documents. In other words, it wasn't just an editor, but a single-source publishing system, with the Web as just one target (along with print and other interactive channels) for published information.

At roughly the same time, CNET created a Web site run on an internal Web publishing system that it later patented and branded as PRISM. Basically, PRISM was a tool that enabled even the most technophobic user to easily create Web pages. CNET wanted to commercialize PRISM, but didn't want to be distracted from its core business, which was publishing content.

Sometime in 1996, along came Ross Garber and Neil Webber, who had founded Vignette in Austin, Texas, with the expressed goal of making Web publishing easier and more personalized. They had been working on a large-scale content management workflow product called StoryBuilder when they teamed up with CNET. They licensed PRISM, offered CNET a stake in the outcome, and transformed it into StoryServer, which shipped in 1997.

The result (built in Tool Command Language, or TCL) was a vastly superior product to the existing CGI/Perl approach to building dynamic Web sites. Companies could buy the Vignette StoryServer product (licenses were in the six-figure range) and build entire applications using the tools provided.

Along the way, the content management space filled up very quickly. BroadVision, InterWoven, Documentum, DynaBase, Future Tense, FileNet, Stellent, and hundreds of others were all actively creating innovative products all centered on different aspects of content publishing: workflow engines, caching technologies, syndication, personalization, and much more. Along with the major corporate players were plenty of others, most notably Phil Greenspun, MIT professor and founder of Ars Digita, who created AOLServer.

Then came the dot-com crash, and the content management marketplace splintered into two major groups, seemingly at opposite ends of the spectrum, with an incredible merger/acquisition frenzy characterizing the marketplace.

On one end were the huge players (the Vignettes, the IBMs, and so on) that played in the enterprise space. Their systems usually involved "Big Iron" (with Oracle on the back end, deployment on a huge server, a lot of redundant backups, and network operations infrastructure), a lot of consultants working for long extended periods, and enormous budgets.

On the other end of the spectrum were the open-source applications that began to evolve in the early years of the new millennium. These systems were mostly browser-based systems that took advantage of the LAMP (Linux, Apache, MySQL, PHP) stack. Some of these systems were commercial (such as Mambo, which, by the way, also has an open-source branch) or open source (such as Joomla!, an offshoot of Mambo), while others were offshoots of earlier systems from the late 1990s (such as TYPO3). The one thing they had in common, though, was that they all stood in sharp contrast to the enterprise systems of the previous era.

For one thing, the new CMSs were either extremely affordable or free. Customers could spend their money not on base software packages, but rather on customizing the front end, the workflow, and the data back ends.

In addition, many of these smaller systems were keenly focused on making one group of users happy. Drupal was originally created as message-board software, and then morphed into an open-source CMS, with 1.4 million downloads from the `drupal.org` site in one calendar year (May 2007 to April 2008). WordPress (which began as a blogging platform) incorporated much of the simpler content management functionality. Joomla! was born when a whole group of Mambo developers jumped ship to build what they felt was a system more true to the open-source movement.

Examples of PHP CMSs

Because this is a book on PHP, it's appropriate to spend most of the focus of this chapter on PHP-based CMSs. You'll learn a little bit about four systems in this section. The first two you've probably heard about, the other two maybe not. These systems were chosen not because they are exemplars in their field, or because of their popularity, but because they each tackle content management in a different way.

It is hoped that after this quick survey, you'll be able to make good choices regarding system selection (when the time comes) or even building your own system (if that's your goal).

Drupal

Drupal is a Web content management framework. As shown in Figure 22-1, it is modular in nature, allowing almost unlimited customization. All content is stored in a database, usually MySQL. The middleware and modules are all written in PHP.

Figure 22-1: A sample Drupal layout

Content in Drupal is stored in individual nodes. You might have a story node, such as an article, or a blog node. Many different node types have been created by developers over the years, each with its own set of rules, metadata, and so forth.

Note that in Drupal, a node is called a node not because it is part of a network. Instead, think of a node as a piece in a puzzle. Nodes can be part of a blog, an online help system, or a forum. Using the Content Construction Kit, users can form their own nodes. At their most basic, all nodes have some universal metadata associated with them, including the following (see Figure 22-2):

❑ Node ID

❑ Content type

❑ Title

❑ Body

❑ Creation date

❑ Body

❑ Author

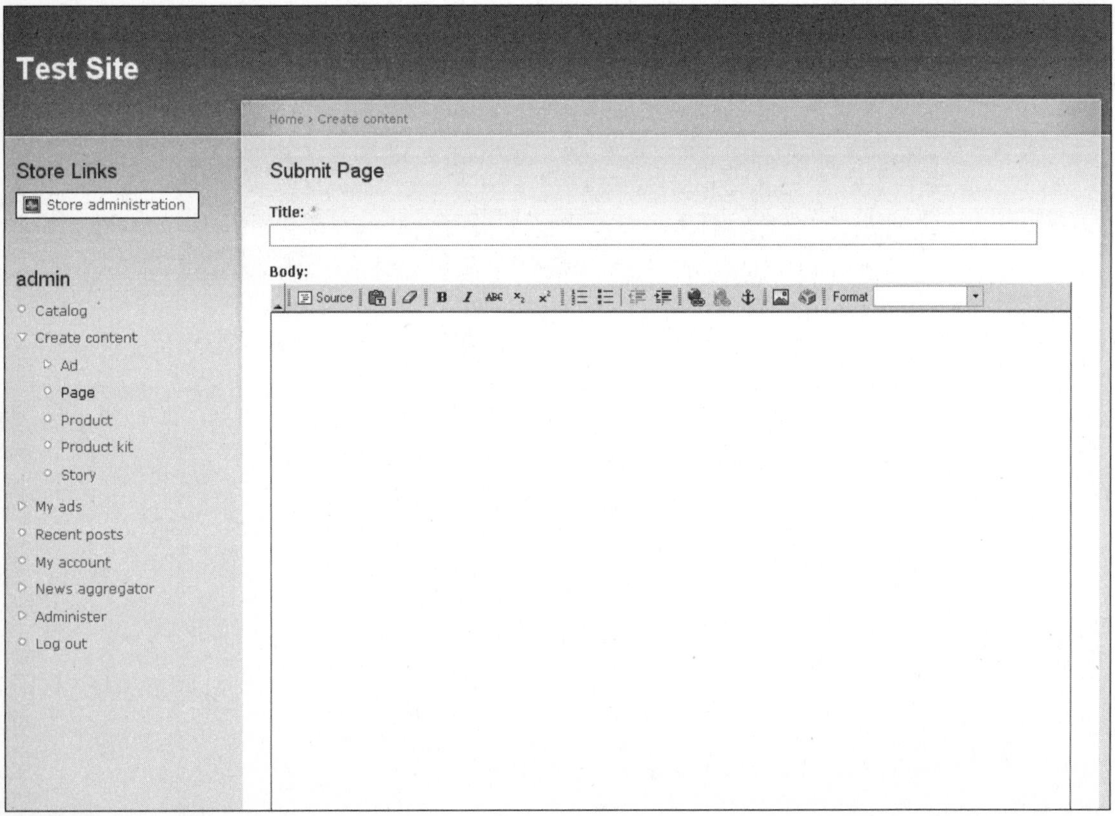

Figure 22-2: Creating content with Drupal

Each node can have any number of relationships with other nodes. If you load a certain node (for example, node 198393), then Drupal will present it to the user and grab all the other nodes associated with it. That particular node, with that particular ID, may be a blog posting with a headline, text body, and so forth, but it will also contain pointers to other nodes — for example, all the comments associated with that blog post, and all the related blog posts listed in a sidebar.

In Drupal, layouts are handled by *themes*. The default theme is a three-column layout, with the center column acting as the "content column" and the sidebar columns providing navigation and contextual links. Each column can contain blocks of information, such as the story being viewed, most recently posted stories, most popular stories, and so on.

Blocks of content may or may not be presented to a viewer, depending on the viewer's role. If you're already logged in, for example, there's no need to show the login block. Different menu items might show up depending on your role, providing some level of personalization.

Nodes can be organized into categories, which in Drupal is called a *taxonomy*. For example, you might have a site organized into five major topic areas (products, services, about us, contact us, and customer service) with subcategories under each (e.g., products ⇨ product 1; services ⇨ service 1; and so on).

Figure 22-3 shows an example of available options when managing content.

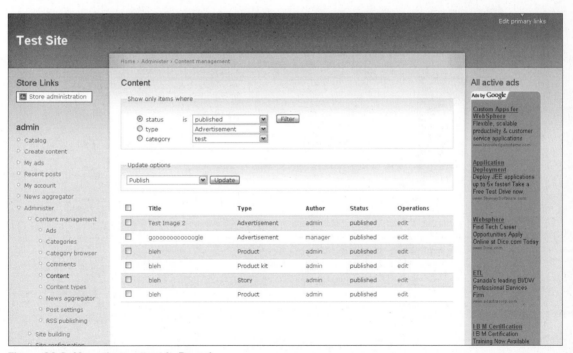

Figure 22-3: Managing content in Drupal

Joomla!

Joomla! came into being when a group of developers defected from Mambo over a disagreement about how the open-source version of Mambo should be handled. Joomla! is the English spelling of the Swahili word that means "all together" or "as a whole."

As shown in Figure 22-4, with Joomla!, you work with articles. Articles can be any kind of content, from Web page copy to blog posts, or whatever you need. Articles can also be assigned to categories and sections. The major difference between a section and a category is simple: *sections* can contain numerous categories, and *categories* can contain numerous articles.

Figure 22-4: Joomla!-powered site

For example, you might have a section called Products, and others called Services, About Us, and Contact. Within each of these sections, you might have categories for each product or service.

Finally, each article can be assigned to a category. As shown in Figure 22-5, each article has a title, a status, a space for content, and other advanced features, such as "Read more" (which displays only part of the article in the normal view) and "Front page" (which features the article on the home page of the site).

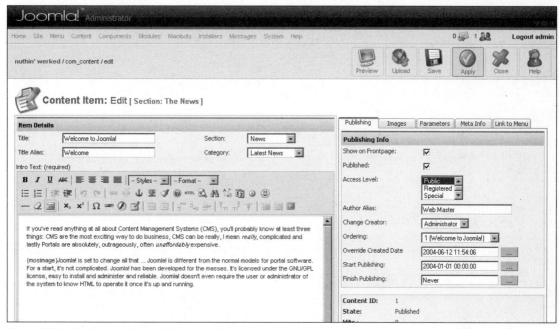

Figure 22-5: Creating content with Joomla!

As with most other systems, Joomla! allows you to create users, each with their specific login, password, and associated privileges. Some users may be able to create and edit articles, while others may be limited to contributing pieces, but not publishing them.

Joomla! also enables the easy creation of Web links (or bookmarks) and news feeds to your site. Each of these content types can be assigned to a particular category, making it very easy to display a unified set of links and feeds for all articles in a given category.

Each category can also be assigned its own layout, with Joomla! giving you control over various parameters (such as category order in menus, page titles, and more), as well as look and feel.

Last but not least, Joomla! supports the addition of various modules, each of which usually focuses on a specific task. For example, there are modules that show breadcrumb links, others that show archived content or custom menus, and still others that syndicate content and show polls.

Figure 22-6 shows the Joomla! Control Panel.

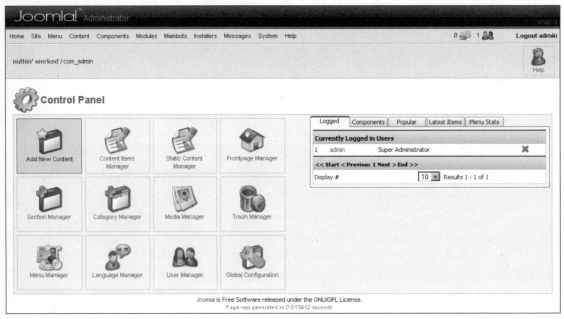

Figure 22-6: The Joomla! Control Panel

ExpressionEngine

ExpressionEngine is the CMS created and marketed by the folks at Ellis Lab, the same group that brought CodeIgniter (a PHP MVC framework) to the market. Of all the major CMSs out there, ExpressionEngine is the most Web 2.0–like, offering many cutting-edge features and an enormous amount of functionality for the price (around $99 for the personal license, $250 or so for the commercial license, but the core system is free to developers). Figure 22-7 shows a Web site featuring ExpressionEngine.

Figure 22-7: ExpressionEngine allows for beautiful Web sites

Within the ExpressionEngine Control Panel (see Figure 22-8), you can manage CMS users, content, and templates. Creating templates (see Figure 22-9) provides you with some fairly granular control over look and feel. Each template can contain XHTML markup and expressions that are parsed by ExpressionEngine (hence, the name of the product).

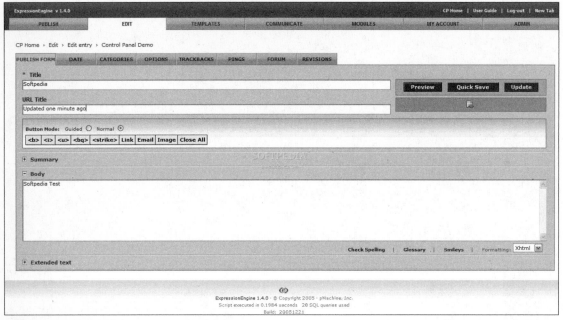

Figure 22-8: Adding content in ExpressionEngine

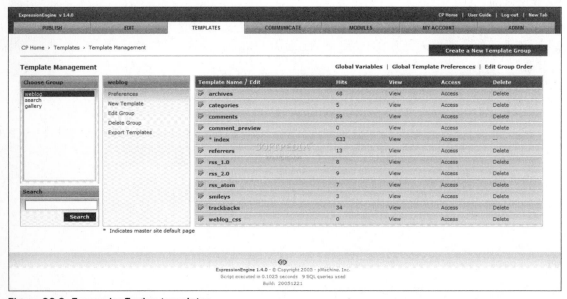

Figure 22-9: ExpressionEngine templates

These expressions can be as simple as adding a custom bit of text, or looping through blog posts in a sidebar. For example, if you were to publish a list of books on your site, you could create custom fields such as Author, ISBN, Title, Publish Year, and Language, all of which can be used by ExpressionEngine in other parts of your site. For example, you could list all books by a certain author, or published in a certain year. You could also designate a certain custom field as a drop-down list or date field, for example.

Furthermore, the way that templates work with the rest of your site is ingeniously simple. You can group your templates in such a way that you create self-explanatory URL paths. For example, you can create a template group called "Services" and place your services-related pages in that template.

Frog CMS

Frog CMS was born as phpRadiant, a PHP version of the popular Rails-based Radiant CMS. Its tagline is "Content Management Simplified" (see Figure 22-10), and anyone who uses it would have to agree. It offers a very elegant user interface, a flexible templating engine, and the bare-bones tools needed for user and asset (file) management (see Figure 22-11).

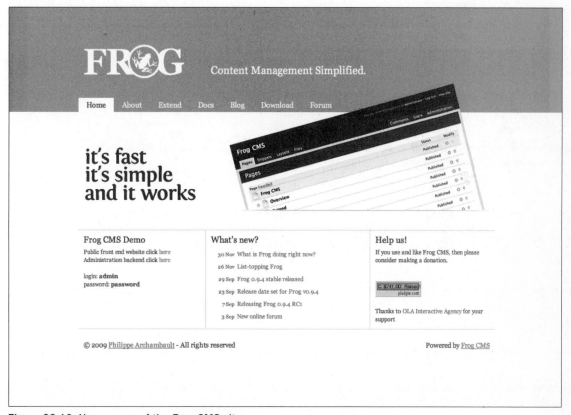

Figure 22-10: Home page of the Frog CMS site

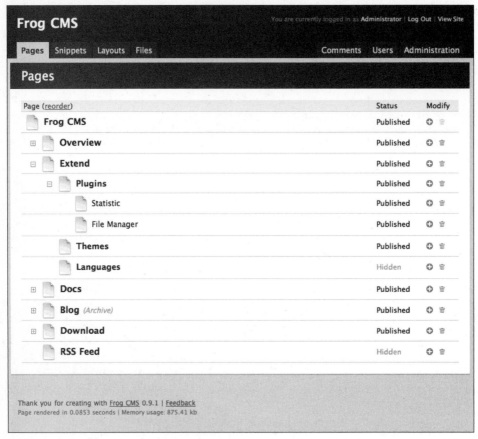

Figure 22-11: Managing pages in Frog CMS

Users can create snippets for their layouts (see Figure 22-12), each of which is a reusable piece of code such as a header or a footer. Snippets can also be pure content, such as a list of links or a graphic. Frog CMS also enables users to create content using a simplified HTML editor.

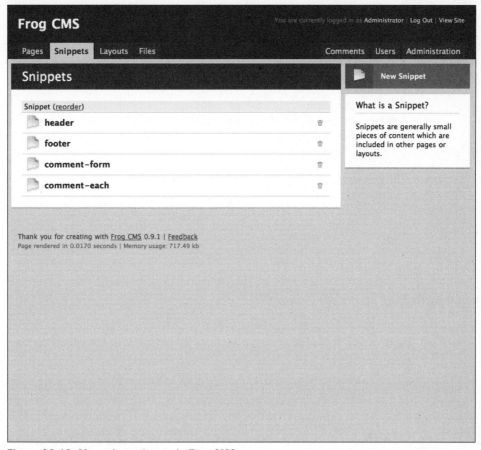

Figure 22-12: Managing snippets in Frog CMS

Last, but not least, you can add modules (usually plug-ins or themes) to Frog CMS, thereby extending it. Core plug-ins include archival features, comments, file management, 404 custom page controls, and SQLite. Already, the user community has created an entire library of plug-ins, including polls, download management, newsletters, contact forms, and more.

Building Your Own System

One of the interesting things about the world of content management is that many organizations have what may be called "unique local requirements" — in other words, they have such one-off needs regarding the creation, publication, management, and syndication of content that no off-the-shelf program (whether free or commercial) is appropriate. Nor will it do to modify any off-the-shelf system.

Instead, a vast percentage of content management projects involve some healthy amount of do-it-yourself programming. If you're participating in one of these ventures, here's a roundup of requirements that will make the short list on any project. Included in this roundup are some technical details to help you clarify your thought process. It's not comprehensive, but it's a good start.

Content-Related Issues

It always seems to be a shocking revelation to some developers, but the whole point of a content management system is to *manage content*. This point is brought up only because most projects seem to devolve into strange quagmires involving workflow engines and database caching.

Content is king. Everything else is subservient to that statement. The beating heart of content is the *content type* — which is just elementary shorthand for how content is structured and used. Most people intuitively understand that a press release is somehow different from a blog post. They not only have different component parts, but different uses and different audiences.

To that end, you could push out a CMS that has a fixed set of content types:

❑   Web page

❑   Article

❑   Blog post

❑   Press release

❑   News feed

Each of these may have its own particular set of data fields (such as title, byline, summary, publication date, and so on). Alternatively, you could push out a system that allows users to define their own content types.

If you pick the former, which always appears to be the easier undertaking (after all, creating a dynamic content construction system is a lot of work), then you must be prepared to live with the constant need to create new content types and alter those that seemed like a good idea during development but have now met the harsh sunlight of after-launch expectations, and have started to fade.

If you pick the latter, and allow administrators to define their own content types, then you must ask yourself how you define a content type. The answer to that question isn't altogether obvious until you've thought about it for a while, and no single answer is 100 percent correct. However, one bit of advice has always led to good outcomes; define a content type as the confluence of two sets of criteria:

❑   What metadata is associated with the content type? (This would be the nouns and adjectives.)

❑   What behaviors are associated with the content type? (This would be the verbs and adverbs.)

Once you have this mental framework in place, the noun/verb metaphor becomes a handy way to express any content type.

Let's take a press release as a starting point. If you think about a press release's morphology (that's fancy talk for "the parts of it"), you can easily translate those parts into metadata. Each press release has the following components (as a rough start):

❑   Headline

❑   Subhead

❑   Date slug

❑ Summary

❑ Body

❑ Contact information

❑ Keywords/tags/categories

Given enough time, you could discover a whole other group of metadata that may or may not be needed by your organization's PR group. Suffice it to say, you have enough to get started.

Stopping the discovery at nouns, however, would give you an incomplete view of what a press release is. Most organizations also need press releases to *function* in a certain way — in other words, a press release also has behaviors associated with it. For example, each press release also has a launch window, usually expressed as a date and time (often after the market closes). It also includes legal language bits that make the regulatory folks happy (if they are present) or unhappy (if they are not).

These "verby" parts of a press release are also embodied as metadata; but the main difference is that the system must be aware of them and do something in response to what is stored there. For example, the legal bits had better be present in order for the press release to be launched. A smart CMS shouldn't allow a press release to go live without alerting someone that the legal bits are missing or incorrect. The same thing applies to the launch window — if the press release is categorized in a certain way (for example, its contents are tagged as financial or market news), then the CMS shouldn't allow posting before market close.

Once you've mapped out what's needed for press releases, do the same for all the other possible content types that the client needs now (and may need later). You'll inevitably find a lot of similarities in both nouns and verbs across all your content types. In fact, you'll note that just about every piece has a headline, a date, an author, keywords, content body, and so on. Some content types will have special needs (such as events, which might also have a signup URL and a reminder widget). For that reason, you should consider nonglobal metadata that can be added to individual types.

Once you have your technical design down for content, you must decide which path you'll take. If you give your client hard-coded content types, then you'll probably end up with different database tables for each content type. If that's the case, make it very easy to add new content types in the future. Here's where a good MVC design comes in, which gives you the capability to easily add a database table for, say, calendar events, along with its model, admin controllers, and any views for CRUD (create, review, update, and delete).

If you go the other route, then you'll probably end up with a centralized table that houses all of your interchangeable blocks of content (a headline block, a byline block, a date block, a content body, and so on), and then give users the capability to reuse, rename, and connect those blocks — in any way they choose — into bigger blocks that are called *content types*.

Don't forget, though, that either way, you must devise some way to tell the CMS what's important about your metadata. In other words, if you hard-code the content types, you must have a way to tell the CMS that no article can be posted without a headline, or a press release must follow certain workflow rules. The same is true if you give administrators the freedom to devise their own content types.

Administrators and Privileges

Speaking of administrators, you will have to account for them. There's no way around it. Make the site's administrators happy, and you'll have a happy team. The more they adopt your system, the more they love working with it, the easier you make things for them, the better off you'll be.

If you have a small installation, with a small group of people (e.g., just one or two administrators), then you probably won't have to expend a lot of energy on managing users and setting up different privileges for them. However, once you get past a certain number (e.g., five administrators) or if the administrators are split into different time zones or geographies (and, certainly, continents or language groups), then you most certainly have to deal with the complexities of privileges.

There are two ways to handle privileges. One is to give the administrators interchangeable building blocks, each of which represents a type of activity: creating content, updating content, reviewing (or reading) only, deleting, publishing, archiving, and so on. There could even be a "super administrator" activity that allows a user to administer other users, add new plug-ins, and so on.

The super administrator could then create a new user in the system (and, of course, each user would have a username, password, real name, e-mail address, phone number, and so on), and then assign building blocks to create a privilege profile. To give the super administrators more granular control, you could also give them building blocks that match up with different content types or sections of the site, as well as activities.

In effect, you could have a new user who has full access when it comes to working with press releases (they are the head of PR, after all!), but only read-only access to articles or blog posts. Other users (such as the CEO) could have read-only access to every single content type, but only create (not publish) authority over a little corner of the blog.

This kind of system is somewhat ingenious, but it requires a whole lot of work, and you'd better get your building blocks right, or you'll be coming back again and again to revise the setup.

Another approach involves levels of access. The levels typically go something like this:

❑   *Subscriber* — This is a person who can log in to see items in read-only view only, or who gets regular reports about what is going on. Think of a C-level executive or senior VP who wants to know what is going on but shouldn't be allowed within ten feet of a blog post.

❑   *Contributor* — This is a base-level content person who can create any content he or she wants, edit anything he or she has written (as long as it is still in draft stage), but must then send it to a higher power in order to see it published.

❑   *Author* — This is a trusted contributor who can write original material and publish it in certain areas of the site.

❑   *Editor* — This is a staff person (typically) who can only edit and revise pieces written by authors and contributors.

❑   *Manager* — This is a supervisory editor who can review anything, write new material, and launch pieces throughout the site. The manager can also set rules for pulling items off the live site, and for archiving material.

❑ *Administrator* — This is usually someone who deals with installing new plug-ins, sets up backups, sets up caching, and figures out the workflow rules and all the other background minutiae. This person also has the right to create new content (and update that content), but usually doesn't just because he or she is too busy.

This second approach is much easier to deal with from the development side, but it leads to some oversimplistic effects on the operations side. For example, a manager might want to bring on a trusted freelancer but have no choice but to give that person a contributor role because the author privileges are just too far-reaching.

Workflow

At its simplest, a *workflow* defines the steps that a piece of content goes through between initial draft and final deletion. In between are stages such as drafting, submitting for approval, legal review, publication, archiving, and, eventually, oblivion.

The heart of a good workflow system is good metadata. Most content types include a mandatory status field, usually a drop-down with a limited set of options. Most administrator roles or privilege sets include the capability to choose different subsets of the status markers — for example, if you are a low-level contributor, you may only be able to have two status markers: draft and pending. You won't be able to make anything live, nor are you able to work on anything that is already live.

Generally speaking, workflows can either be hard-coded into a CMS (easy on the developers, but difficult on the operations staff) or made more flexible, such that content operations staff can define paths for either different content types or different sections of the site (or some combination of the two). For example, for an article, you may have three workflow steps (draft, approve, publish), but an article for the products section of the site may have more approval steps. It may need to be checked by a product manager, a subject matter expert (SME), and the editorial board.

Furthermore, most workflow systems should have some kind of messaging capability. If an editor rejects a draft from a contributor and sends it back to draft status, the editor should be able to send an e-mail to the contributor, explaining why that decision was made.

Alternatively, if you have a complex workflow setup, then you must take into account tracking both parallel and sequential approvals. Most workflows are sequential (drafting, submittal, reviews, and then on to publication); but in the previous example with the SME, product manager, and editorial review board, you would probably want the SME and product manager to review simultaneously, and then pass the material along to the editorial review board.

One other note and then we'll move on. Because workflows are often hard to visualize, the best workflow systems are visual in nature. Either they allow the administrator to graphically add symbols to the screen and pipe them together (much like a UML or process flow) or they use some kind of vertical metaphor (in which the content drops through the pipeline following the rules in each step). Along the way, each step is associated not only with the content item being worked on, but also any other affected groups, such as a certain editor (or maybe the whole editorial group) or even other pieces of content that need to be released at the same time (such as the press release about a product, the five product pages, and the freebie download for that product).

Either way, you must make it easy for an administrator to create and then maintain a workflow. It has to be intuitive enough that you understand it at a glance, but powerful enough to do everything the team needs vis-à-vis their workflows.

Templates

In the early days of content management, it seemed that every Web site run by a CMS was easily identified because of its boxy look and feel. Nowadays, though, the CSS and XHTML wizards on the front end have joined forces with the back-end developers to offer users impressive experiences.

There are at least three ways to handle templates in your CMS.

The quick-and-easy way is to hard-code your look and feel, adding whatever hooks you need in your PHP front-end templates to pull in what you need from the database. For example, if you are working on a template for a press release, you can pull in the headline, body, author byline, contact information, legal bits, and the rest of it.

The problem with this approach is pretty obvious. It's easy on the developers (at first), but a misery for the operations staff. If someone creates a new content type, you must create a new set of templates. No matter how pretty and usable your templates are, this kind of thing can get pretty old.

A second approach is to offer dynamic templates that the administrators control. Again, you can give them the capability to create reusable blocks or snippets to create what they need in terms of sidebars, headers, footers, and content blocks. Then, if you give your templates some smarts and insight into the content types they're supporting, you can enable the administrators to punch out any kind of content they want, using metadata fields as they need them.

For example, let's say that you have a page layout system consisting of four major snippets:

❑   A header snippet, which includes not only the logo, but also the global navigation

❑   A footer snippet, which contains legal/copyright, and so on

❑   A sidebar snippet, for use on either the left or the right, which itself might contain other snippets

❑   A main content snippet, which holds a blog post, article, or whatever

You could make it such that each of these snippets knew about the different content types and the different fields associated with each type, and then use them interchangeably as needed. For example, let's say that you organized content types such that no matter what type is being used, it has a set of universal metadata fields (such as byline, headline, body, date, and so on). You could easily come up with a way to use parsed text in your templates and take advantage of that, as shown here:

```
<h1>[[:content_type:headline]]</h1>
<p>by [[:content_type:byline]]</p>
[[:content_type:body]]
```

The :content_type: expression would be a generic rule that tells the template engine to apply this rule to any content type — for example, because every single one would have a headline. The template engine would be smart enough to deduce that anything between the [[and]] tags requires extra processing before final delivery of HTML to the browser.

Alternatively, if you wanted to create a dedicated template for a press release, for example, you could take a more specific approach:

```
<h1>[[:content_type:headline type='pr']]</h1>
<p>by [[:content_type:byline type='pr']]</p>
[[:content_type:body type='pr']]
```

The third approach involves using an open-source or commercial template system, of which many are available. The most well known is probably Smarty, a fairly robust template engine that enables you to separate your XHTML from your PHP. Your Smarty templates end up having tokens in them that relate back to variables you set in your PHP. Consider the following example:

```
//this is your PHP
include('smarty.php');
$smarty = new Smarty;
$smarty->assign('nickname', 'myerman');
$smarty->assign('realname', 'Thomas Myer');
$smarty->assign('city', 'Austin, TX');
$smarty->display('user.tpl');

//and here is user.tpl
<html>
<head><title>User info for {$nickname|capitalize}</title></head>
<body>
<h1>User info for {$nickname|capitalize}</h1>
<p>Real name: {$realname}</p>
<p>City: {$city}</p>
</body>
</html>
```

Notice two things about this example. First and foremost, any assignment made on the PHP side is easily accessible in {$varname} format on the Smarty side, thus effectively simplifying this work for the front-end developer or designer who is usually terrified of back-end code. The second thing to notice is the opportunity to add operators to different variables — the |capitalize on the end of $nickname enables you to morph data for display as needed.

As with most things in a developer's life, discussions about template engines often descend into religious discussions. In no way are you limited to Smarty (some developers hate it, others love it), so pick the system that best suits your needs as a developer, the needs of the site designers, and the needs of the site's visitors.

Summary

In this chapter, you learned a little bit about content management systems (CMSs). You learned what a content management system is, got a little history lesson, reviewed four exemplars of PHP-based systems, and even got an overview of requirements, just in case you want to build your own.

Chapter 23 provides some tips on handling high traffic and high availability.

23

Handling High Traffic and High Availability

Chapter 22 introduced you to a few PHP-based content management systems (CMSs), platforms that you may well try to incorporate in a large-scale or enterprise-grade Web application. All such CMSs were particularly well-suited to larger or higher traffic sites, where the burden of manual updates would be commercially impractical.

Yet, building large sites has technical as well as commercial implications. Larger sites have two key burdens not found when developing smaller projects: ensuring high availability (that is, a high percentage of uptime when measured over a given period) and the ability to handle exceptionally high levels of traffic without suffering adversely. The insurance techniques involved are often alien to smaller sites, and yet they are surprisingly simple to achieve, especially given that they are not necessarily PHP-specific.

In this chapter, you'll learn about those specialist techniques and how to incorporate them in the architecture of your own applications. In so doing, you'll prove to yourself once and for all that PHP is perfectly suited for such large sites. In addition, you'll sneak a look under the hood at the architecture of some of the Web's highest-traffic commercial sites, including Flickr and Facebook — both proudly built in PHP.

Understanding the Terms

The terms *high traffic* and *high availability* mean different things to different people. Before going any further, it's worth cementing your understanding of what enterprise architects generally consider them to mean.

High Availability

The word "availability" refers to the normal function and operation of an application within acceptable parameters. If the application is broadly usable (even if running a little slower than normal), then it is considered to be available. Availability is generally measured as the percentage of a given period during which the application is available.

There's a fascinating list of the downtime of the top 20 Web sites in 2007 at `http://royal.pingdom` `.com/?p=116`. The only site that manages 100.0 percent over the year is Yahoo!; Google manages an impressive 99.995 percent, and even the Coldfusion-built MySpace manages 99.98 percent. Averaging the top 20 gives an uptime figure of 99.987 percent over the year — that's just six minutes of downtime every month.

Throughout this chapter, you'll also see the word *redundancy*. In this context, redundancy means something very specific — that is, introducing into architectures the ability to cope with unexpected *failures* by providing *failover* onto identical backup equipment. It's largely through the use of redundancy that the top 20 sites achieve the seemingly very high levels of availability that they do, even under high traffic.

For the purposes of this chapter, *high availability* means an uptime of 99.75 percent over a year — perhaps below the expectations of the top 20, but well in excess of a typical PHP Web site.

High Traffic

The metrics used to define "high traffic" can vary a little. The likes of Google, Flickr, and MySpace receive literally tens of billions of page impressions per month. This is certainly "high traffic," but what about the Web site of a large corporation? While not B2C applications, sites such as `unilever.com` and `deloitte.com` still receive millions of page impressions per month. That's nothing compared to the big social networking Web sites, and yet still within the realms of what many Web developers would consider "high traffic."

In practice, though, it's all about perception and positioning. Consider a fast, mainstream, compact automobile such as the MazdaSpeed3. Many would consider it a fast car; the name, the looks, the branding — all point toward an emphasis on performance. And indeed, it's no slouch: 0–60 mph in 5.9 seconds. But compare that to a Bugatti Veyron, which reaches the same speed in well under half the same period of time, or a Formula One car, which can easily reach 140 mph in the same amount of time it takes the Mazda to get to 60.

The point is that all three would be considered *fast* by a layperson. The numbers back this up. The average 0–60 mph time of all cars on the market today is about 13 seconds. Being very black and white about it, you could argue, therefore, that anything under 13 seconds is "fast," and anything above 13 seconds is "slow."

Applying the same rules to the Web, the average number of page impressions received on viable Web sites (discounting closed sites, link farms, scams, and so forth) is around 100,000 per month — just 3,000 per day. That figure is low because of the sheer ubiquity of the Web. For every commercial Web-based operation enjoying millions of hits, there are a thousand more enjoying just a few hundred, if that. It's not exactly what mathematicians would call a normal distribution.

Another way to look at it is to say that any site for whose level of traffic is likely to require special attention to hardware, software, or network architecture could well be considered "high traffic." A site receiving 150,000 page impressions per month can easily be run from a single standard-spec server, probably using a fairly mediocre connection to the Internet. Conversely, it's at around about the 1-million-page-impression-per-month mark that special considerations must be made for the hardware the site is running, the connectivity it has to the Internet, and the manner in which the underlying code is built.

Let's use that as a meter in this chapter, then. Any site exceeding 1 million page impressions per month will be considered a *high traffic* site.

Platforms

You should now understand what this chapter will represent as a site enjoying high traffic and requiring high availability. Indeed, the two are usually inextricably linked. A high-traffic site is generally (although not always) a commercial success for its financial backers, a success that is contingent on an ongoing basis for that site's high availability. Google site revenues for Q1 2008 were $3.40 billion — that's $26,000 per minute. You can see the impact downtime could easily have on Google's bottom line.

Worse still, high availability is usually more difficult to achieve under high-traffic situations. The relentless pounding of equipment under en masse HTTP requests quickly thickens any latent fault lines.

Before considering some of the specific factors affecting availability under high traffic, it's worth briefly identifying and exploring the puzzle pieces that comprise an application's *platform*. As you'll see, it's about far more than just the choice of development language. Many of these components can play a role in frustrating your goal of high availability.

Exterior Network

Any Web site or application accessible over the Internet must, by definition, enjoy some form of connectivity to the outside world. In practice, only company intranets tend to fall outside this obvious and apparent requirement. The *exterior network* refers to the trail of connections between the end user and the internal network — usually from the user's computer right through to the terminating router at the equipment hosting the Web site.

In general, enterprise-grade applications tend to be hosted on either *co-located* or *managed* servers. In a co-located server scenario, the individual, company, or organization behind the site being hosted provides and manages the server, and the Internet Service Provider (ISP) provides the space where it may be placed. In the managed server environment, the ISP provides and manages the server, and the entity behind the site simply uploads its application.

In either case, however, the ISP is responsible for providing suitable connectivity to that server. It should be *high bandwidth* — in other words, a total bandwidth in megabits per second (Mbps) sufficient to accommodate incoming traffic. It's worth keeping in mind that a 10 Mbps connection may sound like a lot, but that's only enough to support five concurrent 2-Mbps end-user connections. Mercifully, the intermittent nature of HTTP means that five concurrent connections doesn't equate to anything like five concurrent users; it's more like a hundred. You'll meet the math behind these assumptions later in this chapter.

Remember, too, that some ISPs meter bandwidth, usually in lieu of providing a specific cap (known as a *committed information rate,* or *CIR*) on bandwidth. Commercially, it often makes more sense for the ISP to sell bandwidth this way. Selling a CIR means keeping that much of their bandwidth permanently free at all times, with no overselling. Instead, many will pool all their available bandwidth and sell it on a first-come, first-served basis, with a monthly limit on how much data may be transferred. This sometimes works in a site's favor, but sometimes not. It is rather the luck of the draw, dependent on how busy the ISP is in general.

Bandwidth these days is fairly cheap, but less so with quality bandwidth. One indicator of quality tends to be *latency* (in layperson's terms, *ping time*). In practice, this is often more important than bandwidth. A well-architected Web site should arguably be more about content than flashy graphics or video. Look at Facebook. It's by and large plain text, and yet one of the most popular and celebrated sites on the Internet because of its usability. That usability, however, can be adversely affected by poor latency, which (in the context of HTTP) will manifest itself as the responsiveness of the site to a user's activity. If it takes half a second for a socket connection to a remote host to open, it doesn't matter how fast that connection can spit data back down to the connecting Web browser. The experience for the end user will be poor, because the responsiveness of the server will be perceived to be poor.

All of this boils down to the ISP, of course, but do keep in mind that in a co-located (as opposed to managed server) environment, some ISPs are predisposed to shifting blame to customer equipment (that is, disputing where in the connectivity chain the fault lies, perhaps claiming that a faulty customer firewall or switch must be to blame). This can be easily proved or disproved as needed, of course, but it does provide yet another hoop through which to jump when problems arise.

It's important, therefore, to keep the interior network as sound as possible, in order to eliminate it from your line of inquiry when addressing connectivity speed and responsiveness issues.

Interior Network

The point at which the ISP hands off to your equipment is generally referred to as a *handoff*. How this is presented depends on the nature of the service you have purchased from your ISP, but it is generally provided in one of two fashions.

In the simplest scenario, it is provided as a single Ethernet port, a range of addresses on the public Internet, and a fixed gateway address within the same network subnet. You would typically connect your firewall's external interface directly to the Ethernet port in question and route traffic to the gateway address given to you. Your firewall's internal interface would then connect to a switch, which would, in turn, provide connectivity to your servers.

In a more complex environment, connectivity may be provided as a single gateway address and a range of addresses on a *different* subnet. In such a scenario, the onus is on you to provide your own router, to which you would bind the gateway address allocated to you. In turn, you would provide your own firewall, with its external interface linked to the secondary interface of that router, which would listen on all the addresses provided to you. Your firewall would then link its own internal interface into your switch, into which your servers would connect in the usual way.

Therefore, your interior network equipment must be capable of shifting the appropriate amount of traffic. The burden depends on where it falls in the chain. A perimeter router handles *all* of your site's traffic, inbound and out. However, it may be configured to quench certain traffic it regards as unroutable. As such, the burden on the firewall is usually slightly less than that of the perimeter router. The firewall, too, will (in most circumstances) filter out large quantities of unwanted traffic, meaning that the internal network switch needs to cope with slightly less traffic than the firewall. In a larger architecture, two or more servers will doubtlessly be used to deliver content, so that individual traffic burden on the network card will be lower still — although internal communication between servers (not via the Internet) can easily push this up again.

A medium-tier router can generally shift about 10 Mbps without any problems. You'd be wise, therefore, to seek out a firewall that can handle about the same amount of traffic. Your switches will almost certainly be 100 Mbps, but you should consider whether internal communication between servers is likely. If your database server and application server are separate, then this will be the case, and providing 1 gigabit per second (Gbps) switching with 1 Gbps network interface cards (NICs) will provide optimum performance.

Hardware

Naturally, your application must run on something, and a typical arrangement for a high-availability/high-traffic Web site will comprise, at a minimum, a separate Web/application server and database server — that's two physical boxes.

In the early days of the Web, sophisticated hardware from the likes of Silicon Graphics, Inc. (SGI) and Sun Microsystems pervaded enterprise architectures across the globe. This wasn't an area of much interest for Intel, whose CPUs were chiefly aimed at the desktop environment. These days, however, server-grade chips based on x86 architecture are readily available — and cheap. In fact, they're so cheap compared to their competitors in other architectures that in 99 percent of applications, it's more cost effective to go the Intel route, even if that involves using twice as many physical boxes.

There are two trends worth considering, however. Moore's law indicates that processing power doubles approximately every two years. As a result, an increasing number of enterprise architects are considering the merits of virtualization. In such a configuration, one or more physical servers in a cluster provide one or more virtual (or *addressable*) servers via software emulation.

The benefits are numerous. The ability to scale an application's hardware base up and down as traffic and load dictates is the most obvious benefit, without the normal cost and lead time associations. A degree of redundancy is also provided by distributing load across multiple physical servers; a single point of failure is eliminated.

A second trend (one championed chiefly by Google) is that of using *commodity hardware* (off-the-shelf, nonspecialist boxes) to provide hosting. It may seem unusual, but consider the math. If 20 boxes costing $500 each can provide the same level of redundancy and performance as 15 boxes costing $1,500 each, it's easy to see why the first option is more attractive. The main benefits of dedicated server hardware — resilience, reliability, and longevity — are negated by sheer volume and economy of scale.

The use of virtualization to combine commodity servers into a single addressable environment provides, in theory, the best of both worlds — although it is worth remembering that it is a relatively young technology, and even in 2009 kinks are still being worked out.

Operating System

Assuming modern application architectures depend largely on Intel-based hardware, the choices of operating system are limited broadly to those that run on Intel architecture, and for which a broad range of suitable application software is available (Web servers, database servers, application servers, and so forth).

Other than specialist and niche operating systems, the bulk of those available are divided chiefly into Windows and a range of UNIX variants.

On the Windows front, only the Windows Server range of operating systems is appropriate for use as a Web server. Built on Microsoft's NT architecture, Windows Server 2003 and 2008 use the same core kernel as Microsoft's desktop operating system equivalents (XP and Vista), but are optimized specifically for a server role. In Windows Server 2008, a new feature known as *Server Core* removes the desktop-oriented Windows Explorer interface, providing a stripped-down, more UNIX-like approach.

As for UNIX and UNIX-like operating systems, the choice is more varied. Of course, Linux is still by far the most pervasive and popular UNIX operating system on Intel hardware, and with good cause. Largely free (depending on distribution) and hugely well supported, it is an excellent "all rounder" — there's little it isn't good at. Having said that, Apple's decision in 2005 to switch to Intel architecture enables the Mac OS X to compete as a viable server operating system for PHP-based architectures. (However, of course, buyers are restricted to purchasing genuine Apple hardware, which generally means an XServe server appliance. These come at a price premium compared to similarly specified generic server equipment from the likes of Dell and HP.)

There are a few "left field" UNIX options, too. Sun has recently released OpenSolaris (available as open source and free of charge), which is essentially Solaris, but with proprietary and closed-source components removed or replaced. FreeBSD is still well supported and is arguably occasionally more stable under load than Linux. OpenBSD has an excellent reputation for security and resilience.

The choice between UNIX and Windows often comes down to personal preference; indeed, it is the subject of numerous religious wars on blogs everywhere. Nonetheless, it's difficult to argue with the facts. As you'll see later in this chapter, the vast majority of high-traffic sites (other than those owned and operated by Microsoft itself) still use some variety of UNIX as their underpinnings — Google, Yahoo!, Wikipedia, YouTube, Facebook, and the list goes on.

Web Server

The importance of choosing the right Web server cannot be understated. Every single request to your site consists of a flurry of HTTP requests for pages and associated assets. Every one of those HTTP requests will pass through the Web server's hands. Choose the wrong one, and the entire site is at risk.

The standard is still Apache. It runs on both UNIX and Windows, although, frankly, is fairly horrendous when run on Windows. A market share of nearly 51 percent means it towers over its nearest rival, Microsoft's Internet Information Server (IIS), at around 35 percent as of this writing. It's achieved that position rather by default — by being free, well supported, and not particularly bad at any one thing. Neither is it particularly good at any one thing; hence, it becomes the "no thinking required" choice.

IIS has come a long way in recent years. Early releases were blighted with security problems. Just as seriously, performance and resilience under load have been called into question in recent years. While these deficiencies now have been largely addressed, one fact still remains: A given level of traffic under IIS on Windows can only be supported with a beefier hardware infrastructure than that required with, perhaps, Apache on UNIX.

Looking elsewhere, certain specialist Web servers can play an important role:

❑ *Squid* (`www.squid-cache.org/`) provides front-end traffic management, caching, and load distribution.

❑ *lighttpd* and *thttpd* are "lightweight" Web servers designed for serving only static assets such as images, CSS stylesheets, and downloadable binaries.

❑ Kernel-level Web servers such as *TUX* and *KHTTPD* provide an even more lightweight solution to the same problem, building the Web-serving capability directly into the operating system itself.

As you'll see later in this chapter, the choice of a Web server is often dependent on the choice of an overall network infrastructure. In a larger setup, multiple servers can often run different Web servers and even different operating systems, all chosen with the laudable goal of maximizing performance in mind.

Application Server

The concept of an *application server* is something not usually familiar to PHP developers. Because most developers run PHP as part of the Web server (be it as a module, compiled in, or, rarely, as a CGI module), the Web server and application server are perceived to be the same thing.

This is, of course, not the case. An application server runs applications; a Web server serves Web pages. The metaphor is aptly expressed in Java 2 Enterprise Edition (J2EE). An application server such as Tomcat, JBoss, or BEA/Weblogic may well accept requests over HTTP, but it's likely to be coupled with a Web server on the front end trafficking requests through to it. Application servers generally support advanced features not found in a Web server (such as resource pooling, diagnostics, and support for advanced deployment techniques). As such, they are rightly considered "overkill" for serving up simple Web pages and other assets.

In the context of PHP, the phrase "application server" refers to the server that handles requests directly into the PHP engine. For optimum performance, this is typically Apache with PHP statically "compiled in" (rather than loaded as a module) such that a single executable serves the application. As shown later in this chapter, the addition of a static assets server and a front-end caching server allows for the smarter distribution of traffic, with each server playing to its strengths.

Database

As you might expect, the choice of underlying database has substantial performance implications in any high-traffic PHP application. It's expected that the bulk of HTTP requests for application pages will invoke some sort of SQL query. As a result, the speed with which each HTTP request can be completed is entirely dependent on the speed with which those SQL queries can be executed, and, if appropriate, data returned.

Much has been made in this book of the fact that well-architected PHP applications are database agnostic, insomuch as abstraction layers such as PDO and SQL generation techniques like ORM provide for a great degree of portability. Indeed, at low traffic levels, there is little to choose between databases.

At high traffic levels, however, everything changes. Much is made of MySQL's performance at running SELECT queries, but with an appropriate use of caching and page generation, the benefit this brings is negated. Of far greater importance is the database's performance in undertaking those transactions that inherently cannot be cached or pre-generated — for example, actions such as user registration, searching, and Web 2.0 functionality (e.g., instant messaging and post commenting).

In addition, application scalability is generally dependent on the ability to "add more of" a particular component. The database is no exception. With your choice of RDBMS, how simple is it to move from a single database server to two, three, four, or more?

That simplicity is governed by two features: clustering and replication. *Clustering* enables multiple physical database servers to represent themselves as a single virtual database server to connecting devices, thus distributing load in the process. *Replication* enables all those database servers to hold identical data sets at all times, thus ensuring that whichever physical server is chosen for a given request, the data returned is identical.

Some RDBMSs are better suited to clustering and replication than others. While this book is a big advocate of PostgreSQL, it is fair to say that its support for clustering and replication is entirely reliant on third-party packages such as Slony-L and Continuent uni/cluster for PostgreSQL. MySQL is somewhat better, but even its much vaunted MySQL Cluster platform is heavily caveated for enterprise deployment.

By contrast, Microsoft's SQL Server and Oracle 11g support extensive clustering and replication out of the box. For that reason, there is, sadly, a realistic expectation that for truly high-traffic applications it's still necessary to get the checkbook out.

Software Architecture

Finally, it's worth considering a human factor — one that, unless given adequate attention, can easily undo all the good work from following best practice across all of the issues previously discussed.

It doesn't matter how much money is spent on excellent server hardware, a first class ISP, carrier-grade network equipment, and so forth, if the application is written poorly. A bad application is deeply vulnerable to cracking under pressure.

In Chapter 13, you were introduced to the fundamentals of designing well-architected PHP applications — builds that will be reliable, secure, extensible, modular, and easy to maintain. But a well-architected application will (more often that not) cope better under pressure, simply because it stops developers from making the human errors that can lead to performance leaks.

Perhaps just as important, the modular nature of well-architected applications means that when performance bottlenecks *are* discovered, they are easier to track down, identify, and address.

Impact Factors

Having considered the core components of any Web application, it's important for you to understand the role each can play in producing adverse performance or poor availability at high levels of traffic.

Remember that non-availability doesn't just mean an application will be completely inaccessible. It can also mean that some core piece of functionality is temporarily disabled. The metric defined at the beginning of this chapter settled on 99.75 percent availability, but that means 99.75 percent of the time *all* functionality is present and correct — not just *some* of it.

Similarly, availability matters not one jot if performance isn't up to scratch. A number of factors manifest themselves as poor performance:

❑ *Socket response time* — This is the time taken between initiating a socket connection to the Web server and that connection being achieved, once local network conditions have been subtracted. A time of around 50 milliseconds (ms) is fine. With a local network latency of 20 ms, this means a connection being opened within 70 ms of that request being made.

❑ *HTTP latency* — This is the time taken between the client issuing its HTTP request (be it GET, POST, or something else) and the server starting to return data to the client, once network delays have been isolated. Anything more than 100 ms is poor. That is, having issued a command such as GET /index.php, the server should start to return data to the client (be it HTML or something else) within 100 ms.

❑ *Transfer rate* — This is the rate (in bits, bytes, or kilobytes per second) at which data transfer can be effected. With connections in the home easily reaching 8 Mbps as of this writing, it's increasingly important that your infrastructure can support a decent transfer rate, especially on larger files such as the binary assets that frequently comprise Flash movies and video (around 2 Mbps at a minimum).

As a rule of thumb, therefore, if under high traffic your application can't respond to socket connections in under 50 ms, respond to HTTP requests within 100 ms, or shift data at at least 2 Mbps, then it's not up to scratch.

With that in mind, what factors can impact availability under load?

Server Load

Every server supporting your application is under *load*. As a rule, the more traffic, the more load. A Web server, application server, and database server will all suffer an increasing burden on their natural resources (memory, CPU, and disk) as traffic levels (in terms of page impressions) increase.

The capability of a computer to carry out more than one operation at a time (*multitasking* and *threading*, in technical terms) is something of a myth. Each CPU can only carry out one instruction at a time. Each hard disk can only read or write to one part of the disk at a time. But smoke and mirrors provided by hardware controllers and the operating system itself allow for the *illusion* of multitasking.

This illusion is, in fact, a simple round-robin. If two tasks are competing for CPU time, the CPU alternates between the two with each clock cycle, although not necessarily on a 50/50 basis. Disks and memory generally work the same way. Requests not currently being serviced are effectively held in a queue. As load increases, that queue gets bigger, and so does the wait to get to the front of the line.

Under heavy load, therefore, tasks take longer to complete, because each server must service a larger number of tasks. Hence, a smaller percentage of the resources are devoted to each task. Depending on which server is the guilty party, load can manifest itself in different ways. An overloaded Web server could provide poor socket response time, whereas an overloaded database or application server could impact HTTP latency. Only an extraordinarily overloaded server would ever run slow enough to impact transfer rate, however. After all, network transfer rates are many orders of magnitude smaller than internal bus transfer rates.

Database servers are often the biggest culprit, here. In a typical PHP application, a single hit may be no great shakes to the Web server, which has to respond to only a single HTTP request. It may be a slightly bigger deal to the application server, which must run the necessary PHP code. But it is a huge deal to the database server, which may have to execute tens of hundreds of queries.

For that reason, the database server is usually the first to fall over. Later in this chapter, you'll meet some appropriate mitigation techniques.

Component Failure

Of course, innumerable physical components in an application's infrastructure can fail — routers, switches, network cards, network cables, motherboards, power supplies, hard drives, memory chips, CPUs, and more.

Should your application's architecture ever feature a *single point of failure,* then the failure of any one component can result in immediate downtime. Thankfully, across virtually every possible point of failure, there is a mitigation strategy.

Only one physical component features mechanical moving parts: the hard disk. For that reason, it is only the hard disk that has a fixed lifetime, a lifetime that is inversely proportional to traffic levels. That said, modern hard disks (even under intense load) last for years.

Network Load

Most of your internal network infrastructure will be capable of throughput speeds far in excess of your external Internet connection. Even a cheap-commodity Ethernet switch can achieve 100 Mbps. You probably won't have anything close to that from your ISP.

However, latency is another matter. The speed with which connections can be opened and closed declines as load on Ethernet devices (switches, routers, and network cards) increases. High traffic can therefore result in excessive latency, diminishing the user experience.

Network Failure

No matter how expensive your ISP, the occasional outage is hard to avoid. If your ISP's core router goes kaput, then no traffic can get to your site, and no traffic can get out. In other words, your site is down — as simple as that.

It's hard to mitigate this when using a traditional ISP, and indeed the majority of downtime suffered by high-profile Web sites is caused by ISP failure, rather than anything more sinister or sophisticated.

Mitigation Techniques

All of the previous discussion seems fairly terrifying at first glance — a whole catalogue of things that can go wrong when your Web site comes under load, all of which can contribute toward non-availability or subpar performance.

Mercifully, there is a whole host of strategies that can be deployed to all but guarantee uptime. The 100 percent achieved by Yahoo! over a year is probably a fluke, but the 99.75 percent mooted earlier in this chapter is certainly achievable, as you'll see.

Load Balancing

For a small-scale Web site serving, perhaps, only a few thousand page impressions per day, a single-server configuration is common. In such a scenario, the Web site's host name (perhaps www.example.com) will resolve in DNS to a single public IP address on the Internet. That IP is then *bound*, either directly to a server or, more usually, to a firewall, which passes traffic onto the server, having filtered it first. That server will run a suitable operating system, Web serving software, a database platform, and an application language. The most common setups are Linux, Apache, MySQL, and PHP, sometimes referred to as LAMP, for short.

In a load-balanced environment, two or more servers are set up to share the burden of HTTP requests arising from traffic to the site. In this way, more traffic than can be successfully served by just one server can be handled by the site.

It is not quite a straight line graph, however. It is very easy to balance Web servers, but as you'll see later, database servers, switches, and the like are more difficult to double up.

Load balancing is traditionally accomplished in two ways: through DNS or using a hardware appliance load balancer.

DNS Load Balancing

Using DNS, it is possible to distribute traffic across two servers by pointing a single hostname (such as www.example.com) to not *one* IP address, but *two* or more. In the DNS zone file, a suitable entry would look like this:

```
$ORIGIN example.com.
www      IN    A     10.0.0.1
www      IN    A     10.0.0.2
www      IN    A     10.0.0.3
```

Each access attempt to your site will result in a DNS lookup against the hostname. Which of the IP addresses associated with that hostname is returned by the name server will be random. As a result, the server that ultimately receives the HTTP traffic associated with the request to access the site will also be random. In theory, if you have two server IP addresses associated with the DNS entry, then each should receive 50 percent of the traffic.

This does have the desired effect of distributing traffic and is certainly inexpensive, but there are a few drawbacks, to say the least. First and foremost, having to assign multiple public IP addresses to a single hostname is wasteful. Authorities that issue IP addresses (especially in the now vastly oversubscribed IPv4 address space) are clamping down on frivolous requests, with most new orders requiring proof of need in very intimate terms. This may not be an issue with a mere two servers, but if your site scales to eight or more, you may well run into trouble.

Another more subtle issue exists, too. DNS lookups are almost always cached — at a minimum for the lifetime of the browser visit to the site. This means that all of the traffic associated with a single session (which, taking into account the existence of the underlying HTML, CSS, JavaScript, imagery, and other external assets, can run to 30 or so requests) will generally hit the same Web server. Hence, a lengthy 10-minute site session could result in 500 HTTP requests, all hitting one server. However, a quick 30-second visit from another visitor could consist of only 50. In such a scenario, you can count two site visits, but certainly not 50/50 traffic distribution between the two. Over the course of several hundred visits, the disparity may become more pronounced.

You must also beware of ISPs that use their own DNS caches. In this case, the DNS servers offered to end users are, in fact, DNS caching appliances. They will perform lookups perhaps only once in a four- or five-day period, and then cache the result. This is, strictly speaking, in violation of what are known as *time-to-live (TTL)* edicts defined in DNS zone files, which often prohibit caching beyond just a few minutes. However, given the sheer volume of DNS requests that must be processed by ISPs on a given day, you can understand why they break the rules.

Breaking the rules yields dividends for the ISP. Far less traffic needs to go "off network" in order to fulfill basic user DNS requests; but DNS load balancing can be broken as a result. A particular host is resolved to a particular IP address, and that single IP address is cached by the ISP. This, therefore, is the sole IP address that is offered to ISP end users until the cache entry "expires." Load balancing for anyone using this ISP simply won't happen.

There's a logistical issue, too. Servers fail from time to time. DNS load balancing doesn't take account of this, because the DNS zone file doesn't "know" which servers are dead and which are live. Taking this to another level of sophistication, servers get "ill." Some will be under higher load than others, and therefore should arguably receive less of the traffic for the Web site.

Hardware Load Balancing

All of these issues can be addressed by using hardware load balancing — a more enterprise-grade approach, with an enterprise price tag to match. In such a scenario, a dedicated device known as a *load balancer* acts as a sentry for all traffic hitting your Web site. It redirects individual HTTP requests on a case-by-case basis to two or more Web servers. This occurs most commonly on a simple "round-robin" basis, but also sometimes takes into account factors such as server availability, server load, and request type — perhaps directing requests for images to an *asset server* (discussed later), but requests for PHP scripts to a dedicated application server.

Enterprise load balancers themselves can be doubled up or clustered, with load shared using a proprietary protocol, connectors, and cable, sometimes called a *heartbeat* link. This provides redundancy should a load balancer fail and can allow exceptionally high traffic sites to share load over multiple balancing devices.

Such an enterprise-grade kit does not come cheaply — $30,000 or more for a dedicated device. That cost isn't usually hardware — load balancers are more often than not simply commodity server PCs — but actually the licensing cost for the software and operating system run on that box. These high costs mean that some architects look closely at rolling their own. Squid (`http://wiki.squid-cache.org/SquidFaq/ReverseProxy`) provides a basic subset of load-balancing functionality and, in practice, will probably be adequate for most readers. Those seeking a commercial solution would be well advised to check out F5 at `www.f5.com`.

Geographic Balancing

There's no doubt that distributing load among servers is a great way of making optimal use of the hardware you have, as well as making it easy to scale up later, simply by adding another server to the mix.

However, as Web sites become more globalized in nature, so, too, does the spread of connecting hosts. A global site can expect traffic from all four corners of the world. As you might expect, the further traffic has to travel, the slower the user experience. A user in Australia connecting to a server in the United Kingdom, for example, must experience traffic making a 20,000-mile round-trip — not exactly nippy.

The obvious solution is to position servers at all four corners of the globe, such that users are never far from a server hosting the content they want. A true global site may well have servers in Los Angeles, New York, London, Tokyo, Sydney, Mumbai, and Shanghai. Such a setup keeps the total number of "hops" down to an absolute minimum for 99 percent of traffic.

Assuming all users will use the same address (say, `www.example.com`) to access the site, how will the traffic get to the server nearest to them? It's a fairly easy task to map a remote user's IP address back to an approximate geographic location. Numerous databases (some of them free) provide developers with a simple resource to achieve such resolution. A good example is MaxMind GeoIP (`www.maxmind.com`); but given such a database, there are a couple of possible approaches to get initial traffic to the right server.

The easiest approach is to accept traffic on `www` in the standard manner, but to then immediately redirect the user to a host specific to them (and geographically nearby). For example, a user from London may access your site at `http://www.example.com`, but then be immediately directed back to `http://london.example.com`.

While this works well enough, there are a few things to keep in mind:

❑ First and foremost, that initial request to `www` is still traveling an appreciable distance, so performance can still be affected.

❑ Second, you're making it tougher for search engines to index your site. Core content under hosts other than `www` isn't a great idea.

❑ Third, there's a risk with people sending links to one another. If a user in London sends a link to a user in Tokyo, it's unlikely the recipient will think of adjusting the URL accordingly.

There is a solution: *geographic load balancing,* whereby DNS is used to distribute load according to the user's location. When a lookup is made for the initial record (`www.example.com`), that is typically made against the DNS server of the user's ISP. Thankfully, that user's ISP is generally located in the same country as the user. Therefore, when that DNS server forwards the request to the name server(s) used by the Web site's domain (that is, example.com), that name server is able to issue a *dynamic* response based on the remote IP address. As such, the IP address to which www.example.com resolves varies according to the remote user's location. Traffic from the very first request, therefore, hits the right server.

There is a challenge in either approach, though — that of keeping content in sync. Assuming users located around the world should get the same content, those servers must constantly replicate against one another. On the code and static content front, this can be accomplished easily enough using scheduled tasks and synchronization software such as rsync. Databases, of course, are more complicated. This is touched upon later in this chapter.

NIC Teaming

In the laudable quest to eliminate single points of failure, the potential for network equipment to fail is often overlooked. If a server must listen and respond on a single IP address, what is the use of having two network cards, two switches, and two firewalls?

By using *NIC teaming* (sometimes known as *link aggregation*), two physical network cards can share a single IP address. In so doing, the two cards can share load. Should one fail, a degree of redundancy is provided. Don't forget, too, that network cables can fail. Such a strategy should mitigate this, too.

In general, each network card links into its own switch so that the switch does not become a single point of failure. Because switches are aware only of hardware addresses (and not of logical addresses), no special configuration is required at the switch level. The two must simply be kept separate and not interconnected. On the server, however, the operating system must be configured to support NIC teaming. Sometimes a BIOS change is required, too. See http://en.wikipedia.org/wiki/Link_aggregation for some useful further reading.

Balancing routers and firewalls is trickier. Generally speaking, a heartbeat connection is required to allow one to "lie in state" as a hot standby while another is active. Should the active device die, the standby device can kick in automatically. The manner in which is this achieved varies from device to device and manufacturer to manufacturer. In most circumstances, your ISP should be able to help you.

Disk Fault Tolerance

Hard disks today are considerably more reliable than they used to be. In typical usage, and under typical levels of traffic, most Small Computer System Interface (SCSI), Serial Attached SCSI (SAS), and Serial Advanced Technology Attachment (SATA) disks will last for five years or more — far longer than the typical life span of the server itself.

Disks do fail from time to time, however; and if your Web application is dependent on a single disk, you're asking for trouble. Not only will failure result in downtime, but manually restoring that lost data from backup (assuming you have backups) can be a major hassle. Remember from earlier in this chapter you learned that Google loses $26,000 of revenue per minute of downtime. That helps keep things in perspective.

The solution is a Redundant Array of Independent Disks (RAID). In such a scenario, multiple physical hard disks are combined to form a single virtual container. The operating system sees just one disk, and the RAID controller takes care of getting data to and from the right disk when required.

Depending on the setup, this can provide numerous advantages. In one of the most common configurations, RAID 5, a *stripe and mirror* approach means that multiple hard disks provide greater opportunities for high capacities, and that any one disk can fail completely with no disruption to the server, and no loss of data. You can rig up the controller to notify you in such a scenario by e-mail or even perhaps Short Message Service (SMS) text message. All you need do is obtain a new disk, remove the old one, and insert the new one. The RAID controller does the rest, gradually bringing the new disk "up to speed" and back online once it is synchronized.

RAID also brings performance benefits. Data is often spread all over a disk's physical platters. If your virtual disk is tasked with reading data from two disparate places in quick succession, then rather than require the disk head to "jump" between the two locations, two physical disks can be charged with delivering each block of data. Hence, the time taken to perform that head jump is eliminated. It might not seem like much, but under heavy traffic it can make a huge difference.

Truly using RAID to your advantage requires being a little smarter than simply declaring "RAID 5 throughout." RAID 5, while providing excellent read speeds, is poor at writing, so it may not be a suitable choice for disks tasked with frequent writes.

By mixing and matching different RAID levels across different disks, optimal performance can be achieved. For example, you may decide to place your operating system boot partition on a single RAID 1 mirror of two disks, providing redundancy and excellent speed, but no incremental capacity. You may then decide to place your swap volume on a single disk with no RAID at all, given that failure of that disk is unlikely to affect anything vital. Application data may sit on another three disks, which may comprise a RAID 5 volume.

Refer to http://en.wikipedia.org/wiki/Standard_RAID_levels for help choosing the RAID levels right for you. Remember that different servers will doubtlessly perform different roles. Web/ application servers should never store variable data; hence, the emphasis should be on performance, rather than redundancy. Database servers need to be both fast and redundant, so RAID 5 or RAID 6 is a better bet.

Monitoring and notification is of huge importance. In the event that a disk has failed (or is failing), it's important to replace it promptly. Putting in place software that can notify you by e-mail should a disk go momentarily offline can provide an early warning system that it is about to fail. You can then reorder and replace without delay. After all, a degraded RAID array is arguably no better than no RAID at all.

Power Redundancy

Most servers feature two power supplies and two power supply connectors, generally IEC60320/C14 type (see http://en.wikipedia.org/wiki/IEC_connector). You should always connect both where possible, while keeping in mind that this may (depending on the manufacturer) double your server's power draw. With this setup, should one power supply fail, the server will continue to function.

Again, you should ensure that whatever utilities at the operating-system level are available to monitor power supplies are installed and set up to notify you should a power supply fail, or voltages start to fall outside of acceptable tolerances (which can indicate an imminent failure).

Ensure, too, that your ISP's data center provides an adequate power supply to your kit. This means power backed up with a regulated uninterrupted power supply (UPS), which should provide short-term cover against spikes and brownouts. Behind that, though, should sit diesel generators that can provide a day or more worth of power in the event of a longer-term outage.

Be careful, though, because as energy prices around the globe rise, ISPs are getting stricter about power. More often than not, it is difficult to fill a 42U rack with servers whose power requirements can actually be fulfilled within the limits your ISP sets per rack. Take care, here. If you place too much of a draw on the rack, then you may find you simply trip a fuse — and bang goes your whole rack.

Multi-segment Topologies

In a typical high-traffic setup, multiple servers will be used as Web servers, database servers, application servers, and asset servers. As shown in Figure 23-1, in a basic multi-server setup, these servers will generally sit on the same single *Ethernet segment*. This means there is a physical link between all the servers, and all can freely communicate with one another.

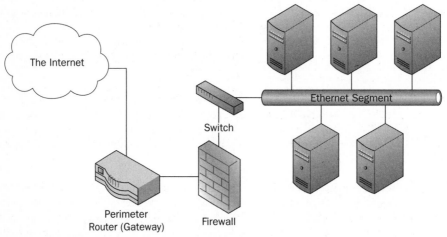

Figure 23-1: Traditional Ethernet segmentation

There is nothing wrong with this setup, strictly speaking, but consider the nature of the servers behind your firewall. Do they really all need access to one another? Similarly, does traffic from the Internet ever need to reach them? If the answer to either question is no, then you may want to consider placing servers on separate Ethernet segments, as shown in Figure 23-2.

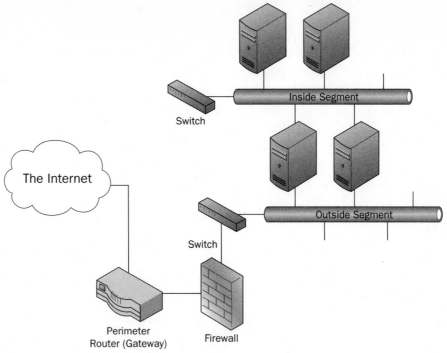

Figure 23-2: Dual Ethernet segmentation

In a dual Ethernet setup, two of the servers in the setup have dual NICs. One NIC connects them into the "outside segment" (which has access to the firewall and, by definition, the Internet), and the second (which has a separate IP address on a different subnet) connects them to the "inside segment" (which does not).

The benefit of such a setup is that it physically precludes communications between servers that do not need to communicate. Typically, database servers would be set up on the "inside segment," meaning that it is physically impossible to access database servers from the outside world, regardless of firewall rules. Security is tightened up by implication. There's no need to worry about getting a firewall rule wrong, because there is no rule to get wrong. However, through that secondary NIC, the Web servers can still speak to the database servers, and vice versa.

Another big advantage is speed. There's a dedicated link between the Web server and the database server, meaning the communications don't have to compete for bandwidth with general Web traffic.

You can take this to yet another tier of segmentation, should you want to do so. If you separate out Web servers, application servers, and database servers, each can sit on its own Ethernet segment. Only the Web servers are publicly accessible to the outside world and sit on an outside segment, and they pass HTTP requests to application servers on a middle segment. Those application servers, in turn, access databases sitting on an internal segment, as shown in Figure 23-3.

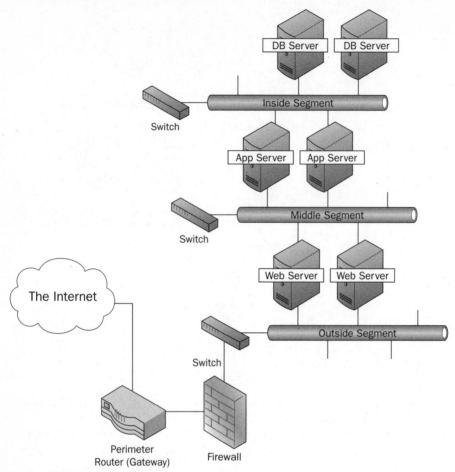

Figure 23-3: Three-tier Ethernet segmentation

This takes the level of isolation even further. The only devices with access to the Internet are the Web servers on the outside segment.

There is one "gotcha" here, though. Your application servers may well need access to the Internet in order to send e-mails and call external Web services. In the preceding schema, they have none and can only talk to database and Web servers. This can be mitigated by providing an HTTP proxy and mail server on the outside segment. Your application servers can then make use of these when they wish.

Database Clustering and Replication

You learned earlier in this chapter that it's relatively easy to load balance between Web servers using hardware load balancers, or even multiple DNS records.

In so doing, you can spread traffic among multiple servers, thereby eliminating a single point of failure. Should one Web server die, the other can pick up the strain, albeit at reduced performance for end users.

Doing the same with database servers is trickier, though. Queries that start with SELECT are easy — you can distribute them using exactly the same kind of methodology used to distribute HTTP traffic among Web servers. But any query that *changes* data (chiefly UPDATE, DELETE, INSERT, and so forth) must go to *all* servers; otherwise, servers will become out of sync.

In addition, should a database server go offline for a few hours, when it comes back, it must be brought back up to date before it's allowed back into the pool; otherwise, its data may be out of sync with its cousins.

All this and more is achieved with a technique known as *clustering and replication*. The term *clustering* refers to the ability to pool several database servers as a single unit, such that connecting applications need only be aware of the cluster, and not the database servers that comprise it. Through clustering, fault tolerance is achieved (in that any one server failing will not affect the availability and integrity of the database), as well as load balancing (in that load is shared, generally evenly, among servers).

By contrast, *replication* refers simply to the act of two disparate database servers keeping part or all of their databases in sync with one another. As you might expect, you can have replication without clustering — but you can't have clustering without replication.

How you achieve either (or both) is very much dependent on the choice of an RDBMS. This is an area where MySQL still isn't that hot. While the newly released MySQL Cluster does provide clustering in the traditional sense of the word, it has significant limitations — chief among which is its memory requirements, as well as the capability for a node to recover automatically upon failure. MySQL replication has been available for years now, but it does not provide load balancing in its own right. Your code has to pick up the slack. It's also asynchronous, meaning there's a built-in delay between changes to databases propagating to peers.

PostgreSQL has recently stormed ahead on this front, after years of very poor support. The likes of pgpool-II support connection pooling, load balancing, replication, and even parallel query processing, meaning that the burden of complex queries can be divided among participating databases. At a commercial level, uni/cluster for PostgreSQL provides virtually turnkey operation.

As you might expect, the two commercial heavyweights — Oracle and MS SQL Server — support both clustering and replication out of the box.

One final thought on this. Database clustering and replication isn't a silver bullet — and more often than not, it can be avoided. The use of caching, code generation, and asset serving means that traffic to your database server can be kept to an absolute minimum, and the real-term impact of the database going offline minimized, too.

Traffic Calculus

The phrase "traffic calculus" has sprung up in recent years. It refers to a branch of mathematics dedicated to the understanding of the shape of Web site traffic.

For example, consider a new Web site being launched for a television channel. The CEO of the network may tell you to expect 10 million page impressions per month. It's reasonable to assume that this traffic is likely to be distributed fairly evenly throughout the calendar month (that is, there's nothing to suggest that week one should have higher traffic than week two, or vice versa). Doing the basic math first, you can determine, therefore, that each week your Web site can expect around 2.3 million page impressions.

You might assume (based on either educated guesses or data available elsewhere) that 40 percent of the site's traffic is likely to occur on the weekend, and 60 percent during the week. This indicates a *bias* toward the weekend. You can, therefore, infer that your busiest day in terms of traffic is likely to be either a Saturday or a Sunday. If each will receive traffic in equal measure, you can assume that on a Saturday or Sunday your site will receive around 461,000 page impressions.

Over the course of a day, though, that traffic is unlikely to be constant. You could use a working theory that 60 percent of the daily traffic is likely to be between 3 P.M. and 6 P.M., since the Web site supports a daily television show that airs at 3 P.M. and finishes at 4 P.M. That means in that three-hour window, the site is likely to receive 60 percent of its daily page impressions, or 276,000 impressions.

You might further hypothesize that in the three-hour slot, 3 P.M. to 4 P.M. is likely to account for 20 percent of that block of peak traffic, 4 P.M. to 5 P.M. (the hour immediately after) 50 percent, and 5 P.M. to 6 P.M. the remaining 30 percent. Your peak hour is therefore 4 P.M. to 5 P.M., when you can expect around 138,000 page impressions.

Using calculus, you might assume that over that hour, the page impressions are likely to be distributed approximately according to the normal distribution, with a peak at five minutes past the hour. By plotting a graph showing a normal distribution, with a mean of five minutes, you can experiment with different values of standard deviation and Y scalar until you find a shape that "fits" your projected traffic. This is neatly illustrated in Figure 23-4.

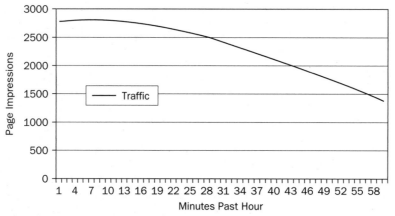

Figure 23-4: Traffic during peak hour

As a normal distribution, the gradient (dy/dx) of the curve will equal zero at the mean point, which has already been stipulated as being five minutes past the hour. Therefore, by calculating the y-value of the curve where x is equal to 5, the peak traffic per minute page impressions can be calculated: approximately 2,800 page impressions per minute. This is backed up by a quick visual check of the graph.

If a page impression consists of one HTTP request for the page, followed by around 20 for images, CSS, JavaScript, and other assets, with a total combined "weight" of 100 KB, you may, therefore, assume a peak transfer of 280,000 KB in that minute. This equates to 37 Mbps. In terms of HTTP requests, if each page impression consists of 21 HTTP requests, you'll need to be able to handle a throughput of 980 HTTP requests per second.

In this exercise, therefore, you've been able to work out your "worst-case scenario" in terms of bandwidth and requests per second for your hypothetical Web site.

How you use this data is up to you. You could, for example, use your peak Mbps figure in the course of your contractual negotiations with your ISP — perhaps asking for a 10 Mbps connection with the ability to "burst" to 100 Mbps when needed without financial penalty.

You might also seek to ensure that your entire infrastructure is capable of handling the peak of 1,000 HTTP requests per second, perhaps using load-testing software such as LoadRunner to achieve this, or even rolling your own test scripts to simulate load.

Either way, you have used a simple mathematical exercise to take a commercial objective — page impressions per month — and map it to a real technical requirement. Sure, you've used assumptions to get there, but businesses use assumptions all the time. At least there's some logic behind the infrastructure you're specifying.

Caching

PHP is fast and lightweight, and properly architected PHP applications run quickly with only fairly modest hardware behind them. Nonetheless, wherever you can save weight, you should, and page caching enables you to do just that, by executing code only when you really need to.

By using some variety of caching, each request to your Web application is inspected carefully, and, if possible, delivered to the client without executing the underlying code in full — indeed, sometimes not executing it at all. As a result, the burden on your application server — and perhaps on your database server — is decreased. This is achieved by *caching* output (that is, storing a copy of it) upon the first request.

Generally speaking, the requested URL, HTTP GET, and POST parameters, as well as cookies are inspected. The combination of the four provides a sort of "unique key." Should an identical request (based on those four parameters) have been generated in the recent past, content will be retrieved from the cache and sent to the end user; if not, the code will be executed as normal, but the output captured and stored in the cache. The word "recent" is almost always defined using a cache expiry constant; something around the two-hour mark is common.

Caching can take place at many points. PHP itself can execute caching. You can easily rig up your code to inspect input parameters by serializing $_POST, $_GET, $_COOKIES, and $_SERVER["REQUEST_URI"] into a unique key using the md5() function. You can equally easily capture output buffer contents using ob_get_contents(). In so doing, you can use simple conditional statements to determine whether or not to proceed with the execution of your script, or whether to serve up content from the cache.

You can also cache at the point of access to the database. You could easily create a wrapper around PDO to, for example, inspect SELECT queries as they are made, and, if an identical query has been made in the past few hours, intercept the call to the database and instead return a cached response retrieved from memory or disk.

It's also not uncommon to use dedicated caching code at the point of request, particularly when combined with load balancing. In such a scenario, the load-balancing appliance determines when to forward a user's request to (one of) the Web server(s). It may simply serve up content from the cache, particularly in the case of HTTP GET requests.

Whatever technique you use for caching, there are potential pitfalls. When deploying new content, it may be frustrating for your content authors if the content is not visible for several hours until the cache has expired. Hence, you may need to provide a manual mechanism to "flush" or otherwise reset the cache to bring forward the visibility of new content. In addition, should you be using caching in a load-balanced environment with multiple servers, you must ensure that their caches are in sync at all times; otherwise, users may not receive a consistent reflection of content from request to request.

These pitfalls aside, caching provides an excellent way to maximize the power of your infrastructure. A good rule of thumb is if you don't really need to run the PHP code, or you don't really need to hit the database, then don't.

Content Generation

In a similar vein to caching, the concept of *content generation* takes account of the fact that plain old Web servers are exceptionally good at serving up static content — that is, files read straight off the hard disk with absolutely no processing whatsoever.

In such a scenario, pages on your Web application are (wherever possible) generated in advance into static `.html` files and associated imagery. Consider the alternative: a complex PHP script that uses the database to dynamically build the page with each and every request. If that page isn't changing much from hour to hour, it makes sense to generate it "offline" and save the results to disk. That way, users don't have to wait while the page regenerates. A database can still be used, of course. The difference is that the database will be accessed only by the script that rebuilds the pages. User requests won't go anywhere near the database — they'll get static HTML.

This technique is used to great effect on the BBC news Web site, `http://news.bbc.co.uk/`, which gets hundreds of million hits a day. Almost everything you see is statically generated using PERL scripts — simple PERL CGI scripts used to provide dynamic functionality *only when it's needed*. It's not exactly high tech, but it certainly copes with the traffic, even during major world news events such as 9/11.

During your development cycle, you may encounter pages on your Web application that are "nearly static" — that is, they are consistent from request to request apart from some small, dynamic area. Maybe there is a news ticker on the bottom right-hand corner of the page, or there's a small login lozenge stating "you're not logged in" or "currently logged in as Ed," or similar. That whole page could be generated statically were it not for that tiny dynamic area.

You have a couple of options here, should you wish to stick to your guns and go the code-generation route. The first is to use IFRAMEs or JavaScript. In such a scenario, the HTML sent to the client is identical, but the client is instructed to request a piece of JavaScript or a separate IFRAME that will always be dynamically generated. There is still server burden in generating these pieces of content, but it is far less than would be involved in generating the whole page. This does have implications for search engine visibility and accessibility, however, as search engines and screen readers are generally incapable of reading JavaScript and will usually ignore IFRAMEs, assuming they are advertising.

The second option is to use server-side includes (SSIs), which is a simple "tag" in the generated HTML that tells the server when to bring in an external resource. Contrary to popular belief, it's perfectly possible to use SSIs to bring in a piece of PHP to generate that dynamic segment. For example, consider how you would include a piece of HTML using SSIs as follows:

```
<!--#include virtual="header.html" -->
```

You could instead include a piece of PHP as shown here:

```
<!--#include virtual="loginstatus.php" -->
```

Keep in mind that this code will be executed server side and not called by the client browser, and as such won't be privy to any cookies passed in the original HTTP request.

Asset Servers

One simple way to improve the performance of your Web site's infrastructure is to use a dedicated *asset server* to serve up pieces of content that are inherently static (that is, they need never be passed through PHP or any other dynamic content-generation engine). When coding your HTML, you simply point your <img> tags and so forth to your asset server, rather than www.

Examples of content that are essentially static include images, CSS stylesheets, JavaScript files, Adobe Flash movies, and simple .html files. As none of these would ever include PHP, why would you deliver them through a server equipped with PHP?

Admittedly, Web servers such as Apache are smart enough not to invoke PHP except when necessary, but Apache is far from the greatest Web server to use to serve up such content in the first place. It's a big piece of code, and far from streamlined — it does a lot of stuff you don't need. For that reason, you may wish to run something else on your asset server — maybe Boa, lighttpd, or thttpd (Google any of them). If you're really focused on squeezing every last drop out of your infrastructure, what about something like the TUX Web server? Built directly into the linux kernel, it enables you to build an entire server that does *nothing but* serve static Web pages — very quickly, indeed.

Content Delivery Networks

A *content delivery network (CDN)* is one of the more expensive tools in the performance tuner's arsenal, but it is also one of the most effective. In practice, CDNs are provided by third-party companies that agree to host large pieces of frequently requested static content on your behalf (typically images, audio, video, and binary downloads) and deliver them directly to end users. This enables you to concentrate on hosting your core infrastructure.

In practice, CDNs are simply niche ISPs that employ many of the techniques explored earlier in this chapter, including geographic load balancing, hardware load balancing, and static asset servers; but by building an infrastructure in bulk, they are effectively conducting aggregated buying, and as such are often able to offer large-scale delivery at a far lower cost than those attempting to do it themselves on a smaller scale. They also have effectively "infinite capacity." As your site gets bigger, you simply pay more.

For large-scale deployments, CDNs make sense, but do your sums first.

Real-World Examples

In closing, it pays to take a look at how a couple of the highest traffic Web sites in the world cope. These sites enjoy traffic probably beyond even the wildest dreams of most readers' own projects (or those of their employers), but nonetheless are notable in demonstrating best practices — and using PHP to boot.

Flickr

Flickr (www.flickr.com) is operated by Yahoo! and is the most successful photo-sharing Web site in the world. It serves tens of millions of users across hundreds of countries and serves more than 2 billion images. In addition to being a popular destination in its own right, it is frequently used by bloggers and other contributors to Web 2.0 experiences as a hosting engine for their own photos, thus saving on potentially expensive bandwidth bills. To this day, Flickr remains (largely) free of charge to use, and that is undoubtedly part of its appeal and popularity.

Database Configuration

Flickr uses a MySQL replication (as opposed to clustering) solution. In this environment, there is a single master database that is "authoritative." When in doubt, the master is *always right*. It uses MySQL replication to replicate asynchronously to a number of slave databases, which carry identical copies of that master database at all times.

A custom-designed hardware load balancer directs traffic between the various database servers. All SELECT traffic goes to one of several slaves; UPDATE, INSERT, and DELETE traffic goes exclusively to the master. This way, there is no need for PHP code to require any kind of special adaptation to route database traffic accordingly.

There is a slight "slave lag," however — the time between when the master is updated and that master replicates to all of its slaves. Because the slaves are used exclusively for all SELECT queries, there is a small chance that the chosen slave won't quite be "in sync." This can have odd effects for Flickr users, such as when uploading a new photo to an album, and it momentarily disappears from view.

Web/Application Servers

As you might expect, there are literally hundreds of servers powering Flickr at the front end. No load balancing is performed in DNS — geographic or otherwise. Resolve www.flickr.com anywhere in the world, and you'll get a single, unique IP address.

In fact, Flickr makes use of front-end caching using Squid. Wherever possible, this caches static content, meaning it is delivered to the end user without ever resorting to consulting the application (PHP) server, or database (MySQL) server.

The stats speak for themselves. Flickr serves up nearly 3,000 images per second, of which 80 percent come from the cache. This keeps the vast majority of traffic completely away from the Web and MySQL servers.

Further Reading

You can find more details about how Flickr handles its ever-growing levels of traffic at www.ludicorp .com/flickr/zend-talk.ppt.

Wikipedia

Still independently owned, Wikipedia is a free, multi-lingual, Web-based encyclopedia with content exclusively contributed and maintained by members of the general public. Despite having spawned countless copies (or "forks"), Wikipedia remains the original — and the most popular. It attracts 638 million annual visitors, who read more than 10 million articles in more than 250 languages, and its traffic continues to grow on a daily basis. As of this writing, it receives between 20,000 and 45,000 requests every second.

Wiki Software

Wikipedia is based on MediaWiki, a free and open-source wiki platform that delivers a sort of lightweight content management platform for delivering wiki content. The MediaWiki platform is written in PHP, and it can make use of any number of corresponding database platforms. Wikipedia, however, chooses MySQL.

Geographic Load Balancing

As touched upon earlier in this chapter, as a global site, Wikipedia makes use of geographic load balancing. In so doing, the DNS resolution of each of its hosts (`en.wikipedia.org`, `fr.wikipedia.org`, and so forth) is dependent on the geographic location of the client computer performing the DNS resolution. In London, for example, `en.wikipedia.org` (the English edition) resolves to 91.198.174.2. In Houston, Texas, it resolves to 208.80.152.2.

The servers at both IP addresses serve up exactly the same content, but both are at quite geographically disparate locations. In this manner, the "trace" to the Web server is kept to a minimum — that is, the number of routers and gateways through which traffic must pass to get from the user's Internet connection to the server is kept to a minimum.

Static File Server

Wikipedia makes excellent use of lighttpd, a lightweight, no-frills database server perfect for serving up static assets such as images and CSS stylesheets. In particular, thumbnail images (as opposed to their full-size variants) are delivered in this way.

In fact, the installation of lighttpd used by Wikipedia is a little more sophisticated than most. It is configured such that if a thumbnail image cannot be found, then the request can be passed to the application server cluster for real-time generation. This enables it to act as more of a content cache than a simple dumb asset server, able to intelligently route requests according to need.

Linux Virtual Server (LVS)

Load balancing in the Wikipedia environment is provided by Linux Virtual Server (LVS). This enables the resources of many physical servers to be pooled, balanced, and exposed to the outside world as a single virtual server.

This has many advantages over traditional load balancing. It is protocol independent, does not require any software-level support, is kernel level for speed, and can also provide no-single-point-of-failure redundancy.

See `www.linuxvirtualserver.org/` for more information. In particular, `http://kb.linuxvirtual server.org/wiki/Load_balancing` has details on its role in providing load balancing.

memcached

Finally, not touched upon earlier in this chapter is memcached. Natively supported in PHP (see `http://uk.php.net/manual/en/intro.memcache.php` for more information), it provides distributed memory caching that enables the results of "expensive" application operations to be cached in memory.

Because memory is almost always faster than, for example, reading from a disk, calling a Web service, or talking to a database server, great speed advantages can be enjoyed and, by extrapolation, a higher load supported.

In the case of Wikipedia, pools of dedicated servers actually function as dedicated caches with large quantities of RAM. There is, therefore, a slight burden in establishing a connection to the cache server in order to lodge or retrieve cached values, so certain heuristics are followed when deciding whether or not to use the cache.

In Wikipedia's case, there is a pool of around 30 servers with 2GB of RAM each — that's more than 60GB worth of caching of textual values.

Further Reading

For further (fairly dense) reading on Wikipedia's infrastructure, visit `http://dammit.lt/uc/workbook2007.pdf`.

Summary

In this chapter, you were finally exposed to the cold, harsh reality of PHP in the enterprise — that is, the need for high application availability under high traffic.

Initially, you explored what these mythical (but oft-used) phrases actually mean and learned about some cold, hard metrics for both. With this in mind, you looked at the architectural factors that affect availability under load, and the relative importance of each. You then explored in some detail an encyclopedia of approaches that can mitigate the risk created by these fault lines.

Finally, you took a look under the hood at two popular Web sites — Flickr and Wikipedia — and learned how they employ some of those mitigation strategies to great effect, and hence cope with enormous volumes of traffic with ease.

In Chapter 24, you'll be forced to ask yourself some pointed questions about whether PHP is actually the right choice for your application in the first place. In so doing, you'll learn some great advocacy techniques — as well as when it's appropriate to look elsewhere.

24

PHP Advocacy

Obviously, you don't set out to write an entire book on a particular programming language without believing that it is the best approach to Web application development. However, PHP suffers from some reputation problems, especially among certain groups of application developers who believe that the simple syntax, weakly typed variables, and lack of a large, complex application server environment relegates PHP to having utility only in very simple applications, and for beginning programmers who lack knowledge of other environments.

It is true that the very low barrier to entry for anyone who wants to build a Web application means that a lot of PHP-based Web sites are poorly built, with gaping security holes, an impenetrable mishmash of business logic and HTML markup, and major performance issues. However, the simplicity of the PHP platform and its accessibility are also major advantages, and the low barrier to entry is something to be celebrated, not denigrated.

Books like this (and other excellent printed and online PHP resources) should encourage beginning developers to increase their knowledge of software development and the craftsmanship of their product. For experienced developers, who are accustomed to working in other environments, these resources should encourage giving PHP a second look and considering it for their next project.

This chapter provides some justification for why PHP is the best programming language selection for even enterprise-class application development. It also provides some counterarguments to those who insist that other platforms have a claim to greater legitimacy.

Low Overhead

One of the most infuriating things about running a Java-based Web application is the amount of setup, installation, configuration, and performance tuning that must take place just to get even the simplest application up and running. After installing Java, a Web server, a J2EE application server, a connector to enable the Web server to talk to the application server, Ant (or other build manager), creating XML files to configure the build manager, compiling the application, packing it up into deployment files (WAR or EAR packages), deploying to the application server, adjusting application configuration files, adjusting the application server configuration files, and then rebooting the application server, you can then find out whether or not the code is working properly.

Ugh!

The simplicity of the PHP environment (that is, just a Web server and the PHP module) makes it very easy to get a PHP application up and running. Unless your application requires some custom modules or other esoterica (which is unusual), there's generally only a small configuration file for the application, usually containing things such as the database connection string and other simple details, and the application is ready to run. Most UNIX platforms (including Mac OS X) now ship with Apache and PHP already installed.

In many applications, you might need cron jobs to run periodically, for which you usually use a command-line application or script. Whereas the basic command-line syntax for running a Java command-line application (and, to a slightly lesser extent, a Python or Ruby application) can be labyrinthine and not at all obvious, PHP command-line applications are generally invoked with only one parameter: the name of the script to be run. Whereas applications have been architected using a clean MVC paradigm, being able to interact with the application from the command line generally only involves a new controller and some new views. While this is true of any well-written application, the simplicity of the invocation in PHP makes this a much more palatable proposition than in other environments.

Whether you are running from the command line or from the Web server, the simplicity of invoking any PHP application is greatly enhanced by the common install locations for systemwide libraries. Compiled modules written in C have a designated install location, and PHP-based extensions installed by PEAR go into a common directory. Unlike the system employed by Perl (which involves many such common folders, all with version-specific names), the PHP structure is incredibly easy to understand and discover, generally by looking at the output of `phpinfo()`. The convoluted classpath of Java (and occasionally Python) does not factor into the configuration of a PHP application.

When new extensions must be installed, there are two very simple approaches to installing them on the Web server: PEAR and PECL. PEAR is the system of utility libraries that are written in PHP, and PECL includes those that are written in C as PHP extensions. The documentation for both repositories is excellent, and available from their respective Web sites (`http://pecl.php.net` and `http://pear.php.net`). While these take their cues from the CPAN repository for Perl, they are far simpler to access, and the documentation is far easier to read. No such repository exists in a meaningful way for .NET or Java.

The preferred practice is to compile new extensions from source, and this is the preference of this book's authors. Many other developers are quite satisfied using their operating system's package manager to add new functionality to PHP. For example, in a Red Hat/Fedora environment, if you should need the PostgreSQL module for PHP, it can be as simple as typing the following from the command line as root:

```
#yum install php-pgsql
```

The near ubiquity of PHP means that the maintainers of the various GNU/Linux distributions ensure that the PHP modules are well-tested and simple to install.

Linguistic Simplicity

PHP's syntax was influenced by a number of popular programming languages, such as Perl, C, and even ASP. As a result, it has the benefit of those languages' older heritage and has been able to incorporate the most useful parts of their syntax and discard those features that were confusing and unnecessary.

Weakly Typed Languages

The primary advantage of strongly typed programming languages such as Java and C# is that some programming errors will be caught by the compiler prior to application deployment, which can catch some bugs that might be otherwise difficult to track down. However, this is done at the expense of the programmer's time spent ensuring that variables are assigned the right type to begin with, and then casting values from one form to another when converting data structures. Like Perl, Python, and Ruby, PHP enables the developer to determine how the data will be used at run-time. This allows for automatic type casting, reuse of variables to hold different types of information at various points in the execution, and generally simpler code.

This feature can, of course, be misused; but there is a primary difference between the philosophies of strongly typed and weakly typed programming languages: The latter *trusts* the developer to know what he or she is doing. The following is arguably sloppy, but perfectly valid in PHP:

```
$words = array('Hello', 'World');
$words = join(' ', $words);
```

Having to create another variable to hold the string representation of the joined array would probably be better practice, but in a strongly typed language such as Java or C#, you must take the time to declare and instantiate the objects to hold the two different values. Likewise, the following is perfectly valid and unambiguous PHP code:

```
$a = 6;
$b = "42";
$c = $a + $b; //48
$d = $a . $b; //"642"
```

Note the advantage here over other weakly typed languages for which the addition operator and the concatenation operator are the same (Perl, JavaScript, and so on). When setting the value of $c, PHP automatically casts the string "42" to its numeric equivalent, 42. When concatenating the two variables to get $d, the 6 is cast to "6". In those languages that overload the operator for the different data types, the value of $c would be ambiguous.

Reduced Punctuation

Languages such as Perl use different sigils to identify variable types (for example, $foo is a scalar, @bar is an array, and %baz is a hash, while $baz is, confusingly, a reference to %baz). A common complaint with such languages is that converting values between the various forms and keeping track of which sigil to use (and when) is enormously time-consuming and a common source of error.

Further adding to the confusion is Ruby's use of those same sigils to indicate variable scope. PHP simplifies all of this by using one syntax for its variables: $myvar.

In general, the PHP developer errs on the side of introducing fewer punctuation symbols to the language, eschewing the shortcut variables of Perl (for example, $_, $?) and the stranger string operators (such as qq) found in Perl and others.

To create an array in PHP, you simply use array(). This is intuitive and does not require remembering whether the array operators are [], (), or {} or something else, as is commonly the case in a number of programming languages. This means that everything must be a bit more explicit, and perhaps occupies more lines of code, but because professional programmers are concerned with the readability of their software to others, this is an advantage, especially as it does not require additional programmer time to implement.

Commonly Understood Syntax

For all of its faults, the C-style syntax of semicolons and braces is well understood and common to a huge variety of programming languages. While the alternative syntaxes found in languages such as Python and Visual Basic are more accessible to new programmers, the rest of us are quite comfortable in a world where whitespace is insignificant, and statements end in a semicolon. Comfort, though not necessarily exciting, is productive.

Anyone with any prior programming experience can very quickly pick up the basic syntax of PHP and understand immediately how to handle basic operations. All operators are simple, one-unit punctuation marks (e.g., assignment is =, concatenation is .), and functions are constructed with the keyword function, with no need to declare them separately, as in C. While many appreciate the simplicity of a visually uncluttered language such as Python, it is a different approach to syntax than what many of us are used to. Programming languages such as Ruby that support multiple programming paradigms (such as functional programming) alongside the imperative programming style of PHP can lead not only to syntactic confusion, but also confusion regarding the intent of a piece of code.

Cross-Platform Support

Like many of the other languages discussed in this section, PHP is supported on nearly every commonly used operating system. Java, with its "write once, run anywhere" philosophy, supports this concept at the level of the language; but this promise starts to rapidly degrade once the various application server environments are brought into the picture. Very often, applications created to run on JBoss don't work properly, or aren't deployed in the same way, as an application written for, say, WebLogic. The complexities of these two environments are such that write-once may work for the application logic (sometimes), but vast amounts of container-specific configuration information must be created for each deployment. This also assumes that the application is written for, and compiled against, Sun's version of Java.

> It is worth mentioning that there is some fragmentation in the implementation of Java with competing JVMs from Microsoft (largely ignored), Apple, and a version more compatible with the open-source licenses from the people at the GNU project. All of these implementations are slightly different.

PHP has a single implementation, with a full free and open-source software license, a very active developer community, and no signs of forks happening anytime soon. The promise of "write once, run anywhere" is realized in the PHP project and, it's worth mentioning, in Python, Ruby, Perl, and several others.

Because PHP only needs a simple plug-in into the Web server to work, with no additional server processes or daemons required to support it, it is readily adaptable to any Web server environment, and SAPI modules exist for nearly any conceivable Web server software you might want to use.

Deployment of a PHP application is usually a trivial matter of uploading some files to the Web server and then performing any application-specific configuration (such as editing the database connection string). There is no complicated deployment of WAR files with server rebooting, and complex XML files dozens of lines long to set up the execution environment. For many installations, the default `php.ini` file included with the source code distribution is nearly (and often completely) correct for the platform on which it is deployed. Moreover, unless new extensions must be added to PHP, this configuration is very often never touched after the initial install.

To deploy a PHP application to the production Web servers, you can use an FTP client to copy files. However, a far better way is to use a Subversion client (or CVS) to deploy from a particular branch of the source code repository. (Appendix A provides a discussion on source code management systems and Subversion.) Because PHP is an interpreted language, there are no compiled, machine-specific binaries to deploy. In addition, unlike J2EE applications, the code is distributed as plain text, rather than ZIP files (which is what WAR and EAR files actually are), facilitating simple and fast incremental updates to only those files that have changed since the last deployment.

One huge advantage over complex GUI application servers such as IIS is the capability to edit the plain-text configuration files remotely using `vi` or `emacs` through an SSH session. Because it is easy to tunnel SSH connections from one machine to another, it is also a simple matter to configure a secure connection to the Web server for administrative purposes. Securely connecting to a Windows Remote Desktop connection to administer security, application settings, user accounts, and other details usually involves a messy process of connecting to a VPN, remoting into a machine in a DMZ, and, from there, connecting to the actual Web server machine, where everything is done through a bandwidth- and memory-hogging GUI.

.NET applications (which are themselves often not simple to deploy) are a "write once, run on one" operating system application environment. Despite the promise of Microsoft's common language run-time and the progress being made by the open-source Mono project, .NET development is still very dependent on the Microsoft application server environment. Though this book doesn't necessarily advocate PHP applications on a Window server running IIS, at least a few applications (especially those with utility across several of the clients of this book's authors) have been quite successfully deployed on UNIX and Windows machines (using MySQL and MSSQL databases, respectively) with almost no modification to the application source, other than some minor changes to the SQL queries.

For .NET development, there's basically only one programming environment to use, which is Microsoft's admittedly quite excellent Visual Studio. However, being tied to one environment for software development is stifling, and the massive overhead of MSVS means that you are limited to doing .NET development on fairly robust hardware, to which you may not always have access. With an SSH client and a copy of `emacs`, you can remotely develop a PHP application from even the most basic computer. For local development, you can essentially run any operating system you like and use any text editor or integrated development environment (IDE) that you like. (See Appendix B for a discussion of some of the better PHP IDEs that are available.)

Ubiquity

PHP's ubiquity and longevity are other reasons that it appears at the top of any list of possible languages to be considered when creating a new application. Because you know that nearly every ISP will support it, and that it will work on any environment you might need to deploy to (including IIS on Windows), you know that you won't need to worry about system support, unlike Java, Python, and Ruby, which are generally not widely supported, even if support for the latter two is growing.

Though Python and Ruby have some support from some very influential users, it remains to be seen how much longevity they will enjoy — especially Ruby, which currently has a trend-of-the-week aura about it, despite being a very capable and robust language. While Ruby on Rails has inspired many programmers to create some innovative applications, the Ruby language itself remains relatively obscure, and the Rails project has scant corporate support.

Python, conversely, has been around for a while, and is widely used at Google (among other heavyweights in the Web world). However, support for Python remains scant at major ISPs and corporate data centers. While that might start to change in the years to come, it remains a specialist application development environment.

The quality of the documentation and the ease by which it is accessed (just go to `http://php.net/`[`function_name`] to get the documentation on any function) make learning PHP a snap. While there is abundant documentation on Python, it is not so easily accessed, and the Ruby documentation still has a way to go. The length of time that PHP has been widely used also means there is an abundance of excellent tutorials and how-to examples on nearly any conceivable programming task. With Python and Ruby fairly new to the scene, the available resources for those languages are not so vast. The documentation for Java is abundant and well-constructed, but the complexity of application development for that platform offsets its utility. The official .NET documentation from Microsoft is middling in quality, though that development community has a very active group of tutorial writers.

Power

It has been said about PHP that while it may work well for your cousin's blog, it's not ready for enterprise-class software development; but just ask any company to show that it is running more processor-intensive, storage-intensive, security-conscious, or mission-critical applications than Wikipedia, Facebook, Yahoo!, and, yes, WordPress, along with countless other Web sites that see far more traffic in an hour than most corporate applications see in a month.

Having said that, it is very, very easy to write really bad applications using PHP. It is really, really difficult to write any application for a full-blown J2EE environment. Where you have excellent software developers, carefully thinking through the software architecture (and planning the execution against established business logic), PHP provides the formalized language and execution environment to create the most robust applications. Where you have inexperienced software developers using amateurish techniques and poor project management, every application will be bad, regardless of the programming language.

Earlier releases of PHP were fairly blamed for the lack of object-oriented support (fixed in PHP 5), the lack of namespaces (fixed in PHP 5.3), and bad application design decisions (such as the presence of `register_globals` in `php.ini`). PHP 5 has now been out for nearly five years, and has proven itself as both a capable language and a robust execution environment. With the default inclusion in PHP 6 of the Advanced PHP Cache (APC), an opcode caching extension covered briefly in Appendix C, you can realize a large performance gain on top of the optimizations to the PHP run-time released in this version.

This discussion has not mentioned some alternative languages, such as ColdFusion, which remains popular in some circles. It is excluded here because it is rapidly waning in popularity, has little support among professional software developers, and is a platform-limited, fairly expensive, and poor-performing environment. Also excluded are some of the higher-level application libraries, such as Struts and Tiles for an MVC implementation in Java, or Catalyst for Perl. The enormous complexity of these systems is laughable in comparison to a PHP-based solution such as Smarty, or the preferred templating system of PHP itself.

Summary

This chapter should have provided some indication of why PHP has the enduring popularity it has, and why the authors of this book are enthusiastic advocates of it. It is hoped that readers who may have decided (as a result of now long-outdated objections) that PHP is "not yet ready for prime time" will reexamine the language and run-time environment, and check out the software architecture of the many great open-source applications written in PHP that are currently serving millions of visitors a day (Wikipedia and WordPress would be great places to start). In addition, consider whether your day is more productive writing XML configuration files for an application server, or writing the business logic for your actual application in PHP.

Now that you're armed with all the information about why PHP is such a fantastic application development platform, Chapter 25 offers some ideas about how to achieve a successful career using it.

25

Your Career As a PHP Professional

If you somehow managed to make it this far without touching a computer, please refer to at least a few of the previous 24 chapters. We humans tend to learn best by physically doing what we have learned. Go back and pick up a chapter (or two) that piques your interest, and feel free to experiment with the code. The adage "You get out of it what you put into it" applies here.

This should ring true even if you've scrupulously read every paragraph and run every application. After all, you're sure to have experienced a thought that starts with, "What happens if . . . ?" Don't know the answer? Can't find it in the documentation? Experiment. There is no shame in breaking code by exploring boundaries, and by now your PHP skills should be up to a critical point. You can dig yourself out of any hole that you've managed to get yourself into.

This is an important distinction. Digging yourself out of a hole by using your technical skills, leveraging unit tests, and pondering the "hows" and "whys" means that your education can continue and, it is hoped, extend itself beyond the technical realm. The ability to determine the likely causes of a problem, and then to develop a short list of likely best solutions (a skill medical doctors call "differential diagnosis"), is a critically important part of your development as a professional technologist. It is a skill that comes only from experience and making a few mistakes along the way.

Motivation

Regardless of why you've purchased this book, the work involved to get here is certainly nontrivial, and you deserve a pat on the back. Getting here probably involved sacrificing at least some time that you would rather have spent playing video games, attending social gatherings, interacting with your family, or just getting enough sleep.

You should now be able to appreciate some of the features and ubiquity of PHP. Go out and apply what you've learned, using baby steps if need be, but apply the lessons you've learned. Install PHPUnit. Cruise through the PEAR archives, and don't just install and run third-party PHP applications, but look at them, read through the source code, figure out what they're doing, and fix them if need be. (Remember that these are open-source libraries; contributions back to the project, especially those that resolve problems, are generally appreciated and sought.)

Even though your skill set may be both deep and wide, you really never stop learning. Contrary to the belief that Wrox is attempting to torture you, every chapter exists for a reason, and none is purely academic. PHP professionals (in the field) have created this book, and everything that was presented to you is used in a professional environment.

That also means that everything has a history. Neither this book nor PHP 6 was created out of the ether, so these functions and practices are worth further exploration. Entire books (even entire companies, and some sub-industries) support the concepts that have been presented to you. Continue reading, because some great resources are coming right up.

Your Career As a Developer

Assuming that you are serious about being a professional software developer (as opposed to being merely someone who gets paid to write code), you should make a conscious effort to further your skills. The shelf life of technical skills is growing ever shorter, and no effort you put forth to keep up-to-date regarding trends and developments can be considered wasted.

How should you spend your precious time? You can't possibly learn everything about everything, and well-rounded technical individuals are considered quite valuable commodities.

More Than Web Development Skills

PHP is more than the details of session management, file downloads, and configuration variables. PHP is a language that grows and changes over time to suit the needs of developers like you who need to have it done by yesterday.

Although the design and implementation of PHP is geared toward Web site development, PHP can be used for more than interacting with a browser. Consider what you can do with a tool that is capable of running seamlessly across Windows and Linux, as well as communicating with file systems and nearly every popular database. What else can you do with it? How about the following:

- ❑   Translate databases
- ❑   Process XML
- ❑   Gather RSS/Atom feeds
- ❑   Test forms/sites from alternative Web development technologies
- ❑   Use Perl-like text processing
- ❑   Run generic utilities

Even if you don't create Web sites every day, you can still find opportunities to leverage your hard-earned and valuable PHP skills.

Soft Skills

Yes, these are also known as the dreaded "people skills." Even PHP geeks must interact with real, live, actual humans from time to time, even if they are other PHP geeks.

Oddly, these abilities are not thought of as standard technical skills, even though most professional software developers spend a significant amount of time interacting with clients and co-workers, gathering functional requirements, determining business logic, coordinating development efforts, and doing postmortem evaluations of work completed. Let's face it, out of the box, most programmers generally do not possess the most effective social skills.

Time invested in enhancing your nontechnical technical skills goes far. Go out of your way to solicit from co-workers and clients feedback on your communications skills, personality traits, and presentation abilities. As a gross overgeneralization, software developers tend to have high intellectual ability, but also tend to have an astounding lack of social awareness, compounded with arrogance.

Your clients and co-workers are not of lesser intellect because they know nothing about technology. (They may be idiots for others reasons, but lack of technical knowledge does not equate to lack of intelligence.) Be sensitive to the fact that technology intimidates most non-technologists. This may be partially because of its complexity, but it may also be attributable to years of experience in dealing with obnoxious technologists who go out of their way to belittle those who lack any knowledge of computer science, and overwhelm them with arcane jargon in an attempt to "explain" a problem. Don't be that obnoxious person. Knowing how to effectively communicate complex topics to non-technologists is a skill that the authors of this book have spent time developing, and one we leverage every day to win and retain clients.

Instead of taking the approach that you are being "bothered" or "distracted" by those who ask questions, instead consider the situation as a teaching opportunity. It actually is an opportunity. The better your clients and co-workers understand what goes in to the creation of an application, the better an appreciation they will have for why various tasks take a certain amount of time, and what sorts of activities are nontrivial.

The goal of this education is not to equip account executives or graphics designers with the knowledge of architecting a database, but rather to help them understand the nature of the various activities that are required to get certain kinds of applications launched.

As an example, the authors of this book regularly hold formal, planned seminars for clients and co-workers, but even more regularly take a little time during the business day to fully explain our answers to certain questions. Both the formal and informal education immensely improves the relationship between clients and co-workers, and helps to ensure that developers are consulted during those phases of the project where their input is essential, and left out of meetings where their time would be wasted. Properly educating everyone makes everyone's life easier.

Academic Skills

The art and science of what we do is continuously evolving. Professional software developers understand that a continuing computer science education is essential to professional development, personal growth, and gains in productivity and application stability. Most of us take some amount of time every day (even if it's only for a hour) to browse the literature, monitor key mailing lists, and keep abreast of industry news and trends (and, no, spending an hour making smarmy comments on Slashdot doesn't count toward a better understanding of your profession). In addition to the abundant online resources and regularly published literature, there are a few classics that should be read, reread, and fully internalized.

A full understanding of what design patterns are, how to implement some of the most common ones in PHP and other programming languages, and learning how to use a design pattern approach to thinking about software architecture almost necessarily results in better overall application design, and better reusability of objects. *Design Patterns: Elements of Reusable Object-Oriented Software* by Erich Gamma, Richard Helm, Ralph Johnson, and John M. Vlissides (often collectively referred to as the "Gang of Four," or "GoF" (Addison-Wesley, 1994)) is a classic; and comes in easy-to-swallow chapters, presented in a carefully typeset, beautifully presented tome (it even has a fancy-pants ribbon for marking your page). Learning just one per week will make half a year fly by in no time.

One way of gaining a richer understanding of how PHP works is to spend some time analyzing and understanding the source code for PHP itself, which is written in C. This is especially useful if you're going to attempt any low-level performance tuning. With *Writing Compilers and Interpreters* by Ronald Mak (Wiley, 1996), knowing how PHP and similar languages do their magic goes a long way when the going gets tough.

Refactoring: Improving the Design of Existing Code by Martin Fowler, Kent Beck, John Brant, William Opdyke, and Don Roberts (Addison-Wesley, 1999) examines the techniques for achieving well-written concise code. *Agile Modeling: Effective Practices for eXtreme Programming and the Unified Process* by Scott Ambler and Ron Jeffries (Wiley, 2002) goes into detail regarding the integration of agile development practices and standard modeling techniques.

Community Skills

PHP exists because it was developed as a community effort. Scores of developers have been involved in the process, if only in the capacity of testing. Another incredibly important contribution one could make to the project of developing the language itself is testing and documentation writing. One of the reasons PHP has succeeded as well as it has is because of the quality and quantity of documentation available; but if you want to contribute to the development of the source code for PHP, one of the PEAR or PECL libraries, or any other open-source project, it's important to understand the culture of those who make up the core of the development effort.

The day will arrive when you find a PHP utility or application that must be repaired, or you might discover someone who might offer a patch for something that you wrote. Either way, a dose of humility goes a great distance in the political process, and this is no exception.

Actively contributing to community projects such as PEAR increases your personal PHP skills, and the value of the effort is multiplied by the time saved by similar developers using your tools. Even if you're not as technically astute as the project may initially require, the act of creating a "How-To" or developer-targeted tutorial is often a great help in learning a new technology. Unfortunately, good documentation is often lacking in the best of projects.

Summary

The technical concepts presented in this book are considered best practices, and you should be prepared to know what they are. As a software developer, you'll most certainly be presented with both good and bad examples of MVCs, refactorings, UML, design patterns, and collections.

Therefore, utilizing your new skills is as important as learning them in the first place. Try to leverage what you know in other areas and be on the constant lookout for interesting tools, development techniques, designs, and projects.

After all, you do share planet Earth with us, the authors, who welcome any help in creating a place where poorly written software is not shockingly easy to find.

Remember, then, young Jedi: "Always in motion is the future" (Yoda).

Part V

Appendixes

Appendix A: Version Control

Appendix B: PHP IDEs

Appendix C: Performance Tuning PHP

Appendix D: Best Practice PHP Installation

Version Control

Many programmers dread big projects, often for a whole host of reasons. However, one particular aspect of big projects can sometimes seem more unappealing than any other: code organization. Six or seven software developers, two software architects, a lead architect, and client-side developers all working on the same project often represent a recipe for disaster.

Mercifully, code organization on big projects has been made much easier in recent years with the advent of readily available, easy-to-use, cross-platform version-control software.

This appendix examines the basic principles of version control, and discusses how to organize a version-control strategy for your project. You'll also learn how these principles are applied in two of the most popular version-control software applications, and how to choose which (if either) best suits your project.

Principles of Version Control

The purpose of version control is twofold. The first is to avoid the version conflicts in development that can arise when multiple programmers work on the same set of project files. The second is to automatically journal changes to key files on a project, which creates a historical record of changes to the code and enables the capability to revert to previous versions.

By requiring programmers to *check out a file* from a central repository when they wish to work on it, a version-control platform can keep a record of who is working on which files, and at what times. Depending on the approach taken, this method can either wholly exclude other developers from working on that file at the same time, or allow other developers to also work on the file and then merge their changes when the file is checked back in again.

Journaling of files in a project involves the retention of previous versions of each file. Whenever a file is checked in to a repository, the version-control platform marks it as current so that anyone retrieving that file from the repository does retrieve that latest version by default. However, a copy is taken of the file in its previous state. Not only does this enable the project administrator or lead architect to roll back a file should a new version prove problematic, it also enables the changes between versions to be easily listed, which, from a project management perspective, is a major boon.

All version-control systems use some variety of a repository for storing a copy (usually verbatim on disk, but sometimes as part of a more complex, and often proprietary, database format) of the file and directory structure of the project. How this repository is accessed varies from system to system. A typical topology is examined later in this appendix.

Concurrent Versus Exclusive Versioning

Version-control platforms differ immensely in their implementations of the principles discussed earlier, especially with respect to how a file is checked out.

In any version-control platform, when a programmer checks out a file, the latest version of that file is retrieved from the central repository, and the user's local version is replaced with that latest version.

However, in a platform employing *exclusive versioning*, a lock is then placed on that file with immediate effect. While the file is checked out, other developers may still retrieve the latest version of that file, but they themselves will not be able to check it out to work on it. This exclusive versioning is usually enforced by marking the developer's local copy of the file as read-only. Of course, this is only notional enforcement, and does require the developer's cooperation to work well in practice. The lock is removed after the developer working on it checks in the file in question. The repository is then updated to reflect the latest version.

Concurrent versioning adopts quite a different approach. The acts of retrieving the latest version of a file and checking it out to work on are combined so that they are essentially one and the same. In other words, in order to work on a file, all a developer must do is ensure that he or she has the latest version of that file and then start working on it. When each developer has finished making changes to the file, he or she will check it in. This is where the magic happens. If a second developer checks out a file after another developer checked it out, and is attempting to check it in after the first developer has checked in a changed version, the two newly submitted versions will be merged.

A Concurrent Versioning Example

To make things a little clearer, consider the following example. This is an imaginary file called `helloworld.php` that prints "Hello World" in the Web browser. Note that line numbers have been included. Of course, these would not be included in the code as it is saved.

```
1: <?php
2: $strToPrint = "Hello World";
3: ?>
4: <html>
5:    <body>
6:       <?php echo $strToPrint; ?>
7:       <br /><br />
8:    </body>
9: </html>
```

You can call this snippet of code version 1.0 of the file.

Suppose that Jane Doe and John Doe are both working on the project. John works out of New York and Jane works out of Los Angeles.

A meeting has been called with the client. They wish to change the code of this particular file so that instead of printing "Hello World" it prints "Goodbye World." John Doe's manager has given John the task of modifying the code to reflect this requirement.

In that meeting, the client also requested that a horizontal rule be drawn underneath the printed text. Jane Doe's manager has given her the task of modifying the code to include that extra line.

In an exclusive versioning setup, it would be impossible for John and Jane to make their changes at the same time. John would have to check out the file, make the change, and check it in again. Jane could then check out the file, make her change, and check it in again.

In a concurrent versioning setup, no such requirement exists. Say that at 12:00 P.M. (Eastern Time) John does a checkout to get the latest version of the file, currently version 1.0. He starts working on making his change. At 12:01 P.M. (Eastern Time), Jane does a checkout as well, also to get the latest version of the file. This is still version 1.0; John hasn't checked anything in yet. Jane starts to work on her change.

At 12:05 P.M., John is done. The code works fine, so he decides to check in his work. He does so, and the repository saves his newly submitted version as the latest version — version 1.1. Version 1.1. now looks like this:

```
1: <?
2: $strToPrint = "Goodbye World";
3: ?>
4: <html>
5:   <body>
6:     <?php echo $strToPrint; ?>
7:     <br /><br />
8:   </body>
9: </html>
```

At 12:09 P.M., Jane is done, too. The code works fine for her, so she now wants to check in her work. Her code now looks like this:

```
1: <?
2: $strToPrint = "Hello World";
3: ?>
4: <html>
5:   <body>
6:     <?=$strToPrint?>
7:     <br /><br />
8:     <hr />
9:   </body>
10: </html>
```

When she checks in, the repository notices that she is checking in a changed edition of version 1.0 — not 1.1, which is now the latest. Her attempt to commit the file will result in an error message indicating that she must first fetch the latest version from the repository and merge it with her changes before she can commit.

The repository now must merge the changes made by John between version 1.0 and 1.1 with the changes made by Jane between 1.0 and her new proposed version.

The repository determines that the change John made was to change line 2 from

```
2: $strToPrint = "Hello World";
```

to this:

```
2: $strToPrint = "Goodbye World";
```

The repository also determines that the change Jane made was to insert the following after line 7:

```
8:    <hr />
```

The repository then simply takes the last version (1.0) and systematically applies both John's and Jane's changes. The merged code now looks like this:

```
1: <?
2: $strToPrint = "Goodbye World";
3: ?>
4: <html>
5:    <body>
6:       <?=$strToPrint?>
7:       <br /><br />
8:       <hr />
9:    </body>
10: </html>
```

As you can see, both developers' changes have been successfully included. The repository now labels this version 1.2, and any subsequent requests for the latest version will yield this version. While both developers are informed of the merge, the software is completely confident that the merge can be made without disruption to Jane's changes, and she need not manually intervene in the merge process.

Concurrent Versioning Conflicts

In some scenarios, two or more developers working on the same version of a file make changes that are not compatible with each other — in other words, a conflict occurs.

Suppose that a further client meeting takes place and two additional requests are made: to include the time of day when saying goodbye to the world, and to include the date. The project manager assigns John the task of implementing the time-of-day requirement, and assigns Jane the task of implementing the date requirement.

John checks out version 1.2 and amends it to read as follows:

```
1: <?
2:    $strTime = time("H:i:s");
3:    $strToPrint = "Goodbye World, it's $strTime";
4: ?>
5: <html>
6:    <body>
7:       <?php echo $strToPrint; ?>
8:       <br /><br />
9:       <hr />
10:    </body>
11: </html>
```

Jane also checks out version 1.2 and amends it to read as follows:

```
1: <?
2:   $strTime = time("Y-m-d");
3:   $strToPrint = "Goodbye World, it's $strDate";
4: ?>
5: <html>
6:   <body>
7:     <?php echo $strToPrint; ?>
8:     <br /><br />
9:     <hr />
10:   </body>
11: </html>
```

The first check-in (whoever gets there first) will cause a version 1.3 to be created. Can you anticipate what will happen when the slower of the two developers checks his or her code in? A new line has been inserted in each case and an existing line modified. Although the version-control platform may well be able to combine the two new lines (by simply incorporating both), it will not know how to combine the changes made to the single line (line 3 in both cases). As PHP developers, you can see the resolution that is required — it's common sense:

```
3: $strToPrint = "Goodbye World, it's $strTime on $strDate";
```

The version-control platform, however, isn't quite as clever as the humans in question, so it raises an error informing the user of the conflict. It is then up to the developer whose most recent check-in attempt has caused the conflict to resolve it. In practice, the version-control system will create a temporary new version, 1.4, which contains details of the conflict. This temporary version will not be issued until the conflict is resolved and that version is made live. The last developer to check in the file will be notified of the conflict by the version-control platform, and invited to edit the temporary version to resolve the conflict. It is the responsibility of the latter of the two developers checking in to resolve the conflict, because the version-control platform views that developer as having caused the conflict.

The temporary version 1.4 created by the repository might look something like this:

```
1: <?
2:   $strTime = time("Y-m-d");
<<<<<<< helloworld.php
3:   $strToPrint = "Goodbye World, it's $strTime";
=======
3:   $strToPrint = "Goodbye World, it's $strDate";
>>>>>>> 1.3
4: ?>
5: <html>
6:   <body>
7:     <?php echo $strToPrint; ?>
8:     <br /><br />
9:     <hr />
10:   </body>
11: </html>
```

You can see the markup that the version-control platform has introduced to show the two different alternatives for line 3.

The previous example is a very simple conflict to resolve. The conflict markup is removed and the line in question is modified to incorporate both developers' changes into the finished version, which is then activated in the repository.

Obviously, in more realistic examples, the resolution of conflicts can occasionally be tedious and time-consuming. However, the productivity gains made by enabling more than one developer to edit a file at the same time usually far exceed any time wasted resolving conflicts. This is the double-edged sword of concurrent versioning. It is useful for two developers to concurrently work on the same file, but they must be prepared to take the responsibility for resolving conflicts when they arise.

Making the Choice

In practice, concurrent versioning is usually the better solution. As strongly encouraged throughout this book, you should divide your project into multiple components and express each of those components as a single file to conform to best practices (which helps to eliminate the amount of work being done by more than one developer on the same file). However, there are generally several files (e.g., the main controller classes in an MVC application) that need to be touched frequently by the developers. Using a system with an efficient merge capability enables maximum productivity.

The previous example is obviously exceedingly trivial, but there are plenty of scenarios in which more than one user might make a minor change like that to the same file. For example, one of the developers in charge of writing the model classes might notice that the exception handling written by another developer displays an error message indicating a grammatical problem. A series of e-mails could be exchanged about the problem, a trouble ticket opened up in the defect-tracking application, and the QA team dispatched to confirm the problem has been resolved; or the model classes developer could just go into the view and fix the mistake.

Having said all that, it is worth pointing out that the principles of concurrent versioning seem to suggest that developers can co-participate in a development project without ever communicating via actual human language. Effective communication and project management is essential to ensuring the success of any project, especially when more than one developer is involved. The source code control system is not a tool for facilitating communication. It is no surprise that concurrent versioning applications such as Concurrent Versioning System (CVS) and Subversion (SVN) are used so frequently in open-source development, which involves thousands of developers, many of whom have never even met, but all of whom are working on the same project; but it is important to realize that mailing lists, e-mail threads, actual voice communications, and the occasional face-to-face meeting are what truly enable those projects to be successful.

The alternative is exclusive versioning, which prohibits two developers from working on the same file at the same time. After a file is checked out, it is physically locked from other developers until such a time as the first developer checks it back in. Accordingly, it is not possible for check-in conflicts to arise, as described previously.

Of course, exclusive versioning has its downsides, too, even if your project is designed to prevent any chance of two people ever needing to work on a file at the same time. One particular bugbear that crops up frequently is the "on vacation" issue. That is, a developer goes on vacation and accidentally leaves a file checked out, which another developer now needs to work on. Sure, you could go into that developer's workstation and check it in, but what if it's a work in progress that isn't ready? Or what if you work in London and that developer works in Los Angeles? If you undo checkout, you risk losing changes that, for all you know, may be 90 percent complete! This is, naturally, a procedural issue as much as anything else, and having suitable policies in place for your development team can avoid this scenario.

The choice is very much up to you. The merging of content is only possible with plain-text sources such as PHP and HTML code. A very binary-heavy application such as a large Flash project with a small PHP back end may be a better candidate for exclusive versioning, whereas a more complex, backend-heavy project that is a PHP and HTML application is always a candidate for a concurrent versioning system. In most contexts, you should choose concurrent versioning.

Version Control Topology

Very shortly you'll be introduced to a few software packages that provide a version-control platform. Before that, it's worth understanding a bit better how a version-control topology works in a real-world setup.

A topology like this will normally apply, regardless of the software you decide to use, and irrespective of whether you opt for concurrent or exclusive versioning for your project. Consider Figure A-1, in which John, Jane, and David are all developers working on the same project — project foo. Each developer has a workstation for his or her use only.

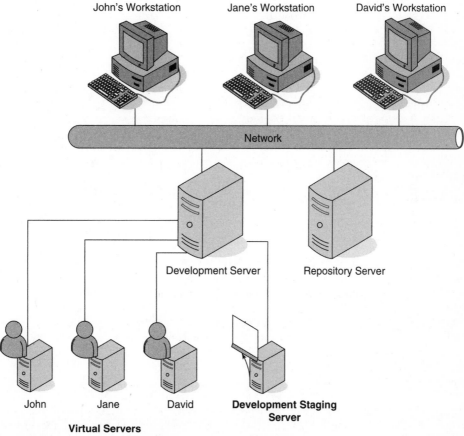

Figure A-1: Version control topology

Obviously, they do not run PHP on each of their workstations, so they all share a powerful central development server. Each developer has his or her own instance of a virtual server representing that developer's own copy of project `foo`, based on source code stored in his or her own home directory on the development server.

For example, John uses `http://john.projectfoo.example.com`, which points to source held in his own home directory on the development server (in `/home/jon/public_html/projectfoo`). Similar setups exist for each developer working on the project.

There is also a staging server that is used by the lead architect as a base for testing and examining the latest version of the project, and possibly for internal demonstrations. An external staging server likely is maintained off-site for external client demonstrations.

When John, Jane, and David want to work on the code for the project, they work on the copies of code in their own home directories, to which nobody else has access. These home directories reside on the server, so they use Samba (see `www.samba.org` for more information) to map a network drive on their workstation to the home directory on the server. They then edit files in their own copy of the project directly. This is their working area. No project files are ever stored on their own workstation, but because the files are exposed through the network drive, developers edit them on the workstation as though they were local.

However, John, Jane, and David must use version-control software on this project. This means that whenever they wish to work on a file, they must perform a check-out action using the version-control software running on their workstation (for the purposes of this example, assume it's Microsoft Visual SourceSafe, which is described shortly). The check-out process downloads the latest version of the file in question from the repository server to the home directory on the development server. This copy of the file is set to writable so that the developer may freely work on it. If John, Jane, or David forgets to check out a file before opening it in their IDE of choice, they will find that it is set to read-only, and that they are unable to save their changes. While the file is checked out, no one else may check it out to work on it.

When they have finished working on the file, they simply check in the file, which records the latest version in the repository. Others who check out the file in the future will then be presented with the latest version, which incorporates the changes just made. The process is similar should one of them wish to add a new file to the repository — a quick press of the Add File button and the file is incorporated permanently.

Because John, Jane, and David are working on the project simultaneously, they need to periodically perform a "get latest versions" operation. This means that the latest versions of all files from the repository will be copied to their local copy in their home directory on the development server, even if they have no intention of ever checking out those files. This is an important practice for two reasons. It may be necessary to have some extra functionality that someone has recently added to the project to make some other component you wish to work on function correctly. In addition, this practice enables developers to quickly see what their colleagues have been working on and, if necessary, point out any errors or provide constructive criticism.

Now and again, Paul, the lead architect, may choose to perform a "get latest versions" into a directory (not his own) on the server marked as staging. This provides him with a snapshot of the project as it currently exists in the repository so that he, too, may provide constructive criticism of his team's work.

With another version-control package, minor variations in this topology and process may exist. For example, with CVS, the developers would be unlikely to use any client software on their workstation. Rather, they would simply create some kind of terminal connection (such as an SSH connection) to the development server, and run the CVS client directly on the server.

It is worth pointing out that the exact role of the repository server varies, too. CVS supports a genuine client/server protocol for the exchange of data, called *pserver*. Visual SourceSafe, however, simply uses a shared data volume on a network drive. As a result, a separate physical repository server may not be necessary, and the development server could quite easily double up in a repository role.

Version Control Software

You can find numerous software applications for handling version control. In this short section, you'll explore three of them, examine the pros and cons, and see how they implement the common functionality and principles of version control.

There isn't enough space in this appendix to go into much detail regarding the setup, installation, and maintenance of each one. Plenty of documentation exists on the Web detailing the ins and outs of each, but this section should at least enable you to make an informed choice regarding which version-control platform is most appropriate for your project.

Microsoft Visual SourceSafe

SourceSafe has been around for a long time, and now comes bundled with copies of Visual Studio .NET. It may seem an unusual package to use in a PHP environment, but for those more comfortable with the Microsoft development environments, it is definitely worth a look.

Although it isn't free, its Windows-based client is easy to use. PHP development folk never shy away from a challenge, but there is little point expending energy on figuring out how to use your version-control client when you could be using it to figure out a neat way to approach an algorithm or object model. SourceSafe is so straightforward to use, you can do just that.

Conversely, SourceSafe uses shared disk space, rather than a proper client/server protocol, for its repository. This has the usual problems associated with shared Access databases, and, accordingly, can be horrifyingly slow to use on larger files with many revisions. It also suffers from difficulty creating and restoring backups; and it has a few irritating facets that largely boil down to differences between Windows and UNIX (such as filename case sensitivity).

SourceSafe uses solely exclusive versioning — that is, when a file is checked out, no one else may check it out. As with many packages that use exclusive versioning, this is enforced using the read-only attribute of the local copy of the file. Because this is a Windows-based client, developers will almost certainly be checking out to a network drive. Strictly speaking, this is slightly inefficient. The workstation is acting as a conduit for the downloaded data rather unnecessarily.

SourceSafe stores its database in a completely arbitrary format, so you can't use its repository storage area as a form of automatic staging server. There is a fairly comprehensive command-line syntax, however, which you could use to build automated scripts for downloading latest versions for a staging server. Such a script, of course, would need to run from a Windows environment, because there is no UNIX client of any description.

This alternative is well worth a look, but keep in mind that the licensing costs may be prohibitive for small projects. You need to pay only for copies of SourceSafe, however. Because it relies on shared disk space, there is no server as such, and you could even use a network drive presented by Samba running on Linux.

CVS

Concurrent Versioning System (CVS), as the name suggests, is one of the better-known examples of a version-control platform that implements concurrent versioning for developer check-outs. CVS has the great advantage of being released under the GNU Public License, which means that it is essentially free to download and use.

It stores its repository in a folder largely mirroring the real directory structure of the project in question, and uses small tag lines in files, hidden files in directories, and minor filename concatenations to store auxiliary data in addition to the latest versions of the files themselves. This starkly contrasts with the manner in which SourceSafe stores its files.

CVS clients can connect to CVS in one of two ways: by simply looking at the repository directly (if it resides on the local machine), or by connecting using the pserver protocol. It would, in theory, be possible to share a network drive (a la SourceSafe) to allow the former connection method, but using the pserver protocol is by far the best way to implement CVS over a client/server environment.

CVS is generally run under UNIX, and typically on the same machine on which the local copies of the files reside. In the previous topology example, CVS was run by each user via a shell connection to the development server. For the more UNIX-savvy, this is probably the preferred route. For the not so UNIX savvy, a SourceSafe-like Windows client called WinCVS exists that replicates most of the UNIX client's own functionality.

Resolving conflicts in CVS is usually relatively straightforward. CVS takes the merger as far as it possibly can, and then presents the user with a new version, annotated to demonstrate the conflict. The user then modifies this new version to resolve the conflict, saves it, and recommits it. CVS then stores this as the latest version. Difficulties do, of course, arise when the conflict is more serious.

CVS can be a good choice, but its concurrent versioning may not be to everyone's taste (for the reasons outlined earlier in this appendix). Consider carefully whether this is appropriate for the project, and whether its presence could encourage poor working practices among your developers.

Subversion

The successor to CVS is the increasingly popular application, preferred by the authors of this book, called Subversion (SVN). Subversion is an attempt to preserve all the things that are great about CVS and to replace all the things that aren't so great. It provides both direct file-system access to the repository where that is useful, but also has an excellent Apache module that enables access to remote users through WebDAV over HTTP. This method does not require any additional ports to be opened in the firewall, or additional daemons to be running on the server, and provides a far more robust permissions system than pserver under CVS. Backup-and-restore is a simple operation, and an entire repository can be exported as a plain text file and migrated to a new server fairly painlessly.

Like CVS, SVN is a concurrent versioning system and is accessible through both command-line and GUI interfaces. For those developing on Windows, the TortoiseSVN extension to Windows Explorer is incredibly simple to use, and incorporates all of the SVN functionality into the Windows Explorer context menu. Similar plug-ins (though less robust at the time of this writing) are available for the Mac OS X Finder.

Other Minor Contenders

A number of other commercial source code control systems are commonly found in large software development shops, including Perforce, BitKeeper, Git (used to manage the Linux kernel), Bazaar, and Microsoft's Team Foundation Server. Some of these use architectures that are seemingly only effective for large open-source applications; others have licensing restrictions and high costs. You should explore the options further and give some of these other applications a try.

Advanced Version Control Techniques

There's a lot more to version control than there is space to cover it in this appendix. As with so much in PHP, the topic can constitute a book in its own right. There are a few interesting techniques, however, that you may wish to employ in your chosen version-control environment.

Branching

Branching involves the divergence of a single project into two parallel projects. This is an immensely useful technique for code reuse. Suppose that you are developing two content-management systems for two different clients, systems that are virtually identical in functionality — the only differences are minor or aesthetic in nature. Obviously, you will want to reuse code from one in the other, but doing so has a pitfall. If you make a major change in the first project, you will want that change to propagate to your second project. Conversely, any changes you make in the second project, you will probably not want to propagate upward to your first project, because these changes represent customizations.

Branching is the solution. By branching the first project to form a second, your version-control software will automatically propagate any changes made to the first project into the second project as (and when) they happen, while retaining changes made in the second project as customizations unique to that project.

Branching can also be used to maintain two different directions for a project. For example, you may want to have one set of developers work on a maintenance release of your product, while another set works on the next big major release. Branching enables you to take a snapshot of your product in time, and then branch off into two distinct development paths, safe in the knowledge that any major changes in the pre-branch product will be propagated into both paths.

Tagging

Not to be confused with the tags CVS places in individual files as mnemonics for its own use, *tagging* involves applying an arbitrary attribute to a given version of each file to create release versions.

For example, you may want to create a beta version of your project. This involves more or less every file in your project being packaged together, but you may want to use different versions of each file — version 1.3 of this file, version 1.5 of that file, and so on. By tagging the right version of each file, you can easily tell your version-control software to deliver a particular version on demand. Individual developers can move tags as (and when) they feel confident; that way, whenever you request a particular version (be it beta, release candidate 1, or whatever), you can be sure that you are getting the latest stable version.

Comments

One frequently overlooked facility of all version-control systems is the application of *comments* at check-in. When checking in a file, the developer will be asked to supply a comment. It is a good idea to ensure that your developers take advantage of this facility and supply a brief description, even if it is something as simple as "fixed bug 21301." When viewing the history of a particular file, this information can be immensely useful.

Binary Files

Care should always be taken when adding *binary files* (such as images) to a repository. Although it is generally a good idea to keep the entire project in one place, many version-control packages are extremely inefficient when handling binary files, and can slow to a crawl when faced with a few dozen JPEGs.

Consider whether there is a third way. For example, consider all those .GIF files containing page titles. Could a single PHP script replace them, one that uses imagefttext to render a caption when required? Such an "outside the box" approach can be of critical importance, because binary files represent only one example of when version control can prove inappropriate or cumbersome (not to mention the productivity gains in having PHP make all those title graphics, rather than a production graphic designer or, worse yet, you).

Summary

In this appendix, you encountered the principles and methodology of version control and its usefulness in larger projects. You learned about the difference between concurrent and exclusive versioning. You looked briefly at the topology of a typical version-control infrastructure, and examined how this infrastructure is implemented in a number of popular version-control packages. Finally, you learned some of the more advanced techniques possible with version control, and how they could be useful with your own projects.

B

PHP IDEs

Using their favorite editor, many developers still tend to program PHP and develop their own preferred methods of debugging their code; but with millions of developers using PHP, it remains a bit of a mystery why integrated development environments (IDEs) are not as widely used as, say, Visual Studio .NET is for ASP .NET. This may be because many people still don't view PHP 6 as a full-fledged programming language in its own right. (Of course, the authors hope that based on what you have seen in this book you believe otherwise.)

At any rate, PHP 6 *is* a full-fledged programming language, and IDEs for it do exist. If you haven't been developing using an IDE that supports PHP 6, this appendix is for you. A host of useful features packed into the IDEs might make the investment worthwhile to you. One of the biggest uses, of course, is the sophisticated debugging facilities that most IDEs provide.

Although this appendix doesn't provide a fully comprehensive rundown of each IDE out there, it will give you an idea of what you can expect from some of the main ones, and an idea of what else is available. For the most part, you should be able to get a deeper understanding of the functionality of each of the IDEs from their documentation. This appendix first takes a detailed look at Zend Studio, because this is the largest PHP-centric IDE on the market. Following this, alternatives such as Komodo are briefly explored.

Choosing an IDE

The aim of an IDE is to give you (the developer) all the support and help you could possibly need to develop robust applications efficiently and accurately. The number of different ways to do this varies wildly from product to product, but there is one thing that you should look for in all of them. As with any software you use, one of the first things to decide before forever developing in one environment is whether that environment benefits you. In other words, does the IDE make it easier for you to develop your applications? If so, then it stands to reason that you should be using that product as your development environment of choice. Simple as that.

However, simplifying the argument to whether you think the IDE of your choice is performing its job ignores one important fact you should bear in mind. As would be true with any other software, it may take some time to fully utilize the power inherent in these IDEs, so it is worth investing the hours finding your way around them. To that end, the following few sections should give you an idea of what to expect.

Zend Studio

Zend's offering should arguably be your first stop when looking for an IDE — assuming that you are willing to fork out the $399 or so that it will set you back. Of course, before purchasing anything, you should really take a close look at it, and you can download a free trial version from www.zend.com/en/products/studio.

As of this writing, the current release version of Zend Studio is 6.1, which does not yet include full support for PHP 6, but is expected to once PHP 6 is officially released. It is available for the Windows, Linux, and Mac OS X platforms, and is based on Eclipse. Other Eclipse-based IDEs include Adobe Flex, and the two integrate tightly to create a compelling platform for creating rich Internet applications using Flex and PHP.

If you are not familiar with IDEs, they can appear a little daunting at first. Keep in mind that they are here to help, not to confuse things. In this case, Zend Studio (ZS) is more than an IDE; it also provides you with features apart from the development environment, including code profiling, integration with JavaScript libraries, SCM integration, and much more. For the purposes of this appendix, we'll concentrate mainly on the tools that enable you to manage and develop your code. With that in mind, the first screen you are presented with in ZS is much like the one shown in Figure B-1 (showing a sample project).

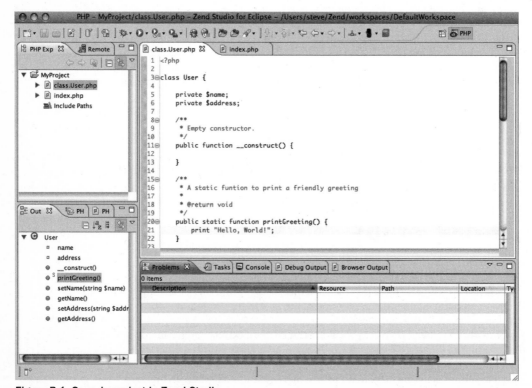

Figure B-1: Sample project in Zend Studio

Plenty of documentation covers all the functionality in ZS, so it is not necessary to cover everything exhaustively here. Instead, let's zero in on the most important features in order to give you a broad idea of what ZS is all about. After playing around with ZS, you can decide whether or not you want to adopt it.

Managing Projects

At the top left of Figure B-1, you will notice the PHP Explorer window. This shows a list of all projects in this workspace. You can think of the workspace as the primary repository of your various projects; in most scenarios, you will only need one workspace on your computer. Within the workspace are one or more projects. Each ZS project corresponds to one of your actual projects. Note that a project need not be physically stored as a child of the folder that contains the workspace.

The MyProject window enables you to navigate any given project you are working on and perform various actions, such as adding and removing files from a particular project. It is probably prudent to mention that the Project menu item on the Zend Development Environment (ZDE) main menu enables you to create, open, save, and close projects, and edit project properties, such as deployment destination.

You use the projects to define a common working environment for files. For example, you may want to have a specific debugging setup while working on a new site for a client. Placing the site's files into a project enables you to do this in an efficient manner.

Figure B-2: Code-completion pop-up

Editing Code

Obviously, you would expect certain editing capabilities to be included with a full IDE like this, and ZS certainly has some neat features. The editing window is the large, central one shown in Figure B-1, and it contains a host of tools designed to make coding easier. One of the major features is code completion, which is available for both PHP and HTML. This enables you to display pop-ups of function parameters, declared functions, keywords, and constants. Figure B-2 shows an example of the pop-up displayed when you begin typing in a PHP 6 array function.

As with most aspects of this IDE, code completion is configurable, and you can check out the options by choosing Tools ⇨ Preferences ⇨ PHP ⇨ Code Assist.

The Preferences window provides you with many other configurable settings, such as editing and debugging options.

ZS also provides you with code-indentation options. You can choose to indent your code either manually (as you type) or all at one time — a nice feature that makes life a bit easier. If you view the PHP ⇨ Editor section of the Preferences dialog, you will see a list of all the available editing features. One of the more useful ones is the matching braces feature, shown in action in Figure B-3.

```
15  /**
16   * A static funtion to print a friendly greeting
17   *
18   * @return void
19   */
20  public static function printGreeting() {
21      print "Hello, World!";
22  }
23
```

Figure B-3: Braces matching

Placing the cursor immediately before the beginning elements or immediately after the closing elements causes the editor to highlight the matching element. A useful trick here is to press Ctrl+Shift+P to jump between matching elements to avoid tiresome scrolling. See the Navigate ⇨ Go To menu for more navigation shortcuts.

Templates are also available to help speed up otherwise repetitive tasks. Several are provided, but you can also add your own or modify the ones that are included. To view the available templates, select the Template tab of the Preferences window. Each template has a given key that denotes its specific template. For example, Figure B-4 shows the results of typing **my** into the Editor window.

Figure B-4: Code-completion templates

The top four options are all templates that come with the IDE. If you click one of them, the template code assigned to that key is automatically added to the Editor window. Figure B-5 shows the results of clicking the second option.

```
while ($row = mysql_fetch_object($query)) {

    }
```

Figure B-5: Result of selecting an option template

Many other useful editing features are available, ranging from HTML tag shortcuts to syntax error highlighting. The only way to really learn your way around these is to play with them. The help files do a good job of outlining all the IDE's features, so use this to find your way around. Let's move on and look at another useful feature of the ZS.

Inspecting Code

Looking back to Figure B-1, the pane on the bottom left is called Outline. This comes with three options: Outline, PHP Project Outline, and PHP Functions. The first option gives you a collapsible list of all the elements of the file with focus in the editor window. You can use this for navigation if you want. Double-clicking any of the elements listed in the Outline window will take the cursor directly to that piece of code in the source file.

You can look at the code from one level up by clicking the Project tab. This gives you an overview of everything in the current project. It works pretty much like the File window in that you can click any file or displayed element of that file in the Project window and it will be opened for editing in the main window.

The final option, PHP Functions, gives you a list of all the PHP functions and their syntax. If you want to know a little more than just a function's usage, you can highlight the function in the Outline window and press F1 to view a slightly more in-depth information file that pops up in a browser window. Incidentally, this also works for PHP functions within your editor window — simply highlight the function you wish to learn about and press F1.

Debugging with the ZDE

For the sake of brevity, let's assume that you have everything running on one machine so that you can debug your applications locally. It is possible to set up a multiuser debugging environment by installing the Zend Platform product on a central, nonlocal server, and you should consult the documentation for more information about this.

One of the biggest advantages you can derive from using IDEs is making use of the innovative debugging features they provide. Plowing through error log files is one way to do it, but that can be quite clumsy in comparison to the more sophisticated methods available. The internal debugger has a list of features designed to help you keep tabs on exactly what is happening in your code. Specifically, its main function is to provide you with the following:

❑ Program flow monitoring

❑ A debug window

❑ A debug messages window

❑ Output rendering

Let's look at these in some detail.

One of the first things with which you need to familiarize yourself is how to go about debugging your code. ZS provides several methods for moving from place to place. Some involve setting breakpoints; others simply trace the flow of the program step by step. Click Run ➪ Debug. When prompted to switch to the PHP Debug Perspective, click Yes. A perspective in Eclipse and in ZS is another set of UI elements customized for a particular task — in this case, debugging.

As shown in Figure B-6, a set of arrows can be used for stepping over and moving between breakpoints, or simply running your code.

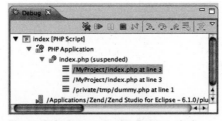

Figure B-6: Arrows in the Debug window

After you have the hang of stepping over your code or following a script's execution, you can use these to find out valuable information about the state of your code. The Debug pane, located by default in the upper-left corner of the ZS PHP Debug Perspective, provides you with five options to monitor and manage your project's debugging. From here, you can view the value of variables, the position of watches, the stack trace, the position of breakpoints, and the buffer. All of these may come in handy, depending on what it is you are trying to determine about your code.

For example, let's say you have stepped over the execution of a very simple PHP script in order to demonstrate how the Variables tab shows you information about all the variables associated with your code (including the global ones). This is shown in Figure B-7.

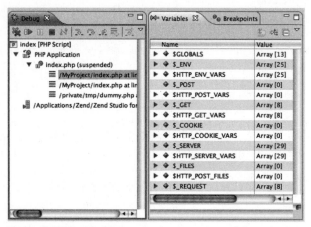

Figure B-7: The Variables tab

If you look at the editor window after invoking the debugger, you will see the first line in the execution of your application highlighted. This is because, at present, the debugger is stopped at this point in the script's execution. The values you see in the Variables pane are the values at this particular point in the program's execution. If you already know the piece of code you want to inspect, you can forgo stepping over all the code line by line and place the cursor on the line you want the debugger to go to. Click Run ➪ Run to Line (or press Ctrl+R) to run the application until it reaches that line of code.

Tracing the execution stack is also a useful way of determining where you are in your code. The Debug pane enables you to view where you are in the program's stack. This can be helpful because if one part of your code calls a function, the program's execution leaves the current place to go off and run the called function. If the function itself makes use of other functions, then the program's execution heads off again to go execute those. Being able to determine exactly where you are in all this is where the stack tracing capability of the debugger comes in.

Figure B-8 shows an example of the Debug pane being used to track a simple script that is in the middle of executing a method in a class, invoked from the `index.php` file.

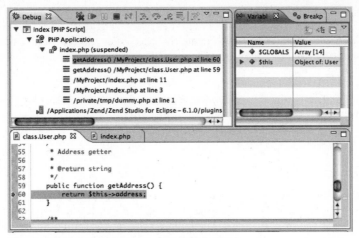

Figure B-8: Viewing the stack in the Debug tab

Rather than step in, over, and around various areas of code, sometimes we just want the application to run until it gets to a certain point in the source code. To get the debugger to stop where you want, you must set *breakpoints*. Breakpoints are simply delimiters that tell the debugger to freeze execution as is so that you can look over whatever you need to.

In Figure B-9, a breakpoint has been set on line 33 by clicking the area to the left of the line number in the editor window. This causes the selected line to be indicated with a dot in the margin, which shows this is now a set breakpoint. Clicking the Breakpoint tab in the PHP Debugger Perspective will verify this for you.

```
26    /**
27     * Set the value of the $name variable
28     *
29     * @param string $name
30     * @return void
31     */
32    public function setName($name) {
33        $this->name = $name;
34    }
35
```

Figure B-9: Setting a breakpoint

With that done, two things are left to mention. The first is the Console pane, which is located (by default) in the bottom-left corner of the window. It displays notices, warnings, and errors that crop up during the debugging of your scripts. Double-clicking the messages in the Console pane enables you to locate their source quite easily by sending the cursor to them in the editor window.

Finally, ZS also renders your script's output in the Debug Output pane. This pops up on the right side of the ZS window as soon as your script creates any output. Use this to keep an eye on whether your scripts are creating the correct headers and HTML output. The rendered HTML can be seen in the Browser Output tab.

Zend provides still other debugging facilities. For example, using remote debugging, you can actually debug your application as it works on the site. This has several advantages, as you can track your application working with input as it would normally. This is often quite difficult to do otherwise. Furthermore, the output from the Debug pane is displayed in the browser. This all requires Zend Server to be running on the Web server. (The details of such an installation are beyond the scope of this book.)

With all the debugging and editing functionality provided, you are encouraged to download a demo copy and play around with it. You never know — you might find that this is the answer to your programming dreams. Before completing this whirlwind tour of Zend's development offering, several other important tools should get a mention.

More Zend Tools

Zend also provides a profiler (click Run ⇨ Profile to enter the PHP Profile Perspective) to help analyze the performance of applications. This profiler can be used to determine how to improve an application's performance by identifying problem areas. Several tabs provide you with different types of information, ranging from pie charts (showing the amounts of time consumed by scripts), tables, and diagrams (displaying statistics for various functions to a call trace to monitor the linear consumption of time from call to call).

In addition, Zend can integrate with CVS and SVN version control, so you should consult the documentation to see how to get this up and running. (Appendix A provides more detail about CVS and SVN.)

Finally, there is also Zend Guard, which enables you to distribute PHP applications using obfuscated code, which prevents others from being able to easily understand the application logic — thus making it possible to distribute closed-source applications without concerns for piracy. For most applications, for which the developers are the only individuals handling the source code, and for anything released to the public under an open-source license, Zend Guard is unnecessary; but if you are planning to sell the application for installation on customers' Web servers, a product like this may be of interest if you're concerned about protecting your intellectual property. Zend Guard also includes implementations for a number of licensing schemes.

Komodo

You can download a trial version of Active State's Komodo from its Web site (www.activestate.com/ Products/Komodo/). The professional version (used for commercial purposes) will set you back $295, so it is certainly a good idea to give the demo version a try before buying. Historically, it has been available for both Linux and Windows, but as of the latest release (4.4) it is now also available on Mac OS X.

Komodo is a highly regarded IDE that supports a number of open-source programming languages (though it is, itself, closed-source commercial software), as opposed to being PHP-specific. It supports (among other things) Perl, Python, Ruby, Tcl, HTML, CSS, JavaScript, and XML. As of this writing, however, the PHP 6 debugger extension is not yet available, so debug support in Komodo is restricted to earlier versions. You should consult the Komodo Web site for any updates about this.

Managing Projects

Komodo provides you with a Project Manager that can be used to perform a large number of actions. By default, it appears down the left side of the IDE window, and project-related functionality can be accessed through the Project main menu item. Among other things, you can do the following:

- ❑ Create and open projects
- ❑ Add files and folders
- ❑ Add commands, templates, URLs, Web services, and dialog boxes
- ❑ Organize, save, and close projects

Additionally, you can access pop-up context menus by right-clicking the project members. Which context menu you get depends on the type of element you have chosen.

Editing Code

Komodo's code editor has some interesting features, as well as the more standard ones such as coloring and indentation. For example, *code folding* is provided to collapse sections of code, enabling you to look at abstracted (or skeleton) versions of your code to get an overview of what is happening. Figure B-10 shows the editor window with collapsed code.

```
<?php
Function one(){
Function two(){
Function three(){
    echo "I am the third function in my script!";
}
?>
```

Figure B-10: Editor with collapsed code

The editor also provides auto-complete functionality for PHP — specifically, for classes, functions, and variables. Classes in the current and included files are displayed when the word **new** is typed in, and class methods are displayed when the -> operator is used. Similarly, all user-defined functions and PHP functions are displayed after four matching characters are typed in.

Another nice feature of the editor is *tips* that tell you what parameters you can use with a function. These display after you have typed in the opening brace for a given function — either user-defined or PHP. Figure B-11 shows the call tip for a user-defined function.

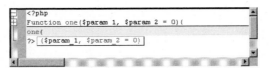

```
<?php
Function one($param_1, $param_2 = 0){
one{
?>  ($param_1, $param_2 = 0)
```

Figure B-11: Call tip for a user-defined function

There are plenty of other features in the editor, but most of them are pretty intuitive to use and need not be covered here in any detail. They include the following:

- ❑ Most Recently Used List
- ❑ Detect Changed Files

❑   Preview in Browser

❑   Background Syntax Checking

❑   Code Commenting

Debugging with Komodo

Komodo's debugger is not examined in too much detail here because the PHP 6 extension has not yet been released. There are some configuration requirements in order to get Komodo's PHP debugger working, and you should consult the documentation for instructions. Apart from this, Komodo provides you with a full-fledged debugger, which includes the following:

❑   Breakpoint control

❑   Stepping

❑   Watching variables

❑   Viewing the call stack

❑   Sending input

❑   Adding command-line arguments

Of course, Komodo comes with a host of other tools to supplement its editor and debugger. Let's take a quick look.

More Komodo Tools

Because Komodo enables a host of items to be added to projects (such as shortcuts, folders, files, commands, and templates), it also provides a toolbox in which to store all these items for easy access. You can work with the toolbox through either the tab in the right pane or the Toolbox main menu item. Figure B-12 shows the sample items available in the toolbox. In this case, the snippet was added to the code window simply by double-clicking it.

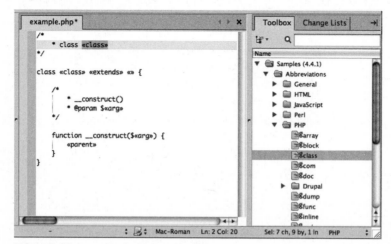

Figure B-12: Items in the Komodo toolbox

Komodo can also be integrated with CVS, SVN, and Perforce. To get this up and running, you click Edit ⇨ Preferences ⇨ Source Code Control from the main menu and then configure your source code control tool of choice.

Again, you should download the demo version to play around with Komodo. One caveat in terms of cost here is that you might find that you are paying extra for functionality that is not really useful to you. For example, some tools included with Komodo are specifically for Perl (such as the Perl Dev Kit). This adds to the development costs of Komodo without providing much value to PHP project management, but it may be of use to you if you routinely develop in other languages.

Other IDEs and Editors

A host of other development environments is available for the professional PHP developer. Some are more useful than others, depending on how you want to use them. For example, PHPEdit (for Windows) offers a bunch of useful editing tools, as well as a debugger. It is available for download free of charge at `www.phpedit.com`. Here, very briefly, are some of its main features:

- ❑ Syntax highlighting
- ❑ Code Hint, Code Insight
- ❑ Integrated PHP debugger
- ❑ Help Generator
- ❑ Customizable shortcuts
- ❑ More than 100 scriptable commands
- ❑ Keyboard templates
- ❑ To-do report generator
- ❑ QuickMarks
- ❑ Plug-ins

Here are some other IDEs and editors you may also want to take a look at:

- ❑ PHPEclipse (`www.phpeclipse.de`)
- ❑ EditPlus (`www.editplus.com`)
- ❑ NuSpherePHPEd (`www.nusphere.com`)
- ❑ PHPCode (`www.phpide.de`)

Of course, simply because this discussion hasn't covered all the options available doesn't mean that they aren't worth looking at. For example, NuSphere's PHPEd provides a ton of advanced features, such as code completion, debugging, profiling, and deployment facilities, among other things. As an IDE, it has received some acclaim, and is well worth investigating.

Summary

This appendix on integrated development environments (IDEs) has given you an idea of what's out there and what you might expect from an IDE with support for PHP. You have learned about the Zend Studio environment as a PHP-specific platform, and Komodo as an open-source environment with support for PHP 6.

Discovering the advantages offered by using an IDE is a rewarding process, as your productivity should increase from using one. Because purchasing a development tool like the aforementioned IDEs represents an investment, you should spend some time looking at the features of each one carefully before you choose.

Performance Tuning PHP

Properly configured, the performance of a well-crafted PHP application can hold its own against any other application environment (such as Java, ASP.NET, Ruby on Rails, and so on)

There are two types of performance to be considered: performance of the programmer, and performance of the application execution. The rest of this book provides a framework for increasing the former. This appendix deals with increasing the latter. Whether you are interested in squeezing the best performance out of a perfectly crafted application of your own design or trying to save a poorly written application written by another party without spending money on new hardware, many of the tricks in this chapter will be of use.

In this appendix, you'll learn to identify the different types of performance bottlenecks, and how to track down their cause. After that, you'll look at how to design and code for optimum efficiency and speed, as well as how to retroactively repair bad code you've been unfortunate enough to inherit.

Introduction to Performance Problems

Typically, the first time you'll hear about an application running slowly is from a user. Unfortunately, users are rarely particularly useful in this respect. The cry of "this thing is so slow" across the office tells you virtually nothing. It's important, therefore, to do a little digging.

Types of Performance Bottlenecks

Let's go back to basics for a minute, and look at the structure of an HTTP GET or POST request. When the user's Web browser makes a request, it makes a socket connection to the Web server, usually on port 80; for SSL connections, port 443. This is a blocking activity in the Web browser, so-called because the browser cannot do anything else until the connection is successfully made. In practice, however, most modern Web browsers allow the user to cancel while the connection attempt is being made, and on faster connections, the connection is made in literally fractions of a second; but if the server is heavily loaded, the connection may take a while to establish. If this is the case, it points to other applications or processes on that server slowing things down (not necessarily the application in question).

After achieving the connection, the Web browser does not wait for any response because the HTTP protocol does not dictate that there should be any. Immediately, it sends a very small request packet, usually not more than a few bytes in size. This request contains (among other data) the document that the Web browser requires, and any GET or POST parameters the user has offered as part of the request.

This request is, in itself, small. The time between the socket connection being established and the request being sent to the Web server is likely to be minimal.

The time between when the Web server has received the request and when it starts to return data is known as the *processing time* for your script. In most cases, PHP will not attempt to send any output to the Web browser until the entire script has finished executing, unless the volume of your output exceeds the value of output_buffering in php.ini. This means that the processing time is roughly equal to the time between when PHP starts executing your script and the time it finishes executing. This is the most likely place for a delay.

The time between when data starts to be returned to the Web browser and when that data is finished transferring is the *delivery time*, and it is not likely to be related to PHP in any way. The amount of time it takes for this data to be transferred is much more likely to be tied to network performance, either at the server side (e.g., an overloaded connection) or the client side (e.g., a horrifyingly slow modem). Unless your page weight exceeds 55 KB (which is generally regarded as the limit for sensible Web pages), this is unlikely to be a cause of delays.

The easiest way to identify where a performance bottleneck is occurring is to use a manual tool, rather than a bona fide Web browser, to make the HTTP request, and then analyze the results yourself.

Differentiating Between Different Types of Bottleneck

Suppose you want to analyze where poor performance might be occurring in requests for the page /example.php, on the server www.example.com, with GET parameter foo equaling bar. This is, of course, equivalent to http://www.example.com/example.php?foo=bar. Start a console session and use telnet as follows:

```
ed@host: $ telnet www.example.com 80
Trying 192.168.1.2...
Connected to www.example.com
Escape character is '^ ]'.
GET /example.php?foo=bar HTTP/1.1
Host: www.example.com
```

A typical response from the server might look like this:

```
<HTML>
 <BODY>
  Hello, World!
 </BODY>
</HTML>
```

In Windows, the same approach applies — start a command prompt and use telnet in exactly the same manner.

To get real-world output, of course, you need to substitute the hostname and URL for real-world examples. Press Enter where you see a blank line, and enter spaces exactly as shown. You may find it easier to write it all out in Notepad and paste it into telnet.

Have a stopwatch handy when you do this. Observe where the delay lies, and infer as follows:

❑ A delay between pressing Enter and observing `Trying 192.168.1.2` indicates a delay in resolving the IP address of the server against a name server. This is unusual. It could indicate unresponsive name servers, either those you are using yourself (typically those of your own ISP) or those serving the domain of the server in question (typically the ISP hosting the server). Why this unresponsiveness exists is outside the scope of this book, but you can at least reassure yourself PHP is not to blame. To a real-world user, this delay would be experienced only once, when first accessing the site, because most Web browsers (and, indeed, operating systems) cache the results of name server lookups.

❑ A delay between the `Trying,...` line and the `Connected` line indicates that the server itself took a while to successfully respond to your requests to connect. A delay here is massively damaging, because a page with several images could easily consist of 20 or 30 HTTP requests. If each one has a delay attached, the page could appear dramatically sluggish even if script execution time is markedly quick. Unfortunately, the delay could exist in one of two places: Either in the network to/from the server, or in the server's capability to respond to connections in a timely manner. The latter could be caused by server load, which could in turn be caused by poorly optimized PHP (not necessarily this script) or other processes bringing the server to its knees. A quick check of memory and CPU utilization on the server can reveal the truth here. If it's the former, then troubleshooting it is outside the scope of this book. If it's the latter, then you should try to track down which script is causing the problem; and if it's PHP, apply the same methods shown here to that script.

❑ A delay between pressing Enter twice after having entered your HTTP request and seeing the HTML of your response almost certainly indicates poor performance at processing time. This can be validated and verified by adding watches in code.

Assuming that the delay can be traced to script processing time, you can now determine what in the script is causing the delay (or delays).

Understanding the Anatomy of a PHP Request

Forgetting the wider edicts on good PHP architecture for just a moment, remember that PHP is a scripting language. Its scripts have a start, a middle, and an end, just like any scripting language. Indeed, at the most basic, simplified level, the pattern of execution of any PHP script looks something like the following:

1. For a request to `index.php`, open `index.php` and perform a lexical analysis of its contents (and the contents of any files included or required by `index.php`). This means interpreting `$x = $y + 2` into something like this:

```
VARIABLE "x" EQUALS VARIABLE "y" PLUS 2
```

2.   Next, parse the lexical representation of the string to create actual executable instructions. This .includes ensuring that the variables $x and $y are valid, that the addition operator can be performed on $y and a constant integer, and then constructing the actual execution instructions, in the form of bytecode.

3.   Pass the bytecode to the PHP virtual machine, and execute the instructions contained therein. This involves the following:

   a.   Read input parameters, be they GET, POST, or COOKIE.

   b.   Use those input parameters to make decisions, consulting external data sources in the process.

   c.   Produce output and send to Apache/IIS for transmission to the requesting client.

Opcode Caching

One of the single biggest performance lags in a large PHP application (aside from those caused by bad application design) happens during the lexing/parsing step, which happens on every file included in the request, and is repeated for each request to that file(s), even though the source code hasn't changed. You can avoid having to repeat these two steps for each request, by using something called an *operations code cache*, or *opcode cache*, for short.

Opcode caching applications preserve the output of the parsing step, the actual instructions to the PHP VM, and save them, typically in memory, to be used on subsequent requests to the same source code files. In a large application containing thousands of lines of PHP code, this can boost performance quite dramatically. Moreover, in PHP 6, one of the best opcode caches is included with the distribution and is enabled (though not turned on) by default. Alternative PHP Cache (APC) has long been available through PECL as an optional (though highly recommended) PHP module. However, its utility, performance, configuration flexibility, and simplicity have promoted it to a first-class citizen in the PHP source code base, and it is now included with the PHP 6 source code.

To enable APC, set apc.enabled = 1 in your php.ini file. You will need to configure a few other parameters, such as how much memory should be allocated for the cache, what type of caching should be used, and any filters to exclude files from being cached. The available documentation on APC is reasonably good. A Google search should turn up a lot of useful material on how to properly configure APC. For the basic documentation, see www.php.net/manual/en/book.apc.php.

Other Sources of Performance Problems

The remaining source of performance issues (once the lexing/parsing step has been eliminated, where possible) comes down to application design and systems engineering.

These delays will boil down to one of three things:

❑   *Poor algorithms* — Inefficient code resulting in high execution time

❑   *Poor hardware* — The code is not unreasonable, but the hardware it's running on is elderly or overworked.

❑   *External bottlenecks* — A database causing holdups

Hardware is rarely the problem. Except in extreme cases (such as intense usage of Gd for graphics rendering, intense number crunching, or large reporting applications), the overhead imposed by PHP itself does not require significant system resources.

Tracking Down the Bottleneck

There are straightforward steps to resolving each different variety of identifiable bottleneck, as discussed in the remainder of this appendix. However, your first task is to determine where the bottleneck can be found and into which of the three categories described previously it falls.

Database Queries

The easiest offenders to track down are slow database queries. Almost all enterprise-class PHP applications depend on a database of some kind. This book has heavily advocated PostgreSQL, but many applications (particularly those you will encounter that are written by third parties) will make use of the more popular MySQL.

You must eliminate database bottlenecks before attempting to optimize code. Because most code is dependent on the database in some respect (even if only for the supply of data), looking at code before its data source is optimized is not time well spent.

The simplest way to determine whether database bottlenecks exist in a script is to temporarily adapt your database interaction code to add a timer method.

Consider the query method of your abstraction layer for PostgreSQL. By adding error log stamps before and after each query, you can show how long each query took and easily produce an analyzable log for your page. The following excerpt shows an example, demonstrating how you might measure the time taken to perform a query in the database abstraction layer by sandwiching the execute query statement as follows:

```
$intTimeNow = microtime();
$q_handle = pg_exec($this->link_ident, $sql);
$intTimeTaken = microtime() - $intTimeNow;
error_log("DEBUG: QUERY: $sql\n");
error_log("DEBUG: TIME TAKEN: $intTimeTaken\n");
```

This will yield error log output similar to the following:

```
[Sun May 16 22:10:19 2004] [error] DEBUG: QUERY: SELECT id,logged_in,user_id FROM
        "user_sessions" WHERE session_id='98ce552be0a2ea6b6f69fbebcd14997c' AND
        user_agent='Mozilla/4.0 (compatible; MSIE 6.0; Windows NT 5.1)' AND
        ip_address='192.168.4.3'
[Sun May 16 22:10:19 2004] [error] DEBUG: TIME TAKEN: 0.003752
```

Executing a typical PHP script with your database abstraction layer doctored as shown in the preceding example will then yield a series of DEBUG: QUERY xx and DEBUG: TIME TAKEN statements as shown.

The pattern of queries will be easier to analyze if you can ensure that no other warnings, error messages, or code-initiated debug statements are writing to the error log, and that the analysis of the time being taken by your query has exclusivity for now.

You should easily be able to spot the slow performers. In typical setups, anything lasting more than half a second should raise a red flag. Also note the sum total of the duration of queries for a page. Anything totaling more than three seconds is considered incredibly bad form and will drive your users nuts.

Algorithms

After any database bottlenecks have been addressed, you may safely look at the code itself. PHP is very fast, so algorithmic holdups are certainly less likely to be a factor than poor database performance.

However, by seeding your script with timestamp output similar to that used in tracking down database problems, you can determine where bottlenecks might lie.

You cannot do this in one fell swoop, for obvious reasons. The burden is on you to place "start the clock" and "stop the clock" statements at either side of blocks of code you feel might be troublesome. If you do find one, you can always drill down and add more start/stop statements within that block of code to find the precise culprit. Don't be afraid to output variable values in your `error_log` statement, too — such as providing a clue as to progress in `for` loops.

This approach can be automated to some extent by using a package such as APD, the Advanced PHP Debugger (`http://pecl.php.net/package/apd`), though for smaller applications and those built in a "best practices" modular fashion, its immense functionality may well prove to be overkill.

Progress between steps should be nearly instantaneous in PHP, as long as an external data source is not involved. Delays of more than fractions of a second between logical blocks point to serious problems in your code.

Patching for Performance

Now that you know what's to blame and where it is, you can concentrate on patching your code to improve performance. Mercifully, there is one thing of which you can be certain: You won't be the only PHP developer who's ever encountered bottlenecks like yours. As a result, there are some tried-and-tested techniques you can follow to try to patch them.

Fixing Database Holdups

Earlier, you saw how to identify which queries were holding up execution of your script. Why a query is running badly could be a result of any number of factors. Optimizing SQL statements is a massive topic, and there simply isn't the space to go into much detail here. You can find numerous excellent volumes on PostgreSQL, MySQL, and other databases that deal with query optimization. However, the following points are worth bearing in mind:

❑ Primary keys that are numbers will always be faster as a primary index than primary keys that are alphanumeric, even if there are unique alphanumeric values that would ordinarily be an obvious candidate for primary key. In general, an "id" column is what is required.

❑ Ensure that columns and, perhaps more important, combinations of columns by which you will filter or order in SELECT statements have corresponding indices defined.

❑ Scheduled scripts to clean up tables (using, for example, the VACUUM statement in PostgreSQL) whose contents are updated frequently may well prove to be sound investments.

❑ Never use SELECT *. If you know the names of the columns you want, specify them. This will improve performance.

❑ Subselects are easier to put together than INNER or OUTER joins, but nowhere near as efficient. Avoid them if possible (this will also, as a side effect, increase RDBMS portability). If you suspect that subselects may be slowing down your application, try replacing them with either INNER or OUTER joins as appropriate. Consult the documentation of your preferred flavor of database for more information.

Most tips such as the preceding increase speed by only fractions of a second but this really is a case of every little bit helping, especially when you are dealing with pages with a large number of queries.

Don't forget that you will almost certainly need to look outside the PHP script itself to track down the offending SQL query, particularly if you are following the best practice principles described in this book. If you have devised an object model that is heavily dependent on a database back end, you may find that performance tweaks in queries used in that model have unexpected performance gains elsewhere. By the same token, however, when changes are being made to such high-level classes, care should be taken to thoroughly test all components that depend on them to ensure that functionality and behavior remain consistent with expectations.

Fixing Code Holdups

Ultimately, the same principles that apply to optimizing database queries apply here. It's not good enough to know simply which block of code is causing a holdup; you need to work out which PHP statement is being slow and under what circumstances.

Logic Errors

However, sometimes simple errors in application logic are to blame. In such cases, the application does function as expected, so ordinary QA techniques have not registered a bug, but some human error in the code has caused performance to be adversely affected. These are the easiest to fix.

Consider the following example:

```
switch ($i) {
 case 0:
  array_pop($arMediumArray);
  break;
 case 1:
  array_reverse($arAnotherHugeArray);
 case 2:
  $arHugeArray = array_unique($arHugeArray);
  break;
};
```

As you can probably spot, this code is missing a break statement under the case where $i is equal to 1. This means that the case where $i is equal to 2 will also be executed when $i is equal to 1. In that case, it is only necessary to reverse $arAnotherHugeArray. However, $arHugeArray is also being made unique, as a side effect. It is quite possible that $arHugeArray will never be used again after this switch statement should $i equal 1, so this method being erroneously called may not cause a malfunction per se. What it likely does, however, is double the execution time for the block. Adding the `break` statement stops the redundant method call and speeds execution as a result.

The methods alluded to previously should still allow you to track down such problems. By printing the execution time for the entire block, and the execution time for the statements you think should be getting executed, you will often see a discrepancy between the two. Although this discrepancy may be the result of any number of problems, it is entirely possible that a logic error is to blame. Accordingly, it is worthwhile to check for such problems, particularly when using prone constructs such as the `switch` statement, before getting too far with query optimization and other more intense performance tuning.

Bottleneck Avoidance

At all other times, judicious use of the techniques met earlier should enable you to narrow your bottleneck down to a single offender, or at least a collection of offenders.

The most common methods built into PHP (which can be very slow for one reason or another) include the following:

❑ Any method that relies on an external source for data. This appendix has looked at databases as a bottleneck separately, but consider, for example, disk access to a busy disk or network drive, HTTP and FTP requests, IP address resolution, and communication with other objects via Web services protocols such as SOAP and XML-RPC.

❑ Memory-intensive methods may have no problems when called in isolation, but when fighting for physical memory with other instances of the script, and forced to use virtual memory (that is, disk) as a result, such methods can grind to a halt. Typically, anything related to the built-in graphics library Gd is likely to be an offender, especially when working with large images. Consider whether implementing caching techniques, or performing offline generation using scheduled tasks, is feasible.

❑ Anything involving sockets is heavily dependent on network performance. Again, an approach whereby socket conversations are made offline and the user is advised as to his or her status when a request is made, rather than initiating a socket conversation as a direct consequence of a request being made, is a better approach. Consider, therefore, maintaining an e-mail queue database table, which is processed every five minutes, and inserting into that queue from within your script instead of sending mail directly from within a script.

❑ Exercise extreme caution when using shared network drives (over NFS, in particular) as sources for large binary files. For example, a community Web site may allow users to upload a JPEG photograph of themselves for use in their profiles. In a multiple-server environment, this JPEG needs to be accessible by all Web servers. It makes sense to use disk-based file storage rather than the database (databases are still awful at storing binary data), but shared network disk protocols are notoriously slow. Instead, consider replicating binary data across each server using rsync or similar tools. A sync script might run as a background process every five minutes, redistributing data between servers, so a local copy is always available within five minutes of the initial upload.

There are many more examples of methods that can cause bottlenecks. The PHP online documentation often refers to potential performance problems in its entries for particular methods and classes.

When you're relying on PEAR classes, it is also worth checking that your server is installed with the latest supported versions. As with all distributed components, bugs do crop up, so ensure that you have the latest versions to rule out any performance problems that might arise from those bugs.

Testing

Any changes you make to your code or SQL queries as a result of the discoveries discussed previously need to be tested thoroughly. Ensure that you apply the same basic first principles of QA discussed in Chapter 20 when testing the scripts and components you have changed, just as you would when testing the application as a whole.

This includes testing not just the input parameters and usage scenarios you used while making your changes, but all conceivable parameters and scenarios for which it is conceivably possible that your changes could have an impact. Err on the side of overtesting rather than undertesting.

If you have made changes on a development environment, rather than a live environment, try to snatch a copy of your live database or data store and test locally. If this is not possible, try to set up a virtual server in Apache (or your preferred Web server) to use as a temporary staging environment, using your new code base against the live database, but running distinctly from the live environment.

Either way, be sure that when you go live, you are confident not only that your changes will have the desired effect in improving performance, but also that they will not adversely affect functionality in any way.

Preemptive Avoidance

Everything discussed so far refers to fixing an existing application. This is all well and good, but these ad hoc solutions rely on having the end users of your product point out the poor performance they are experiencing, which can have quite serious commercial ramifications.

A more productive (as well as professional) approach is to design with performance in mind from the outset. This is, of course, a whole book in its own right. Generally speaking, the principles set out in this book have had performance as a priority, so it is hoped that none of them will adversely affect your application if used appropriately and with reasonable volumes of data. It is in your own architecture that you need to be careful.

Tips for High-Performance Architecture

Here are a few useful tips you can employ when architecting your application, which should help to ensure fast, efficient design from the outset:

❑   *Get the hardware right* — The fastest PHP in the world will still run like molasses on the wrong hardware. Serving Web pages is relatively simple, so put your weaker hardware to work as Apache workhorses. Keep the big guns for running databases. In addition, try to equip all servers with high-performance SCSI disks in a RAID configuration where possible.

❑   *Use caching at the lowest level possible* — If some of your more intensive scripts are repeatedly producing the same output, should you really hit the database every time? True, the database will cache the responses to queries at some level, but if the HTML remains the same each time, why not cache the HTML itself? Various third-party caching packages of variable quality are available in PECL, but you can easily write your own using the serialization of GET, POST, and COOKIE parameters passed to your script. By comparing that serialization to those made on previous requests, you can determine the "uniqueness" of each request. Requests that are identical to those made previously can be satisfied using cached data, rather than having to hit the database again.

❏ *Perform unpredictable processes offline* — If a process in one of your scripts is dependent on some unpredictable third party, strongly consider taking it offline. The most obvious example is processing credit cards through a payment service provider. If you must have real-time authorization (for example, if customers can purchase access to online content), then use a simple, automatically refreshing page that diverts to a success page after the database has been updated to indicate authorization. Assign an external script (run as a scheduled task, even if once every 60 seconds) the task of batch-processing requests to authorize cards, and update the database to reflect the successful authorization, or otherwise, of those requests.

❏ *Use databases judiciously* — Not all data must be stored using a database. For example, a content-management system that stores its content in XML may be better off storing that data on disk, rather than in a database. Databases are not efficient for storing large chunks of text.

❏ *Optimize database queries* — Learn what does and doesn't run quickly in your particular flavor of database, and err toward the quicker techniques. PostgreSQL, for example, is noticeably slow when handling subselects, and INNER joins are likely to prove a more efficient choice. In addition, ensure that all necessary indices are in place and, equally important, remove any unnecessary indices, because these will actually slow down the database.

❏ *Load test* — Load test individual components using realistic traffic levels and data sets to ensure that real-world performance will match performance at development time. This is addressed in more detail shortly.

Load Testing

Functional testing is an important part of QA, but load testing is of equal importance in ensuring the overall quality of your finished project.

In a nutshell, load testing entails simulating a number of simultaneous connections to the Web server, and carrying out typical user flow scenarios in each case. At the same time, you should measure the performance of the scripts as load increases, as well as the overall impact on the server as a whole.

A table of data can then be produced that, properly analyzed, can advise that, at a given number of simultaneous users, response time will be n. Of course, n will obviously tend toward infinity as the number of simultaneous users increases, but at what point does it reach an unacceptable value and, hence, what is the maximum number of simultaneous users that can be supported on the setup in question?

Excellent packages such as ApacheBench (http://codeflux.com/ab/) can simulate the very simplest of scenarios, but more sophisticated commercial software such as LoadRunner can recreate more realistic scenarios by randomly deviating the interval between the requests of each user, and requesting randomly altering sequences of pages to more realistically match the behavior of a real human user.

When load testing, endeavor to use another server (or, ideally, servers) to act as clients connecting to the live Web server(s). This ensures that the load test software itself is not a burden on your Web server. In addition, always try to use the live server running in a staging mode or, if not feasible, an accurate recreation of the live environment and configuration on another server, to ensure that the results are representative.

It can often be helpful to present the results of your tests (assuming that they are positive) in a nontechnical manner to your client. It will help the client plan for future expansion against his or her own commercial or operational objectives.

Summary

In this appendix, you learned how to spot the different types of bottlenecks that may occur in your code, how to pinpoint them one by one, and how to quickly amend them.

You also learned how to avoid performance bottlenecks in the first place by avoiding some common pitfalls of software and systems architecture, and leveraging opcode caching software to avoid unnecessary lexing/parsing.

Finally, you were introduced to load testing and some of the factors that must be considered when it is carried out on your own projects.

Best Practice PHP Installation

These days, it seems anyone can handle a simple installation. Even your mom and dad could probably handle popping the latest version of Windows on their PC.

The exception to this rule seems to be server applications such as PHP. Although the PHP Web site and supplied documentation do touch on how to get it up and running, they never really go as far as explaining exactly that. Having a usable installation is quite a different matter and requires some inside knowledge.

This appendix examines the ins and outs of getting PHP properly set up in a configuration best suited to the kind of enterprise development detailed in this book. You'll learn about the differences between PHP on Windows and PHP on UNIX, and discover which is better suited for enterprise development.

Introduction to PHP Installation

PHP is an application language. It is not a server in its own right, or a piece of software in the traditional sense. Nor is it a compiler such as Pascal or C++. It must be installed — wrapped, if you like — in a Web server. With this in mind, for every installation of PHP, you need some kind of Web server, such as Apache.

The phrase "installing PHP," therefore, is perhaps not quite accurate. The phrase "installing PHP and Apache" would be better, but that omits the fact that PHP is heavily dependent on third-party libraries and applications for any of its more sophisticated functionality.

To make things worse, most applications that this book introduces you to, as well as anything useful you'll write yourself, require some kind of a back-end database. This book advocates PostgreSQL over MySQL, but they are much the same in practice.

In fact, the actual steps for a PHP installation look something more like this:

1. Install and configure the various external libraries.

2. Install and configure your database platform.

3. Install and configure your Web server.

4. Install and configure PHP.

As you can see, it's far from child's play. To make matters a lot worse, the exact manner in which the preceding steps are accomplished varies, depending on your chosen operating system (UNIX or Windows), your chosen Web server (Apache, IIS, Zeus, etc.) and your chosen database platform (MySQL, PostgreSQL, MS SQL Server, Oracle, IBM DB2, Informix).

Presenting the lowdown on every possible permutation in this appendix would not only affect the number of trees required to produce this book, it would be madness, because there's a very convincing argument for one particular combination over any others.

The Winning Platform

To be clear about something, this book is not about operating system wars. Those of you interested in the great Windows versus UNIX debate can find literally thousands of pages of well-considered, informed dialogue among the ever-rational and well-spoken denizens of *Slashdot* (www.slashdot.org).

However, we do proffer the following bold statement: "Windows is bad at being an Internet application server, just as UNIX is bad at being a workstation operating system."

This is somewhat of a sweeping generalization, and there are exceptions to the rule, but tens of thousands of ISPs and big businesses in the United States alone can't be wrong. Although Windows is frequently found in the corporate environment as an Exchange server or domain controller, it is UNIX that hosts Web sites and DNS, and routes mail at the SMTP level across the whole of the Internet. Similarly, although there are those who choose to use Linux with X window managers such as Enlightenment, Gnome, and KDE on their laptops, they represent a minority. Most people recognize that Windows excels on the desktop, while UNIX excels as a server environment.

> We are acutely aware of the fact that UNIX is a trademarked name, and refers to a specific operating system that is not the GNU/Linux distribution that most of us use on a daily basis. What we mean by using the commonly known appellation UNIX is a POSIX-compliant operating system, such as the various GNU/Linux distributions, FreeBSD, OpenBSD, Solaris, and so on, sometimes collectively referred to as *nix systems. However, *nix isn't readily pronounceable and GNU/Linux, FreeBSD, OpenBSD, Solaris, and so on, is a lot to type. Therefore, we have chosen to use UNIX.

The reasons for this distinction are really quite simple. The Windows interface is optimized for the desktop because it has undergone year after year of development with GUI desktop applications as a primary focus. Many thousands of hours have gone into researching and evolving the Windows user interface to make it intuitive and efficient. It's not perfect, but it is better than what is offered by its UNIX counterparts.

As of this writing, Microsoft's Internet Information Services (IIS) is the default and most popular choice for hosting Web sites on the Windows platform. Although it is vastly better than it used to be, IIS still suffers from an ongoing discovery of major and widely publicized security flaws on a fairly regular basis, as well as often being regarded as unstable and unreliable by systems administrators. In addition, the massive overhead of the Windows environment means that dedicated Windows servers on the Internet still carry enormous amounts of unnecessary baggage. A server with 2GB of RAM could easily have 512MB chewed up by the operating system and its various services, with only 64MB of that being used to actually power the Web server running on it.

In contrast to that, most production UNIX servers are running no GUI at all, which enables them to devote more system resources to applications, with less taken up by the operating system. Admittedly, it's not quite as easy to configure, but it's infinitely quicker, more stable and reliable, and a greater "respecter" of resources.

You can probably see where this is going. There is an argument for using IIS/Windows-based Web servers for ASP-based Web sites, of course, because ASP.NET on UNIX (which does exist) is incredibly difficult to get working successfully; but this is a PHP book, and it is fair to say that PHP on Windows is every bit as bad an idea as is ASP.NET on UNIX.

There may be legitimate exceptions — for example, you are developing an intranet platform for a client whose setup is entirely Windows-based, and he or she insists you deploy onto the existing Windows-based environment. With this in mind, you can find notes at the end of this appendix to help you deal with the differences. This will be the exception, however, not the rule. The vast majority of Web sites are hosted on a machine (or cluster of machines) operated by a hosting company whose choice of operating system, Web server, and programming language is limited to some predefined configurations; for PHP, this will almost always be GNU/Linux and Apache.

With that in mind, this book assumes that your PHP installation is on UNIX, not Windows. This assumption is applied uniformly throughout, and is evident in all the examples demonstrated, without exception. PHP on UNIX is the choice of the professional, and this is a professional's book.

Don't panic. This does not mean that you need to use UNIX yourself. Indeed, Appendix B (which examines various development environments such as Zend Studio) suggests that Windows is the best platform to use on your desktop, and indeed it is. The development server you will use, which could be situated just a couple of inches away from your own PC, needs to run UNIX — but your workstation won't. There are also a number of excellent virtualization options available today that enable a reasonably powerful workstation to quite happily run UNIX as a virtual server with a Windows or Mac OS host operating system. This is an option the authors of this book have used quite successfully.

The Winning Web Server

By choosing the operating system at this stage, you have a number of options regarding which Web server software to use on UNIX: Apache, lighttpd, Zeus, and others.

There are two main manners in which PHP can be compiled and installed: as a CGI executable or as an integral part of the Web server (known as a *SAPI module*). The latter option is a great deal faster and can handle many more concurrent connections. A CGI binary requires an instance of the PHP interpreter to load with every single HTTP request, which is very inefficient. All the previous options stated support

PHP as a SAPI module. The authors do not recommend that any production or development environment run PHP as a CGI module.

Although all the preceding options are perfectly valid, so prevalent is the Apache server that it is practically unavoidable. It is running fully half of the Web sites in existence. Recall from earlier in this appendix that the ISPs to whom you will be deploying will almost certainly be running Apache in preference to any of the other alternatives. You will make your life considerably easier if you stick to Apache.

It's a good choice in its own right. Apache has proven to be stable, secure, and very well supported; it is also being further developed on an ongoing basis. As an open-source application, it is free of charge, and free of commercial license encumbrance.

With all this in mind, the instructions in this section relate to getting PHP up and running on Apache on UNIX. Thankfully, the Web server in use, in contrast to the operating system, doesn't really affect PHP syntax at all, so the examples in this book, although they may be specific to UNIX, aren't specific to any particular Web server.

The Winning Database

Although you've restricted your PHP/Web server to the UNIX platform, there's nothing to stop your database server from being a completely different physical machine. In fact, many of the more high-traffic sites and applications you build will almost certainly require a separate database server — in some cases, two or three.

With this in mind, therefore, the doors are flung wide open. You have to choose between PostgreSQL, MySQL, SQLite, Oracle, Informix, DB2, Microsoft SQL Server, SAP DB, and many more.

Indeed, all the aforementioned options would be excellent choices. They are all highly accomplished and frequently updated. Because database servers are not exposed to the Internet, any security flaws discovered are of little importance. As long as a proper firewall is in place, they are all as secure as one another.

There are minor discrepancies in their notional reliability, but in all honesty, for every champion of, say, SQL Server, there is also a champion of MySQL, Oracle, DB2, and so on.

They're all fast, too. Any real difference in performance is often related to how you have structured your database, rather than the database server itself.

With this in mind, you might struggle to choose. So have we, but this book encourages the use of PostgreSQL for a number of reasons:

❑   You probably want to stick to free software as much as possible, because Apache and PHP are both free to download and use. PostgreSQL is, too, so it passes the first test.

❑   PostgreSQL is about as close to industry standard heavyweights such as Oracle as you can get without actually being Oracle. Its syntax is largely ANSI compliant, meaning that porting an application away from PostgreSQL to another database is a relatively straightforward job.

❑ The rich environment for writing stored procedures and functions far surpasses the limited environment offered by MySQL 5, and supports standard programming languages such as Perl and even PHP itself for writing stored procedures, unlike the proprietary languages used by SQL Server and Oracle; and the vast array of libraries for more complex functions such as Geographic Information Services makes it far superior to many of the other alternatives for enterprise-class database services.

❑ It's great all around. In addition to being free and standards-compliant, it's also extremely fast, extremely stable, and pretty easy to set up and install. It's also very well supported by PHP, which is a huge bonus, given the topic of this book.

The Installation Itself

Now that you understand the background, it's time to start the installation. The following assumes that you have a working UNIX machine, installed and ready to go.

If you don't already have a UNIX machine and want a good place to start, GNU/Linux is the ideal UNIX-based operating system for PC-based hardware. Just make sure to tell it to install all the developer utilities during installation, because you'll need these to get PHP up and running.

This installation assumes that your UNIX machine is networked, has a private IP address assigned, and can be pinged from your workstation (and your workstation from it). It is also assumed that you are familiar with basic UNIX commands and utilities.

If all this looks good to you, then you can get started. Log in to your UNIX machine as `root` (or become `root` from a normal user account using `su`), and you can begin.

Downloading and Installing PostgreSQL

Because your development environment is for your own use only, you don't need to worry about putting PostgreSQL on a separate machine. You can use the same machine to run Apache, PHP, and your database without any real performance implications.

Mac OS X users have it easy, and need not follow this section. Instead, download the wizard-driven installer from http://www.postgresql.org/download/macosx which will install, configure and start PostgreSQL for you with virtually no intervention required.

Ensure that you get the complete archive of PostgreSQL from `www.postgresql.org` and that you download the source code — not any binaries. You'll compile it yourself for maximum speed and resilience. The filename of your downloaded file will look something like `postgresql-8.3.3.tar.gz`. To find the URL, go to `www.postgresql.org`, click Downloads, and find the link for the source code.

You can download the file using Lynx or FTP if you must, but the authors' preferred route is `wget`:

```
# wget ftp://ftp.postgresql.org/pub/latest/postgresql-8.3.3.tar.gz
```

After you've downloaded it, unpack PostgreSQL in the normal way:

```
# tar -xzvf postgresql-8.3.3.tar.gz
```

This will create a directory called `postgresql-8.3.3` that contains the source files for PostgreSQL. Change into that directory:

```
# cd postgresql-8.3.3
```

Run the configure script to generate a `Makefile` appropriate to your particular UNIX environment:

```
# ./configure
```

With luck, you won't see any errors and you'll get a string of checks passed, with the last line reading as follows or similarly:

```
config.status: linking ./src/makefiles/Makefile.linux to src/Makefile.port
```

If this all looks good, you can start the compilation process by simply typing the following:

```
# make
```

It may take quite a while for PostgreSQL to compile, so go have a cup of coffee at this point. When you return, PostgreSQL should have compiled without incident (it is hoped), and you can install it as follows:

```
# make install
```

Strictly speaking, PostgreSQL is now installed, but a certain amount of configuration is still required. You must create the user account under which the daemon will run, set permissions on the data directory so that user owns it, and then initialize the data directory. Follow these steps to get your database working directory set up (where all your data will be stored):

```
# adduser postgres
# mkdir /usr/local/pgsql/data
# chown postgres /usr/local/pgsql/data
# su - postgres
# /usr/local/pgsql/bin/initdb -D /usr/local/pgsql/data
```

You're almost ready to start the PostgreSQL daemon (server) now. One final step: You have to tell PostgreSQL from where to allow connections. Normally, this will just be from the same server or, in a pinch, from other machines on the same network.

Suppose that your server's IP address in this case is 192.168.1.1 and you want to allow access from that IP address only. Edit the file `/usr/local/pgsql/data/pg_hba.conf` using your favorite editor, adding this line to the very bottom of the file:

```
Host  all  all  192.168.1.1  255.255.255.255  trust
```

Save the file and quit the editor. You can now start PostgreSQL using the following syntax:

```
# su - postgres
# /usr/local/pgsql/bin/postmaster -i -D /usr/local/pgsql/data &
```

The first line is very important. The postmaster process must run as your new `postgres` user and not as `root` or whomever you may have been logged in as. The `-i` directive when starting is important too, because it tells PostgreSQL to allow TCP/IP connections — something it disallows by default.

That's it. You can create a database as follows, again as the user `postgres`:

```
# /usr/local/pgsql/bin/createdb databasename
```

Now you can manipulate it using the PostgreSQL console as follows:

```
# /usr/local/pgsql/bin/psql databasename
```

Finally, you can create new users as follows:

```
# /usr/local/pgsql/bin/createuser username
```

This concludes your crash course in PostgreSQL installation. There are plenty of variations in the process, depending on your operating system and functional requirements. More advanced setups and further details on the required libraries are covered in the PostgreSQL documentation.

Installing the Various Support Libraries

In an ideal world, you could now press on and install PHP and Apache. Unfortunately, life is unfair, and you'll need to install a few support libraries for PHP.

PHP 6 has drastically reduced the number of external libraries needed to get the core functionality up and running. The major GNU/Linux distributions have also become much better at handling binary distributions of these libraries, and, for the first time, the authors now recommend installing the few needed libraries from the binary distributions. Install the following using your favorite package manager (such as `yum`, `apt-get`, and so on):

❑   `libicu`

❑   `libicu-devel`

These two libraries contain the code for the International Components for Unicode, which provide some of the software infrastructure that supports the new Unicode support in PHP 6. Which additional libraries you need (if any) depends on exactly what functionality you require.

With `libicu` installed, you're ready to get onto PHP and Apache themselves.

Installing PHP and Apache

PHP and Apache must be installed in tandem, so they are covered in one section here. It will become clear exactly why very shortly.

Mac OS X users can once again bail out at this step, and download and install MAMP from http://www .mamp.info/en/index.php. It will create a working PHP 6 installation for you using a simple 'wizard' process. Once done, you'll find you have an installation of PHP at http://localhost:8080.

First, download the latest versions of Apache and PHP from their respective Web sites —
httpd.apache.org and www.php.net.

The two files you'll download will be named something like httpd-2.2.9.tar.gz and
php-6.0.0.tar.gz. Uncompress them in the normal manner.

```
# tar -xzvf httpd-2.2.9.tar.gz
# tar -xzvf php-6.0.0.tar.gz
```

The first step is to do an initial configure on Apache. Change into the Apache directory (probably
httpd-2.2.9) and run the configure script with the default parameters, and then compile and install:

```
# ./configure
# make && make install
```

When it's done, go ahead and configure PHP. Change back out of the Apache directory and into the PHP
directory:

```
# cd ..
# cd php-6.0.0
```

You now configure PHP using a remarkably simple configure statement, compared to the requirements
of previous versions of PHP:

```
./configure -with-aspx2=/usr/local/apache/bin/aspx -with-pgsql --with-pdo-pgsql.
```

Note that if you installed Apache to a different prefix, or used one of the -enable-layout options, you
will need to amend the -with-aspx2 directive to point to the installation location of the aspx
executable.

It may well take a few minutes to configure, but assuming that you've followed this appendix correctly
up until now, you shouldn't receive any error messages, and everything should configure okay.

You can then build PHP:

```
# make
# make install
```

Note that the make may well take a few minutes, depending on the hardware and load of your server.
The make install probably won't take long at all. If it fails, you may need to retrace your steps. In
particular, confirm that all the support packages mentioned in the previous section have been configured
correctly.

The PHP compile and install process creates a module in your Apache modules directory; you can now
configure and install Apache to make use of that module. You must tell the Apache configuration file
how to handle the .php extension. Modify the file /usr/local/apache/conf/httpd.conf (again,
depending on your configure parameters, this path can vary, but this is the default) and add the
following lines:

```
AddType application/x-httpd-php .php
AddType application/x-httpd-php-source .phps
```

These lines can be added virtually anywhere, but should be placed near all the other `AddType` and `AddHandler` directives in the file in order to keep things clean. Note that PHP should already have edited this file to add the following line:

```
LoadModule php6_module       lib/apache/libphp6.so
```

Confirm that the preceding line is already in your `httpd.conf` file. If not, add it.

Testing Your Installation

All that remains is to test your installation. Start Apache using the following syntax:

```
# /usr/local/apache/bin/apachectl start
```

Now create a file in `/usr/local/apache/htdocs` called `test.php` containing the following code:

```
<?php
phpinfo();
?>
```

Save it and, in your workstation's Web browser, point it to the IP address of your UNIX machine, followed by `/phpinfo.php`. For example, if your server is 192.168.1.1, point it to `http://192.168.1.1/phpinfo.php`. You should see a screen showing the full details of your PHP installation.

If so, congratulations. Your PHP installation has been successful! You will probably want to create virtual server entries for each project that you work on, however. Much more information on this can be found in Chapter 21.

When Windows Is Needed

Scenarios do crop up for which you will simply have to use Windows. The most classic example is for the installation of a closed system onto a large company's IT infrastructure, which is already Windows-based, and management has resolutely refused to install a UNIX server.

With some adaptation, the examples in this book will all still work just fine. The following pointers may help you transfer your PHP from UNIX to Windows.

Changing Paths

Don't forget that paths on Windows look very different from paths on UNIX. References to paths such as `/data/res/1230.jpg` on disk need to be changed to a Windows equivalent, such as `C:\ data\res\1230.jpg`.

PHP is kind and allows you to keep the slashes oblique (/). If you avoid drive letters by using relative paths, you may be able to keep your application more portable.

External Libraries

Because Windows does not come with a built-in and highly pervasive C/C++ compiler in the same way UNIX does, PHP does not require a myriad of external libraries to work under Windows. Instead, PHP supplies with its Windows installations a huge set of precompiled DLLs for the various extensions discussed in this appendix. Note that these DLLs are only supplied with the ZIP distribution of the Windows binaries. You should not install PHP on Windows using the .msi installer.

To enable such extensions, ensure that the PHP extensions directory is in the system PATH (such as C:\php\ext), ensure that the extension_dir directive is set properly in php.ini (it is *not*, by default, set to a useful value for a Windows installation), and restart your Web server. You should find that the relevant functionality becomes available to PHP right away.

Using PEAR

Using the PEAR repository to install library packages in Windows is a little different from how it is accomplished under UNIX. Before you can use PEAR, you must set it up using the following bundled script:

```
C:\php\PEAR>..\php go-pear.php
Welcome to go-pear!
Go-pear will install the 'pear' command and all the files needed by
it. This command is your tool for PEAR installation and maintenance.
```

This script will ask you various questions about proxy servers and so forth, but creates a single pear command as a batch file, which you can then use in exactly the same manner as its UNIX counterpart.

Summary

In this appendix, you learned the key reasons why this book has opted for UNIX, Apache, and PostgreSQL in its examples, and why you might want to consider doing the same in your own PHP enterprise development.

You then learned the fundamental steps involved in setting up a working, practical installation of Apache, PHP, and PostgreSQL on a UNIX platform from start to finish.

Finally, you learned some of the key differences between PHP on Windows and UNIX, and how to circumnavigate them effectively in your own development.

Index

A